A DICTIONARY OF KLEINIAN THOUGHT

A Dictionary of
Kleinian Thought

R. D. HINSHELWOOD

*'an association in which the free development of
each is the condition of the free development of all'*

Free Association Books / London / 1991

First published in Great Britain 1989 by
Free Association Books
26 Freegrove Road
London N7 9RQ

Second edition, revised
and enlarged, 1991

British Library Cataloguing in Publication Data

Hinshelwood, R.D.
  A dictionary of Kleinian thought.
  1. Psychoanalysis. Kleinian system
  I. Title
  150.19′5′0942

  ISBN 0–946960–82–8
       0–946960–83–6 pb

Typeset by Columns of Reading, England

Printed and bound in the United States by Haddon Craftsmen, Scranton,
Pennsylvania.

To my father, who did not understand very much of this way of thinking but who would have been proud of my effort.

Contents

PUBLISHER'S FOREWORD

I have felt for some time that psychoanalysis would benefit from a clear and accessible account of Kleinian and post-Kleinian concepts and of the work of the main figures in this tradition. This would be particularly helpful with respect to Klein's writings, since they are often found obscure, as are those of Bion. It is often said that these ideas are best grasped in supervision, where they are conveyed in the light of clinical material.

It occurred to me one day that Raymond Williams's *Keywords* (Fontana, 1976), which traces the historical evolution of concepts in cultural studies, could serve as a model for such a book, along with Laplanche and Pontalis, *The Language of Psycho-Analysis* (Hogarth, 1983). I shared the idea that day with Bob Hinshelwood, with whom I had been working for some time – tutoring him on the history of ideas and being supervised by him on clinical cases. He rang me a day later and agreed to undertake the project. I had no idea just how ambitious he would be, and what a thorough and comprehensive book he would write.

I cannot overstate how proud I am to have edited and published this book, which I believe will be a landmark in psychoanalysis. Henceforward, I believe, no one can dismiss Kleinian ideas merely because they are difficult of access, while many will find, as I have, that their own experience and that of their patients will benefit from a flood of subtle and multilevel illumination. As I anticipated, certain essays required revision for this edition though, in fact, the book has been widely acclaimed. A basis for clarity and accessibility has been laid. I remain grateful and admiring.

Robert M. Young

PREFACE TO THE SECOND EDITION

This revised edition of *A Dictionary of Kleinian Thought* has been a fortunate opportunity to consider the clamour of response to the first edition. It was extremely heartening to have so large a response – so much of it favourable.

But not all those who responded were in agreement with one another, and that gave me pause to reflect further on the geography of the field. As a result I have added some new material and rewritten a number of passages. Mercifully, the amount that is rewritten and that had to be modified from the first edition is very small. I am pleased about that, both because of the satisfaction in having produced a substantially acceptable version of Kleinian thought, and also because the amount of rereading required of anyone who has studied from the first edition is not great. What is more important about this second edition is the additional material.

The major critiques have been around two issues: certain aspects of the death instinct and envy; and the recent developments in technique associated with the name of Betty Joseph.

The first of these criticisms has led me to make some alterations in the entries DEATH INSTINCT, ENVY, AGGRESSION and PERVERSION.

The second criticism – that I had undervalued and under-represented the work of Betty Joseph – was more difficult to assess. The publication of her collected papers in 1989, edited by Michael Feldman and Elizabeth Spillius, brings this issue out more strongly. Her book is a remarkable collection of papers about a remarkable development in the work of a significant group of London Kleinians – work that is admired and acknowledged by the whole Kleinian group. It concerns the phenomenon of 'acting-in', as Betty Joseph calls it. She describes this as the clinical manifestation most strongly encountered within the analytical treatment of certain kinds of particularly difficult patients, those who are 'difficult to reach'. 'Acting-in' is the clinical counterpart to the theoretical problems referred to by other Kleinian analysts as 'pathological organizations'. I have emphasized this work more in this edition by introducing new entries, PATHOLOGICAL ORGANIZATIONS and, to cover Betty Joseph's work, PSYCHIC CHANGE and PSYCHIC EQUILIBRIUM (terms adopted by Feldman and Spillius to give Betty Joseph's writing more technical clarity) and PSYCHIC PAIN and ACTING-IN. It has also entailed some modifications to the existing entries TRANSFERENCE and COUNTERTRANSFERENCE. I was able to give a fuller account of my own impressions of the place of Betty Joseph's work when I was invited to review her book for *Free Associations* 22.

There is an additional small entry – MEMORY AND DESIRE – in order to highlight one key aspect of Kleinian technique. The bibliography has been updated from 1987 to 1989; and I have attempted to keep track of the republication of previously published papers by Kleinians, which seems at present to be becoming a major industry in its own right.

I have corrected some minor errors such as spelling which I am grateful to friends and colleagues for having pointed out. It is to the credit of the original editor at Free Association Books, Selina O'Grady, that so few slipped past her careful eye. I am grateful for the time Hanna Segal spent in commenting on and discussing the first edition of this book; and also for a detailed correspondence with Elizabeth Spillius following her review of the first edition ('On Kleinian language', *Free Associations* 18: 90–110). And as always Bob Young has been very encouraging with the work, and very perceptive over what is needed.

August 1990

INTRODUCTION

Kleinian concepts are about very primitive elements of the human mind, remote from common sense and rather like those ungraspable particles of subatomic physics. The basic building blocks are few but built into phantastically rich complexity. Unlike subatomic particles, however, the matter of the mind is potentially knowable by the individual person. He *is* a mind in a different sense from the way in which he is a massive structuring of electrons and protons. Something of this is knowable to those who can enquire within themselves with or without the help of their own analyst. It is impossible in the written word to pass on a sense of understanding – merely a *knowing about* the concepts which the reader must take further with himself on his own.

Much of the inaccessibility of Kleinian thought comes about not only because it is framed in the patient's own experiences but because those experiences are so very remote from conscious and verbal thought, and so difficult to communicate in a manner that is verifiable outside the particular analyst–patient partnership: 'The description of such primitive processes suffers from a great handicap, for these phantasies arise at a time when the infant has not yet begun to think in words' (Klein, 1946, p. 8n). These are issues with which all psychoanalytic writing has to contend. This dictionary is no exception, and I have tried to go about the business of describing concepts without shirking the fact of their great complexity and their remoteness.

To a degree the definitions can be brought to life by conveying the cut and thrust of the debate out of which they have come, but there is an inherent difficulty in bringing psychoanalytic concepts to life in this way – particularly Kleinian concepts, which are especially closely linked to the clinical grounding of psychoanalysis. To a major extent Kleinian theory *is* clinical theory; and the theories that patients have about their own minds are the basis of Kleinian theories of the mind. This emphasis on taking the patient's subjective experience seriously has often tended to cause confusion, specifically because the language of the subject and the language of the observer are traditionally separate discourses in 'scientific' psychology.

There are several main characteristics to the formation of Kleinian thought:

1. Klein came into professional life, and into psychoanalysis, late in life and because of that – and probably for reasons set in her own personality – she fought continually to establish herself securely, a

position which constantly evaded her. Kleinian psychoanalysis remains a body of knowledge carefully kept by a group of people (the Kleinian Group) with the same aloof sense of insecurity and a worry about what others who come to possess the knowledge might do with it. Debate with other schools of psychoanalysis has been either nonexistent or, when it has happened, has degenerated into dispute of a quite personal kind.

2. All the same Klein was, like all innovators, fortunate in finding herself in possession of a new technique that allowed her a much further reach in her area of discovery than anyone before her. She was thrilled by the power of her play technique and enthusiastic to demonstrate its usefulness. But the newness and power of her technique failed to give her the secure position she sought; in fact, the reverse: her exceptional results made her an awkward and deviant member of the orthodox psychoanalytic community.

3. Another major strand in Klein's thought was the importance of 'object-relations', which emerged slowly out of the growing emphasis on the special aspect of the analytic relationship: the transference. Klein's professional life spanned the slow realization of the concrete reality of internal object-relations, the process of comprehending these through the play of children and the madness of psychotics, and the eventual radical revision of the nature and use of the transference as a result of these discoveries.

Klein's thinking did not always progress in a single direction. The steps can be listed in roughly chronological order:

   1919 Importance of the content (rather than instinctual origin) of anxiety
   1922 Play therapy
   1923 Unconscious phantasy
   1923 Violence and sadism in phantasy life
   1925 Relinquishing the timetable of developmental phases
c. 1925 Cycles of persecution
   1926 Internal objects
   1926 Guilt and the early superego
   1927 Introjection of phantastical images of parents
   1928 Symbolization, personification and externalization
   1930 Primitive defence mechanisms
   1933 Death instinct
   1935 The importance of the loved object
   1935 Depressive position
   1946 Pre-depressive-position persecution and defences (paranoid-schizoid position)
   1957 Envy

I have regarded some of these concepts as so fundamental that the first section of this dictionary (*Part A*) consists of *13 Main Entries* dealing with these basic concepts. These Main Entries are set out in a chronological order. Some concepts emerge and fade away (like the *Femininity phase*); others remain powerfully central (particularly *Unconscious phantasy* and *Internal objects*); one (*Technique*) concerns the important tool from which all the discoveries came. Possibly these 13 entries could be read as the chapters of an introductory work on Kleinian psychoanalysis.

The last of these Main Entries (*Projective identification*) is the springboard for most of the development that colleagues have contributed in the later part of her career (1945–60) and subsequently.

The second part of the dictionary (*Part B*) consists of the *General Entries* arranged in conventional alphabetical order. They are all intended to give adequate access through cross-referencing to the matrix of concepts, and the determined reader should be able to follow his own path of interest. The General Entries also amplify the developments that came after Klein. Like Freud, Klein left a legacy that remained richly endowed for others to take further. There are many later developments, in particular:

(i) *Developments in the concept of projective identification:* Differentiating normal from pathological projective identification (Bion, 1959); Symbol-formation and its abnormalities (Segal, 1957); Theories of containing and thinking (Bion, 1962, 1970); Development of the concept of countertransference into a theory of therapeutic action (Money-Kyrle, 1956).

(ii) *Clinical manifestations of the death instinct:* Investigation of negative narcissism (Rosenfeld, 1971); Pathological structuring of the personality (Meltzer, 1968; Joseph, 1975).

(iii) *Direct observation of infants in the earliest phases of life:* The skin and adhesive identification (Bick, 1968; Meltzer, 1975); Autism (Meltzer *et al.*, 1975; Tustin, 1981).

In the course of writing this dictionary I have become more than ever convinced that Kleinian concepts arose from the context of Freudian thinking. Some description of the Freudian framework has therefore been essential, and I have had to try to judge how much of the Freudian background it is necessary to explain. For some readers I may have described too much that is familiar already; for others too little, and they may need more background, in which case I can only refer them to Laplanche and Pontalis's *The Language of Psycho-Analysis* and Charles Rycroft's excellently simple *Critical Dictionary of Psycho-Analysis*.

The Kleinian tradition has always emphasized clinical work, and one could say virtually no Kleinian paper appears without a substantial amount of clinical material to back up argument. Klein, being such an outstanding observer in the consulting room, always fell back on this strength when she felt, during the years of contention between 1926 and 1946, that she was pressed to argue her case. Her basis was always in the psychological content of her patients' minds as it emerged in the material. It is curious to write a nonclinical account of Kleinian thought, yet it is the central pillar in the purpose of this dictionary to draw together the theoretical strands.

Although Kleinian concepts came out of earlier classical psychoanalysis they exist now in contrast to *ego-psychology*, which is currently the dominant tradition deriving from classical Freudian psychoanalysis. I have made, where possible, references to the divergent paths between these two schools.

Finally I have compiled a fairly comprehensive *Bibliography* for my own purposes in working on this dictionary and, since there is a fairly clear boundary between those who work rigorously with Kleinian psychoanalysis and those who do not, it seemed worth including this compilation.

I have felt awkward about the use of third-person pronouns. The neuter 'it' is unpleasantly impersonal, in my view, for descriptions of such intensely human and personal material. To qualify constantly the pronoun by using the phrase 'he or she' or 'his or hers' makes for a laboured style. I have on occasions therefore used 'he', 'him' and 'his' where it may refer to both male or female identities, and no offence is meant by this. In fact it is my view – and that of psychoanalysis in general – that gender is skin-deep; we are all an amalgam of both gender stereotypes and the use of 'he' or 'she' reduces the identity to a part-object, a point which might be clarified from looking at the entry for FATHER.

I want to thank my own Kleinian analyst, my teachers in psychoanalysis and my patients, from whom I have learned how to wield these difficult conceptual tools, and also a number of people who have helped me with the preparation of this book: Gillian Beaumont, Joe Berke, Susanna Isaacs Elmhirst, Karl Figlio, Selina O'Grady, Frank Orford, Hanna Segal, Elizabeth Spillius, Victor Wolfenstein, Bob Young. I must particularly mark the constant support that I gratefully received from Bob Young; and the rigorous intellectual testing that Karl Figlio put my manuscript through which helped me to make a much more meticulous product than I would otherwise have achieved.

Finally, let me acknowledge someone who had nothing directly to do with this dictionary except for the following important advice:

> Some people, when they see a word, think the first thing to do is to define it. Dictionaries are produced, and, with a show of authority no less confident because it is usually so limited in place and time, what is called a proper meaning is attached. But while it may be possible to do this, more or less satisfactorily, with certain simple names of things and effects, it is not only impossible but irrelevant in the case of more complicated ideas. What matters in them is not the proper meaning but the history and complexity of meanings: the conscious changes, or unconsciously different uses: and just as often those changes and differences which, masked by a nominal continuity, come to express radically different and often at first unnoticed changes in experience and history. (Williams, 1972, pp. 67–8)

I have tried, perhaps falteringly, to bear in mind this warning about complex ideas. In so far as I have made their complexity clear, I am indebted to Raymond Williams's advice; in so far as I have not, then I can only direct the reader to the original sources to explore for himself.

Bick, Esther (1968) 'The experience of the skin in early object relations', *Int. J. Psycho-Anal.* 49: 484–6; republished (1987) in Martha Harris and Esther Bick, *The Collected Papers of Martha Harris and Esther Bick.* Perth: Clunie, pp. 114–18.

Bion, Wilfred (1959) 'Attacks on linking', *Int. J. Psycho-Anal.* 40: 308–15; republished (1967) in W. R. Bion, *Second Thoughts.* Heinemann, pp. 93–109.

—— (1962) *Learning from Experience.* Heinemann.

—— (1970) *Attention and Interpretation.* Tavistock.

Joseph, Betty (1975) 'The patient who is difficult to reach', in Peter Giovacchini, ed. *Tactics and Techniques in Psycho-Analysis,* vol. 2. New York: Jason Aronson, pp. 205–16.

Klein, Melanie (1946) 'Notes on some schizoid mechanisms', in *The Writings of Melanie Klein,* vol. 3. Hogarth, pp. 1–24.

Meltzer, Donald (1968) 'Terror, persecution, dread', *Int. J. Psycho-Anal.* 49: 396–400; republished (1973) in Donald Meltzer, *Sexual States of Mind.* Perth: Clunie, pp. 99–106.

—— (1975) 'Adhesive identification', *Contemporary Psycho-Analysis* 11: 289–310.

Meltzer, Donald, Bremner, John, Hoxter, Shirley, Weddell, Doreen and Wittenberg, Isca (1975) *Explorations in Autism.* Perth: Clunie.

Money-Kyrle, Roger (1956) 'Normal counter-transference and some of its deviations', *Int. J. Psycho-Anal.* 57: 360–6; republished (1978) in *The Collected Papers of Roger Money-Kyrle.* Perth: Clunie, pp. 330–42.

Rosenfeld, Herbert (1971) 'A clinical approach to the psycho-analytical theory of the life and death instincts: an investigation into the aggressive aspects of narcissism', *Int. J. Psycho-Anal.* 52: 169–78.

Segal, Hanna (1957) 'Notes on symbol-formation', *Int. J. Psycho-Anal.* 38: 391–7; republished (1981) in *The Work of Hanna Segal.* New York: Jason Aronson, pp. 49–65.

Tustin, Frances (1981) *Autistic States in Children.* Routledge & Kegan Paul.

Williams, Raymond (1972) 'Ideas of nature', in (1980) *Problems in Materialism and Culture.* Verso, pp. 67–85.

A   Main Entries

1 TECHNIQUE

DEFINITION. Klein's work on children emphasized the function of phantasy and her technique used toys in the psychoanalytic setting to enhance the expression of phantasies. Play, like free associations, dreams and acting out, were all regarded as expressions of phantasy. Klein showed that the technique of early and deep interpretation resulted in a modification of anxiety, a finding which strongly supported deep and early interpretation; it also emphasized the mutative quality of transference interpretations.

All the material of the patient's utterances in an analytic session, even in an adult who is free-associating, refers to aspects of the transference relationship to the analyst. Those associations that refer to external figures in the patient's life are regarded as aspects of transference that have been split off in order to reduce the anxiety of the immediate moment with the analyst to a tolerable level.

Countertransference was always viewed with some suspicion by Klein, as also by Freud; however, Bion's model of a mother–baby interaction brought countertransference into the centre of psychoanalytic technique. Understanding the countertransference is equivalent to the mother's understanding of her infant's bodily needs, and builds up the capacity of the patient/infant to understand himself. Kleinian analysts do not interpret a countertransference feeling on its own; the analyst's own experience is interpreted *in the light* of the relationships described in the patient's material.

CHRONOLOGY
1918 Working with children.
1919 Interpreting unconscious questions about sexuality.
1921 Using toys and play (Klein, Melanie, 1920, 'The development of a child'; Klein, Melanie, 1955, 'The psycho-analytic play technique: its history and significance').
1926 Confrontation with Anna Freud (Klein, Melanie, 1926, 'The psychological principles of early analysis').
1934 Strachey's emphasis on the transference (Strachey, James, 1934, 'The nature of the therapeutic action of psycho-analysis').
1956 Emphasis on countertransference and cycles of projective and introjective identifications (Money-Kyrle, Roger, 1956, 'Normal countertransference and some of its deviations'; Bion, Wilfred, 1959, 'Attacks on linking').

Freud had discovered the psychology of childhood (notably the phases of childhood sexuality, and the theory of repressed trauma) from his psychoanalysis of adults [see 3. AGGRESSION; LIBIDO]. When he wanted to check his theories with actual children, he asked acquaintances and colleagues to collect observations of their own sons and daughters. The resulting 'case history' of Little Hans (Freud, 1909) was an analysis of the father's shorthand notes of daily conversations with the four-and-a-half-year-old Hans. The 'analysis' of Little Hans did two things. First, it confirmed Freud's theories of childhood development, but second, his pessimism about working directly with children seemed to deter anyone else from working with children, either therapeutically or for research purposes. It took another fifteen years until there was again an interest in studying children, this time to check the newer theories of narcissism (Freud, 1914) [see NARCISSISM]. From that grew an attempt to institute a more therapeutic (rather than research) form of analysis of children. This was linked at first with education (Hug-Hellmuth, 1921; Pfister, 1922; Hoffer, 1945). Hug-Hellmuth regarded psychoanalysis as best used to inform the education of children – psychoanalytic teachers. Klein, however, was the first analyst to attempt a rigorous form of psychoanalysis with children which excluded all pedagogic elements.

KLEIN'S CONTRIBUTION TO PSYCHOANALYTIC TECHNIQUE.

All Klein's developments in technique and practice stem from her primary interest in anxiety, and in particular in the *content* of anxiety:

> For her it has been throughout the touchstone, the guiding thread that has led her through the maze . . . To Freud himself anxiety was of very great significance . . . his approach to it was to some extent from the physiological angle, as a condition of tension which must be investigated and understood, and he did not concern himself with the psychological content of the fear (phantasies) to the extent that Melanie Klein did. (Riviere, 1952, p. 8)

Klein's technique emphasized the *content* of the mind [see 2. UNCONSCIOUS PHANTASY] rather than the underlying driving forces – the instincts – which classical analysts had hitherto studied. This led to many far-reaching modifications which continue to mark the difference between Kleinian and orthodox (ego-psychology) psychoanalysis:

I The play technique

(1) children's play was regarded as the equivalent of free association in adults;

(2) interpretations that addressed the unconscious anxiety visibly modify it;

(3) the activity of play is a form of externalization into the analytic setting of internal preoccupations, in particular a preoccupation with relationships with objects believed to exist internally.

II Adult psychoanalysis

(1) free associations of adults came to be seen as play with objects (with the analyst or with the parts of his mind);

(2) an emphasis developed on the *child in the adult patient*;

(3) the significance of the negative transference;

(4) the 'total situation' (that is, all associations) refer to the transference to the analyst;

(5) the analyst, his bodily parts and the functions of his mind may all be experienced as part-objects;

(6) the infant in the patient.

I THE PLAY TECHNIQUE. Melanie Klein first saw Freud in 1918 when she attended the International Congress in Budapest, where Freud read 'Lines of advance in psycho-analytic therapy' (Freud, 1919). She must have been inspired and encouraged to contribute to the new developments. Klein started to practise psychoanalysis with children at the suggestion of her own psychoanalyst, Ferenczi, in Budapest, probably in 1917 – her first subject was one of her own children (Petot, 1979). This is somewhat shocking today; however, it was in line with Little Hans's analysis by his father, and indeed Freud's own analysis of his daughter, Anna (Young-Bruehl, 1989); and Abraham's analysis of his daughter. These early trials led Klein to specialize in the analysis of children.

The development of the technique: Over a period of some five years Klein developed a specific technique which she called *play technique*, with which she could analyse children who were younger than three; in this way, she felt, she was able to reach back into the grey area of infancy further than anyone else.

The technique did not come about all at once, but in a series of steps. She started by setting aside time to talk to the children, she answered their questions, and especially those concerned with the sexual life of the parents. She was frank and open and modelled what she did on the way that Freud had approached the handling of the problems with Little Hans (Freud, 1909). She found that there was a generally positive effect on a child who was confronted with an open and totally frank adult, so that play and phantasy life were visibly enriched.

However, when she reported her work at a meeting of the Hungarian Psycho-Analytical Society in Budapest in 1919, a colleague, Anton von Freund, complained that she addressed only the conscious questions the child was puzzling over, not the unconscious ones. Her interpretations, he said, were not psychoanalytic, even though the way she formulated her observations was.

Thereupon, she did begin to address the *unconscious* questions [see 2. UNCONSCIOUS PHANTASY]. At first she was very cautious with these interpretations; even so, she was amazed by the far-reaching changes that occurred. A quite astonishing upsurge of phantasies and play resulted: '. . . quite spontaneously he began to talk, and from then on he told longer or shorter phantastic stories . . . Hitherto the child had shown as little tendency to tell stories as to play' (Klein, 1920, p. 31). She seems to have been almost alarmed by the sudden endless production of phantasies – not least, perhaps, because she found they were so often violent. However, the potency of the technique was immediately confirmed for her.

Little toys introduced (1923): To enhance the expression of these phantasies, Klein began to use very personal sets of toys:

> In a session in which I again found the child unresponsive and withdrawn I left her, saying that I would return in a moment. I went into my own children's nursery, collected a few toys, cars, little figures, a few bricks, and a train, put them into a box and returned to the patient. The child, who had not taken to drawing or other activities, was interested in the small toys and at once began to play. (Klein, 1955, p. 125)

Klein took as her model Freud's interpretations of an infant of eighteen months playing with a cotton reel (Freud, 1920).

(1) **Play as free associations.** Klein's approach to analysing very young children was simple and refreshing – freedom of play could substitute for free association, and the phantasies expressed are 'the same language, the same archaic, phylogenetically acquired mode of expression as we are familiar with from dreams' (Klein, 1926, p. 134). Each child had his own locker, and this remains an important feature of the play technique. The locker contained small toys, water and a basin, paper, scissors, glue, etc. Klein watched and, when necessary, took part in the child's play.

The new setting: This was a *new setting* involving toys and actual objects. Thus transference involved all the objects in this setting, not just the analyst [see 'the total situation', below]. She adoped a strict, orthodox method. By this she meant that she exclusively interpreted the unconscious and refrained from other interventions which Hug-Hellmuth and Anna Freud were promoting at that time.

She interpreted the elements of play and respected their symbolic value as if they were elements in a dream. She used the words commonly used by the child, but she talked explicitly and frankly about sexual matters, and parts of the body, and about the prominent aggressive and sadistic relations as well as the loving sexual ones. It seems that Klein herself was quite active in her play with her little patients, willing to play parts in their phantasies – thus enacting the dramas also played out with toys. She interpeted the *relations between objects* as the psychological content of the mind. Looking back, she contrasted this with the standard technique:

> . . . it was an established principle that interpetations should be given very sparingly. With few exceptions psychoanalysts had not explored the deeper layers of the unconscious – in children such exploration being considered dangerous. (Klein, 1955, p. 122)

Play and object-relationships: The little person's possessed objects within the analytic setting left their mark, not only on the technique of child psychoanalysis but also on the kinds of observations that Klein began making, and subsequently on the theories she developed. The playroom is an arena in which the toys are manipulated and of necessity arrange themselves into spatial relationships with each other. The sense of a set of active relationships between objects, within a clearly demarcated space, is already apparent from the setting of Klein's discovery of object-relations. The idea of the internal world was already prompted by her choice of setting [see 5. INTERNAL OBJECTS]. By a happy chance, she had stumbled upon an ideal medium for bringing to light the object-relations view of the human mind [see 5. OBJECT-RELATIONS SCHOOL].

(2) **Interpretation as modifying anxiety.** Klein found that interpretation modified anxiety. In an analysis conducted in 1924, Ruth (four years and three months) refused to relate to the analyst and would stay in the room only if her older sister was present. Klein was defeated over many sessions, in her efforts to make a positive contact with the child: 'I therefore found myself forced to take other measures – measures which once again gave striking proof of the efficacy of interpretation in reducing the patient's anxiety and negative transference.' She goes on to describe how she used material from several sessions to formulate an interpetation of the child's anxiety about mother's insides, and the fear of a baby coming. She was amazed at the immediate change: 'The effect of my interpretation was astonishing. For the first time Ruth turned her attention to me and began to play in a different, less constrained way' (Klein, 1932, pp. 26–7).

Anxiety and the negative transference: The negative aspects of the child's relationship with the analyst (negative transference) were of considerable importance, since the play that Klein witnessed was so suffused with aggressive phantasies and the fear and alarm to which they

seemed to give rise. It became obvious to her that the act of
interpretation had to deal first and foremost with the negative aspects
of the child's phantasies, both because that was the maximum point of
anxiety and also because she found it definitely shifted the feelings for
the analyst in a positive direction. Isaacs (1939) confirmed the effect of
interpreting the *point of maximum anxiety*. However, other child
analysts at that time, alarmed by explicit and deep interpretations,
strongly disapproved (Anna Freud, 1927) [see below; also CHILD
ANALYSIS].

(3) **Play as expulsion.** The importance of play led Klein to take an
interest in its nature; by expulsion an internal conflict was externalized,
and in that way made more tolerable. Searl (1929) commented that
'Phantasies are always better or worse than reality' (p. 289); so that,
whereas we tend to be conscious of the ones that are better
(daydreams), the ones that are worse tend to be externalized in order to
mitigate them. Play therefore has an aspect which is desperate and in
fact a form of defence – expulsion or projection [see PROJECTION].

This function of play is rather grim and pessimistic. It is no fun. It is
to provide relief from these persecuting internal states:

> By the division of roles the child succeeds in expelling the father
> and mother whom, in the elaboration of the Oedipus complex, it has
> absorbed into itself and who are now tormenting it inwardly by their
> severity. The result of this expulsion is relief, which contributes in
> great measure to the pleasure derived from the game. (Klein, 1926,
> p. 133)

Externalization and unconscious guilt: Freud (1916) had shown how
criminals with a harsh unconscious sense of guilt externalize persecution [see UNCONSCIOUS GUILT]. This was linked with the eventual
development of his later theory of the superego. Freud had also
considered children's play, and described it in similar form: 'As the
child passes over from the passivity of the experience to the activity of
the game, he hands on the disagreeable experience to one of his
playmates' (Freud, 1920, p. 17). Klein regarded herself as making
significant contributions to the externalization of unconscious guilt,
since she was analysing children at or before the age when Freud
supposed the superego was forming (four to six years old) [see 7.
SUPEREGO].

II KLEINIAN TECHNIQUE WITH ADULTS. In Kleinian technique with adult psychoanalysis the idea, derived from child analysis,
of an externalized internal state has been developed much further.

Klein's use of play technique, and the assumptions which lay behind it, influenced the development of psychoanalytic technique with adults.

(1) Free associations as play. Although play in the child was originally taken to be equivalent to free associations in the adult, it gave a new emphasis if the free associations of adults were, conversely, seen as a similar externalization with the analyst. Free associations themselves can be a form of acting out (expulsion) of internal conflicts, states of mind, and parts of the self.

The very act of interpreting may itself offer an opportunity for the patient to engage in defensive manoeuvres, a process that Kleinians have increasingly noticed (Joseph, 1975; O'Shaughnessy, 1981; Riesenberg-Malcolm, 1981; Brenman, 1985) [see STRUCTURE; PERVERSION]. This acting out in the transference situation is a function of projective identification in which certain aspects of the patient's experience and impulses are projected into the analyst, to which he or she may respond either (i) by reacting to them or (ii) by verbalizing them. This aspect of the countertransference has been progressively developed and has greatly sensitized the analyst to the nonverbal aspects of the patient's communications [see COUNTER-TRANSFERENCE; and below].

(2) Transference as unconscious phantasy. Klein came to recommend a very much more rigorous view of transference:

> From my work with children I came to certain conclusions which have to some extent influenced my technique with adults. Take transference first. I found that with children the transference (positive or negative) is active from the beginning of analysis, since for instance even an attitude of indifference cloaks anxiety and hostility. With adults too I found that the transference situation is present from the start in one way or another, and I have come, therefore, to make use of transference interpretations early in analysis. (Klein, 1943)

The relation to the analyst is seen as having meaning for the patient in accordance with the active impulses in the patient at the moment [see 2. UNCONSCIOUS PHANTASY].

Externalization of unconscious phantasy: It is not therefore merely a repetition of old attitudes, events and traumas from the past; it is an externalization of unconscious phantasy 'here and now'. The primacy of externalization (projective) processes gives a spatial as well as temporal significance to the concept of transference as opposed to a merely temporal one [see TRANSFERENCE].

The Kleinian tradition has emphasized the importance in the

transference of anxiety and negative attitudes in the 'here-and-now'. Strachey (1937) extended this on theoretical grounds that derived from the theory of internal objects and the superego [see 5. INTERNAL OBJECTS; 7. SUPEREGO]:

> Let us suppose that the analyst gives a woman patient an interpretation to the effect that on some occasion she had a wish that her husband should die. Now the effect that (according to our theory of interpretation) should be produced here is that the patient, by being made conscious of this particular id-impulse, will be in a position to discriminate between her actual object (a father imago, perhaps) and thus will be able to make a correction in her attitude to external reality and ultimately to make an internal readjustment. But what *actually* happens is something quite different. When the interpretation is given, the whole conflict is transferred from the situation which the analyst is talking about to another situation which he is *not* talking about. The patient may, it is true, agree that she wished her husband to die, but her emotional interests have automatically passed over to another problem – this time about the analyst and his interpretation. She is now filled with conflicting feelings about *him* – anger, fear, suspicion, gratitude and many more. And the whole of this new conflict is for the time being out of the analyst's sight and reach. (Strachey, 1937, pp. 142–3)

These views in turn strengthened Klein's own emphasis on internal objects and coincided with her thinking out the depressive position [see 10. DEPRESSIVE POSITION].

(3) **The significance of the negative transference.** The importance of the immediate conflicts in the relationship with the analyst was further emphasized when a psychoanalytic technique with schizophrenics developed in the 1940s. Rosenfeld (1947) and others found that a truly psychoanalytic technique could be used with psychotic patients, provided that a proper, immediate and deep enough attention was paid to the transference, especially in the negative phases.

The negative transference had been so prominent in children that Klein was alert to its frequently hidden nature in adults, a point to which Abraham (1919) and others had occasionally drawn attention. The negative transference is also important on theoretical grounds. Since derivatives of the death instinct are the problem, aggression and destructiveness need to be brought into the transference for investigation and interpretation.

(4) **The total situation as a transferential one.** Attention to hidden manifestations of deeply negative aspects as well as the positive ones reveals the transference as a whole:

> We are accustomed to speak of the transference *situation*. But do we always keep in mind the fundamental importance of this concept? It is my experience that in unravelling the details of the transference it is essential to think in terms of *total situations* transferred from the past into the present, as well as of emotions, defences, and object-relations. (Klein, 1952, p. 55)

Klein laid down that the total of all free associations that come into a patient's mind can be referred to the transference, however remote from consciousness the link may be:

> For many years transference was understood in terms of direct references to the analyst in the patient's material. My conception of transference as rooted in the earliest stages of development and in deep layers of the unconscious is much wider and entails a technique by which from the whole material presented the *unconscious elements* of the transference are deduced. (Klein, 1952, p. 55)

This has developed as an emphasis on the total situation. Classical analysis, in contrast, is wary of such 'deep' interpretations [see below].

This is a crucial mark of Klein's approach, to which she has returned again and again:

> The principle at issue is the quite fundamental one of the significance of the unconscious in conscious life. When we realize this fundamental difference in outlook we understand why some analysts see so little in their patients' material, interpret so little, do not even recognize a transference-situation until the patient himself expresses something of it in conscious and direct reference to the analyst. (Riviere, 1952, p. 17)

Klein emphasized how the patient will turn away from the analyst with his aggressive and negative impulses and phantasies, and turn them towards other figures, who appear in the patient's account (or play) as extraneous:

> . . . the patient is bound to deal with conflicts and anxieties re-experienced towards the analyst by the same methods he used in the past. That is to say, he turns away from the analyst as he attempted to turn away from his primal objects; he tries to split the relations to him, keeping him either as a good or as a bad figure: he deflects some of the feelings and anxieties experienced towards the analyst on to other people in his current life, and this is part of 'acting out'. (Klein, 1952, pp. 55–6)

This repeats the primary splitting activity of the infantile ego [see SPLITTING]. Thus all figures appearing in play or free associations should be considered as aspects of the analyst that have been split off and projected [see PROJECTION]; it is a splitting designed to regulate the relationship with the analyst to controllable levels of anxiety. This is the importance of the *total situation* (Joseph, 1985).

(5) **Part-objects in the transference.** Many aspects of the transference can be missed unless the whole of the material that is produced can be interpreted as an important light thrown on the transference, especially the unconscious elements: '. . . it does not carry us far enough if we realize that the analyst stands for the actual father or mother, unless we understand which aspect of the parents has been revived' (Klein, 1952, p. 54). In the deepest levels of the mind the infant experiences separate maternal functions – feeding, cleaning, holding, etc. – as if performed by separate objects [see PART-OBJECTS]; and in particular the good aspects of the mother (who feeds, for instance) and her bad aspects (she keeps the baby waiting in a state of desperation for his feed, for instance) are attributed to separate objects. Which function mother is or is not performing at any one moment is clarified in the transference. The analyst '. . . is not only standing for actual people in the patient's present and past, but also for the objects which the patient has internalized from the early days onwards' (Klein, 1943). The internalized parent has undergone distortion in the patient's mind through '. . . projection and idealization, and has often retained much of its phantastic nature' (Klein, 1952, p. 54).

It is because of this technique of taking every association in a patient's train of thought as referring unconsciously to the analyst that the Kleinians achieved their breakthrough with schizophrenics. Freud had thought schizophrenics unanalysable, which was why he tried to analyse Schreber from the published book of memoirs (Freud, 1911). Freud held this view because he was not in a position to understand the idea of split-off aspects of the transference. He did not really grasp the phenomenon of splitting until much later, and its importance in understanding schizophrenics was not developed by Klein until 1946 [see PSYCHOSIS].

(6) **The infant in the patient.** These ideas became more pointed when Bion (1959, 1962) distinguished normal from abnormal projective identification [see 13. PROJECTIVE IDENTIFICATION; CONTAINING] and showed that 'acting out' in the transference was related to the containing of infantile fears, and dependence. In its normal form projective identification has a communicative function at a non-symbolic level. This view of the transference drama enacted between mother and infant has drawn attention, in recent years, to the countertransference [see below and COUNTERTRANSFERENCE]. Through maternal understanding and containing, the infant, and the

patient, can accumulate experiences of being understood, and this, as Segal puts it, '. . . is a beginning of mental stability' (1975, p. 135). The maternal container model of therapeutic action makes a priority of understanding the infant in adult patients [see CHILD].

THERAPEUTIC EFFECTS. Klein justified her method by the remarkable effects it had in reducing anxiety – the dissolving of inhibitions of play, the reduction of immediate anxiety, and a change to a more positive relation with the analyst:

> I have again and again seen how rapidly the interpretations take effect . . . though there are numerous unmistakable indications of this effect; the development of play, the consolidation of the transference, the lessening of anxiety, etc., nevertheless for quite a long time the child does not consciously elaborate the interpretations . . . My impression is that the interpretation is at first only unconsciously assimilated. It is not till later that its relation to reality gradually penetrates the child's understanding . . . the first thing that happens in analysis is that the emotional relation with the parents improves; conscious understanding only comes when this has taken place. (Klein, 1926, p. 137)

She noticed that the *reactions* of the patient were more significant than his *conscious* responses. The unconscious meaning of the association that comes immediately after an interpretation is more important than any conscious agreement or argument.

Klein gradually came to formulate the therapeutic effects:

(i) the development of the subject's awareness of his psychic reality; and

(ii) balancing the currents of love and hate which run in him.

She expressed this in terms of the very first anxieties he suffers: '. . . my approach to the problem of terminating both child and adult analyses can be defined as follows: persecutory and depressive anxiety should be sufficiently reduced, and thus – in my view – presuppose the analysis of the first experiences of mourning' (Klein, 1950, p. 45). In terms of her later theories of the depressive and paranoid-schizoid positions, this meant the establishment of a more secure internal good object.

The mutative interpretation: Strachey (1934) was very influential in developing the theory that the therapeutic effect comes from the satisfactory internalization of a good object. Through splitting, the analyst may be one or other of two archaic figures – an exceptionally good figure, or a phantastically bad one. The introjection of the analyst in either of those forms would not result in therapeutic benefit. It would enhance the splitting of internal objects into these *exceptionally* and *unrealistically* good or bad forms.

He elaborated a theory of immediate interpretation of the *here-and-now* which took the analyst outside these transference distortions and enabled the patient to introject an image that was more realistic – a mixture of good and bad. Thus the analyst, through interpretation, becomes a moderating influence that can ameliorate the internal situation and mediate between the unrealistic, archaic internal objects through forming the basis of a new internal object: less archaic, more realistic. These interpretations are mutative.

His is, in effect, a theory of how the external object can come to modify the primary harshness of the superego – and Strachey refers, in fact, to the analyst as an 'auxiliary superego'. It is a structural model of intrapsychic change, as opposed to an economic model [see ECONOMIC MODEL].

Strachey's thinking was deeply embedded in the Kleinian framework of ideas and showed how extensively Klein had influenced the analysts of the British Psycho-Analytical Society. In effect his paper is a remarkable contribution towards systematizing Kleinian theory and is, in some respects, comparable to Klein's theory of the depressive position which she was thinking out at the same time. It is still regarded as an important cornerstone in the understanding of the therapeutic action of psychoanalysis (Rosenfeld, 1972; Etchegoyen, 1983).

Countertransference: The emphasis on the transference has gathered momentum over the years, and has been supplemented and enhanced by an increased understanding of the countertransference. Joseph (1985), in her account of the *total* transference situation, brought out the importance of the analyst's reactions to the patient – she even described in her paper the reactions that the members of a post-graduate seminar had to a patient reported to them!

Klein did not go along with this emphasis on countertransference, but the theory of countertransference nevertheless rests on her descriptions of the paranoid-schizoid position, and projective identification in particular. The analyst who is in contact with the patient will in most cases receive the projection of the patient's own experiences into himself; and then either experience the projected feelings of the patient in himself, or the results of his own defensiveness against such feelings. For instance, if the patient projects guilt the analyst may himself feel guilt, responsibility, inadequacy; or, because of his defensiveness, he may feel self-justifying and want to protest [see COUNTERTRANSFERENCE].

The analyst is in a position to have a 'first-hand' knowledge of his patient's experiences, albeit one which is easily clouded by his own defensive distortions:

Over the past fifty years, psychoanalysts have changed their view of their own method. It is now widely held that, instead of being about the patient's intrapsychic dynamics, interpretations should be about the *interaction* of patient and analyst *at an intrapsychic level*. (O'Shaughnessy, 1983, p. 281) [see COUNTERTRANSFERENCE]

The analytic situation of transference and countertransference is an interaction of separate intrapsychic processes through introjection and projection. The analyst in this sense has the function of accepting the patient's own experiences, and is thus more of an *auxiliary ego* (contrasting with Strachey's view, above, in which he described the newly internalized object, the internal analyst, as an auxiliary superego). This view had begun with Heimann (1950): 'My thesis is that the analyst's emotional response to his patient within the analytic situation represents one of the most important tools for the work . . . an instrument for research into the patient's unconscious' (p. 81). She argued against the analyst who believes he should remain stonily unmoved by his patient.

The analyst's mind is an element of the patient's environment, perhaps the most significant element:

The [analyst's] understanding of the roots of the anxiety will be rudimentary at the start, but the perception of the anxiety *per se* need not be rudimentary. It is through the willingness to contact the patient's anxieties, not to be overwhelmed by them, to work with them, that the analyst forges a working therapeutic relationship. (Jaques, 1982, p. 503)

The patient's mind seeks out a *containing function* in the analyst who, having experiences and working them through in his own mind, is the important aspect of the 'total situation'. So the analyst's mind, its capacities and its fallibilities, becomes in the analysis the crucial containing object which, if reintrojected by the patient into his own mind, forms an internal object that functions as the basis of mental stability [see CONTAINING]. An interpretation is mutative in so far as the analyst works, psychically, to contain *himself* as distinct from acting the role of one or other archaic figure (Elmhirst, 1978).

Normal and abnormal countertransference: Money-Kyrle (1956) and Bion (1959) formulated the clearest picture of the projective and introjective containing of the patient's experiences. Money-Kyrle (1956) elaborated Strachey's theory. Whereas Strachey looked at the problem of the patient's introjection of his analyst, and described the way in which the patient's projections assigned primitive aspects of the object to the analyst, Money-Kyrle described the situation from two intrapsychic points of view – the patient's and the analyst's. If the patient projects on to the analyst and then reintrojects the analyst as distorted by the projection, there is also the situation of the analyst who introjects the patient's projection and what he does with it inside him before returning it to the patient for reintrojection. In this normal process the analyst takes in what the patient says and, in the form of an interpretation, he or she calmly projects a modified version of the patient's communication [see MEMORY AND DESIRE]. The conversion of the patient's projection, while it resides inside the analyst, should, in normal circumstances, be in line with Strachey's view that the interpretation presents the analyst as neither of the polarized archaic objects ('good' or 'bad'). Money-Kyrle calls this *normal countertransference*. However, all is not so straightforward. 'Abnormal' uses of the analyst come about from impairment of the process, with mounting forcefulness of the projections into the analyst [see COUNTERTRANSFERENCE; LINKING].

There are situations when the process of introjection from the patient causes trouble for the analyst's mind, and then projection back to the patient gets stuck. The analyst may suffer prolonged states of holding on to an introjected patient, thinking about him after the session in a preoccupied way, etc.; or prolonged states of projection in which his own infantile self is attributed exaggeratedly to the patient. This then requires the psychoanalyst to resort to internal work to unstick the situation. He has in fact to work out what it is in him which is disturbed by what the patient projects into him [see COUNTERTRANSFERENCE].

Precautions!: Klein, like Freud, objected to this use of countertransference because it could be a licence for the analyst to project any of his feelings into the patient defensively, thus seeming to 'blame' the patient for 'putting your feelings into me'. It is important to remember this mistake (Finell, 1986). The analyst's own feelings are only a guide to the patient's experience. The difficulty the analyst must have in distinguishing his own unconscious investment in the setting means that he needs to check his own feelings by using the details of the patient's associations to *make sense of* his own experience with the patient.

In the same vein it is possible for the analyst to make interventions that sound like transference interpretations but in a mechanical manner, and:

> . . . relate all the material presented to him in a vague way to the transference such as 'You feel this about me now' or 'You are doing this to me' or they repeat the words of the patient parrot-like and relate them to the session. I think this stereotyped kind of interpretation, which is supposed to be an interpretation, of the here-and-now situation, changes Strachey's valuable contribution of the mutative interpretation into something absurd. (Rosenfeld, 1972, p. 457)

The patient experiences this mechanical form of interpreting as the analyst defending himself against the patient and the anxieties the patient is projecting.

Contemporary Kleinian technique: Kleinian technique today emphasizes (i) the immediate here-and-now situation, (ii) the total of all aspects of the setting, (iii) the importance of understanding the content of the anxiety, (iv) the consequence of interpreting the anxiety rather than the defences only (so-called deep interpretation). These fundamental principles come from the practice of child analysis and were reinforced by the analysis of schizophrenics in the 1940s and 1950s. At that time the realization of the importance of splitting and projective identification had a significant theoretical influence on the practice, enhancing the blunt and extensive use of words denoting part-objects (referred to as breast, penis, nipple, etc.). A change in the last two decades, based on the understanding of projective identification and of acting out in the transference [see ACTING-IN; PSYCHIC CHANGE], has focused instead on the way these processes in the analytic setting defend against the patient's experience of dependency and envy in the here-and-now (Spillius, 1983):

> Gradually, though rather unevenly, four trends of change emerge in . . . the 1960s and 1970s: (1) Destructiveness began to be interpreted in a more balanced way. (2) The immediate use of part-object language tended to be replaced by a more step-by-step approach to the bodily expressions of unconscious phantasy. (3) The concept of projective identification began to be used more directly in analysing the transference. (4) Arising from the third trend there has been increasing emphasis on acting out in the transference and on pressure being put on the analyst to join in. (Spillius, 1983, p. 325)

Classical technique and Kleinian technique: Klein's interest in anxiety drove her to make interpretations that described the early anxiety-situation [see 8. EARLY ANXIETY-SITUATIONS], and were therefore deep in the sense of trying to touch the anxiety underneath the defences. In contrast, classical technique, as developed in Vienna, was quite different. Here the technique was to identify the impulses as they were emerging into the preconscious as derivatives of the drives in the unconscious, to identify for the patient the immediate impulse – almost on the surface – that is struggling to *come through*; and to interpret the final defensiveness that resists its percolation through into consciousness. Thus classical analysts, in describing the most surface derivative of the instincts that is not yet quite conscious, believed they maintained a co-operation based on a positive transference (later termed the treatment alliance (Zetzel, 1956)); and prevented a damaging negative transference being stirred up through challenging the defences beyond a certain minimal level that can be controlled (see Fenichel, 1941). The classical method of interpreting from the surface and only cautiously moving deeper systematically through the layers of the mind is based on Freud's 'physiological' approach to mental energy [see LIBIDO; ECONOMIC MODEL]. For a clear summary of the divergence between the two techniques, see Payne (1946).

THE DEBATE WITH ANNA FREUD. In 1926 Anna Freud gave a series of lectures in Vienna on her experience of analysing children. The core of her lectures was a criticism of Klein's work and her play technique (Anna Freud, 1927). Although these criticisms were later mitigated somewhat, they form the basis of the deep gulf between the technique as described in this entry and the classical technique that has become adopted by the school of psychoanalysis known as ego-psychology [see EGO-PSYCHOLOGY].

In 1927, the year after Anna Freud's lectures, there was a symposium at the 10th Congress of Psycho-Analysis in Innsbruck, at which Anna Freud gave a brief summary of her lectures, and Klein (1927) gave a full rebuttal of Anna Freud's criticisms.

Anna Freud's early criticisms. Anna Freud made a number of specific criticisms, couched in uncompromising language. They conveyed that Klein was seriously at fault in the theoretical underpinning of her approach. These criticisms can be considered under several headings: (i) the preparatory phase; (ii) the changed analytic situation; (iii) the transference of children; and (iv) play and free association.

(a) The preparatory phase: Anna Freud started by pointing out that the child does not come to analysis of his own volition, but arrives because of others – family, school – who suffer because of his symptoms. The child starts without an understanding of what analysis is for and the analyst must engage the child's interest, showing how in one form or another the analyst may be of use to the little patient as an ally. She advocated a 'preparatory phase' to bind the child to the analyst in an emotional attachment of an affectionate kind. This argued against Klein's view of the importance of sticking with the prime psychoanalytic strategy of interpretation of the unconscious.

(b) The changed analytic situation: Anna Freud thought that the analyst can no longer present himself as a shadowy figure for the child patient but is a personality in his own right if the child is going to develop an affectionate bond: 'The analyst accordingly combines in his own person two difficult and diametrically opposed functions: he has to analyse and educate' (Anna Freud, 1927, p. 49). Since it was common practice at the time that the analyst had to present a blank screen in order not to interfere with the development of the patient's transfer-

ence, it seemed that a proper transference could not develop in a child analysis, and so a classical analytic technique of interpreting the transference resistances could not go on.

(c) The transference of children: According to the theory of transference at the time the child was still in the care of his primary objects (father or mother) and when the child still has exactly those objects, the primary ones, he or she will not transfer affects and impulses from those relationships to form 'a new edition' with the analyst. To develop a transference would entail taking the child away from home to a residential school of some kind. In fact such a step is adopted by, for instance, the Orthogenic School in Chicago established by Bettelheim for severely autistic children (Bettelheim, 1975; Sanders, 1985).

(d) Play and free association: Anna Freud particularly criticized Klein's view that the child's play is equivalent to the adult's free association. The child does not play for this purpose. She therefore regarded Klein's method of interpreting as wild because it lacked associations that could confirm the meanings of the play. In 1937 Waelder was still critical of Klein's technique, and he believed her findings resulted from faulty technique, a criticism repeated more recently by Greenson (1974).

Klein's rebuttals. Klein (1927) argued exhaustively against all these criticisms. There was a degree of impatience and sarcasm in the way she presented her evidence against Anna Freud:

> My experience has confirmed my belief that if I construe the dislike at once as anxiety and negative transference feeling and interpret it as such in connection with the material which the child at the same time produces and then trace it back to its original object, the mother, I can at once observe that the anxiety diminishes. This manifests itself in the beginning of a more positive transference and, with it, of more vigorous play . . . By resolving some part of the negative transference we shall then obtain, just as with adults, an increase in the positive transference and this, in accordance with the ambivalence of childhood, will soon in its turn be succeeded by a re-emerging of the negative (Klein, 1927, pp. 145–6)

She ruthlessly demonstrated Anna Freud's inconsistent manner of dealing with the negative transference.

> As far as I can understand from her [Anna Freud's] book . . . she tries by every means to bring about a positive transference, in order to fulfil the condition, which she regards as necessary for her work, of attaching the child to her personality . . . [But] we have another excellent and well-tried weapon which we use in an analogous

fashion to that in which we employ it in the analyses of adults . . . I
mean that we interpret. (Klein, 1927, pp. 145–6)

Klein claimed Anna Freud's method was nonanalytic, and went on to
make the ultimate accusation against another analyst: 'The examples
which Anna Freud gives do in fact show no analysis of the Oedipus
complex' (Klein, 1927, p. 141). The Oedipus complex being the core
of psychoanalytic theory and practice, Klein was claiming that Anna
Freud's technique could not be classed as psychoanalysis. Klein was
moved to this fierce retort because Anna Freud had claimed to be
more orthodox in her theoretical approach.

In brief, Klein's views on Anna Freud's approach can be summarized under the same headings:

(a) The preparatory phase: Klein contended that children do not need to
be coaxed or persuaded but will immediately understand (unconsciously) the benefits of analysis from the first interpretation. She
argued that the patient's unconscious sense of being understood
becomes his motivation.

(b) The changed analytic situation: Klein (1927) used detailed clinical
examples in an attempt to demonstrate that the setting does not have to
be changed from one based on the interpretation of the unconscious.
Interpretation of the negative transference (hostile feelings), while they
were being displayed, had quite astonishing results which enabled the
child to turn immediately to the analyst. She stuck to her claim that
there was no need to change the analytic situation from an
interpretative one to include teaching or to coax a positive attitude out
of the patient.

(c) The transference of children: Klein also produced clinical examples in
which the analyst, or the toys, are specially linked with, and represent,
the parents. The evidence that primary objects [see PART-OBJECTS]
are represented all the time in this way led her eventually to recognize
them as internal objects, constantly externalized on to external objects,
including the actual parents. *In practice*, whatever the theory, a
resolution of conflicts in the analytic transference resulted in a better
relationship with the parents. There is not, as Anna Freud supposed, a
conflict between analysis and home. Klein agreed that the analyst who
sets out to establish a particular relationship with the child cannot form
a transference. She and other English analysts commented wryly that
there is something self-contradictory about Anna Freud's deviation
from classical technique and then her complaint that she could not use
transference interpretations.

(d) Play and free association: Klein denied making wild interpretations
of the meaning of the symbols in play and claimed that she always had

evidence of the link between the figure in the play and the primary object before interpreting, though in her papers she frequently does not give the actual links that come out in the sessions.

The highly critical nature of these exchanges tended to polarize opinions on each of these points, entrenching either side in their own views.

Anna Freud's later technique. Anna Freud's 1926 lectures were not published in Britain until 1946, a fact which led to some bitterness and suspicion that the English were boycotting the Viennese. But by the time they were published Anna Freud's technique had changed somewhat – and in the direction of Klein's. She commented to this effect in the preface to the English edition of her book, and Klein rather triumphantly noted this in a later (1948) edition of her own 1927 paper. Geleerd (1963) also confirmed that the 'preparatory phase' was no longer required, and that much of the educative role was not necessary. She acknowledged that many of Klein's

> . . . criticisms of Anna Freud are valid today: e.g. the manipulative preparation of the child for child analysis as then proposed by Anna Freud is outdated. A systematic analysis of the defences and affects has taken its place. (Geleerd, 1963, p. 496)

Levels and depth. Nevertheless, Geleerd was profoundly critical of Klein's method of interpretation, in which the various levels were constantly muddled or chosen seemingly at random, since in classical technique the level of the active impulse – oral, anal or genital – must be discerned exactly [see LIBIDO].

Although Klein's early work was to make clear from extensive clinical evidence that the phases of libido (oral, anal or genital level) are not actually clear-cut, concern about the *level of interpretation* has remained constant [see 4. OEDIPUS COMPLEX]. Greenson (1974) was very critical of the claim by Kleinians (for instance Rosenfeld, 1965) that schizophrenics could be analysed without change in classical technique when Kleinian technique had seemingly abandoned classical technique altogether. This is reflected too in the repeatedly critical papers of Kernberg (for instance 1969, 1980). They were also scathing about interpretations which are considered deep because there is a danger that the patient will experience them as intrusive. It is not surprising, they claim, that Kleinians so frequently encounter persecutory anxiety in their patients – their interpretations provoke it. In response, Rosenfeld (1987) has tried to distinguish in clinical material those occasions when the patient is hurt by an incorrect interpretation from those paranoid responses that derive from other sources. He has also emphasized the important relief of paranoid feelings that correct 'deep' interpretation can give.

The nature of play. Because Anna Freud was critical of Klein's assumption of the equivalence of play and free association, Klein began a long-term interest in the nature of symbolization. She constantly returned to the importance of externalization as symbolizing the content of anxious phantasies and as a form of turning to new objects [see SYMBOL-FORMATION]. In contrast Viennese analysts, supportive of Anna Freud, regarded play as a more innocent activity; although Waelder (1933), after Freud (1920), regarded play as a repetition, in which a painful situation or incident is replayed constantly for the purpose of coming to terms with the trauma; the anxiety-situation is controlled by switching the roles around so that the subject is no longer passive but in the active role. Anna Freud (1936) later adopted the term 'identification with the aggressor' [see also 13. PROJECTIVE IDENTIFICATION] for that process. Thus play is to change the ending into a pleasurable outcome instead of a painful one. The crucial difference was that for Klein the externalization of phantasy is a defensive manoeuvre, whereas in classical psychoanalysis phantasy is used for working through the trauma [see PSYCHO-LOGICAL DEFENCE].

CONCLUSIONS. By temperament Klein bolstered her views, when she felt under attack, by resort to her observations in the clinical situation rather than engaging in theoretical elucidation. She was assisted in this by being naturally a very astute clinical observer and by the good fortune of stumbling upon a powerful technique for working with children. Her technique was an immense asset in supporting her views, but it was also a burden as she moved into a completely new field of work while so junior. Inevitably this brought her up against the views of many of her seniors. Klein was never shy to have an opinion of her own, and this led to much affront, bitterness and pain in her professional career, for herself and for those who worked as colleagues (Grosskurth, 1986). There is a noticeable difference in the writings of Anna Freud and those of Melanie Klein. The former approached her work with children on the basis of the theory of child development at the time, whilst Klein more simply observed clinical situations and the effect of her interpretations.

The power of Klein's original technique for psychoanalysis with children gave impetus to all the later developments in her theory, and to her technique of psychoanalysis with adults. Kleinian writings continue to reflect the clinical emphasis; very few papers are published without detailed case reports to substantiate their point.

Abraham, Karl (1919) 'A particular form of neurotic resistance against the psychoanalytic method', in Karl Abraham (1927) *Selected Papers on Psycho-Analysis*. Hogarth, pp. 303–11.

Bettelheim, Bruno (1975) *Home for the Heart*. Thames & Hudson.

Bion, Wilfred R. (1959) 'Attacks on linking', *Int. J. Psycho-Anal.* 40:308–15; republished (1967) in W. R. Bion, *Second Thoughts*, Heinemann, pp. 93–109.

—— (1962) *Learning from Experience*. Heinemann.

Brenman, Eric (1985) 'Cruelty and narrow-mindedness', *Int. J. Psycho-Anal.* 66:273–81.

Brenman Pick, Irma (1985) 'Working through in the counter-transference', *Int. J. Psycho-Anal.* 66:157–66.

Elmhirst, Susanna Isaacs (1978) 'Time and the pre-verbal transference', *Int. J. Psycho-Anal.* 59:173–80.

Etchegoyen, Horatio (1983) 'Fifty years after the mutative interpretation', *Int. J. Psycho-Anal.* 64:445–59.

Fenichel, Otto (1941) *The Psycho-Analytic Theory of the Neuroses*. New York: Norton.

Finell, Janet (1986) 'The merits and problems with the concept of projective identification', *Psychoanal. Rev.* 73:103–20.

Freud, Anna (1927) *The Psycho-Analytic Treatment of Children*, English edn, 1946. Imago.

—— (1936) *The Ego and the Mechanisms of Defence*. Hogarth.

Freud, Sigmund (1909) 'Analysis of a phobia in a five-year-old boy', in James Strachey, ed. *The Standard Edition of the Complete Psychological Works of Sigmund Freud*, 24 vols. Hogarth, 1953–73. vol. 10, pp. 1–149.

—— (1911) 'Psycho-analytic notes on an autobiographical account of a case of paranoia'. *S.E.* 12, pp. 1–82.

—— (1914) 'On narcissism'. *S.E.* 14, pp. 67–102.

—— (1916) 'Some characters met with in psycho-analytic work: III Criminals from a sense of guilt'. *S.E.* 14, pp. 332–3.

—— (1919) 'Lines of advance in psycho-analytic therapy'. *S.E.* 17, pp. 157–68.

—— (1920) *Beyond the Pleasure Principle*. *S.E.* 18, pp. 1–64.

—— (1926) *Inhibitions, Symptoms and Anxiety*. *S.E.* 20, pp. 77–175.

Gedo, John (1986) *Conceptual Issues in Psycho-Analysis*. New York: Analytic Press.

Geleerd, Elisabeth R. (1963) 'Evaluation of Melanie Klein's *Narrative of a Child Analysis*', *Int. J. Psycho-Anal.* 44:493–506.

Greenson, Ralph (1974) 'Transference: Freud or Klein?', *Int. J. Psycho-Anal.* 55:37–48.

Grosskurth, Phyllis (1986) *Melanie Klein*. Hodder & Stoughton.

Heimann, Paula (1950) 'On counter-transference', *Int. J. Psycho-Anal.* 31:81–4.

Hoffer, Willi (1945) 'Psycho-analytic education', *Psychoanal. Study Child* 1:293–307.

Hug-Hellmuth, Hermine (1921) 'On the technique of child analysis', *Int. J. Psycho-Anal.* 2:287–305.

Isaacs, Susan (1939) 'Criteria for interpretation', *Int. J. Psycho-Anal.* 20:148–60.

Jaques, Elliott (1982) 'Review of *The Work of Hanna Segal*', *Int. J. Psycho-Anal.* 63:502–4.

Joseph, Betty (1975) 'The patient who is difficult to reach', in Peter Giovacchini, ed. *Tactics and Techniques in Psycho-Analytic Therapy*, vol. 2. New York: Jason Aronson, pp. 205–16.

—— (1985) 'Transference: the total situation', *Int. J. Psycho-Anal.* 66:447–54.

Kernberg, Otto (1969) 'A contribution to the ego-psychology critique of the Kleinian school', *Int. J. Psycho-Anal.* 50:317–33.

—— (1980) *Internal World and External Reality*. New York: Jason Aronson.

Klein, Melanie (1920) 'The development of a child', in *The Writings of Melanie Klein*, vol. 1. Hogarth, pp. 1–53.

—— (1926) 'The psychological principles of early analysis', *The Writings of Melanie Klein*, vol. 1. Hogarth, pp. 128–38.

—— (1927) 'Symposium on child analysis', *The Writings of Melanie Klein*, vol. 1. Hogarth, pp. 139–69.

—— (1932) *The Psycho-Analysis of Children*, *The Writings of Melanie Klein*, vol. 2. Hogarth.

—— (1943) 'Psycho-analytic technique', paper presented to the Training Committee, Institute of Psycho-Analysis, London (unpublished).

—— (1950) 'On the criteria for the termination of a psychoanalysis', *The Writings of Melanie Klein*, vol. 3. Hogarth, pp. 43–7.

—— (1952) 'The origins of transference', *The Writings of Melanie Klein*, vol. 3. Hogarth, pp. 48–56.

—— (1955) 'The psycho-analytic play technique: its history and significance', *The Writings of Melanie Klein*, vol. 3. Hogarth, pp. 122–40.

Money-Kyrle, Roger (1956) 'Normal counter-transference and some of its deviations', *Int. J. Psycho-Anal.* 37:360–9; republished (1978) in *The Collected Papers of Roger Money-Kyrle*. Perth: Clunie, pp. 330–42.

O'Shaughnessy, Edna (1981) 'A clinical study of a defence organization', *Int. J. Psycho-Anal.* 62:359–69.

—— (1983) 'On words and working through', *Int. J. Psycho-Anal.* 64:281–9.

Payne, Sylvia (1946) 'The theory and practice of psycho-analytical techniques', *Int. J. Psycho-Anal.* 27:12–19.

Petot, Jean-Michel (1979) *Melanie Klein: Premières Découvertes et premier système 1919–1932*. Paris: Bourdas/Dunod.

Pfister, Oscar (1922) *Psycho-Analysis in the Service of Education*. George Allen & Unwin.

Riesenberg-Malcolm, Ruth (1981) 'Technical problems in the analysis of a pseudo-compliant patient', *Int. J. Psycho-Anal.* 62:477–84.

Riviere, Joan (1952) 'General introduction', in Melanie Klein, Paula Heimann and Joan Riviere, eds *Developments in Psycho-Analysis*. Hogarth, pp. 1–36.

Rosenfeld, Herbert (1947) 'Analysis of a schizophrenic state with depersonalization', *Int. J. Psycho-Anal.* 28:130–9; republished (1965) in Herbert Rosenfeld, *Psychotic States*. Hogarth, pp. 13–33.

—— (1965) *Psychotic States*. Hogarth.

—— (1972) 'A critical appreciation of James Strachey's paper on the nature of the therapeutic action of psycho-analysis', *Int. J. Psycho-Anal.* 53:455–61.

—— (1987) *Impasse and Interpretation*. Hogarth.

Sanders, Jacqui (1985) 'The Sonia Shankman Orthogenic School', *Int. J. Therapeutic Communities* 6:181–9.

Searl, Mina (1929) 'The flight to reality', *Int. J. Psycho-Anal.* 10:280–91.

Segal, Hanna (1972) 'The role of child analysis in the general psycho-analytic training', *Int. J. Psycho-Anal.* 53:157–61.

—— (1975) 'A psycho-analytic approach to the treatment of schizophrenia', in Malcolm Lader, ed. *Studies in Schizophrenia.* Ashford: Headley Brothers, pp. 94–7.

Spillius, Elizabeth Bott (1983) 'Some developments from the work of Melanie Klein', *Int. J. Psycho-Anal.* 64:321–32.

Strachey, James (1934) 'The nature of the therapeutic action of psycho-analysis', *Int. J. Psycho-Anal.* 15:127–59; republished (1969) *Int. J. Psycho-Anal.* 40:275–92.

—— (1937) 'The theory of the therapeutic results of psycho-analysis', *Int. J. Psycho-Anal.* 18:139–45.

Waelder, Robert (1933) 'The psycho-analytic theory of play', *Psychoanal. Q.* 2:208–24.

—— (1937) 'The problem of the genesis of psychical conflict in earliest infancy', *Int. J. Psycho-Anal.* 18:406–73.

Winnicott, Donald (1971) *Playing and Reality.* Tavistock.

Young-Bruehl, Elisabeth (1989) *Anna Freud.* Macmillan.

Zetzel, Elisabeth (1956) 'Current concepts of transference', *Int. J. Psycho-Anal.* 37:369–76.

2 UNCONSCIOUS PHANTASY

DEFINITION. Unconscious phantasies underlie every mental process, and accompany all mental activity. They are the mental representation of those somatic events in the body which comprise the instincts, and are physical sensations interpreted as relationships with objects that cause those sensations. Erupting from their biological instigation, unconscious phantasies are slowly converted in two ways: (i) by change through the development of the organs for distance perception of external reality; and (ii) by emergence into the symbolic world of culture from the primary world of the body. Phantasies can be elaborated for the alleviation of internal states of mind by either manipulation of the body and its sensations (masturbation phantasies), or direct phantasizing. Phantasy is the mental expression of the instinctual impulses and also of defence mechanisms against instinctual impulses.

CHRONOLOGY
1920 Conscious phantasy and sexual curiosity (Klein, Melanie, 1920, 'The development of a child').
1921 Pregenital phantasies (Klein, Melanie, 1923, 'The role of the school in the libidinal development of the child').
1925 Masturbation phantasies (Klein, Melanie, 1925, 'A contribution to the psychogenesis of tics').
1948 Instinct and phantasy (Isaacs, Susan, 1948, 'The nature and function of phantasy').

The idea of phantasy as an unconscious activity was present for Klein from the beginning of her work. By taking an interest in the *content* of anxiety she inevitably put play phantasies to the fore. The importance of phantasy in Klein's thinking was reinforced by two factors:

(1) The extraordinary proclivity in children to produce phantasies in their play, and especially their worried construction of sexual theories about the relationships between their own organs and their parents [see 3. AGGRESSION]. Klein was impressed at this form of narrative thinking with objects, and she challenged the theory of primary narcissism. Ferenczi (1921) discovered in the psychological symptom of tic clinical evidence of primary narcissism. The motor activity in the tic was simply a discharge of psychic energy. In contrast, Klein (1925) set out to show that even with this prototype of the objectless impulse, there were underlying phantasies in the unconscious part of the children's minds [see NARCISSISM].

(2) The striking effects that interpretation had on the production of

phantasies [see 1. TECHNIQUE]. Klein was bewildered by the scale of phantasy-production after the freeing of inhibition, but she was astute enough to realize that a release of phantasy and a relaxing into a more positive attitude to the analyst were crucial therapeutic indicators and denoted an important marker of a healthily functioning mind. This basic clinical importance of unconscious phantasy has remained unchanged all through Kleinian thought.

There have, however, been several steps in understanding its theoretical importance: (I) phantasy activity in the pregenital phases and, in fact, from birth; (II) phantasy as the mental representation of biological instincts; (III) unconscious phantasy and defences; (IV) the distinction from Freud's classical theory of fantasy (phantasy and reality); and (V) the developmental role of unconscious phantasy.

I EARLY PHANTASY ACTIVITY. In support of Freud's (1914) paper on narcissism, Abraham (1921) and Ferenczi (1921) both described psychoanalytic cases of tic in which no sexual object was connected with the motor discharge. The tic was therefore a simple substitute for masturbation. Libidinal impulses are simply discharged and satisfied. The notion of a phase of primary narcissism or autoerotism in which there is no relationship with objects as such was confirmed.

The array of phantasy production elicited by the new play technique impressed Klein by this form of narrative thinking with objects, and she challenged the theory of primary narcissism. She showed that even with tic, the apparent prototype of the objectless impulse, there were underlying phantasies in the unconscious part of the children's minds (Klein, 1925). She found that she could interpret phantasy activities that were symbolically represented in the tic: phantasies of doing something to objects, or passively having things done to the subject. These phantasies which accompanied the involuntary action of the tic were described as masturbation phantasies [see MASTURBATION PHANTASIES] and were *unconscious*, though the term 'unconscious phantasy' appears almost to be a contradiction. Such phantasies (denoted in the literature by spelling with a 'ph-' rather than an 'f-') are evidenced through derivatives of one kind or another, just like the unconscious itself. They are known by inference on the basis of clinical evidence.

Pregenital phantasies: Adding to this confidence was the fact that the children Klein was analysing had oral and anal phantasies about intercourse. Such pregenital phantasies are not explained in Freud's theory of primary narcissism, in which there are no true others (objects) until the genital phase. Such phantasies, expressing horrific sadistic impulses from pregenital sources, are evidence against primary narcissism.

II INSTINCT AND UNCONSCIOUS PHANTASY. Isaacs formulated the concept of unconscious phantasy most clearly on behalf of the Kleinian Group in 1943, in a paper designed to crystallize the controversies between Klein's views and the classical psychoanalysts from Vienna. She stated the kernel of her paper as 'Phantasy is the primary content of unconscious mental processes' (Isaacs, 1948, p. 82). This is a far-reaching idea: all mental activity takes place on the basis of phantasied relations with objects, including the activity of perception, phantasied as a concrete incorporation through the perceptual apparatus, and thoughts as objects [see BION]. Unconscious phantasy, being the mental representation of instinctual impulses, is the nearest psychological phenomenon to the biological nature of the human being.

Primary phantasies: Innate, instinctually derived phantasies are primarily unconscious. They include knowledge of the nipple and the mouth, innately conceived by the newborn for sucking. Isaacs deals with a common objection:

> It has sometimes been suggested that unconscious phantasies such as that of 'tearing to bits' would not arise in the child's mind before he had gained the conscious knowledge that tearing a person to bits would mean killing him or her. Such a view does not meet the case. It overlooks the fact that such knowledge is *inherent* in bodily impulses as a vehicle of instinct, in the *aim* of instinct, in the excitation of the organ, i.e. in this case, the mouth. (Isaacs, 1948, pp. 93–4) [see INNATE KNOWLEDGE]

Somatic origins: The unconscious is made up of relationships with objects. An unconscious phantasy is a belief in the activity of concretely felt 'internal' objects [see 5. INTERNAL OBJECTS]. This is a difficult concept to grasp. A somatic sensation tugs along with it a mental experience that is interpreted as a relationship with an object that wishes to cause that sensation, and is loved or hated by the subject according to whether the object is well-meaning or has evil intentions (i.e. a pleasant or unpleasant sensation). Thus an unpleasant sensation is mentally represented as a relationship with a 'bad' object that intends to hurt and damage the subject. For instance, a baby that is hungry will, let us say, experience unpleasant feelings of hunger in his stomach. This is mentally represented by the baby feeling a malevolently motivated object actually concretely in his tummy that wants to cause him the discomfort of hunger there. When we say colloquially, 'Hunger is gnawing at my stomach', we revert to this primitive animistic and concrete form of experiencing, though we do not suspend our knowledge that the hunger is something to do with our physiology. The baby does not have this sophisticated knowledge but is absorbed in primitive interpretations of his reality [see INTERNAL REALITY]. Conversely, when he is fed, the infant's experience is of an object, which *we* can identify as mother, or her milk, but which *the infant* identifies as an object in his tummy benevolently motivated to cause pleasant sensations there. After feeding, the full sensations contribute to the blissful phantasy in which a wonderful benevolent object resides inside his tummy.

Reflexes and phantasies: When we see that in the first instances of life the baby can be made to turn his head and suck if his cheek is touched, we can think of this as a biological endowment: instinctual, and probably a reflex based on the early neuronal link-ups in his little nervous system. However, we can ask the question whether he also *experiences* this incident as one that involves the skin of his cheek, his lips and an object that comes in contact with them. If so, what sort of experience is he having? In this way the biological and the psychological are both united in one incident, although they are distinguishable conceptually. Isaacs describes this as a '. . . single undifferentiated experience of sucking and phantasying' (Isaacs, 1948, p. 92n).

The baby's rising crescendo of rage and fear as his hunger goes unsatisfied derives, of course, from instinctual responses, but he experiences it in his own way as the rising threat of an increasingly hostile persecutor successfully attacking his tummy and making the pain worse and worse. This is a fearful situation, and babies appear to have the capacity to feel fear and rage from the start. It is this belief that there is something inside the tummy that is malevolently attempting to damage and destroy that is the content of the rage. These fearful phantasies are the nearest to a direct manifestation of the death instinct, experienced as deflected on to an object [see DEATH INSTINCT].

III UNCONSCIOUS PHANTASIES AND DEFENCES

Elaborated phantasy: The infant, right from the start, is beset by these situations in which he fears being damaged by something right inside him. As a result he will try to take some steps to avoid this damage and this situation. There is not much he can do, and mostly he is dependent on mother to relieve the situation by presenting herself as the equally phantastical 'good' object [see 5. INTERNAL OBJECTS]. However, there are certain phantasies that the infant can use – phantasies that can function, as it were, as a defence [see PSYCHO-LOGICAL DEFENCE; 9. PRIMITIVE DEFENCE MECHANISMS]. Segal (1964) has pointed out that phantasy is not only the mental representation of an instinct, but can be elaborated to represent defensive actions against anxiety [see 8. EARLY ANXIETY-SITUATIONS]. The infant's unconscious phantasy is linked with bodily sensations, but through bodily sensations and through manipulating bodily sensations he can come to stimulate his phantasy world into more tolerable situations. The externalization of the 'bad' object [see PROJECTION] and the internalization of the 'good' object [see INTROJECTION] are the prototype defence mechanisms and relate to processes in which substances pass through the ego-boundaries. For example, the expulsion of excrements gives rise to sensations in the anus and the urethra which are interpreted as objects passing out of the internal world into the external. Later, phantasy comes to be less connected with bodily sensations as, with the depressive position, the internal world comes to be populated more with symbolic, rather than concretely actual, objects [see 10. DEPRESSIVE POSITION]. However, remnants of the primitive concrete objects survive and are occasionally experienced as somatizations and psychosomatic conditions. Anxiety is still expressed, and even experienced, as 'butterflies in the stomach', or sadness as 'a lump in the throat'.

A rather complex arrangement has arisen in which primary instinctual impulses and defence mechanisms are represented by similar phantasies in the unconscious [see PSYCHOLOGICAL DEFENCE; 9. PRIMITIVE DEFENCE MECHANISMS].

IV UNCONSCIOUS PHANTASY AND FREUD'S THEORY OF FANTASY. Freud had previously described hallucinatory wish-fulfilment as the mental activity of the infant in frustration. Klein modified this and claimed that it was an incessant accompaniment of the child's activity at all times. So Klein's theory of unconscious phantasy radically extended Freud's, or – as Glover (1945) bitterly remarked – deposed it. Freud held that fantasies were substitute gratifications when instinctual impulses did not find satisfaction. When frustration and tension build up, the energy is discharged back towards the memory and the perceptual apparatus rather than into muscular discharge and action. Thus fantasy came into play only when gratification was suspended – a much more restricted view than Klein's.

From a very early point in her work, Klein described extraordinary phantasy life that was actually an accompaniment of reality-orientated behaviour. Symbolic elements of play and enactment expressed all kinds of relations between all kinds of objects and people:

> For Fritz when he was writing, the lines meant roads and the letters rode on motor-bicycles – on the pen – upon them. For instance, 'i' and 'e' ride together on a motor-bicycle that is usually driven by 'i'

and they love one another with a tenderness quite unknown in the real world. Because they always ride together they become so alike that there is hardly any difference between them, for the beginning and the end of 'i' and 'e' are the same, only in the middle the 'i' has a little stroke and the 'e' has a little hole. (Klein, 1923, p. 64)

These phantasies of the male and female genitals together in love are simply part of the experience of being at school. Of course, especially fearful phantasies at school could lead to a disturbance of learning because of the fear. In a case report, Isaacs (1943b) stressed '. . . how intimately external and internal reality are intertwined in the symptoms, the developmental history and the analytic responses' (p. 31). In their notion of unconscious phantasy, Klein and her followers claimed to respect Freud's concept of the unconscious by adding to and elaborating it.

Unconscious phantasies, being ubiquitous, are a completely different category of events. The distinction in the views on phantasy is a radical one, upon which each analyst has to decide. On the one hand there is the view of orthodox psychoanalysis that there is *either* reality *or* phantasy; on the other there is the view that unconscious phantasy accompanies all experience of reality. All through Klein's work, as well as that of her colleagues, the investigation has been into the way in which internal unconscious phantasy penetrates and gives meaning to 'actual events' in the external world; and at the same time, the way the external world brings meaning in the form of unconscious phantasies.

Freud's seduction theory: The seduction theory was an attempt to put into physiological form the abnormality of a psychological neurosis (Freud, 1896). A trauma in childhood caused a *physical* trauma to part of the electrical circuitry of the brain, with an ensuing build-up of tensions. Freud's replacement of this theory by one in which the trauma resulted from an *imagined* (distorted) event introduced the notion of unconscious phantasy. It is the child's phantasy of a seduction that is the disturbing trauma, not the actual physical event to his/her body. (Freud's idea of some physical interference with the electro-circuitry of the brain has survived in general psychiatry in the form of electrical and other physical treatments even though psychoanalysis has now dropped this (Caper, 1988).)

Phantasy or reality: The recent controversy instigated by Masson (1984) is based on a claim that Freud actually suppressed his theory of a physical seduction leading to a neurological trauma. The implication is that the 'actual event' should be rescued from oblivion. The either/or nature of the problem (either actual seduction or phantasy), which originally expressed the conflict between physiology and psychology, has migrated to a conflict between external reality and the internal world (in fact sociology versus psychology) [see MIND–BODY PROBLEM; SUBJECTIVITY], with the idea of a subtle interpenetration of external and internal worlds.

V UNCONSCIOUS PHANTASY AND DEVELOPMENT. One further confusing problem is that certain mechanisms, especially introjection and identification, result in the accretion to the ego of new skills and attributes. Like all other mental processes, these introjections and identifications are also represented by phantasies, incorporation and assimilation, which underlie defence mechanisms and primitive oral impulses. Unconscious phantasies about incorporation or expulsion therefore have an influence on the experience of what the subject contains, and what he or she identifies with and actually becomes like. In this sense the phantasy is felt to be actual reality and in fact its effects are real enough. Unconscious phantasy in this sense is *omnipotent* [see OMNIPOTENCE].

The philosophical problem of how a biological entity can transform from a world of bodily gratifications and needs to a world of symbolic gratifications and meanings remains unsolved [see MIND–BODY PROBLEM]. The key position of unconscious phantasy on the borderline between the physiological instinct and the psychological representation has led Kleinians to search with confidence for greater understanding of symbols in their clinical work [see SYMBOL-FORMATION]. Phantasies *about* the bodily contents stand for the actual primary bodily sensations. Subsequently, the infant emerges into the social world of symbols in which phantasies are composed of non-bodily and non-material objects [see SYMBOL-FORMATION]. The movement from a concretely felt experience of an object, constructed in unconscious phantasy, to a non-physical symbolic object is a major developmental step; it represents giving up the idiosyncratic and innate forms of representation by means of unconscious phantasy, and investing such meanings in socially offered objects (symbols).

This movement involves another change: from omnipotence of phantasy to a recognition of the object as separate and different from the thing symbolized (Segal, 1957) [see SYMBOLIC EQUATION].

Susan Isaacs, with her academic background and her formidable capacity for intellectual debate, dealt with *the nature of* unconscious phantasy. She showed that it was the basis for a completely new view of the nature of mind – as a small society of relationships with objects. Being closely connected with the biological nature of man, unconscious phantasy provides a clinically workable bridge to the mind–body problem [see MIND–BODY PROBLEM].

THE CONTROVERSIAL DISCUSSIONS 1943–4. No other topic occupied more time – and generated more heat – in the Controversial Discussions of the British Psycho-Analytical Society than 'unconscious phantasy' [see CONTROVERSIAL DISCUSSIONS]. The first set of five discussions were in response to a paper by Susan Isaacs, 'The nature and function of phantasy' (later published, 1948). This was a clear statement of the concept, supported heavily by quotations from Freud and some interesting comments trawled from Anna Freud's recent writing which, it was claimed, had moved towards the Kleinian position following the earlier controversy (1926–7) over child analysis [see 1. TECHNIQUE; CHILD ANALYSIS].

A number of issues emerged from the emotional heat, and they will be summarized under seven headings: (1) the method of inference; (2) primary narcissism; (3) sophistication in the first year of life; (4) secondary process; (5) confusion of terms; (6) concepts and phantasies; (7) regression.

(1) **The method of inference.** One of the arguments used against Klein was that there was no method of investigating or checking the existence of phantasies in the first year of life – or from the beginning of life, as Klein held (Waelder, 1937). Isaacs gave detailed accounts of the current psychological research on the first year of life, emphasizing especially the work of Middlemore (1941). It demonstrated, she claimed, that signs of anxiety and distress in the newborn were more varied and more frequent than signs of pleasure or contentment. The latter occurred only after feeding. She claimed that these proportions changed after some three to four months, indicating a change from the paranoid phase into the depressive position as love for the object becomes more mobilized. The observations were challenged on several grounds: (i) that the proportions of anxious moments versus contented moments were incorrect, and that since the major amount of time in the first few months is occupied in feeding, the contented times outweigh the anxious ones; (ii) these direct observations of feeling states in infants cannot be corroborated by psychoanalysis, a method applicable only to much older children. Isaacs's reply (developed fully in the published version of her paper in 1948) was that all scientific knowledge was inferential and that inference was a method valid enough in Freud's descriptions of children's development. She made a plea that psychoanalytic conclusions can and need to be tested against direct observation of infants.

There has continued to be a profound doubt about the method by which Kleinians acquire their theories, with the suspicion that the method of deep interpretation itself creates artefacts in the observations.

(2) **Primary narcissism.** According to orthodox analysts, the first years of life are occupied by autoerotic and narcissistic gratification in which any object is merely an instrument for instinctual satisfaction. There is only 'pleasure without meaning'. Object-love does not appear until the third to fifth year, and only then can there be phantasies of relations to objects: 'Phantasy as the imaginal corollary of instinct takes the place of the sensorial corollary (pleasure pain)' (A. Freud, 1943), a view which follows in orthodox manner from Freud's own view that the qualities of pain or pleasure were all the infant can appreciate, and there is no capacity for imagining the sources that give pain or pleasure. Barbara Lantos (1943), contesting Isaacs's descriptions of her evidence of unconscious phantasy in the first year of the infant's life, said:

> The fact that he [the infant] is able to recognize persons, that he is aware of their coming or going and afraid of their loss and that he reacts accordingly, is in our opinion bound up with the development of the sensory and mental apparatus without suggesting the existence of phantasies.

The dispute here seemed to revolve around the distinction between mere perceptual and mnemic registering of objects on the one hand and the ability to conceive of wished-for activities with or by them. This issue then became a debate over the time at which the infant makes connections between these perceived and remembered images and the emotional recognition of them as loved or hated sources of pleasure or pain.

(3) **Sophistication in the first year of life.** There was much dispute about the age at which a function as sophisticated as phantasying starts.

Retrospective sophistication: It was argued, against Isaacs's view, that because children at an older age do have these phantasies, the Oedipus complex has been affected by a regression. The child of three or four who is occupied with anxieties about the parents' relation and under the pressure of frustration regresses to oral desires and impulses, which then colour his theories of what his parents are doing together. This is a form of 'retrospective sophistication'. It was one of the bitterest arguments against Klein's view of phantasy in the first year of life. Waelder (1937) ground the point home with the comment: '. . . this argument seems to me no more convincing than it would be to insist that Shakespeare's *Hamlet* or *Lear* must have already existed in his mind in childhood' (p. 429). However, Ernest Jones (1943) responded scathingly:

> A regression backwards into the blue has no meaning for me. Thus when Waelder talks of extraordinary cannibalistic phantasies being

familiar at the age of three or four, but ascribes them to regression, this conveys nothing at all to me if it does not mean a re-animating of corresponding oral phantasies at the age of say six months; why a child of four should suddenly be seized for the first time with the desire to eat breasts passes my comprehension.

His point is that regression to oral phantasies of this kind implies oral phantasies at the oral phase to regress back to.

Cognitive sophistication: It was argued that the phantasies of biting into bits, killing, drowning the mother and so on are far too sophisticated for the mind of an infant in the first year. The infant cannot possibly know what killing and dying mean at that age. Isaacs (1948) took great pains to describe the primitiveness of the phantasies – nonverbal, nonvisual, a somatically experienced phantasy – and she claimed that there is a phylogenetically endowed knowledge. By this she meant that in the make-up of the body and its impulses there is already an inherent or innate knowledge – bodily sensations are a form of *postulating in the form of action* [see INNATE KNOWLEDGE].

Following the furious debates in the 1940s, the issue of the infant's capacity for cognitive sophistication has remained restricted to academic psychologists and a good deal of academic research into infant psychology has accumulated (Trevarthen, 1980; Chamberlain, 1987). The processes that Trevarthen calls 'primary intersubjectivity' do suggest that there is a very early sophistication in relations with objects, which goes against the detractors of Klein. The research also suggests that there is a very good reality sense of the emotional context of the infant–mother relationships, which tends to go against Klein's descriptions of the almost solipsistic relations with phantasy objects. The evidence is that infants are actually more sophisticated than either Klein or her Viennese critics claim. Lichtenberg (1983) and Stern (1985) have begun to survey this literature for its psychoanalytic implications.

(4) Secondary process. Orthodox psychoanalysts define the mental activity of the unconscious as primary-process – that is, a process depending on condensation and displacement, as in the logic and symbolism of dreams. They claim that the Kleinian concept of unconscious phantasy showed signs of negation, a conception of time, and an interaction of impulses – all qualities of secondary-process mental activity, which is not supposed to occur in the unconscious, or certainly not in the first year of life. Anna Freud argued against an integrated 'early pleasure ego' that appeared to be implied in the theory of unconscious phantasy which must presuppose an ego to have the phantasies. In contention, Isaacs quoted passages of Freud suggestive of her point of view that a psychic apparatus possessing only a primary process is a fiction (Freud, 1900) and that some organization of functioning of the unconscious exists. She claimed that to allow oral wishes in the first year with conscious memory of the experiences, as Anna Freud had described in her writings, but to deny the function of phantasy was theoretically inconsistent. This debate seems to boil down to a somewhat sterile dispute over what Freud really said, extended to what Freud really meant.

(5) **Confusion of terms.** There was a good deal of concern that the precision of established psychoanalytic terminology was being eroded – for instance Anna Freud's criticism, described above, over primary process and the nature of the unconscious. Glover (1945) dismissed the theory of unconscious phantasy because it conflated more or less all known psychoanalytic terms into one, thus reducing psychoanalytic theory to nothing. What gets lost, he believed, includes the concepts of the progression of the libidinal phases, regression and fixation, and the Oedipus complex.

Marjorie Brierley was also concerned. Although she agreed that Isaacs's argument on the basis of genetic continuity was a cogent one, extending the term phantasy to cover all aspects of mental activity in the past and as underlying all mental activity of patients in the present obscured important distinctions between early stages and later ones – between, for instance, the early stages of the Oedipus complex and the later ones [see 4. OEDIPUS COMPLEX].

Isaacs challenged this by saying that the discovery of factors which are important in the development of a particular psychic state or organization, such as the Oedipus complex, do not diminish the importance of the concept of the Oedipus complex; indeed, they enhance the understanding of it. For instance, she said, Klein had greatly increased the importance of the Oedipus complex by showing that its influence was earlier and that important aspects of the pregenital infant were related to the Oedipus complex.

(6) **Concepts and phantasies.** Glover described what he called Klein's 'addiction . . . to a sort of psychic anthropomorphism . . . namely of confusing concepts of the psychic apparatus with psychic mechanisms' (Glover, 1943). If the mechanisms of introjection and projection are also made to convey the meaning of phantasies (of incorporation and expulsion) then there is a conflation of objective observation with the subjective experience of the patient.

Brierley was also concerned with the elision of experiences with concepts and argued strongly for keeping 'the description of experience as lived distinct from the description, inferred from experience, of the objective conditioning of experience' (Brierley, 1943). This debate, though only touched upon in the Controversial Discussions, has deep ramifications in the philosophy of science and the special position of those sciences which concern human subjects as opposed to inanimate objects. Heimann (1943), for instance, pointed out that the kind of work a psychoanalyst is engaged in is a special case; it is an objective science of the subjective [see SUBJECTIVITY].

Brierley wanted to suggest an alternative term, 'meaning', which would give clarity to the distinction between objective and subjective descriptions, since phantasy confuses them. The term 'meaning' locates the subjective quality of unconscious phantasy and keeps it apart from the instinctual and objective aspects (see also Rycroft, 1966). Isaacs disagreed with this and decided to stick to the term 'phantasy', partly because the power of the concept seems to be that it does encompass both the biological and psychological aspects of the basis of mental functions. However, Meltzer (1973) has commented on the need to emphasize this change in metapsychology:

> As Freud's original neuropsychological frame of reference changed to a purely psychological one, the quasi-physiological idea of 'psychic energy' has needed to be replaced by purely mental concepts of 'meaning' and 'vitality'. (p. 131)

(7) Regression. Prior to Klein phantasy had meant a regression of the libido that resulted from frustration, which excites the perceptual apparatus causing hallucinations, or developing fantasies for thinking. Isaacs acknowledged that the theory of unconscious phantasy altered the significance of regression, if the unconscious phantasies of early life are continuously active and underlie (and give meaning to) all later developmental stages. Although Freud and Abraham and classical psychoanalysis held that early instinctual drives exert their later influences as a result of regression, Isaacs emphasized that in recognizing the pervading influence of these early stages, the functioning and context of the very early defence mechanisms were seen in the later repetitions [see 9. PRIMITIVE DEFENCE MECHANISMS]; therefore the importance of regression lies in including the defensive configurations at the early stages to which regression takes place.

Glover was adamant that expanding the meaning of the term phantasy beyond regressive and hallucinatory satisfactions made other terms redundant. Continuously active unconscious phantasy of a primitive kind would seem to dispose of the concept of fixation points, and of the regression of the libido or the regression of object-relations from later to earlier forms.

Permanent fixation: By claiming the importance of unconscious phantasy at every stage from the earliest, and emphasizing the primal phantasies of the oral stage (incorporation, introjection, etc.), it was argued, Klein's metapsychology amounted to a permanent fixation at the earliest stages. The occurrence of phantasies connected to oral, anal and genital impulses was believed to dispose of regression altogether, since Klein had thrown out the concept of progression through these phases [see LIBIDO].

The employment of phantasies against other phantasies – for instance, the development of genital phantasies as a means of dealing with pregenital sadism [see DEVELOPMENT] – in effect disposes of the economic model of qualitative conservation of energy [see ECONOMIC MODEL].

Glover's 'enclave': Glover was insistent that the idea of continuously active phantasies of a primitive kind in the unconscious was un-Freudian. He conceptualized this as an *enclave* of primitive mental activity that continued in some separated way in the unconscious. He emphasized the heretical quality of these ideas by the argument that if pre-eminence is given to this primary enclave, the Oedipus complex is automatically demoted from its key psychoanalytic position. This criticism of the displacement of the Oedipus complex is dealt with later [see 4. OEDIPUS COMPLEX]. No other analyst supported this particular criticism, and the Kleinian respondents in the Controversial Discussions gave little time to serious debate with Glover and dismissed his criticisms on the whole as *ad hominem*.

However, in an ironic way, time may have been kinder to Glover. The idea of a separate (split-off) enclave returned – in the Kleinian literature. Klein herself came to entertain the view that there is an extremely primitive area of archaic objects (Klein, 1958) [see 7. SUPEREGO]. Later, Rosenfeld (1971), in his investigations of the clinical manifestations of the death instinct, described a sort of internal 'Mafia gang' not integrated with the rest of the personality. This kind of structuring of the personality has become a prominent focus of contemporary Kleinian thought in Britain [see STRUCTURE].

In spite of the heat, hurt pride and retaliatory point-scoring in these discussions, there are numerous issues of fundamental importance. Although the sense one gets from reading the records of the Controversial Discussions is that Isaacs's sharp, academically trained method of debate got the better, by and large, of her opponents, in fact these issues were not really resolved. As is well known, a 'Gentlemen's Agreement' was concocted in the British Psycho-Analytical Society for the alignment of members into separate groups (eventually Kleinians, the Independent Group and the 'B' Group of orthodox Freudians) and their power-sharing in all the committees of the Society (Steiner, 1985; Grosskurth, 1986). Instead the Discussions served to bury 'scientific' debate between the groups, with very little subsequent engagement. Consequently many of these issues, though for each party seemingly long forgotten, are still at the roots of current divergences between Kleinians and classical or ego-psychology psychoanalysts.

Abraham, Karl (1921) 'Contribution to a discussion on tic', in Karl Abraham (1927) *Selected Papers on Psycho-Analysis*. Hogarth, pp. 323–5.

Balint, Michael (1943) 'Contribution to the Controversial Discussions 1943–1944 of the British Psycho-Analytical Society' (unpublished).

Brierley, Marjorie (1943) 'Contribution to the Controversial Discussions 1943–1944 of the British Psycho-Analytical Society' (unpublished).

—— (1951) *Trends in Psycho-Analysis*. Hogarth.

Caper, Robert (1988) *Immaterial Facts: Melanie Klein's Development of Psycho-Analysis*. New York: Jason Aronson.

Chamberlain, David (1987) 'The cognitive newborn', *Br. J. Psychother.* 4:30–71.

Ferenczi, Sandor (1921) 'Psycho-analytic observations on tic', in S. Ferenczi, *Further Contributions to the Theory and Technique of Psycho-Analysis*. Hogarth.

Freud, Anna (1943) 'Contribution to the Controversial Discussions 1943–1944 of the British Psycho-Analytical Society' (unpublished).

Freud, Sigmund (1896) 'The aetiology of hysteria', in James Strachey, ed. *The Standard Edition of the Complete Psychological Works of Sigmund Freud*, 24 vols. Hogarth, 1953–73. vol. 3, pp. 189–221.

—— (1900) *The Interpretation of Dreams*. vols 4, 5.

—— (1914) 'On narcissism'. *S.E.* 14, pp. 67–107.

—— (1915) 'The unconscious'. *S.E.* 14, pp. 159–215.

—— (1926) *Inhibitions, Symptoms and Anxiety*. *S.E.* 20, pp. 77–175.

Glover, Edward (1932) 'On the aetiology of drug addiction', *Int. J. Psycho-Anal.* 13:300–7.

—— (1943) 'Contribution to the Controversial Discussions 1943–1944 of the British Psycho-Analytical Society' (unpublished).

—— (1945) 'An examination of the Klein system of child psychology', *Psychoanal. Study Child* 1:3–43.

Grosskurth, Phyllis (1986) *Melanie Klein*. Hodder & Stoughton.

Heimann, Paula (1943) 'Contribution to the Controversial Discussions 1943–1944 of the British Psycho-Analytical Society' (unpublished).

Isaacs, Susan (1943a) 'Contribution to the Controversial Discussions 1943–1944 of the British Psycho-Analytical Society' (unpublished).

—— (1943b) 'An acute psychotic anxiety occurring in a boy of four years', *Int. J. Psycho-Anal.* 24: 13–32.

—— (1948) 'The nature and function of phantasy', in Melanie Klein, Paula Heimann, Susan Isaacs and Joan Riviere, eds (1952) *Developments in Psycho-Analysis*. Hogarth, pp. 67–221; originally read in 1943 in the Controversial Discussions of the British Psycho-Analytical Society 1943–44; published *Int. J. Psycho-Anal.* 29: 73–97.

Jones, Ernest (1943) 'Contribution to the Controversial Discussions 1943–1944 of the British Psycho-Analytical Society' (unpublished).

Klein, Melanie (1920) 'The development of a child', in *The Writings of Melanie Klein*, vol. 1. Hogarth, pp. 1–53.

—— (1923) 'The role of the school in the libidinal development of the child', *The Writings of Melanie Klein*, vol. 1, pp. 59–76.

—— (1925) 'A contribution to the psychogenesis of tics', *The Writings of Melanie Klein*, vol. 1, pp. 106–27.

—— (1929a) 'Personification in the play of children', *The Writings of Melanie Klein*, vol. 1, pp. 199–209.

—— (1929b) 'Infantile anxiety-situations reflected in a work of art and in the creative impulse', *The Writings of Melanie Klein*, vol. 1, pp. 210–18.

—— (1958) 'On the development of mental functioning', *The Writings of Melanie Klein*, vol. 3, pp. 236–46.

Lantos, Barbara (1943) 'Contribution to the Controversial Discussions 1943–1944 of the British Psycho-Analytical Society' (unpublished).

Lichtenberg, J. D. (1983) *Psycho-Analysis and Infant Research*. Hillsdale, NJ: Analytic.

Masson, Jeffrey (1984) *Freud: The Assault on Truth*. Faber & Faber.

Meltzer, Donald (1973) *Sexual States of Mind*. Perth: Clunie.

Middlemore, Nerrell (1941) *The Nursing Couple*. Hamish Hamilton.

Rosenfeld, Herbert (1971) 'A clinical approach to the psycho-analytical theory of the life and death instincts: an investigation into the aggressive aspects of narcissism', *Int. J. Psycho-Anal.* 52:169–78.

Rycroft, Charles (1966) 'Introduction: causes and meaning', in Charles Rycroft, ed. *Psycho-Analysis Observed*. Constable, pp. 7–21.

Segal, Hanna (1957) 'Notes on symbol-formation', *Int. J. Psycho-Anal.* 38: 391–7; republished (1981) in *The Work of Hanna Segal*. New York: Jason Aronson, pp. 49–65.

—— (1964) *Introduction to the Work of Melanie Klein*. Heinemann; republished (1973) Hogarth.

Steiner, Riccardo (1985) 'Some thoughts about tradition and change arising from an examination of the British Psycho-Analytical Society's Controversial Discussions 1943–1944', *Int. Rev. Psycho-Anal.* 12:27–71.

Stern, Daniel (1985) *The Interpersonal World of the Infant*. New York: Basic.

Trevarthen, C. (1980) 'The foundations of intersubjectivity: development of interpersonal and co-operative understanding in infants', in Olson, ed. *The Social Foundations of Language and Thought*. New York: Norton.

Waelder, Robert (1937) 'The problem of the genesis of psychical conflict in earliest infancy', *Int. J. Psycho-Anal.* 18:406–73.

3 AGGRESSION, SADISM AND COMPONENT INSTINCTS

DEFINITION. In Freud's theory of sexuality there are a number of components to the libido – oral, anal and genital love; heterosexuality and homosexuality; sadism and masochism; voyeurism and exhibitionism. Libidinal impulses were a complex mixture of these components, with different emphases towards one or other at different stages of development. Klein showed that the sequential development as seen from adult analysis was greatly exaggerated and that there was a squeezing-up of all the components into the first year of life. This did not preclude a phase dominance, in which one component will predominate over the others, but she described a situation in which more or less all kinds of impulses were present at most stages.

She showed also that sadism has enormous importance in the child. In this she followed Abraham who studied the aggressive phases of early life. Klein regarded aggression eventually as *the* critical factor in development, or the inhibition of it. She came to see it as the manifestation of the death instinct. The other component instinct which became important to her was the epistemophilic impulses (connected with voyeurism and exhibitionism).

CHRONOLOGY
1920 The finding of enormous sadism in the young child (Klein, Melanie, 1922, 'Inhibitions and difficulties in puberty'; Klein, Melanie, 1927, 'Criminal tendencies in normal children').

1927 The early origins of the superego, guilt and remorse (Klein, Melanie, 1933, 'The early development of conscience in the child').

1929 Infantile anxiety-situations (Klein, Melanie, 1929, 'Infantile anxiety-situations reflected in a work of art and in the creative impulse').

1932 Sadism as a manifestation of the death instinct (Klein, Melanie, 1932, *The Psycho-Analysis of Children*).

1935 Depressive position (Klein, Melanie, 1935, 'A contribution to the psychogenesis of manic-depressive states').

When Klein started her work in 1918–19, orthodox Freudian theory rested heavily on the developmental model of the infantile sexual phases. There were several component instincts to sexuality and several phases in the sexual development of childhood (Freud, 1905).

(a) The components – oral, anal and genital love; heterosexuality and homosexuality; sadism and masochism; voyeurism and exhibitionism. All these groups can merge with each other, and each has an active and a passive mode.

(b) The phases – (a) first year, orality; (b) second year, anality; (c) third

to fifth or sixth year, genitality; (d) from sixth year to puberty, the latency phase, and (e) from puberty onwards until adulthood, adolescence. These loving phases of the libido progress naturally. Other components of the libido appeared on top of this basic chronology. Particularly significant were the sadism/masochism components, which Abraham tried to sort out into similar phases. These phases of sadism overlapped with the oral, anal and genital phases, splitting each of them into two in fact, thus setting out what he called a 'timetable' of the development of the libido (Abraham, 1924) [see SADISM; LIBIDO].

KLEIN'S CONTRIBUTION TO THE THEORY OF INSTINCTS.

At the beginning of her work Klein accepted the theory of component instincts, but as she went on her observations on children showed differences from the developmental timetable worked out from the analysis of adult patients. She made four main contributions:

(1) First, she noticed the problem set for the child by his own curiosity (she called this the epistemophilic component – equivalent to Freud's voyeurism/exhibitionism). She thought this was basically the curiosity about the primal scene, the parents' sexuality and their sexual organs.

(2) Second, and closely connected, was the sadistic component. This shocking manifestation of horrifying phantasy in children appeared to be brought out by the frustrated sexual curiosity. It has, however, profound consequences which include the underlying factor in paranoia and psychosis. The term 'sadism' took its meaning, in Klein's writings, from Freud and especially from Abraham. At that time (about 1923) it was believed to derive from the sexual perverse impulse, especially at the oral or anal level. Increasingly in Klein's thinking 'sadism' became synonymous with any extreme form of aggression.

(3) Unlike Abraham, who refined the timetable of the libidinal phases more and more precisely, Klein found that when she looked at the development in children as it happened, the phases were imprecisely ordered, and in fact often overlapping.

(4) Finally, in 1932, Klein unhooked the sadistic phantasies that had shocked her so much and had led her to clash with Freud. Sadism was no longer seen as a component of the libido, but as a separate instinct endowed from birth. In this she was adopting Freud's theory of the death instinct. However, whereas Freud regarded the death instinct as clinically silent, Klein claimed the sadistic phantasy life of children as a clinical manifestation of the death instinct.

(1) **Epistemophilia.** In her early work, Klein showed how interpretations

of the child's questions and phantasies of the primal scene released a powerful uprush of phantasy. She viewed this as the release of inhibited phantasy about the primal scene. The desire for knowing, curiosity, seemed evidently to be a powerful primitive and primal drive [see EPISTEMOPHILIA]. She became interested in this for two theoretical reasons. First, her technique, using toys and play as symbols, led her to concentrate on the nature of symbolism [see 1. TECHNIQUE; SYMBOL-FORMATION]. Secondly, she found herself confronted in some cases with a massive absence of symbolic functioning (Klein, 1930); these led her to suppose that she might have stumbled upon the nature of psychosis [see PARANOIA; PSYCHOSIS].

The inhibition of curiosity was especially strong in psychotic or near-psychotic children. This discovery seemed of great importance in understanding the disorders of psychosis, which were known to include difficulties in the proper formation of symbols. Freud distinguished word-presentations from thing-presentations (Freud, 1915) and he had hypothesized this from the disorders of schizo-phrenics:

> If now we put this finding [the peculiarly concrete form of symbols in schizophrenics] alongside the hypothesis that in schizophrenia object-cathexes are given up, we shall be obliged to modify the hypothesis by adding that the cathexis of *word*-presentations of objects is retained. (Freud, 1915, p. 201)

Klein realized that she could look at the roots of this problem in the child as it was happening.

In seeking to express phantasies of one kind or another in play or any other symbolic activity, there is a process of externalization. Externalization is bound up with the process of expulsion, or projection, as a defence against intolerable internal conflicts and sadistic superego punishment. The cruelty of this kind of internal situation was borne in upon Klein when she wrote:

> This defence, in conformity to the degree of sadism [in the internal situation], is of a violent character and differs fundamentally from the later mechanism of repression. In relation to the subject's own sadism the defence implies expulsion, whereas in relation to the object it implies destruction. The sadism becomes a source of danger because it offers an occasion for the liberation of anxiety and also because the weapons employed to destroy the object are felt by the subject to be levelled at his own self as well . . . the wholly undeveloped ego is faced with a task which at this stage is quite beyond it. (Klein, 1930, p. 220)

(2) Sadism. The early connection between the epistemophilic impulse and sadism is very important for the whole of mental development. This instinct . . . at first mainly concerns the mother's body, which is assumed to be the scene of all sexual processes and developments. The child is still dominated by the anal-sadistic libido-position which impels him to wish to appropriate the contents of the body. He thus begins to be curious about what it contains, what it is like etc. So the epistemophilic instinct and the desire to take possession come quite early to be most intimately connected with one another. (Klein, 1928, p. 188)

Learning, Klein was saying, represents an intrusion into mother's body (1931) and therefore touches on the anxieties arising from the phantasy of penetrating mother sadistically [see 8. EARLY ANXIETY-SITUATIONS]:

The child expects to find within the mother (a) the father's penis, (b) excrement, and (c) children, and these things it equates with edible substances. According to the child's earliest phantasies (or 'sexual theories') of parental coitus, the father's penis (or his whole body) becomes incorporated in the mother during the act. Thus the child's sadistic attacks have for their object both father and mother, who are in phantasy bitten, torn, cut or stamped to bits. The attacks give rise to anxiety lest the subject should be punished by the united parents, and this anxiety also becomes internalized in consequence of the oral-sadistic introjection of the objects and thus is already directed towards the early superego. (Klein, 1930, p. 219)

The clear evidence of the infant's aggression was a troubling finding for her:

The idea of an infant of from six to twelve months trying to destroy its mother by every method at the disposal of its sadistic trends – with teeth, nails and excreta and with the whole of its body, transformed in phantasy into all kinds of weapons – presents a horrifying, not to say unbelievable picture to our minds. And it is difficult, as I know from my own experience, to bring oneself to recognize that such an abhorrent idea answers to the truth. (Klein, 1932, p. 130)

Because it was such an unexpected finding for her she concentrated on it more or less exclusively for the first fifteen years of her clinical practice.

Vicious circle: The especial preoccupation with aggression, and the vengeful consequences which arouse fear and more aggression, are self-perpetuating. The attacks on the persecutors render them more harmful, rather than less, because they are supposed, in phantasy, to be enraged further to retaliatory violence; '. . . when the objects are introjected, the attack launched upon them with all the weapons of sadism rouses the subject's dread of an analogous attack upon himself from the external and the internalized objects' (Klein, 1929, p. 212). This kind of vicious circle represents a paranoid state of hostility, with intense suspicion of any 'good' figures [see PARANOIA].

(3) Pregenital phases. Klein originally followed Abraham in assigning sadism to a period late in the first year of life, and she tended to refer back the phantasies she found in older children to that time as a fixation point. She eventually came to the conclusion that all the various libidinal impulses coincide, though one or other will be in the ascendant at any one time: 'The libidinal phases overlap from the earliest months of life onwards. The positive and inverted Oedipus tendencies are from their inception in close interaction' (Klein, 1945, p. 416). The sadistic phantasies are largely attributed to the oral and anal phases, and the pregenital impulses are at first more dominant than the genital ones. Thus the child in his earliest moments has to struggle against the anxiety caused by these sadistic impulses. Klein came to understand that there was some stirring of genital impulses (i.e. towards both parents as a couple) from the first year of life, but later the genital impulses strengthen and enhance the child's loving.

Often Klein seems to write as if pregenital (sadistic) impulses are opposed to the genital, loving ones:

> ... sadism is overcome when the subject advances to the genital level. The more powerfully this sets in, the more capable does the child become of object-love, and the more able he is to conquer his sadism by means of pity and sympathy. (Klein, 1929, p. 214)

She considered that one of the ways in which the aggressive impulses influence development is that they promote a movement forward by the ego towards genital impulses (stimulations) in order to mobilize the loving feelings. Thus the aggressive feelings may strengthen as well as inhibit developmental movement; or even, at times, the movement forward may be impelled prematurely, with different consequences. So Klein evolved the controversial view that it was the impact of the aggressive impulses in these very early stages that determined the course of development or its hindrance [see LIBIDO; DEVELOPMENT].

It was on the evidence of pregenital phantasies that Klein began to revise the classical view of the Oedipus complex and the origin of the superego [see 4. OEDIPUS COMPLEX; 7. SUPEREGO].

(4) The death instinct. Later (from 1932) Klein regarded the whole of the first year as the time of maximal sadism. That extension of her views came as a result of her adoption, in 1932, of the death instinct as a primary source of aggressive impulses from the beginning: '... a deflection of the death instinct outwards influences the relations of the child to his objects and leads to the full development of his sadism' (Klein, 1932, p. 128); and:

> . . . his destructive instincts have aroused anxiety in him as early as the first months of life. In consequence, his sadistic phantasies become bound up with anxiety, and this tie between the two gives rise to specific anxiety-situations . . . Libidinal satisfaction, as an expression of Eros, reinforces his belief in his helpful imagos and diminishes the dangers which threaten him from his death instinct and his superego. (Klein, 1932, p. 201) [see DEATH INSTINCT]

From this point on, Klein's view of the mind and its development turns on the inherent conflict between the death instinct and the libido (life instincts) and the manner in which the external world can assist in the development of the awareness of external and internal realities. When the death instinct predominates then the mixture (or fusion) of the instincts results in envy, masochism or other forms of perversion and various other states of pathological aggression. Health, and normal development, rely upon the dominance of the life instincts [see DEATH INSTINCT].

From birth, the infant reacts to experiencing his own needs by demanding satisfactions, and ultimately seeking satisfying objects and loving them (life instincts); or by obliterating the experience (or the perception of the object that is longed for) or the perceptual apparatus that has the experience or perceives the object (death instinct) [see 12. ENVY]. In evading the effects of the early destructiveness the death instinct is usually projected (Freud's original term was 'deflection') outwards into an external object which embodies the destructive threat to the self; and an element of destructiveness is retained inside and turned towards the threatening external object.

Depressive position: The conflict of feelings which was originally seen between the pregenital and genital impulses came to be seen as conflicts between the positive and negative Oedipus complex, which exists in unconscious phantasies in pregenital as well as genital forms [see 4. OEDIPUS COMPLEX]. These confusing elisions of theoretical categories became less problematic as Klein moved on theoretically, in 1935, to develop the idea of the depressive position, which became steadily more prominent than the Oedipus complex and the phase sequences [see 10. DEPRESSIVE POSITION] since it formed the underpinning on which these classical developmental steps take place.

Schizoid annihilation: In 1946 Klein reviewed her theory of the intense sadistic and paranoid period at the outset of life (called by then the *paranoid position*). She found that aggressive impulses operated against the ego of the subject as well as towards objects. The self-destructiveness was as if the death instinct (promoting the slipping back of the individual into dissolution and death) had not properly been turned outwards from birth [see 7. SUPEREGO]. In her theory of the death instinct she followed Freud's view of the outward deflection of the death instinct. In schizoid states, there is an initial failure of that deflection [see 11. PARANOID-SCHIZOID POSITION; 12. ENVY]. Hence the schizoid individual is afraid of an annihilating force from within, and fears for himself and the dissolution into fragments of his own ego and identity (Klein, 1946). At this time Klein described the *prototype of an aggressive object-relationship* in which these fragments of the ego may be expelled into external objects [see 13. PROJECTIVE IDENTIFICATION].

Envy: In 1957 Klein made her last contribution to her theory. Like the very earliest preoccupations, it was to do with the enormous quantities of sadistic aggression in human beings. Not only had she found, early on, vast quantities of aggression in children at play, but later in her career she could confirm this excessive sadism and aggression in clinical material from adult psychotic patients. Primary envy is an innate aggression and sadism towards the good objects or their good attributes, as opposed to the more paranoid aggression towards bad objects that seem threatening to the subject [see 12. ENVY]. Envy and the death instinct are similar in that both attack life and loved objects. In envy the death instinct impulses are in fusion with the life instincts in such a way that the death instinct is dominant. This is a pathological form of fusion in which (a) the object is attacked as a satisfaction of the death instinct, and (b) it is, at the same time, attacked as a defence against envy by obliterating the object that gives rise to the need. The destructiveness concerns an object that excites a need (and therefore love) and which is also the satisfaction of that need.

A primary form of envy seemed to represent one of the most primitive manifestations of the aggressive impulses, and Klein thought that at the outset the infant was endowed with an innate discrepancy in the quantities of life and death instinct, together with, in schizophrenics, other defects, especially a difficulty in separating aggressive from libidinal impulses (and weak tolerance of frustration, unfavourable environment for development, etc.).

DEBATE ABOUT THE DEATH INSTINCT. There is no real dispute about there being sadistic phases in childhood, but there is about their origin in the death instinct. There were four main objections to the usefulness of the concept of the 'death instinct': (a) Freud's descriptions had largely been speculative and he referred to it as clinically 'silent'; (b) it is unnecessary to postulate the projection of the death instinct as a source of aggression, since the frustration of libido is quite adequate to account for aggression; (c) there is no evidence for a self-directed destructiveness working inside the personality; and (d) the importance given by Klein to the death instinct demotes libido from its central importance in psychoanalytic theory.

(a) The silent instinct: It is a widely held view that Freud came upon the idea of the death instinct from biological examples, his reflections on the mortality of organisms and the universal tendencies for living matter to return to the inanimate state, and for inanimate matter to degenerate to lower levels of organization. Linking this second law of thermodynamics, or entropy, to Freud's model of the mind threatened to bring a tone of mysticism into psychoanalysis. Consequently most psychoanalysts have failed to give it a serious place in their clinical thinking. It proved possible to consign the death instinct to oblivion, because Freud had referred to it as 'a mute and silent instinct'. This inaudibility explained for Freud why he had neglected it in his earlier work.

However, Klein argued vigorously that the 'death instinct' is a clinical concept, because Freud (1920) began his arguments with data from clinical work on the transference (the repetition compulsion), from the dreams of patients suffering traumatic neuroses, and from the observation of infants at play. It was indeed the clinical problem of repetition compulsion that gave rise to his choice of name for that work in 1920 – *Beyond the Pleasure Principle*. Because patients seem compelled to repeat painful experiences, the pleasure principle is breached. There must be something beyond pleasure.

(b) Frustrated libido: Equally, in its projected form the death instinct is far from silent – it is noisy and raucous [see DEATH INSTINCT]. It is often argued that the aggressive impulses are not in themselves evidence of the death instinct, as these may be derivatives of libidinal impulses that have been frustrated. The argument at its most benign is that it is impossible to isolate the different instinctual components by psychoanalytical investigation. The disagreements amongst psychoanalysts over the death instinct are replete with ingenious *a posteriori* arguments on this point from both sides [see 2. UNCONSCIOUS PHANTASY; GENETIC CONTINUITY].

(c) Internal destructiveness: Klein showed that, in children at least, the death instinct was not mute and silent; there was a sense in which the ego, or some part of what it contained, remained within to exert a deathly influence on the personality. This is the 'bad' internal objects that give rise in the course of development to the harsh superego [see 7. SUPEREGO]. In adults the experience of a destructive object inside

the ego is conveyed by the patient who has a phobia for cancer which represents an internal devouring object. Indeed, the general fear of cancer is similarly linked with unconscious phantasies of an oral-sadistically conceived 'bad' object. Other forms of hypochondria may be equivalent illustrations.

A clinically manifest internal destructiveness was examined by Rosenfeld (1971) and recently by many others in response to the complaint that Kleinians have not responded to the criticisms of their employment of the concept of the 'death instinct'. The structure of borderline patients consists of the organization of 'bad' parts of the self which attack the 'good' self with seductive or intimidating strategies [see STRUCTURE].

(d) The relative importance of death instinct and libido: In another direction it has been argued that Klein asserted that the death instinct predominates in influence over the libido, and that the drive to relate to objects derives from the death instinct! This would be quite contrary to Freudian theory. Complaints that Klein had disposed of Freud's theory of progression of libidinal phases reached a crescendo when the Viennese analysts came to London in 1939 [see CONTROVERSIAL DISCUSSIONS]. The complaint was overwrought, but it is true that Klein saw the problems and inhibitions in development of the libido (as well as in intellect) as due to the anxiety caused by the aggressive impulses. She did not really jettison the libido theory and the sequence of infantile sexual phases. She stuck to it formally while pointing to the fact that the phases no longer progress like a railway timetable (Abraham's own analogy). They are squeezed up all the time, but still exhibit a sequence of dominance of impulses – at first oral impulses dominate over anal, then anal impulses begin to assert themselves and become dominant over oral and genital. Klein's emphasis was on the *interference* of libidinal development by sadism which marks the fixation points of the libido.

The problems therefore remain. For the Kleinians the death instinct is not silent but active as an important factor that greatly disturbs and modifies the natural progression of the libidinal development through the early phases; whilst classical psychoanalysts minimize the *clinical* importance of the death instinct and emphasize the epigenetic development of the libido and the ego [see EGO-PSYCHOLOGY]. What critically decisive situations in clinical practice would lead to deciding these issues is yet to be given serious attention.

Abraham, Karl (1924) 'A short study of the development of the libido', in Karl Abraham (1927) *Selected Papers on Psycho-Analysis*. Hogarth, pp. 418–501.
Freud, Sigmund (1905) *Three Essays on Sexuality*, in James Strachey, ed. *The*

Standard Edition of the Complete Psychological Works of Sigmund Freud, 24 vols. Hogarth, 1954–73, vol. 7, pp. 125–245.

—— (1915) 'The unconscious'. *S.E.* 14, pp. 159–215.

—— (1920) *Beyond the Pleasure Principle*. *S.E.* 18, pp. 3–64.

Klein, Melanie (1922) 'Inhibitions and difficulties in puberty', in *The Writings of Melanie Klein*, vol. 1. Hogarth, pp. 54–8.

—— (1927) 'Criminal tendencies in normal children', *The Writings of Melanie Klein*, vol. 1, pp. 170–85.

—— (1928) 'Early stages of the Oedipus complex', *The Writings of Melanie Klein*, vol. 1, pp. 186–98.

—— (1929) 'Infantile anxiety-situations reflected in a work of art and in the creative impulse', *The Writings of Melanie Klein*, vol. 1, pp. 210–18.

—— (1930) 'The importance of symbol-formation in the development of the ego', *The Writings of Melanie Klein*, vol. 1, pp. 219–32.

—— (1931) 'A contribution to the theory of intellectual inhibition', *The Writings of Melanie Klein*, vol. 1, pp. 236–47.

—— (1932) *The Psycho-Analysis of Children*, *The Writings of Melanie Klein*, vol. 2.

—— (1933) 'The early development of conscience in the child', *The Writings of Melanie Klein*, vol. 1, pp. 248–57.

—— (1935) 'A contribution to the psychogenesis of manic-depressive states', *The Writings of Melanie Klein*, vol. 1, pp. 262–89.

—— (1945) 'The Oedipus complex in the light of early anxieties', *The Writings of Melanie Klein*, vol. 1, pp. 370–419.

—— (1946) 'Notes on some schizoid mechanisms', *The Writings of Melanie Klein*, vol. 3, pp. 1–24.

—— (1957) 'Envy and gratitude', *The Writings of Melanie Klein*, vol. 3, pp. 176–235.

Rosenfeld, Herbert (1971) 'A clinical approach to the psycho-analytical theory of the life and death instincts: an investigation into the aggressive aspects of narcissism', *Int. J. Psycho-Anal.* 52:169–78.

Segal, Hanna (1987) 'The clinical usefulness of the concept of the death instinct' (unpublished).

4 OEDIPUS COMPLEX

DEFINITION. Klein's clinical findings eventually modified Freud's theory of the Oedipus complex. By emphasizing the phantasy content of the instinctual impulses, Klein showed especially the pregenital components (oral and anal) of oedipal phantasies. She took that as evidence of the early, and pregenital, origin of the Oedipus complex. Klein was always ill at ease with Freud's theory that the superego was the 'heir to the Oedipus complex' because its timing did not tally with her own clinical observations, and she had eventually to go against Freud.

The very early terrifying and 'psychotic' phantasy life of the child lies beneath the classical Oedipus complex and she emphasized *the early stages of the Oedipus complex*. Klein thought that she was emphasizing the importance of the Oedipus complex by showing the intensity of the underlying early stages.

Klein also emphasized the importance of the negative (inverted) Oedipus complex, and the intricate interaction between the positive and negative complexes; and later on this became absorbed into her theory of ambivalence in the depressive position. Subsequently her own developing theory of ambivalence and the depressive position resulted in an implicit reformulation of the Oedipus complex in terms of the coming together of phantasy 'good' and 'bad' figures (the 'good' and 'bad' part-objects). In the transference situation of a psychoanalysis this often entails the patient's relation to the coming together of parts of the analyst's mind.

CHRONOLOGY

1920 The classical Oedipus complex in children (Klein, Melanie, 1920, 'The development of a child').

1928 Pregenital forms of the Oedipus complex and the inverted Oedipus complex (Klein, Melanie, 1928, 'Early stages of the Oedipus complex').

1932 Disconnecting the superego from the Oedipus complex (Klein, Melanie, 1932, *The Psycho-Analysis of Children* (Part II); Klein, Melanie, 1933, 'The early development of conscience in the child').

1935 The Oedipus complex and the depressive position (Klein, Melanie, 1940, 'Mourning and its relation to manic-depressive states'; Klein, Melanie, 1945, 'The Oedipus complex in the light of early anxieties').

Orthodox psychoanalysis at the time when Klein started her work had established that the nuclear problem of all neuroses was the Oedipus complex. Klein never questioned that. She did, however, look at the Oedipus complex from an increasingly divergent point of view.

The Oedipus complex in the 1920s: In the classical Freudian view the infant has sexual feelings from its body which it attempts to discharge as desires towards its parents, but without success – and with prohibition. This leads to masturbation, which attracts similar prohibitions. Freud described this at the genital level, and explored the child's sexual theories (phantasies). He discerned the little boy's castration anxiety due to the threats he experiences from his father; the little girl suffers penis envy.

In a paper Freud published in 1918 – about the time Klein first started analysing children – he described extremely carefully the identifications the child makes with each of the parents in intercourse, and at a very early age (as young as eighteen months). In that case he had been trying to work out clinically some of the implications of the ideas he had published the year before in 'Mourning and melancholia' (Freud, 1917), in which he described for the first time the mechanism of identification (through introjection). These papers must have provoked excited and intense discussion in all the psychoanalytical societies at just the time when Klein was formulating her first cases.

KLEIN'S CONTRIBUTION TO THE OEDIPUS COMPLEX.
Klein's work with children at play showed her the variety of these phantasies and the ways in which children seemed to identify with the toy figures in all sorts of ways. This kind of multiple identification seemed to produce the creative flourishing of play itself, with the child looking at the events of the play from the viewpoint of one figure and then another [see 1. TECHNIQUE]. She, too, emphasized the identifications with each of the parents, as well as the simple form of the Oedipus couple, a hatred for one parent and a love for the other:

> I found out what Werner called his 'fidgeting thoughts'. He told me that he fidgeted about Tarzan's animals. The monkeys are walking through the jungle; in his phantasy he walks behind them and adapts to their gait. Associations showed clearly his admiration for his father who copulates with his mother and his wish to participate as a third person. This identification, again with both mother and father, also formed the basis of his other numerous 'fidgeting' thoughts, all of which could be recognized as masturbation phantasies. (Klein, 1925, p. 118)

On the basis of these infantile *phantasies*, Klein made four main clinical discoveries about the Oedipus complex in the period 1919 to 1935. Each of these steps was of such magnitude that the theory had eventually become a quite different one – the theory of the depressive position.

The steps were:

(1) the particular quality of sadism that is attached to the phantasies of the oedipal couple, giving rise to great anxiety [see 8. EARLY ANXIETY-SITUATIONS];

(2) the clinical evidence for pregenital phantasies and therefore of a pregenital origin, which is quite different from Freud's view that the Oedipus complex arises in the genital phase at the third to fifth year [see LIBIDO; 7. SUPEREGO];

(3) the conception of the oedipal parents in terms of individual organs – the penis in the vagina (the nipple in the breast) – which gives rise to a fearful phantasy of the parents eternally conjoined making up a combined parent figure [see COMBINED PARENT FIGURE]; and

(4) the ambiguity of the positive and inverted Oedipus complexes which, in existing together, create ambivalent feelings towards each parent [see 10. DEPRESSIVE POSITION].

(1) Anxiety. Klein added to the orthodox theory of the Oedipus complex by concentrating upon the *content* of the anxieties that arose from phantasies about the oedipal objects (mother and father):

> The little boy who hates the father as a rival for the love of the mother, will do this with the hate, the aggression and the phantasies derived from his oral-sadistic and anal-sadistic fixations . . . In this case [of Gerard] the father's penis was to be bitten off, cooked and eaten. (Klein, 1927, p. 172)

She remarked that ' . . . such a manifestation of primitive tendencies is invariably followed by anxiety' (Klein, 1927, p. 175). These sadistic impulses create great fear and remorse in young children, who fear what will happen to the actual parents and also fear their retaliation against the child [see 3. AGGRESSION; PARANOIA].

(2) The early origins of the Oedipus complex. Freud regarded the pregenital impulses as simply being discharged, while true oedipal phantasies commence only with the genital phase (around the age of three to five). Klein, however, showed oedipal phantasies at pregenital ages: ' . . . children often show, as early as the beginning of their second year, a marked preference for the parent of the opposite sex and other indications of incipient Oedipus tendencies' (Klein, 1926, p. 129). Pregenital impulses occur in children's reactions to their parents and to their parents' sexual relationship and their play revolves around ideas, phantasies and anxieties connected with the primal scene; in the child's ignorance of the facts, these phantasies are based on interpretations of his own needs (oral or anal) and their cruel frustration:

> According to the oral- and anal-sadistic stage which he is going through himself, intercourse comes to mean to the child a performance in which eating, cooking, exchange of faeces and

sadistic acts of every kind (beating, cutting up, and so on) play the principal part. (Klein, 1927, p. 175)

With this mass of clinical evidence of pregenital phantasies Klein found herself pressed to the conclusion that the Oedipus complex arises *before* the genital phase.

Thus the parents are mutually feeding, incorporating each other, biting each other to pieces, messing each other inside, controlling each other, as well as genital phantasies of penetrating, cutting, caring or protecting each other:

> . . . early analysis has shown that it [the child] develops such theories much earlier than this, at a time when pregenital impulses still predominantly determine the picture though its as yet concealed genital impulses have some say in the matter. These theories are to the effect that in copulation the mother is continually incorporating the father's penis via the mouth, so that her body is filled with a great many penises and babies. All these the child desires to eat up and destroy. In attacking mother's inside, therefore, the child is attacking a great number of objects. (Klein, 1933, p. 254)

(3) **Part-objects.** Much of the phantasy life of the child is conceived in terms of part-objects: that is to say, he imagines organs in relation to each other – hardly visualized, imagined objects with a single function, but coming together in intercourse. In particular there is mother's breast, which will engage with father's penis, or father's penis inside mother's vagina: '. . . at this early stage of development the principle of *pars pro toto* holds good and the penis also represents the father in person' (Klein, 1932, p. 132) [see PART-OBJECTS]. Involved too in this world of organs are the babies which mother's creative body also contains, which evoke other phantasies, again predominantly aggressive. All these primitive notions of organs, not yet connected together, are probably innate propensities for imagining such things – unconscious phantasies [see 2. UNCONSCIOUS PHANTASY; INNATE KNOWLEDGE].

The combined parent figure: Central to the early stages of the Oedipus complex is a picture of the parents as a fearful joint couple locked in violent intercourse that will destroy themselves and the infant (Klein, 1932). Thus the combined parents (or their organs) destroy each other in a world disaster for the infant that leaves nothing for him; at the same time the figure turns on him because of his own omnipotent phantasies against the parents and subjects him to the same destructive forces that he believes they wreak upon each other [see COMBINED PARENT FIGURE].

(4) **Inverted Oedipus complex.** Because Klein was analysing very young children she was in a particularly good position to show that the Oedipus complex is not simply a love for the parent of the opposite sex and a hatred for the rival parent of the same sex. In fact she found very mixed feelings, and therefore came to emphasize the inverted Oedipus complex in which little girls both love and identify with mother, and boys both love and identify with father, to the exclusion of the opposite-sex parent. This is in line with Freud's view of inherent bisexuality. The oscillations between positive and inverted oedipal complexes became of increasing importance, and contributed eventually to Klein's development of the concept of the depressive position [see 10. DEPRESSIVE POSITION].

THE THEORETICAL CONSEQUENCES OF KLEIN'S CONTRIBUTIONS. Klein's contributions led in several directions:

(1) a new origin of the superego;

(2) the 'secondary' quality of the classical anxieties connected with *castration* and *penis envy*;

(3) the depressive position theory of the loss of the loved object;

(4) rather later, Klein's most original follower, Bion (1962), developed the important notion of part-objects coupling like a container with its contents [see CONTAINING].

Klein's difficulty was that her clinical observations on children had far-reaching implications that conflicted with the clinical observation of adult psychoanalysts. Trouble was always in store for anyone who challenged Freud's own findings. The psychoanalytic world in the 1920s was not a forgiving one. Only in the 1930s could she develop her own theories independent of Freud. By that time, her view of anxiety and the oedipal situation had changed as a result of her incorporation of Freud's concept of the death instinct into her understanding of her clinical evidence, and that led to her concept of the depressive position.

(1) **The early superego.** The aggression that is evoked in these pregenital phases of the complex creates already complicated relations with the primary figures even before the genital impulses take over. These complex, ambiguous and terrifying figures, when introjected, become internal persecutors. Klein argued that internalized versions of parents which attack the ego are clearly phenomena in the same category as the superego as described by Freud. Consequently the superego must also arise at a much earlier age than Freud stated (in 1923) when he proposed it as the 'heir to the Oedipus complex' and

therefore as the main outcome of the Oedipus complex. Thus an early origin of the superego suggested an earlier origin of its precursor, the Oedipus complex. As this was in line with her discovery of pregenital phantasies of the oedipal couple, she believed the clinical facts demonstrated that the general sequence of events which Freud had defined could be sustained, if it was to be advanced to an earlier age in development. As she pursued her observations she found herself putting both the superego and the Oedipus complex earlier and earlier. At first she clung to the sequence Freud had laid down: the superego is the result of the Oedipus complex. However, unlike Freud's view, the two processes of working through the Oedipus complex and the formation of the superego are not wholly in sequence because the '. . . analysis of very young children shows that, as soon as the Oedipus complex arises, they begin to work through it and thereby develop the superego' (Klein, 1926, p. 133). Then, eventually, both processes became so bunched up in the first year or so of life that she finally unhooked one from the other and made them independent – the superego advancing, in effect, to the earliest moments of life [see 7. SUPEREGO].

(2) **Castration anxiety and penis envy.** Klein was at pains to reinforce all aspects and anxieties described in the classical theory of the Oedipus complex, and constantly claimed that her discovery of these phantasies was merely filling out accepted theory. She was therefore in a position to claim that the enormous anxieties she had been describing are deeply involved in the frightfulness of the 'orthodox' anxieties. So, castration anxiety is reinforced and multiplied by the boy's phantasies of violent assaults on mother's body to destroy the penis that resides there with the terror of the mutilating retaliation, brought about in kind, on his own penis. Penis envy in little girls is more clearly related to the anxiety Klein described as the raid that the girl makes on her mother's body as the receptacle of the father's penis and the babies it brings to life there. Penis envy is a narrower concept than Klein's descriptions of the variety of phantasies that beset the little girl [see 6. FEMININITY PHASE].

In spite of the claim that she was filling out Freud's theories with more detailed phantasies that are observable if one works with children at the time when the Oedipus complex is at its height, in fact the anxieties she was describing were not those that Freud described. Klein in the 1920s had described a new anxiety – that of violently invading mother's body, and the fear of a comparable retaliation on the child's own body. Her allegiance to Freud, however, required her to endorse his view of the prime anxieties by putting her own findings forward as underlying amplifiers of castration anxiety and penis envy.

(3) Loss of the loved object. Freud thought that the oedipal parents had to be given up eventually, and that this loss was achieved like other losses as he had described in 1917: by an introjection of the object. In 1923 he defined the internal object that resulted as the superego. However, towards the end of the 1920s, once Klein had installed herself in the supportive framework of the British Psycho-Analytical Society, she was freer to allow her own theoretical deductions to go ahead.

The internal objects resulting from the oedipal parents became, for Klein, the important psychological figures, more important than the external ones from which, of course, the internal ones nevertheless derive. She believed that the oscillations between the positive and negative Oedipus complexes in the course of infant development resulted in both loved internal objects and hated ones. Eventually a confluence develops between the loved and hated figures, resulting in an internal object (parent) which is both loved and hated. This confluence of love with sadistic attacks gives rise to a special constellation of affects, attitudes, object-relations, anxieties and defences which she called the depressive position [see 10. DEPRESSIVE POSITION].

THE DEPRESSIVE POSITION. The advent of the depressive position in Klein's thinking necessitated a rearrangement of her theories. First, she no longer referred so confidently to weaning as the most important frustration, emphasizing instead the vicissitudes of the *internal* object and the feared loss of it, rather than the fate of the external object (the actual breast). Secondly, the turning to father, attributed previously to the reaction against mother at weaning, was seen more as inherent in inevitable frustrations and conflicts of ambivalence towards mother, which set in from the outset. This conflict is seen as inherent, inevitable and embedded within the conflictual nature of the instincts – a conflict between the positive oedipal complex (wanting the love of the parent of the opposite sex against the rivalry with the parent of the same sex) and the inverted Oedipus complex (loving, and identifying with, the parent of the same sex, with opposition towards the parent of the opposite sex). Thus there is some correspondence between the coming together of the parents in the oedipal situation, and the coming together of the 'good' part-object with the 'bad' one:

> Each object, therefore, is in turn liable to become at times good, at times bad. This movement to and fro between various aspects of the primary imagos [parental figures] implies a close interaction between the early stages of the inverted and positive Oedipus complex. (Klein, 1945, p. 409) [see 10. DEPRESSIVE POSITION]

Reparation: The importance of reparation comes through, too, in some oedipal phantasies. Reparation is involved in enhancing the loving aspects of the Oedipus situation. The genital oedipal impulses represent a move towards a strengthening of the loving feelings; these are important in the acts of reparation, to mitigate the triumphant possibility of omnipotent reparation based on manic mechanisms [see REPARATION].

The paranoid-schizoid position: With the understanding of the splitting of the infantile mind into parts or fragments, together with the associated splitting of the objects, the coming together of these parts and fragments took over the role of the classical oedipal object [see SPLITTING; 11. PARANOID-SCHIZOID POSITION]. In the infant's experience the good and satisfying mother disappears when he is unsatisfied, and a different object intrudes. In his only partly perceived external world, father, a sibling, a visitor or the family dog do as well as anything else to represent this intrusive and damaging third figure. At this stage, however, these figures are kept separate in time to minimize the experience of a triangular configuration. The infant, in moments of experiencing his good object, is in full possession of it – an internal and external possession. However, as cognitive and emotional potentials develop, the objects come together and the onset of the depressive position creates a situation in which the infant no longer possesses the 'good' object but *witnesses* the possession of two objects by each other (Britton, 1989).

The Oedipus complex in this version is one which gives little account of the *actual parents and their actual* intercourse, for it is founded on the *way in which the infant makes use of* the actual objects to 'listen in' to his own phantasy world and to manipulate them (defensively) for his own relief [see PSYCHOLOGICAL DEFENCE].

This capacity to stand aside and observe a relationship between two objects requires the ability to sustain feeling left out and therefore the full impact of the classical oedipal pain. It is this moment, in which the capacity for love and hate is joined by the capacity to observe and know, which is one of the great characteristics of the depressive position [see LINKING; 10. DEPRESSIVE POSITION]. Thus the depressive position is more than the attaining of the Oedipus complex. It involves the capacity to begin a better knowledge of the internal and external worlds:

> The stronger and more coherent ego . . . again and again brings together and synthesizes the split-off aspects of the object and of the self . . . All these developments lead to a growing adaptation to external and internal reality. (Klein, 1952, p. 75)

'Mother' and 'father' parts of the analyst's mind: In the clinical situation

the use of this 'part-object' interpretation of the Oedipus complex has greatly influenced the understanding of the transference [see 1. TECHNIQUE]. The patient's reaching for the analyst's state of mind frequently includes the way in which the patient experiences the parts of the analyst's mind as separate or as linked together. Thus the analyst may be experienced as sympathetic, but in so doing another part of the analyst – his sterner, analysing part, which the patient feels will criticize him – is split off. Such aspects of the analyst's mind may be experienced in gender terms, as a maternal part and a paternal one, which the patient wishes to keep apart. Or, similarly, a feeling and intuitive part of the analyst may be felt to be missing when the analyst interprets using, as the patient believes, his own intellectual functions. The coming together of the parts of the analyst's mind may be greatly resisted, and fiercely attacked by the patient.

EARLY STAGES VERSUS PRECURSORS – THE DISPUTE.

There has been continuing reluctance to accept Klein's conclusions that the Oedipus complex commences before the genital phase (phase of genital primacy) [see also 7. SUPEREGO]. Fenichel articulated this most clearly:

> It is undoubtedly true that at a far earlier period the child is attached to the parent of the opposite sex, and feels jealousy and hatred towards the other parent. But, these preliminary phases differ in certain fundamental points from the Oedipus complex at the time of its zenith. The preliminary phases have contents (not genital) other than those of the true Oedipus complex; they are still competing with autoerotic tendencies; the jealous hatred still exists without conflict side by side with love for the parent of the subject's own sex. (Fenichel, 1931, pp. 141–2)

The argument is based on there being no links between the jealousy and the love. In fact Fenichel described a number of separate and different pregenital situations: the prohibition of autoerotic impulses; the enhancing of castration anxiety from the loss of mother's breast (weaning); pregenital love impulses; the equation of the penis with the breast or with faeces; the equation of mother's children with the breast or with faeces; and the equation of coitus with oral incorporation. All these components eventually influence the Oedipus complex when the genital phase is eventually reached, and would seem actually to weigh against Fenichel's argument and in favour of the importance of the earliest stages of the Oedipus complex.

This stands against a Kleinian view of contrasting emotional states (for example, the jealousy and the love) which would regard the separation as secondary (a splitting of the objects and the relationship) rather than a primary unintegration before the ego begins to function

as an integrating force. Classical Freudian analysts viewed the'
pregenital phantasies of parental intercourse and the oedipal situation
as arising retrospectively from a later working over in the genital phase
of the oedipal couple *in terms of* pre-oedipal impulses that were
brought out through regression. The Kleinian claim that impulses
from all the phases (oral, anal, genital) tended to coincide seemed to
abolish the psychoanalytic phenomenon of regression.

The Kleinian response was to emphasize the principle of genetic
continuity [see GENETIC CONTINUITY]; phenomena in adulthood, or
even in childhood, grow inevitably from something earlier, an argument used at the same time about the *early superego*. And that
regression has to be regression back *to* something; that is to say, the
early oral or anal phantasies of parental intercourse have to have
existed in order to regress back to them. The issue between regression
to phantasy activity of an early stage and retrospective elaboration of
earlier impulses is a difficult one to decide on clinical evidence and,
like so many of the disputes, this issue has tended to fade out of
discussion rather than to have reached a resolution.

The cut and thrust, hurt esteem and entrenched positions of the
Controversial Discussions in 1943 illustrated the difficulties of
pursuing a wholly scientific attitude to these topics [see CONTRO-
VERSIAL DISCUSSIONS]. The temperature rose especially over the key
concept of the Oedipus complex, as this was central to the classical
theory of Freud at the time. The accusation by Klein (1927) that Anna
Freud did not interpret the Oedipus complex [see 1. TECHNIQUE]
brought heart-rending agony and bitterness, expressed painfully
carefully in a correspondence between Freud himself and Ernest
Jones, respective patrons of the warring women (Steiner, 1985) [see 1.
TECHNIQUE].

However, the development of the Kleinian theory of the Oedipus
complex did move it away from the classical notion of the 'actual'
parents and into the phantasy world of part-objects in the paranoid-
schizoid position. In practice, in the consulting room, it is the analyst's
marriage and devotion to psychoanalysis, or the joining together of the
analyst's thoughts or the parts of his mind, which are the crucial
couples the psychoanalytic patient reacts to. To some (classical
analysts) the theory is now unrecognizable; to Kleinians it is the
continuity between the phantasies of part-objects in the *early stages of the
Oedipus complex* and the later (classical) oedipal stage that is the
relevant issue [see GENETIC CONTINUITY].

Bion, Wilfred (1962) *Learning from Experience*. Heinemann.
Brierley, Marjorie (1934) 'Present tendencies in psycho-analysis', *Br. J. Med.
Psychol.* 14:211–29.
Britton, Ronald (1989) 'The missing link: parental sexuality in the Oedipus

complex', in Ronald Britton, Michael Feldman and Edna O'Shaughnessy *The Oedipus Complex Today: Clinical Implications*. Karnac, pp. 83–101.

Fenichel, Otto (1931) 'The pre-genital antecedents of the Oedipus complex', *Int. J. Psycho-Anal.* 12:138–70.

Freud, Sigmund (1917) 'Mourning and melancholia', in James Strachey, ed. *The Standard Edition of the Complete Psychological Works of Sigmund Freud*, 24 vols. Hogarth, 1953–73. vol. 14, pp. 67–107.

—— (1918) 'From the history of an infantile neurosis', *S.E.* 17, pp. 3–123.

—— (1923) *The Ego and the Id. S.E.* 19, pp. 3–66.

Glover, Edward (1933) 'Review of Klein's *Psycho-Analysis of Children*', *Int. J. Psycho-Anal.* 14:119–29.

—— (1943) 'Contribution to the Controversial Discussions 1943–1944 of the British Psycho-Analytical Society' (unpublished).

—— (1945) 'An examination of the Klein system of child psychology', *Psychoanal. Study Child* 1:1–43.

Isaacs, Susan (1943) 'Contribution to the Controversial Discussions 1943–1944 of the British Psycho-Analytical Society' (unpublished).

Klein, Melanie (1920) 'The development of a child', in *The Writings of Melanie Klein*, vol. 1. Hogarth, pp. 1–53.

—— (1925) 'A contribution to the psychogenesis of tics', *The Writings of Melanie Klein*, vol. 1, pp. 106–27.

—— (1926) 'The psychological principles of early analysis', *The Writings of Melanie Klein*, vol. 1, pp. 128–38.

—— (1927) 'Criminal tendencies in normal children', *The Writings of Melanie Klein*, vol. 1, pp. 170–85.

—— (1928) 'Early stages of the Oedipus complex', *The Writings of Melanie Klein*, vol. 1, pp. 186–98.

—— (1932) *The Psycho-Analysis of Children*, *The Writings of Melanie Klein*, vol. 2.

—— (1933) 'The early development of conscience in the child', *The Writings of Melanie Klein*, vol. 1, pp. 248–57.

—— (1940) 'Mourning and its relation to manic-depressive states', *The Writings of Melanie Klein*, vol. 1, pp. 344–69.

—— (1945) 'The Oedipus complex in the light of early anxieties', *The Writings of Melanie Klein*, vol. 1, pp. 370–419.

—— (1952) 'Some theoretical conclusions regarding the emotional life of the infant', *The Writings of Melanie Klein*, vol. 3, pp. 61–93.

Kohut, Heinz (1971) *The Analysis of the Self*. New York: International Universities Press.

Rosenfeld, Herbert (1971) 'A clinical approach to the psycho-analytic theory of the life and death instincts: an investigation into the aggressive aspects of narcissism', *Int. J. Psycho-Anal.* 52:169–78.

Steiner, Riccardo (1985) 'Some thoughts about tradition and change arising from an examination of the British Psycho-Analytical Society's Controversial Discussions 1943–1944', *Int. Rev. Psycho-Anal.* 12:27–71.

Winnicott, Donald (1962) 'Providing for the child in health and crisis', in (1965) *The Maturational Processes and the Facilitating Environment*. Hogarth, pp. 64–72.

5 INTERNAL OBJECTS

DEFINITION. This term denotes an unconscious experience or phantasy of a concrete object physically located internal to the ego (body) which has its own motives and intentions towards the ego and to other objects. It exists within the ego, and in a greater or lesser extent of identification with the ego (a phantasy of absorption, or assimilation, to the ego). The experience of the internal object is deeply dependent on the experiencing of the external object – and internal objects are, as it were, mirrors of reality. But they also contribute significantly, through projection, to the way the external objects are themselves perceived and experienced.

CHRONOLOGY
1927 Expulsion as a means of managing the internal world (Klein, Melanie, 1927, 'Criminal tendencies in normal children').
Multiple internal objects (imagos making up superego) (Klein, Melanie, 1929a, 'Personification in the play of children').
1935 Loss of good internal object (Klein, Melanie, 1935, 'A contribution to the psychogenesis of manic-depressive states').
1946 Splitting of objects and self (Klein, Melanie, 1946, 'Notes on some schizoid mechanisms').

The idea of the internal object is one of Klein's most important discoveries, yet one of the most mysterious. The experience that the subject has of an object inside himself gives him a sense of existence and identity. Our relations with objects comprise what we are. Klein's awareness of this phenomenon started very early on. However, the deepening of the theory was a prolonged process involving a number of conceptual steps:

(1) the introjected object (the term 'object' and the way it is used by Kleinian and other object-relations psychoanalysts is described elsewhere [see OBJECTS]);

(2) externalization;

(3) the internal world;

(4) the superego;

(5) helpful figures;

(6) the internal reality of objects; and

(7) omnipotence and concreteness.

(1) **The introjected object.** In her analysis of Rita in 1923, Klein realized the importance of an introjected object that came to terrorize

the child. This realization came from elucidating the phantasy involved in bedtime rituals – the 'fear that a mouse or a butty might come through the window and bite off her butty (genital)' (Klein, 1926, p. 132). This fear of the internal persecuting object was a violent prohibition that did not emanate '. . . from the *real* mother, but from an introjected mother' (Klein, 1926, p. 132). Klein found that part of the bedtime ritual involved putting an elephant, standing for father, beside the bed:

> The elephant (the father-imago) was intended to take over the part of the hinderer. This part the introjected father had played within her since the time when [fifteen months] she had wanted to usurp her mother's place with her father, to steal from her mother the child with which she was pregnant, and to injure and castrate the parents. (Klein, 1926, p. 132)

(2) Externalization. Klein continued by describing how '. . . the game of acting a part serves to separate those different identifications', and '. . . the child succeeds in expelling the father and mother whom, in the elaboration of the Oedipus complex, it has absorbed into itself and who are now tormenting it inwardly by their severity' (Klein, 1926, p. 133).

(3) The internal world. Like his concept of the superego, Freud's concept of the internal world was greatly amplified by Klein. She attempted to illustrate the dramatic preoccupations of the child's mind in a strange paper based on a Berlin newspaper review of an operetta by Ravel, performed in Vienna (Klein, 1929b). The nightmare world of a child formed a kind of narrative full of persecutors, feared and attacked, which is enacted on the stage, with an ensuing poignant state of pity. She also linked this with a process of visual creativity (the story of a painter). She strove to re-create the dramatic effect in order to convey the quality of a whole world of phantasy in which the child is involved.

As early as 1923 she had been absorbed in studying the way in which children were preoccupied with the insides of bodies, their own and mother's:

> The little girl has a sadistic desire, originating in the early stages of the Oedipus conflict, to rob the mother's body of its contents, namely, the father's penis, faeces, children, and to destroy the mother herself. This desire gives rise to anxiety lest the mother should in her turn rob the little girl herself of the contents of her body (especially of children) and lest her body should be destroyed or mutilated. (Klein, 1929b, p. 217)

The child thus has a conception of objects inside her own body, pictured, Klein says here, as her own children. It is not just girls; about the little boy she says:

> It is, however, not only his penis he feels he must preserve, but also the good contents of his body, the good faeces and urine, the babies which he wishes to grow in the feminine position and the babies which – in identification with the good and creative father – he wishes to produce in the male position. (Klein, 1945, p. 412)

With this attention to the inside of mother, Klein termed this the femininity phase [see 6. FEMININITY PHASE]. She viewed children as having an absorbing interest, from very early on, in their own insides, which they felt to contain good and enriching objects and which they felt to be threatened and often damaged by attack from bad objects, either inside themselves or from outside.

(4) **The superego.** At the time when Klein was investigating children's ideas about a world inside themselves, Freud produced his own theory of the structure of the personality – id, ego and superego. In effect the superego is the only introjected and internal object Freud described. Klein's interest, then, was to connect the observations she was making on the children's introjected objects with Freud's new model of the mind. In the play of one little child, she says:

> Erna often made me be a child, while she was the mother or teacher. I then had to undergo fantastic tortures and humiliations ... I was constantly spied upon, people divined my thoughts, and the father or teacher allied themselves with the mother against me – in fact, I was always surrounded by persecutors. I myself in the role of the child had constantly to spy upon and torment others ... In this child's phantasies all the roles engaged could be fitted into one formula: that of two principal parts – the persecuting superego and the id or ego, as the case may be, threatened, but by no means less cruel. (Klein, 1929a, pp. 199–200)

Thus the dramas enacted in the playroom are equally, in Klein's interpretation, dramas internal to the child's mind, and she ingeniously linked them to the structure Freud had recently described.

(5) **Helpful internal objects.** However, it was not just the terrifying and harsh superego: Klein also noted helpful figures:

> George had always consciously felt himself surrounded and threatened (by magicians, witches and soldiers) but ... he had tried to defend himself against them by the aid of helping figures ... Three principal parts were represented in his games: that of the id

and those of the superego in its persecuting and its helpful aspects. (Klein, 1929a, p. 201)

'The helping figures thus invented are mostly of an extremely phantastic type' (Klein, 1929a, p. 203). Whereas the first impressions she had obtained from child analysis were of frightening struggles with horrific persecutors, distorted versions of the parents, she had now '. . . come to realize that the operation of such imagos, with phantastically good and phantastically bad characteristics, is a general mechanism in adults as well as children' (Klein, 1929a, p. 203).

At this stage Klein thought the helpful figures were conjured up as a defence against the persecutors, and she continued, by elaborating these imagos, to point out the problems that ensue from an '. . . excessively strong influence exerted by these extreme types of imagos, the intensity of the need for the kindly figures in opposition to the menacing, the rapidity with which allies will change into enemies' (Klein, 1929a, p. 204). This view of very varied 'imagos' is in stark contrast to the very limited relations Freud described between the superego and the ego and id. Later she came to describe these helpful figures as 'good' objects, especially the good internal object.

Multiple internal objects: The realization of the two sides of the superego – harsh and helpful – expressed as different objects, and then the objects from the different libidinal levels – oral, anal and genital – led to a view of the internal world as populated by a large number of varied objects, derived from the actual environment and history of the infant. In loyalty to Freud, Klein wrote: '. . . the superego as a whole is made up of the various identifications adopted on the different levels [phases] of development' (Klein, 1929a, p. 204); and in order to make her own observations conform to Freud's view of a monolithic amalgam of father and mother internally, she described a process of '. . . synthesizing the identifications into a whole superego'. However, in the course of time Kleinian thought has come to accept that the internal world is a full arena of varied objects in various degrees of synthesis and separateness in different contexts and at different times.

(6) **The internal reality of objects.** The concept of the internal object subsequently became a subject of great mystification – and repeated elucidations. The difficulty is that the internal objects described from the clinical evidence of children's play (and subsequently from the analysis of schizophrenics) were of a very concrete kind. It is of course true that children (and adults, too) have very concrete phantasies about what is inside their body. However, the *unconscious* phantasies of those contents are quite extraordinary. Internal objects are not 'representations', as they might be in memories or in conscious phantasies

(daydreams). They are felt to make up the substance of the body and of the mind.

During the 1930s and 1940s a group of Kleinians formed what they called the Internal Objects Group in order to try to clarify this mysterious concept. Searl (1932, 1933) and Schmideberg (1934) attempted to give descriptive accounts. Karin Stephen stated lucidly and categorically: '... the belief in these fantastic internal objects originates in actual bodily experiences of very early childhood, connected with violent, often uncontrollable, discharges of emotional tension' (Stephen, 1934, p. 321). Isaacs (1940) reported a case for demonstration purposes, to show the clinical evidence for internal objects; and Heimann (1942) reported in detail a case in which the clinical material showed the introjection of a hostile maternal object that interfered with the capacity of the ego; the patient's creative skills returned when the object could be identified with (assimilated).

The internal object and identification: The internalized object is normally, though not always, felt to belong to the ego. For instance, if we expand the ego boundaries for the sake of clarification, I could say that within the boundaries of my house I have 'my wife', or 'my lodger'. These objects are not denied their own identity, but they actually make up my identity as well – as husband, landlord – through being part of my household. It is different with other objects that come into my house – I would not refer to 'my burglar', nor 'my swarm of bees' if either of these objects intruded. Although they would be internal to the boundaries of my house, they are not felt to belong there.

The same is true of the boundaries of the ego: objects are normally felt to belong to (identified with) it but they may reside there as alien objects [see below; and ASSIMILATION].

(7) **Omnipotence and concreteness.** The object is firstly an *emotional* object because it comes from the infant's sensations of pleasure or pain. But because these sensations are bodily, the infant experiences these objects as actual concrete entities, as concrete as his body itself – the sensations are there, so the objects causing them must be there too. At the very beginning, objects are not known in terms of their physical attributes, but this in no way prevents the belief in their actual physical presence – because the child 'knows' the effects of them: his own bodily sensations are proof.

Heimann (1949) summarized the bodily relation to internal objects:

... instinct is object-seeking ... The situation would then appear as follows: Under the sway of hunger and oral desires the infant in some way conjures up the object that would satisfy these impulses. When this object, the mother's breast, is in reality offered to him he accepts it and in phantasy incorporates it. (Heimann, 1949, p. 10)

The experience is felt as concretely real; the phantasy is omnipotent and produces actual results in the ego, changing it and forming the basis of ego-development.

The representational world and the internal world: The earliest and most concrete level of phantasy is overlaid in later development by the world of object- and self-representations, but never actually replaced. The concrete world of the internal object persists as a bedrock layer of the personality, to surface in dreams, delirium, hallucination, hypochondria and the lesser delusion states of prejudices and preferences. The metaphor of a 'lump in the throat' for an emotional moment of sadness corresponds to a reality made up of an actual bodily experience of sensations in the throat [see OBJECTS].

Freud's notion of representations (Freud, 1900) is that they have the function of personal symbols, since they are not confused with the actual external object. When such representations *are* confused with the external object, as a result of the operation of omnipotent phantasy, the experience is of a completely real object existing inside the subject (Rosenfeld, 1964). Similarly in the *representation of the self*, if the phantasy is omnipotent in kind the self becomes actually fused or confused with the object [see ASSIMILATION].

Internal objects are conceived at a quite separate (and earlier) level of development and based on the omnipotent phantasy of incorporating an object into the ego and identifying with it. The latter results in a radical change in the ego because of the confusion of the external object with the actual introject resulting from the omnipotent quality of primitive phantasy. In the same manner, omnipotent projection results in the experience of a real loss of parts of the internal world or of the self which are believed to be in the external object [see 13. PROJECTIVE IDENTIFICATION].

INTERNAL OBJECTS AND THE BODY. Kleinian usage of the term 'internal object' refers mostly to this very primitive experience of internal objects as concretely real. Schilder and Wechsler (1935), in a pilot empirical study, elicited from children what they thought was inside their bodies, and demonstrated an astonishing variety of concretely imagined objects. In Schmideberg's (1934) case bodily symptoms were derived from psychological causes (conversion symptoms and hypochondria): '. . . her conversion symptoms and anxiety were determined largely by her anxiety of the incorporated object. She felt that the dangerous object inside her was in opposition to her ego' (p. 263); and as the patient's condition improved: '. . . the contrast between the incorporated object and the ego became less forcible and she identified herself with the object inside her' (p. 263).

This mode of experiencing internal objects is carried through development and throughout life; however, it becomes overlaid by a progressive set of additional modes of experiencing. The experience of the body, with the development of distance receptors, takes on the possibilities of a more objective appreciation. It results in what are then called 'representations' in the mind of internal and external objects. Representations are therefore a developmentally advanced ability of the infant. Later comes the substitution of other objects for the primary one, and this is the development of symbol-formation. This step-by-step progress in the experiencing of objects is sketched by Money-Kyrle (1968), who distinguished three stages: (i) concrete belief in a physically present object; (ii) the representation of an object in mind and memory; and (iii) a symbolic representation in words or other symbols [see SYMBOL-FORMATION]. The emergence from the concrete experience of objects to a more representational mode complements the views of Piaget (1954; see also Matthews, 1980) and is linked to the phenomenon that Bion called alpha-function [see THINKING; ALPHA-FUNCTION].

EXPERIENCING OBJECTS. The special experience of these concretely felt primitive internal objects is obscure, but we can take, for example, the infant who is hungry. His bodily sensations given by his physiology are also experienced mentally as a relationship with an object. The discomfort is attributed to the motivation of a malevolent object actually located in his tummy that intends to cause the discomfort of hunger. Bion ambiguously referred to this object as a 'no-breast', recognizing that objectively there is an absence, but for the infant there is no such thing as an absence, merely the presence of something causing the pain.

In this example the object is located inside the ego, in his tummy. This *internal object* is a 'good' one when he experiences being fed and feels the warm milk giving satisfying sensations in his tummy [see 2. UNCONSCIOUS PHANTASY]. Internal objects derive their character-istics from the instinctual impulses which are active (frustrating or 'bad' objects), or are being satisfied (satisfying or 'good' objects), depending on the bodily sensations that are at the centre of attention at the moment. The object is thus limited to relevance of only one kind: in connection with the sensations of the moment – eating, warmth, comfort, messing, wetting, etc., etc., and also in terms of whether the object allows some satisfaction, or is frustrating of these impulses. Each object represents only a very partial slice of the infant's world, and indeed only a part of the person who looks after him ('mother'), who is his external world. Technically this is known as a *part-object*. Only later can the child win through to a more complete picture of his objects through his more advanced perceptions, and then his objects come to have multiple intentions and mixed feelings, as well as physical attributes and consistency in time.

So the object's main characteristic is its motivation to cause the bodily sensation. Being drastically reduced to a single motivated entity, these objects are, from an objective point of view, at best partial. They are known as *part-objects* [see PART-OBJECTS; 11. PARANOID-SCHIZOID POSITION].

The first concrete objects have only emotional attributes. That creates an animistic world in which everything feels and has intentions. It is only later with the development of further perceptual skills, especially distance receptors, that an objective set of attributes can come to be known and assigned to the already existing emotionally real objects. Only with great sophistication can the world of feeling objects and the world of inanimate objects be finally and accurately separated out, and a representation in memory, or eventually in symbols, can take place.

THE FIRST OBJECT-RELATIONS. At birth, Klein believed, the infant relates to objects that are primitively distinguished from the ego – 'there are object-relations from birth'. These relations derive from the infant's innate capacity to interpret his bodily sensations – good objects that want to cause pleasant, enjoyable feelings (say, a sense of completeness with the nipple filling out his mouth; or the tummy full of warm milk); bad objects that want to cause the unpleasant feelings (the biting object, for instance, that causes the pain in the mouth when the teeth are coming through; or the one that gnaws away at his tummy causing the feeling of hunger).

By 1935 Klein had gone as far as postulating that introjective processes were active and created internal objects from birth: '. . . from the beginning the ego introjects objects "good" and "bad" for both of which the mother's breast is the prototype' (Klein, 1935, p. 262). Introjection of objects was no longer to be understood as having been brought about by the loss of a loved object, nor dependent on the resolution of the Oedipus conflict. Introjection and the achievement of a 'good' object inside the ego is a defence against the death instinct. The terrifying imagos, however,

> . . . are a phantastically distorted picture of the real objects [external parents] upon which they are based, [they] become installed not only in the outside world but, by the process of incorporation, also within the ego . . . Very soon, too, the ego tries to defend itself against internalized persecutors by the processes of expulsion and projection. (Klein, 1935, p. 262)

This happens with both the terrifying (now called 'bad') objects and the helpful ('good') ones. These states of being in relation to phantastically bad or good objects are generated by vicious or benevolent circles through the repeated projection of the phantastical internal object on to an external object and a reintrojection of the distorted object to augment the internal one: 'It seems that here we have two circles, the one benevolent and the other vicious, both of which are based on the interplay of external or environmental and internal psychical factors' (Klein, 1936, p. 292). The installation of these phantastical internal objects, starting from birth, entailed giving up the attempt to bring her observations into line with Freud's view of the superego. It allowed her, in fact, much greater freedom to explore the vicissitudes of the internal objects, and she postulated in 1935 and 1940 the main outline of the depressive position [see 10. DEPRESSIVE POSITION].

Narcissism: Part of the results of the 'Internal Objects Group' was a new view of narcissism which Heimann (1952) elaborated from the idea, previously suggested by Schmideberg (1931) and Riviere (1936), that narcissism represented the withdrawal of libido from the external object *to an internal object* identified with the ego [see NARCISSISM], and not simply to the ego itself.

In fact, in an early formative paper Klein (1925) analysed two boys with tics which had hitherto been thought of

> ... as a primary narcissistic symptom ... Experience has convinced me that the tic is not accessible to therapeutic influence as long as the analysis has not succeeded in uncovering the object-relations on which it is based. (Klein, 1925, p. 121)

The tic is not just an autoerotic satisfaction like masturbation, but '... masturbation phantasies are also bound up with it' (Klein, 1925, p. 124), and she postulated that these masturbation phantasies consist of parts of the infant's body that are involved in the movements of the tic, being identified with one or other parent that had been introjected and identified with. This intensely emotional relationship, composed of introjection and identification with objects, exists from very early in development – and in fact from birth. When, for instance, an infant sucks his thumb, the psychology is complicated. He has already introjected the feeding breast in such a way that it is at least partially secured inside through an identification with a part of the infant's body. In this case the identification of the breast is with his thumb. So, when he sucks it, he is in relationship with the internalized breast, identified with a part of the ego (Heimann, 1952).

Assimilation of the object: One of the difficulties about the concept of internal objects was to picture the actual relations between the introjected object, the ego and the other internal objects. Freud had assumed in 1917 that introjection implied an identification of the object with the ego. In fact he used the term 'identification' to describe the internalization by a manic-depressive patient of their ambivalently loved object. Later in 1923 he described the internalization of the superego, which has a different outcome since it remains separate from the ego, or separates out from the ego. This appears to be contradictory and had been noted by other psychoanalysts (e.g. Rado, 1928) [see ASSIMILATION]. The point, however, is that Klein's descriptions of children's play showed that the child may at one moment identify with one part of the relationship (say the superego) and at another moment become the guilty and errant child, scolded by the superego. This fluid arrangement of identifications (introjective identification) suggests that internal objects *are available for* the ego to identify with, and exist as a repertoire of identities, attitudes, roles, etc., for the ego at any one time or in any particular context.

There are, however, certain other, more pathological, kinds of internal objects which seem to exist as alien intruders (like the internal objects described by Schmideberg, 1934, and Heimann, 1942). Heimann (1942) described them as foreign bodies which cannot be *assimilated*. Klein (1946) later described this problem, acknowledging Heimann's clinical material. She described the ego as having been weakened by excessive projective identification; that is to say, large numbers of fragments of the self have been located in external objects, so the ego experiences itself as a depleted – even depersonalized – self, weak and vulnerable. When the ego is in this state, introjected objects, even if they are felt as good objects, are experienced as overwhelming and cannot be identified with and thus assimilated to the ego.

OBJECTS IN THE DEPRESSIVE POSITION. Achieving the depressive position is thus more than winning greater perceptual ability. It involves an intense emotional situation concerned with the *emotional part-objects* and gives rise to a special emotional change and turmoil: the depressive position.

The change in the object: Klein's initial description of the depressive position rested on the distinction between part- and whole objects:

> . . . the loss of the loved object takes place during that phase of development in which the ego makes the transition from partial to total incorporation of the object . . . The processes which subse-quently become clear as the 'loss of the loved object' are determined by the subject's sense of failure (during weaning and in the periods which precede and follow it) to secure his 'good, internalized' object . . . One reason for his failure is that he has been unable to overcome his paranoid dread of internalized persecutors. (Klein, 1935, p. 267)

The depressive position arises when the object provokes a confluence of love and hate. It is stimulated, therefore, by the integration of good objects with bad ones, so that the anguish of hating the object that is loved risks the object altogether. 'Not until the object is loved as a whole', Klein says, 'can its loss be felt as whole' (1935, p. 264). By this she means that previously the loss was felt as an active deprivation *by* a bad object – the good object becomes a persecutor; whereas in the depressive position the object is felt as a whole to be missing, lost, damaged, etc., and 'pined' for.

Internal objects and the external world: With the beginning of an appreciation of the external object as a 'whole object' the infant is required to accept a more realistic view of its nature. The animistic world of the concrete internal object gives way, and the internal world gradually becomes separated out more accurately. The concrete identification of parts of the self and objects gives way to an ability to represent objects to oneself and the depressive position brings in a crucial change in the accuracy of the perception of the external object [see EXTERNAL WORLD].

The concrete internal object continues to be linked to an external object through projection and under the influence of bodily demands. The external object remains partially constructed from internal sources; this part of the construction gradually diminishes, but can hardly be said to disappear. Equally, the construction of the internal world of objects through introjection of external objects continues, perhaps with lessening intensity, throughout life.

The importance of the good object: Before 1935, Klein had emphasized the importance of the persecuting object that created the paranoid vicious circles [see PARANOIA]. But with the depressive position, her emphasis changed to the importance of the good object – one that is needed, depended upon and loved, one that has to be sustained. In normal development the individual is protected from the bleak and paranoid relations with the persecuting bad object by having, internally, a good and supporting object. The sense of having a good object inside is the basis of confidence in oneself, and disturbances to self-confidence result from problems in sustaining an internal good object. For instance, she says of Richard, as his analysis progressed:

> The belief in the internal good mother was his greatest support. Whenever this belief was strengthened, hope and confidence and a greater feeling of security set in. When this feeling of confidence was shaken – either by illness or other causes – then depression and hypochondriacal anxieties increased. (Klein, 1945, p. 391)

Maintaining the internal object: The importance of the internal object is greater in Klein's subsequent work, since the struggle to attain a secure and stable good internal object inside – one that is identified with – is seen as the core of a stable personality that can weather much emotional disturbance. Abraham's extension of Freud's work on mourning and manic-depressive illness showed how precarious the possession of objects introjected into the ego is in pathological states. This precariousness lies at the bottom of much psychological illness and disturbance. The internal good object has to be sustained against the phantasies of attack and damage which are brought out by the unwelcome 'bad' side of the 'whole object'.

Mourning: The discovery of the depressive position, then, enabled Klein to make a significant contribution to the nature of mourning. In the later depressive position paper in 1940 she says:

> The poignancy of the actual loss of a loved person is, in my view, greatly increased by the mourner's unconscious phantasies of having lost his 'internal good' objects as well. He then feels that his internal 'bad' objects predominate and his inner world is in danger of disruption. We know that the loss of a loved person leads to an impulse in the mourner to reinstate the lost loved object (Freud, Abraham). In my view, however, he not only takes into himself (reincorporates) the person whom he has just lost, but also reinstates his internalized good objects (ultimately his loved parents) . . . These too are felt to have gone under, to be destroyed, whenever the loss of a loved person is experienced. Thereupon the early depressive position, and with it anxieties, guilt and feelings of loss and grief, are reactivated. If, for instance, a woman loses her child through death, along with sorrow and pain her early dread of being robbed by a 'bad' retaliating mother is reactivated and confirmed. (Klein, 1940, p. 353) [see 10. DEPRESSIVE POSITION]

INTERNAL OBJECTS AND THE PARANOID-SCHIZOID POSITION.

The anxiety of the paranoid-schizoid position mostly concerns the fear of the fragmentation and loss of the ego. This is intimately connected with the fate of the internal object – a part-object, highly unstable, switching from 'good' to 'bad'. If the object is attacked at this position, it is fragmented; the ego is felt to be identically fragmented [see 11. PARANOID-SCHIZOID POSITION]. In descriptions of the paranoid-schizoid position there is an exquisite sensitivity to the fate of objects, both internal and external. Fears that the good internal object will be lost through forceful projections, as if by mistake (throwing the baby out with the bath water), or that bad objects will be introjected along with good objects (the Trojan horse) are persistent anxieties at the early stages.

THE STRUGGLE TO COMPREHEND INTERNAL
OBJECTS. Not all analysts interested in internal objects followed Klein in her view that internal objects are features in the normal development of the ego through the central importance of the good internal object, its loss and its reinstitution in the depressive position. Brierley struck out on a new line: 'Internalized objects only announce themselves as such in clinical practice in cases in which it is obvious that normal ego-synthesis is defective' (Brierley, 1939, p. 241). She was making the point here that the appearance of an internal object is a mark of severe psychopathology and in effect said that it comes out of the work with manic-depressive and other psychoses. She based her idea on Glover's theory of ego-nuclei (Glover, 1932). Glover described the ego as forming from nuclei, each one of which formed around the separate bits of bodily sensations that the infant experiences. These ego-nuclei gradually draw together to integrate into the ego as development progresses. However, in states of severe disturbance they do not all integrate, or under tension there may be a regression to a less integrated state of the ego, leaving some separate nuclei which give rise, in Brierley's theory, to the sense of something separate inside. Brierley, in intending to support this theory, pointed out that Klein had endorsed Glover's theory of ego-nuclei. However, later Klein (1946) changed her view [see 10. DEPRESSIVE POSITION]. Here Brierley was developing ideas about the abnormal states of the ego and virtually ignored the object Klein described.

Fuchs (1937), in a paper that took the English analysts seriously (but was ignored by them), developed a somewhat similar idea. He attempted to clarify the phenomena by distinguishing two forms of identification, depending on the character of the internalization processes – on the one hand there is a pregenital form of identification with an object, based on introjection and as a defence against the actual loss of an external object, leading to a *narcissistic* identification; on the other hand a partial identification with an object as a result of genital impulses, with preservation of the external object, leading to a *hysterical* identification.

In a related theory, Matte-Blanco (1941) hypothesized that the internal object fails to be assimilated if it has been split by aggression; otherwise objects are assimilated into the ego harmoniously and unobtrusively.

The various attempts at theoretical solutions did not lead to a general acceptance of the Kleinian position as defined by Klein (1935, 1946), Isaacs (1940) and Heimann (1942, 1952). In fact the confused position was displayed by Alix Strachey (1941), who discerned three separate usages of the term 'internal' – (a) mental; (b) imaginary; (c) inside. Kleinian publications over ten years indicated that they were moving towards the third of these usages, the belief of something inside – although Brierley still remained uncertain in 1942 and requested that the Kleinians decide which of Alix Strachey's usages they adhered to.

Endopsychic structure: Fairbairn, in a series of papers in the 1940s (collected in 1952), began to describe a new structural model of the mind in which three parts of the ego engage in separate internal relations with three internal objects [see FAIRBAIRN]. According to Fairbairn, the object that is introjected is only the 'bad' object, internalized as a means of controlling it. The structure was then described in stable form in the way that Freud's structural model is fixed. In both these ways, Fairbairn's structural model contrasted with Klein's fluid and subjectively described model.

Internal objects and representations: Freud described the establishing of representations when he was working out the theory of dreams (Freud, 1900). In classical psychoanalytic theory the only internal object is the superego. All other objects are 'represented' in perception or in memory. Many analysts have therefore decided that Klein's concept of internal objects is a translation of the classical term 'object-representation'; however, it is not so. The distinction between a concrete object experienced, in phantasy, as active inside the personality (body) and a representation in memory of an object is a significant one. They are distinguished by, in the one, an omnipotent belief in the concrete presence of the object and, in the other, a representation that symbolizes it to the ego but is not confused with it [see INTERNAL REALITY]. This distinction corresponds to the one between symbolic equation and true symbols [see SYMBOL-FORMATION; SYMBOLIC EQUATION]. Sandler and Joffe (1969) exploiting the distinction between 'ego' and 'self-representation' made by Hartmann (1950) and Jacobson (1954) [see EGO-PSYCHOLOGY] developed the concept of the representational world (Sandler and Rosenblatt, 1962) into a model for mapping other conceptual frameworks on to the classical psychoanalytical one. Latterly Sandler (1989) has used this model for understanding the term 'internal object' which he proposed should stand for a theoretical construction, by the analyst, of an underlying structure in the patient (rather than to denote an aspect of the patient's experience).

The concept of the 'internal object' shares with 'unconscious phantasy' the role of the most original and innovative aspects of Klein's work, and both concepts deepen Freud's view of the unconscious. The concept of the 'internal object' remains a potent force for understanding the most severe mental disorders, and it is an equally potent weapon for the most severe misunderstandings between Kleinian and other psychoanalytic schools.

We have today a situation in which the mysteriousness of 'internal

objects' which so preoccupied analysts in the 1930s and 1940s has
been overshadowed (not solved) in the 1970s and 1980s by the
mysteries of 'projective identification'. Perhaps it would be more
useful, in attempting to evaluate the relative merits of the Kleinian
school and ego-psychology, if the distinction between internal objects
and representations were made a focus of attention, instead of the
more usually theoretical contests that take place over the effectiveness
of the concept of 'projective identification'.

Brierley, Marjorie (1939) 'A prefatory note on "internalized objects" and
    depression', *Int. J. Psycho-Anal.* 20:241–7.
—— (1942) ' "Internalized objects" and theory', *Int. J. Psycho-Anal.* 23:
    107–12.
Fairbairn, Ronald (1952) *Psycho-Analytic Studies of the Personality.* Routledge &
    Kegan Paul.
Freud, Sigmund (1900) *The Interpretation of Dreams*, in James Strachey, ed.
    The Standard Edition of the Complete Psychological Works of Sigmund Freud, 24
    vols. Hogarth, 1953–73. vols 4, 5.
—— (1917) 'Mourning and melancholia', *S.E.* 14, pp. 237–60.
—— (1923) *The Ego and the Id. S.E.* 19, pp. 3–66.
Fuchs (Foulkes) S.H. (1937) 'On introjection', *Int. J. Psycho-Anal.* 18:
    269–93.
Glover, Edward (1932) 'A psycho-analytical approach to the classification of
    mental disorders', *Journal of Mental Science* 78:819–42.
Hartmann, Heinz (1950) 'Comments on the psycho-analytic theory of the
    ego', *Psycho-Analytic Study of the Child* 5:74–96.
Heimann, Paula (1942) 'A contribution to the problem of sublimation and its
    relation to processes of internalization', *Int. J. Psycho-Anal.* 23:8–17.
—— (1949) 'Some notes on the psycho-analytic concept of introjected
    objects', *Br. J. Med. Psychol.* 22:8–17.
—— (1952) 'Certain functions of projection and introjection in early infancy',
    in Melanie Klein, Paula Heimann, Susan Isaacs and Joan Riviere, eds
    (1952) *Developments in Psycho-Analysis.* Hogarth, pp. 122–68; originally read
    1943 in the Controversial Discussion, British Psycho-Analytical Society.
Isaacs, Susan (1940) 'Temper tantrums in early childhood and their relation to
    internal objects', *Int. J. Psycho-Anal.* 21:280–93.
Jacobson, Edith (1954) 'The self and the object world', *Psycho-Analytic Study of
    the Child* 9:75–127.
Klein, Melanie (1925) 'A contribution to the psychogenesis of tics', in *The
    Writings of Melanie Klein*, vol. 1. Hogarth, pp. 106–27.
—— (1926) 'The psychological principles of early analysis', *The Writings of
    Melanie Klein*, vol. 1, pp. 128–37.
—— (1927) 'Criminal tendencies in normal children', *The Writings of Melanie
    Klein*, vol. 1, pp. 170–85.
—— (1929a) 'Personification in the play of children', *The Writings of Melanie
    Klein*, vol. 1, pp. 199–209.
—— (1929b) 'Infantile anxiety-situations reflected in a work of art and in the
    creative impulse', *The Writings of Melanie Klein*, vol. 1, pp. 210–18.

—— (1935) 'A contribution to the psychogenesis of manic-depressive states', *The Writings of Melanie Klein*, vol. 1, pp. 262–89.

—— (1936) 'Weaning', *The Writings of Melanie Klein*, vol. 1, pp. 290–305.

—— (1940) 'Mourning and its relation to manic-depressive states', *The Writings of Melanie Klein*, vol. 1, pp. 344–69.

—— (1945) 'The Oedipus complex in the light of early anxiety', *The Writings of Melanie Klein*, vol. 1, pp. 370–419.

—— (1946) 'Notes on some schizoid mechanisms', *The Writings of Melanie Klein*, vol. 3, pp. 1–24.

Matte-Blanco, Ignacio (1941) 'On introjection and the processes of psychic metabolism', *Int. J. Psycho-Anal.* 22:17–36.

Matthews, Gareth (1980) *Philosophy and the Young Child.* Cambridge, MA: Harvard University Press.

Money-Kyrle, Roger (1968) 'Cognitive development', *Int. J. Psycho-Anal.* 49: 691–8; republished (1978) in *The Collected Papers of Roger Money-Kyrle.* Perth: Clunie, pp. 416–33.

Piaget, Jean (1954) *The Construction of Reality in the Child.* Routledge & Kegan Paul.

Rado, S. (1928) 'The problem of melancholia', *Int. J. Psycho-Anal.* 9:420–38.

Riviere, Joan (1936) 'On the genesis of psychical conflict in earliest infancy', *Int. J. Psycho-Anal.* 17:395–422; republished (1952) in Melanie Klein, Paula Heimann, Susan Isaacs and Joan Riviere, eds *Developments in Psycho-Analysis.* Hogarth, pp. 37–66.

Rosenfeld, Herbert (1964) 'On the psychopathology of narcissism: a clinical approach', *Int. J. Psycho-Anal.* 45:332–7; republished (1965) in Herbert Rosenfeld, *Psychotic States.* Hogarth, pp. 169–79.

Sandler, Joseph (1989) 'Internal relationships and their externalization', paper given to *Conference on Transference and Internal Object Relationships,* University College, London, April 1989.

Sandler, Joseph and Joffe, Walter (1969) 'Towards a basic psycho-analytic model', *Int. J. Psycho-Anal.* 50:79–90; republished in Sandler (1987) *Safety and Superego.* Karnac, pp. 235–54.

Sandler, Joseph and Rosenblatt, Bernard (1962) 'The concept of the representational world', *Psycho-Analytic Study of the Child* 17:128–45; republished in Sandler (1987) *Safety and Superego.* Karnac, pp. 58–72.

Schilder, Paul and Wechsler, David (1935) 'What do children know about the interior of their body?', *Int. J. Psycho-Anal.* 16:355–60.

Schmideberg, Melitta (1931) 'A contribution to the psychology of persecutory ideas and delusions', *Int. J. Psycho-Anal.* 12:331–67.

—— (1934) 'The play analysis of a three-year-old girl', *Int. J. Psycho-Anal.* 15:245–64.

Searl, M.N. (1932) 'A note on depersonalization', *Int. J. Psycho-Anal.* 13: 329–47.

—— (1933) 'Play, reality and aggression', *Int. J. Psycho-Anal.* 14:310–20.

Stephen, Karin (1934) 'Introjection and projection: guilt and rage', *Br. J. Med. Psychol.* 14:316–31.

Strachey, Alix (1941) 'A note on the use of the word "internal" ', *Int. J. Psycho-Anal.* 22:37–43.

6 FEMININITY PHASE

DEFINITION. Klein described the early relationship to the breast as inherently fraught. At first it has oral characteristics, and the phantasies – sadistic and paranoid ones of sucking, biting or being bitten – result in the earliest form of anxiety. Both boys and girls turn away from the first object (mother) to the father and his penis. In this sense they adopt a position of *femininity*.

The turning away from the primary object, mother – or, at the primitive level, her breast – was originally thought to be a response to weaning, but later Klein saw it as more fundamental and realized that a deep ambivalence resides in human nature, resulting in the features of the depressive position. With the deflection of interest from one object to the next goes a step in development – giving rise to the importance of the father, as is characteristic of Freud's theories. Alternatively the degree of ambivalence may be so great as to inhibit developmental steps. Klein thought she was describing important observations which did not contradict Freud's views, but underlay them and gave them more meaning.

CHRONOLOGY
1928   Anxiety connected with attacks on mother's body (Klein, Melanie, 1928, 'Early stages of the Oedipus conflict'; Klein, Melanie, 1932, *The Psycho-Analysis of Children*).
1945   Feminine phase and the depressive position (Klein, Melanie, 1945, 'The Oedipus complex in the light of early anxieties').

During the mid-1920s Klein became convinced that her technique allowed her new insights because of the much closer observations that she could make with young children, rather than extrapolations from the psychoanalysis of adults or older children. However, she was hesitant about making the modifications to the orthodox psychoanalytic theory of the Oedipus complex, and later the superego, which were implied by her observations. She had to be uncharacteristically reticent, but there was a contribution which she could make: this was to the contemporary interest in female psychology.

KLEIN'S CONTRIBUTIONS TO EARLY SEXUALITY. At that time, in the 1920s, this was a wide-open field. She did not have to be hesitant about her results, and she was not. She announced her discoveries as comparable in importance to the castration anxiety in little boys.

There were two important discoveries:

(1) the ferocity and frequency of phantasy *attacks upon mother's body* by

the little girl (and also the little boy) which led to fear about losing mother, and also fears of retaliation from her; and

(2) the important process of finding new objects to relate to, with the aim of avoiding the painful constellation of ambivalence and fear that has developed with an old object. Turning to the father as the new object represents a normal phase of development in which a *feminine attitude* with which to relate to father is brought out.

(1) Attacks on mother. The early analyses Klein conducted began to show her a particular phantasy of violence:

> Then she came out of the particular corner which she called her room, stole up to me and made all sorts of threats. She would stab me in the throat, throw me into the courtyard, burn me up, or give me to the policeman. She tried to tie my hands and feet, she lifted the sofa-cover and said she was making *po-kaki-kucki* [buttocks/ faeces] . . . At that time she had already wished to rob her mother, who was pregnant, of her children, to kill her and to take her place in coitus with father. These tendencies to hate and aggression were the cause of her fixation to her mother, as well as of her feelings of anxiety and guilt. (Klein, 1926, p. 131)

This whole discovery was later summarized with great clarity:

> My observation of the cases of Trude, Ruth and Rita . . . [has] led me to recognize the existence of an anxiety, or rather – anxiety- situation, which is specific for girls and the equivalent of the castration anxiety felt by boys. This anxiety-situation culminates in the girl's idea that her mother will destroy her body, abolish its contents and take the children out of it . . . It is based upon the child's impulses of aggression against the mother and her desires, springing from the early stages of the Oedipus conflict, to kill her and steal from her. (Klein, 1932, p. 31)

When Klein found these anxious phantasies in the analyses of 1923–4, they were new to psychoanalysis. The attack on mother's body and its contents was vivid in the manipulations of toys in the playroom. Riviere described the effect of weaning:

> In consequence of disappointment or frustration during sucking or weaning, coupled with experiences during the primal scene which is interpreted in oral terms, extremely intense sadism develops towards both parents. The desire to bite off the nipple shifts, and desires to destroy, penetrate and disembowel the mother and devour her and the contents of her body succeed it. These contents include the father's penis, her faeces and her abdomen – all her

possessions and loved objects, imagined as within her body. The desire to bite off the nipple is also shifted, as we know, on to the desire to castrate the father by biting off his penis. (Riviere, 1929, pp. 309–10)

(2) **New objects**. The result of the aggression towards mother is that the child turns to father with a feminine attitude: *the femininity phase*. At first Klein thought this was driven by an actual affront to the child by mother (weaning): 'I regard the deprivation of the breast as the most fundamental cause of the turning to the father' (Klein, 1928, p. 193). Later, however, she thought it arose from the inherent ambivalence towards objects.

Turning away to new objects is the beginning of one of the most important developmental steps: the capacity to substitute symbols for primary objects of interest [see SYMBOL-FORMATION]. The impetus to explore new objects and to enlarge the infant's world results from hurt, loss and their attendant fearful phantasies. Symbols have the quality, therefore, of defending against the anxieties of the early aggression and form part of the working through of the depressive position [see 10. DEPRESSIVE POSITION].

FEMALE SEXUALITY. The interest in the development of girls was very high during the 1920s. With the increasing emancipation of women following the First World War and their acceptance into the professions, there were a number who were able to challenge Freud's view of the 'shadowy area' of the girl's sexual development:

> Nevertheless the conclusion so far drawn from the investigations – amounting as it does to an assertion that one-half of the human race is discontented with the sex assigned to it, and can overcome this discontent only in favourable circumstances – is decidedly unsatisfying, not only to feminine narcissism but also to biological science. (Horney, 1924, p. 52)

Horney threw down the glove and followed with progressively more strident dissociations from the male-dominated psychoanalytic view of women (Horney, 1926). Freud (1925, 1931) and Jones (1927) tried to keep up, but the pace was set by women analysts (Lampl de Groot, 1928; Riviere, 1929; Deutsch, 1930; Klein, 1932; Horney, 1932, 1933).

In 1930 Deutsch delivered a series of lectures on *The Psychic Development of Women* to the Vienna Psycho-Analytic Institute, and Horney (1933), growing more provocatively independent, announced her agreement with Klein's discovery of the furious and retaliatory relation with mother's inside. Riviere (1934) took the opportunity offered by the publication of Freud's *New Introductory Lectures* to criticize his view of female psychology, in the midst of an otherwise laudatory review. Jones (1935) reviewed the 'new understanding' of women's psychology in a lecture he delivered to the Vienna Psycho-Analytical Society. This was the first in a series of Exchange Lectures between London and Vienna, arranged because of the theoretical divergences between the two main centres of psychoanalysis at the time. It is significant that Jones, in confronting the growing differences and threatening divorce, took female sexuality as his central theme. He was daring to take to Vienna one of the most important divergences from Freud's views that remained within the psychoanalytic world [see CONTROVERSIAL DISCUSSIONS].

THE PSYCHOLOGICAL DEVELOPMENT OF GIRLS.

Crucial, as a stage in the development of her later work, was Klein's interest in the development of the female child. She concurred with the many criticisms about Freud's views on the role of penis envy in the development of the little girl. In this view a woman is no more than a man who lacks something, and the little girl's development is determined by the painful slight she feels at this discovery about her body, and then a search for the object to blame – usually mother.

Criticism of Freud: Freud's view of women is historically relative, deriving from nineteenth-century social relations. In the social reality of the time women were socially, morally, economically and anatomically inferior.

The emphatic chorus of protest against Freud was that he underplayed the little girl's awareness of her internal space, and the life-creating potential of her body – 'the denial of the vagina'.

The prior relationship with mother: Klein was particularly intent on displaying a truly psychoanalytic account of the development of femininity. She took this to be the content of the child's anxieties as she goes through the various twists and turns of instinctual development, especially in the pregenital phases. It was Klein's contribution to show the importance of the relationship to mother before that to father, and this has led some writers to counterpose Klein to Freud (e.g. Chodorow, 1978). However, Klein's position is actually more subtle, in that she does not deny the denigratory attitude detectable in Freud but attributes it instead to the phantasies of the patient, who is caught between her destructive impulses towards mothers and women, and impulses of love and identification.

Freud himself, in a late paper, granted the strength of these corrections:

Our insight into this early, pre-Oedipus, phase in girls comes to us as a surprise, like the discovery, in another field, of Minoan-

Mycenaean civilization behind the civilization of Greece. Everything in the sphere of this first attachment to the mother seemed to me so difficult to grasp in analysis – so grey with age and shadowy and almost impossible to revivify – that it was as if it had succumbed to an especially inexorable repression. But perhaps I gained this impression because the women who were in analysis with me were able to cling to the very attachment to the father in which they had taken refuge from the early phase that was in question. (Freud, 1931, p. 226)

This is a gracious acknowledgement of his willingness at least to consider the greater possibilities open to women analysts in this sphere. He acknowledged the turning to a phase of feminine attachment to father.

The terrifying conflict of castration anxiety, which leads to maturational processes and also to the infantile amnesia in the little boy, has its equivalent in the little girl. Klein came to this discovery early in her work with children, and stated this categorically as 'the equivalent of castration anxiety in the little boy' in her London lectures in 1925 (see *The Psycho-Analysis of Children* – Klein, 1932). In her view the girl is very preoccupied with the inside of her mother's body, attracted there by the evidence of mother's creativity in producing further children, and in witnessing the change and size of mother's tummy during pregnancy. The interest in mother's body is determined by many factors, and Klein postulates an inherent awareness of father residing in mother's insides [see COMBINED PARENT FIGURE]. These are complex phantasies and entail relations with and between parts of mother's and father's bodies: breast, tummy, bottom and penis [see PART-OBJECTS]. These are not just perceptions or imaginings, but are felt with an intensity of emotion of a very mixed kind. The phantasy of father's penis inside mother's tummy, or her breast, creates enormously powerful feelings of exclusion and rage that is experienced as a relationship of hate, damage and being damaged. The little girl's feelings amount to a wish to enter, rob and destroy mother's tummy and her creativity, and the relationship which exists there with father's penis. This primitive, mystifying and unconscious phantasy is then matched by the fear that mother and the damaged and angry remains of her insides, of her children and of father's penis will come back at her to destroy her own body and her own children with exactly the same kind of attack. The little girl fears her mother as full of damaged and now hostile objects; and at the same time feels the loss of her mother as the great love and protector.

It is the little girl's phantasies of the mutual destruction of each other's insides that create an intensely problematic relationship with her mother. It results in a need, similar to the boy's, to maintain amnesia for this childhood period of development, and sets in train a prolonged working over of hostile feelings towards mother and the parents in union. It lays the seeds for the adult woman's anxieties about her bodily attractiveness, or lack of it, and the ravages of the ageing process.

The underpinning of penis envy: These horrifying anxieties underlie the belief in a damaged body that is eventually expressed as the classical problem of penis envy. The girl suffers from the fear that there is something wrong with her body (symbolized by the small external genital), which will be manifest in the fears, during pregnancy, of giving birth to deformed babies, all of which matches the deformities to the babies and the penis which the little girl has attacked in phantasy, inside mother.

THE DEVELOPMENT OF BOYS. Following these discoveries about little girls and the basis of their penis envy, Klein extended the theory to the little boy. Freud's acknowledgement of the difficulty of extending so far back as to the first attachment to the mother in the little girl suggests it may be just as true that the early attachment of the little boy to his mother was equally neglected by classical psychoanalytic theory – and was an equally grey area of doubt.

Klein summarized the feminine phase:

> It has its basis on the anal-sadistic level and imparts to that level a new content, for faeces are now equated with the child that is longed for and the desire to rob the mother now applies to the child as well as to the faeces. Here we can discern two aims which merge with one another. The one is directed by the desire for children, the intention being to appropriate them, while the other aim is motivated by jealousy of the future brothers and sisters whose appearance is expected, and by the wish to destroy them inside mother. (A third object of the boy's oral-sadistic tendencies inside the mother is the father's penis.) (Klein, 1928, pp. 189–90)

Thus the boy, too, has a feminine phase:

> As in the castration complex of girls, so in the femininity complex of the male, there is at bottom the frustrated desire for a special organ. The tendencies to steal and destroy are concerned with the organs of conception, pregnancy and parturition, which the boy assumes to exist in the mother, and further with the vagina and breasts, the fountain of milk . . . The boy fears punishment for his destruction of his mother's body, but, besides this, his fear is of a more general nature, and here we have an analogy to the anxiety associated with the castration wishes of the girl. He fears that his body will be mutilated and dismembered, and this dread also means castration

... This dread of the mother is so overwhelming because there is combined with it an intense dread of castration by the father. The destructive tendencies whose object is the womb are also directed with their full oral- and anal-sadistic intensity against the father's penis, which is supposed to be located there ... Thus the femininity phase is characterized by anxiety relating to the womb and the father's penis, and this anxiety subjects the boy to the tyranny of a superego which devours, dismembers and castrates and is formed from the image of father and mother alike. (Klein, 1928, p. 190)

The underpinning of castration anxiety: In this way Klein investigated the factors underlying castration anxiety. However, she quite neglected the fact that she brutally tore the concept of castration anxiety from its intricate theoretical attachments to the Oedipus complex. Indeed, these hypotheses pushed her further and further into modifying the Oedipus complex [see 4. OEDIPUS COMPLEX].

The femininity phase is charged with a particular attention to internal matters and to a particular need to mobilize compensating solidarity, love and identification with women and women's concerns. This focusing on the internal was an important realization which resulted in the full-scale theory of the internal world and objects. It comprised also an understanding of the characterological development of women's interest in their bodily interiors – and, for that matter, men's interest in women's bodily interiors.

EARLY STAGES OF THE OEDIPUS COMPLEX. The importance of the femininity phase gradually faded after Klein described the depressive position. Her interest in the effects of the ambivalence in relationships no longer depended so heavily on keeping in line with classical theories. The painful experience of attacking mother, her breasts, her body and everything in her became subsumed under the general anxiety of attacks on, and damage to, the loved object.

The turning to father represented the feminine phase in both boys and girls, and the relationship which is turned to him is one of inherent ambivalence. Thus the pain and suffering of the depressive position is involved here, too.

These anxieties [see DEPRESSIVE ANXIETY], in 'the early stages of the Oedipus complex', are powerful forces for promoting development, as well as for causing difficulties and the arrest of growth (fixations):

The gratification experienced at the mother's breast enables the infant to turn his desires towards new objects, first of all towards his father's penis. Particular impetus, however, is given to the new desire by frustration in the breast relation. (Klein, 1945, p. 408)

The relation to the breast is twofold. Both the positive aspect of it as a spur to develop new experiences and relationships, and also the negative aspects may enhance (the latter probably prematurely and anxiously) a developmental step forward [see DEVELOPMENT]. This dual (ambivalent) attitude is eventually transferred to the penis:

> Frustration and gratification from the outset mould the infant's relation to a loved good breast and to a hated bad breast. The need to cope with frustration and with the ensuing aggression is one of the factors which lead to idealizing the good breast and the good mother, and correspondingly to intensifying the hatred and fears of the bad breast and bad mother, which becomes the prototype of all persecuting and frightening objects. The two conflicting attitudes to the mother's breast are carried over into the new relation to father's penis. The frustration suffered in the earlier relation increases the demands and hopes from the new source and stimulates love for the new object. (Klein, 1945, p. 408)

The two conflicting attitudes to mother – with the third object (father) – are taken into the complexity of the coexisting positive and inverted Oedipus complexes [see 4. OEDIPUS COMPLEX].

ABNORMAL SEXUAL DEVELOPMENT. The development of sexual identity depends upon the successful negotiation of these early persecutory anxieties. Deviations from heterosexual development result, according to Klein, from the persistence of intense persecutory and paranoid anxiety. In this she developed the ideas from classical psychoanalysts. Freud had attributed homosexuality to a rebuff by the loved parent of the opposite sex, with a consequent turning to the parent of the same sex as a loved object. Abraham began to look at homosexuality in terms of the identifications based on introjections of the parents. Klein looked at homosexuality from both points of view. Her particular contribution was that the turning away to a new object, and the satisfactory introjection of an object to identify with, resulted from the balance of sadistic and loving forces, in a complicated interplay with the actual external objects: 'When his fear of the castrating father is mitigated by trust in the good father, he can face his Oedipus hatred and rivalry' (Klein, 1945, p. 411). In this passage she was conveying that the boy looks for a good father whom he can introject as an internal support that strengthens his confidence in himself as a man, and helps him to face his own hatred of his father. This in turn rests to a major extent on the actual father being able to withstand the son's hatred without leaving the son bereft of support from him.

In contrast to Freud's view that latent homosexuality underlies paranoia – for example, in Freud's analysis of Schreber (Freud, 1911)

– Klein pointed to the possibility that paranoid fears underlie homosexuality. Rosenfeld (1949) explicitly examined this revision.

The sexual perversions, even the sado-masochistic ones, have been very little studied by Kleinians. Hunter (1954) and Joseph (1971) both analysed fetishists and showed the turning to a substitute object which, being inanimate, relieved some of the painful ambivalence of human loved ones. Joseph was particularly meticulous in defining the need of the object as a feverish urge to get right inside it, a concrete form of projective identification. In general the perversions are typically regarded as having the form Rosenfeld (1949) described, in which the turning away to sexual substitutes derives from a paranoid persecutory anxiety. The interest is therefore not so much in the specific form of perverse sexuality, but the underlying paranoia or envy to which the analyst has traced the conflict back (Gallwey, 1979) [see PERVERSION].

The idea of the femininity phase of girls and boys, characterized by great jealousy and aggression, was important to Klein at the time (the 1920s and 1930s) because it was one hypothesis that pointed to the power of her play technique in uncovering greater detail of childhood sexual development and its aberrations underlying the psycho-pathology of childhood (and adults) with which classical psycho-analysts had hitherto been occupied. However, after Klein adopted the death instinct as having equal importance to the sexual libido (1932) her attention to the development of sexual objects and identifications faded somewhat, as the importance of primary aggression came to the fore. However, the specific phantasy of intrusion with damage into the inside of the object did come back into its own. In 1957 the theory of primary envy [see 12. ENVY] emphasized this as an innate phantasy representing the death instinct; however, the specific connotations with the sexual development had fallen away.

Chodorow, Nancy (1978) *The Reproduction of Mothering*. Berkeley: University of California Press.

Deutsch, Helene (1930) 'The significance of masochism in the mental life of women', *Int. J. Psycho-Anal.* 11:48–60.

Freud, Sigmund (1911) 'An autobiographical account of a case of paranoia', in James Strachey, ed. *The Standard Edition of the Complete Psychological Works of Sigmund Freud*, 24 vols. Hogarth, 1953–73. vol. 12, pp. 3–82.

—— (1925) 'Some psychical consequences of the anatomical distinction between the sexes'. *S.E.* 19, pp. 243–58.

—— (1931) 'Female sexuality'. *S.E.* 21, pp. 223–43.

Gallwey, Patrick (1979) 'Symbolic dysfunction in the perversions', *Int. Rev. Psycho-Anal.* 6:155–61.

Horney, Karen (1924) 'On the generation of the castration complex in women', *Int. J. Psycho-Anal.* 5:50–65.

—— (1926) 'The flight from womanhood', *Int. J. Psycho-Anal.* 7:324–9.

—— (1932) 'The dread of women', *Int. J. Psycho-Anal.* 13:348–66.

—— (1933) 'The denial of the vagina', *Int. J. Psycho-Anal.* 14:57–70.

Hunter, Dugmore (1954) 'Object relation changes in the analysis of fetishism', *Int. J. Psycho-Anal.* 35:302–12.

Jones, Ernest (1927) 'The early development of female sexuality', *Int. J. Psycho-Anal.* 8:459–72.

—— (1935) 'Early female sexuality', *Int. J. Psycho-Anal.* 16:263–73.

Joseph, Betty (1971) 'A clinical contribution to the analysis of a perversion', *Int. J. Psycho-Anal.* 52:441–9.

Klein, Melanie (1926) 'The psychological principles of early analysis', in *The Writings of Melanie Klein*, vol. 1. Hogarth, pp. 128–38.

—— (1928) 'Early stages of the Oedipus conflict', *The Writings of Melanie Klein*, vol. 1, pp. 186–98.

—— (1932) *The Psycho-Analysis of Children*, *The Writings of Melanie Klein*, vol. 3.

—— (1945) 'The Oedipus complex in the light of early anxieties', *The Writings of Melanie Klein*, vol. 1, pp. 370–419.

—— (1957) *Envy and Gratitude*, *The Writings of Melanie Klein*, vol. 3, pp. 176–235.

Lampl de Groot, J. (1928) 'The evolution of the Oedipus complex in women', *Int. J. Psycho-Anal.* 9:332–45.

Riviere, Joan (1929) 'Womanliness as a masquerade', *Int. J. Psycho-Anal.* 10:303–13.

—— (1934) 'Review of Freud's *New Introductory Lectures*', *Int. J. Psycho-Anal.* 15:329–39.

Rosenfeld, Herbert (1949) 'Remarks on the relation of male homosexuality to paranoia, paranoid anxiety and narcissism', *Int. J. Psycho-Anal.* 30:36–57; republished (1965) in Herbert Rosenfeld, *Psychotic States*. Hogarth, pp. 34–51.

7 SUPEREGO

DEFINITION. Klein's work challenged the classical theory of the superego, which consisted of the internalized parents (imagos) who represent social standards, the capacity for self-assessment, and the origin of certain states of mind such as guilt, worthlessness, self-esteem. In Klein's view the superego is analysable into a number of internal figures, known as internal objects, which are themselves in relation to each other as well as to the ego. During the first period of her work (1920–32) Klein was much preoccupied with the superego and its origins, which appeared earlier than Freud's theory allowed. Eventually, after a long, uneasy acceptance of the classical theory of Freud, she evolved her own radically different view on its origins in the initial deflection of the death instinct.

CHRONOLOGY
1926 Unconscious guilt and the harsh superego (Klein, Melanie, 1927, 'Criminal tendencies in normal children').
1929 Multiple internal objects.
1932 The superego and the death instinct (Klein, Melanie, 1932, 'Early stages of the Oedipus conflict and of superego formation' (Chapter 8 of *The Psycho-Analysis of Children*); Klein, Melanie, 1933, 'The early development of conscience in the child').
1935 Guilt and the depressive position (Klein, Melanie, 1935, 'A contribution to the psychogenesis of manic-depressive states').

From the beginning of her work until 1932, Klein was struggling to understand the experience of remorse and guilt in her child patients; and from 1923, when Freud produced his own theory of the superego as the source of guilt, Klein not only had to struggle to understand her patients; she also found herself in opposition to orthodox views. She constantly tried to place her findings in the 'correct' theoretical framework of the superego, but with diminishing success as time went on. She finally made a break from the orthodox view in 1932 when she adopted the superego as the manifestation of the death instinct, a view which remains opposed to classical psychoanalysis now as then. However, the importance of the concept of the superego has diminished in Kleinian thought since 1935, when Klein's concept of the depressive position intervened and became her full-scale theory of guilt.

The problem: The main problem was that Klein had, from the beginning of her work in 1918, discovered the intense feelings of remorse in children, some as young as two years and a few months. But five years later, in 1923, Freud described guilt as arising from the superego, which is formed *after* the Oedipus complex in the genital

position, giving the superego a developmental date of around four or
five years. Klein's views came to diverge in three main ways: (i) the
early forms; (ii) multiple constituents; and (iii) a specific developmental
history of the superego from harsh to softer.

REMORSE. Klein dated her realization of the importance of guilt to
1923 (Klein, 1955) when she analysed Rita, a child of only two years
and nine months: 'the cause of these common phenomena was a
particularly strong sense of guilt underlying *pavor nocturnus* [night
terrors]' (Klein, 1926, p. 131). Rita was troubled by her own
aggression and was stricken with remorse and guilt way back to the age
of fifteen months, when her symptoms began.
    In this same year, 1923, Freud described guilt as the result of an
internal conflict between the instincts (the id) and the 'superego'. For
some time Freud had been occupied with a phenomenon he called the
unconscious sense of guilt or the unconscious need for punishment
(Freud, 1916, 1920). With the emergence of his theory of the superego
in the same year (Freud, 1923), guilt was clearly on the agenda for
discussion throughout the psychoanalytic community [see UNCON-
SCIOUS GUILT].

Freud's theory of guilt and the superego. At this point Freud had no
knowledge of Klein or of her evidence of early remorse. She must have
been both excited and dismayed by his new theory – excited because it
gave her own work a theoretical framework and importance, and she
could provide clinical evidence for the great man, but dismayed
because the theory stated categorically that the internal moral agency,
the superego, was formed at about the age of four or five. Freud
confirmed the importance of his views the next year with his paper on
the dissolution of the Oedipus complex (Freud, 1924b). The mould
was then set for a new orthodoxy in psychoanalysis, which has
persisted to this day.

The heir to the Oedipus complex. In this view the superego is the
'heir to the Oedipus complex' (Freud, 1923, p. 48). It is formed by the
introjection of the oedipal loved objects (mother and father) – the
introjection of the 'primary identifications'. They are taken inside the
ego (inside the personality) and set up as part of the internal, watchful,
self-critical agency. Freud's view of the superego built on his
discoveries about mourning (1917) by describing the resolution of the
Oedipus complex as a process of introjecting the childhood (sexual)
loved ones, in the act of giving them up due to castration anxiety. The
result was an internal relationship with a figure moulded on the
parents with the same kind of guardian/censorship role. That work
came out of a persisting collaboration with Abraham (working in

Berlin), who developed his own views in a long paper in 1924 – the year when Klein was in her own psychoanalysis with him.

Klein's struggle. Once the theory of the superego had been fully elaborated, Freud was then able to make a lot more sense of unconscious guilt, linking it, also, with masochism (Freud, 1924a). The new theory made unconscious guilt and the need for punishment a topic of considerable interest and confusion (for example Glover, 1926; Fenichel, 1928). Where there was perplexity and confusion in the psychoanalytic world, Klein was not far behind, showing how child analysis could throw light on the most obscure points. Her first reference to the superego was in 1926, and the next year she investigated Freud's original theory (Freud, 1916) that unconscious guilt was the driving force behind criminal behaviour (Klein, 1927).

However, Freud's concept of the superego had posed problems for Klein at a time when she was also in analysis with Freud's closest collaborator, Abraham. She never questioned the existence of the superego; it was a matter of dating. The source of guilt in Freud's theory arose as a resolution of the Oedipus complex at about the age of four or five, yet Klein had evidence of guilt and remorse in her patients well back into the second year.

Her position, in the Berlin Psycho-Analytical Society, was precarious as a young and inexperienced – and perhaps quite difficult – new-comer. This was especially so following the death in 1925 of her own mentor and analyst, Abraham. As a result she insisted desperately that she was not in conflict with Freud. She wrote hopefully (in her own first reference to the superego):

> In the cases which I have analysed the inhibitory effect of feelings of guilt was clear at a very early age. What we here encounter corresponds to that which we know as the superego in adults. The fact that we assume the Oedipus complex to reach its zenith round about the fourth year of life and that we recognize the development of the superego as the end-result of the complex, seems to me in no way to contradict these observations. (Klein, 1926, p. 133)

She maintained until 1932 that there was no real disagreement with Freud, a view hotly disputed by Anna Freud in the inflammatory contest (1926–7) between these two women [see ANNA FREUD; CHILD ANALYSIS; 1. TECHNIQUE].

In spite of her disclaimers, Klein did significantly alter and contribute to Freud's theory:

> Those definite, typical phenomena, the existence of which in the most clearly developed form we can recognize when the Oedipus complex has reached its zenith and which precede its waning, are

merely the termination of a development which occupies *years*. The analysis of very young children shows that, as soon as the Oedipus complex arises, they begin to work it through and thereby to develop the superego. (Klein, 1926, p. 133)

What she was getting at here was that the fully fledged superego is all that is properly recognized from the distance of adult analyses, but from the vantage point of child analysis the early formation process of the superego could be described in much finer detail. In fact, before Freud's new structural theory there had been hints of early 'moral' agencies inside the mind: Abraham (1924) described the internal inhibition of oral greed, and Ferenczi (1925) had introduced the notion of a 'sphincter morality' deriving from the anal phase.

Support from the British Society: Inconveniently, Abraham died in 1925 and the Berlin Psycho-Analytical Society had to choose whether to endorse the views of this challenging but as yet insignificant new analyst, or to dismiss her and her untested work with children. She had already presented challenging and unpopular papers, for instance her paper on tics (Klein, 1925) [see 2. UNCONSCIOUS PHANTASY]. The Berlin Society did not give her the immediate recognition and support which she desired and needed, so she was therefore vulnerable to the overtures from Britain. She had set her mind to analysing the early forms of mental life and anxiety, and to give herself space to do this without harassment she moved to London (1926), where she was granted considerable support for her findings (Jones, 1926, 1927; Isaacs, 1929).

It is not clear why Ernest Jones, someone of high standing in the international psychoanalytic world, should have made these overtures to a little-known 'upstart'. It may have been his surreptitious wish to try to wrest some scientific initiative from Vienna for London; it may have been that he needed someone to treat a young member of his own family. In continuing her own line of development behind the defensive moat of the English Channel, Klein provoked conflict across the continent of Europe with her rival, Anna Freud [see ANNA FREUD]. The conflict between them was at its height between 1926 and 1943 and it centred, in the first instance, around the nature and timing of the origin of the superego.

Jones himself was quite critical of Freud's concept and shortly after the original descriptions (Freud, 1923) he wrote, in a mixture of obsequiousness and incisive criticism:

When, however, we leave these valuable broad generalizations and come to a closer study of the problems involved, a considerable number of awkward questions present themselves. To mention only a few at this point: How can we conceive of the same institution as being both an object that presents itself to the *id* to be loved instead of the parents and as an active force criticizing the ego? If the superego arises from incorporating the abandoned love object, how comes it that in fact it is more often derived from the parent of the same sex? If it is composed of elements taken from the 'moral' non-sexual ego-instincts, as we should expect from the part it plays in the repression of the sexual incestuous ones, whence does it derive its sadistic, i.e. sexual nature? (Jones, 1926, p. 304)

KLEIN'S DIVERGENT VIEWS. Klein's views on the superego diverged from Freud's in three main respects:

(1) the origin of the superego is much earlier than Freud suggested;

(2) the constituents of the superego are multiple and varied and not a monolithic amalgam of introjected oedipal parents; and

(3) because of the much longer developmental course, the superego passes through processes of modification, in particular a softening of its harshness and an integration of its contradictory parts.

(1) The origin of the superego. Although Klein accepted Freud's description of the superego, she did not agree with its origin as late as the fourth or fifth year; her clear evidence of the early feelings of guilt showed the origins of the superego to be in the second year of life at the latest. What was her evidence?

(a) Direct evidence: The analysis of young children before the age of four to five showed direct evidence of remorse and guilt.

(b) The evidence of continuous symptoms: The underlying phantasies involved in symptoms can be supposed to be operating at the time when the symptoms started, for instance:

> Rita's case clearly showed that the *pavor nocturnus* which appeared at the age of eighteen months was a neurotic working over of her Oedipus complex . . . [and was] very closely connected with strong feelings of guilt arising from that early Oedipus conflict. (Klein, 1932, p. 4)

Schmideberg expresses the logic clearly:

> I assume that the determinants for the symptoms I found at three years had been continuously at work from the time the symptoms first occurred. This is not susceptible of proof. But the same assumption was made by Freud when he used the factors revealed in the analysis of adults to explain symptoms which had occurred in childhood. (Schmideberg, 1934, pp. 257–8)

(c) The harshness of the child's superego: One thing to which Klein continually pointed was the *quality* of the guilt, which suggested an extremely harsh superego, much more so than in adults – the only feature of Klein's work which Freud ever referred to (Freud, 1930). For example, Erna had experienced a very early potty training at twelve months, '. . . in reality accomplished without any sort of harshness', but the little girl experienced it '. . . as a most cruel act of coercion' from which her symptoms developed, indicating '. . . her sensitivity to blame and the precocious and marked development of her sense of guilt' at that age (Klein, 1926, p. 136n).

In fact Klein showed that the younger the child, the harsher the superego, suggesting that in the development of the child there is a process of continuous modification and softening of an earlier sadistic superego, which persecutes the child with the ideas of horrifying punishments. The implication is that the harsh superego is related to pregenital phases of sadism as described and dated by Abraham (1924).

In 1927 she strengthened this view of the harsh superego when, following Freud (1916), she took an interest in criminal features in children, and their relation to guilt and the sadism to which guilt gave rise (Klein, 1927) [see CRIMINALITY].

(d) The pregenital superego: The fourth form of evidence is in the pregenital character of the phantasies involved, indicating an origin in the pregenital phases. The particular harshness of the superego in some children (Erna, for instance) '. . . bear[s] the stamp of the pregenital impulses' (Klein, 1929, p. 204):

> . . . the child then dreads a punishment corresponding to the offence: the superego becomes something that bites, devours and cuts. The connection between the formation of the superego and the pregenital phases of development is very important from two points of view. On the one hand, the sense of guilt attaches itself to the oral- and the anal-sadistic phases, which as yet predominate; and on the other, the superego comes into being while these phases are in the ascendant, which accounts for its sadistic activity. (Klein, 1928, p. 187)

(2) The constitutents of the superego. The superego, forming in the context of oral and anal impulses, results in various internalized figures based on both mother and father:

> the analysis of little children reveals the structure of the superego as built up of identifications dating from very different periods and strata in mental life. These identifications are surprisingly contradictory in nature, excessive goodness and excessive severity existing side by side. (Klein, 1928, p. 187)

These imagos (internalized figures based on the parents) therefore represent to the child oral activities or anal activities directed towards the child himself. These internal relations can be represented by phantasies of being fed, or being devoured, bitten, or feeding the object, etc. (the 'gnawing of one's conscience', for instance); equally so with anal impulses. Klein described this catalogue of relations in fabulous detail in children's play with all sorts of objects.

From then on, the superego is seen as a whole set of internal objects, each endowed with specific phantasy functions [see 2. UNCONSCIOUS PHANTASY], and Kleinian psychoanalysis, in practice, became increasingly an analysis of these internalized objects. This was a broadening tendency to the concept and in contrast to Freud who, in replacing 'the ego-ideal by the superego has tended to narrow intrapsychic object-relationships down to the relation between the ego and the superego' (Heimann, 1955, p. 251).

The internal community of objects: The mind of the child is occupied by many 'objects' that could be called superegos [see 5. INTERNAL OBJECTS]. Klein refers to them as imagos, and their variety gives a great richness to the characteristics of the mind:

> ... two main 'characters': that of the doll, which embodied the id, and that of the deterring elephant, which represented the super-ego ... The 'characters', as in George's case, consist of three principal roles: that of the ego or the id, that of a figure who helps and that of a figure who threatens or frustrates. (Klein, 1929, pp. 202–3)

This variety is amplified by a distinction between good and bad: 'I have come to realize that the operation of such imagos, with phantastically good and phantastically bad characteristics, is a general mechanism.' The imagos are also different in respect of which pregenital level they represent: 'The imagos adopted in this early phase of ego-development bear the stamp of the pregenital instinctual impulses, although they are actually constructed on the basis of the real Oedipus objects', she adds loyally, and continues:

> These early levels are responsible for the phantastic imagos which devour, cut to pieces, and overpower and in which we see a mixture of the various pregenital impulses at work. Following the evolution of the libido, these imagos are introjected under the influence of the libidinal fixation points. But the superego as a whole is made up of the various identifications adopted on the different levels of development whose stamp they bear. (Klein, 1929, p. 204)

Helpful figures: Increasingly Klein noticed that these figures included helpful ones as well as the terrifying, sadistic ones. The helpful ones correspond to those that give satisfaction of the pregenital impulses. However, the importance of the helpful figures seems to have been secondary for Klein at this stage of her thinking, since the observations of the aggressiveness in children's play and the guilt and remorse about it had been so prominent and so shocking. It was not until 1935 that the importance of the helpful internal figures came properly to the fore, and then, with the introduction of the depressive position, the good internal object and its preservation became the all-important factor [see 5. INTERNAL OBJECTS].

(3) Modification of the superego. The harshness of the superego is progressively modified mainly by the influence of the actual external object:

> Compared with the preceding stage in which play was completely inhibited, this was progress, for now the superego did not merely threaten in a meaningless and terrifying way but tried with menaces to prevent the forbidden actions. (Klein, 1929, p. 202)

Helping figures also come into effect. They 'are mostly of an extremely phantastic kind' (Klein, 1929, p. 203) and derive, partly at least, from a surge forward to the genital impulses which give access to more positive feelings and the possibility of more helpful figures to mitigate the harshness.

Synthesis of internal objects: Klein was acutely aware of the divergence of her views from those of Freud. Freud had described a relatively unified object at the age of four or five, and Klein hung her own theory on to this by thinking in terms of the coming together of the various imagos into some sort of unitary object which was later observable as the superego described by Freud: 'The necessity for a synthesis of the superego arises out of the difficulty experienced by the subject in coming to an understanding with a superego made up of imagos of such opposite natures' (Klein, 1929, p. 205). This idea of an ego driven towards a unifying effort upon the internal objects appears at this time (1929) to be in the context of her own concerns about diverging from Freud's views. However, the unifying idea comes back in a very different and very powerful form in 1935, as part of the development she called the depressive position [see 10. DEPRESSIVE POSITION].

The external object: In summarizing her views at this stage, Klein wrote:

> In the adult, it is true, we find a superego at work which is a great deal more severe than the subject's parents were in reality . . . in the small child we come across a superego of the most incredible and phantastic character. . . I have no doubt from my own analytic

observations that the real objects behind those imaginary, terrifying figures are the child's own parents, and that those dreadful shapes in some way or other reflect the features of its father or mother, however distorted and phantastic the resemblance may be. (Klein, 1933, p. 249)

Here she was hitching herself to the classical theory of the origin of the superego in the character of the parents. It was, however, the extreme distortion of those figures which worried her; the investigation of the processes involved in such extreme distorting has become the hallmark of Kleinian psychoanalysis.

By viewing the superego as an interaction of external figures introjected under the distorting influence of early sadistic impulses, Klein deepened the theory of the origins of the superego beyond a mere correspondence between some external object and the resulting introjection.

The superego and therapeutic effect: James Strachey (1934) outlined a formal theory of the therapeutic action of psychoanalysis based on the idea that the external object, the analyst, is introjected to become an *auxiliary superego*. The special advantage of this new internal object is that through the function of interpreting the transference, the analyst avoids being distorted by primitive unconscious phantasy and is not then identified with the primitively good internal object or the primitively bad (the primitive imagos). In this case the patient is then able to sustain an internal object-relationship which is not based on horrific self-condemnation or extreme idealization [see 1. TECHNIQUE].

RELINQUISHING THE CLASSICAL THEORY. Strachey's celebrated paper was written at a critical moment in Kleinian thought. His ideas partly connected up with the radical change of direction that Klein was making: (1) in 1932, she relinquished the orthodox theory of the superego and made it a clinical and intrapsychic manifestation of the death instinct; and (2) in 1935, she published her theory of the depressive position dealing with the developmental history of the primitive imagos that Strachey was also conceptualizing.

(1) The superego and the death instinct. Klein was continually pushed away from her allegiance to classical theory. Her 'small' modification to Freud's view of the origins of the superego – that the superego arises from the moment when the Oedipus complex appears – did actually have deeper significance than she exposed at the time [see 4. OEDIPUS COMPLEX]. In particular, she implied that introjection of the parents does not come after the 'loss of the loved objects' of infancy but is a process that goes on in the course of – and in fact from the beginning of – an active relationship. This implication is much more in line with Abraham's views – introjection and projection are constantly active processes linked with oral and anal impulses, and they are active continuously from the beginning and throughout life [see 9. PRIMITIVE DEFENCE MECHANISMS].

By 1932 attitudes had hardened, with little prospect of the views of Klein and Anna Freud being reconciled. Klein was securely in the patronage of Ernest Jones, and there is an interesting correspondence between Jones and Freud about the conflicts between their respective protégées (Steiner, 1985). So there was less and less to prevent Klein from taking the fateful step of relinquishing the classical theory of the superego, as laid down by Freud. Her book *The Psycho-Analysis of Children*, published in 1932, was a collection of clinical papers (Part 1), originally lectures given in 1925, and theoretical chapters (Part 2) on the implications of the clinical observations for the theories of the Oedipus complex, the early development of boys and girls and the superego, rewritten from lectures given in 1927. The theoretical part had been revised, and is in some respects inconsistent: 'It is her fullest account of her first series of findings and conceptions, but written at a moment of transition. It puts forward views which only partially accord with its main theoretical basis' (Melanie Klein Trust, 1974). One of the most fateful of the new developments, sketchily introduced here and there in the text, was the entirely new view of the origin of the superego in the death instinct.

The superego and the death instinct: Klein elaborated the theory of the origin of the superego in the death instinct more systematically in 1933. In breaking with the classical views, she ingeniously found passages in Freud which she could claim to be following. Relying on Freud's descriptions of the death instinct in *Beyond the Pleasure Principle* (Freud, 1920), she employed his view that the earliest function of the ego is to deflect the death instinct outwards, towards an object in the external world. This first act brings the ego into being:

> In order to escape from being destroyed by its own death instinct, the organism employs its narcissistic, or self-regarding libido to force the former outward, and direct it against its objects . . . I should say, moreover, that parallel with this deflection of the death-instinct outward against objects, an intrapsychic reaction of defence goes on against that part of the instinct which could not be thus externalized. For the danger of being destroyed by this instinct of aggression sets up, I think, an excessive tension in the ego, which is felt by it as anxiety . . . A division takes place in the id, or instinctual levels of the psyche, by which one part of the instinctual impulses is directed against the other. This apparently earliest measure of

defence on the part of the ego constitutes, I think, the foundation-stone of the development of the superego, whose excessive violence in this early stage would thus be accounted for by the fact that it is an offshoot of very intense destructive instincts. (Klein, 1933, p. 250) [see 3. AGGRESSION; DEATH INSTINCT]

In this way, resting her case on Freud's own theories (albeit highly selected), she showed the early origin of the superego (at birth in fact), the reasons for its extreme harshness, and the need to revise the relation of the superego to the Oedipus complex. Thus the superego arises *before* the Oedipus complex.

The intricacy of her argument was to cover herself against the criticism that her theory was not really psychoanalytic, because it deviated from Freud. In fact the exact details of the formation of the superego, which she was describing, are as speculative as Freud's theories, and having at this point disconnected the superego from the Oedipus complex, she hardly came back to these arguments again – the exception being in 1958 when she was exploring certain phenomena in schizophrenics [see below]. In fact, once she had relinquished the classical theory of the superego, the importance of the superego itself declined in Klein's theories. It became a much less obtrusive concept. Instead Klein brought into much greater prominence the idea of internal objects, a much richer world that she then explored in its own right [see 5. INTERNAL OBJECTS].

(2) **The depressive position.** With the loss of its precision, the term 'superego' has been retained as a general description of internal objects that have a harsh and self-criticizing character. Often its use seems to be more adjectival – 'superegoish'. For the Kleinian Group, 'one could say that the superego is not finally settled' (Segal, 1987). First, it means the integration of the ideal and persecutory objects. Second, 'it means an aspect of internal objects that exerts moral pressure; for instance the internal parents in intercourse. We don't know how that contributes to the superego, maybe as an influence on how to make love' (Segal, 1987).

Searl (1936), a one-time supporter of Klein, made an attempt to rescue the concept of the superego by describing a structure of two ideals – based partly on Strachey's (1934) description of good and bad objects. She suggested making the term 'superego' refer to the 'negative ideal' (the 'thou-shalt-not' imperative) and the ego ideal as the positive ('thou shalt'). Searl was by this time already moving away from the Kleinian Group and shortly afterwards she resigned from the British Psycho-Analytical Society. This idea was resurrected much later by Meltzer (1967) and Mancia and Meltzer (1981) to distinguish the depressive position (in which the move from persecutory towards helpful internal figures predominates) from envy (the reason for being stuck with a persecutory superego).

The greatest effect of relinquishing the classical theory of the superego was to allow developments in quite different directions – in particular, in 1935, the depressive position [see 10. DEPRESSIVE POSITION]. This gave Money-Kyrle (1951) the possibility of using the distinction between the depressive position and the paranoid-schizoid position to separate out two broad categories of superego. He applied this psychoanalytic formulation in Germany in the aftermath of the Second World War, in an attempt to predict those Nazis capable of rehabilitation to responsible jobs (people with a more enhancing superego – in the depressive position) and those with a sadistic and authoritarian superego who had flourished best under the Nazi regime, based on obedience and persecution rather than personal responsibility (paranoid-schizoid functioning). Grinberg (1978) emphasized the different kinds of guilt: persecutory (or harshly punitive) and depressive (with possibilities of reparation) [see DEPRES-SIVE ANXIETY]. Common to these writings is an emphasis upon the sequence of changing affect in the course of development – (i) perse-cution; (ii) persecutory guilt; (iii) guilt and reparation [see DEPRESSIVE ANXIETY].

FURTHER DEVELOPMENTS

(1) Assimilation. An issue explored especially by Heimann was the interesting question of whether the external object was introjected into the ego or into the superego (Heimann, 1952) [see ASSIMILATION]. In a late and rare summary of the origins of the superego Klein wrote:

> the ego, supported by the internalized good object and strengthened by identification with it, projects a portion of the death instinct into that part of itself which it has split off – a part which comes to be in opposition to the rest of the ego and forms the basis of the superego. (Klein, 1958, p. 240)

The importance of this passage is that it is describing introjection as a process that identifies an external object with the ego. But a different process was investigated by Heimann (1955), who had reported a case of a masochistic patient whose excitement at being beaten on the buttocks resulted from the introjection of a hated and hostile father imago which became identified with the part of his ego to be beaten, his buttocks. The external object is identified with only a part of the ego which is then, as it were, disowned, not properly assimilated by the ego but, in contrast, depleting it. This is a way of describing, in terms of internal object-relations, the specific nature and development of the harsh form of the superego.

The contrasting process is 'a progressive assimilation of the superego by the ego' (Klein, 1952, p. 74). Klein is vague about this process: 'the increased capacity of the ego to accept the standards of the external objects . . . is linked with the greater synthesis within the superego and the growing assimilation of the superego by the ego' (Klein, 1952, p. 87). The unassimilated object is described by Klein and Heimann – 'the internal objects act as foreign bodies embedded within the self' (Klein, 1946, p. 9n). This results from a weakening of the ego (resulting from excessive projective identification) which is no longer strong enough to assimilate the object without being over-whelmed and dominated by it. Riesenberg-Malcolm (1981) described a form of pseudo-compliance that results. However, the independent, alien object resembles somewhat the superego originally described by Freud.

(2) **The superego and schizophrenia.** The increasing psychoanalytic work with schizophrenics in the 1940s and 1950s, by younger psychoanalysts with medical qualifications (Scott, Rosenfeld, Segal, Bion) – for example Rosenfeld's paper on the superego of the schizophrenic (Rosenfeld, 1952) – led Klein to refer back to her previous work with schizophrenic children. She described something previously unnoticed.

Split-off persecutors: She now described extremely hostile objects with which schizophrenics are preoccupied:

> These extremely dangerous objects give rise, in early infancy, to conflict and anxiety within the ego; but under stress of acute anxiety they, and other terrifying figures, are split off in a manner different from that by which the superego is formed, and are relegated to the deeper layers of the unconscious . . . the superego is normally established in close relation with the ego and shares different aspects of the same good objects. This makes it possible for the ego to integrate and accept the superego to a greater or lesser degree. (Klein, 1958, p. 241)

Even at the time of the latency period, and thereafter, these especially violent figures remain:

> . . . the organized part of the superego, although very often harsh, is much more cut off from its unconscious part . . . when we penetrate to deeper layers of the unconscious, we find that dangerous and persecutory figures still coexist with idealized ones. (Klein, 1958, p. 242)

Although the persistence of a deeply unconscious set of primal objects was recognized in schizophrenics it was not entirely new, as it resembles a return to the descriptions of children (some of them latency) in the early period of Klein's work – and Strachey (1934), for one, had made use of the notion of archaic objects, persecutors and idealized imagos.

The persistence, in a separated-off state, of relations with especially archaic objects has been used by Bion in a distinction between psychotic and non-psychotic parts of a personality [see 13. PROJECTIVE IDENTIFICATION]. Rosenfeld also took this idea further in terms of an internal domination of the personality by cruel, split-off parts that terrorized the good parts of the personality like a Mafia gang (Rosenfeld, 1971); and a similar line of thinking has been developed by Sidney Klein in describing encapsulated autistic aspects of neurotic personalities (Sidney Klein, 1980) [see STRUCTURE].

OBJECTIONS TO KLEIN'S MODIFICATIONS OF THE SUPEREGO. At the outset, Anna Freud (1927) disputed, on theoretical grounds, Melanie Klein's description of the superego at the earlier stages. This set the scene for a prolonged disagreement between Kleinians and orthodox Freudians tracing their lineage from the Viennese analysts [see 1. TECHNIQUE]. Fenichel (1928, 1931) made a distinction between the superego as described by Freud, and precursors of the superego which may be found at the pregenital levels, similar to his critique of Klein's modification to the Oedipus complex [see 4. OEDIPUS COMPLEX]. Oral and anal harshness and sadism, he thought, may give rise to masochistic self-punishment but cannot be confused with the fully formed superego, which has a 'moral' component derived from the genital love of the parents. Fenichel's arguments concerning the 'precursors of the superego' go along with his similar arguments concerning the early, pregenital components of the Oedipus complex [see 4. OEDIPUS COMPLEX]. The several objects from the pregenital phases which Fenichel was willing to accept go into the make-up of the superego, becoming integrated only when the ego begins and its integrating function comes into operation – this contrasts with Klein's view that the early components are actively kept apart and manipulated by an ego that has functions and operates defences.

The distinction is again over the occurrence of early functioning of an ego in the first year of life. In Fenichel's view the dating of the superego must follow the beginnings of ego and its integrative functions; for Klein the superego is dated from the first act of splitting, when the ego has to deal with the death instinct. Waelder (1937) reiterated these objections, but like so many of the controversies between Kleinians and classical psychoanalysts, the issue died away without being resolved.

Another issue concerned the especial harshness of the superego, even in adults, and typically in criminals. Freud had explained this harshness as the result of the introjection of the parents' superego, rather than the whole of the parents' personalities. However, that explanation merely put off the question of the nature of the superego in relation to the development of the id-impulses, and Freud's later thinking moved closer to Klein's (see footnote to Klein, 1933, p. 250). But the issue here concerns the explanation of the harshness as a retrospective distortion in the memory of older children and adults of their parental handling, as opposed to the direct observation of the phantasies and remorse in children as young as two years of age. This issue surfaced strongly in the Controversial Discussions over unconscious phantasy [see 2. UNCONSCIOUS PHANTASY] and whether the phantasies of later children and adults are those that have persisted since very early stages of the ego (the first six months) or a retrospective sophistication resulting from the regression of later hostility to oral and anal phantasies.

The evidence from very young children was strong, and Waelder (1937) conceded that the harshness of the superego came partly from internal sources, though he remained opposed to the view that this indicated an earlier origin of the superego. In spite of this these disagreements have not, on the whole, been properly resolved but have tended to fade out of sight, partly because Kleinians have laid less stress on the superego as their own interest moved to examining the depressive position and then the paranoid-schizoid position and projective identification.

The story of the superego is integral to the story of Melanie Klein. It placed her in opposition to orthodox opinion – a position in which she struggled to remain true to her findings, but at the same time enjoyed being slightly scandalous. She failed in her struggle to remain loyal to orthodox Freudian theory at the time (1930s) and suffered for it. Her own theoretical progression more or less bypassed Freud's structural theory of id, ego and superego. It is not too extreme to describe Klein's development of the idea of the superego as a new structural theory. The blossoming out of a whole set of internal objects creates a truly internal world populated by imagos of external figures and the subsequent recognition of hidden organizations of the personality (the psychotic part, the perverse part, etc.) which engage in internal relations that constantly destroy or pervert the experiences of the ego [see STRUCTURE].

Many of the issues over which Kleinian theory diverged from classical psychoanalysis meet in the history of the 'superego' concept – the squeezing-up of the early libidinal phases versus their clearly timed progression; the manifestation of the death instinct internal to the personality versus the death instinct as clinically silent; the initial functioning of the ego at birth versus the development of the ego much later; the ego's first act of splitting and deflection (projection) versus its initial integrative function; the phenomenology and the subjective experience of concretely felt internal objects of various kinds versus the experience of symbolic representations in the mind. These erupted in heated atmospheres of controversy between Melanie Klein and Anna Freud, between the British and Viennese Psycho-Analytical Societies and eventually between different groups within the British Society. This atmosphere was not conducive to resolving these debates so the issues remain with us, now often unrecognized by a new generation which seems to have inherited the heat, but not the clarity of the issues. Further dispute has tended to be conducted over later developments in theory on both sides [see 13. PROJECTIVE IDENTIFICATION; EGO-PSYCHOLOGY] without tracing these to their roots in the earlier unresolved issues of the 1920s and 1930s.

Abraham, Karl (1924) 'A short study of the development of the libido', in Karl Abraham (1927) *Selected Papers on Psycho-Analysis*. Hogarth, pp. 418–501.

Fenichel, Otto (1928) 'The clinical aspect of the need for punishment', *Int. J. Psycho-Anal:* 9:47–70.

—— (1931) 'The pregenital antecedents of the Oedipus complex', *Int. J. Psycho-Anal.* 12:412–30.

Ferenczi, Sandor (1925) 'Psycho-analysis of sexual habits', in (1950) *Further Contributions to the Theory and Technique of Psycho-Analysis*. Hogarth, pp. 259–97.

Freud, Anna (1927) *Psycho-Analytic Treatment of Children*, English edn, 1946. Imago.

Freud, Sigmund (1916) 'Some character-types met with in psycho-analytic work: III Criminals from a sense of guilt', in James Strachey, ed. *The Standard Edition of the Complete Psychological Works of Sigmund Freud*, 24 vols. Hogarth, 1953–73. vol. 14, pp. 332–3.

—— (1917) 'Mourning and melancholia'. *S.E.* 14, pp. 237–60.

—— (1920) *Beyond the Pleasure Principle. S.E.* 18, pp. 3–64.

—— (1923) *The Ego and the Id. S.E.* 19, pp. 3–66.

—— (1924a) 'The economic problem of masochism'. *S.E.* 19, pp. 157–70.

—— (1924b) 'The dissolution of the Oedipus complex'. *S.E.* 19, pp. 173–9.

—— (1930) *Civilization and its Discontents. S.E.* 21, pp. 59–145.

Glover, Edward (1926) 'The neurotic character', *Int. J. Psycho-Anal.* 7:11–29.

Grinberg, Leon (1978) 'The "razor's edge" in depression and mourning', *Int. J. Psycho-Anal.* 59:145–54.

Heimann, Paula (1952) 'Certain functions of introjection and projection in early infancy', in Melanie Klein, Paula Heimann, Susan Isaacs and Joan Riviere, eds *Developments in Psycho-Analysis*. Hogarth, pp. 122–68.

—— (1955) 'A combination of defence mechanisms in paranoia', in Melanie Klein, Paula Heimann and Roger Money-Kyrle, eds *New Directions in Psycho-Analysis*. Tavistock, pp. 240–65.

Isaacs, Susan (1929) 'Privation and guilt', *Int. J. Psycho-Anal.* 10:335–47.

Jones, Ernest (1926) 'The origin and structure of the superego', *Int. J. Psycho-Anal.* 7:303–11.

—— (1927) 'The early development of female sexuality', *Int. J. Psycho-Anal.* 8:459–72.

Klein, Melanie (1925) 'A contribution to the psychogenesis of tics', in *The Writings of Melanie Klein*, vol. 1. Hogarth, pp. 106–27.

—— (1926) 'The psychological principles of early analysis', *The Writings of Melanie Klein*, vol. 1, pp.128–37.

—— (1927) 'Criminal tendencies in normal children', *The Writings of Melanie Klein*, vol. 1, pp. 170–85.

—— (1928) 'Early stages of the Oedipus complex', *The Writings of Melanie Klein*, vol. 1, pp. 186–98.

—— (1929) 'Personification in the play of children', *The Writings of Melanie Klein*, vol. 1, pp. 199–209.

—— (1932) *The Psycho-Analysis of Children, The Writings of Melanie Klein*, vol. 2.

—— (1933) 'The early development of conscience in the child', *The Writings of Melanie Klein*, vol. 1, pp. 248–57.

—— (1935) 'A contribution to the psychogenesis of manic-depressive states', *The Writings of Melanie Klein*, vol. 1, pp. 262–89.

—— (1946) 'Notes on some schizoid mechanisms', *The Writings of Melanie Klein*, vol. 3, pp. 1–24.

—— (1952) 'Some theoretical conclusions regarding the emotional life of the infant', *The Writings of Melanie Klein*, vol. 3, pp. 61–93.

—— (1955) 'The psycho-analytic play technique: its history and significance', *The Writings of Melanie Klein*, vol. 3, pp. 122–40.

—— (1958) 'On the development of mental functioning', *The Writings of Melanie Klein*, vol. 3, pp. 236–46.

Klein, Sidney (1980) 'Autistic phenomena in neurotic patients', *Int. J. Psycho-Anal.* 61:393–402.

Mancia, Mauro and Meltzer, Donald (1981) 'Ego ideal functions and the psycho-analytical process', *Int. J. Psycho-Anal.* 62:243–9.

Melanie Klein Trust (1974) 'Explanatory note to *The Psycho-Analysis of Children* in *The Writings of Melanie Klein Volume 2*'. Hogarth, pp. 283–5.

Meltzer, Donald (1967) *The Psycho-Analytic Process*. Heinemann.

Money-Kyrle, Roger (1951) 'Some aspects of state and character in Germany', in George B. Wilbur and Warner Muensterberger, eds *Psycho-Analysis and Culture*. New York: International Universities Press; republished (1978) in *The Collected Works of Roger Money-Kyrle*. Perth: Clunie, pp. 229–44.

Riesenberg-Malcolm, Ruth (1981) 'Technical problems in the analysis of a pseudo-compliant patient', *Int. J. Psycho-Anal.* 62:477–84.

Rosenfeld, Herbert (1952) 'Notes on the psycho-analysis of the superego conflict in an acute schizophrenic patient', *Int. J. Psycho-Anal.* 33:111–31; republished (1955) in Melanie Klein, Paula Heimann and Roger Money-Kyrle, eds *New Directions in Psycho-Analysis*. Tavistock, pp. 180–219; and (1965) in *Psychotic States*. Hogarth, pp. 63–103.

—— (1971) 'A clinical approach to the psycho-analytical theory of the life and death instincts: an investigation into the aggressive aspects of narcissism', *Int. J. Psycho-Anal.* 652:169–78.

Schmideberg, Melitta (1934) 'The play analysis of a three-year-old girl', *Int. J. Psycho-Anal.* 15:245–64.

Searl, M. N. (1936) 'Infantile ideals', *Int. J. Psycho-Anal.* 17:17–39.

Segal, Hanna (1987) personal communication.

Steiner, Riccardo (1985) 'Some thoughts about tradition and change arising from an examination of the British Psycho-Analytical Society's Controversial Discussions (1943–1944)', *Int. Rev. Psycho-Anal.* 12:27–71.

Strachey, James (1934) 'On the therapeutic effect of psycho-analysis', *Int. J. Psycho-Anal.* 15:127–59.

Waelder, Robert (1937) 'The problem of the genesis of psychical conflict in earliest infancy', *Int. J. Psycho-Anal.* 18:406–73.

8 EARLY ANXIETY-SITUATIONS

DEFINITION. Klein took this term from Freud's reference to early situations of anxiety or danger for the infant and applied it to her own discovery of the fears arising from sadistic phantasies of attacking mother's body, and the retaliation expected from it. The intensity of the anxiety and the relevance in children of both sexes led to the discovery of the femininity phase in both boys and girls. In 1935 Klein introduced the depressive position; at this point she reverted to Freud's view of the loss of the loved object as the crucial anxiety, but it was significantly modified from Freud's idea. Klein focused on the loss of the *internal* loved object. Later, from 1946, the description of the paranoid-schizoid phase of very early splitting indicated a different anxiety-situation – a fear of annihilation of the ego (resulting from the inherent death instinct operating in the internal world); and in writings after Klein, anxiety has been conceived predominantly in this sense (persecutory anxiety).

CHRONOLOGY
1927 Attacks on mother's body with retaliation (Klein, Melanie, 1928, 'Early stages of the Oedipus conflict'; Klein, Melanie, 1929, 'Infantile anxiety-situations as reflected in a work of art and in the creative impulse').

1935 A non-paranoid anxiety connected with loss of the internal good object (Klein, Melanie, 1935, 'A contribution to the psychogenesis of manic-depressive states'; Klein, Melanie, 1945, 'The Oedipus complex in the light of early anxieties').

1946 The fear of annihilation of the ego, due to death instinct working within (Klein, Melanie, 1946, 'Notes on some schizoid mechanisms').

One aspect of the unique way in which Klein approached psychoanalysis was her particular attention to anxiety, rather than to the derivatives of instincts. Psychoanalysis started with an interest in symptoms and moved to an interest in defence mechanisms. Klein started on a different trajectory: 'From the beginning of my psychoanalytic work, my interest was focused on anxiety and its causation' (Klein, 1948, p. 41). She was aware that in this she only just escaped being dismissed as heretical: 'I deviated from some of the rules so far established, for I interpreted what I thought to be most urgent in the material the child presented to me and found my interest focusing on his anxieties and the defences against them' (Klein, 1955, p. 122).

Freud's 1926 work, *Inhibitions, Symptoms and Anxiety*, had a remarkable and far-reaching effect on Klein's theoretical development. She repeatedly returned to it to help her with her own theoretical formulations. She took up four main ideas, with far-reaching effect:

(a) Freud introduced the term 'infantile situations of danger and anxiety', which confirmed for Klein the correctness of her approach to the *content* of anxiety, rather than the more orthodox interest in the transformations of libido.

(b) Freud discussed birth trauma and the general nature of the '. . . loss of the loved object', which was later to be an important theoretical base for her theory of the depressive position [see 10. DEPRESSIVE POSITION].

(c) Freud's remarks on the special nature of defences in relation to the death instinct gave Klein support, at last, for her own observations of children. His views were the instrument for her soon to cast adrift from the classical theories of the superego and the Oedipus complex [see 7. SUPEREGO; 4. OEDIPUS COMPLEX].

(d) The formation of the superego from an outward deflection of the death instinct and a division in the id was the '. . . earliest measure of defence on the part of the ego' (Klein, 1933, p. 250) [see 7. SUPEREGO; DEATH INSTINCT].

So the influence of this paper extended to the radical climax of Klein's theoretical break from orthodox psychoanalysis in 1932 (the superego as the clinical manifestation of the death instinct); and in the development of the concept of the depressive position. What started her on this confident journey of her own was the support she felt for an interest in the *content* which led directly to a radical change in the view of the nature of anxiety – from a physiological transformation to a psychological content. This represents one of the most important distinctions, even today, between the Kleinian School and other psychoanalysts.

KLEIN'S VIEW OF ANXIETY. Freud's 1926 paper on anxiety was to have a remarkable and far-reaching effect on Klein's own theoretical development. In introducing the term 'infantile situations of danger and anxiety', Freud confirmed for Klein the correctness of her approach to the content of *anxiety*. In fact Freud was responding to Rank's book which argued that all anxiety was due to one cause – birth trauma. Freud argued instead that the anxiety-situation changed at different stages of life. In doing so he was in effect endorsing the importance of the phantasy, or reality, *content* which gives meaning to anxiety.

Klein's unorthodox approach, which gave priority to the content of anxiety, resulted in specific contributions to anxiety:

(1) anxiety in children linked with aggression revealed in play;

(2) anxiety as instinctual conflict;

(3) the emphasis on the phantasy content of anxiety;

(4) attacks on mother's body;

(5) psychotic anxieties; and

(6) technique.

(1) Play and sadism. Klein discovered that the cruelty and aggression of play led to an extremely harsh form of remorse and guilt that stemmed from the aggression. She herself was shocked by the violence of children's phantasies: '... it is difficult, as I know from my own experience, to bring oneself to recognize that such an abhorrent idea answers to the truth' (Klein, 1932, p. 130).

It was increasingly apparent to Klein that it was their sadism that frightened little children and made them fearful of an equally sadistic retribution. Although she stuck at first to the view that anxiety and guilt arose from the sexual libido and the Oedipus complex, it was clear that she interpreted the children's efforts to control their aggression, not just their sexuality. In 1927 (especially in her paper on criminality) the emphasis on aggression and sadism increased. She had discovered just how far-reaching an effect guilt and anxiety could have on children's play, resulting in severe inhibitions of phantasy, which correlated with equally severe inhibitions of development in general (1930) and of the intellect in particular (1931) [see 1. TECHNIQUE].

(2) Instinctual conflict. When she started, Klein's interpretations, like Freud's, concerned the way phantasy life was inhibited by the repression of libido, which was touched off especially by frustrations in the quest for knowledge of the primal scene. The classical view of anxiety at the time (1920s) was of a central conflict over the child's sexual instincts arising at a premature age, and in a society which prohibited free satisfaction of the sexual impulses.

Freud's version of this theory in 1926 was important for Klein (see (3) below), and in about 1932 her views underwent a radical change. She began to accept the death instinct as a clinically useful concept [see DEATH INSTINCT]. Clinically, she understood that the anxiety she was dealing with in young children was concerned with a very primitive conflict between aggression and the remorseful reaction to it. She suddenly went quite beyond her previous theory of anxiety by describing the propensity for the death instinct, in its projected form as aggression, to come into conflict with the loving instincts. Such conflict becomes inevitable, because it springs from the contradictory, inherited endowment of life and death instincts. The idea of a primordial conflict of the instincts was quite compatible with her view of psychotic anxiety as a self-perpetuating vicious circle of aggression and fear. The classical view of anxiety, she believed, referred to a later form which arises on the basis of the already preceding conflict between instincts.

(3) **Infantile situations of danger and anxiety.** Freud (1926) had begun to emphasize the *psychological content* of anxiety. That is to say, anxiety represented a psychologically experienced situation, a dangerous one, real or imaginary (anxiety-situation). At that time (1926), when Klein was embroiled in dispute with Anna Freud [see CHILD ANALYSIS], she was grateful to be able to latch on to Freud's writing as a support for her own approach. She embraced the term 'early anxiety-situation' with enthusiasm because she thought it strengthened her position on the map of classical psychoanalytic theory.

Freud had suggested that in a general way there were specific anxiety-situations at different periods of development. Klein put forward her own discoveries to fill in the detailed psychological content to Freud's outline. She first adopted Freud's term 'anxiety-situation' in 1929, in an extraordinary paper based on the review in a Berlin newspaper of an operetta by Ravel, performed in Vienna, which she had not herself seen. Using Freud's term guarded against the accusation that she diverged from Freud (a common accusation from Vienna):

> I wanted to recall these concepts of mine to your minds because I can make a bridge from them to a concept of Freud's: one of the most important of the new conclusions which he has put before us in *Inhibitions, Symptoms and Anxiety* (1926), namely the hypothesis of an early infantile situation of anxiety or danger. (Klein, 1929, p. 212)

She went on to elaborate:

> Freud assumes that the infantile danger-situation can be reduced ultimately to the loss of the beloved (longed-for) person. In girls, he thinks, the loss of the object is the danger-situation which operates most powerfully, in boys it is castration. My work has proved to me that both these danger-situations are a modification of yet earlier ones. I have found that in boys the dread of castration by the father is connected with a very special situation which, I think, proves to be the earliest anxiety-situation of all. As I pointed out, the attack on the mother's body, which is timed psychologically at the zenith of the sadistic phase, implies also the struggle with the father's penis in the mother. (Klein, 1929, p. 213) [see 6. FEMININITY PHASE; COMBINED PARENT FIGURE]

(4) Attacking mother's body. The anxiety-situation Klein first described was, crucially, the infantile attacks on the mother's body with a
fear of retaliation in kind [see 6. FEMININITY PHASE]. Klein had
already discovered a specific anxiety in several analyses – Rita in 1923,
and Trude and Ruth in 1924:

> My observation of the cases of Trude, Ruth and Rita, together with
> the knowledge I have gained in the last few years, have led me to
> recognize the existence of an anxiety or rather an anxiety-situation,
> which is specific for girls and the equivalent of the castration anxiety
> felt by boys . . . It is based upon the child's impulses of aggression
> against her mother and her desires, springing from the early stages
> of her Oedipus conflict, to kill her and steal from her. These
> impulses lead not only to an anxiety or to a fear of being attacked by
> mother, but to a fear that her mother will abandon her or die.
> (Klein, 1932, p. 31)

This anxiety-situation arises from the oedipal provocation to extreme
aggression against the inside of mother's body, with the consequent
fear of retaliation by mother and father, whose penis resides within the
attacked body of mother and who is also attacked for his residence
there. These infantile phantasies are extraordinarily rich (Searl, 1929)
and the intense enthusiasm to add to Freud's theory of anxiety in this
way must have been met by an equally intense stoniness on the part of
Anna Freud and the continental analysts who were opposed to this
approach [see CONTROVERSIAL DISCUSSIONS].

Destroying persecutors: One of the defences against these horrendously
harsh parental imagos (such as the combined parents) is to launch
direct attacks against them to destroy them, with the result that the
object is then feared even more because of its powers of retaliatory
violence. There ensues the vicious circle of paranoia [see PARANOIA].
The intensity of fear that can mount up comes to such a pitch that
Klein began to refer to the anxiety as a psychotic one, and eventually
reviewed her theory of their origin in the Oedipus complex.

(5) Psychotic anxieties. Klein showed in her 1935 paper how anxiety
becomes modified in the most significant of ways by entry into the
depressive position [see 10. DEPRESSIVE POSITION]. At this point in
development (about four to six months) the good object and the bad
object become less severely separated, and one begins to contaminate
the other. The good object particularly is no longer as completely
good. This *whole object* is a new experience [see WHOLE OBJECT]. Its
less than complete goodness gives rise to a serious fear *for* it and its
survival; an acute sense of responsibility for it and for the possibility of
having contaminated or damaged the good object. These are the

earliest manifestations of the feeling of responsibility and guilt, and are the reason for Klein's view that the superego is apparent at a very early age [see 7. SUPEREGO; DEPRESSIVE ANXIETY]. This guilt is of an especially painful kind – raw, as it were, with the persecuting feelings of the paranoid-schizoid position. It has an intensely persecuting quality and gives rise to desperate feelings that the damage is beyond repair [see REPARATION].

Libido and the depressive position: The characteristic anxiety of the depressive position – fear for the loved object – came in 1935 to be *the* anxiety-situation. At this time Klein realized that depressive anxiety contributed to the development of the libido in various ways: in general (i) by posing an intolerably painful internal state, it inhibited development of the libido and the personality as a whole, which depends on the libido developing; and (ii) the depressive position can be alleviated by a movement towards the genital stage, in which the loving feelings for the object are greater and will mitigate the sadistic impulses, sometimes with premature eroticization and ensuing later erotic perversions.

The paranoid-schizoid position: In 1946 Klein went back to Freud's postulate of the death instinct and added new discoveries which threw the emphasis back from the depressive position and the importance of the good object to paranoia and the working of the bad object and impulses [see 11. PARANOID-SCHIZOID POSITION]:

> Freud stated that no fear of death exists in the unconscious, but this does not seem compatible with his discovery of the dangers arising from the death instinct working within. As I see it, the primordial anxiety which the ego fights is the threat arising from the death instinct. (Klein, 1958, p. 237)

The death instinct's first manifestation is from birth as the fear of persecution by the bad object and the mobilization of hatred against that object, creating the first paradigm for 'a bad object-relation' – thus 'Part of the death instinct is projected into the object, the object thereby becoming a persecutor; while that part of the death instinct which is retained in the ego causes aggression to be turned against that persecutory object' (Klein, 1958, p. 238n). The paranoid element of these bad-object-relations is clear, and they were clarified through work with paranoid and schizophrenic patients and children by Klein and by her close workers (Segal, Rosenfeld).

   This kind of anxiety is referred to as persecutory anxiety and it is the hallmark of what was eventually described as the paranoid-schizoid position [see 11. PARANOID-SCHIZOID POSITION]. In 1946 the early anxiety-situation was described as a new fear, an *annihilation of the ego*, a fragmentation which results from the death instinct at work internally.

Internal world: Depressive anxiety (concerned with the loss of the *internal* loved object) and persecutory anxiety (concerned with the fear of the annihilation of the self) are deeply personal predicaments and relate to the person's own troubled phantasies about what he or she is in him- or herself, what is inside, what he or she consists of. The 'anxiety-situations', from 1935 onwards, were *internal* situations.

The primitive defence mechanisms (or psychotic mechanisms) are concerned primarily to alleviate the fears about these internal states, and in fact initiate the ego as a function controlling this internal world. The defences against psychotic anxieties are splitting, denial, projection, introjection, identification and idealization [see 9. PRIMITIVE DEFENCE MECHANISMS] and they are gradually overshadowed as the anxieties change and as more mature defences come into prominence. Repression takes over from splitting, obsessional defences from manic ones, etc.

Primary envy: In rounding out her theoretical system in 1957 with her theory of primary envy, Klein described a particular phantasy relationship with an object. She returned to the specific phantasy of intruding into a 'good' object and spoiling the inside contents. Klein's original contribution – the attack on mother's body – was initially regarded as an oedipal one. In 1957 it returned as primary envy traced to an inherent and instinctual conflict [see 12. ENVY].

(6) **Technique.** Klein started by observing the change in anxiety as a result of her interpretative interventions. This has continued to be an important indicator of analytic work. Joseph (1978, 1981) has shown in fine detail the importance of following the shifts in anxiety that occur during a psychoanalytic session. She has pointed out that the movement of the anxiety between persecutory and depressive is the important one, rather than simply the overall diminution. These movements between the paranoid-schizoid and depressive positions, Klein came to believe, were the important steps in maturation [see 1. TECHNIQUE; PARANOID DEFENCE AGAINST DEPRESSIVE ANXIETY]. The oscillations between the depressive and paranoid-schizoid positions were raised to a comprehensive theory of development and of thinking by Bion [see Ps-D; BION].

CONTROVERSIES OVER KLEIN'S VIEW OF ANXIETY. The classical view of anxiety continues to be held in ego-psychology. Anxiety is a signal warning of a libidinal conflict which will result in dammed-up charges of psychic energy, finding outlets in nonspecific states of bodily and mental tension. Klein's view that it is a state of tension between love and aggression (life and death instincts) implied radical changes to Freud's 'economic model' of the mind [see

ECONOMIC MODEL]. These implications of Klein's theory for the concept of psychic energy and the economic model were not properly addressed by her or by subsequent Kleinians. However, it does seem that the physical analogizing of the economic model is not, in practice, compatible with a psychological view of the phantasy content of anxiety.

Anxiety and development: Anna Freud (1927) and Glover (1945) believed that Klein's theory of anxiety as a tension between the instincts had disposed of Freud's theory of the development of the libido, elevated to a pre-eminent position the importance given to aggression (death instinct), and demoted the role and importance of the libido. If anxiety is an interaction between sadism and libido and thus libido and aggression are on an equal footing, then this demotes libido as the crucial element of instinctual life; and if excessive anxiety inhibits or distorts development through the interference with the natural progress of the libido, then aggression is the real motor of development [see 3. AGGRESSION; LIBIDO]. Anna Freud came to view the natural unfolding (epigenesis) of the phases of the libido as an inherent quality of the organism which leads to a normal drive towards adaptation and aspects of the ego which are outside its conflict with the other agencies of the mind [see EGO-PSYCHOLOGY]. Development is thus seen in two quite different lights – the ego-psychological one of a natural unfolding and adapting versus a troubled push forward impelled by instinctually derived anxiety.

Death instinct: Klein's emphasis on the manifestations of the death instinct have been persistently disputed on three main grounds:

(a) the death instinct according to Freud is largely silent clinically (Freud, 1920);

(b) it is unnecessary to postulate that aggression is a manifestation (through projection) of the death instinct, since aggression as the frustration of life instincts as described by Freud (1915) is quite sufficient; and

(c) evidence for an internal process of self-directed destructiveness, offered by Kleinians – Klein's theory of the superego (Klein, 1933) and later theories of the structure of borderline personalities (Heimann, 1952; Rosenfeld, 1971) [see STRUCTURE] – is disputed [see DEATH INSTINCT].

Anxiety and technique: Klein's interest in the content of anxiety led to her technique of deeply penetrating interpretations. In contrast, the classical technique evolved by the ego-psychologists was concerned with analysing the ego's defence mechanisms (and adaptation mechanisms) and led to criticism of Klein that her deep interpretations were themselves the cause of anxiety because they must be experienced by the patient as intrusive and therefore persecutory, with the result that Kleinians are confronted with a great deal of persecutory anxiety (Geleerd, 1963; Greenson, 1974) [see 1. TECHNIQUE].

Freud, Anna (1927) *The Psycho-Analytical Treatment of Children*, English edn, 1946. Hogarth.

Freud, Sigmund (1915) 'Instincts and their vicissitudes', in James Strachey, ed. *The Standard Edition of the Complete Psychological Works of Sigmund Freud*, 24 vols. Hogarth, 1953–73 vol. 14, pp. 109–40.

—— (1916) 'Some character-types met with in psycho-analytic works: III Criminals from a sense of guilt'. *S.E.* 14, pp. 332–3.

—— (1920) *Beyond the Pleasure Principle. S.E.* 18, pp. 13–64.

—— (1924) 'The economic problem of masochism'. *S.E.* 19, pp. 157–70.

—— (1926) *Inhibitions, Symptoms and Anxiety. S.E.* 20, pp. 77–175.

Geleerd, Elizabeth (1963) 'Evaluation of Melanie Klein's *Narrative of a Child Analysis*', *Int. J. Psycho-Anal.* 44:493–506.

Glover, Edward (1945) 'An examination of the Klein system of child psychology', *Psychoanal. Study Child* 1:3–43.

Greenson, Ralph (1974) 'Transference: Freud or Klein?', *Int. J. Psycho-Anal.* 55:37–48.

Grosskurth, Phyllis (1986) *Melanie Klein.* Hodder & Stoughton.

Heimann, Paula (1952) 'Notes on the theory of the life and death instincts', in Melanie Klein, Paula Heimann, Susan Isaacs and Joan Riviere, eds *Developments in Psycho-Analysis*. Hogarth, pp. 321–37.

Joseph, Betty (1978) 'Different types of anxiety and their handling in the analytic situation', *Int. J. Psycho-Anal.* 59:223–8.

—— (1981) 'Towards the experiencing of psychic pain', in James Grotstein, ed. *Do I Dare Disturb the Universe?* Beverly Hills: Caesura.

Klein, Melanie (1927) 'Criminal tendencies in normal children', in *The Writings of Melanie Klein*, vol. 1. Hogarth, pp. 170–85.

—— (1928) 'Early stages of the Oedipus conflict', *The Writings of Melanie Klein*, vol. 1, pp. 186–98.

—— (1929) 'Infantile anxiety-situations as reflected in a work of art and in the creative impulse', *The Writings of Melanie Klein*, vol. 1, pp. 210–18.

—— (1930) 'The importance of symbol-formation in the development of the ego', *The Writings of Melanie Klein*, vol. 1, pp. 219–32.

—— (1931) 'A contribution to the theory of intellectual inhibition', *The Writings of Melanie Klein*, vol. 1, pp. 236–47.

—— (1932) *The Psycho-Analysis of Children, The Writings of Melanie Klein*, vol. 2.

—— (1933) 'The early development of conscience in the child', *The Writings of Melanie Klein*, vol. 1, pp. 248–57.

—— (1935) 'A contribution to the psychogenesis of manic-depressive states', *The Writings of Melanie Klein*, vol. 1, pp. 262–89.

—— (1945) 'The Oedipus complex in the light of early anxieties', *The Writings of Melanie Klein*, vol. 1, pp. 370–419.

—— (1946) 'Notes on some schizoid mechanisms', *The Writings of Melanie Klein*, vol. 3, pp. 1–24.

—— (1948) 'On the theory of anxiety and guilt', *The Writings of Melanie Klein*, vol. 3, pp. 25–42.

—— (1955) 'The psycho-analytic play technique: its history and its significance', *The Writings of Melanie Klein*, vol. 3, pp. 122–40.

—— (1957) *Envy and Gratitude*, *The Writings of Melanie Klein*, vol. 3, pp. 176–235.

—— (1958) 'On the development of mental functioning', *The Writings of Melanie Klein*, vol. 3, pp. 236–46.

Rosenfeld, Herbert (1971) 'A clinical approach to the psycho-analytical theory of the life and death instincts: an investigation into the aggressive aspects of narcissism', *Int. J. Psycho-Anal.* 52:169–78.

Searl, M. N. (1929) 'Danger situations of the immature ego', *Int. J. Psycho-Anal.* 10:423–35.

9 PRIMITIVE DEFENCE MECHANISMS

DEFINITION. The primitive (or psychotic) defence mechanisms are ranged against anxieties that derive from the activity of the death instinct; they are to be contrasted with the neurotic defences, notably repression, against libido. They make up the character of the psychotic (depressive and paranoid-schizoid) positions and comprise denial, splitting, excessive forms of projection and introjection, related identifications, and idealization. Mostly these mechanisms were described by classical psychoanalysts but are given special significance by Klein as characterizing the earliest phases of development, filling in the period otherwise regarded as the objectless phase of primary narcissism.

At first Klein emphasized, in line with Freud, the obsessional defences as specific against sadism. But she was driven more and more, by her clinical observations, to notice the primitive defence mechanisms that affected the character of the object-relations and defined the fundamentals of identity. Thus she substituted the primitive defence mechanisms for obsessional ones as the typical defences against sadism and destructiveness. In particular, Klein took early and massive (omnipotent) projection as a manifestation of the process, hypothesized by Freud, by which the ego defends itself against the death instinct.

The two forms of psychotic anxieties, depressive and persecutory, arouse different sets of defences whose components are the primitive defence mechanisms. The earliest (against persecutory anxiety) comprise annihilation of persecutors, expulsion (projection, including projective identification), denial, flight to the good object, and splitting. In the depressive position the manic defences – omnipotence, denial, triumph and contemptuous control – are characteristic.

CHRONOLOGY

1895 Freud (projection).

1911 Ferenczi (introjection).

1924 Abraham's introjection–projection cycles.

1930 Klein's development of expulsion and incorporation as (a) ego-development, and (b) perception and action (Klein, Melanie, 1930, 'The importance of symbol-formation in the development of the ego').

1932 Primary projection of the death instinct (Klein, Melanie, 1932, *The Psycho-Analysis of Children*).

1946 Projective identification and splitting of the ego (Klein, Melanie, 1946, 'Notes on some schizoid mechanisms'; Bion, Wilfred, 1957, 'Differentiation of the psychotic from the non-psychotic personalities').

When Klein became interested in psychological defences, in about 1930, she developed the notion of two categories: the 'psychotic' defences and the 'neurotic'. She concerned herself only with the former, and these became increasingly important as she went deeper into the severe disorders and the very early stages of infantile development. Her views about defences fall into several phases:

(i) 1930–5: specific defences against aggression;

(ii) 1935–46: the special constellation of defences in the depressive position;

(iii) 1946 onwards: the special defences against the anxiety of annihilation in the paranoid-schizoid position, especially projective identification; and

(iv) 1957: the defences against envy.

Because Klein's original discovery was the method of modifying anxiety by direct interpretation at the level of maximum anxiety, she was less interested in the defences used against anxiety than in the content of the anxious phantasies; in fact this was a point of contention between herself and Anna Freud, who was more interested in the defences than in the anxiety underneath.

SPECIAL DEFENCES AGAINST AGGRESSIVE IMPULSES.

In 1930, however, Klein developed her interest in the manifestation of psychosis in children and realized that the quality of the defensiveness was extreme. So when she found the passage in Freud (1926) in which he wondered about the possibility of special, early defences, she was challenged to show that her play technique could clarify this query about childhood development:

> It may well be that before its sharp cleavage into an ego and an id, and before the formation of the superego, the mental apparatus makes use of different methods of defence from those which it employs after it has reached these stages of organization. (Freud, 1926, p. 164)

So Klein filled out this early period with actual clinical data from the analysis of children. 'This defence,' she writes, linking it with the passage from Freud, 'in conformity with the degree of sadism, is of a violent character and differs fundamentally from the later mechanism of repression' (Klein, 1930, p. 220). She linked the special quality of the child's paranoid anxieties to special defences operating early in life – defences that are quite different from repression, with which most adult analysis was concerned:

> It is only in the later stages of the Oedipus conflict that the defence

against the libidinal impulses makes its appearance; in the earlier stages it is against the accompanying destructive impulses that the defence is directed . . . This defence is of a violent character, different from the mechanism of repression. (Klein, 1930, p. 232)

This was an important moment in Klein's own theoretical development.

From then on she took a great deal of interest in the earliest defences and remained relatively uninterested in repression and the 'neurotic defences'. In contrast, she called the very early defences 'psychotic defences' or *primitive defence mechanisms*. She linked this up with her own discovery of intense anxieties in some children which approached a psychotic intensity and had a psychotic quality, paranoia [see PARANOIA]. She became more enthusiastic about these primitive defences when she could see that Freud's theory of a special early operation of projection could solve the problem of the origin of the superego which had caused her so much heart-searching and ostracism. Her observations on the superego enabled her to demonstrate this '. . . apparently earliest measure of defence on the part of the ego' (Klein, 1933, p. 250) [see 7. SUPEREGO].

Omnipotence: One of the most important characteristics of the primitive defence mechanisms is the quality of omnipotence, which gives rise to major changes in the structure of the mind and personality. These mechanisms are connected with the operation of primitive and unconscious phantasies about the contents of the self and the external world, such as denial, projection and introjection [see OMNIPOTENCE].

PSYCHOTIC ANXIETY. Klein's early discovery that the phantasies enacted in play were derived from early (especially oral) phases, dominated by sadism, led her to discover paranoid states in children, suffused with an anxiety about a primitive internal violence akin in its character and consequences to psychotic conditions in adults [see PARANOIA; 8. EARLY ANXIETY-SITUATIONS]. She described vicious circles as the basis for this paranoia. Retaliatory attacks on the persecutors render them more harmful rather than less, because they are supposed, in phantasy, to be further enraged to retaliatory violence. This kind of vicious circle represents a paranoid state of hostility, with intense suspicion of any 'good' figures. The operation of these mechanisms gives rise to further excessive use of the primitive defence mechanisms, depletion of the ego and a fixation with this structure of defences which contributes a permanent risk of a regression to a psychosis.

Special defences: At first, following Abraham (1924), the most suitable candidate for the role of special defence against sadistic impulses seemed to be the *obsessional defences* [see OBSESSIONAL DEFENCES]. It was clear from Klein's clinical observations that her little patients used obsessional forms of controlling and mastering their anxieties and impulses through all kinds of rituals. However, she quite soon noted the psychotic quality behind these obsessional symptoms. For example, in the analysis of little Erna, conducted around 1925, 'As the analysis went on I discovered that the severe obsessional neurosis masked a paranoia' (Klein, 1927, p. 160n). She therefore became more interested in the mechanism of projection which Freud had shown to be involved in paranoia (Freud, 1911), and also the mechanism of introjection (Abraham, 1924).

Early mental processes. Whereas obsessional mechanisms provided control, the mechanisms of projection and introjection were fundamental to developing a sense of the self and the personality and, in fact, of the very composition of the internal world [see PROJECTION; INTROJECTION]. Klein relied on a passage of Freud's (1925) which succinctly expressed this development of a sense of self, and the nature of the two mechanisms of projection and introjection:

> The function of judgement is concerned in the main with two sorts of decisions. It affirms or disaffirms the possession by a thing of a particular attribute; and it asserts or disputes that a presentation has an existence in reality. The attribute to be decided about may originally have been good or bad, useful or harmful. Expressed in the language of the oldest – the oral – instinctual impulses, the judgement is: 'I should like to eat this', or 'I should like to spit it out'; and, put more generally: 'I should like to take this into myself and to keep that out.' That is to say: 'It shall be inside me' or 'it shall be outside me'. As I have shown elsewhere, the original pleasure-ego wants to introject everything that is good, and to eject everything from itself which is bad. (Freud, 1925, p. 237)

The whole effect of the mechanisms of projection and introjection contributes to the building up of an internal world of objects [see INTERNAL REALITY] and a sense of self.

THE PRIMITIVE MECHANISMS OF DEFENCE. Klein was not the only analyst to follow up Abraham's investigation of projection and introjection (for instance, Hárnik, 1932). However, her development of these ideas was quite original and eventually deviated from the classical concepts. Klein emphasized the links between the mechanisms and phantasies, and Stephen (1934) summarized, in outline, the connections of these mechanisms to states of feeling, and to objects, rather than to impulses.

Projection. There are various ways in which the term 'projection' is used [see PROJECTION]: in particular, the externalizing of an internal conflict or the externalizing of a deathly hostile object so that the aggression is turned outwards:

(i) Klein, following Freud, assigned a primary role in the existence of the ego to projection: 'Projection . . . originates from the deflection of the death instinct outwards and in my view helps the ego to overcome anxiety by ridding it of danger and badness' (Klein, 1946, p. 6). It is thus crucial to the initial defence of the ego against anxiety that arises from the outset about survival.

(ii) In the course of her researches on symbolization, Klein realized that one urge to play is the relief gained from externalizing painful internal situations. At first these were regarded theoretically as torturing relations between the ego and the superego:

> By the division of the roles the child succeeds in expelling the father and mother whom, in the elaboration of the Oedipus complex, it has absorbed into itself and who are now tormenting it inwardly by their severity. (Klein, 1926, p. 133)

The importance of projection as an externalization of internal conflicts (Klein, 1927) confirmed Freud's view of criminality from an unconscious sense of guilt (Freud, 1916). Externalizing the internal conflict (into play, for instance) evades the torturing cruelty of the internal objects [see 7. SUPEREGO]:

> His anxiety enhances the repetition-compulsion, and his need for punishment ministers to the compulsion (now grown very strong) to secure for himself actual punishment in order that the anxiety may be alleviated by a chastisement less severe than that which the anxiety-situation causes him to anticipate. (Klein, 1929, p. 214)

Introjection. Ferenczi (1909) thought of introjection as coming about *through* identification, a usage Freud seemed to adopt in his paper on mourning (1917), where he used the term identification to mean what we would now call introjection. Introjection and identification are now regarded as independent mechanisms, which at times combine. However, the attempts to disentangle introjection and identification have not always been consistent and have sometimes been idiosyncratic (Fuchs, 1937; de Saussure, 1939; Alice Balint, 1943). The development, in the Kleinian tradition, of the internal world as a space in which objects came and went and related in their own right became highly formalized [see 5. INTERNAL OBJECTS] (Klein, 1935, 1940).

Freud described the defensive function of introjection in 1917, when he showed that an external object can come to be identified with the ego, or a part of the ego, and a relationship with it can be set up internally. Freud originally called this identification, though it would now be called *introjective identification*. This is one kind of introjection, when the internalized object is identified with a part of the ego. However, there is an alternative situation in which the object remains separate within the internal world '. . . as a foreign body' (Klein, 1946, p. 9n). There is an important distinction to be made between the internal (i.e. introjected) object that has been assimilated and the one that has not [see INTROJECTION; ASSIMILATION].

Also, 'Closely connected with projection and introjection are some other mechanisms . . . splitting, idealization and denial' (Klein, 1946, p. 6).

Splitting. There are a number of forms of splitting. It is a mechanism loosely defined at first, but it can now be systematically described with the help of two discriminations: (i) there is a splitting of the object, or of the ego; (ii) and the splitting may be coherent (as in good versus bad), or it may be fragmenting. There are thus four possible kinds of splitting: a coherent split in the object, a coherent split in the ego, a fragmentation of the object, and a fragmentation of the ego [see SPLITTING]. The distinction of these forms may be less clear in practice, since as Klein says: '. . . the ego is incapable of splitting the object without a corresponding splitting taking place within the ego' (Klein, 1946, p. 6) [see SPLITTING].

Idealization. Idealization involves several defensive steps:

> It is typical to find an idealization of the good object so that it can be kept as far away as possible from the persecuting bad object and thus avoid confusion with it. This defensive process is combined with the mechanism of denial which in its turn is backed up by omnipotence: it is omnipotent denial which can completely deny the existence of bad objects . . . In the unconscious this process is equivalent to the annihilation of the whole disturbing object-relationship, so that it is clear that it involves the denial not only of the bad object but of an important part of the ego, which is in a relationship with the object. (Rosenfeld, 1983, p. 262) [see IDEAL OBJECT]

One of the associated problems is the impossibility of the ideal object remaining perfect. Any imperfection that occurs (a sensation of pain or frustration) leads to an abrupt switch to a 'bad' object. This enormous precariousness abates only when the depressive position is approached and there develops some tolerance of a 'good' object that is not perfect.

Denial. As part of idealization, denial is an important mechanism. However, it also has an independent function. In the very early stages of the ego, denial represents the phantasy of annihilating perceptions and parts of the ego [see LINKING].

Identification. This is a profoundly important mechanism for the establishment of a sense of a personal world, internal and external. The ability to recognize a personal link of identity, of a belongingness of the objects to the ego, is the basis of psychological existence, and a sense of self. Identification, according to Klein, may be through the associated mechanisms of introjection or projection [see IDENTIFICA-TION; 13. PROJECTIVE IDENTIFICATION].

DEFENCES AGAINST PARANOIA. At the time when Klein was using the idea of a paranoid position (until 1946) she regarded the main defence against the anxiety arising out of the threats of bad objects as the impulse to destroy the object: '. . . defences against these fears are predominantly the destruction of the persecutors by violent or secretive and cunning methods' (Klein, 1940, p. 348) [see 8. EARLY ANXIETY-SITUATIONS]. Klein had described the powerful aggression in children's play, and their struggles to cope with this, as the manifestation of the bad-object-relationship. The aggression itself, however, leads to further anxieties – typically about retaliation – and sets up further expectations of increased violence from the objects, resulting in spiralling hostility:

> . . . the defence, in conformity with the degree of the sadism, is of a violent character . . . In relation to the subject's own sadism it implies expulsion, whereas in relation to the object it implies destruction . . . The object of the attack becomes a source of danger because the subject fears similar – retaliatory – attacks from it. (Klein, 1930, p. 220)

This is the grounding for a vicious circle in which hostile relations breed fear and aggression, promising retaliation and an increase in fear: 'Thus, the wholly undeveloped ego is faced with a task which at this stage is quite beyond it – the task of mastering the severest anxiety' (Klein, 1930, p. 220).

The hostile attack aimed at annihilating the persecutor may be reinforced by expelling the internal state into the external world, to annihilate the (now external) object: 'In the baby, processes of introjection and projection . . . are dominated by aggression and anxieties which reinforce each other' (Klein, 1940, p. 348); this gives rise to further attempts to defend against these phantasy situations: '. . . various typical defences of the early ego, such as the mechanisms of splitting the object and the impulses, idealization, denial of inner and outer reality and the stifling of emotions' (Klein, 1946, p. 2). All these potentially violent defensive mechanisms in the very early period actually aggravate the sense of persecution, giving rise to a vicious circle.

THE ORGANIZATION OF PRIMITIVE DEFENCES. After 1932 Klein's theory became more systematic, through identifying the primitive defence mechanisms as those ranged against the death instinct. Typically the anxieties arising from the death instinct take two forms: (1) the depressive anxieties associated with the depressive position, an anxiety that includes a high degree of guilt; (2) the paranoid anxieties of being attacked or of falling apart in bits (schizoid). There are specific defences and constellations of defences (positions) against each of these anxieties. In addition, there is the anxiety that derives from envy – aggression towards the *good* object, as opposed to the paranoid aggression towards the bad object. Recently there has been increasing interest in the structure of defences, stimulated by the presentation of borderline, narcissistic or schizoid personalities for analysis [see STRUCTURE].

Defences in the depressive position. Klein's interest in the very early paranoid fears abated in 1935, when she realized the importance of the 'good' internal object and its fate. The pivotal issue in her descriptions of an internal world populated by internal objects [see INTERNAL REALITY; 5. INTERNAL OBJECTS] was the need to sustain a good and secure internal object [see 10. DEPRESSIVE POSITION] (Klein, 1935). The anxiety of losing the loved internal object provoked special forms of defence – in particular the paranoid defence against depressive anxiety, the manic defences, and reparation.

The anxiety of the depressive position is about '. . . the dangers which await the object inside the ego' (Klein, 1935, p. 265) because '. . . the ego becomes identified with its good internalized objects'. Furthermore, '. . . the ego makes a greater use of introjection of the *good* object as a mechanism of defence. This is associated with another important mechanism: that of making reparation to the object' and, incidentally, '. . . the mechanisms of expulsion and projection lose value'. *Introjection* is thus very characteristic of this phase, as well as the crucial urge to restore: *reparation*.

The paranoid defence against the depressive position: Klein's evidence that the depressive position occurs so close to, and arises out of, the preceding states of paranoia suggested to her a fluctuating process in which there is, repeatedly, a retreat from the depressive position when depressive anxieties become too strong. In that case, '. . . paranoid fears and suspicions were reinforced as a defence against the depressive position' (Klein, 1935, p. 274) [see PARANOID DEFENCE AGAINST DEPRESSIVE ANXIETY]. Then later, advance takes place once more towards the depressive position and the sustaining of depressive anxiety (Joseph, 1978, 1981) [see PS-D].

Suicide is a drastic form of 'defence', aimed at '. . . destroying the . . . part of the ego which is identified with the bad objects and the id' (Klein, 1935, p. 276). It is a little surprising, in view of the dispute with classical psychoanalysts over evidence for the death instinct as a self-directed destructiveness, that Kleinians have not paid more attention to suicidal ideas, phantasies and behaviour.

Manic defences: The manic defences, like the paranoid one, are an attempt to evade the exquisite pain of guilt in the early depressive position. The defence is really a collection of defences involving a denial of psychic reality and therefore of the importance of the objects that are loved and taken in, a denigrating contempt for the objects that are loved so that their loss will not be experienced as important, and a triumphant and omnipotent form of putting everything right. These are all means of minimizing the feelings of loss and guilt [see MANIC DEFENCES].

Reparation: To a significant extent the concept of reparation took over in Klein's thinking from the obsessional defences, in particular the defence known as 'undoing', in which there is an attempt to retrace exactly a destructive action (real or imagined) and thus restore a pre-existing situation. Reparation also supplanted, to a significant extent, the notion of sublimation – that is, the healthy discharge of instincts in mutated form through socially accepted, and socially provided, channels. To put it another way: *the* form of sublimation for Klein was reparation, the 'sublimation' of guilt into constructive action [see REPARATION].

Defences in the paranoid-schizoid position. In 1946 Klein described the paranoid-schizoid position [see 11. PARANOID-SCHIZOID POSITION]. She pinpointed the fear of annihilation as the primary anxiety – this is the fear of the death instinct working from within to annihilate the ego. There is a failure of deflection of the death instinct outwards on to an external object, and the result is the fear of an internal persecutor working for the death of the subject from within. The results of these phantasies – when they are particularly strong, and when the defences are not adequately coping with the anxiety – are a variety of experiences of falling to pieces and fragmentation of the self, or of hypochondriacal fears of a deathly object inside, e.g. cancer phobia. The predominant defensive manoeuvre is projection in order to accomplish the deflection of the death instinct, and then to relocate the persecutor in the outside world – in contrast to the depressive position, where introjection comes to the fore.

Klein emphasized splitting in the paranoid-schizoid position, but in a particular form – splitting of the ego. This is in contrast to the splitting of objects [see SPLITTING], in which the object is reduced to a single function (part-object) or is attributed only good (or only bad) characteristics – idealized object (or persecutor). To some extent the problems of this early period are actually aggravated by the employment of splitting processes:

> ... the early ego splits the object and the relation to it in an active way, and this may imply some active splitting of the ego itself. Thus one consequence is the experience of the ego being fragmented and in pieces. (Klein, 1946, p. 5)

Many of these defensive processes result in the weakening or fragmentation of the ego itself, especially (i) splitting and the impulses behind it which derive from the oral impulse to bite up and chew to pieces; (ii) the idealization of the good remaining fragments, with denial and annihilation of bad objects and their expulsion:

> Omnipotent denial ... is in the unconscious equal to annihilation by the destructive impulse. It is, however, not only a situation and an object that are denied and annihilated – *it is an object-relation* which suffers this fate; and therefore a part of the ego, from which the feelings towards the object emanate. (Klein, 1946, p. 7)

and (iii) projective identification leads to parts of the self being lost:

> Together with these harmful excrements, expelled in hatred, split-off parts of the ego are also projected on to [into] the mother. These excrements and bad parts of the self are meant not only to injure but also to control and to take possession of the object. (Klein, 1946, p. 8) [see 13. PROJECTIVE IDENTIFICATION]

Other defences in the paranoid-schizoid position are linked with projective identification – particularly splitting of the object and of the ego. Linked also with that is the primary splitting into a good object and a bad object. The primary instincts (libido and death instinct) are defused to give these polarized states of love and hate. In the primitive mechanism of *idealization*, there is a division of the object into supposed good and bad parts. The bad parts are then projected and/or denied, so that for the ego only a good object with no bad aspects (idealized object) survives, while the threat to the ego from any bad object is eliminated (denial and projection) (Rosenfeld, 1983) [see IDEALIZATION].

Defences against envy: In 1957 Klein introduced her last great theoretical concept, envy [see 12. ENVY]. This came out of her interest in schizophrenics and concerned the very primitive forms of aggression against the good (or idealized) object [see OBJECTS]. Part of her interest was in the defensive manifestations that the infant has to adopt right at the outset of ego-formation. Envy results from the inherited endowment of libido and death instinct, and a degree of confusion between them results. The infant urgently needs to separate these two contrasting impulses at the beginning and does so by using the earliest splitting process. This represents the earliest moment for things to go wrong, giving rise to certain forms of pathology [see PSYCHOSIS; CONFUSIONAL STATES; NARCISSISM]. Prominent among these defences is the prompt separation of the two kinds of instinctual impulses which amounts to a normal form of splitting, essential for survival.

Klein (1957, pp. 216–19) detailed other defences [see 12. ENVY] – omnipotence, denial and splitting, and confusion; flight from the primal object, devaluation of the object and, paradoxically, devaluation of the self; greedy internalization of the object, stirring up envy in others, stifling of feelings of love and corresponding intensification of hate; and finally a special form of acting out described by Rosenfeld (1952). Somewhat related to the latter is a defence described by Segal (1962) which she described as splitting-off of primary envy into an unintegrated state [see 12. ENVY]. This list of defences compiled by Klein are characteristic organizations of the typical primitive defence mechanisms which may be found in the depressive or paranoid positions.

FIXATION AND DEVELOPMENT. Klein frequently made the point that the defence mechanisms may have consequences of a deleterious kind. She described vicious circles, especially in connection with the very early paranoid states, in which the hostile measures taken by the ego to rescue itself from danger only enhance the danger [see 8. EARLY ANXIETY-SITUATIONS; PARANOIA].

Defences and impulses. A more intricate problem is that processes which appear to be a normal psychological expression of an instinctual impulse are also described as defences against the instinctual impulses. This relation between the ego's defences and the id-impulses is of great importance in some branches of psychoanalysis, but the Kleinian school is not one of them. The terms projection and introjection are used without reference to whether they refer to a manifestation of a normal process (incorporation or expulsion, to be found in the normal processes of perception) or to defensive manifestations, or abuse (as Freud called it).

Such a stance is complicated, partly because psychoanalytic theories of 'normal' psychology are squeezed out of view by theories of the abnormal. Although in ego-psychology there is a theory of normal adaptation, it is still designated as conflict-free and outside the domain of psychoanalytic interest. The unravelling of normal and abnormal remained a bugbear of Kleinian theories, as of the other psychoanalytic schools. Bion contributed to the significant distinction between omnipotent mechanisms and the more benign operation of defence mechanisms [see OMNIPOTENCE].

How a psychic mechanism is devoted to a defensive use or impulse satisfaction has to be unravelled by reference to the clinical material itself. For instance, projection of an internal persecutor into the external world of the playroom was a very important defence as Klein understood it, by making an internal threat into a more manageable external one. However, at the same time projection may itself be an attack on an external persecutor.

Defences and development. In addition these mechanisms, both instinctual impulses and defences, are the building blocks of ego-development. Introjection, for instance, is the single most important developmental mechanism in that it is the means by which the good object, '. . . a precondition for normal development . . . comes to form a focal point in the ego and makes for cohesiveness of the ego' (Klein, 1946, p. 9):

> However, the infant's oral-sadistic desires, which are active from the beginning of life and are easily stirred by frustration from external and internal sources, inevitably again and again give rise to a feeling that the breast is destroyed and in bits inside him, as a result of his greedy devouring attacks upon it. These two aspects of introjection exist side by side. (Klein, 1952, p. 67)

The introjections actually build the ego on the basis of accumulating the attributes of the object in the self; and projection divests the ego in phantasy (and then by effect in reality) of certain disowned attributes.

Normal and abnormal projective identification. At a later date, Bion (1959) explored projective identification to reveal both a normal and an abnormal form, depending on the degree of hostility and destructiveness inherent in the state of mind in which the projective identification is accomplished. In its more normal form projective identification establishes the basis of a communication, to an object, of the subject's state of mind. This is important in the interpersonal field of the infant with mother and the patient with his analyst [see 13. PROJECTIVE IDENTIFICATION].

Thus these primitive defence mechanisms perform four ego-functions:

(i) defence against anxiety and pain;

(ii) discharge of pregenital impulses, oral and anal;

(iii) a step in ego-development through introjective identification with an object, often moulded by projective processes; and

(iv) nonverbal communication of emotional states.

Repression. From time to time Klein made reference to the distinction between primitive defence mechanisms and repression. She saw repression as a later modification of the splitting mechanism, the splitting of consciousness from the unconscious mind. At one point she described varied degrees of this split, leading to more or less permeable forms of repressions [see REPRESSION]. The change is one from a vertical form of splitting of the mind, each part having an element of the ego in a partial relationship with a part-object, towards a horizontal division of the mind in unconscious, preconscious and conscious layers (the topographical model) [see REPRESSION].

MAIN CRITICISMS OF KLEIN'S VIEW OF DEFENCES. The emphasis on these primitive mechanisms depends on the acceptance of the importance of primary destructiveness as a determining factor (a) in the creation of anxiety, and (b) in the inhibition or precocious enhancement of the normal progression of the libido.

The early ego. Since they had set themselves the task of analysing the structures and functions of the ego (Anna Freud, 1936; Hartmann, 1939), the ego-psychologists found themselves somewhat out-manoeuvred by the Kleinians' concentration on these early ego-functions. Klein's descriptions of the earliest aspects of the ego in the remote and misty period of the first year of life undercut ego-psychologists' concentration on the later phases when the ego was more behaviourally apparent [see EGO-PSYCHOLOGY].

Ego-psychologists argue that the first year of life is occupied with autoerotic and narcissistic states during which ego-function is more or less absent. Hence there were no object-relations, no integrative functions of the ego and phantasy life had not commenced; there was no ego.

The assertion of a negative proposition has been difficult. Academic psychology research on the early weeks and months of life has tended to suggest considerable early cognitive sophistication in the infant (Chamberlain, 1987). Indeed, a good deal was also known of this in the 1940s (Middlemore, 1941, and see Chapter 3, note 2 of Isaacs, 1952). Mahler *et al.* (1975) have made comprehensive studies with a psychoanalytic background, though their interpretations of their observations have been questioned (Stern, 1985). This does not necessarily favour the Kleinian view, since the theory of unconscious phantasy is much more to do with affective development in relation to an object than with cognitive or perceptual sophistication. The mass of literature requires further reviewing and elucidation before it can bear weight on the issue of the objectless world or otherwise of the infant. Murray's work on the affective perturbations of the mother–infant relationship promises a possible discrimination (see, for instance, Murray and Trevarthen, 1985; Murray, 1987).

Downgrading of later development. Ego-psychologists complain of the downgrading and neglect of later defence mechanisms and the later developmental aspects of the ego, its structure and functions, by constantly referring all later processes back to the forms in the early mechanisms. With the emphasis on these primitive ego-functions there was a concern that the whole of psychoanalytic theory and terminology might go out of the window, as everything is redrawn in terms of these early processes. There was a good deal of complaint about the elision of terms, which condensed everything back into these primitive processes. Glover (1945) was particularly incensed that a process giving rise to the ego and its development (introjection) should itself be an ego-function, and scorned the internal inconsistency of this.

The psychotic infant. Schmideberg (1931) considered that the primitive defence mechanisms were hangovers in psychotic patients (e.g. Abraham's [1924] manic-depressives) of early mechanisms normally absorbed into the later ego-functions with no further significance. There was a suspicion that essentially psychotic processes were being attributed to the normal infant; moreover a frankly psychotic character was being attributed to the unconscious of adults: a residual, untouchable psychotic 'enclave' (Glover, 1945).

Klein (1946) was sensitive to the charge that she confused 'primitive' with 'psychotic' and that she could be construed as believing that all children are psychotic (Klein, 1929, 1930). The Kleinian descriptions of the constellations of these primitive defences in the depressive and paranoid-schizoid positions remained vulnerable to the charge that infants were regarded as psychotic until Bion, and others, distinguished the psychotic from the non-psychotic use of these primitive mechanisms [see OMNIPOTENCE; LINKING; 13. PROJECTIVE IDENTIFICATION].

Abraham, Karl (1924) 'A short study of the development of the libido', in Karl Abraham (1927) *Selected Papers on Psycho-Analysis*. Hogarth, pp. 418–501.

Balint, Alice (1943) 'Identification', *Int. J. Psycho-Anal.* 24:97–107.

Bion, Wilfred (1957) 'Differentiation of the psychotic from the non-psychotic personalities', *Int. J. Psycho-Anal.* 38:266–75; republished (1967) in W. R. Bion, *Second Thoughts*. Heinemann, pp. 43–64.

—— (1959) 'Attacks on linking', *Int. J. Psycho-Anal.* 40:308–15; republished (1967) in *Second Thoughts*, pp. 93–109.

—— (1962) *Learning from Experience*. Heinemann.

Chamberlain, David (1987) 'The cognitive newborn: a scientific update', *Br. J. Psychother.* 4:30–71.

Ferenczi, Sandor (1909) 'Introjection and transference', in Ferenczi (1952) *First Contributions to Psycho-Analysis*. Hogarth, pp. 35–93; previously published (1908) as 'Introjektion und Übertragung', *Jahrbuch der Psychoanalytische und Psychopathologische Forschung* 1:422–57.

Freud, Anna (1936) *The Ego and the Mechanisms of Defence*. Hogarth.

Freud, Sigmund (1911) 'Psycho-analytic notes on an autobiographical account of a case of paranoia', in James Strachey, ed. *The Standard Edition of the Complete Psychological Works of Sigmund Freud*, 24 vols. Hogarth, 1953–73. vol. 12, pp. 3–82.

—— (1916) 'Some character-types met with in psycho-analytic work: III Criminals from a sense of guilt'. *S.E.* 14, pp. 332–3.

—— (1917) 'Mourning and melancholia'. *S.E.* 14, pp. 237–60.

—— (1925) 'Negation'. *S.E.* 19, pp. 235–9.

—— (1926) *Inhibitions, Symptoms and Anxiety. S.E.* 20, pp. 77–175.

Fuchs (Foulkes), S.H. (1937) 'On identification', *Int. J. Psycho-Anal.* 18: 269–93.

Glover, Edward (1945) 'An examination of the Klein system of child psychology', *Psychoanal. Study Child* 1:3–43.

Hárnik, J. (1932) 'On introjection and projection in the mechanism of depression', *Int. J. Psycho-Anal.* 13:425–32.

Hartmann, Heinz (1939) *Ego Psychology and the Problem of Adaptation*. New York: International Universities Press.

Heimann, Paula (1955) 'Certain functions of introjection and projection in early infancy', in Melanie Klein, Paula Heimann, Susan Isaacs and Joan Riviere, eds *Developments in Psycho-Analysis*. Hogarth, pp. 122–68.

Isaacs, Susan (1952) 'On the nature and function of phantasy', in Melanie Klein, Paula Heimann, Susan Isaacs and Joan Riviere, eds *Developments in Psycho-Analysis*. Hogarth, pp. 67–121; previously published (1948) *Int. J. Psycho-Anal.* 29:73–97.

Joseph, Betty (1978) 'Different types of anxiety and their handling in the analytic situation', *Int. J. Psycho-Anal.* 59:223–8.

—— (1981) 'Toward the experiencing of psychic pain', in James Grotstein, ed. (1981) *Do I Dare Disturb the Universe?* Beverly Hills: Caesura, pp. 93–102.

Klein, Melanie (1926) 'The psychological principles of early analysis', in *The Writings of Melanie Klein*, vol. 1. Hogarth, pp. 128–38.

—— (1927) 'Symposium on child analysis', *The Writings of Melanie Klein*, vol. 1, pp. 139–69.

—— (1929) 'Infantile anxiety-situations reflected in a work of art and in the creative impulse', *The Writings of Melanie Klein*, vol. 1, pp. 210–18.

—— (1930) 'The importance of symbol-formation in the development of the ego', *The Writings of Melanie Klein*, vol. 1, pp. 219–32.

—— (1932) *The Psycho-Analysis of Children, The Writings of Melanie Klein*, vol. 2.

—— (1933) 'The early development of conscience in the child', *The Writings of Melanie Klein*, vol. 1, pp. 248–57.

—— (1935) 'A contribution to the psychogenesis of manic-depressive states', *The Writings of Melanie Klein*, vol. 1, pp. 262–89.

—— (1940) 'Mourning and its relation to manic-depressive states', *The Writings of Melanie Klein*, vol. 1, pp. 344–69.

—— (1946) 'Notes on some schizoid mechanisms', *The Writings of Melanie Klein*, vol. 3, pp. 1–24.

—— (1952) 'Some theoretical conclusions regarding the emotional life of infants', *The Writings of Melanie Klein*, vol. 3, pp. 61–93.

—— (1955) 'On identification', *The Writings of Melanie Klein*, vol. 3, pp. 141–75.

—— (1957) *Envy and Gratitude*, *The Writings of Melanie Klein*, vol. 3, pp. 176–235.

Mahler, Margaret, Pine, Fred and Bergman, Anni (1975) *The Psychological Birth of the Human Infant*. Hutchinson.

Middlemore, Merrell (1941) *The Nursing Couple*. Hamish Hamilton.

Murray, Lynne (1987) 'Effects of post-natal depression on infant development: direct studies of early mother–infant interactions', in I.F. Brockingham and R. Kumar, eds (1982) *Motherhood and Mental Illness*, vol. 2. Academic.

Murray, Lynne and Trevarthen, Colin (1985) 'Emotional regulation of interactions between two-month-olds and their mothers', in Tiffany Field and Nathan Fox, eds *Social Perception in Infants*. Norwood, NJ: Ablex, pp. 177–97.

Rosenfeld, Herbert (1952) 'Notes on the psycho-analysis of the superego conflict in an acute catatonic schizophrenic', *Int. J. Psycho-Anal.* 33:457–64; republished (1955) in Melanie Klein, Paula Heimann and Roger Money-Kyrle, eds *New Directions in Psycho-Analysis*. Tavistock, pp. 180–219; and (1965) in Herbert Rosenfeld *Psychotic States*. Hogarth, pp. 52–62.

—— (1983) 'Primitive object relations and mechanisms', *Int. J. Psycho-Anal.* 64:261–7.

de Saussure, R. (1939) 'Identification and substitution', *Int. J. Psycho-Anal.* 20:465–70.

Schmideberg, Melitta (1931) 'A contribution to the psychology of persecutory ideas and delusions', *Int. J. Psycho-Anal.* 12:331–67.

Segal, Hanna (1962) 'Curative factors in psycho-analysis', *Int. J. Psycho-Anal.* 43:212–17; republished (1971) in *The Work of Hanna Segal*. New York: Jason Aronson, pp. 69–80.

Stephen, Karin (1934) 'Introjection and projection: guilt and rage', *Br. J. Med. Psychol.* 14:316–31.

Stern, David (1985) *The Interpersonal World of the Infant*. New York: Basic.

10 DEPRESSIVE POSITION

DEFINITION. The confluence of hatred and love towards the object gives rise to a particularly poignant sadness that Klein called depressive anxiety (or 'pining'). This expresses the earliest and most anguished form of guilt due to ambivalent feelings towards an object. The infant, at some stage (normally at *four to six months*), is physically and emotionally mature enough to integrate his or her fragmented perceptions of mother, bringing together the separately good and bad versions (imagos) that he or she has previously experienced. When such part-objects are brought together as a whole they threaten to form a contaminated, damaged or dead whole object.

Depressive anxiety is the crucial element of mature relationships, the source of generous and altruistic feelings that are devoted to the well-being of the object. In the depressive position efforts to maximize the loving aspect of the ambivalent relationship with the damaged 'whole object' are mobilized (reparation). But so also are the defence mechanisms. These comprise the constellation of paranoid defences (originally called by Klein the 'paranoid position', but later dropped) and the manic defences.

CHRONOLOGY

1935 The definitive statement of change on reaching whole objects (Klein, Melanie, 1935, 'A contribution to the psychogenesis of manic-depressive states).

1945 Mourning the loss of the *internal* loved object (Klein, Melanie, 1940, 'Mourning and its relation to manic-depressive states').

Around 1932 Klein finally accepted that she was on an increasingly divergent trajectory from classical psychoanalysis, although she rightly maintained that her views were not divergent from much of Freud's later writing. At that point she espoused Freud's later theory of the death instinct. Her own theoretical journey began in 1935 with a radical reappraisal of guilt [see UNCONSCIOUS GUILT], setting off from the point that Abraham and Freud had reached before the description of the superego and the structural model: Freud's (1917, 1921) discovery that the ego internalizes an external object; Abraham's (1924) observations on the fate of the object in melancholic and obsessional states.

Precursors: Klein was aware of depression in children and its connection with their aggression and guilt: 'After her sadism had spent itself in these phantasies, apparently unchecked by any inhibition, reaction would set in in the form of deep depression, anxiety and bodily exhaustion' (Klein, 1929a, p. 200). Like Freud, she knew that guilt and depression were to do with losing and mourning an ambivalently loved object: 'At a later stage of development the content of the dread changes from that of an attacking mother to the dread that the real, loving mother may be lost and that the girl will be left solitary and forsaken' (Klein, 1929b, p. 217):

> ... as soon as the child's sadism is diminished and the character and function of its superego changed so that it arouses less anxiety and more sense of guilt, those defensive mechanisms which form the basis of a moral and ethical attitude are activated, and the child begins to have consideration for its objects and to be amenable to social feeling. (Klein, 1933, p. 252)

There is a movement from sadism [see SADISM] into depression, the fear of losing the mother who is also loved, and this gives rise to moral and ethical attitudes.

THE GREAT THEORETICAL LEAP. Klein added, in 1935, that at the moment when the great phase of sadism in childhood begins to be resolved, a new relation to objects begins – a *whole-object-relationship*. Then loving impulses come more into the picture, and deep remorse and concern fill the child. She now understood that the concern is the result of a confluence of love and hatred (instinctual and inherited) towards the same person (object), with both 'good' and 'bad' aspects.

The features of the depressive position: The depressive position was the first of the major theoretical developments in Klein's work. It can be considered from five points of view:

(1) it integrated in a remarkable way all the major theoretical aspects of the preceding phases of her work;

(2) the core of the new development is the notion of the coming together of part-objects which are superseded in the experience of the developing infant by whole objects at the age of four to six months;

(3) in contrast to her persistent interest in the bad-object-relationship and paranoid anxiety, Klein suddenly emphasized in a new way the importance of the good object and of the loving impulses;

(4) the good object that is lost is the *internal* object; and

(5) the depressive position represented a change in emphasis in development from projection, in the preceding paranoid states, to introjection.

(1) **The theoretical integration.** Klein's emphasis on phantasy life, as opposed to the classical economics of instinctual energy, opened a new world: a world of objects experienced as concretely located inside the personality. The phantasies of sadism and aggression had contributed

to a new theory of the Oedipus complex and had focused psychoanalytic controversy on the first year of life. The conflation of the libidinal phases, the Oedipus complex and the formation of the superego had changed the significance of each. The upshot was the contesting aspects of the superego (persecutors and helpful figures) and of the Oedipus complex (positive and reverse [negative] complexes), and the tension between the libidinal instincts (mostly regarded as genital) and the aggressive instincts (mostly pregenital). This had reached its theoretical focus previously in the femininity phase and the specific anxiety-situation in which the child raids, soils, steals from and destroys mother's body and father's penis, which resides inside mother [see 6. FEMININITY PHASE; 8. EARLY ANXIETY-SITUATIONS].

However, Klein's increasing awareness of the importance for the child of the insides of people led her to give increasing significance to the processes of projection and introjection and the constant movement, in phantasy, between the internal and the external worlds. With the realization of the importance of the good object, and damage to it, she could see the internal world as centred around the internal good object, and the problems posed for the infant as he finds his aggressive impulses for that object as well as his love. Thus the depressive position is formed out of the mounting appreciation of the poignancy of ambivalent impulses [see LOVE; GRATITUDE]; the importance of the internal world in the founding of the personality itself; and the developing awareness of an internal world of good and bad objects and impulses (insight).

(2) **Whole objects.** For various reasons, including the lack of perceptual development, the very young infant at first recognizes only very polarized objects, good people or bad ones. Because of this lack of perceptions the infant does not even recognize whole people, but only parts of people – the breast especially, mother's face eventually: 'The loss of the loved object takes place during that phase of development in which the ego makes the transition from partial to total incorporation of the object' (Klein, 1935, p. 267). Klein was referring to Freud's use of the phrase 'loss of the loved object', which comes from his paper on anxiety (Freud, 1926), where he defined this as the typical primary anxiety-situation faced by every infant. Klein linked this in a totally original way with Abraham's theory of part- and whole objects [see WHOLE OBJECT]. The crucial loss of the loved object is the infant's experience of losing the wonderfully perfect, ideal object (mother) when he discovers her imperfections. The breast that feeds him is also the mother that makes him wait.

These early objects have very little physical presence or attributes, simply because the infant is not in a position to recognize such attributes [see 5. INTERNAL OBJECTS]. As development progresses, the infant develops the capacity to perceive people as whole objects, especially as the visual apparatus comes into use. This is not just a capacity of the perceptual apparatus, it is an emotional accomplishment as well. Since separate objects are defined for the infant largely in terms of their benevolent or malevolent feelings and intentions, to bring these parts together into something wholer means merging into one an object that has a mixture of intentions.

This step (at about four to six months of age) poses intense emotional issues that are quite new and very painful. There are two aspects:

(a) The good object is now changed in the child's mind to something both more realistic (in an objective sense) and more suspect. This is a new relation to mother, one in which the very and exceptionally good and wholly well-intentioned mother (a part-object) comes to be a mixed figure, particularly hostile, and therefore contaminated, damaged, and no longer the perfection the child desires. This new relation to mother is the core of the depressive position and is the source of many painful phantasies about what has happened to her. She may seem to be depleted drastically of her goodness, or to have been contaminated with badness, or to have been harmed, damaged or brutally mutilated. All these phantasies, based on the kinds of impulses the infant knows in himself, lead to an intense feeling of responsibility as well as an exquisite sorrow [see DEPRESSIVE ANXIETY]. The infant has to contend with the fact that he hates, with the most unrestrained and paranoid intensity, the mother whom he can now see is the same person he loved for feeding and caring for and loving him [see LOVE].

In short, the object becomes properly separate and potentially a character of her own. The omnipotence of phantasy diminishes, and the ego comes painfully to find a smaller place in its own growing world. Objects come and go in spite of it.

(b) With this step comes a new capacity to love. Concern, sorrow and love for the whole object are *for* the object itself, not merely for the gratification it gives. Abraham (1924) first described 'true-object-love' in contrast to desire for partial objects. This new form of love brings new consequences to hate and loss [see LOVE]. Klein regarded this as important for the understanding of the psychotic conditions: 'I believe that the main difference between incorporation in paranoia and in melancholia is connected with changes in the relation of the subject to the object' (Klein, 1935, p. 263). In the depressive position the object is loved in spite of its bad parts, whereas in the paranoid-schizoid position awareness of the bad parts changes the good object abruptly into a persecutor. Thus love can be sustained in the depressive position, giving the beginnings of stability.

The confluence of emotions is extremely disturbing and this step forward from the paranoid state may be resisted, so that the infant grows up with an unusually strong propensity for paranoid relations (that is, a psychotic potential is fixed in the personality). Klein described the reversion to paranoid relations as a *paranoid defence against depressive anxiety.*

(3) **The importance of the good object.** Up to this point (1935) Klein's focus had always been drawn towards the paranoid relations – the fear and hatred – and the object of those impulses – the bad object. It was the bad object that dominated the child's world and the internal world and controlled the normal or abnormal development of the libido. But at this point Klein began to realize the importance of the good object, the need to sustain it and the relationship to it, and the poignancy and the pain of the love for it.

The realization of the relationship with the good object began a whole new rearrangement of the child's developmental struggles. Instead of the conflicts over controlling the libido which Freud described, and instead of the struggles to control the aggressive impulses, Klein now saw the basis of the struggles as the impetus to protect and repair the good object. She described the insecurity as especially significant with the *internal* good object – a sense of there being a good, helpful figure inside the personality, felt to reside there, and so closely loved as to constitute the basic primary identification around which the whole of an identity is formed. The good internal object provides the continual internal dialogue of encouragement and self-esteem on which confidence and psychological security are based.

(4) **The internal object.** With her theory of internal objects, Klein was in a position to define which object's loss is important. As in Freud's theory of melancholia, it is the loss of the good object internally which is important. The loss of the internal good object is closely connected with the external. An external rebuff, or a bereavement, also threatens the phantasy of a good internal object nourishing the person with psychological support from inside. Klein saw the mourning of the bereaved person as only a gross and overt manifestation of a process which is constantly being carried out in smaller and internal ways throughout life whenever rebuffs and losses of a lesser kind are suffered.

Mourning: Klein's concept of the depressive position is a direct development of Freud's (1917) and Abraham's (1924) discoveries on melancholia and the central importance that the 'fear of the loss of the loved object' has in human development and experience.

Freud discovered the link between mourning (loss of the external object) and melancholia, in which an abnormal and persecuting relationship to an 'internal object' is set up because of ambivalence. Abraham later recognized that both mourning and melancholia are part of the same phenomenon. Klein defined the importance of a balance – melancholia tended more to hate than love; mourning, more to love than hate.

The infant is beset with the work of mourning. For Klein, the work of the depressive position is the work of mourning: 'My contention is that the child goes through states of mind comparable to the mourning of the adult' (Klein, 1940, p. 344). However, she was making a radical new suggestion about mourning itself: '... this early mourning is revived whenever grief is experienced later in life' (Klein, 1940, p. 344). Mourning is an internal mourning for something dead inside, a dead or dying internal object; and a repetition of innumerable earlier occasions.

Klein emphasized the importance of the correspondence between the external and internal objects, especially in terms of fears of the loss of one or the other: 'From the beginning of psychic development there is a constant correlation of real objects with those installed within the ego' (Klein, 1935, p. 266). In recovering from the mourning state, the mourner '... not only takes into himself (reincorporates) the person whom he has just lost, but also reinstates good objects (ultimately the loved parents)' (Klein, 1940, p. 353).

This is an important addition to Freud's view of the work of mourning in which the mourner introjects, and identifies with, the lost actual person. Klein is now saying that this is part and parcel of a process of reinstatement of a *primal object*, a parent, which has been felt to be damaged, destroyed and lost, in correspondence with the death of the external object.

'Many mourners can only make slow steps in re-establishing the bonds with the external world because they are struggling against the chaos inside ... this gradual development in the baby's object-relations ... is also due to the chaotic state of his inner world' (Klein, 1940, p. 361). The infant has an experience that everything inside himself is in turmoil and chaos. It is not just that his feelings are chaotically mixed up. Because his feelings are always represented in his mind as phantasies, he believes that the object resides concretely inside him, or in his own body, so that his own internal state is one that becomes confused and mixed up, with a mixture of 'good' and dangerously 'bad' objects, loved and hated all at once. In particular, he feels that his hatred damages his loved actual mother, and this comes also to be reflected in the experience that the object inside him is also damaged or dead, and he may identify with this internal deadness. An internal chaos comes about through the introjection of an object already damaged or dead externally. In fact, Klein went further:

'. . . any pain caused by unhappy experiences, whatever their nature, has something in common with mourning' (Klein, 1940, p. 360).

Rather later, when there was more understanding of the unintegrated states of the ego [see 11. PARANOID-SCHIZOID POSITION], Grinberg (1978) noted that the mourning for the loss of the loved object must include a form of mourning for the part of the self that is linked with that object.

(5) **The balance of projection and introjection.** The attaining of the depressive position is a developmental step, an uncertain one, and one which is therefore a lifelong task. It takes over from the preceding paranoid states and the paranoid-schizoid position. In those previous states the ego maintains separation of the good and the bad in the object and in itself, through a persistent use of the mechanism of projection for dealing with these bad things. But when it comes to the depressive position, the balance changes. Projection itself gives rise to fears, for example, that the good internal object will be lost through projecting it outwards (as in the clinical details Abraham reported). As a result there is a greater emphasis on introjecting good things into the internal world, and a relaxing of the impulse to project bad things out. With the decline in reliance on projection there is a greater opportunity for awareness of the state of the internal world and, in turn, of the external world – the first entails acknowledging unwelcome aspects of oneself; the latter entails recognizing the better qualities of the external world.

DEPRESSIVE ANXIETY. The first anxieties come from a fear of the aggressive impulses, ultimately a fear of the death instinct. These are the *psychotic anxieties*, and there are two kinds – persecutory and depressive – (i) fear for oneself, and (ii) fear for the loved object, respectively. With the change in the relation to the object (at four to six months), the predominant anxiety changes: 'The dread of persecution, which was felt on the ego's account, now relates to the good object as well' (Klein, 1935, p. 264). The phantasy life of the infant is beset with the idea that the hate has done actual harm to the loved person, and he is thrown into a state Klein refers to (following Freud and Abraham) as the *loss of the loved object*, the emotional turmoil over the idea that the wonderful 'good' object (mother, breast) has gone [see DEPRESSIVE ANXIETY]. In a useful summary, Joseph said:

> Freud [1926] . . . brought together the various types of anxiety, in relation to the impulses and the superego, thus including feelings of guilt as a type of anxiety. In addition, he stressed that the very existence of the life and death instincts and the awareness of them together, in the form of ambivalence, produced, as he described it,

'the fatal inevitability of a sense of guilt'. Klein's work is in line with these findings. She stressed that once the individual is aware that the object he loves is also the one against whom he rages and feels anger, then guilt is fatally inevitable, and she stressed the pain and anxiety caused by such guilt and by the reproaches of the objects towards whom guilt is felt, internal and external, in the depressive position. In her view, before this position is achieved the death instinct gives rise to anxieties which are of a persecutory nature. (Joseph, 1978, pp. 223–4)

The infant fears that the loved mother has been killed or destroyed:

> ... only when the ego has introjected the object as a whole ... is it able to fully realize the disaster created though its sadism and especially through its cannibalism ... The ego then finds itself confronted with the psychic reality that its loved objects are in a state of dissolution – in bits – there is anxiety how to put the bits together in the right way and do away with the bad ones; how to bring the object to life when it has been put together; and there is the anxiety of being interfered with in this task by bad objects and by one's own hatred, etc. (Klein, 1935, p. 269)

The concern about repairing something irretrievably damaged or dead is the core: 'The processes which subsequently become clear as "the loss of the loved object" are determined by the subject's sense of failure to secure his good, internalized object, i.e. to possess himself of it' (Klein, 1935, p. 267) [see LOVE].

In these earliest moments of the appreciation of the whole object, the pain is particularly exquisite. It comes in on top of the old paranoid anxieties:

> ... the ego feels constantly menaced in its possession of internalized good objects. It is full of anxiety lest such objects should die. Both in children and adults suffering from depression, I have discovered the dread of harbouring dying or dead objects (especially the parents) inside one and an identification of the ego with objects in this condition. (Klein, 1935, p. 266)

The anguish of the subject is personal, a fear for his own survival without the supporting mother, and also a genuine concern for her [see 8. EARLY ANXIETY-SITUATIONS; LOVE].

The early period of Klein's writing referred to 'anxiety and a sense of guilt', but this was resolved in 1935 by a clear-cut distinction between a paranoid anxiety of persecution and guilt associated with the depressive position, which is referred to as depressive anxiety. Persecutory anxiety is a fear for the ego; depressive anxiety is a fear for the survival of the loved object:

> There are thus two sets of fears, feelings and defences, which, however varied in themselves and however intimately linked together, can, in my view, for purposes of theoretical clearness, be isolated from each other. The first set of feelings and phantasies are the persecutory ones, characterized by fears relating to the destruction of the ego by internal persecutors by violent or secretive and cunning methods . . . The second set of feelings . . . go to make up the depressive position. (Klein, 1940, p. 348)

But the anxiety, in practice, is a mixed one. The interplay of persecutory anxiety and guilt (now termed 'depressive anxiety') is extremely complex, and is managed with intricately woven combinations of introjection and projections of objects between the internal world and the external. The preceding paranoid anxieties do not disappear but remain as a prominent background colouring for the depressive position, involving

> . . . the depressive state as being the result of a mixture of paranoid anxiety and of those anxiety-contents, distressed feelings and defences which are connected with the impending loss of the whole loved object. (Klein, 1935, p. 275)

Persecutory and depressive anxieties interact – in particular the interference in the depressive position of the vicious circle that creates persecutory anxiety through projection and reintrojection: 'One reason for his failure is that he has been unable to overcome his paranoid dread of internalized persecutors' (Klein, 1935, p. 267). Guilt is a term which then refers to the combination of the two anxieties in a variety of different proportions.

The intensity of guilt varies over time. With a reasonably consistent external object, some confidence in restoration and repair develops. The persecuting, punishing kind of guilt gradually gives way to a form that is more enhancing of realistic efforts [see DEPRESSIVE ANXIETY; GUILT].

DEFENCES AGAINST DEPRESSIVE ANXIETY. The infant has other resources for trying to deal with the burdensome feelings of the depressive position. That is, he can establish psychological defences. With the new form of relationship (to whole objects) there is a new anxiety (depressive anxiety) and this evokes new defences. There are two main defensive forms of evasion of the depressive anxiety (paranoid and manic defences). Klein thought that normally there was constant fluctuation both (i) between the depressive position and the paranoid states, and (ii) between the depressive and manic defences. Consequently, she talked at first of all three positions – depressive, paranoid and manic. However, she later reserved the term position for the depressive position, while the other two are really constellations of defences [see POSITION].

The paranoid defence. First there is a defensive retreat from the depressive position, back to the more straightforward paranoid forms of relating: 'I have found that paranoid fears and suspicions were reinforced as a defence against the depressive position' (Klein, 1935, p. 274). This involves ensuring that objects are seen as part-objects – wholly good or wholly bad [see PARANOID DEFENCE AGAINST DEPRESSIVE ANXIETY]. There is an often arbitrary splitting of the object to avoid the confluence of hatred with love. This gives protection against depressive anxiety (guilt).

Suicide: Klein wrote only in the briefest way about suicide, a topic about which analysts have in general been reticent. However, she devoted one paragraph to it:

> . . . in some cases the phantasies underlying suicide aim at preserving the internalized good objects and that part of the ego which is identified with good objects, and also at destroying the other part of the ego which is identified with bad objects and the id. Thus the ego is enabled to become united with its loved objects. In other cases . . . the same phantasies . . . relate to the external world and real objects, partly as substitutes for the internalized ones. (Klein, 1935, p. 276)

The manic defence. Central to the manic defence is the omnipotent notion that the object-relations are not of great importance. The ego tells itself that the loved object, which is felt to be dead or damaged, inside or out, is not really of any great importance; he can manage perfectly well without being dependent on anyone:

> . . . in this state the source of the conflict is that the ego is unwilling and unable to renounce its good internal objects and yet endeavours to escape from the perils of dependence on them as well as from its bad objects . . . It succeeds in this compromise by *denying the importance* of its good objects and also of the dangers with which it is menaced from its bad objects and id. (Klein, 1935, p. 277)

The manic defence is really a collection of defences, involving a denial of psychic reality and therefore the importance of the objects that are loved and taken in, a denigrating contempt for the objects that are loved so that their loss will not be experienced as important, and a triumphant and omnipotent form of putting everything right. These are all means of minimizing the feelings of loss and guilt [see 9. PRIMITIVE DEFENCE MECHANISMS; MANIC DEFENCES].

Klein emphasized that the manic defences are aimed at both the depressive feelings and the paranoid ones which exist in the depressive position: 'In mania the ego seeks refuge not only from melancholia but also from a paranoid condition which it is unable to master' (Klein, 1935, p. 277).

Obsessional defences: Because the anxieties of the depressive position are so closely connected at the early stages with the paranoid anxieties, the defences specific for the depressive position are mixed with the defences against the persecutory anxiety resulting from the sadistic phases. This includes the specific defence of destroying the persecutors; and also the obsessional defences. At various times Klein perceived different relations between the manic defences and the obsessional ones [see OBSESSIONAL DEFENCES]. Both kinds involve mastery and control over the objects. This comes out particularly in the kinds of reparation that are attempted. Often the subject phantasizes repair to the object, but if these are too mixed in alongside the defences against persecution (manic or obsessional), the reparation will be carried out with all the hatred characteristic of the paranoid state – mastery and control will have a hateful, spiteful quality and lead to anxiety that the objects have been further damaged in the process of repair.

REPARATION. Reparation is not a separate position; it is a progressive modification of the depressive anxiety. It is not a defence mechanism either, since it is a modification rather than an evasion of the anxiety. It is to be placed alongside sublimation as a method of managing the impulses rather than defending against them – an 'acceptance mechanism', in Grotstein's terminology (Grotstein, 1983).

Klein first explored the idea in a note on artistic creation (1929b) and in the same year Riviere was clearly thinking along joint lines (Riviere, 1929). Another colleague at the time, Ella Freeman Sharpe (1930), began to explore reparation, following Klein's lead by examining the material of patients as dramatizing conflicts and object-relations in the same way as a child does in its play.

The experience of reparation is a tolerance of the loss, and guilt and responsibility for the loss, while at the same time feeling that not all is lost. The possibility of retrieving the disaster remains a hope. This is based on the sense of an internal world in which some goodness survives, whatever paroxysms of bad feelings sweep across it. It is the confidence for optimism after all.

Klein realized that normally guilt gives rise to concern, and that this is a more hopeful reaction to the depressive position. Concern promotes efforts to put things right, and she adopted the term 'reparation':

One moment after we have seen the most sadistic impulses, we meet with performances showing the greatest capacity for love and the wish to make all possible sacrifices to be loved . . . It is impressive to see in analysis how these destructive tendencies can be used for sublimation . . . how the phantasies can be liberated for most artistic and constructive work. (Klein, 1927, p. 176)

Later, when Klein relaxed her commitment to classical theory, the idea of sublimation fell away somewhat, whereas the idea of reparation developed and became the cornerstone of the maturational processes that forge a way out of the depressive position [see LOVE].

Reparation is called out specifically by the anxieties of the depressive position, and together with reality-testing forms one of the two main methods of getting over the depressive anxiety. Klein stressed that the concern is more than just the child needing to ensure its own survival through maintaining a mother to support and care for it – though that is one aspect of the anxiety. Reparation also comes out of real concern for the object, a pining for it, and may involve great self-sacrifice. For example, in describing maternal feelings

. . . the mother is capable of putting herself in the child's place . . . being able to do so with love and sympathy is closely bound up, as we have seen, with feelings of guilt and the drive to reparation . . . [and] may lead to an entirely self-sacrificing attitude. (Klein, 1937, p. 318)

The issue is complex, however, because the theory of the depressive position is that the concern is as much about the internal object, which for so much of the time is identified with the ego. So reparation devoted to restoring the good mother (external object) has as a corresponding aspect the effect of restoring at the same time an internal state within the subject [see NARCISSISM].

DEVELOPMENT. How does the infant struggle towards this secure internalized good object? Four main factors are involved:

(i) The actual nature of the mother is crucial in enabling the child to progress through the pain of the depressive position.

(ii) The capacity to repair (see above) comes from tolerating painful guilt and remorse to the extent of finding a way to make reparation.

(iii) The predisposition to feel secure comes from the preceding phase which provides a resource for the infant when he first approaches the depressive position. This was not dealt with until a later point in Klein's theoretical working out of her material when, in 1946, she turned to a close examination of this earliest phase of mental life [see 11. PARANOID-SCHIZOID POSITION].

(iv) The depressive position is in one sense a way out of the paranoid position, yet the pain and turmoil of the depressive position do not seem an attractive invitation. The way the child manages this depends on his ability to build up and sustain a sense of his own lovingness, as balanced against his own hate. However, the infant is impelled towards the depressive position by the maturation of his perception of the external object and also by the natural unfolding of the phases of the libido. Mobilizing genital impulses for whole-object-love gives a new strength to love and repair. And, in short, this means his ability to sustain a feeling of love for an 'object' that is good and is felt to be concretely inside him, making up a part of his personality. A secure personal confidence, Klein claims, comes down finally to a sense of a secure loving core for the personality.

Klein saw the depressive position as the threshold of enormous developmental potential, as it is based on the emerging recognition of the reality of objects. However phantastical the good and bad components, if the perceptual development can be sustained, then discriminations about the objects as they actually are in reality can be won, and ultimately a growing knowledge of internal reality and self-knowledge and understanding. In turn, a true assessment of internal reality (the capacity for honest self-assessment) develops as well. The capacity for concern is deeply stimulated by the depressive anxiety, and leads to the drive for social and interpersonal engagement with other actual people. The developmental potential of concern is the Kleinian substitute for the superego: by contrast with genuine concern the superego drives the subject to social considerations through threats of punishment; while the concern to repair is an act of love out of sadness.

LATER MODIFICATIONS. Klein, like Freud, was forever trying out new ideas and making modifications. To some extent the concept of the depressive position has been overshadowed, like so much else of her early thinking, by the development of the concept of the paranoid-schizoid position, and particularly projective identification. The years after the introduction of the depressive position were disturbing for Klein, as a number of people began to disagree with her – including Glover and Melitta Schmideberg (Klein's daughter). There seemed little interest in developing the idea, though Scott (1947) produced an important detailed case history.

Riviere was one of the few people to take up the idea of the depressive position immediately and she used it to understand how depression and guilt, comprising withdrawal into a preoccupation with internal objects (narcissism), could express itself as a negative therapeutic reaction to analysis:

To my mind it is *the love for his internal objects*, which lies behind and produces the unbearable guilt and pain, the need to sacrifice his life to theirs and so the prospect of death, that makes this resistance so stubborn. And we can counter this resistance only by unearthing this love and so the guilt with it. To these patients the analyst represents an internal object. So it is the positive transference in the patient that we must bring to realization; and this is what they resist beyond all, although they know well how to parade a substitute 'friendliness'. (Riviere, 1936, p. 319) [see NEGATIVE THERAPEUTIC REACTION]

There were two other small, though important, additions to Klein's theory of the depressive position [see DEPRESSIVE ANXIETY]. First, in 1948, Klein described the possibility of the integration of objects at the part-object level, though she adds that this is transitory:

for from the beginning of life the ego tends towards integrating itself and towards synthesizing the different aspects of the object. There appear to be transitory states of integration even in very young infants – becoming more frequent and lasting as development goes on. (Klein, 1948, p. 34)

This was intended to explain further clinical observation on schizoid patients who appeared to show the effects of having to defend themselves against depressive anxiety.

The second development of the theory is similar. It was some observations made by Hanna Segal in the course of a pioneering analysis of a severely ill schizophrenic (Segal, 1956). She showed that there was some evidence of depression in a schizophrenic, but that it is not felt by him. Instead, there is a process in which the depression is felt by other people – in the course of the analysis, it is in the analyst. Klein was impressed by this work of one of her young students (Klein, 1960) [see PSYCHOSIS].

THE RECEPTION OF THE THEORY OF THE DEPRESSIVE POSITION. The great leap in theory embodied in the description of the depressive position put a distance between Klein and her critics. There were very few outside the Kleinian circle who could comment. Other analysts were mostly bemused by the notion of internal objects which had suddenly been hoisted from obscurity into the central plank of her psychoanalytic theory and practice. Much of the criticism of this area of Kleinian theory therefore appears under other entries [see 5. INTERNAL OBJECTS].

At a general level, Brierley (1950), in attempting a balanced review of Klein's collection of papers (published as *Contributions to Psycho-Analysis*, 1948), had reservations about the depressive position on two counts: first, it ousted the Oedipus complex from the central axis of psychoanalytic theory, as she did not recognize the fluctuations between the positive and inverted Oedipus complex as the prototype of the coming together of the good and bad objects in the depressive position; and secondly, she complained that the idea of the depressive position discounts the importance of regression, while emphasizing the importance of the 'progressive' move into the greater awareness of reality (internal as well as external) and the development of reparation.

Reparation: Glover (1945) dismissed reparation as a mere obsessional mechanism, which indeed had been the precursor idea – the attempt to undo a wrong. However, as Klein pointed out, the obsessional undoing has magical properties and consists of a precise reversal of action (turning off the tap that has been turned on) [see MANIC REPARATION], whereas reparation involves a more imaginative repair of the situation, very often in symbolic form, which itself may entail extremely creative or artistic processes [see SYMBOL-FORMATION].

The similarity of reparation to reaction-formation has been pointed out, yet again the reality-based quality of reparation makes it different. Omnipotent (or magical) reparation does indeed incorporate phantastical aims and delusional achievements comparable to obsessional undoing or reaction-formation, often termed 'manic reparation'. Although there was complaint about the introduction of another term, 'reparation' does have the virtue of setting these various mechanisms, realistic and unrealistic, in a context with each other.

The relation between reparation and defence mechanisms such as undoing and reaction-formation is similar to the relation between reparation and sublimation. In both cases there is the difference between managing an impulse (undoing, reaction-formation and sublimation) as opposed to loving an object. Strictly speaking, they are two emerging vocabularies that do not have strict rules of translation between them. The link, in Klein's view, was that reparation was related to the primitive defence mechanisms and the depressive anxiety which is an underlying substratum upon which the later personality develops, which can then be described in terms of orthodox Freudian terminology.

Depressive anxiety: The crucial feature of the depressive position, the anguishing over the state of the object, was criticized from a self-psychology point of view by Grotstein (1983):

> Klein has placed too much emphasis on the welfare of the object by the infant and has seemingly sacrificed the right of the infant to have a 'self' of his or her own and/or to have recognition of the self's needs independent of consideration of the object's welfare. (p. 529)

However, what he is describing is exactly the pain of the depressive position in its early stages when the guilt has a strongly persecutory tone that demands extreme self-sacrifice and slavery [see DEPRESSIVE ANXIETY]. It is because of this developmentally early quality to depressive anxiety that the person evades it, defends against it or retreats to the paranoid-schizoid position. It is only by working through this that the infant and older individuals can come to an easier adjustment between their concern for their object and the normal degree of self-respect (a sort of normal narcissism) required to look after themselves (see Rosenfeld, 1987).

Fairbairn and futility: The most telling critique of the depressive position was in fact quite a sympathetic one, and one which, uncharacteristically, Klein took seriously. Fairbairn (1941) regarded the depressive position as merely a logical development of Freud's views once he and Abraham had diverted their attention from hysteria to melancholia. Fairbairn regarded this as a mistake and argued that the structure described as the superego was in fact a defensive organization of the ego that concealed beneath it a fundamentally different structure, characterized by splits within the ego and the object. By returning to a study of hysteria, states of dissociation and schizoid individuals, he claimed, it was possible to investigate this prior position, which he called the schizoid position. The clue to this was in the affects.

He pointed out that often what is called depression is in fact a quite different affect, one which he called *futility*. He linked it with hysterical states of mind, typically the affectless *belle indifférence* characterized by a seemingly missing affect. Fairbairn attributed this emptiness to a splitting of the mind, and argued strongly for more attention to be paid to the dissociative phenomena. With that Klein duly complied (1946) [see 11. PARANOID-SCHIZOID POSITION]. Fairbairn considered that depressive phenomena masked those of the schizoid states, and in particular it masked the splitting of the ego and the consequent fear for the self, points which Klein took seriously.

So far as Klein and her immediate followers were concerned, the depressive position immediately became central, and it has undergone remarkably little modification. The attaining of the depressive position, with a balanced view of the reality of objects, is still regarded as the hallmark of psychological progress. James Strachey (1934), in his theory of the modification of unrealistically good and bad objects, was clearly treading close on her heels in understanding the therapeutic significance of modifying the archaic good and bad objects. Stephen (1934), no doubt from close acquaintance with Klein, also explored the relation between internalization of objects, destructiveness and guilt.

However, after the publication of the papers on the depressive position (1935, 1940), the psychoanalytic world was embroiled in the political situation in Europe and then the infighting in the British Psycho-Analytical Society. When it emerged, Klein had moved on to her discovery of the paranoid-schizoid position.

Abraham, Karl (1924) 'A short study of the development of the libido', in Karl Abraham (1927) *Selected Papers on Psycho-Analysis*. Hogarth, pp. 418–501.

Brierley, Marjorie (1950) 'Review of Klein's *Contributions to Psycho-Analysis*', *Int. J. Psycho-Anal.* 31:209–11.

Fairbairn, Ronald (1941) 'A revised psychopathology of the psychoses and psychoneuroses' in Ronald Fairbairn (1952) *Psycho-Analytic Studies of the Personality*. Routledge & Kegan Paul.

Freud, Sigmund (1917) 'Mourning and melancholia', in James Strachey, ed. *The Standard Edition of the Complete Psychological Works of Sigmund Freud*, 24 vols. Hogarth, 1953–73. vol. 14, pp. 237–60.

—— (1921) *Group Psychology and the Analysis of the Ego*. S.E. 18, pp. 67–143.

—— (1926) *Inhibitions, Symptoms and Anxiety*. S.E. 20, pp. 77–175.

Glover, Edward (1945) 'An examination of the Klein system of child psychology', *Psychoanal. Study Child* 1:3–43.

Grinberg, Leon (1978) 'The "razor's edge" in depression and mourning', *Int. J. Psycho-Anal.* 59:245–54.

Grotstein, James (1983) 'The significance of Kleinian contributions to psychoanalysis: IV Critiques of Klein', *Int. J. Psycho-Anal. Psychother.* 9:511–35.

Joseph, Betty (1978) 'Different types of anxiety and their handling in the analytic situation', *Int. J. Psycho-Anal.* 59:223–8.

Klein, Melanie (1927) 'Criminal tendencies in normal children', in *The Writings of Melanie Klein*, vol. 1. Hogarth, pp. 170–85.

—— (1929a) 'Personification in the play of children', *The Writings of Melanie Klein*, vol. 1, pp. 199–209.

—— (1929b) 'Infantile anxiety-situations reflected in a work of art and in the creative impulse', *The Writings of Melanie Klein*, vol. 1, pp. 210–18.

—— (1933) 'The early development of conscience in the child', *The Writings of Melanie Klein*, vol. 1, pp. 248–57.

—— (1935) 'A contribution to the psychogenesis of manic-depressive states', *The Writings of Melanie Klein*, vol. 1, pp. 262–89.

—— (1936) 'Weaning', *The Writings of Melanie Klein*, vol. 1, pp. 290–305.

—— (1937) *Love, Guilt and Reparation*, *The Writings of Melanie Klein*, vol. 1, pp. 306–43.

—— (1940) 'Mourning and its relation to manic-depressive states', *The Writings of Melanie Klein*, vol. 1, pp. 344–69.

—— (1945) 'The Oedipus complex in the light of early anxieties', *The Writings of Melanie Klein*, vol. 1, pp. 370–419.

—— (1946) 'Notes on some schizoid mechanisms', *The Writings of Melanie Klein*, vol. 3, pp. 1–24.

—— (1948) 'On the theory of anxiety and guilt', *The Writings of Melanie Klein*, vol. 3, pp. 25–42.

—— (1960) 'A note on depression in the schizophrenic', *The Writings of Melanie Klein*, vol. 3, pp. 264–7.

Riviere, Joan (1929) 'Magical regeneration by dancing', *Int. J. Psycho-Anal.* 10: 340.

—— (1936) 'A contribution to the analysis of the negative therapeutic reaction', *Int. J. Psycho-Anal.* 17:304–20.

Rosenfeld, Herbert (1987) *Impasse and Interpretation.* Tavistock.

Scott, W. Clifford M. (1947) 'On the intense affects encountered in treating a severe manic-depressive disorder', *Int. J. Psycho-Anal.* 28:139–45.

Segal, Hanna (1956) 'Depression in the schizophrenic', *Int. J. Psycho-Anal.* 37:339–43; republished (1981) in *The Work of Hanna Segal.* New York: Jason Aronson, pp. 121–9.

Sharpe, Ella Freeman (1930) 'The technique of psycho-analysis: seven lectures', in (1950) *Collected Papers on Psycho-Analysis.* Hogarth.

Stephen, Karin (1934) 'Introjection and projection: rage and guilt', *Br. J. Med. Psychol.* 14:316–31.

Strachey, James (1934) 'The nature of the therapeutic action of psycho-analysis', *Int. J. Psycho-Anal.* 15:127–59.

11 PARANOID-SCHIZOID POSITION

DEFINITION. In the earliest state of mind, persecutory anxiety is met by processes which threaten to (and do) fragment the mind. Its severity affects the move onwards into the depressive position because the integrity of the mind is severely disrupted. The splitting processes typically lead to projection of parts of the self or ego (projective identification) into objects, with a depleting effect on the self. The depleted self then has difficulties with introjection and with introjective identification. This position was described in 1946, and was a profound modification of Klein's previous descriptions of paranoid and persecutory states. These descriptions in 1946 led on to major developments (especially of projective identification) by her contemporary colleagues and by her students.

CHRONOLOGY
1929 Early precursor ideas.
1946 The paranoid-schizoid position (Klein, Melanie, 1946, 'Notes on some schizoid mechanisms'; Rosenfeld, Herbert, 1947, 'Analysis of a schizophrenic state with depersonalization').

The paranoid states of infancy had been Klein's old preoccupation, until in the decade between 1935 and 1946 she and her co-workers explored the concepts of unconscious phantasy, internal objects and especially the importance of the good internal object in the depressive position [see 10. DEPRESSIVE POSITION]. The depressive position was barely contested as yet, nor was it greatly elaborated by Kleinians. Then, in 1946, Klein was suddenly influenced by Fairbairn, someone completely outside her immediate circle of co-workers.

Fairbairn provoked a question: Why do some people manage to get through the eruption of guilt in the depressive position more or less well, while others do not? – and he answered that

> The moral situation which results belongs, of course, to a higher level of mental development than the original situation ... guilt must be regarded as partaking of the nature of a defence. In a word, *guilt operates as a resistance in psychotherapy.* (Fairbairn, 1943, pp. 68–9)

He regarded that original situation as an experience which 'is not so much guilty as simply "bad" ' (Fairbairn, 1943, p. 63). Klein concluded that this distinction was correct:

> If persecutory fears are very strong, and for this reason (amongst

others) the infant cannot work through the paranoid-schizoid position, the working through of the depressive position is in turn impeded. (Klein, 1946, p. 2)

Schizoid states: Remote from the rest of the psychoanalytic community, Fairbairn lived and worked in Scotland, but he had been influenced by Klein's work on the paranoid states [see FAIRBAIRN]. He argued, though, that the paranoid position was not merely defensive against the depressive position [see PARANOID DEFENCE AGAINST DEPRESSIVE ANXIETY]. He made a plea for the importance of processes that split the ego, and against the relative neglect of hysteria and dissociative mechanisms which had been the original grounding of psychoanalysis. He drew attention to schizophrenics and schizoid states in contrast to manic-depressive illness, which had been so predominant (Abraham, 1911, 1924; Freud, 1917):

> It will be seen that some of the conclusions which I shall present in this paper are in line with Fairbairn's conclusions, while others differ fundamentally. Fairbairn's approach was largely from the angle of ego-development in relation to objects, while mine was predominantly from the angle of anxieties and their vicissitudes . . . The particular emphasis he laid on the inherent relation between hysteria and schizophrenia deserves full attention. His term schizoid would be appropriate if it is understood to cover both persecutory fear and schizoid mechanisms. (Klein, 1946, p. 3)

Schizophrenia, Fairbairn declared, might be better understood if more reference were made to hysteria and dissociative phenomena. Schizophrenia means a mind split into fragments, and Fairbairn therefore postulated a schizoid position which is prior to – and fundamental to – Klein's depressive position. It explained and determined the future pathology of the personality, and he went on to describe a systematic categorization of conditions on the basis of splits within the ego and the object. Klein took the point – and understood that schizophrenia was about an experience of a mind in bits. How, she must have asked herself, can it come to experience itself as in bits? Klein found herself impressed, and at once also determined to incorporate this into a properly Kleinian framework. She realized that she had not yet paid enough attention to the first few months of life, since she had placed the onset of the depressive position in the second quarter of the first year of life.

Klein had in one sense weathered the attacks upon her views in the early 1940s [see CONTROVERSIAL DISCUSSIONS], the result being an unhappy but stable stalemate. There was no reason to wait for other analysts outside her group to catch up with her views; she simply pushed ahead by returning to her old interest in psychosis. Previously it had been children and their inhibited and fragmented states of thinking (Klein, 1930, 1931). She had always emphasized the paranoid fear that inhibited the development of thought and symbolization. So without abandoning the importance of the depressive position, she agreed with Fairbairn that the onset of the depressive position was dependent on an adequate prior working through of another kind of anxiety, not of the depressive type. She also agreed that this concerned schizoid mechanisms and a prime place for the mechanism of splitting. Consequently she acknowledged Fairbairn's contribution by combining his term 'schizoid position' with her own term 'paranoid position' to produce the fair but somewhat cumbersome term 'paranoid-schizoid position'.

FEATURES OF THE PARANOID-SCHIZOID POSITION.

There were a number of features which Klein described clinically:

(1) **Fragmentation and the death instinct.** Klein was able to accept Fairbairn's criticism because she had hit on an elegant idea: the experience of being in bits might be something to do with the working of the death instinct inside the ego. She could look, therefore, for more clinical evidence of the death instinct in the analysis of the most disturbed of all patients, the disintegrated schizophrenic. She therefore investigated the hypothesis with the aid of her own students who were treating schizophrenics [see KLEINIAN GROUP; PSYCHOSIS].

(2) **The early ego.** The ego, at first, alternates between states of integration and disintegration: '. . . the early ego largely lacks cohesion, and a tendency towards integration alternates with a tendency towards disintegration, a falling to bits' (Klein, 1946, p. 4). This was described later by Bick (1968) from direct observation of infants in their first week of life [see ADHESIVE IDENTIFICATION]. Whereas classical analysis focuses upon the ego as an organ that seeks discharge of the instinctual tensions in some form of satisfaction and can be described objectively in terms of its structure and function, Klein saw the ego in a different way: as the function it has of experiencing itself. She described this, characteristically, in terms of the phantasies the ego has of struggling with anxieties experienced in the course of its relations with objects.

From early on, the states of persecution and paranoia in young children were regarded as of paramount importance in the relatively smooth (or otherwise) progress of development. Searl (1932), one of Klein's closest colleagues at the time, described how such states of mind might form a '. . . drive to early and advanced ego-formations, e.g., in the precocious child, which impoverish the libidinal life precisely because they are in the service of a reduction of feeling and sensations of tension' (Searl, 1932, p. 346). She described the phenomenon of a child who disposed of his feeling states, '. . . becoming still and hard' (p. 334), which presaged the descriptions Klein gave in 1946, and Bick in 1968.

(3) **The anxiety.** The ego's struggle is to maintain its own integrity in the face of its painful experiences of objects that threaten annihilation. Klein started, therefore, with the *experience* of the split ego, the anxiety of being split up in bits. She significantly modified Freud's view of the deflection of the death instinct as the first act of the ego. Although she continued to pay lip-service to it, she indicated that an adequate projection of the death instinct is accomplished only by an ego which has already been formed from, and is assisted by, a secure internal good object. Therefore the deflection of the death instinct is not the primary event that brings the ego into existence, but may instead be an ongoing process of deflecting and splitting that happens repeatedly, or indeed may sometimes fail.

Previously Klein had followed Freud's hypothetical idea of a primary deflection of the death instinct, with a splitting of the id [see 7. SUPEREGO]. This allowed her to abandon classical psychoanalysis while sticking to Freud, a skilful contortion. She had done this by offering clinical evidence for the death instinct. The description of the paranoid-schizoid position gives further evidence of the death instinct by filling in the details of the early moments of the ego. The early anxiety is '. . . a fear of annihilation (death) and takes the form of a fear of persecution . . . experienced as a fear of an uncontrollable overpowering object . . . the anxiety of being destroyed from within' (Klein, 1946, pp. 4–5).

The experience of one's mind in bits, she argued, has something to do with the action of the death instinct within the internal world. It may have to do with some degree of failure of the primary deflection of the death instinct outwards. She came down to saying that this is a primary anxiety which underlies all other anxieties – is, in fact, just the very one evoked by the action of the death instinct: an object within is about to annihilate the ego [see 8. EARLY ANXIETY-SITUATIONS].

This differs from her previous descriptions of the early anxiety-situation, when she enthusiastically took over the idea from Freud and used her own clinical material to fill in the idea for him; then (in 1927) she had regarded the anxiety as derived from the raids on mother's body, in phantasy, and the feared retaliation in kind by mother or her damaged contents. This is one specific content to the anxiety, connected with genital impulses and at that time recognized by her as part of the orthodox Oedipus complex. In 1932 Klein adopted Freud's hypothetical description of the deflection of the death instinct outwards, and the feared reintrojection of an internal persecutor. It was in her description of the paranoid-schizoid position in 1946 that she filled in the *experience* of the death instinct, in terms of phantasies of objects that threaten death *from within*, which have pregenital sadistic qualities as well as oedipal.

(4) **The absence of anxiety.** Often the schizoid or schizophrenic patient, stuck to a greater or lesser extent in the paranoid-schizoid position, appears to feel little or no anxiety, or feelings of any kind. Klein (1946) showed that this did not mean that there were none, only that the method of dealing with anxiety was extreme. That is to say, it was projected elsewhere, leaving the subject apparently affectless and emotionally depleted. This was confirmed by the observations of Segal (1956), who showed how depression *in* the schizophrenic was most often not actually in the schizophrenic but invariably ended up *in* the analyst (Klein, 1960). Understanding this state in which affects are missing, and indeed similarly missing aspects of the transference, has been an important influence on Kleinian technique with psychotic and borderline adult patients [see 1. TECHNIQUE] and also on the theory of the psychodynamics of groups, especially large ones [see SOCIAL DEFENCE SYSTEMS].

Mastering the persecutory anxiety: The paranoid-schizoid position is the struggle to achieve and sustain an adequate deflection of the death instinct, in order to feel confident of not falling to pieces. What Klein described were various ego-states in which the dominant preoccupation is whether the ego is in pieces or not. She suggested that the ego actively splits itself:

> . . . some active splitting processes within the ego [may] occur at a very early stage [leading to] . . . the primary anxiety of being annihilated by a destructive force within, with the ego's specific response of falling to pieces or splitting itself. (Klein, 1946, p. 5)

Suicide itself may represent the action of the death instinct in which the ego attacks itself. It is also a defence against the internal bad objects and bad self by destroying them through destroying the whole of the ego.

Later, Bion (1957) showed this active splitting process in clinical material from cases of schizophrenics; in particular, he showed the active destruction of their perceptual apparatus, because it presents them with their own pain, which they cannot tolerate (the messenger who brings bad news is killed) [see PSYCHOSIS; THINKING; LINKING]. Rosenfeld's concept of negative narcissism, which he described clinically as the manifestation of a death-dealing object inside, like a Mafia gang, shows a similar active threat going on internally (Rosenfeld, 1971) [see NARCISSISM; PERVERSION].

(5) The first introjection. Before 1946 Klein had followed Freud in regarding the first act of the ego as a projection; the death instinct is projected outwards, followed by the risk of introjecting a tormenting and frightening persecutor. But in 1946 she described the first introjections differently: they are much more primitive. On the basis of the importance attributed to the good internal object, which she had worked out in the depressive position, she described the introjection of the good and loved object as a primary activity to create an internal good object which comes to form the focus of the fragile ego, and around which it can integrate:

> The first internal good object acts as a focal point in the ego. It counteracts the process of splitting and dispersal, makes for cohesiveness and integration, and is instrumental in building up the ego. (Klein, 1946, p. 6)

The integrative good object: Alternating states of integration and disintegration are connected with the appearance and disappearance of the external good object. States of frustration develop with the loss of the introjected good object, and are mitigated only when the infant is presented with an external good object for continued introjection. The object needed at the outset by the infant is an object that can hold or *contain* his experiences [see CONTAINING; REVERIE]. Bick (1968) was even more categorical in saying that the first act of the ego is an introjection – an introjection of an object that gives a capacity for holding things together internally to give the primary sense of self [see SKIN].

Omnipotent introjection in the paranoid-schizoid position: It is important to distinguish between the introjection of the good object in the paranoid-schizoid position – which comes to be a core of the ego, drawing it together – and the introjection of the good object in the depressive position, which is loved and worried over by an ego *in relation to* it. The difference is effected by the quality of the introjection. When this is accomplished in phantasy with a degree of omnipotence (Rosenfeld, 1964) there is a dissolving of the boundary between the ego and the internal object, which is possessed by the ego as simply a part of the self. The depressive position marks a waning of this omnipotent narcissistic dissolution of ego-boundaries, and objects are more realistically experienced as whole in themselves [see NARCISSISM].

Often the ego is greatly weakened by the splitting and unable adequately to introject and identify, resulting in unassimilated internal objects [see ASSIMILATION]; also, omnipotent phantasies of incorporation may involve considerable aggression and result in the loss of any undamaged object inside [see GREED]. In fact introjection may be greatly impaired in this position, due to the fear of introducing good objects into a disastrously destructive internal world.

THE DEFENCE MECHANISMS IN THE PARANOID-SCHIZOID POSITION. Fairbairn's criticism had been that Klein had

placed too much emphasis on depression and also followed Abraham with his interest in obsessional mechanisms and manic-depressive states. Having assumed in her early work (1920s) that the specific defences against sadism and paranoid anxiety were obsessional, she began to realize that there was a whole class of primitive defence mechanisms of a quite different nature [see 9. PRIMITIVE DEFENCE MECHANISMS]. As late as 1940 she had still been trying to find a place for the obsessional mechanisms in her scheme of the depressive position. But she seems from then on to drop their importance altogether, and in later years Kleinians have come to regard obsessional neurosis as a particular and later manifestation of certain of the manic defences of mastery and control.

Fundamental to the whole paranoid-schizoid position is the mechanism of splitting [see SPLITTING], but Klein was particularly concerned with projection and introjection in relation to splitting:

> The phantasied onslaughts on the mother follow two main lines: one is the predominantly oral impulse to suck dry, bite up, scoop out and rob the mother's body of its good contents. The other line of attack derives from the anal and urethral impulses and implies expelling dangerous substances (excrements) out of the self and into the mother. (Klein, 1946, p. 8)

These are the mechanisms of introjection and projection expressed in terms of phantasy experiences.

Projective identification: Klein's dominant interest was in the violent expulsion of excrements. In association with these violent projections the splitting of the ego results in the associated expulsion of disowned, bad parts of the self:

> Together with these harmful excrements, expelled in hatred, split-off parts of the ego are also projected on to the mother, or as I would rather call it, *into* the mother. These excrements and bad parts of the self are meant not only to injure but also to control and to take possession of the object. In so far as the mother comes to contain the bad parts of the self, she is not felt to be a separate individual but is felt to be *the* bad self . . . This leads to a particular form of identification which establishes the prototype of an aggressive relation. (Klein, 1946, p. 8)

and the sentence 'I suggest for these processes the term "projective identification" ' was added in 1952 to the text at this point. The intention of this form of projection is various, but invariably involves violent control of the object; the results are severe psychotic symptoms and the profound sense of a depleted or weakened ego, producing depersonalization [see 13. PROJECTIVE IDENTIFICATION].

This prototype aggression is complicated, since '. . . if this projective process is carried out excessively, good parts of the personality are felt to be lost' (Klein, 1946, p. 9). Especially if the good parts of the self are lost, there is '. . . a weakening and impoverishment of the ego'. This is the particular dilemma of the schizoid personality for whom love depletes, because of the invariable use of projective identification.

The expulsions are aimed at an object, and the composite projectile of an internal object plus a part of the self is inserted violently right into the external object. Klein emphasized the interiority of the object, and this linked back to her previous interest in the early anxiety-situation comprising the invasion of mother's body, in phantasies of aggressive control, robbery and spoiling [see 6. FEMININITY PHASE].

The ego is thus split and dispersed, not only within its own internal world but also into the external world. There, objects that are subsequently believed, in phantasy, to contain the part of the self that has been expelled now resemble the ego. The hatred with which the object is attacked in this way makes the ego feel that its parts are in danger, and this enhances its states of anxiety. As a result of this fragmentation of the ego, it feels itself to be the weaker. Although these processes occur in phantasy, the conviction with which they are held, and the infant's lack of resources for in any way testing the reality of himself and others, results in the ego actually being affected by the phantasy as if it had happened – in Freud's terms, an 'alteration of the ego' (Freud, 1940) [see OMNIPOTENCE]. So the dispersal in phantasy comes, in effect, to be a reality, a psychic or emotional reality. The ego becomes weakened by the loss of its parts. This may make introjections more difficult to handle, and they may seem to dominate completely a now weakened ego within its own internal world, and it can feel merely a shell for an alien object inside, so that the ego feels overwhelmed and 'compulsively subordinated' even to the good internal object. There are many processes in these descriptions that clearly resemble the bizarre states of identity suffered by the schizophrenic patient [see PSYCHOSIS].

LATER DEVELOPMENTS. In the last four decades there has been a major industry in keeping the term 'projective identification' alive and full of meaning. Although Klein thought and described persecutory anxiety as the hallmark of the paranoid-schizoid position, projective identification has almost come to take over that role. It is particularly important since it covers the strange states of confused identity and depersonalization that are found in psychotic or borderline conditions. The bizarre experiences of schizophrenics – not only their disintegration, but also the externalization of parts of their own mind into hallucinations and ideas of reference – are encompassable in the term 'projective identification'. It has been described in an increasing number of situations, including the not unreasonable claim that it is the underlying mechanism of the capacity for empathy (putting oneself in someone else's shoes). So the history of Kleinian thought, from the mid-1950s or so onwards, has been largely the development of the concept of projective identification [see 13. PROJECTIVE IDENTIFICATION] and to a lesser extent of the concept of envy [see 12. ENVY].

Other forms of identification: In the 1970s, on the basis of minutely detailed observations of mother–baby interaction from birth onwards, there developed the notion of adhesion or adhesive identification (Bick, 1986; Meltzer, 1975) [see ADHESIVE IDENTIFICATION].

Bleger, a South American Kleinian, described (Bleger, 1971) a position which is prior to the paranoid-schizoid and depressive positions (see Amati (1987) for the only account in English, at present, of Bleger's views), but which survives as nuclei (*agglutinated nuclei*). These are agglutinated in that conflicting affects and impulses are undifferentiated and therefore not conflictual. Such agglutinated nuclei may be deposited in the external world – not into an object, since there is no properly distinguished object, though there seems to be a world outside the self. This depositing is not quite a projective identification, since there is no object into which to project and with which to identify. It might resemble the leakage into empty space described by Bick (1968), and the idea of undifferentiated feelings resembles Rosenfeld's descriptions of the confusion of libido with destructive impulses in primary envy.

RESPONSES TO THE THEORY OF THE PARANOID-SCHIZOID POSITION.

Most critics of Klein had ceased to follow her by the time she developed the notion of the depressive position, so when she advanced from there to describe the paranoid-schizoid position, few apart from her own group were in a position to comment. However, Fairbairn, who had initiated further discussion of the prior position, bears comparison. Fairbairn had consistently said that the depressive position was a logical extension of Freud's train of thought, but that it misdirected attention. The oral organization of the superego structure masked, and was a defence against, the prior position which was characterized by splitting.

He differed from Klein in his view that the introjective processes are used only in defence; and therefore, he said, only the 'bad' object is internalized. He then emphasized the importance of the fate, at the hands of splitting, of the bad object internally. This is radically different from Klein, who thought that development of the ego was a process that depended entirely on cycles of projection–introjection of both the 'good' and 'bad' objects.

Fairbairn attributed the problems of early splitting processes to an inclement environment, and completely eschewed Klein's view of the innate and therefore primarily internal conflict within the instincts. This led Klein to place much more emphasis on phantasy, a direction that Fairbairn did not follow.

Some of Klein's group did not follow her theoretical developments and moved away. Winnicott, for instance, although accepting the importance of the depressive position (1945), produced a completely different view of the early period which reverted back to the classical notion of a period of autoerotism in which there is no distinction between self and object. He called this primary infantile omnipotence, and any environmental impingement on this creates a profound disruption of the self.

The other great defection from the Kleinian camp was Paula Heimann, who in the mid-1950s disengaged herself from Klein in a way that may have resembled that of Klein's own daughter, Melitta Schmideberg, some two decades before. Heimann never employed the idea of projective identification and seems to have had a very different view of the divisions of the ego, based on her ideas of assimilated and unassimilated objects (indicated in Heimann, 1955).

Projective identification: In recent years there has been a considerable interest in projective identification outside the Kleinian Group which, as might be expected, has therefore given rise to a wide degree of concept variance and simple confusion. An attempt to disentangle this is made elsewhere in this dictionary [see 13. PROJECTIVE IDENTIFICATION].

Abraham, Karl (1911) 'Notes on the psycho-analytical investigation and treatment of manic-depressive insanity and allied conditions', in Karl Abraham (1927) *Selected Papers on Psycho-Analysis*. Hogarth, pp. 137–56.
—— (1924) 'A short study of the development of the libido', in *Selected Papers on Psycho-Analysis*, pp. 418–501.
Amati, Sylvia (1987) 'Some thoughts on torture', *Free Assns* 8:94–114.
Bick, Esther (1968) 'The experience of the skin in early object relations', *Int. J. Psycho-Anal.* 49:484–6.
—— (1986) 'Further considerations on the function of the skin in early object relations', *Br. J. Psychother.* 2:292–9.
Bion, Wilfred (1957) 'Differentiation of the psychotic from the non-psychotic personalities', *Int. J. Psycho-Anal.* 38:266–75.
Bleger, J. (1971) *Simbiosis y Ambiguedad*. Buenos Aires: Paidos.
Fairbairn, Ronald (1943) 'The repression and the return of bad objects', *Br. J. Med. Psychol.* 19:327–41; republished, with amendments (1952) in Ronald

Fairbairn, *Psycho-Analytic Studies of the Personality*. Routledge & Kegan Paul, pp. 59–81.

Freud, Sigmund (1917) 'Mourning and melancholia', in James Strachey, ed. *The Standard Edition of the Complete Psychological Works of Sigmund Freud*, 24 vols. Hogarth, 1953–73. vol. 14, pp. 237–60.

—— (1940) 'Splitting of the ego in the process of defence'. *S.E.* 23, pp. 271–8.

Heimann, Paula (1955) 'A combination of defences in paranoid states', in Melanie Klein, Paula Heimann and Roger Money-Kyrle, eds *New Directions in Psycho-Analysis*. Tavistock.

Klein, Melanie (1927) 'Criminal tendencies in normal children', in *The Writings of Melanie Klein*, vol. 1. Hogarth, pp. 170–85.

—— (1930) 'The importance of symbol-formation in the development of the ego', *The Writings of Melanie Klein*, vol. 1, pp. 219–32.

—— (1931) 'A contribution to the theory of intellectual inhibition', *The Writings of Melanie Klein*, vol. 1, pp. 236–47.

—— (1932) *The Psycho-Analysis of Children*, *The Writings of Melanie Klein*, vol. 2.

—— (1940) 'Mourning and its relation to manic-depressive states', *The Writings of Melanie Klein*, vol. 1, pp. 344–69.

—— (1946) 'Notes on some schizoid mechanisms', *The Writings of Melanie Klein*, vol. 3, pp. 1–24.

—— (1960) 'A note on depression in the schizophrenic', *The Writings of Melanie Klein*, vol. 3, pp. 264–7.

Meltzer, Donald (1975) 'Adhesive identification', *Contemporary Psycho-Analysis* 11:289–310.

Rosenfeld, Herbert (1947) 'Analysis of a schizophrenic state with depersonalization', *Int. J. Psycho-Anal.* 28:130–9; republished (1965) in Herbert Rosenfeld, *Psychotic States*. Hogarth, pp. 13–33.

—— (1954) 'Considerations regarding the psycho-analytic approach to acute and chronic schizophrenia', *Int. J. Psycho-Anal.* 35:138–40; republished (1965) in *Psychotic States*, pp. 117–27.

—— (1964) 'On the psychopathology of narcissism: a clinical approach', *Int. J. Psycho-Anal.* 45:332–7; republished (1965) in *Psychotic States*, pp. 169–79.

—— (1971) 'A clinical approach to the psycho-analytical theory of the life and death instinct: an investigation into the aggressive aspects of narcissism', *Int. J. Psycho-Anal.* 52:169–78.

Searl, Mina (1932) 'A note on depersonalization', *Int. J. Psycho-Anal.* 13:329–47.

Segal, Hanna (1956) 'Depression in the schizophrenic', *Int. J. Psycho-Anal.* 37:339–43; republished (1981) in *The Work of Hanna Segal*. New York: Jason Aronson, pp. 121–9.

Winnicott, D. W. (1945) 'Primitive emotional development', *Int. J. Psycho-Anal.* 26:137–43.

12 ENVY

DEFINITION. Klein and her co-workers described a precise form of envy from their work in analysing schizophrenics. It is a destructive attack on the sources of life, on the *good* object, not on the bad object, and it is to be distinguished from ambivalence and from frustration. It is held to be innate in origin as part of the instinctual endowment, and requires the mechanism of splitting as an initial defence operating at the outset.

CHRONOLOGY
1952 Rosenfeld's clinical descriptions (Rosenfeld, Herbert, 1952, 'Notes on the psycho-analysis of the superego conflict in an acute schizophrenic').
1957 Klein's theoretical exposition (Klein, Melanie, 1957, *Envy and Gratitude*).
1971 Envy and structure of the ego (Rosenfeld, Herbert, 1971, 'A clinical approach to the psycho-analytic theory of the life and death instincts: an investigation into the aggressive aspects of narcissism').

The term 'envy' has a long history in psychoanalysis, but the meaning has varied. Freud introduced the concept with 'penis envy' as the specific problem in the psychological development of women. However, many analysts and others have since challenged Freud's descriptions of women's psychology [see 6. FEMININITY PHASE].

Oral envy: Klein (1929) recognized its origins in very early stages of development of both boys and girls, and described it in the oral phase: 'Oral envy is one of the motive forces which make children of both sexes want to push their way into mother's body and which arouse the desire for knowledge allied to it' (Klein, 1932, p. 131).

With the new technical ability to understand the transference of schizophrenics that came from the use of the concepts of the 'paranoid-schizoid position' and 'projective identification', envious material was steadily drawn to the attention. In such patients the phantasy of *entering a 'good' object and spoiling it and its contents* is very prevalent. This phantasy is a primary expression of an instinct – the death instinct. Whereas previously the death instinct was supposed to have been deflected outwards to an object, perhaps arbitrarily chosen, as a 'bad' object with intentions against the subject, Klein described a different deployment of the impulses of the death instinct. These were now seen as directed towards the 'good' object so that 'good' and 'bad' impulses and 'good' and 'bad' objects appear to be confused. This state, which the infant inevitably suffers, has to be immediately dealt with, though the efforts turn into a lifelong struggle to discriminate between what is good and bad in oneself and in the external world around.

PRIMARY ENVY. In beginning to analyse adult schizophrenic patients (late 1930s and 1940s), it appeared that the problems and transferences encountered were the remnants of the earliest stages of psychic activity, the very earliest moments of life. Klein had always accepted Freud's hypothetical descriptions of the deflection of the death instinct at birth, but the group of analysts associated with Melanie Klein in the 1940s found themselves confronted with an apparently innate propensity for conflict and confusion, in which the good object is attacked for its goodness. This phenomenon was repeated over and over again, in the most primitive ways, in the transferences of adult chronic schizophrenics (Rosenfeld, 1947, 1952; Segal, 1950) [see PSYCHOSIS].

The features of primary envy: Klein was describing an entity with specific features which distinguish it from related mental states of frustration or rivalry:

(i) the phantasy is innate;

(ii) the attack is upon the 'good' object because of its goodness;

(iii) consequently the awareness of being separate from the 'good' object which arouses envy is intolerable.

This constellation of features leads to two more:

(iv) there is a necessary and immediate need to keep 'good' objects and 'bad' objects separate, and equally the good and bad impulses of the infant. This is a form of 'normal' splitting, which fails in schizophrenic disturbances;

(v) the intolerance of dependent separateness leads to a tendency towards a confusion (merger) with the 'good' object, a process (projective identification) which brings out the features of the paranoid-schizoid position: the difficulty of achieving a sense of reality, and a potential narcissistic personality structure.

Envy and frustration: It is important to distinguish this phantasy of attacking, entering and spoiling the good object *because it is good* from other forms of attack and hatred. It is not the hatred towards a frustrating object which withholds what it has, nor is it the violence of feelings towards a rival that has occupied the good object for itself.

Precursors. Abraham (1919) had written clinically about exasperating patients who cannot respond to the efforts and skills of the analyst and stubbornly remain unhelped, and Klein had originally regarded envy, theoretically, as a manifestation of oral sadism (Klein, 1929). Riviere (1932), in an account of jealousy, described '... envy and the spoliation of the object' without distinguishing it clearly from jealousy. Horney (1936) had begun to describe envy in some detail as implicated in the negative therapeutic reaction [see NEGATIVE THERAPEUTIC REACTION].

The concept was around within the Kleinian Group for some time before the work on *Envy and Gratitude* (1957). In 1952 Rosenfeld began exploring the idea. He described detailed clinical material demonstrating primal envy in a schizophrenic patient:

> He then said, 'The world is round', and continued clearly and deliberately, 'I hate it because it makes me feel burnt up inside'. And later he added, as if to explain this further, 'Yellow' – 'envy'. I interpreted to him that the round world represented me felt as a good breast, and that he hated the external me for arousing his envy, because his envy made him feel he wanted to kill and burn me inside himself. So he could not keep me good and alive himself, and felt he had a bad and burning me inside. (Rosenfeld, 1952, p. 92)

In 1952 Klein, in commenting on greed, claimed:

> My analytic work has shown me that envy (alternating with feelings of love and gratification) is first directed towards the feeding breast. To this primary envy, jealousy is added when the Oedipus situation arises. (Klein, 1952a, p. 79)

She also recognized that envy, though typical of the earliest phases (the oral-sadistic), is nevertheless responsible for forms of projection into objects, and described:

> ... the ways in which internal persecutions influence, by means of projection, the relation to external objects. The intensity of her [Erna's] envy and hatred unmistakably showed its derivation from the oral-sadistic relation to mother's breast. (Klein, 1955a, p. 135)

and in another paper that year she described envy as one of the prime movers of aggressive phantasies: '... these emotions urge Fabian to get hold of other people's possessions, both material and spiritual; they drive him irresistibly towards what I described as projective identifications' (Klein, 1955b, p. 154). She gave envy considerable importance as a factor promoting projective identification [see 13. PROJECTIVE IDENTIFICATION].

The death instinct. Envy was a late addition to Klein's theoretical framework. It derived from the work begun with the paper on the paranoid-schizoid position (1946) and her efforts to take the death instinct and what it meant seriously. She had taken the idea of the deflection of the death instinct from Freud (1926) as an underpinning for her new theory of the superego, and the harshness of the superego in the very young child was clinical evidence of the death instinct manifesting itself as a sadistic conscience (Klein, 1933) [see 7. SUPEREGO]. Introjection of the good object, which consistently provides basic satisfactions of the libidinal impulses, becomes the stabilizing core of the ego, which integrates itself by taking the good object into its heart and by fending off the death instinct, which is experienced as a persecutor [see 11. PARANOID-SCHIZOID POSITION]. It was clear to Klein – and she communicated it vividly – that much can go wrong in this process. Various forms of imbalance in the systems of projections and introjections can leave behind disastrous propensities in the personality to collapse into fragmentation and psychosis later in life (Klein, 1946).

The concept of envy was designed to fill in why some infants should be beset by problems in integration. The answer, Klein found, lay in the innate confusion that the baby cannot manage to sort out. Envy is the tendency to establish hostile relations with the good object – not with the bad and feared persecutor. The satisfier of libidinal impulses comes to be attacked, as if by mistake, but actually because it is good.

Fusion of the instincts: Recently Segal (1987) reviewed the relation between envy and the death instinct [see DEATH INSTINCT]. From birth the death instinct is manifest in various forms including a projection (in Freud's original terms, a 'deflection') of the death instinct so that an external object threatens the self, an element of destructiveness that remains inside and is turned towards the threatening external object, and another element that internally threatens and destroys the perceiving self or the perceptions of objects.

Though envy and the death instinct are both attacks upon life instincts and the objects of those impulses, in the envious state the death instinct is fused with the life instincts. Then the destructiveness is directed at an object that excites a need and therefore love. It is hated for its capacity to excite, but is also the satisfaction of the need which is excited. Envy therefore involves both life instincts (the recognition of needs and the urge towards the object) and the death instinct (attacks upon the object and the capacity to perceive it).

The fusion in persistent envy, dominated by the death instinct, contrasts with the more normal and healthy forms of integration which are dominated by the life instincts. In the latter case libidinal urges succeed in establishing loving object-relations [see LOVE] and pursue the development through the libidinal phases [see LIBIDO].

Envy is one form of fusion under the dominance of the death instinct but there are others – masochism and other perversions, [see PERVERSIONS, NEGATIVE NARCISSISM, PATHOLOGICAL ORGAN-IZATIONS].

The struggle for the good object: Klein, on the basis of the tendency to attack the good object, established as the first and necessary act of the ego a discrimination between good and bad states of mind and good and bad objects. This is a form of splitting which appears to be healthy: that is to say, without too much hatred. When too much hatred is present this form of splitting is disrupted and confusions remain between the good and bad impulses and objects.

If the infant cannot allow the good object to be safe from attack, he cannot properly introject it safely and undamaged. He cannot disentangle it from bad objects which he needs to escape, and so will start with the basic inability to put his own experiences into the most primitive order. In normal development a form of normal splitting separates the good object from the bad so that the process of integrating the ego based on a loved and protected good object can get going. The elements of envy, the attack on people with special advantages and qualities simply for the sake of their goodness, can gradually be modulated to jealousy, and eventually a more honest state of competition.

Envy and persecutory anxiety. Envy leads to various paranoid anxieties through the characteristic vicious circles which Klein had described from early on in her work [see PARANOIA]:

(i) Forced introjection: As a result of the envious forcing (projection) of the self into the object to occupy it and spoil it, there may be equally fearful phantasies of a retaliatory entry into the infant for spoiling, once the infant has reached the stage of awareness of separate objects not omnipotently owned and controlled. Indeed, this fearful retaliatory forced introjection is an inhibition on the emerging recognition of separateness.

(ii) Greed: Envy is a phantasy of forced entry (by projective methods) and destructive attacks on the *good* object, just because of its goodness. When envy is strong there may be an equally omnipotent phantasy of an *introjective* aggression – taking in with a damaging violence so that the object is spoiled through a violent form of possession and control. The internal state then remains unnourished with a continually unsatisfied hunger. Greed may result in an accumulation of damaged objects inside, each provoking a greater demand and hunger for a good object to be taken in to alleviate the steadily worsening internal state.

Gratitude and gratification. Klein opposed the sense of gratitude to
envy. Gratitude is the specific feeling for an object that is a source of
gratification. In Freud's view instincts require gratification by an
object; the object itself remains merely an incidental addendum to
the gratification so long as it does not hinder satisfaction. Gratitude is
not the same as satisfaction and enjoyment but arises out of them:

> If the undisturbed enjoyment in being fed is frequently experi-
> enced, the introjection of the good breast comes about with
> relative security. A full gratification at the breast means that the
> infant feels he has received from his loved object a unique gift
> which he wants to keep. This is the basis of gratitude. (Klein,
> 1957, p. 188)

Klein saw the object as at least as important as the drive – in fact she
thought the object was inherent in the drive [see 2. UNCONSCIOUS
PHANTASY]. As a result the object is experienced, in her view, entirely
differently. This sense of an object being available and freely given
arouses care, consideration and gratitude for the object itself as part of
the life instinct [see LOVE]. Envy is directed against the object that
provides gratification, and is thus quite different from the attack on the
object that frustrates.

This specific sense of gratitude for the object characterizes object-
relations theory and is a sense of love and appreciation that becomes
especially poignant in the depressive position, in a relationship with a
whole object [see 10. DEPRESSIVE POSITION; LOVE].

Defences against envy. The defence mechanisms against envy were
described specifically by Klein, and included those encountered in the
descriptions of the paranoid-schizoid position –omnipotence, denial,
splitting and idealization. They are subtle: 'There is often a mixture of
the actual expression of envy and defences against that envy. It is not
always possible to say whether a thing is an envious attack or whether it
is a defence' (Joseph, 1986, p. 18). She described a number of others
specific to envy: (i) one of the most important is *confusion*: 'By
becoming confused as to whether a substitute for the original figure is
good or bad, persecution as well as the guilt about spoiling and
attacking the primary object by envy is to some extent counteracted'
(Klein, 1957, p. 216); (ii) 'The *flight from the mother to other people*, who
are admired and idealized in order to avoid hostile feelings towards
that most important envied object, the breast' (Klein, 1957, p. 217);
(iii) *devaluation of the object*: 'The object which has been devalued need
not be envied any more' (Klein, 1957, p. 217); (iv) *devaluation of the
self*: '. . . whenever there is danger of rivalry with an important
figure . . . [by] devaluing their own gifts they both deny envy and
punish themselves for it' (Klein, 1957, p. 218); (v) *greedy internalizing of*

the breast, so that '. . . in the infant's mind it becomes entirely his possession and controlled by him, he feels that all the good he attributes to it will become his own' (Klein, 1957, p. 218); (vi) *envy may be projected*: 'A frequent method of defence is to stir up envy in others by one's own success, possessions, and good fortune, thereby reversing the situation' (Klein, 1957, p. 218); (vii) the *stifling of feelings of love and corresponding intensifying of hate* '. . . is less painful than to bear the guilt arising from the combination of love, hate and envy. This may not express itself as hate but takes on the appearance of indifference' (Klein, 1957, p. 219); (viii) finally, a defence operates specifically to avoid the coming together of a split that has hitherto kept envy at bay. This defence was described originally by Rosenfeld (1952), and is an '. . . *acting out* used to avoid integration' (Klein, 1957, p. 219; see also Rosenfeld, 1955). Somewhat later, Segal (1962) described in detail (ix) the *splitting-off* of envy resulting in depletion of the ego: in effect, projective identification.

LATER DEVELOPMENTS. In the subsequent discussion of Kleinian theory, envy has taken second place to projective identification. It has nevertheless been considerably amplified, though virtually no comment outside the Kleinian Group has been relevant. Joffe's (1969) paper dealt only with Klein's own work and ignores later developments.

Confusion between self and object: One of the most primitive and immediate effects of the confusion of impulses towards the 'good' object is the dissolving of the boundaries between the separate object and the self. The phantasy of envy involves getting into the object and taking it over for spoiling purposes (projective identification). The omnipotence involved in this phantasy destroys the separateness of the object and the pain of envying it. Rosenfeld (1965) described this omnipotent confusion of self and object in various forms of severe disturbance.

As the destruction, in phantasy, of the relationship with an external 'good' object goes ahead, an omnipotent narcissistic state arises which may become protracted as a narcissistic personality structure (Rosenfeld, 1987) [see NARCISSISM; STRUCTURE]. Rosenfeld (1965) regarded the confusion in the object-relations at birth as an inherent endowment. A specially inherited potential for confusing the instinctual impulses in this way may well conform to the evidence for a genetic factor in schizophrenia which has amassed from psychiatric sources [see CONSTITUTIONAL FACTOR].

Envy is thus one of several factors which Klein regarded as constitutional. This does not mean that envy is unmodifiable, although this criticism is levelled at the concept. It is noticeable in the schizophrenic, where indeed it has not been modified, but in the normal course of development the human infant does in fact modify it sufficiently to be able to take nourishment and to develop a normally developing psyche. It is only in the severe mental disorders where modification has failed, and in some split-off states it remains primitively active.

Envy and narcissism: Klein says little in her paper (1957) about the structure and phantasy systems of narcissism. She stresses the detail of observation of the defences, and it is clear from this that she is describing an elaboration of the paranoid-schizoid position. As this is concerned with the state of the ego, it is a narcissistic position (in fact Segal [1983] called it 'the narcissistic position'):

> Finding the object becomes a fundamentally frustrating experience only if the subject wants *to be* the object instead of *to have* it . . . intolerance to object-relations implies envy and every theory which defines object-relations as frustrating introduces envy into theory in an underhand way. (Etchegoyen *et al.*, 1987, pp. 54–5)

Envy is an attack upon object-relations *per se*, in order to preserve omnipotence and self-idealization [see NARCISSISM], not simply an attack on the object for its frustrating behaviour. 'Envy and narcissism are closely connected as two sides of the same coin' (Etchegoyen *et al.*, 1987).

Negative narcissism: In 1971 Rosenfeld described in detail considerable *clinical* evidence for the death instinct internally within the internal object-relations [see NARCISSISM]. He described an internal object, rather like a Mafia gang, which dominated and intimidated the better parts of the personality and which idealized aggression and destruction. He had found this kind of internal object (structure) in borderline patients. He located a phantasy life concerning an internal conflict in which the death instinct remains a potent force idealizing the bad parts of the self, its impulses and bad objects. These split-off states of psychotic-like phenomena were amplified by Sidney Klein (1980), who described autistic phenomena even in neurotic patients and traced them to internal objects that were felt to survive in a walled-off state, as if surrounded by a carapace [see STRUCTURE]. This internal psychotic organization was described again by Steiner (1982), showing the perverse quality of internal relationships.

In a related approach, Joseph (1971, 1975) described clinical manifestations of the death instinct in the form of perversions – or, more precisely, in the form of a perversion of character (in contrast to the sexual perversions) in which the destructive aspects are deviously concealed, often in the guise of good aspects of the self, and good object-relations. The perverse quality suffuses the transference and is extremely important in severely disturbed patients.

CRITIQUES OF KLEINIAN ENVY. The general criticisms of the death instinct are applicable to the concept of 'envy' [see 3. AGGRESSION]. The complaint that Kleinians have failed to respond to these criticisms – '. . . their failure to respond to criticisms of these concepts bespeaks of either their inability to do so or their dogmatism' (Kernberg, 1980, p. 41) – is not actually true. Clinical evidence arises from the observation of children (Klein, 1952b; Bick, 1964, 1968, 1986) and also on psychoanalytic evidence (notably Riviere, 1936; Meltzer, 1963, 1973; Rosenfeld, 1971, 1987), especially concerning the negative therapeutic reaction [see NEGATIVE THERAPEUTIC REACTION].

The temptation – often indulged in by inexperienced analysts – to attribute all untoward reactions to an envious negative therapeutic reaction is not valid, as Kernberg (1969) and Greenson (1974) have scathingly pointed out. Kernberg (1980, p. 49) acidly commented on the perverse transference arising directly as a consequence of Kleinian technique. In reply, Rosenfeld (1987) has attempted to give detailed clinical data to distinguish negative reactions arising from mistaken interpretation and defective technique from those arising from an envious backlash.

Joffe (1969) made a meticulous study of envy, describing the concept from a clinical point of view. He showed that the idea of constitutional envy was put forward as early as 1921 (Eisler, 1921, who acknowledged the important link with Abraham, 1919). But Joffe became adamant that in his own framework the concept is untenable. He repudiated Klein's views on the grounds that 'envy implies object-relations and must come after the primary phase of narcissism'. It is not primary and is, in fact, a complex of affects rather than a unitary drive inherent in the id – 'Although certain id elements are necessary components of envy, its specific quality lies in the contribution of the ego' (1969, p. 540) – and the ego does not come into existence until after the narcissistic stage (age two, he guessed). He distinguished four ego-components: (i) the capacity to distinguish between self and object; (ii) some capacity to fantasy, (iii) the capacity to distinguish between a fantasied wish-fulfilment and a hallucinatory gratification (i.e. between internal reality and the external world); and (iv) the existence of an enduring feeling-quality – 'We should perhaps speak of an "envy-organization" of a permanent or semi-permanent kind' (p. 540).

It is not quite right to say that Joffe has criticized the Kleinian concept. Joffe mistook the Kleinian concept, assuming it to be related to the frustration of instinctual impulses, since what he said is envied is '. . . the feeding breast . . . seen *from birth* as deliberately withholding gratification for its own benefit' (p. 538). In fact, envy is the spoiling of something good because of its goodness and not because it frustrates by withholding its goodness: often in analysis because the analyst has *not* withheld his interpretation but has actually given it to the patient. It is this idea of a confusion of bad feelings towards a good object which has passed Joffe by.

Joffe has definitely shown that the Kleinian concept of envy is not compatible with the ego-psychology framework of concepts, but he has not mounted a critique from a position which would give a perspective on it. It becomes merely a choice between two whole frameworks. In fact, since about 1946 Kleinian theory has moved so far away from ego-psychology that it is hard for those of one camp to grasp the important features and nuances of the conceptual framework of the other and therefore accurately to distinguish the points from which divergences have arisen. Consequently, useful dialogue between the two has tended to die away.

To those outside the Kleinian Group, the concept of 'envy' has supported the view that Kleinian psychoanalysis is profoundly pessimistic. Since envy is constitutional it is assumed to be unchangeable, and this leads to attempts to reduce it to more congenial concepts. That human beings have aggression and wanton destructiveness so fundamentally ingrained into our nature is a grim realization that nobody welcomes. In fact there may be some truth in the view that Klein was pessimistic about this work:

> Both she and I came to recognize the importance of her destructive envy towards me, and, as always when we reach these deep strata, it appeared that whatever destructive impulses were there, they were felt to be omnipotent and therefore irrevocable and irremediable. (Klein, 1957, p. 207)

Those who were in a position to make informed criticisms of Klein's concept of 'envy' – notably Heimann and Winnicott – had already moved away from Kleinian thinking to a considerable extent after the introduction of the theory of the paranoid-schizoid position. Heimann never used the concept of projective identification or the ideas of splitting as they were described in the paranoid-schizoid position and she left no published version of her opinion of 'envy'. Winnicott, having accepted the importance of the depressive position and the love for the good object, diverged from Klein's emphasis on destructiveness in the paranoid-schizoid position, used the concept of projective identification only meagrely, and seems to have hotly disagreed with the concept of 'envy' as Klein described it. There is not a published account of his criticisms but it seems that innate envy dismissed, for him, the importance of the environment and the unique mother–infant bond (reported in Grosskurth, 1985, p. 417).

Abraham, Karl (1919) 'A particular form of neurotic resistance against the psycho-analytic method', in Karl Abraham (1927) *Selected Papers on Psycho-Analysis*. Hogarth, pp. 303–11.

Bick, Esther (1964) 'Notes on infant observation in psycho-analytic training', *Int. J. Psycho-Anal.* 45:558–66; republished (1987) in Martha Harris and Esther Bick, *The Collected Papers of Martha Harris and Esther Bick*. Perth: Clunie, pp. 240–56.

—— (1968) 'The experience of the skin in early object relations', *Int. J. Psycho-Anal.* 49:484–6; republished (1987) in *The Collected Papers of Martha Harris and Esther Bick*, pp. 114–18.

—— (1986) 'Further considerations of the function of the skin in early object relations', *Br. J. Psychother.* 2:292–9.

Eisler, M.J. (1921) 'Pleasure in sleep and the disturbed capacity for sleep', *Int. J. Psycho-Anal.* 3:30–42.

Etchegoyen, Horatio, Lopez, Benito and Rabih, Moses (1987) 'Envy and how to interpret it', *Int. J. Psycho-Anal.* 68:49–61.

Freud, Sigmund (1926) *Inhibitions, Symptoms and Anxiety*, in James Strachey, ed. *The Standard Edition of the Complete Psychological Works of Sigmund Freud*, 24 vols. Hogarth, 1953–73. vol. 20, pp. 77–175.

Greenson, Ralph (1974) 'Transference: Freud or Klein?', *Int. J. Psycho-Anal.* 55:37–48.

Grosskurth, Phyllis (1985) *Melanie Klein*. Hodder & Stoughton.

Horney, Karen (1936) 'The problem of the negative therapeutic reaction', *Psychoanal. Q.* 2:29–44.

Joffe, Walter (1969) 'A critical review of the envy concept', *Int. J. Psycho-Anal.* 50:533–45.

Joseph, Betty (1971) 'A clinical contribution to the analysis of a perversion', *Int. J. Psycho-Anal.* 52:441–9.

—— (1975) 'The patient who is difficult to reach', in Peter Giovacchini, ed. *Tactics and Techniques in Psycho-Analytic Therapy*, vol. 2. New York: Jason Aronson, pp. 205–16.

—— (1986) 'Envy in everyday life', *Psycho-Analytic Psychotherapy* 2:13–30.

Kernberg, Otto (1969) 'A contribution to the ego-psychological critique of the Kleinian School', *Int. J. Psycho-Anal.* 50:317–33.

—— (1980) *Internal World and External Reality*. New York: Jason Aronson.

Klein, Melanie (1929) 'Personification in the play of children', in *The Writings of Melanie Klein*, vol. 1. Hogarth, pp. 199–209.

—— (1932) *The Psycho-Analysis of Children*, *The Writings of Melanie Klein*, vol. 2.

—— (1933) 'The early development of conscience in the child', *The Writings of Melanie Klein*, vol. 1, pp. 248–57.

—— (1946) 'Notes on some schizoid mechanisms', *The Writings of Melanie Klein*, vol. 3, pp. 1–24.

—— (1952a) 'Some theoretical conclusions regarding the emotional life of infants', *The Writings of Melanie Klein*, vol. 3, pp. 61–93.

—— (1952b) 'On observing the behaviour of young infants', *The Writings of Melanie Klein*, vol. 3, pp. 94–121.

—— (1955a) 'The psycho-analytic play technique: its history and significance', *The Writings of Melanie Klein*, vol. 3, pp. 122–40.

—— (1955b) 'On identification', *The Writings of Melanie Klein*, vol. 3, pp. 141–75.

—— (1957) *Envy and Gratitude*, *The Writings of Melanie Klein*, vol. 3, pp. 176–235.

Klein, Sidney (1980) 'Autistic phenomena in neurotic patients', *Int. J. Psycho-Anal.* 61: 395–402.

Meltzer, Donald (1963) 'A contribution to the metapsychology of cyclothymic states', *Int. J. Psycho-Anal.* 44:83–96.

—— (1973) *Sexual States of Mind*. Perth: Clunie.

Riviere, Joan (1932) 'Jealousy as a mechanism of defence', *Int. J. Psycho-Anal.* 13:414–24.

—— (1936) 'A contribution to the analysis of the negative therapeutic reactions', *Int. J. Psycho-Anal.* 17:304–20.

Rosenfeld, Herbert (1947) 'Analysis of a schizophrenic state with depersonalization', in Herbert Rosenfeld (1965) *Psychotic States*. Hogarth, pp. 13–33; originally published *Int. J. Psycho-Anal.* 28:130–9.

—— (1952) 'Notes on the psycho-analysis of the superego conflict in an acute schizophrenic', in *Psychotic States*, pp. 63–103; originally published *Int. J. Psycho-Anal.* 33:111–31; republished (1955) in Melanie Klein, Paula Heimann and Roger Money-Kyrle, eds *New Directions in Psycho-Analysis*. Hogarth, pp. 180–219.

—— (1955) 'An investigation of the need of neurotic and psychotic patients to act out during analysis' [quoted in Klein, 1957], in *Psychotic States*, pp. 200–16.

—— (1965) *Psychotic States*. Hogarth.

—— (1971) 'A clinical approach to the psychoanalytic theory of the life and death instincts: an investigation into the aggressive aspects of narcissism', *Int. J. Psycho-Anal.* 52:169–78.

—— (1987) *Impasse and Interpretation*. Tavistock.

Segal, Hanna (1950) 'Some aspects of the analysis of a schizophrenic', *Int. J. Psycho-Anal.* 31:268–78; republished (1981) in *The Work of Hanna Segal*. New York: Jason Aronson, pp. 101–20.

—— (1962) 'The curative factors in psycho-analysis', *Int. J. Psycho-Anal.* 43:212–17; republished (1981) in *The Work of Hanna Segal*, pp. 69–80.

—— (1983) 'Some clinical implications of Melanie Klein's work', *Int. J. Psycho-Anal.* 64:321–32.

—— (1987) 'The clinical usefulness of the concept of the death instinct' (unpublished).

Steiner, John (1982) 'Perverse relationships between parts of the self', *Int. J. Psycho-Anal.* 63:241–52.

13 PROJECTIVE IDENTIFICATION

DEFINITION. Projective identification was defined by Klein in 1946 as the prototype of the aggressive object-relationship, representing an anal attack on an object by means of forcing *parts of the ego* into it in order to take over its contents or to control it and occurring in the paranoid-schizoid position from birth. It is a 'phantasy remote from consciousness' that entails a belief in certain aspects of the self being located elsewhere, with a consequent depletion and weakened sense of self and identity, to the extent of depersonalization; profound feelings of being lost or a sense of imprisonment may result.

Without a concomitant introjection by the object projected into, increasingly forceful attempts to intrude result in extreme forms of projective identification. These excessive processes lead to severe distortions of identity and the disturbed experiences of the schizophrenic.

In 1957 Klein suggested that envy was deeply implicated in projective identification, which then represents the forced entry into another person in order to destroy their best attributes. Shortly afterwards Bion (1959) distinguished a normal form of projective identification from a pathological one, and others have elaborated this group of 'many distinct yet related processes'. The further understanding of projective identification has been the major area subsequently developed by Kleinians.

CHRONOLOGY

1946 Klein's classical description (Klein, Melanie, 1946, 'Notes on some schizoid mechanisms').

1957 Post-Kleinian extensions of the concept as containing, etc. (Segal, Hanna, 1957, 'Notes on symbol formation'; Bion, Wilfred, 1957, 'Differentiation of the psychotic from the non-psychotic personalities'; Bion, Wilfred, 1959, 'Attacks on linking'; Bion, Wilfred, 1962b, *Learning from Experience*).

Early on, Klein described parts of the self and its impulses being located in the external world: 'Gerard proposed to send it [a toy tiger] off into the next room to carry out his aggressive desires on his father . . . This primitive part of his personality was in this case represented by the tiger' (Klein, 1927, p. 172). However, only in 1946 was the concept fully described and placed in its theoretical framework [see 11. PARANOID-SCHIZOID POSITION]. At that point Klein was describing the severe pathology in the ego-development of the schizophrenic.

When Klein republished her 1946 paper in *Developments in Psycho-Analysis* in 1952 she made an addition to suggest the term 'projective identification' as a name for this process. From then on the concept of 'projective identification' has come more and more to centre stage in Kleinian psychoanalysis. The foremost developments that have taken place after Klein's death in 1960 have been in the understanding of the far-reaching importance of this concept. The origins and framework of the concept are discussed elsewhere [see 11. PARANOID-SCHIZOID POSITION; PROJECTION]. This entry will describe problems in the definition of the term; the main developments in the use of the concept (with reference to more extended discussions under specific general entries); and some of the non-Kleinian usages and critiques of the concept.

PROJECTION AND PROJECTIVE IDENTIFICATION.

Because of its long history of use in psychoanalysis, the term 'projection' has become confused with 'projective identification'. The distinction between these terms is often a great mystery to many approaching this topic for the first time. The truth is that historically both terms have been used in overlapping ways to cover phenomena that are not fully distinguished [see PROJECTION].

Freud's initial use of the term projection referred to '. . . an abuse of the mechanism of projection for purposes of defence' (Freud, 1895, p. 209); he described how one person's ideas may be attributed to someone else, thus creating a state of paranoia. A very similar concept turns up in Rosenfeld (1947) when he describes the projection of a patient's sexual impulses:

> Her whole anxiety turned on whether she could control *his* wishes and arguments. She repeated some of his arguments to me, and it was clear that Denis stood for her own greedy sexual wishes which she had difficulty in dealing with and which she therefore projected on to him. (Rosenfeld, 1947, p. 18)

In the mean time other meanings of 'projection' came to the fore.

Abraham: In 1924 Abraham formalized a view of manic-depressive states, the basis of which was the detailed clinical evidence of cycles of projection followed by recuperative introjection of objects. The anal elimination of objects (typically faeces and what they represent) became an important aspect of the developing view of object-relations, especially in Britain, since many analysts from London had been to Berlin for their own analysis with Abraham (James and Edward Glover, Alix Strachey, and Klein herself came to London following Abraham's death). Hence, as the detailed understanding of object-relations flowered during the 1920s and 1930s, Abraham's view of projection became established: the *projection into the external world of an internal object.*

Projection of the superego: Klein contributed to this considerably during the important consideration of the nature of play and symbolism [see 1. TECHNIQUE; SYMBOL-FORMATION]. The externalization into the external world was initially couched in terms of the externalization of the superego or parts of it, since at that time the psychoanalytic world was preoccupied with assimilating Freud's (1923) new theory of the superego [see 7. SUPEREGO]; for instance, about George (six years old): 'Three principal parts were represented in his games: that of the id and those of the superego in its persecuting and its helpful aspects' (Klein, 1929, p. 201).

Self or object: At this stage Klein was uncomfortably trying to couple Abraham's idea of objects expelled from inside with Freud's theory of the superego (the only internal object Freud recognized). However, her clinical material was not so tidy: '. . . in thus throwing them [some toys] out of the room he was indicating an expulsion both of the damaged object and of his own sadism' (Klein, 1930b, p. 226). Thus both object and a part of the self (his own sadism) were being projected.

Until 1946 the emphasis in Klein's work was on the fate of the object. This was greatly enhanced in 1935 by the theory of the depressive position [see 10. DEPRESSIVE POSITION]. The fate of parts of the self was less in evidence in Klein's thinking until Fairbairn pointed this out. Klein then concentrated on the fragmentation of the ego in schizoid processes, and the projective fate of those fragments [see 11. PARANOID-SCHIZOID POSITION]. They could be seen to be identified with external objects through a process of projection of some kind, which she called 'projective identification'. She chose this term because for some time there had been a prolonged debate amongst Kleinians and others over the relation between introjection and the form of identification based on incorporation [see ASSIMILATION]. Projective identification seemed to offer the possibility of a symmetrical meaning. However, its ramifications have not realized that hope.

It might at this point be tempting to consider using the term 'projection' in Abraham's sense of projecting objects, and 'projective identification' in Klein's sense of projecting parts of the self. Again, such a neat solution falls down.

First of all, as the above quotation (Klein, 1930b, p. 226) makes clear, parts of the ego (self) are projected *with* the internal object. This is emphasized in Klein's definition of projective identification: 'Together with these harmful excrements, expelled in hatred, split-off parts of the ego are also projected' (Klein, 1946, p. 8). In the later ideas on projective identification also, the projection of an object capable of containing a projection is a prerequisite for projecting part of the self into the external object [see SKIN].

Secondly, the way in which objects and the ego are *psychologically* constructed makes for difficulty.

The construction of the ego and the objects: The development of the ego is in large part through the introjection of objects into it which comes to be an integration, more or less stable, of introjected objects assimilated into, and felt to belong to, the ego, which is largely structured by them. At the same time, external objects are constructed through projections into the external world of objects derived partly from unconscious phantasy and partly from previous experiences of objects. These objects in the external world are thus constructed in part from inherent aspects of the ego (unconscious phantasy) together with actual characteristics of the present and past objects. This amalgam, when introjected, may then be assimilated as a part of the ego [see ASSIMILATION]; or it may remain an internal object apparently separate from – even alien to – the ego.

Thus both the ego and its objects are constructed from varying degrees of mixture and integration of the self and the external world. The experiences of when they are part of the self or when separated off as objects internally – or externally – are very fluid and vary in time, requiring constant analysis of the process of internal and external object-relations.

The upshot is that there is no clear distinction between projection and projective identification:

> I do not think it useful to distinguish projection from projective identification. What Klein did, in my view, was to add depth and meaning to Freud's concept of projection by emphasizing that one cannot project impulses without projecting part of the ego, which involves splitting, and, further, that impulses do not just vanish when projected; they go into an object, and they distort the perception of the object. (Spillius, 1983, p. 322)

However, Freud did occasionally refer to this deeper aspect of projection. In writing about children's play in a reference which undoubtedly influenced Klein at the outset of her work, he described how children attempt to work through traumatic experiences: 'As the child passes over from the passivity of the game, he hands on the disagreeable experience to one of his playmates and in this way revenges himself on a substitute' (Freud, 1920, p. 17). He is demonstrating how an experience of the subject is transferred to become the experience of an object (in substitution).

Projective identification and the countertransference: The proprietorial claim made by Kleinians over the term 'projective identification' contrasts with the extreme difficulty in making clear how to recognize it when you meet it: 'The description of these processes suffers from a great handicap, for these phantasies arise at a time when the infant has not yet begun to think in words' (Klein, 1946). Joseph, for instance, in a number of papers (1975, 1981, 1982) has adopted a mode of description that depends upon indicating the process in clinical material, as opposed to an attempt to derive a definition; no amount of defining the colour red to someone who has never seen it before will substitute for pointing to some red object. She described how a patient may *use* the analyst, and the excitement it gives him to succeed in this use. It is not a use of the analyst to represent something – a parental figure, etc. – but a use to evade a committed link with the analyst, from which the patient runs the risk of painful experiences and a destabilizing of his personality structure. After reporting an inter-change in some clinical material, Joseph commented:

> I think it probable that I made a technical error in interpreting the cow fantasy too fully, or rather, prematurely, in terms of the mother's body, and that this encouraged my patient unconsciously to feel that he was actually succeeding in pulling me into his exciting fantasy world and thus encouraged him to proliferate his fantasies. (Joseph, 1975, pp. 215–16)

The analyst has momentarily been caught off guard and sucked into performing *like* an analyst, which the patient immediately enjoys as a mastery over the analyst because he can feel that the analyst performs according to the patient's control. Such lapses in the analyst which lead to a playing into the patient's phantasies may well be engineered by the patient who knows his analyst well. The problem is to define what is happening in the analyst when, as in the patient, it is not happening in words. The analyst's subjective experience is difficult to grasp:

> the experience of countertransference appears to me to have a quite distinct quality that should enable the analyst to differentiate the occasion when he is the object of a projective identification from the occasion when he is not. The analyst feels he is being manipulated so as to be playing a part, no matter how difficult to recognize, in someone else's phantasy – or he would do if it were not for what in recollection I can only call a temporary loss of insight, a sense of experiencing strong feelings and at the same time a belief that their existence is quite adequately justified by the objective situation. From the analyst's point of view, the experience consists of two closely related phases: in the first there is a feeling that whatever else one has done, one has certainly not given a correct interpretation; in the second there is a sense of being a particular kind of person in a particular emotional situation. I believe ability to shake oneself out of the numbing feeling of reality

that is a concomitant of this state is the prime requisite. (Bion, 1961, p. 149)

Although he was referring to the analyst working in a group, Bion was trying to convey both the intensity and numbingness of the subjective quality of receiving a powerful projective identification. Although Bion's is one of the best attempts at describing projective identification, it is a subjective quality that is more easily pointed out than defined.

NORMAL AND ABNORMAL PROJECTIVE IDENTIFICATION.
Bion (1959, 1962a,b) established that the concept is a complex one and that it could be categorized into normal and abnormal projective identification. The difference depends on the degree of violence in the execution of the mechanism. There are two alternative aims of projective identification:

(i) one is to evacuate violently a painful state of mind leading to forcibly entering an object, in phantasy, for immediate relief, and often with the aim of an intimidating control of the object [see BIZARRE OBJECTS; PSYCHOSIS]; and

(ii) the other is to introduce into the object a state of mind, as a means of communicating with it about this mental state [see CONTAINING].

The difference between evacuation and communication is crucial, though it may be that in any one instance there is a mixture. In practice, however, it is important to distinguish these two *motives*.

Omnipotence and fusion: Evacuation and communication are connected with different defensive functions and different effects, in phantasy, upon the object and the ego. What characterizes the pathological form is the great violence and omnipotence with which it is carried out:

> When Melanie Klein speaks of 'excessive' projective identification I think the term 'excessive' should be understood to apply not to the frequency only with which projective identification is employed but to excess of belief in omnipotence. (Bion, 1962a, p. 114)

The object ceases to be independent (Rosenfeld, 1964b). A fusion of the self with the object takes place and this represents, amongst other things, a defence against separateness, need and envy [see 12. ENVY].

Projective identification as communication: In elaborating Klein's theory of the development of the ego through repeated cycles of introjection and projection Bion took it further by recognizing that these cycles were of projective identification and introjective identification. He presented his model in mature form in 1959:

Throughout the analysis the patient resorted to projective identification with a persistence suggesting it was a mechanism of which he had never been able sufficiently to avail himself; the analysis afforded him the opportunity for the exercise of a mechanism of which he had been cheated . . . there were sessions which led me to suppose that the patient felt there was some object that denied him the use of projective identification . . . the patient felt that parts of his personality that he wished to repose in me were refused entry by me . . . When the patient strove to rid himself of fears of death which were felt to be too powerful for his personality to contain he split off his fears and put them into me, the idea apparently being that if they were allowed to repose there long enough they would undergo modification by my psyche and could then be safely reintrojected. On the occasion I have in mind the patient had felt . . . that I evacuated them so quickly that the feelings were not modified but had become more painful . . . he strove to force them into me with increased desperation and violence. His behaviour, isolated from the context of analysis, might have appeared to be an expression of primary aggression. The more violent his phantasies of projective identification, the more frightened he became of me. There were sessions in which such behaviour expressed unprovoked aggression, but I quote this series because it shows the patient in a different light, his violence a reaction to what he felt was my hostile defensiveness . . . the analytic situation built up in my mind a sense of witnessing an extremely early scene. I felt that the patient had witnessed in infancy a mother who dutifully responded to the infant's emotional displays. The dutiful response had in it an element of impatient 'I don't know what's the matter with the child.' My deduction was that in order to understand what the child wanted the mother should have treated the infant's cry as more than a demand for her presence. From the infant's point of view she should have taken into her, and thus experienced, the fear that the child was dying. It was this fear that the child could not contain. He strove to split it off together with the part of the personality in which it lay and project it into mother. An understanding mother is able to experience the feeling of dread that this baby was striving to deal with by projective identification, and yet retain a balanced outlook. This patient had had to deal with a mother who could not tolerate experiencing such feelings and reacted either by denying them ingress, or alternatively by becoming a prey to the anxiety which resulted from introjection of the baby's bad feelings . . . To some this reconstruction may appear to be unduly fanciful; to me it . . . is the reply to any who may object that too much stress is placed on the transference to the exclusion of a proper elucidation of early memories . . . Thus the link between patient and analyst, or infant and breast, is the mechanism of projective identification. (Bion, 1959, pp. 103–4)

If the analyst is closed or unresponsive, 'The result is excessive projective identification by the patient and a deterioration of his developmental processes' (p. 105).

In the schizophrenic,

> ... the disturbance is twofold. On the one hand there is the patient's inborn disposition to excessive destructiveness, hatred and envy: on the other the environment which, at its worst, denies to the patient the use of the mechanisms of splitting and projective identification. (p. 106)

Bion is describing both inherited and environmental disturbances of normal projective identification.

The distinction between psychotic and non-psychotic was important. Klein had frequently been criticized for claiming that children normally went through a period of psychosis in their development (Waelder, 1937; Bibring, 1947; Kernberg, 1969). This distinction clearly refuted that criticism, and described clinical features to demarcate (i) a use of psychotic mechanisms in 'normal' development from (ii) the psychotic character of their use. The hallmarks of the *abnormal*, pathological use of projective identification (sometimes referred to as 'massive' or 'excessive' projective identification) are

(a) the degree of hatred and violence of the splitting and the intrusion;

(b) the quality of omnipotent control and therefore fusion with the object;

(c) the amount of the ego that is lost; and

(d) the specific aim of destroying awareness, especially of internal reality. In contrast, 'normal' projective identification has the aim of communication and empathy, and plays its part in the participation of the social reality [see EMPATHY].

THE PHANTASIES OF PROJECTIVE IDENTIFICATION.

Klein was aware of the problem of finding a term: 'The description of such primitive processes suffers from a great handicap, for these phantasies arise at a time when the infant has not yet begun to think in words' (Klein, 1946, p. 8n), and this concern continues to be echoed: projective identification '... may have to be changed eventually to something like "intrusive identification" if only someone could find a word to express a phantasy function so remote from consciousness, save in fairy tales' (Meltzer, 1967, p. xi).

The problem has been defined in other ways, perhaps more

profitably: 'Projective identification is an overall name for a number of distinct yet related processes connected with splitting and projection' (O'Shaughnessy, 1975, p. 325). Rosenfeld (1983), after long experience, eventually began a catalogue of the kinds of phantasies involved. It comprised the following:

(i) Projective identification for defensive purposes such as ridding the self of unwanted parts.

    (a) Omnipotent intrusion leading to fusion or confusion with the object.

    (b) The concrete phantasy of passively living inside the object (parasitism).

    (c) The belief in a oneness of feeling with the object (symbiosis).

    (d) Expulsion of tension by someone who has been traumatized as a child by violent intrusions.

(ii) Projective identification used for communication.

    (a) A method of getting through to an object believed to be aloof.

    (b) Reversal of the child/parent relationship.

    (c) Identifying with similarities in the object for narcissistic purposes.

(iii) Projective identification in order to recognize objects and to identify with them (empathy).

Phantasy consequences: Projective identifications, being a phantasy function involved in constructing the identity of the self and objects, has major consequences for the experiences of the individual. The dislocation of the self is experienced in a number of ways:

(i) the underlying splitting gives the sense of being in pieces [see SPLITTING];

(ii) the experience of a depleted and weakened ego leads to a complaint of having no feelings or drives, and a sense of futility;

(iii) this loss to the ego can be experienced as a sense of not being a person at all (depersonalization);

(iv) the identification with the object leads to a confusion with someone else;

(v) the ego may feel that parts of itself have been forcibly removed, imprisoned and controlled (claustrophobia);

(vi) the identification may result in a peculiarly tenacious clinging to the object in which parts of the self are located;

(vii) anxieties arise about damage to the object as a result of the intrusion and control;

(viii) there may be severe anxieties about retaliation by the object for the violent intrusion;

(ix) the fate of the object in pathological projective identification *is* the fate of the lost self, which may come to be felt as alien and persecuting [see STRUCTURE].

LATER DEVELOPMENTS: 1952–87. The understanding of projective identification led immediately to a much greater understanding of the psychotic's experiences. Rosenfeld (1952) described detailed sessions with a schizophrenic patient, with many references to the patient's phantasy of intruding into the analyst. These ideas were also taken up with child analyses (Rodrigue, 1955). However, from the mid-1950s onwards projective identification gave rise to enormous and radical developments in Kleinian psychoanalytic theory.

The scope of these discoveries has overshadowed and even eclipsed other investigations. The relative neglect of certain introjective problems (forced introjection, for instance) is quite noticeable. The main points of development will be considered in turn:

(i) Psychosis;

(ii) Linking;

(iii) Thinking;

(iv) Symbol-formation;

(v) Containers and change;

(vi) Countertransference;

(vii) Adhesive identification;

(viii) Structure; and

(ix) The social container.

(i) Psychosis [see PSYCHOSIS]: Klein became interested in psychosis almost by accident. The pressure on her to justify the play technique and the nature of the symbolization process inherent in the production of play led her to study children who failed to play and were inhibited in their capacity to form and use symbols. Thus she stumbled upon psychosis in children, and remarked on its frequency (Klein, 1930a). Others were equally interested. Melitta Schmideberg, Klein's daughter, was influenced early and made her own mark (Schmideberg, 1931).

However, the new ideas on splitting and projective identification went much further. Rosenfeld first reported the analysis of a schizophrenic in 1947. The analysis was commenced about 1944–5, at a period when Klein was herself writing her own paper on schizoid mechanisms (Klein, 1946) and while Rosenfeld was in his own analysis with her. He and Segal (1950) demonstrated in the clinical situation the processes of splitting up of the ego so that various functions and pieces of knowledge were not brought into contact with each other. In one instance, knowing how long it took to get to the analyst's house was not connected with the knowledge of the time of the session, so the patient could not leave sufficiently before the appointment time to get there punctually. In another instance (quoted earlier) the patient's sexual impulses were encountered in a sexual partner and controlled there rather than in the patient herself.

In 1956 Segal described the schizophrenic's projection of depression into the analyst, leading to the characteristic despair in those in charge of the care of schizophrenics. From 1953 Bion began to study schizophrenics from the point of view of their thinking disorder. He showed that the schizophrenic splits a certain part of the ego, the perceptual apparatus. This gives rise to a pathological form of projective identification in which the functions of perception seem, to the schizophrenic, to be performed by external objects around him [see BIZARRE OBJECTS].

(ii) Linking [see LINKING]: Bion extended the theory of schizophrenia to become one of generalized attacks on awareness, especially the awareness of internal reality. Severance of thoughts within the mind, as described by Rosenfeld and Segal, are active attacks on the links between mental contents. Bion likened this to oedipal linking; the attack on the link between mental contents is an attack on the parental couple experienced as part-objects. This, in its most basic form, is the linking of the mouth with the breast, or the vagina with the penis.

Bion was able to establish a general theory of linking as a theory of the mind itself in which the highest functions of thought are composed of very basic emotional building blocks, the core of which is the oedipal link. Thus thinking is based on the bodily experienced phantasies of sucking and sex [see INNATE KNOWLEDGE]. He referred to this link by one of its key properties – one element fitting inside another – as the container–contained relationship. By focusing on the coupling of the two objects, one going inside the other, he began to expand the idea of projective identification to a quite ubiquitous function [see CONTAINING].

From here Bion accomplished a theoretical *tour de force* which took him on a wide-ranging examination of very many problems in the psychological, philosophical, religious and social spheres [see BION; ALPHA-FUNCTION; CONTAINING]. Foremost amongst these were his theories of thinking and of the container–contained relationship.

(iii) Thinking [see THINKING]: Bion employed the notion of 'normal'

projective identification as the basic building block for generating thoughts out of experiences and perceptions.

Klein's work had considered theories of knowledge, including the notion of innate knowledge, particularly knowledge of the pairing oedipal couple [see COMBINED PARENT FIGURE]. There is an inherent expectation that the union of two objects makes a third which is more than a sum of the two parts. In the generation of thoughts out of experience an innate *pre-conception*, like the neural and anatomical expectancy of the mouth for a nipple, meets a *realization* (the real nipple enters the mouth) and the result is a conception. Conceptions result from satisfying conjunctions in which a pre-conception meets an adequate realization (Bion, 1959). Conceptions are then available for thinking.

This is one model of thinking that Bion proposed, but he goes further. He seems to suggest altogether three models of thinking (Spillius, 1988).

In the second model Bion considered the state of affairs when a pre-conception does not meet an actual realization. A pre-conception then has to mate with a frustration; emotional work is done. The conception resulting when a pre-conception mates with a frustration is a thought useful for thinking with, so that rational action for seeking a satisfaction can be planned. Higher-level thinking repeats the model by taking conceptions as new pre-conceptions for mating with new realizations – for instance, 'facts' (realizations) generate a theory (conception) which can then function as a new pre-conception to seek further 'facts' (realizations) to create a more general theory.

In a third model, the acquisition of meaning is a function which Bion wanted to explore free from all prior expectations, similar to investigating mathematical functions. So he found a 'neutral' term – *alpha-function* [see BION; ALPHA-FUNCTION] and let it mean the separation of elements of perception into those usable for thinking and dreaming (alpha-elements) and others, unconsciousness and unassimilable raw data, which he called beta-elements [see BETA-ELEMENTS]. This function is performed in the first instance for the infant by a mother who, in a receptive state of mind called *reverie*, contains the infant's intolerable experience through her own use of *alpha-function*, putting it into suitable action or words [see REVERIE; CONTAINING]. This later model of containing and alpha-function is the most complete of the models:

> Bion did not do as much as he might have to link his three models. It is surely repeated experiences of alternations between positive and negative realizations that encourage the development of thoughts and thinking. (Spillius, 1988, p. 156)

(iv) Symbol-formation [see SYMBOL-FORMATION]: Freud's view of

symbolization was relatively undeveloped, but based on sublimation. It was elaborated by Jones (1916) and others. However, they made no real attack on the complex problem of the special modification of a biological organism from a world of physical gratifications into the symbolic world of human society. Klein herself did not make large inroads into understanding the difference between these two worlds, but she did implicitly point to the importance of further study of thinking and in particular symbol-formation as a uniquely human achievement. As her colleague Searl puts it: 'Klein has made it abundantly clear that symbolism plays a most important part in providing the libidinal bridge on which the ego can build its relations of familiarity with the material world' (Searl, 1932, p. 330).

However, it fell to Klein's followers to develop an explicit theory of symbol-formation. They relied on Klein's description of projective identification. While Bion examined the difference between normal and pathological projective identification, Segal described a comparable difference that clarified the nature of 'symbolic equation', distinguishing it from symbols proper. In the *symbolic equation* there '. . . was no distinction between the symbol and the thing symbolized . . . It was not merely a symbolic expression of his wish to bring me his stool. He felt that he had actually offered it to me' (Segal, 1950, p. 104). Later (1957) she systematized her views more clearly, and showed that this confusion between the symbol and the object symbolized is a result of projective identification. This accords with the variety of projective identification that is conducted with omnipotence and violence aimed at removing separateness [see SYMBOLIC EQUATION].

(v) Containers and change [see CONTAINING]: The theory of the container–contained is an attempt to raise the concept of projective identification to a general theory of human functioning – of the relationships between people, and between groups; of the relationships with internal objects; and of the relationships in the symbolic world between thoughts, ideas, theories, experiences, etc. The container–contained relationship exists between two elements, one containing the other, with the production, or otherwise, of a third element. The attributes of this relationship are various, and were extensively explored by Bion (1970). The prototype is the sexual union, one part contained within another. However, it is not to be restricted to the sexual union, but typically can be a marriage which *contains* the sexual activity. It is also a containing of meaning in language.

Bion categorized various types of container–contained relationship and used, somewhat confusingly, two separate sets of categories rather indiscriminately:

(a) The first set consists of relationships which do damage to one or other of the elements in the relationship. Either the contained is so forceful that it blows the container apart; or the container is so strong and inflexible that it constricts '. . . by compression or denudation' the element it contains. These are in contrast with the relationship in which each enhances the other with mutual growth.

(b) Separately, Bion classified the relationship as *commensal, symbiotic* or *parasitic*. Briefly he defined these:

> By 'commensal' I mean a relationship in which two objects share a third to the advantage of all three. By 'symbiotic' I understand a relationship in which one depends on another to mutual advantage. By 'parasitic' I mean to represent a relationship in which one depends on another to produce a third, which is destructive of all three. (Bion, 1970, p. 95)

Bion had been interested for a long time in the fact that both therapy and thinking depend on psychic change. Psychoanalysis must be concerned with the possibilities and conditions for change. Mental activity is contained within a framework of thoughts and expectations which he called conjunctions. Change therefore demands destructuring of the existing, internal, containing theories and the re-establishing of new conjunctions. Bion liked to think of this process as one of minor mental breakdown ('catastrophic change') followed by recovery. Destructuring is a process of fragmentation akin to Klein's descriptions of the problems of the paranoid-schizoid position, while the restructuring is in line with the depressive position. These are constant oscillations to which Bion gave the term *Ps-D* [see Ps-D].

(vi) Countertransference [see COUNTERTRANSFERENCE]: Normal projective identification has given rise to an understanding of empathy and of the therapeutic effect of psychoanalysis. 'Putting onself in someone else's shoes' is a description of empathy, but it is also a phantasy of the projective identification type – inserting oneself into someone else's position.

Heimann's (1950) seminal paper urged that countertransference should be taken seriously. The countertransference is a *specific* response to the patient, and may therefore function as a unique instrument for probing his mind. This significant idea was rejected by Klein herself, who remained suspicious of analysts who might then attribute all their feelings to the patient. Nevertheless it has become a cornerstone of Kleinian technique since Klein [see 1. TECHNIQUE]. The aim is that the analyst should come *to receive* the patient's projective identifications (Money-Kyrle, 1956).

The theory goes further by suggesting that the analyst then modifies the part of the patient which he now contains, by direct mental activity of his own going on inside himself. Then, eventually, he re-projects (in the utterance of an interpretation) back into the patient a modified form of the projection. The patient then has the benefit of introjecting not only this part of himself but an aspect of the analyst, the understanding part of the analyst's mind which can then become an *internal* resource for the patient in making sense of himself.

This process described by Money-Kyrle clearly has the elements of a cycle: a projective identification into the analyst, followed by the analyst's modification, and the reintrojection by the patient in the form of the analyst's interpretation. Thus the interaction between analyst and patient comes to be illuminated by the concept of projective identification. This idea was not developed by Klein herself, and it is difficult to be clear who has the major credit for it, since Heimann, who made the initial plea about countertransference, never took up the idea of projective identification. The idea comes through in Rosenfeld's clinical paper in 1952, though not explicitly stated; it is explicit, but in a rather different context, in Jaques's (1953) paper on the way people project into social groups [see SOCIAL DEFENCE SYSTEMS; and below].

In the instance when the analyst does not manage to contain the projective identification of the patient he or she may respond by a reactive projective identification into the patient, a common enough occurrence [see Money-Kyrle, 1956; Brenman Pick, 1985; and 1. TECHNIQUE]. This sad but common occurrence was given the name *projective counteridentification* by Grinberg (1962).

(vii) Adhesive identification [see SKIN]: Because of the quarrels in the 1930s and 1940s (Waelder, 1937; Isaacs, 1948) about the validity of Klein's conclusions about the first year of life, attempts were made in the early 1950s to get direct evidence of this developmental period. Klein (1952) reported some observations on infants, but this interest suffered from a lack of a rigorous method until Bick began, in 1948, systematic observations of infants with their mothers on a weekly basis (Bick, 1964). She recognized that the first object gives the infant the feeling of being in existence, having an identity. The personality is kept together passively by this first object (Bick, 1968).

Bick believed that the struggle to sustain the internal good object was preceded by an *introjection of the capacity to introject*. She showed the baby struggling for the capacity to introject and that this is a function of the skin, or rather a function of skin sensations which arouse phantasies of a containing object.

He has to develop a concept of a bounded space into which things can be put, or from which they can be removed. The first achievement is to win the concept of a space that holds things. This concept is gained in the form of the experience of an object which holds the personality together. The infant, in gaining the nipple in his mouth, has an experience of acquiring such an object – an object that closes the hole (the mouth and other orifices) in the skin boundary. The first introjection is the introjection of an object which provides a space into which objects can be introjected. Before projection can happen there has to be an internal object capable of containing which can be projected into an object before that object can be felt to contain a projection.

When that first achievement fails, the infant is unable to project or introject. Without such an internal object that holds the personality together, it cannot be projected into an external object to give projections a container. The personality is felt simply to leak uncontainedly out into a limitless space. The infant has to find other methods of holding his personality together, a *second-skin* formation. Meltzer (Meltzer *et al.*, 1975; Tustin, 1981, 1986) found these ideas important for an analytic technique with autistic children, who typically engage in a form of mechanical mimicry, experienced, in phantasy, as sticking *to* the object – an adhesive form of identification.

(viii) Structure [see STRUCTURE]: Klein originally tried to retain the classical view of the internal agencies of id, ego and superego. However, with her modifications to the theory of the superego [see 7. SUPEREGO; 5. INTERNAL OBJECTS] the internal world came to be viewed as much more fluid. The internal objects are varied, loving and hating, and include the particularly important 'combined parent figure'. The personality is structured by relationships with all these internal objects.

Important in the structural view of the internal world is the state of identification, or otherwise, between the ego and the objects. Some objects will be closely assimilated to the ego, while others are less close. In fact some objects may fail to be assimilated in any respect and exist as alien objects, or foreign bodies [see 5. INTERNAL OBJECTS; ASSIMILATION].

The ego is not always permanently in a state of identification with its objects. This varies from time to time, according to the context. At work a person may strongly identify with some superior, whereas back at home the same man may identify with his father when playing with his children. The fluidity of such a structure conforms to the adaptability of people to their immediate context. This represents 'the other end of a continuum from fragmentation' (Orford, 1987).

Rather differently, the ego may tend to split in more violent ways. Thus different sets of ideas or feelings may exist contemporaneously and incompatibly. Under stress the ego tends to come apart – commonly along the lines of cleavage, as it were, of the objects that have been assimilated. However, more active processes of splitting may take place with considerable fragmentation, and disorders of thinking and all other functions [see PSYCHOSIS].

The structure of the internal world is strongly influenced by projective identification, when parts of the ego are projected into external objects. This creates a narcissistic structure in which the ego is in identification with external objects that are considered to *be* the ego or a part of it.

The internal world can come, in borderline personality disorders, to be structured according to the primary instincts. The negative aspects of the personality come together and are held, as if by violence, in the form of a sort of Mafia gang (Rosenfeld, 1971). This negative internal structure is an internal organized and enduring form of the negative therapeutic reaction [see NEGATIVE THERAPEUTIC REACTION; 12. ENVY]. This organization tyrannizes the personality, and especially its good parts which are often felt to be imprisoned, intimidated and inactivated. Often this shows itself by the motivation for treatment becoming hidden or unconscious. The transference comes to be perverse, and used, as if for the good, but in fact for twisted ends devoted to spoiling the treatment and frustrating change [see PERVERSION].

(ix) The social container [see SOCIAL DEFENCE SYSTEMS]: Bion's use of the concept of projective identification to describe a containing function between people lends itself to becoming an interpersonal one. Jaques (1953), early on, described social structures in terms of projective and introjective identifications. Whole groups may develop concordant phantasy systems about themselves and their work, and about other groupings. Just as in individuals, groups may act to absorb the states of mind of one or more individuals. Funerals are occasions in which the bereavement of some is shared by many. A group that maintains a solidarity on the basis of a common external enemy is clearly projecting, as a group, into the enemy. Similarly a group that sustains its coherence by common allegiance to a single leader is again a condition in which the members are collectively projecting qualities into him; and a successful leader reciprocates with a projection of complementary qualities that his followers collectively introject and with which they then identify.

Projective identification was thus expanded by Jaques to show the important process of group cohesion and the tenaciously glue-like quality of allegiances to groups which individual members develop. This described Le Bon's mysterious 'contagion' effect in groups, which Freud (1921) had explained as the power of the hypnotist over his subject under trance. Although Freud's explanation is only substituting one mystery (of hypnosis) for another, it could be followed up by showing that the processes of projective and introjective identification are the underlying processes in hypnotism.

NON-KLEINIAN USAGE AND CRITIQUES. As psychoanalysis in the United States has begun to lose ground and status, new aspects of ego-psychology have developed. One area of interest has been in the experience of the 'self'; another related interest has been in object-relations (Greenberg and Mitchell, 1983). As a result some interest has turned to the British School of psychoanalysis with an examination, amongst other things, of 'projective identification'. In the process the concept has been taken from the overall framework of Kleinian theory and used in the theoretical framework developed in the United States.

In the process there has been a neglect of all sorts of aspects of projective identification – the particular variety of projective identification that is in operation, its specific intrapsychic purpose, whether the projection is made in hatred or not, the degree of omnipotence in the phantasies and, in fact, a neglect of the phantasy nature of the mechanism. The danger is of a rapidly declining usefulness as the concept comes to be a catch-phrase for all interpersonal phenomena. Unfortunately the concept of projective identification has proved to be as potent a source of confused thinking as the mechanism it indicates.

The different development of psychoanalysis in the United States [see EGO-PSYCHOLOGY] came to emphasize the adaptational aspects of the ego and the interpersonal or cultural influences in development. Consequently 'projective identification' has been adopted for its value (1) as descriptive of the states of fusion between the ego and its objects encountered in psychotic or borderline patients, or (2) as an interpersonal concept that contributes to the psychoanalytic understanding of adaptational processes and the influence of the social context.

(1) **The intrapsychic mechanism.** Interest in projective identification as an *intrapsychic* concept has been particularly in terms of the origin and development of ego-boundaries across which projective identification takes place.

Kernberg: Kernberg (1975) is perhaps the nearest of the ego-psychologists to the British object-relations view. His is a genuine attempt to forge an alloy between ego-psychology and British object-relations theory. Specifically he attempted an integration with Kleinian views and 'projective identification' was used as an important bridging concept between ego-psychology and object-relations theory. He attempted to establish that 'objects' have a primary role which tends to dispose of the notion of primary narcissism:

> . . . in contrast to the traditional psychoanalytic viewpoint according to which there first exists a narcissistic investment of libido and later an object investment of libido . . . it is my belief that the development of normal and pathological narcissism always involves

the relationship of the self to object-representations and external objects . . . The general implication is that the concept of 'primary narcissism' no longer seems warranted because 'metapsychologically', 'primary narcissism' and 'primary object investment' are in effect coincidental. (Kernberg, 1975, p. 341)

Projective identification, being the process of seeing parts of the self in the other, must depend upon and therefore reinforce the self–other boundary. Kernberg, therefore, implicated projective identification in this process from which the ego-boundaries eventually emerge.

Kernberg proposed projective identification as an early mechanism based on splitting processes; projection, in contrast, relied on the later and more sophisticated defence of repression. Another distinction concerned the 'identification' aspect, which he described as an 'empathy with' component of projective identification, which in his definition 'is a primitive form of projection . . . "empathy" is maintained with the real object on to which the projection has occurred, and is linked with an effort to control the object' (Kernberg, 1975, p. 80). Projection is the misperception of the object without any further involvement in it. This pinpointed the quality in projective identification of being able to affect the 'inside' of the object and make it feel something under the control of the subject, and is similar to Klein's insisting on referring to projection *into* the object, as opposed to *on to* the object (Klein, 1946, p. 8n). Kernberg regarded projective identification as arising only when the ego-boundary has been formed, and postulated that since projective identification, being the process of seeing parts of the self in the other, must depend upon the self–other boundary it may be deeply involved in forming it and reinforcing it. Curiously, this places projective identification in an unaccustomed position, since it was originally described from clinical material in which it was implicated in the confusion between self and object (Rosenfeld, 1965). Such conflicting views need to be reconciled.

However, when Kernberg attempted to implant the concept into his theoretical framework, his explanations were couched in terminology of a deeply alien form: '. . . what is projected in a very inefficient way is not "pure aggression", but a self-representation or an object-representation linked with that drive derivative' (Kernberg, 1975, pp. 80–1). 'Self-' and 'object-representations' are not contemporary in development with projective identification in its original form. A 'drive derivative' is substituted for 'a split-off part of the self'. The phantasy notion of concretely felt objects and parts of the self is missing. The effect is a curious hybrid of theoretical terms, in which the concepts of ego-psychology and object-relations theory have become distorted into quite different shapes. What seems to have happened is that there has been an inevitable clash between psychic processes and structures objectively described and unconscious phantasies subjectively experienced. The Kleinian metapsychology couched in terms of the patient's own phantasies has been partially translated into the terminology of an objective science [see SUBJECTIVITY].

Grotstein: At times Grotstein (1981) writes with a strongly Kleinian perspective but also has difficulties shaking off the ego-psychology frame of reference. He, too, attempted to bridge the theoretical divide. Kleinians, he said, have used the concept of projective identification and other primitive defence mechanisms '... to account for the formation of psychotic states rather than seeing them as primitive neurotic mechanisms and, as a consequence of this, they often overlook the normal or neurotic aspects of splitting and projective identification' (Grotstein, 1983, pp. 529–30).

Grotstein's attempts to bring the two theories together did not involve mixing up a cocktail of concepts to see what came out. He used the idea of a 'dual track' development in which primitive and other aspects of the ego exist harmoniously alongside each other.

He tried also to deal in the same relaxed way with the early moments of life when projective identification is most significantly operative; the essential incompatibility between Klein's dismissal of primary narcissism and Mahler's espousal of it could, he thought, be resolved:

> Klein's concept of initial infant mental separateness collides with Mahler's (and others') conception of continuing postnatal primary narcissism or primary identification. The dual track theory allows for each to be correct on two tracks. (Grotstein, 1981, p. 88)

Mahler's (Mahler *et al.*, 1975) experimental confirmation of the classical Freudian view that there is not a separateness in the early weeks and months of life has always been a problem for British object-relations psychoanalysts [see NARCISSISM]. Klein stuck to the logic of her own trajectory and stated categorically that there are 'object-relations at birth'. Only on this basis do the primitive defence mechanisms have any meaning. Projective identification represents the struggles of the infant with those very early relations. Grotstein's efforts to have it both ways at the same time leave an unsatisfying result.

Grotstein was also concerned to distinguish between projection and projective identification, suggesting: '"projection" is the mechanism dealing with the drives which are projected on to objects; whilst the parts of the self, connected with these drives, are dealt with by "projective identification"' (Malin and Grotstein, 1966).

Jacobson: Jacobson (1967) ruled out projective identification as a primitive mechanism on the grounds that the ego does not exist in these very primitive stages. For her, projective identification is a useful concept but one which can only be a sophisticated response in the adult patient and not a repetition of the infantile mechanisms. Rosenfeld (1987) discussed this point of view and argued that Jacobson did not understand that the problem of interpreting to psychotic patients is due to the recurrence of infantile concrete thinking based on projective identification.

The critique of the concept of projective identification as too sophisticated is an important and telling one and points to a significant and profound difference between theories of the earliest functions of the ego. It is true that the ability to get *into* an object and control the way it feels and responds sounds very sophisticated. It is clearly possible to perceive this occurring in both adult patients and child patients in psychoanalysis. But could such a phantasy exist at birth? The answer to this depends on what sort of object it is that the infant is relating to when he begins functioning. On the one hand, those who hold that the ego does not function at birth view the first objects as external objects that are constructed with physical properties when the infant can perceive them when he has the use of his distance receptors, particularly eyes and ears; however, on the other hand the theory of unconscious phantasy would have it that the first objects are constructed as primitive interpretations of basic bodily sensations giving pain or pleasure and the object is therefore an emotional one with motivations but without physical qualities. The question we are left with is whether objects first have an emotional meaning which is later linked with physical objects, or whether they have physical attributes in which an emotional life is eventually discovered.

There must be some validity in the criticism that infants cannot perform their projective identifications in as sophisticated a way as adult patients. The extraordinarily subtle methods of using the analyst that Joseph (1975), for instance, describes are a long way from the simple screaming of an infant which engages mother in his world. The Kleinian description of projective identification as primitive has to be qualified when describing such sophisticated interpersonal manoeuvring, and restricted to the primitive quality of the concreteness of the phantasies behind the subtle methods.

(2) **The interpersonal process.** Projective identification displays a potential for describing interactions between people (Money-Kyrle, 1956) [see COUNTERTRANSFERENCE]. The stressing of this aspect of projective identification above the intrapsychic phantasy functions (Ashbach and Shermer, 1987) can be called the *interpersonal* concept of projective identification.

Ogden: A number of similar concepts in the literature of classical psychoanalysis were noted by Ogden (1979, 1982). He (1982, p. 80) specified them – Anna Freud (1936) 'identification with the aggressor'; Brodey (1965) 'externalization'; Wangh (1962) 'evocation by proxy'; Sandler (1976) 'role actualization' – lumped them all together as a single clinical manifestation, and termed it 'projective identification'.

In this formulation the term covers a complex clinical event of an interpersonal type: one person disowns his feelings and manipulatively induces the other into experiencing them, with consequent visible changes in the behaviour of both. While acknowledging the intra-psychic backdrop, Ogden emphasized observable interpersonal events, the 'interpersonal actualization' (Ogden, 1982, p. 177). These inter-personal happenings are observable and cannot be denied and might therefore introduce some clarity, since the behavioural nature of the term is potentially verifiable in an objective manner. For this reason Ogden's formulation has certainly become popular in the field of interpersonal therapies such as family therapy (Bannister and Pincus, 1965; Zinner and Shapiro, 1972; Box, 1978) and group therapy (for instance Main, 1975; Rogers, 1987).

However, a difference exists between a definition such as Ogden's and the original concept. This difference is difficult to pinpoint: 'The description of these processes suffers from a great handicap, for these phantasies arise at a time when the infant has not yet begun to think in words' (Klein, 1946). Ogden's formulation downgrades the subjective experiencing of the subject and his unconscious phantasies in a fashion similar to other ego-psychological formulations. Nevertheless, the difference is more than that. Joseph (1975 and in many papers), for instance, has adopted a way of describing these phenomena that is quite different from those of Ogden, Kernberg, Grotstein, etc (Sandler, 1988). It is an attempt to *indicate* in clinical material as opposed to an attempt to derive a definition. It is to do with the subjective experience of the *analyst* about which it is also very difficult to think in words, the use to which the analyst is put in being unwittingly drawn into the patient's phantasy world.

The broadening of the concept: A number of people have noted a great broadening of the concept of projective identification. Kernberg, for instance, wrote (1980): 'Projective identification is broadened to include the reaction of the object, that is, an interpersonal process is described as part of an intrapsychic mechanism . . . [This] shift in the definition of the underlying concept creates clinical as well as theoretical problems' (p. 45). He attributed this broadening of the concept to Rosenfeld (1964a). Meissner (1980) attributed the broadening to Bion (1962a and b) and Segal (1957). On the other hand, Spillius (1983) attributed it to Americans such as Ogden (1979):

. . . the concept is now used by non-Kleinians, and papers are even being written about it in the United States. In the course of such general popularity the concept has been widened and is sometimes used loosely. (Spillius, 1983, p. 321)

What Kleinians call a loose use of the term results in large measure from the complaint by non-Kleinians against keeping the concept tied into the whole package of the paranoid-schizoid position. Others have disposed of a fair amount of Kleinian baggage: distinctions between (a) pathological or normal projective identification; (b) omnipotent phantasy or empathy; (c) part-objects or whole objects; and the acceptance of (a) secondary, defensive fusions described by Rosenfeld as opposed to primary narcissism, and (b) unconscious phantasy and subjective meaning as opposed to objective mechanisms and structures. Whether the resulting concept that is 'written about in the United States' is a useful one is no longer perhaps a Kleinian issue, but judging by the profusion of papers, both for and against, opinion is very divided.

Meissner: The most testing of the ego-psychology critiques of projective identification is the paper by Meissner (1980). In part his arguments deal with the Kleinian concept [see SYMBOLIC EQUATION] and in part with the American broadening towards an interpersonal concept: '. . . overextension and application of the term have led to a situation in which it has acquired multiple and at times inappropriate meanings, resulting in evacuation of the meaningfulness of the term' (p. 43).

He agreed that projective identification includes diffusion of ego-boundaries, loss of self–object differentiation and taking the object as a part of the self, all of which are key elements of the ego-psychology view of psychosis, and the term is meaningful on this strictly limited basis. It is when the term is used outside its reference to psychotic patients, Meissner believed, that trouble begins. His various points may be listed:

(a) The description (Klein, 1959) of empathy as based on projective identification is one such broadening of the term to which Meissner objected, since there is no loss of ego-boundaries during moments of empathy.

(b) Bion's theory of containers [see CONTAINING] is, Meissner argues, a sloppy extension of the term:

> . . . projective identification becomes a metaphor, translated loosely into the terms of container and contained, which applies to almost any form of relational or cognitional phenomenon in which the common notes of relation, containment or implication can be appealed to. (1980, p. 59)

It loses its precise reference to psychotic experience. If projective identification is not strictly confined to psychosis, Meissner complained, but is described in conditions in which there is good reality appreciation of self and object, then the term collapses into simple 'projection' and therefore generates confusion.

(c) Similarly Meissner argued that the significance Segal gives in symbolic equation (Segal, 1957) is equally unwarranted, and he mounts specific arguments to the effect that the concrete use of symbols which Segal described is not necessarily a result of projective identification. He appealed to the 'palaeological' pre-Aristotelian forms of thinking described by Von Domarus (1944) [see SYMBOLIC EQUATION].

(d) Meissner then dealt with the mushrooming use of the term 'projective identification' as an interpersonal description (Zinner and Shapiro, 1972; Greenspan and Mannoni, 1975; Slipp, 1973). In these he noted that the term refers to complex projective–introjective processes in family systems, *among* people:

> The basic question that must be raised in objection to the use of projective identification in these contexts is whether complex interactions addressed by these concepts in fact involve anything more than complex interactions of projection and introjection. (1980, p. 62)

He condemned the extrapolation to *inter*personal contexts on the grounds that it again moves away from the phenomena of psychosis.

(e) Meissner, correctly, pointed out that the use of the term 'projective identification' implied a set of unexpressed assumptions – the nature of instinctual conflict, the earliest stages of processing these instinctual elements, object–self confusion as a defence. Consequently, the term has become distorted by being grafted on to other sets of assumptions – primary narcissism, object–self confusion as a primary anxiety, the objectivity of psychoanalytic observation.

Countertransference: The development of the concept of projective identification coincided with the new appreciation of countertransference. In Britain at least both developments were probably interlocking and enhanced each other. Because of the interpersonal aspect of projective identification it has a bearing on the transference–countertransference relationship. However, it can lead to simplistic methods of conducting analysis. To interpret projective identification in clinical material on the basis of the analyst's reactions can lead to the suspicion that the analyst is merely attributing his own feelings, without further thought, to the patient, and omnipotently 'knows' the patient's feelings in this directly intuitive way. Such a rationalization for wild analysis was condemned by Finell (1986). She used vignettes offered by both Ogden and Grotstein to show the analyst's evasions and defensive omnipotence. This criticism of a simplistic use of 'projective identification' in the countertransference is valid, as Rosenfeld (1972) also indicated. Superficial interpretations of this kind lead the patient to act on the assumption that the analyst is defending himself against the patient's projections; and Grinberg (1962) pointed out that in some instances of this kind the patient may feel that he is being forced to receive the analyst's projective identifications [see COUNTERTRANSFERENCE]. Along these lines, Dorpat (1983) argued that the term be put out of use altogether.

There is often an agreement between Kleinians and non-Kleinians at the clinical level about certain extreme moments in the transference–countertransference situation which are characterized by the analyst finding himself off guard and caught into some movement *with* the patient away from the analytic situation. Joseph (1975) described some extremely subtle manifestations of this by attending to the way patients *used* the analyst, and the excitement it gave the patient to succeed in this use. It is not a use of the analyst to represent something – a parental figure, etc. – but a use to avoid certain experiences of dependence, jealousy, separation, envy. This use needs to be displayed to the patient in order to help him with his excitement and triumph. Kernberg (1988) described a situation in which a patient fully believed that the analyst had acted outside the session in a way that was detrimental to the patient, and became more and more angry when the analyst would not admit to such an act until the analyst himself became frightened of being physically attacked by the patient. In this case the patient's powerful invitation to be drawn into enacting something was resisted. The analyst's recourse in this case was to step outside the analytic setting by stating that the analysis could not proceed unless the patient could give a guarantee that he would not assault the analyst physically. Kernberg defended his non-interpretative handling of these attempted projections into himself on the grounds that with certain especially aggressive patients it is necessary to introduce such a parameter into the analysis. These alternative techniques – either pursuing interpretations or introducing parameters – require further comparative assessment.

Kernberg's procedure is based on the view that the extreme aggressiveness represents a primary ego-defect, a regression to the barely formed state of the ego as it begins to emerge through projective identification. In this sense the violence displayed towards the analyst is a very different phenomenon from the Kleinian view of the destructive effects of projective identification upon the analyst aimed at dissolving boundaries by controlling him. Kernberg's assertion of control of the session was required, in his view, to make up for his patient's uncertain control.

This raises an important debate which was also hinted at in Meissner's last point ((e) above): in what context of assumptions should the term 'projective identification' be used? Does 'projective identification' remain the same concept if psychotic ego-defects are assumed to arise from the primary absence of ego-boundaries (primary narcissism) as opposed to the view that psychotic ego-defects arise from the omnipotent phantasies involved in projective identification? Quite different views of the origins of psychosis lead to quite different assessments of the meaning and value of the term and of what to do about it. There appears to be no consensus on the value of the term 'projective identification' outside the Kleinian conceptual framework.

Abraham, Karl (1924) 'A short study of the development of the libido', in Karl Abraham (1927) *Selected Papers on Psycho-Analysis*. Hogarth, pp. 418–501.

Ashbach, C. and Shermer, Vic (1987) 'Interactive and group dimensions of Kleinian theory', *Journal of the Melanie Klein Society* 5:43–68.

Bannister, K. and Pincus, L. (1965) *Shared Phantasy in Marital Problems*. Hitchin: Codicote.

Bibring, E. (1947) 'The so-called English school of psycho-analysis', *Psycho-Anal. Q.* 16:69–93.

Bick, Esther (1964) 'Notes on infant observation in psycho-analytic training', *Int. J. Psycho-Anal.* 45:558–66; republished (1987) in Martha Harris and Esther Bick, *The Collected Papers of Martha Harris and Esther Bick*. Perth: Clunie, pp. 240–56.

—— (1968) 'The experience of the skin in early object relations', *Int. J. Psycho-Anal.* 49:484–6; republished (1987) in *The Collected Papers of Martha Harris and Esther Bick*, pp. 114–18.

Bion, Wilfred (1957) 'Differentiation of the psychotic from the non-psychotic personalities', *Int. J. Psycho-Anal.* 38:266–75; republished (1967) in W. R. Bion, *Second Thoughts*. Heinemann, pp. 43–64.

—— (1959) 'Attacks on linking', *Int. J. Psycho-Anal.* 40:308–15; republished (1967) in *Second Thoughts*, pp. 93–109.

—— (1961) *Experiences in Groups*. Tavistock.

—— (1962a) 'Theory of thinking', *Int. J. Psycho-Anal.* 43:306–10; republished (1967) in *Second Thoughts*, pp. 110–19.

—— (1962b) *Learning from Experience*. Heinemann.

—— (1970) *Attention and Interpretation*. Tavistock.

Box, S. (1978) 'An analytic approach to work with families', *Journal of Adolescence* 1:119–33.

Brenman Pick, Irma (1985) 'Working through in   ounter-transference', *Int. J. Psycho-Anal.* 66:157–66.

Brodey, Warren (1965) 'On the dynamics of narcissism: I Externalization and early ego development', *Psychoanal. Study Child* 20:165–93.

Dorpat, T. L. (1983) 'Book review of *Splitting and Projective Identification* by J. S. Grotstein', *Int. J. Psycho-Anal.* 64:116–19.

Finell, Janet (1986) 'The merits and problems with the concept of projective identification', *Psychoanal. Rev.* 73:104–20.

Freud, Anna (1936) *The Ego and the Mechanisms of Defence.* Hogarth.

Freud, Sigmund (1895) 'Draft H – paranoia', in James Strachey, ed. *The Standard Edition of the Complete Psychological Works of Sigmund Freud*, 24 vols. Hogarth, 1953–73. vol. 1, pp. 206–12.

—— (1920) *Beyond the Pleasure Principle.* S.E. 18, pp. 3–64.

—— (1921) *Group Psychology and the Analysis of the Ego.* S.E. 18, pp. 67–143.

—— (1923) *The Ego and the Id.* S.E. 19, pp. 3–66.

Greenberg, Jay and Mitchell, Stephen (1983) *Object Relations in Psycho-Analytic Theory.* Cambridge, MA: Harvard.

Greenspan, S. I. and Mannoni, F. V. (1975) 'A model for brief intervention with couples based on projective identification', *American Journal of Psychiatry* 131:1103–6.

Grinberg, Leon (1962) 'On a specific aspect of counter-transference due to the patient's projective identification', *Int. J. Psycho-Anal.* 43: 436–40.

Grotstein, James (1981) *Splitting and Projective Identification.* New York: Jason Aronson.

—— (1983) 'The significance of Kleinian contributions to psycho-analysis: IV Critiques of Klein', *Int. J. Psycho-Anal. Psychother.* 9:511–35.

Heimann, Paula (1950) 'On counter-transference', *Int. J. Psycho-Anal.* 31:81–4.

Isaacs, Susan (1948) 'The nature and function of phantasy', *Int. J. Psycho-Anal.* 29:73–97; republished (1952) in Melanie Klein, Paula Heimann, Susan Isaacs and Joan Riviere, eds *Developments in Psycho-Analysis.* Hogarth, pp. 67–121.

Jacobson, Edith (1967) *Psychotic Conflict and Reality.* Hogarth.

Jaques, Elliott (1953) 'On the dynamics of social structure', *Human Relations* 6:3–23; republished (1955) as 'Social systems as a defence against persecutory and depressive anxiety', in Melanie Klein, Paula Heimann and Roger Money-Kyrle, eds (1955) *New Directions in Psycho-Analysis.* Tavistock, pp. 478–98.

Jones, Ernest (1916) 'The theory of symbolism', *Br. J. Psychol.* 9:181–229.

Joseph, Betty (1975) 'The patient who is difficult to reach', in Peter Giovacchini, ed. *Tactics and Techniques in Psycho-Analytic Therapy*, vol. 2. New York: Jason Aronson, pp. 205–16.

—— (1981) 'Towards the experiencing of psychic pain', in James Grotstein, ed. (1981) *Do I Dare Disturb the Universe?* Beverly Hills: Caesura, pp. 93–102.

—— (1982) 'On addiction to near death', *Int. J. Psycho-Anal.* 63:449–56.

Kernberg, Otto (1969) 'A contribution to the ego-psychological critique of the Kleinian school', *Int. J. Psycho-Anal.* 50:317–33.

—— (1975) *Borderline Conditions and Psychological Narcissism.* New York: Jason Aronson.

—— (1980) *Internal World and External Reality.* New York: Jason Aronson.

—— (1988) 'Projection and projective identification: developmental and clinical aspects', in Joseph Sandler, ed. (1988) *Projection, Identification, Projective Identification*. Karnac, pp. 93–115.

Klein, Melanie (1927) 'Criminal tendencies in normal children', in *The Writings of Melanie Klein*, vol. 1. Hogarth, pp. 170–85.

—— (1929) 'Personification in the play of children', *The Writings of Melanie Klein*, vol. 1, pp. 199–209.

—— (1930a) 'The psychotherapy of the psychoses', *The Writings of Melanie Klein*, vol. 1, pp. 233–5.

—— (1930b) 'The importance of symbol-formation in the development of the ego', *The Writings of Melanie Klein*, vol. 1, pp. 219–32.

—— (1935) 'A contribution to the psychogenesis of manic-depressive states', *The Writings of Melanie Klein*, vol. 1, pp. 262–89.

—— (1946) 'Notes on some schizoid mechanisms', *The Writings of Melanie Klein*, vol. 3, pp. 1–24.

—— (1952) 'On observing the behaviour of young infants', *The Writings of Melanie Klein*, vol. 3, pp. 94–121.

—— (1955) 'On identification', *The Writings of Melanie Klein*, vol. 3, pp. 141–75.

—— (1957) *Envy and Gratitude*, *The Writings of Melanie Klein*, vol. 3, pp. 176–235.

—— (1959) 'Our adult world and its roots in infancy', *The Writings of Melanie Klein*, vol. 3, pp. 247–63.

Mahler, Margaret, Pine, Fred and Bergman, Anni (1975) *The Psychological Birth of the Human Infant*. Hutchinson.

Main, T. F. (1975) 'Some psychodynamics of large groups', in Lionel Kreeger, ed. (1984) *The Large Group*. Constable, pp. 57–86.

Malin, A. and Grotstein, James (1966) 'Projective identification in the therapeutic process', *Int. J. Psycho-Anal.* 47:26–31.

Meissner, W. W. (1980) 'A note on projective identification', *J. Amer. Psychoanal. Assn.* 28:43–65.

Meltzer, Donald (1967) *The Psycho-Analytical Process*. Heinemann.

Meltzer, Donald, Bremner, John, Hoxter, Shirley, Weddell, Doreen and Wittenberg, Isca (1975) *Explorations in Autism*. Perth: Clunie.

Money-Kyrle, Roger (1956) 'Normal counter-transference and some of its deviations', *Int. J. Psycho-Anal.* 37:360–6; republished (1978) in *The Collected Papers of Roger Money-Kyrle*. Perth: Clunie, pp. 330–42.

Ogden, Thomas (1979) 'On projective identification', *Int. J. Psycho-Anal.* 60:357–73.

—— (1982) *Projective Identification and Psychotherapeutic Technique*. New York: Jason Aronson.

Orford, Frank (1987) personal communication.

O'Shaughnessy, Edna (1975) 'Explanatory notes', in *The Writings of Melanie Klein*, vol. 3. Hogarth, pp. 324–36.

Rodrigue, Emilio (1955) 'The analysis of a three-year-old mute schizo-phrenic', in Melanie Klein, Paula Heimann and Roger Money-Kyrle, eds (1955) *New Directions in Psycho-Analysis*. Tavistock, pp. 140–79.

Rogers, Cynthia (1987) 'On putting it into words: the balance between projective identification and dialogue in the group', *Group Analysis* 20: 99–107.

Rosenfeld, Herbert (1947) 'Analysis of a schizophrenic state with depersonalization', in Herbert Rosenfeld (1965) *Psychotic States*. Hogarth, pp. 13–33; originally published *Int. J. Psycho-Anal.* 28:130–9.

—— (1952) 'Notes on the psycho-analysis of the superego conflict in an acute schizophrenic', in *Psychotic States*, pp. 63–103; originally published *Int. J. Psycho-Anal.* 33:111–31.

—— (1964a) 'Object relations of the acute schizophrenic patient in the transference situation', in Solomon and Glueck, eds *Recent Research on Schizophrenia*. Washington: American Psychiatric Association.

—— (1964b) 'On the psychopathology of narcissism: a clinical approach', *Int. J. Psycho-Anal.* 45:332–7; republished (1965) in *Psychotic States*, pp. 169–79.

—— (1965) *Psychotic States*. Hogarth.

—— (1971) 'A clinical approach to the psycho-analytical theory of the life and death instincts: an investigation into the aggressive aspects of narcissism', *Int. J. Psycho-Anal.* 52:169–78.

—— (1972) 'A critical appreciation of James Strachey's paper on the nature of the therapeutic action of psycho-analysis', *Int. J. Psycho-Anal.* 53:455–61.

—— (1983) 'Primitive object relations and mechanisms', *Int. J. Psycho-Anal.* 64:261–7.

—— (1987) *Impasse and Interpretation*. Tavistock.

Sandler, Joseph (1976) 'Dreams, unconscious phantasies and "identity of perception"', *Int. Rev. Psycho-Anal.* 3:33–42.

—— ed. (1988) *Projection, Identification, Projective Identification*. Karnac.

Schmideberg, Melitta (1931) 'A contribution to the psychology of persecutory ideas and delusions', *Int. J. Psycho-Anal.* 12:331–67.

Searl, Mina (1932) 'A note on depersonalization', *Int. J. Psycho-Anal.* 13: 329–47.

Segal, Hanna (1950) 'Some aspects of the analysis of a schizophrenic', *Int. J. Psycho-Anal.* 31:268–78; republished (1981) in *The Work of Hanna Segal*. New York: Jason Aronson, pp. 101–20.

—— (1956) 'Depression in the schizophrenic', *Int. J. Psycho-Anal.* 37:339–43; republished (1981) in *The Work of Hanna Segal*, pp. 121–30.

—— (1957) 'Notes on symbol formation', *Int. J. Psycho-Anal.* 38:391–7; republished (1981) in *The Work of Hanna Segal*, pp. 49–65.

Slipp, S. (1973) 'The symbiotic survival pattern', *Family Process* 12:377–98.

Spillius, Elizabeth Bott (1983) 'Some developments from the work of Melanie Klein', *Int. J. Psycho-Anal.* 64:321–32.

—— (1988) *Melanie Klein Today: Volume 1 Mainly Theory*. Tavistock.

Stern, Daniel (1985) *The Interpersonal World of the Infant*. New York: Basic.

Tustin, Frances (1981) *Autistic States in Children*. Routledge & Kegan Paul.

—— (1986) *Autistic Barriers in Neurotic Patients*. Karnac.

Von Domarus (1944) 'The specific laws of logic in schizophrenia', in Jacob Kasanin, ed. *Language and Thought in Schizophrenia*. Berkeley: University of California Press.

Waelder, Robert (1937) 'The problem of the genesis of psychical conflict in earliest infancy', *Int. J. Psycho-Anal.* 18: 406–73.

Wangh, Martin (1962) 'The "evocation of a proxy": a psychological maneuver, its use as a defence, its purposes and genesis', *Psychoanal. Study Child* 17:451–72.

Zinner, J. and Shapiro, R. (1972) 'Projective identification as a mode of perception and behaviour in families of adolescents', *Int. J. Psycho-Anal.* 53:523–30.

B General Entries

Note: In references, *S.E.* = James Strachey, ed. *The Standard Edition of the Complete Psychological Works of Sigmund Freud*, 24 vols. Hogarth, 1953–73.

WMK = *The Writings of Melanie Klein.* Hogarth.

Karl Abraham

Biography. Born in Germany, 1877, Abraham became interested in psychoanalysis while a trainee psychiatrist in Zurich with Jung. In 1907 he began a psychoanalytic practice in Berlin, the first in Germany, and he founded the German Psycho-Analytical Society in 1910. He became President of the International Psycho-Analytical Association in 1924, but then died at the height of his professional abilities and reputation in 1925 (Hilda Abraham, 1974).

He was persuaded by Melanie Klein to analyse her in 1924, though this was interrupted some fifteen months later by his ill-health. He also analysed a number of English analysts including James Glover, Edward Glover and Alix Strachey. He had a special position within the psychoanalytic movement as he, with Jung (in Zurich), Ferenczi (in Budapest) and Jones (in London), was one of the first pioneers of psychoanalysis outside Vienna. But more than that, his importance is as an outstanding clinical observer.

SCIENTIFIC CONTRIBUTIONS. Abraham's main contributions were in his collaboration with Freud in trying to understand the psychoses (Abraham, 1911). Since these conditions were so narcissistic, psychotic patients did not make a typical transference and contemporary psychoanalysts could not work with them. Their investigation of psychosis was therefore an investigation of narcissism [see NARCISSISM]. However, Abraham exploited the fact that manic-depressive psychosis went through phases of remission in which the patients were, on the surface, normal enough. He analysed patients during these 'normal' phases with a view to finding the underlying predispositions for the psychotic phases.

Pregenital phases of development: Abraham confirmed clinically that there were *fixation points* specific to the psychoses in the very early phases of the libidinal development (oral and anal phases). This had been expected on the grounds that narcissism was postulated as the primary state of the infant, and that the narcissism of psychotic regression resulted from a fixation at that early period. Abraham showed clear evidence of the oral and anal impulses in these conditions, and he described these magnificently in his great summary work (Abraham, 1924). In particular, he found that the oral and anal phases are represented by the prominence of *introjection* (oral taking in) and *projection* (anal expelling) [see INTROJECTION; PROJECTION]. The manic-depressive psychosis seems to be a preoccupation with repeated cycles of incorporating and expelling, connected with extreme anxiety about the objects taken in or expelled.

At the same time he also confirmed that these phases were especially scarred by profoundly aggressive and *sadistic* impulses. As a result he refined the 'timetable' of the libidinal phases [see LIBIDO]. The idea of sadistic forms of introjection and projection was later greatly enhanced by Klein [see 3. AGGRESSION].

Abraham's interest, therefore, was in the multiple manifestations of sadism and aggressiveness – for instance, his paper (1919) on difficult patients is a celebrated description of the hidden manifestations of aggression.

Narcissism and object-relations: However, Abraham's death left his work incomplete. Although he was investigating the phase of primary narcissism, which he and Freud thought at the time lasted from birth to about the age of two, he was actually describing the incorporation and expulsion of objects or bits of objects. There still remains today disagreement about the nature of object-relations during the period of primary narcissism [see NARCISSISM]. Abraham's work, in a rather sketchy way, suggested that the infant does relate to objects at this primary stage but they are very odd sorts of objects, which he called partial, or *part-objects*; and he was at pains to describe the development at a later stage of true object-love [see PART-OBJECTS; WHOLE OBJECT; LOVE]. This distinction was of great importance in Klein's development of the idea of the depressive position [see 10. DEPRESSIVE POSITION].

Klein's debt to Abraham is enormous, not just in analysing her but in giving her a background of soundly based theory to develop. Klein was important to Abraham, too, since her work with children was bringing confirmatory evidence about his postulates of the sadism of the early pregenital phases and of the importance of introjection and projection [see CHILD ANALYSIS]. Though Abraham, like Freud, barely mentions Klein, it is possible that his own observations in 1924 drew from the material Melanie Klein was reporting from 1919 onwards.

Abraham, Hilda (1974) 'Karl Abraham: an unfinished biography', *Int. Rev. Psycho-Anal.* 1:17–72.

Abraham, Karl (1911) 'Notes on the psycho-analytic investigation and treatment of manic-depressive insanity and allied conditions', in Karl Abraham (1927) *Selected Papers on Psycho-Analysis*. Hogarth, pp. 137–56.

—— (1919) 'A particular form of neurotic resistance against the psycho-analytic method', in *Selected Papers on Psycho-Analysis*, pp. 303–11.

—— (1924) 'A short study of the libido, viewed in the light of mental disorders', in *Selected Papers on Psycho-Analysis*, pp. 418–501.

Acting-in

Relations between the analyst and the patient may enact primitive impulses, object relations or defences and form a resistance to the work of analysis (Freud, 1914). That enactment in the transference has been called 'acting-in' (Sandler, Holder and Dare, 1973). In Freud's time resistance and defence were assumed to express themselves in the transference as a disturbance to the free associations. But Betty Joseph makes the transference important in another way. It is for 'looking at the way in which patients use us – analysts – to help them with anxiety' (Joseph, 1978, p. 223) [see COUNTERTRANSFERENCE].

Working with severe borderline personalities, Joseph (1975) described a form of impasse encountered in analysis as an *unreachability*. She was drawn towards detailed examination of the way the patient uses the analyst for his own purposes in order to help him with his anxiety [see PSYCHIC EQUILIBRIUM].

The kind of contact engaged in with the analyst is one in which the analyst and patient together talk *about* the patient. He is not emotionally moved by the analyst's interpretations but may be very thoughtfully co-operative. An alliance forms but it 'turns out to be inimical to a real alliance and what is termed understanding is actually anti-understanding' (Joseph, 1975, p. 49). Joseph conceptualized this in terms of two separate parts of the patient. One part 'may appear to be working and co-operating with the analyst but [this] part of the personality that is available is actually keeping another more needy or potentially responsive and receptive part split off' (Joseph, 1975, p. 48). The available and essentially observing part of the personality is 'used to ward off the analyst' (Joseph, 1975, p. 52). The purpose of this structure is to create a 'kind of balance ... Repeatedly we experienced a sequence in which within one session he made progress, became deeply involved and moved by what was going on, but the following day it was a mere flat memory' (Joseph, 1975, p. 55).

Sometimes this is achieved by projecting into the analyst an interested or concerned part of the patient so that the analyst is expected to act out the concern and wish to get something done. Sometimes the understanding part of the patient is projected into the analyst and the patient expects omnipotent and omniscient understanding from the analyst; sometimes large parts of the ego are projected so that the patient becomes very apathetic; sometimes the sane part of the patient is projected and he then appears stupid [see 13. PROJECTIVE IDENTIFICATION].

The character of this impasse appeared to give rise to specific features of the transference [see TRANSFERENCE]:

> Much of our understanding of the transference comes through our understanding of how our patients act on us for many varied reasons; how they try to draw us into their defensive systems; how they unconsciously act out with us in the transference, trying to get us to act out with them; how they convey aspects of their inner world built up from infancy – elaborated in childhood and adulthood, experiences often beyond the use of words, which we

can only capture through the feelings aroused in us, through our counter-transference. (Joseph, 1985, p. 62)

In the transference something is *constantly* going on, the analyst is constantly being used. This is not the analysis of resistance and defence, it is the playing out, in the relationship with the analyst, of subtle and often extremely obscure object-relations. The analyst is subjected to unconscious manoeuvring (of his unconscious) in order that the patient can organize the parts of himself, and his internal objects, to 'help him with his anxiety'. The patient's words have therefore to be listened to, not firstly for their content, but more for what they are aimed at doing to the analyst and his mind.

Other Kleinian analysts have recently supported these conclusions:

The patient does not only express himself in words. He also uses actions, and sometimes words and actions. The analyst listens, observes and feels the patient's communications. He scrutinizes his own responses to the patient, trying to understand the effects the patient's behaviour has on himself, and he understands this as a communication from the patient (while being aware of those responses which come from his own personality). It is this, comprehended in its totality, that is presented to the patient as an interpretation. (Riesenberg-Malcolm, 1986, p. 434)

Segal (1982) putting it succinctly wrote 'early infantile development is reflected in the infantile part of the transference. When it is well integrated it gives rise to underlying non-verbal communication which gives a depth to other communications. When not integrated it gives rise to acting in as a primitive mode of communication' (Segal, 1982, p. 21).

Joseph showed that patients attempt to preserve a psychic equilibrium, poised uncertainly between the paranoid-schizoid position and the depressive position (Joseph, 1989) [see PSYCHIC EQUILIBRIUM]. Movement towards the depressive position seems particularly blocked, by a specific form of psychic pain [see PSYCHIC PAIN].

Borderline personalities especially seem to feel their equilibrium is precarious and they resort to an organization of their defences that is extremely rigid. These states are associated with development under the dominance of the death instinct and destructiveness [see DEATH INSTINCT] and these organizations often involve the dominance of 'bad' parts of the self over 'good' ones [see PATHOLOGICAL ORGANIZATIONS].

Freud, Sigmund (1914) 'Remembering, repeating and working-through', *S.E.* 12, pp. 145–56.
Joseph, Betty (1975) 'The patient who is difficult to reach', in Peter

Giovacchini, ed. *Tactics and Techniques in Psycho-Analytic Therapy*, vol. 2. New York: Jason Aronson, pp. 205–16.

—— (1978) 'Different types of anxiety and their handling in the analytic situation', *Int. J. Psycho-Anal.* 59:223–8.

—— (1985) 'Transference – the total situation', *Int. J. Psycho-Anal.* 66:291–8.

—— (1989) *Psychic Equilibrium and Psychic Change*. Routledge.

Riesenberg-Malcolm, Ruth (1986) 'Interpretation: the past in the present', *Int. Rev. Psycho-Anal.* 13:433–43.

Sandler, Joseph, Dare, Christopher and Holder, Alex (1973) *The Patient and the Analyst*. George Allen & Unwin.

Segal, Hanna (1982) 'Early infantile development as reflected in the psycho-analytic process: steps in integration', *Int. J. Psycho-Anal.* 63:15–21.

Adhesive identification

The concept of 'adhesive identification' was described by Bick in the early 1970s (Bick, 1986) and by Meltzer (1975). Bick's work in developing a rigorous method of infant observation (Bick, 1964, 1968) produced new ideas about the very earliest moments of life, the first object and the first introjection [see INFANT OBSERVATION; SKIN]. In cases where this fails the earliest stages of development go wrong, as projective identification cannot be properly employed because of an absent sense of internal space [see INTERNAL REALITY]. Meltzer (Meltzer *et al.*, 1975) took up these ideas and found them important in research into a child-analytic technique with autistic children. Meltzer described a child who

> ... tended to draw pictures of houses, in which there was a house on this side of the paper, and there was a house on the other side of the paper and when you held it up to the light, you saw that the doors were superimposed, you know, a kind of house where you open the front door and step out the back door at the same time. (Meltzer, 1975, p. 300)

In the course of this collaboration, Bick and Meltzer began to recognize a pattern in these 'second-skin' formations [see SKIN]. Bick typically called it an act of mimicry. However, what they began to realize was that the mimicry represented the experience, and phantasy, of sticking *to* an object as opposed to projecting *into* it [see 13. PROJECTIVE IDENTIFICATION]. A lapse in developing a sense of internal spaces leads to a tendency to relate to objects in a two-dimensional way, without depth [see AUTISM]:

> This baby had to make the most of his mother just touching him so that he could go to sleep again. During the bath when mother took off the clothes he started quivering and shivering ... perhaps he was cold because the clothes were taken off, but that was made

unlikely by the fact that when mother touched him with a piece of wet cotton wool he also stopped shivering. I would suggest that this touching derives its power from its significance as an adhesion, as a re-establishment of feeling stuck on to mother. (Bick, 1986, p. 297)

See SKIN

Bick, Esther (1964) 'Notes on infant observation in psycho-analytic training', *Int. J. Psycho-Anal.* 45:558–66; republished (1987) in Martha Harris and Esther Bick, *The Collected Papers of Martha Harris and Esther Bick*. Perth: Clunie, pp. 240–56.
—— (1968) 'The experience of the skin in early object relations', *Int. J. Psycho-Anal.* 49:484–6; republished (1987) in *The Collected Papers of Martha Harris and Esther Bick*, pp. 114–18.
—— (1986) 'Further considerations of the function of the skin in early object relations', *Br. J. Psychother.* 2:292–9.
Meltzer, Donald (1975) 'Adhesive identification', *Contemporary Psycho-Analysis* 11:289–310.
Meltzer, Donald, Bremner, John, Hoxter, Shirley, Weddell, Doreen and Wittemberg, Isca (1975) *Explorations in Autism*. Perth: Clunie.

Aggression

Shortly after the First World War, Freud (1920) belatedly admitted the importance of aggression. At that point, the evidence of the deep well of destructiveness in human beings drove him to give it equal priority to the libido [see DEATH INSTINCT]. Heated dispute has raged since then. Some (e.g. Glover, 1933) believe an instinctual source of aggressiveness to be pessimistic; they regard aggression as deriving from frustration of libido and other instincts. However, it is generally accepted that aggression – whether of internal (instinctual) origin or of environmental origin (frustration of the libido) – is of an importance rivalling that of sexuality.

Klein was foremost amongst those who regarded aggression as instinctual [see 3. AGGRESSION; DEATH INSTINCT]. However, by emphasizing unconscious phantasies she was supporting Freud's view that the instincts in human beings are extraordinarily malleable. Therefore the multiple manifestations of aggression demonstrate its changeability and its potential for contributing to the development of the mind, as well as its disorders. Klein thought that the inevitability of aggression in itself was neither optimistic nor pessimistic; each individual engages in his or her own personal struggle against his or her own aggressive impulses. In fact, Klein was of the view that this destructiveness was an important factor in the development of the libido, a view which led her to be criticized, incorrectly, as demoting the core theories of psychoanalysis – the phases of the libido, sexuality and the Oedipus complex (Glover, 1945; Yorke, 1971).

With the development in later years (especially following Rosenfeld,

1971) of an understanding of negative narcissism, Kleinian clinical practice tends now to have a primary focus on the organization of destructiveness in the personality [see STRUCTURE].

Freud, Sigmund (1920) *Beyond the Pleasure Principle. S.E.* 18, pp. 3–64.
Glover, Edward (1933) *War, Sadism and Pacifism.* George Allen & Unwin.
—— (1945) 'An examination of the Klein system of child psychology', *Psychoanal. Study Child* 1:3–43.
Rosenfeld, Herbert (1971) 'A clinical approach to the psycho-analytic theory of the life and death instincts: an investigation into the aggressive aspects of narcissism', *Int. J. Psycho-Anal.* 52:169–78.
Yorke, Clifford (1971) 'Some suggestions for a critique of Kleinian psychology', *Psychoanal. Study Child* 29:129–55.

Alpha-function

Bion's descriptions were influenced by his interest in mathematics, and he was intent on deriving similar general theorems within psychoanalysis. In a curious, obscure and intensely stimulating theoretical leap, Bion (1962a, 1962b) generated the neutral term 'alpha-function' as a kind of psychoanalytic algebraic notation that was to be defined by practical results but was initially devoid of meaning:

> It seemed convenient to suppose an alpha-function to convert sense data into alpha-elements and thus provide the psyche with the material for dream thoughts and hence the capacity to wake up or go to sleep, to be conscious or unconscious. (Bion, 1962a, p. 115)

The concept came from Bion's investigations of the schizophrenic's problem of applying meaning to his experiences. When Isaacs called unconscious phantasy the 'mental representative of instinct' she conveyed a conversion process of some kind across the body/mind discontinuum. Bion gave the conversion process the name 'alpha-function' and began to fill in the clinical detail – when it works adequately, and when not [see BION]. The term 'alpha-function' stands for the unknown process involved in taking raw sense data and generating out of it mental contents which have meaning, and can be used for thinking. These resulting products of alpha-function are *alpha-elements* (or alpha-particles).

When alpha-function does not work, the sense data remain unassimilated *beta-elements* which are developed by expulsion of a violent kind (projective identification) [see BETA-ELEMENTS]. As elements of alpha-function Bion postulated (i) a pre-existing 'pre-conception', a kind of anticipation, possibly even inherent, which, he says, must meet (ii) a 'realization', some occurrence in actual reality, which fits, hand in glove, with the pre-conception; this union of the one within the other creates (iii) a 'conception' which is mentally usable for further thought [see LINKING]. This paradigm of the union of two elements to create a third is the basic building block of mind, of thoughts, of theories [see CONTAINING]. Integral with this process is an emotional one in which splits join into a whole, a process he cryptically denotes 'Ps-D', which is related to Klein's theory of the depressive position [see Ps-D]. The accumulation of alpha-elements (thoughts) creates an apparatus for thinking (concepts, theoretical structures, etc.); rather than, as in other theories of thinking, the apparatus for thinking creates thoughts. The failure of alpha-function [see BETA-ELEMENTS] gives rise to the accumulation of beta-elements and the creation of an apparatus for ridding the mind of unwanted contents.

See CONTAINING; THINKING; REVERIE

Bion, Wilfred (1962a) 'A theory of thinking', in W. R. Bion (1967) *Second Thoughts*. Heinemann, pp. 110–19; previously published (1962) *Int. J. Psycho-Anal.* 43:306–10.
—— (1962b) *Learning from Experience*. Heinemann.
—— (1970) *Attention and Interpretation*. Tavistock.

Ambivalence

Psychoanalysis has always been theoretically based in the notion of mental conflict, and *ambivalence* means the holding of contradictory feeling states in the relationship towards one object. Freud had described the bisexuality of the human organism, giving rise to both normal and reversed oedipal complexes, with the result that love and hate can be felt about both parents. This idea was greatly enhanced by Freud's postulate of a duality of instincts (libido and death instinct). Klein elevated this state of ambivalence to a central place in the key concept of the depressive position [see 10. DEPRESSIVE POSITION].

Conflicting feelings may, in contrast, be alternated, in states that are dissociated mentally from each other, or split [see SPLITTING], giving rise to considerable instability as love and hate abruptly give way to each other [see IDEAL OBJECT]; or impulses may be fused: for example the mixture of libido and destructiveness (sadism), giving rise to an excited sexual sadistic perversion.

See CONFLICT; INSTINCTS

Annihilation

The history of psychoanalysis has been one of trying to understand the core anxiety of the human condition. Freud (1926) enshrined this search in the term *early anxiety-(danger) situation* [see 8. EARLY ANXIETY-SITUATIONS], and noted that it differs with the stage of development. At the time he was arguing against Rank's theory of birth trauma as the only and ubiquitous anxiety underlying all others; thus the birth trauma may be superseded by the loss of the breast, loss of love, and ultimately castration anxiety.

Klein, in 1946, took the view that central to the earliest experience is the fear of personal annihilation similar to that felt by psychotic patients and that this is the way the death instinct is experienced as working within the personality.

Fear of annihilation has been postulated by several psychoanalysts. Jones (1927), for instance, postulated a catastrophic loss, *aphanisis*, a fear that extended beyond castration anxiety to a deprivation of all possible instruments of pleasure and therefore of existence.

Impingement: Winnicott (1960) believed that the experience of annihilation derived from impingement of the environment on infantile omnipotence, which destroyed the infant's 'continuity of being'. In the earliest stages of infancy the mother is charged with supporting the infant's view that there is no separate object beyond the self. By bringing the needed breast to exactly the right place at exactly the right moment when the infant is hallucinating it she protects the infant from a true understanding of how his needs are met. If the mother fails to support the infant's notion of satisfying himself, then he suffers a particular experience described by Winnicott as impingement, leading him to feel annihilated in himself. Winnicott changed the significance that Klein gave to the experience of annihilation: instead of an internal destructive object, Winnicott saw the destruction as the effect of an external agent. The failure of the environment (mother) to facilitate the infant's sense of his own omnipotence results in a break in his 'sense of continuity of being'. Thereafter the developing personality can assume a feeling only as if he or she existed – a *false self* [see SKIN].

Tustin (1981) followed Winnicott in describing the consequences of an impingement upon the infant that is not yet ready to give up the primary state (she called it 'primary autism') [see AUTISM]. Bick (1968), on the other hand, described the relationship with the external object that holds the infant together as truly a relationship with an object, experienced sensually through skin contact, and capable of containing the parts of the personality [see SKIN].

Klein described annihilation (or fragmentation of the ego) as the typical fear in the paranoid-schizoid position.

(i) Anxiety in the paranoid-schizoid position: The annihilation of the ego (of the self), especially by an object within, the earliest fear of all, is due to the working of the death instinct at the outset. Annihilation includes a fragmentation and disintegration of the ego as an active process of the ego upon itself, and gives rise to the phenomenology of the schizophrenic condition [see 11. PARANOID-SCHIZOID POSITION].

The fear of being annihilated is part of the unconscious phantasy experiences with which the infant is endowed at birth. It is also represented within the primitive defence mechanisms by *denial*, which is experienced as annihilating the denied aspect of the object or of the self. It is both a defence and a contributory factor in the fear of annihilation, forming the vicious circle of paranoia [see PARANOIA].

(ii) Defences against the fear of annihilation: Many Kleinians, notably Bion (1958), Segal (1972), Sidney Klein (1974), have described the clinical manifestations of defences against the experience of catastrophic annihilation. As well as denial these defences include the omnipotent forms of the primitive defences of projection, introjection, projective identification, splitting and idealization.

(iii) The containing skin: On the basis of the observation of infants from birth [see INFANT OBSERVATION], Bick (1964) described the observational evidence for a primary experience of annihilation. She demonstrated the usually somatic and sensory methods by which the environment can enable the infant to survive such experiences, phenomena which she referred to as the *function of the skin*. She also described omnipotent bodily methods by which the child can survive in the absence of adequate containment by the external object, methods which she called the *second skin* [see SKIN; ADHESIVE IDENTIFICATION].

(iv) Catastrophic change: Giving emphasis to Klein's view that there is a constant wobbling between the paranoid-schizoid position, with its anxiety of annihilation, and the depressive position, with its typical anxiety of concern and guilt, Bion regarded the fear of annihilation as a persistently threatening experience all through life.

Any change brings out the threat, yet change is a necessary part of life and thought; Bion focused on the need to change and develop thought, and his views apply to all forms of personality change. The consequence of his view is that all development brings in its train the threat of *catastrophe* to the mind, and development rests upon small oscillations between the paranoid-schizoid fragmentation and depressive position concern, to which he gave the notation 'Ps-D' [see Ps-D].

Bick, Esther (1964) 'Notes on infant observation in psycho-analytic training', *Int. J. Psycho-Anal.* 45:558–66; republished (1987) in Martha Harris and Esther Bick, *The Collected Papers of Martha Harris and Esther Bick*. Perth: Clunie, pp. 240–56.
—— (1968) 'The experience of the skin in early object relations', *Int. J. Psycho-Anal.* 49:484–8; republished (1987) in *The Collected Papers of Martha Harris and Esther Bick*, pp. 114–18.
Bion, Wilfred (1958) 'On arrogance', *Int. J. Psycho-Anal.* 39:144–6; republished (1967) in W. R. Bion, *Second Thoughts*. Heinemann, pp. 86–92.
Freud, Sigmund (1926) *Inhibitions, Symptoms and Anxiety*. S.E. 20, pp. 77–175.
Jones, Ernest (1927) 'The early development of female sexuality', *Int. J. Psycho-Anal.* 8:459–72; republished (1948) in Ernest Jones, *Papers on Psycho-Analysis*. Hogarth, pp. 438–51.

Klein, Sidney (1974) 'Transference and defence in manic states', *Int. J. Psycho-Anal.* 55:261–8.

Segal, Hanna (1972) 'A delusional system as a defence against the re-emergence of a catastrophic situation', *Int. J. Psycho-Anal.* 53:393–403.

Tustin, Frances (1981) *Autistic States in Children*. Routledge & Kegan Paul.

Winnicott, Donald (1960) 'The theory of the infant–parent relationship', *Int. J. Psycho-Anal.* 41:585–95.

Anxiety

Psychoanalytic theories of anxiety have proliferated over the years. They are largely to do with conflict.

(i) In the first instance, Freud described the conflict between the individual and the demand for civilized (desexualized) behaviour.

(ii) This was modified to a conflict between the libido and self-preserving instincts or 'ego-instincts'. In this theory, dammed-up libido became converted into manifestly felt anxiety.

(iii) Then, with Freud's change in his theory of instincts (to adopt a dualistic theory of libido and death instinct), the conflict became located (by Klein) as an internal conflict between the instincts. According to Klein, such a conflict develops two forms: depressive anxiety and persecutory anxiety [see ANNIHILATION; PERSECUTION; DEPRESSIVE ANXIETY].

(iv) Freud's late paper on anxiety (Freud, 1926) described *signal anxiety*, not directly a conflicted instinctual tension but a signal occurring in the ego of an *anticipated* instinctual tension. Freud described the ego as appreciating certain situations that would give rise to anxiety. These anxiety-situations were not therefore instinctual in themselves, but might reside within purely ego-functions such as memory.

(v) Klein often pointed to Freud's term *early anxiety-situation* as a confirmation that she was on the right lines in looking at the phantasy *content* of anxiety rather than the energy from which it is derived [see 8. EARLY ANXIETY-SITUATIONS].

Freud, Sigmund (1926) *Inhibitions, Symptoms and Anxiety. S.E.* 20, pp. 77–175.

Assimilation

During the prolonged period of the 1930s and 1940s when the concept of the internal object was being worked out, Heimann (1942) began to discuss the question: What is the fate of the external object once it has been introjected? Does it go into the ego or into the superego? Rado (1928) had previously been troubled by this problem in Freud's and Abraham's work with manic-depressive patients. Freud (1917) originally described how the object 'cast its shadow upon the ego', calling this process an identification. Later (1921) he tried to sort out these confusions by describing the fate of the object as either '. . . put in the place of the ego or of the ego ideal' (p. 114) and subsequently (1923) he formalized the concept of the superego. He also described the state of being in love '. . . as "fascination" or "bondage" . . . [the ego] is impoverished, it has surrendered itself to the object, it has substituted the object for its own most important constituent' (Freud, 1921, p. 113).

Difficulties in understanding the Kleinian discovery of *internal objects* [see 5. INTERNAL OBJECTS] derive from the confusing quality of these early attempts to understand identification and introjection. When, for example, Klein wrote:

> . . . the ego, supported by the internalized good object and strengthened by identification with it, projects a portion of the death instinct into that part of itself which it has split off – a part which comes to be in opposition to the rest of the ego and forms the basis of the superego. (Klein, 1958, p. 240)

she was describing a number of different internal relations between the ego and its objects: (i) the ego has a relationship of support with an internal object; (ii) the ego is enhanced and supported by identification with the object; (iii) a split-off part of the ego becomes a hostile internal object.

Assimilation to the ego: Heimann's (1942) use of the term 'assimilation' is helpful in sorting out these confusions, since it allows us to conceive of internal objects that become a part of the ego, enhance it, and provide skills, attitudes, qualities, constituents, and defences which the ego subsequently has at its disposal by identifying with this internal object. In contrast are unassimilated objects that remain alien inside the personality and '. . . act as foreign bodies embedded in the self. Whilst this is more obvious with regard to the bad objects, it is true even for the good ones, if the ego is compulsively subordinated to their preservation' (Klein, 1946, p. 9n).

Heimann (1942) had reported a case history of a woman artist in which the material demonstrated the introjection of a hostile object that then resulted in an internal persecution of the ego and diminution of her creative ability. In the course of the psychoanalytic process this hostile internal mother became modified and could be assimilated as a support and strength to the ego. A similar modification of a hostile internal object was described by Schmideberg (1934) in a child patient.

Later, Heimann (1955) described a case in which the hostile internal object was identified with a part of the ego (an anatomical part) and treated then as an alien object. This was the case of a masochistic patient whose excitement at being beaten on the buttocks resulted from the introjection of a hated and hostile father imago and an identification of that imago with the part of his ego to be beaten, his buttocks. This internal object, regarded as 'bad', was an internal persecutor endowed with similar sadistic impulses with which it was attacked, and was indistinguishable from the internal object known as the superego.

Heimann (1955) also illustrated the typical situation of an object that has been assimilated and becomes an additional resource for the ego, with the child who introjects mother's breast after feeding and identifies it with his thumb, and then when hungry can suck that internal object in the form of his thumb in order, at a later point, to generate phantasies of satisfaction to protect him from a hostile hunger-generating object [see 5. INTERNAL OBJECTS].

In the course of development there is '. . . a progressive assimilation of the superego [hostile internal object] by the ego' (Klein, 1952, p. 74); '. . . the increased capacity of the ego to accept the standards of the external objects . . . is linked with the greater synthesis within the superego and the growing assimilation of the superego by the ego' (Klein, 1952, p. 87). As whole objects develop in the depressive position they become more available for support and identification internally, and the internal world becomes less of a hostile collection of alien internal objects.

See 5. INTERNAL OBJECTS

Freud, Sigmund (1917) 'Mourning and melancholia'. *S.E.* 14, pp. 237–60.
—— (1921) *Group Psychology and the Analysis of the Ego. S.E.* 18, pp. 67–143.
—— (1923) *The Ego and the Id. S.E.* 19, pp. 3–66.
Heimann, Paula (1942) 'A contribution to the problem of sublimation and its relation to processes of internalization', *Int. J. Psycho-Anal.* 23:8–17.
—— (1955) 'A combination of defences in paranoid states', in Melanie Klein, Paula Heimann and Roger Money-Kyrle, eds (1955) *New Directions in Psycho-Analysis.* Tavistock, pp. 240–65; early version published (1952) as 'Preliminary notes on some defence mechanisms in paranoid states', *Int. J. Psycho-Anal.* 33:208–13.
Klein, Melanie (1946) 'Notes on some schizoid mechanisms', in *WMK* 3, pp. 1–24.
—— (1952) 'Some theoretical conclusions regarding the emotional life of the infant'. *WMK* 3, pp. 61–93.
—— (1958) 'On the development of mental functioning'. *WMK* 3, pp. 236–46.
Rado, S. (1928) 'The problem of melancholia', *Int. J. Psycho-Anal.* 9:420–38.
Schmideberg, Melitta (1934) 'The play analysis of a three-year-old girl', *Int. J. Psycho-Anal.* 15:245–64.

Autism

The severe disturbance in children known as autism was studied (Meltzer *et al.*, 1975; Tustin, 1981, 1986) following successful psychoanalytic work with adult psychotic patients [see PSYCHOSIS]. The theoretical interest is in the very early psychological states of mind when the predisposition for autism is provoked. The condition is held, therefore, to be one access to the very earliest stages of development – in fact, the moments immediately before and after the birth experience.

Frances Tustin: Tustin described how Klein '. . . as long ago as 1930, showed that she had anticipated Leo Kanner's differentiation of "Early Infantile Autism" from mental deficiency by thirteen years' (Tustin, 1983, p. 130). She postulated (1981, 1986) a primary state of 'normal autism' which she linked with the autoerotism that Freud described, a non-object-related search for pleasurable body sensations. She also accepted Winnicott's view of primary infantile omnipotence as equivalent to her term. She proceeded then to distinguish two kinds of autism: (i) one in which the 'normal autism' has been interrupted prematurely for the infant who, in a state of hypersensitivity to experiencing separation, reacts by retreating impenetrably into a preoccupation simply with his bodily sensations, with a permanent, psychotic *fusion* with the environment (mother); and (ii) another form in which the infant, less severely traumatized, resorts to a permanent reliance on pathological projective identification, with a permanent *confusion* with external objects. Both forms result in a lack of development of the internal world and a preoccupation with bodily sensations. The first of these kinds of autistic states is clearly seen in Winnicott's notion of impingement by external objects prior to the developmental stage at which separation can be tolerated [see ANNIHILATION]. Tustin's views therefore bridge the divide between Klein's and Winnicott's views of the earliest states of infantile psychology.

Donald Meltzer: In a slightly different direction, Meltzer *et al.* (1975) followed Bion's understanding of the growth of the mental apparatus, and the aberrant forms into which the mental apparatus can dissolve. The reversal of the normal process of mental integration brings about a disintegration into fragments of sense data [see THINKING; BETA-ELEMENTS], resulting in a lack of the proper development for thinkable thoughts (Meltzer, 1978). He also linked this with Bick's work on adhesive identification deriving from the observation of 'normal' infants from birth [see ADHESIVE IDENTIFICATION]. There seems to be a significant correspondence between observations of autistic children and of normal infants from the earliest days (Meltzer, 1975). Bick (1968) showed the way in which the infant first comes to acquire the sense of being held together, through the stimulation of the skin. Where this does not adequately happen, the infant is left with a defective sense of integration, pictured as an inability to hold a sense of a containing space. The absence of a containing space, either internal to himself or external, characterizes the autistic child [see SKIN]; as a result the child looks to intense perceptual and other bodily sensations as mechanisms for holding himself together.

As usual with new understandings of the early experiences of infancy, they can be used to understand the later problems in adult disorders. Sidney Klein (1980) demonstrated autistic aspects of patients who presented with neurotic problems. These were encapsulated in rigid structural isolation, and often conceived in dreams as hard insects or animals with carapaces, reminiscent of the hard, muscular secondary defensiveness described by Bick (1968). These split-off parts of the personality may be related to the organization of deeply narcissistic elements described by Rosenfeld (1971) [see STRUCTURE].

Bick, Esther (1968) 'The experience of the skin in early object relations', *Int. J. Psycho-Anal.* 49:484–8; republished (1987) in Martha Harris and Esther Bick, *The Collected Papers of Martha Harris and Esther Bick*. Perth: Clunie, pp. 114–18.

Klein, Sidney (1980) 'Autistic phenomena in neurotic patients', *Int. J. Psycho-Anal.* 61:395–402.

Meltzer, Donald (1975) 'Adhesive identification', *Contemporary Psycho-Analysis* 11:289–301.

—— (1978) 'A note on Bion's concept of reversal of alpha-function', in *The Kleinian Development, Part III*. Perth: Clunie, pp. 119–26; republished (1981) in James Grotstein, ed. *Do I Dare Disturb the Universe?* Beverly Hills: Caesura, pp. 529–35.

Meltzer, Donald, Bremner, John, Hoxter, Shirley, Weddell, Doreen and Wittenberg, Isca (1975) *Explorations in Autism*. Perth: Clunie.

Rosenfeld, Herbert (1971) 'A clinical approach to the psycho-analytical theory of the life and death instincts: an investigation into the aggressive aspects of narcissism', *Int. J. Psycho-Anal.* 52:169–78.

Tustin, Frances (1981) *Autistic States in Childhood*. Routledge & Kegan Paul.

—— (1983) 'Thoughts on autism with special reference to a paper by Melanie Klein', *Journal of Child Psychotherapy* 9:119–31.

—— (1986) *Autistic Barriers in Neurotic Patients*. Karnac.

Babies

Freud showed that the significance of babies was very important and deep. They represent the girl's exultant substitute for a penis, and a triumph for her creativity.

Attacks on mother's body: In Klein's early views (Klein, 1932), mother's babies, believed to reside inside her body, are an extreme provocation to jealousy and envy from early infancy. This gives rise to violent attacks, in phantasy, on mother's body and its contents and dreadful fears of retaliation [see 6. FEMININITY PHASE; 8. EARLY ANXIETY-SITUATIONS]. The little girl's phantasies of her own babies are therefore a reassurance against the paranoid anxiety of mother's retaliation.

It is much the same for the little boy, who is moved to violence (and paranoid fear) by the added phantasy of mother's body containing father's penis [see COMBINED PARENT FIGURE]. In both sexes the idea of babies in mother's body (and also father's penis) produces aggression and paranoid fears [see PARANOIA] which enhance the normal castration anxiety and penis envy described by Freud; these greatly affect the sexual development of the child, with possible resultant inhibitions in adulthood; and, in turn, influence adults' relations with their own babies as mothers or fathers.

See CHILD

Klein, Melanie (1932) *The Psycho-Analysis of Children. WMK* 2.

Baby observation See INFANT OBSERVATION

Bad object
In early phantasy life [see 5. INTERNAL OBJECTS; 2. UNCONSCIOUS PHANTASY] objects are attributed, in an animistic way, with motives towards the subject. An unpleasant bodily sensation is interpreted as deriving from the intentions of a *bad* (evilly motivated) object. Such an object at this stage has a very powerful sense of reality for the infant; but it is a reality of the existence and location of a motive, rather than the sense of a physically identified object as usually conceived by adults.

The bad object contrasts with its polar opposite – and coexistent – 'good' object, which derives from pleasant bodily sensations and is supposed to be benignly motivated. For example, in the feeding sensations a frustrating, hunger-inducing object ('bad' object) is matched by a satisfying, hunger-relieving object. These primitive conceptions are indicated by the notation: 'good' breast, 'bad' breast; and 'good' mother, 'bad' mother; and likewise for father, penis, etc. [see BREAST; MOTHER; FATHER].

At first these pairs of objects are perceived as strictly split apart and quite separate, though gradually more realistic perceptions develop so that objects with mixed 'good' and 'bad' characteristics and motivations come to be perceived [see 10. DEPRESSIVE POSITION].

See PART-OBJECTS

Basic assumptions

Bion's work with groups (Bion, 1948–51; Rioch, 1970), before his training as a Kleinian analyst, is often included in the Kleinian canon. He did subsequently develop part of his results with a strong Kleinian emphasis (Bion, 1955, and later, 1970); but 'A Kleinian interpretation of the basic assumptions does not necessarily follow from his data, though its plausibility is considerable' (Trist, 1987); Meltzer (1984) has elevated this work by describing it as '... the momentous formulations of Bion on Basic Assumption Groups' (Meltzer, 1984, p. 89). Wilson (1983) pointed out in some detail how Bion's model of basic assumptions is a 'metapsychology of groups which is equivalent in many respects to the system Freud devised' (Wilson, 1983, p. 157), and in particular Freud's topographical model.

Analysis of the group: Bion (1961) dealt with groups as an analyst sitting down with a patient. The 'group-as-a-whole' exhibits a transference to the group leader in the form of a group culture which, he showed, was suffused with unspoken and unconscious assumptions shared by all the group members. The set of assumptions about the nature of the group, of its leader, of the task of the group, and of the role expected of the members, has three variants. The three *basic assumptions* are detected in the feeling tone in the atmosphere of the group:

(i) first, the *dependent basic assumption (BaD)* gives rise to a group of members each hanging, often disappointedly, on the words of wisdom of the group leader, as if they assumed that all knowledge, health and life is located in him and is to be derived by each member individually from him;

(ii) secondly, in the *fight/flight basic assumption (BaF)*, the members gather around the excited and violent idea that there is an enemy to be identified, and that the members will be led in a conformist phalanx by the leader against this enemy, or alternatively in flight from it. Such an enemy may be 'neurosis' itself in the therapy group, or one of the members of the group, or some suitable object outside the group (an external enemy);

(iii) finally, the *pairing basic assumption (BaP)* suffuses the group with a mysterious kind of hope, often with behavioural pairing between two members, or a member and the leader, as if all share the belief that some great new idea (or individual) will emerge from the intercourse of the pair (a messianic belief).

The work groups: Bion contrasted the basic-assumption state of a group with what he called the work group, in which the members address the consciously defined and accepted task of the group. In this state the group functions with secondary-process sophistication and attends to an examination of the reality inside and outside the group. Bion's reliance on the psychoanalytic model of a sophisticated functioning of the mind based on a seething unconscious was noted by Wilson (1983). The work-group state usually shows signs of active basic-assumption states and Bion thought of the basic assumptions as 'valencies' which drew people inevitably together and established group belonging.

Bion attempted to relate basic-assumption characteristics to the working of social institutions: the army, for instance, clearly represented the fight/flight assumption, and the Church, he believed, represented the dependency assumption. The pairing assumption he saw in the aristocracy, an institution concerned with breeding.

This view of the triadic nature of group assumptions has become widespread outside psychoanalysis (de Board, 1978; Pines, 1985). Although Bion made an initial attempt to relate his findings to Klein's concept of projective identification (Bion, 1955) he subsequently dropped these ideas, and his work on groups. But later (Bion, 1970; Menzies Lyth, 1981) he remoulded the idea of the pairing assumption to make it more or less basic to group life in general, seeing it as the principal method for examining the *containing function* of groups and an appropriate way of understanding the relationship between the individual and society – the mystic and the establishment [see CONTAINING].

Bion, Wilfred (1948a) 'Experiences in groups I', *Human Relations* 1:314–20; republished in Bion (1961) *Experiences in Groups*. Tavistock, pp. 29–40.

—— (1948b) 'Experiences in groups II', *Human Relations* 1:487–96; republished (1961) in *Experiences in Groups*, pp. 41–58.

—— (1949a) 'Experiences in groups III', *Human Relations* 2:13–22; republished (1961) in *Experiences in Groups*, pp. 59–75.

—— (1949b) 'Experiences in groups IV', *Human Relations* 2:95–104; republished (1961) in *Experiences in Groups*, pp. 77–91.

—— (1950a) 'Experiences in groups V', *Human Relations* 3:3–14; republished (1961) in *Experiences in Groups*, pp. 93–114.

—— (1950b) 'Experiences in groups VI', *Human Relations* 3:395–402; republished (1961) in *Experiences in Groups*, pp. 115–126.

—— (1951) 'Experiences in groups VII', *Human Relations* 4:221–8; republished (1961) in *Experiences in Groups*, pp. 127–37.

—— (1955) 'Group-dynamics: a review', in Melanie Klein, Paula Heimann and Roger Money-Kyrle, eds (1955) *New Directions in Psycho-Analysis*. Tavistock, pp. 440–7; republished (1961) in *Experiences in Groups*, pp. 141–91.

—— (1961) *Experiences in Groups*. Tavistock.

—— (1970) *Attention and Interpretation*. Tavistock.

de Board, Robert (1978) *The Psycho-Analysis of Organizations*. Tavistock.

Meltzer, Donald (1984) 'A one-year-old goes to nursery: a parable of confusing times', *Journal of Child Psychotherapy* 10:89–104; republished (1986) in Meltzer, *Studies in Extended Metapsychology*. Perth: Clunie, pp. 136–53.

Menzies Lyth, Isabel (1981) 'Bion's contribution to thinking about groups', in James Grotstein, ed. (1981) *Do I Dare Disturb the Universe?* Beverly Hills: Caesura, pp. 661–6.

Pines, Malcolm, ed. (1985) *Bion and Group Psychotherapy.* Routledge & Kegan Paul.

Rioch, Margaret (1970) 'The work of Wilfred Bion on groups', *Psychiatry* 33:56–66.

Trist, Eric (1987) 'Working with Bion in the 1940s', *Group Analysis* 20:263–70.

Wilson, Stephen (1983) '"Experiences in Groups": Bion's debt to Freud', *Group Analysis* 16:152–7.

Beta-elements

In generating a theory by which a biological organism becomes an experiencing psyche, Bion (1962a) described a process he called *alpha-function*, the essential feature of which is the process of generating 'meaning' out of sensations. The end results of alpha-function are *alpha-elements*, which are the furniture for dreams and for thinking [see ALPHA-FUNCTION]. When alpha-function goes wrong or fails, another (abnormal) kind of mental content is generated, which Bion called *beta-elements*. 'Beta-element' is one of Bion's 'meaning-free' terms intended to be filled up from the experience of using the concept in practice [see BION]; there are several features of the term:

(i) Raw sense data: Experience is generated from raw sense data (a realization) by meeting with some pre-existing expectation (a preconception) which results in a 'meaning-full' conception [see PRE-CONCEPTION; THINKING]. On occasion, however, such a meeting may fail (failure of alpha-function), with the result that particles of 'undigested' sense data accumulate. These are *beta-elements*.

(ii) Evacuation: Beta-elements may agglomerate into collections (like a schizophrenic's 'word salad' type of speech). These accumulations are processed by evacuation, not by thinking thoughts into dreams and theories. The process of evacuation is that described by Klein as projective identification in its pathological form [see 13. PROJECTIVE IDENTIFICATION].

(iii) The mental apparatus: Under the pressure of the accumulation of beta-elements, the mind develops as an apparatus for '. . . ridding the psyche of accumulations of bad internal objects', not as an apparatus for thinking (Bion, 1962a, p. 112).

See THINKING

Bion, Wilfred (1962a) 'A theory of thinking', in Bion (1967) *Second Thoughts*. Heinemann, pp. 110–19; previously published (1962) *Int. J. Psycho-Anal.* 43:306–10.
—— (1962b) *Learning from Experience*. Heinemann.

Esther Bick

Biography. Born **1901** in Poland, Esther Bick studied psychology in Vienna with Charlotte Buhler, but came as a refugee to England, eventually embarking on a psychoanalytic career after the Second World War. She then worked at the Tavistock Clinic and developed the method of infant observation as a training tool for child psychotherapists. However, her interest was in testing Klein's conclusions about the first year of life by direct observation. In the course of this she made her own original discoveries. In spite of her loyalty to Klein, Bick's views, since her death in **1983**, have been left behind by the main Kleinian stream of development.

SCIENTIFIC CONTRIBUTIONS. Bick contributed a method out of which came four main results concerning the very early stages of development in the first days and weeks of life (Harris, 1984).

(i) Infant observation: Bick started a rigorous method of weekly observations of mothers with babies in their own homes (Bick, 1964). Originally this was a method of teaching child psychotherapists and trainee psychoanalysts to observe rather than to intervene. However, the observations produced immediate results [see INFANT OBSERVATION].

(ii) Primary skin sensation: Bick's most significant observation concerned the infant's *passive* experience of being held together by an external object sensed through the skin sensations [see SKIN]; and of passively *falling apart* if this object failed (Bick, 1968). The skin is crucial in its function of giving evidence of such an object. This is in contrast to the experiences described by Bion and others, working with schizophrenics, of an active process of splitting and annihilation of the self.

The idea that the experience of internal space has to be acquired implies the possibility of a failure to acquire it and therefore of compensatory measures, the most primitive of all defences, which Bick (1968) called 'second-skin' phenomena [see SKIN].

(iii) The primary object: Bick obtained evidence in much greater detail of the nature of this first object that binds the personality together [see 11. PARANOID-SCHIZOID POSITION] and has to be introjected in order to give a sense of space into which introjections can be put. The view that the experience of an internal space is one that is *acquired*, through adequate experience, contrasts with the idea of an innate experience of internal space implied in Bion's theories.

(iv) Adhesive identification: The possible failure to develop such an integrating primary object (space) appears to be confirmed in work with autistic children (Meltzer *et al.*, 1975) [see AUTISM]. Bick and Meltzer (Meltzer, 1975, 1986) collaborated in describing the ways in which autistic children develop *without* a sense of internal or external space. Their relationship with objects appears to be a 'sticking on to' the object, a mechanism called adhesive identification [see ADHESIVE IDENTIFICATION].

Bick, Esther (1964) 'Notes on infant observation in psycho-analytic training', *Int. J. Psycho-Anal.* 45:558–66; republished (1987) in Martha Harris and Esther Bick, *The Collected Papers of Martha Harris and Esther Bick*. Perth: Clunie, pp. 240–56.

—— (1968) 'The experience of the skin in early object relations', *Int. J. Psycho-Anal.* 49:484–6; republished (1987) in *The Collected Papers of Martha Harris and Esther Bick*, pp. 114–18.

—— (1986) 'Further considerations of the function of the skin in early object relations', *Br. J. Psychother.* 2:292–9.

Harris, Martha (1984) 'Esther Bick', *Journal of Child Psychotherapy* 10:2–14.

Meltzer, Donald (1975) 'Adhesive identification', *Contemporary Psycho-Analysis* 11:289–310.

—— (1986) 'Discussion of Esther Bick's paper "Further considerations of the function of the skin in early object relations"', *Br. J. Psychother.* 2:300–1.

Meltzer, Donald, Bremner, John, Hoxter, Shirley, Weddell, Doreen and Wittenberg, Isca (1975) *Explorations in Autism*. Perth: Clunie.

Wilfred Bion

Biography. Bion was born in India in 1897 and had a dangerous career in the First World War as a tank commander (winning the DSO) before settling down to study medicine and eventually psychoanalysis in the 1930s and 1940s. In the 1940s he made dazzling discoveries in the social psychology of groups, which he quickly dropped to join in the forefront of the psychoanalytic investigation of schizophrenia. His extraordinary ability to distinguish himself in whatever setting he happened to be was matched by a continual disappointment at the resistance which he felt met his efforts. This led him to leave Britain in an attempt to implant himself in the California of the 1970s, which again misfired. He returned to support a move to create a psycho-analytic group (of Kleinian persuasion) in Oxford. This final move turned out to be only months before his death in 1979. His geographical searching to the end of his life for a place to make his home was a metaphor for his equally restless theoretical strivings in psychoanalysis. His achievements were second only to those of Klein herself, though some (Meltzer *et al.*, 1982) would say their potential far outstrips those of Klein. If there is yet a post-Kleinian school or tradition, Bion is it.

Bion's contributions are very extensive, and to be found in detail in other entries in this dictionary, to which reference will be made. His writings appear gnomic, irritating and intensely stimulating, and this style has been responsible for a tendency to sanctify him while not really understanding him. All Kleinians today regard their present practice and theory as having been significantly moulded by his work (O'Shaughnessy, 1981).

SCIENTIFIC CONTRIBUTIONS. While training as a psycho-analyst, Bion conducted therapy in groups (Bion, 1961) [see BASIC ASSUMPTIONS]. Despite the fact that his interest lasted only a few years, his imaginative approach led to: (i) the development of a tradition of *group therapy* known as the Tavistock style (Menzies Lyth, 1981; Gosling, 1981); (ii) the creation of a form of psychiatric practice known as the *therapeutic community* (Main, 1946; Hinshelwood, 1987); (iii) the formation of the Tavistock Institute working and researching in *organization development* (Rice, 1963; Menzies Lyth, 1988, 1989); (iv) the introduction of a novel and lasting method of *officer selection* in the forces (Bion, 1946); (v) the understanding of the social psychology of *large groups* (Turquet, 1975); and (vi) the development of *teaching methods* in groups (Gosling *et al.*, 1967).

Bion's contribution to psychoanalysis can be briefly summarized under the headings below and further exposition appears in the entries referred to:

(1) Psychosis. As a psychoanalyst, Bion joined the group of Kleinian analysts who were exploiting the breakthrough in understanding schizophrenia that came from Klein's (1946) paper on schizoid mechanisms. A new development in practice came out of the discovery of split-off aspects of the transference that was described in that paper. In his first paper on this topic, in 1954, Bion based his view of the schizophrenic as '. . . either splitting or getting in or out of his objects' (Bion, 1954, p. 24). At the symposium to which he contributed that paper, there was also one by Katan which described criteria for distinguishing psychotic from non-psychotic parts of the personality, which seems to have resulted in Bion's classic statement, in 1957, on differentiating the psychotic from the non-psychotic. In 1959 Bion described the crucial difference between a *normal* and a *pathological* form of projective identification [see 13. PROJECTIVE IDENTIFICATION; BIZARRRE OBJECTS]. This brought a great deal more order into the confused concept of projective identification.

In the pathological form the process is achieved with maximal violence and sadism, resulting in an invaded external object suffused with retaliatory hatred, a *bizarre object*. This notion was at the basis of all further developments of his theories [see PSYCHOSIS].

(2) Empathy. Once a pathological form of projective identification had been separated off, a more 'normal' form, conducted with less hatred, could be understood. Such benign processes as empathy, which involves 'putting oneself in the object's shoes', became important features in understanding the therapeutic effect of psychoanalysis [see 1. TECHNIQUE].

(3) Thinking. The violence and omnipotence of the schizophrenic's intrusiveness is the cause of his or her difficulty in thinking. However, once the abnormalities of schizophrenic thinking were discerned it became clear how the more normal processes of thinking are also based on projective identification (a more normal form). Bion experimented with paradigms for the *linking* of thoughts [see LINKING]. Interpenetration of one element within another could be built up into very complex structures of abstraction with serial repetitions of this kind of emotional linking [see THINKING]. This is a process that *generates meaning* out of sensations and experiences [see ALPHA-FUNCTION; EPISTEMOPHILIA].

(4) Containing. Bion (1962a) described a new theory of relationships which advances beyond the traditional paradigm of sexuality. However it may be stated the other way round: that the Oedipus complex and its disturbance can come to invest any one of these interpenetrating contacts. Contact can be thought of as a process of *containing*. One thing becomes jammed into another, with or without violence. Bion then described a whole phenomenology of the container–contained relationship, in which the contained might explode the container, or in turn might be constricted and suffocated by the container; or alternatively there could be a mutual adaptation between the two. He described *symbiotic, parasitic* and *commensal* forms of the relationship (Bion, 1970). Although Bion described this interpenetrating form of contact first of all in the process of developing thoughts and theories, he extended it to all kinds of phenomena: getting thoughts into words; the thought, or the feeling, in the individual's mind; the individual in his social group; the infant in mother's consciousness (reverie), etc. [see CONTAINING].

Psychoanalytic technique: The theory of containing contributed to the revision of psychoanalytic technique that was under way in the 1950s (Racker, 1948; Heimann, 1950; Rosenfeld, 1952; Money-Kyrle, 1956) through Bion's characteristic gift of vivid and challenging descriptions [see 1. TECHNIQUE; COUNTERTRANSFERENCE].

Memory and desire: In approaching an analysis, Bion thought, both analyst and analysand fear the experience of change and development which it brings about. They are small *catastrophes* in the peace of mind of both [see Ps-D; ANNIHILATION]. Bion enjoined the analyst to avoid certain mental manoeuvres that will obstruct his approach to the potential catastrophe of development in the analysis [see MEMORY AND DESIRE; CONTAINING]. He thought that the major obstacles were the cluttering of the analyst's mind with previously learned knowledge of the patient or of psychoanalysis (rather than being patent to the immediate experience) and a therapeutic zeal that wanted to plan future development without allowing it to emerge in the mutual experience. These escape routes from the immediate present into the past or the future could be closed off by Bion's injunction (1965, 1970) to 'abolish memory and desire'. Clearing the mind in this way is a strenuous activity on the analyst's part, although, like the theory of countertransference, it may be abused and taken as an excuse for 'ignorance and indolence' (Spillius, 1988).

(5) **The communicability of psychoanalytic thinking.** Later in his career Bion began to be interested in the way in which psychoanalysts understand – or misunderstand – one another. First of all he invented a *grid* (Bion, 1963) in which he plotted all the possible kinds of communications on two co-ordinates. One co-ordinate was a serial *cascade* of containing relations at different levels of abstraction, from very primitive sense data right up to general theories of the most abstract kind (from dreams and phantasies to concepts, to theoretical systems to algebraic calculus). The other co-ordinate displayed the way these mental elements could be used. Thus Bion attempted to bring a precision into communication about psychoanalysis and, indeed, a rigour into the thinking that is to be communicated.

Vertices: In another attempt to bring order into all the misunderstanding, Bion (1970) tried to generate a theory of different points of view: vertices. The levels of containment give different points of view – mythical, scientific, etc. This leads to religious, individual, sociological vertices, which he hoped could be reconciled with each other.

Social phenomena: His thoughts about communication and points of view (vertices) led Bion to speculate upon social phenomena from a psychoanalytic framework (Bion, 1970) [see BASIC ASSUMPTIONS; SOCIETY]. The tension between an individual and his society was worked out in terms of containing; it reflected an idea that Pichon-Riviere (1931) had considered a long time before.

Bion's style of writing: Bion's curious writing style seems to be connected with the content of the ideas he is writing about. In his early writing it is terse, even slightly irascible – aimed, it seems, at challenging with new ideas. However, later, when he understood better his own theory of thinking and communicating with others, his style evolved to a demand on the reader to do his own thinking. He perfected a trick of describing certain psychic processes, while at the same time engaging in just that process during the act of describing it. For instance, his term 'alpha-function' was sought to describe the mental process of acquiring meaning for sense impressions; at the same time the term was selected for its meaning-free quality and was, in the course of Bion's writings, in the process itself of acquiring a meaning. The conflation of the process with the method of describing it compares with the schizophrenic's inability to distinguish communication from action. But Bion's conflation is no inability; it is a calculated attempt to give a meaning through experience as well as through didactic exposition: 'The advantage of employing a sign . . . is that it at least indicates that the reader's comprehension of my meaning should contain an element that will remain unsatisfied until he meets the appropriate realization' (Bion, 1962b, pp. 95–6). The reader is required to fill Bion's words with his or her own experience.

Bion's significance. It is impossible, in a summary entry, to convey the scale of Bion's impact on Kleinian thinking. The character of Kleinian psychoanalysis has developed significantly from Klein's paper on schizoid mechanisms (Klein, 1946), but the following-up of those ideas was done largely by her group of followers [see KLEINIAN GROUP; 13. PROJECTIVE IDENTIFICATION] and Bion has emerged as the most original of them. The most far-reaching developments are: (a) the recognition of normal and omnipotent projective identification; (b) the theory of the emotional containing of the personality; and (c) the theory of thinking that derives meaning itself from the most primitive infantile configurations of emotions [see ALPHA-FUNCTION; BETA-ELEMENTS; BIZARRE OBJECTS; CONTAINING; COUNTER-TRANSFERENCE; LINKING; NAMELESS DREAD; PRE-CONCEPTION; Ps-D; THINKING]. In all these developments Bion has been the foremost figure.

A major point in contemporary Kleinian debate is how to allot Bion his significance: whether he has moved beyond Klein to be acknowledged as, in effect, the founder of a new school of psychoanalysis, as Meltzer and some of his colleagues have begun to suggest (Meltzer *et al.*, 1982; Harris, 1982; Meltzer, 1986); or whether the developments with which Bion has been especially associated are part and parcel of a general development of Kleinian thought that also includes (a) Segal's development of a Kleinian theory of symbolism and the aesthetic experience [see SYMBOL-FORMATION; SYMBOLIC EQUATION], (b) the developments made by Rosenfeld, Joseph and others on personality structure [see NEGATIVE NARCISSISM; PERVERSION; STRUCTURE] and (c) the continuing study of children and infants by Bick and others, developing the theory of internal spaces and adhesive identification [see ADHESIVE IDENTIFICATION; AUTISM; INFANT OBSERVATION; SKIN].

Bion, Wilfred (1946) 'Leaderless groups', *Bulletin of the Menninger Clinic* 10:77–81.

—— (1954) 'Notes on the theory of schizophrenia', in W. R. Bion (1967) *Second Thoughts*. Heinemann, pp. 23–35; previously published (1954) *Int. J. Psycho-Anal.* 35:113–18; and expanded as 'Language and the schizophrenic', in Melanie Klein, Paula Heimann and Roger Money-Kyrle, eds (1955) *New Directions in Psycho-Analysis*. Tavistock, pp. 220–39.

—— (1957) 'Differentiation of the psychotic from non-psychotic personalities', *Int. J. Psycho-Anal.* 38:266–75; republished (1967) in W. R. Bion, *Second Thoughts*, pp. 43–64.

—— (1961) *Experiences in Groups*. Tavistock.

—— (1962a) 'A theory of thinking', *Int. J. Psycho-Anal.* 43:306–10; republished (1967) in W. R. Bion, *Second Thoughts*, pp. 110–19.

—— (1962b) *Learning from Experience*. Heinemann..

—— (1963) *Elements of Psycho-Analysis*. Heinemann.

—— (1965) *Transformations*. Heinemann.

—— (1970) *Attention and Interpretation*. Tavistock.

Gosling, Robert (1981) 'A study of very small groups', in James Grotstein, ed. (1981) *Do I Dare Disturb the Universe?* Beverly Hills: Caesura, pp. 633–45.

Gosling, Robert, Miller, D. H., Turquet, P. M. and Woodhouse, D. (1967) *The Use of Small Groups in Training*. Codicote.

Harris, Martha (1982) 'Growing points in psycho-analysis inspired by the work of Melanie Klein', *Journal of Child Psychotherapy* 8:165–84.

Heimann, Paula (1950) 'Counter-transference', *Int. J. Psycho-Anal.* 31:81–4.

Hinshelwood, R. D. (1987) *What Happens in Groups*. Free Association Books.

Katan, M. (1954) 'The importance of the non-psychotic part of the personality in schizophrenia', *Int. J. Psycho-Anal.* 55:119–28.

Klein, Melanie (1946) 'Notes on some schizoid mechanisms', in *WMK* 3, pp. 1–24.

Main, Tom (1946) 'The hospital as a therapeutic institution', *Bulletin of the Menninger Clinic* 10:66–70.

Meltzer, Donald (1986) *Studies in Extended Metapsychology*. Perth: Clunie.

Meltzer, Donald, Milana, Giuliana, Maiello, Susanna and Petrelli, Diomine (1982) 'The conceptual distinction between projective identification (Klein) and container–contained (Bion)', *Journal of Child Psychotherapy* 8:185–202.

Menzies Lyth, Isabel (1981) 'Bion's contribution to thinking about groups', in James Grotstein, ed. *Do I Dare Disturb the Universe?* Beverly Hills: Caesura, pp. 661–6.

—— (1988) *Containing Anxiety in Institutions*. Free Association Books.

—— (1989) *The Dynamics of the Social*. Free Association Books.

Money-Kyrle, Roger (1956) 'Normal counter-transference and some of its deviations', *Int. J. Psycho-Anal.* 37:360–6; republished (1978) in *The Collected Papers of Roger Money-Kyrle*. Perth: Clunie, pp. 330–42.

O'Shaughnessy, Edna (1981) 'A commemorative essay on W.R. Bion's theory of thinking', *Journal of Child Psychotherapy* 7:181–92.

Pichon-Riviere, Eduardo (1931) 'Position du problème de l'adaptation réciproque entre la société et les psichismes exceptionels', *Revue française de Psychanalyse* 2:135–70.

Racker, Heinrich (1948) 'A contribution to the problem of counter-transference', published in English (1953) *Int. J. Psycho-Anal.* 34:313–24; republished as 'The counter-transference neurosis', in Heinrich Racker (1968) *Transference and Counter-Transference*. Hogarth, pp. 105–26.

Rice, A.K. (1963) *The Enterprise and its Environment*. Tavistock.

Rosenfeld, Herbert (1952) 'Notes on the analysis of the superego conflict of a catatonic schizophrenic', *Int. J. Psycho-Anal.* 33:111–31; republished (1955) in Melanie Klein, Paula Heimann and Roger Money-Kyrle, eds *New Directions in Psycho-Analysis*. Tavistock, pp. 180–219; and (1965) in *Psychotic States*. Hogarth, pp. 63–103.

Spillius, Elizabeth Bott (1988) *Melanie Klein Today: Volume 1 Mainly Theory*. Tavistock.

Turquet, Pierre (1975) 'Threats to identity in the large group', in Lionel Kreeger, ed. *The Large Group*. Constable, pp. 87–144.

Bizarre objects

During the 1950s Bion began to elaborate a comprehensive theory of schizophrenic thought disorder, based on the consequences of a fragmentary splitting of the ego. He demonstrated that the schizophrenic suffers from a splitting of a certain part of the ego – the perceptual apparatus:

> . . . attacks are directed against the apparatus of perception from the beginning of life. This part of his personality is cut up, split into minute fragments, and then, using projective identification, expelled from the personality. Having thus rid himself of the apparatus of conscious awareness of internal and external reality, the patient achieves a state which is felt to be neither alive nor dead. (Bion, 1956, p. 39)

The personality is thus depleted, but the ejected fragments of the perceptual apparatus continue an alienated existence as *bizarre objects*. They intrude omnipotently into an external object to form a particularly persecutory object that has an awareness of the schizophrenic's own mind:

> Each particle is felt to consist of a real external object which is encapsulated in a piece of personality that has engulfed it. The character of this complete particle will depend partly on the character of the real object, say a gramophone, and partly on the character of the particle of the personality that engulfs it. If the piece of the personality is concerned with sight, the gramophone when playing is felt to be watching the patient. The object, angered at being engulfed, swells up, so to speak, and suffuses and controls the piece of personality that engulfs it: to that extent the particle is felt to have become a thing. (Bion, 1956, pp. 39–40)

Through the repeated evacuation of these parts of his or her mind, the schizophrenic's thought and capacity to attend to reality are progressively whittled away. The accumulation of bizarre objects builds up a persecutory egocentric world in which the schizophrenic is destined to remain trapped.

See PSYCHOSIS; THINKING; BION

Bion, Wilfred (1956) 'Development of schizophrenic thought', *Int. J. Psycho-Anal.* 37:344–6; republished (1967) in W. R. Bion, *Second Thoughts.* Heinemann, pp. 36–42.
—— (1957) 'Differentiation of the psychotic from non-psychotic personalities', *Int. J. Psycho-Anal.* 38:266–75; republished (1967) in W.R. Bion, *Second Thoughts*, pp. 43–64.

Breast

The part of mother with which the infant is first in contact is her breast. Klein became aware that the infant has only partial perceptions of the objects in his world, for reasons that depend on his neurophysiology and also his emotional development. She consequently described the part-object as 'the breast'.

Although at first it was imagined that the physical breast was experienced as physically present and separate from the rest of the physical mother, the term has come to acquire the general meaning of the first part-object [see PART-OBJECTS], which, latterly, means the containing maternal object and contrasts with the paternal penis, and rival babies.

As a part-object the 'breast' has various possible characteristics according to the needs of the infant at any one moment. Some of the baby's experience will feel good, and the breast is then conceived as a good one (the 'good' breast), while bad experience leads to a conception of the 'bad' breast.

See OBJECTS; PART-OBJECTS

Castration

Classically, Freud's view was that the core of the oedipal problem was that sexual (libidinal) desires brought with them the risk of the little boy being castrated by his father. There were certain problems with this theory, not least the problem of understanding the little girl's Oedipus complex. Klein described (1932) an anxiety in girls which was the counterpart of castration anxiety – the fears aroused by the girl's phantasy attacks on her mother's insides, and on the objects she believes reside there: mother's babies and also father's penis which, she believes, forms a permanent coitus inside mother. The combined object of mother-with-penis or penis inside breast is extremely violent and frightening [see COMBINED PARENT FIGURE]. The little girl fears retaliation, in kind, for her invading, spoiling and robbing attacks on her mother's body and its contents [see 6. FEMININITY PHASE; 8. EARLY ANXIETY-SITUATIONS]. The little boy, too, has similar phantasies of attacking mother, but these centre to a major extent on the father's penis, which is accommodated inside her.

Klein believed she had discovered a forerunner of castration anxiety which, based in the very sadistic pregential phases, gives a particularly strong fear to the castration anxiety. Thus her contribution at this time (in the 1930s) was to reinforce the classical view of the anxieties that beset the infant and child by showing the especially primitive elements that underlie, and are drawn into, the genital configuration from earlier developmental phases. Thus she thought she was enhancing classical theory by extending it back to earlier periods with which it has genetic continuity, a method Freud had always himself employed [see GENETIC CONTINUITY].

Klein, Melanie (1932) *The Psycho-Analysis of Children. WMK* 2.

Child

Child analysis drew attention to the childlike wishes and fears as living issues actually in the analysis [see CHILD ANALYSIS]. Deriving from this is an emphasis on seeing the child in the analysis of adults. The child part of the personality is often felt to be extremely valuable, because of its life and its embodiment of the emotions and feelings; at the same time it is extremely vulnerable, humiliating and therefore repudiated. In practice the split between the child part of the personality and the adult is important. In the Kleinian framework, strictly speaking, it is the infant in the patient, including the infant in the child patient, which is addressed by the analysis.

See BABIES

Child analysis

When Freud, in 1905, had worked out the details of his theory of childhood sexuality, he had done so on the evidence he gained from the analysis of adult patients. He then sought direct evidence of the development of sexuality from the observation of children, and he put out the request for parents, in his circle in Vienna, to record their children's activity and conversation. The outcome of this was the Little Hans 'case', which served beautifully to confirm the provisional theories. A similar situation arose later when Freud had refined his theories further, particularly as a result of the interest he and Abraham had taken in psychotic patients, which gave rise to the theory of *narcissism* (Freud, 1914) and subsequently the place of the mechanisms of *introjection* and *projection* (Freud, 1917) and the development of the structural model (Freud, 1923). There was a further turning to a psychoanalytic interest in children from 1917 onwards [see 1. TECHNIQUE].

Psychoanalysis and education: In Vienna Hug-Hellmuth (1921) started a psychoanalytically inspired form of pedagogic child instruction. She did not, however, use interpretations as in adult analysis, or even, for that matter, as Little Hans's father had done. Hug-Hellmuth believed that the child, unlike the adult, was not motivated to come for analysis; therefore interpretations would mean nothing. It was, she thought, the family that suffered and not the child. In addition she thought that the ego had not developed sufficiently in strength to withstand the added burden of psychoanalytic interpretation. She believed, too, that the children should be seen in their own home; and hence there was no chance of developing a transference with children.

The first child patients: In Budapest Klein (1918–19) started to practise a different form of child analysis. This, we now know, was first of all with her own children, an activity that would now be frowned upon (and she appears to have suppressed the fact after the publication of her first paper in 1919 (Petot, 1979; Grosskurth, 1986)), though at the time, with the evidence of Little Hans's successful treatment, it seemed much more straightforward. She had been encouraged by Abraham, who analysed his daughter (Abraham, 1974); and indeed Freud also analysed his own daughter (Gay, 1988).

Klein fairly soon came to different conclusions from Hug-Hellmuth. She believed (Klein, 1927) that children could, once they had experienced interpretations of their anxieties, be motivated (unconsciously) within themselves for the analysis. In fact she believed that children had a much greater unconscious understanding of their own problems and the nature of interpretative help than was apparent (reported by Alix Strachey, 1924).

Klein's first practice was to answer frankly and openly the request for sexual knowledge that the children presented. In this she was influenced by Freud's advice to Little Hans's father (Freud, 1909) and also by his case history of the Wolf man, whose pregenital sexual phantasies were traumatic, because they coincided with witnessing the primal scene of intercourse between his parents (Freud, 1918). However, when Klein presented her work to a meeting of the Hungarian Psycho-Analytical Society in 1919, von Freund advised her that she was not addressing the unconscious questions that the child was *not* asking. Klein took the point and from then on was an enthusiast for interpreting the unconscious. Later she began to use toys and the standard play technique was evolved [see 1. TECHNIQUE].

A technique with children: Klein then rapidly produced a series of papers, all aiming to show the importance of child analysis and her play technique in understanding the early forms of adult neuroses, and she lectured in Vienna in 1924 on her method, which had now grown completely away from Hug-Hellmuth's. Hug-Hellmuth had recently died, murdered by her own nephew (whom she had brought up!), but

Anna Freud had taken up the mantle in Vienna. The difference in technique created an atmosphere of resentment in Vienna which was exacerbated by the prickly and forceful quality of Klein's personality.

Friction became warfare during 1926–7. When Anna Freud delivered a detailed and swingeing attack on Klein's technique to the Berlin Society in 1926, Klein had already moved to London. But battle had commenced, and the next clash was a symposium held by the British Psycho-Analytical Society in the following year to discuss a book of the lectures given by Anna Freud (published in England only in 1946!).

The arguments dwelt largely on Anna Freud's assertions of the general principles that she had learnt from Hug-Hellmuth in Vienna. By now, Klein had sufficient clinical evidence to push aside and demolish these objections [see 1. TECHNIQUE].

The arguments of the British symposium did not unsettle the Viennese, but entrenched them further behind Anna Freud; a stalemate which endures today in the systematized theories of ego-psychology [see EGO-PSYCHOLOGY] and Kleinian psychoanalysis.

Abraham, Karl (1974) 'Little Hilda: daydreams and a symptom in a seven-year-old girl', *Int. Rev. Psycho-Anal.* 1:5–14.

Freud, Anna (1946) *The Psycho-Analytical Treatment of Children*. Imago.

Freud, Sigmund (1909) 'Analysis of a phobia in a five-year-old boy'. *S.E.* 10, pp. 3–149.

—— (1914) 'On narcissism'. *S.E.* 14, pp. 67–102.

—— (1917) 'Mourning and melancholia'. *S.E.* 14, pp. 237–60.

—— (1918) 'From the history of an infantile neurosis'. *S.E.* 17, pp. 3–123.

—— (1923) *The Ego and the Id*. *S.E.* 19, pp. 3–66.

Gay, Peter (1988) *Freud: A Life for our Time*. Dent.

Grosskurth, Phyllis (1986) *Melanie Klein*. Hodder & Stoughton.

Hug-Hellmuth, Hermine von (1921) 'On the technique of child analysis', *Int. J. Psycho-Anal.* 2:287–305.

Klein, Melanie (1927) Symposium of child analysis'. *WMK* 1, pp. 139–69.

Petot, Jean-Michel (1979) *Melanie Klein: Premières découvertes et premier système 1919–1932*. Paris: Bourdas/Dunod.

Strachey, Alix (1924) 'Alix's report of Melanie Klein's Berlin lecture', in (1986) *Bloomsbury Freud: The Letters of James and Alix Strachey 1924–1925*. Chatto & Windus, pp. 325–9.

Classical psychoanalysis

See EGO-PSYCHOLOGY

Coitus   A child's play shows the numerous sexual theories he or she is trying to explore. Klein discovered (in the 1920s) that many of these theories derived from pregenital phantasies – mutual sucking, biting, feeding with milk, with faeces, beating, etc.

The implications, for her, were that phantasies of the primal scene commenced very early in life, and that there must be some genital stirrings (premonitions of a parental couple) even in the oral and anal stages. This contrasted with the orthodox theory at the time in which ideas of parental intercourse were normally delayed until the genital phase, and were the basis for the Oedipus complex. The result was that Klein found herself describing pregenital forms of the Oedipus complex and dating earlier and earlier the timing of its origins [see 4. OEDIPUS COMPLEX].

Klein also described an object which she termed 'the combined parent figure', which is the infant's phantasy of the parents as locked together in mutual preoccupation with each other.

See COMBINED PARENT FIGURE; LINKING

Combined parent figure One of the infant's most

profound experiences is the wish to penetrate mother's body out of anger and frustration and do harmful things to the organs and objects found there, partly out of jealousy of her and of them, partly because the child wants to steal them for himself. This raiding and robbing is the nuclear core of a terrifying phantasy of the maternal body containing the father's penis.

The profound and escalating terror is that mother and the objects inside her will retaliate against the infant. It arises from the oral wishes which led to wanting to incorporate all these things for himself and the infant ends up in the midst of a phantasy that all these retaliatory wounded objects are now marauding – as internal persecutors in his own insides after being introjected there, and as the persecuting external figure. Thus the aggressive phantasies about parental sexual intercourse arouse huge amounts of paranoia [see 8. EARLY ANXIETY-SITUATIONS].

The phantasy of the combined parent figure is that the parents, or rather their sexual organs [see PART-OBJECTS], are locked together in permanent intercourse. It is the earliest and most primitive phantasy of the oedipal situation: 'A special intensity is imparted to this danger-situation by the fact that a union of the two parents is in question . . . these united parents are extremely cruel and much dreaded assailants' (Klein, 1929, p. 213). The combined parent figure is expressed as mother with the father inside her: '. . . the idea of the maternal penis, and indeed of one concealed inside the vagina' (Klein, 1923, p. 69).

The infant's fury and rage lead him or her to imbue this intercourse with as much violence between the parents as he or she is feeling towards them:

. . . these sadistic masturbation phantasies . . . fall into two distinct, though interconnected, categories. In those of the first category the child employs various sadistic means to make a direct onslaught upon the parents either combined in coitus or separately; in those of the second . . . its belief in its sadistic omnipotence over its parents finds expression in a more indirect fashion. It endows them with instruments of mutual destruction, transforming their teeth, nails, genitals, excrements and so on, into dangerous weapons and animals, etc., and pictures them, according to its own desires, as tormenting and destroying each other in the act of copulation. (Klein, 1932, p. 200)

The intercourse the parents perform is dangerous to themselves and there are horrendous hostilities between the child and this particularly menacing figure. The combined parent figure is one of the most terrifying persecutors in the *dramatis personae* of childhood.

Envy: The combined parent figure was an early conception of Klein's, and later the source of the especially strong violence and sadism connected with this infantile phantasy figure derived from the envy of the parental intercourse and the exclusion from it of the separate infant [see 12. ENVY].

Meltzer (1973) described the development of sexuality and creativity in the personality in terms of the struggle to move beyond this part-object figure to reconstruct it in whole objects with more realistic versions of the mother and father, a process inherent in the depressive position. Internally such a realistic parental intercourse forms an internal object that is the basis – or felt to be the fount – of personal creativity: sexual, intellectual and aesthetic.

Klein, Melanie (1923) 'The role of the school in the libidinal development of the child'. *WMK* 1, pp. 59–76.
—— (1929) 'Infantile anxiety-situations reflected in a work of art and in the creative impulse'. *WMK* 1, pp. 210–18.
—— (1932) *The Psycho-Analysis of Children. WMK* 2.
Meltzer, Donald (1973) *Sexual States of Mind.* Perth: Clunie.

See COITUS

Concern See GRATITUDE; LOVE

Confusional states
Confusional states are common in schizophrenic patients, and their origins have been described by Rosenfeld (1965). He showed that there may be a primary *confusion of instincts* which is extremely troubling. If the death instinct dominates the libido then the good object is hated and destroyed by mistake, as it were, leading to

intense insecurity and inability to sort out internal states and impulses. This confusion of the instincts is a pernicious result of *envy* in which the good object is hated for being good [see 12. ENVY].

Confusion of self and object: Rosenfeld also described various forms of confusion that formed defences against envy – a complicated situation to disentangle in the psychoanalysis of schizophrenics. The ego is confused with the objects as a result of omnipotent forms of projection and introjection which are aimed at denying separation and dependency [see NARCISSISM]. In particular huge parts of the self are put into the object through the massive and violent operation of the mechanism of projective identification.

A form of fusion of the self with the external world may be achieved in some autistic states of retreat into a sole occupation with bodily sensations [see AUTISM].

This kind of confusion between self and object is secondary and for the purpose of defence. It contrasts with a primary state of fusion and regressive confusion described by ego-psychologists (typically Mahler *et al.*, 1975), who follow the orthodox theory of primary narcissism [see NARCISSISM]. *Primary narcissism* is a quite different theoretical framework, which asserts that there is no primary experience of 'me' and 'not-me', no boundary to the ego at birth and therefore no ego at the outset of life. This is not accepted by Kleinians, who accept an ego, ego-functions and an ego-boundary as present and active from birth. Confusion of ego and object is thus secondary and the result of omnipotent primitive defence mechanisms.

Mahler, Margaret, Pine, Fred and Bergman, Anni (1975) *The Psychological Birth of the Human Infant*. Hutchinson.
Rosenfeld, Herbert (1965) *Psychotic States*. Hogarth.

Constitutional factor

Immediately after birth constitutional factors are compounded by environmental factors, and the deeply intertwined relationship between nurture and nature from the outset makes the two extremely difficult to disentangle. The problem is aggravated because of the enormous amount of interaction that has taken place in the development of an individual before any direct symbolic communication with him is possible. Study of the very early states of interaction between the constitutional factor and the environment depends on observational approaches such as infant observation [see INFANT OBSERVATION] or academic psychological studies of early cognition; or else on a psychoanalytic study of these early conditions through the 'frozen sections' of development that are presented by states of autism (Meltzer *et al.*, 1975; Tustin, 1981) [see AUTISM]. There is no doubt that many psychological characteristics, like bodily ones, are inherited.

The genetics of schizophrenia, for instance, shows satisfactorily that there is a definite inherited precondition, which is acted upon by environmental (psychological) factors to bring out the psychosis (Gelder, 1983).

Biological pessimism: Much criticism of Klein has arisen from her emphasis on 'internal' factors, arising from the pessimistic supposition that anything endowed within the biological constitution is unchangeable. This was not Klein's view, and indeed is manifestly untrue biologically, since human beings are endowed with a psychology that is especially adaptable. It is in fact the hallmark of Freud's theories that human instincts are typically extraordinarily plastic. The endowment of a sexual instinct, for instance, does not prevent the sexual attractiveness of a seemingly unlimited array of all sorts of partners, as well as all kinds of fetish objects that are rivetingly attractive to certain appetites. The impulsiveness of the fashion industry would not exist without an extraordinary willingness on the part of the biologically endowed sexual make-up to adapt and reach after novelty. In fact part of the human biological endowment is to be attracted to change and towards new objects [see DEVELOPMENT].

Klein is often criticized for being unduly biological when accepting the concept of the death instinct from Freud. However, the plasticity of the death instinct, leading to the variety, ingenuity and adaptability of human destructiveness under psychological and social influences, is no less than those of the sexual instinct.

Envy: However, Klein did emphasize that the relative proportions of libido and destructiveness may be determined by heredity. A constitutional factor has received mounting evidence from twin studies of a genetic factor in schizophrenia. A balance of instincts weighted in favour of the death instinct is a constitutional predisposition to particularly severe envy from the outset (see Rosenfeld, 1965), which disturbs both child and mother and ultimately leads to a schizoid child, a desperate mother and a schizophrenogenic interpersonal environment in the family. A preponderance of destructive impulses may be matched by an inherent weakness of the ego, leading to a very low threshold for frustration [see 12. ENVY].

It is implicit in the concept of unconscious phantasy that there is constitutional grounding for the development of a mind [see MIND], and for that development to be in the form of representing all sensations and experience as relationships with objects [see INNATE KNOWLEDGE]. That there must be some biological grounding in the body for the development of a mind would hardly be challenged by ordinary scientific and psychological opinion. The problem is where to set the limit of the psychological self which struggles with the biological endowment [see SUBJECTIVITY]. Klein, without denying the importance of the social environment, went a long way towards a picture of a purely psychological self grappling with its own internal states, with constitutional factors (like social ones) acting only as constraining limits.

See EXTERNAL WORLD; INNATE KNOWLEDGE

Bion, Wilfred (1956) 'Development of schizophrenic thought', *Int. J. Psycho-Anal.* 37:344–6; republished (1967) in W. R. Bion, *Second Thoughts*. Heinemann, pp. 36–42.

Gelder, John (1983) *Oxford Textbook of Psychiatry*. Oxford: Oxford University Press.

Meltzer, Donald, Bremner, John, Hoxter, Shirley, Weddell, Doreen and Wittenberg, Isca (1975) *Explorations in Autism*. Perth: Clunie.

Rosenfeld, Herbert (1965) *Psychotic States*. Hogarth.

Tustin, Frances (1981) *Autistic States in Children*. Routledge & Kegan Paul.

Containing

The notion of 'containing' has become a decisive concept for most British forms of analytic psychotherapy inside and outside the Kleinian Group of psychoanalysts. It derives from Klein's original description of projective identification [see 13. PROJECTIVE IDENTIFICATION] in which one person in some sense contains a part of another. This has given rise to a theory of development based on the emotional contact of infant with mother and, by extension, a theory of the psychoanalytic contact.

The concept gradually formed in the literature as Kleinian analysts groped to explore projective identification:

> The patient . . . showed that he had projected his damaged self containing the destroyed world, not only into all the other patients, but into me, and had changed me in this way. But instead of becoming relieved by this projection he became more anxious, because he was afraid of what I was then putting back into him, whereupon his introjective processes became severely disturbed. (Rosenfeld, 1952, pp. 80–1)

Here Rosenfeld is using the theory that Klein established of the development of the ego through repeated cycles of introjection and projection; but he is taking it further by recognizing that it is not just projection of the object, but also projection of parts of the self – projective identification in cycle with introjective identification. Jaques (1953) was similarly experimenting with these kinds of ideas at the same time [see SOCIAL DEFENCE SYSTEMS].

Bion (1959) is normally credited with the mature form of this model:

> Throughout the analysis the patient resorted to projective identification with a persistence suggesting it was a mechanism of which he had never been able sufficiently to avail himself; the analysis

afforded him the opportunity for the exercise of a mechanism of which he had been cheated ... there were sessions which led me to suppose that the patient felt there was some object that denied him the use of projective identification ... there are elements which indicate that the patient felt that parts of his personality that he wished to repose in me were refused entry by me ... When the patient strove to rid himself of fears of death which were felt to be too powerful for his personality to contain he split off his fears and put them into me, the idea apparently being that if they were allowed to repose there long enough they would undergo modification by my psyche and could then be safely reintrojected. On the occasion I have in mind the patient had felt ... that I evacuated them so quickly that the feelings were not modified but had become more painful ... he strove to force them into me with increased desperation and violence. His behaviour, isolated from the context of analysis, might have appeared to be an expression of primary aggression. The more violent his phantasies of projective identification, the more frightened he became of me. There were sessions in which such behaviour expressed unprovoked aggression, but I quote this series because it shows the patient in a different light, his violence a reaction to what he felt was my hostile defensiveness. The analytic situation built up in my mind a sense of witnessing an extremely early scene. I felt that the patient had witnessed in infancy a mother who dutifully responded to the infant's emotional displays. The dutiful response had in it an element of impatient 'I don't know what's the matter with the child.' My deduction was that in order to understand what the child wanted the mother should have treated the infant's cry as more than a demand for her presence. From the infant's point of view she should have taken into her, and thus experienced, the fear that the child was dying. It was this fear that the child could not contain. He strove to split it off together with the part of the personality in which it lay and project it into mother. An understanding mother is able to experience the feeling of dread that this baby was striving to deal with by projective identification, and yet retain a balanced outlook. This patient had had to deal with a mother who could not tolerate experiencing such feelings and reacted either by denying them ingress, or alternatively by becoming a prey to the anxiety which resulted from introjection of the baby's bad feelings. (Bion, 1959, pp. 103–4)

If the analyst is closed or unresponsive, 'The result is excessive projective identification by the patient and a deterioration of his developmental processes' (p. 105). Although he says that the schizophrenic's disturbance '... finds its main source in the inborn disposition' (p. 105), Bion believed that both genetic and environmental influences disturb normal projective identification.

Maternal reverie: Bion (1962) described the mother's state of mind when she can take in the infant's projected terror as *reverie*. This was expressed succinctly by Segal as a summary of Kleinian technique with schizophrenics [see 1. TECHNIQUE]. It describes, she indicated, the way in which a patient's ego may be built up through introjection of an object that can contain and *understand* his experiences:

> ... the nearest I can come to it is to explain it by a model, based on Melanie Klein's concept of the paranoid-schizoid position and Bion's concept of the 'mother capable of containing projective identification'. In this model, the infant's relation to his first object can be described as follows: When an infant has an intolerable anxiety, he deals with it by projecting it into the mother. The mother's response is to acknowledge the anxiety and do whatever is necessary to relieve the infant's distress. The infant's perception is that he has projected something intolerable into his object, but the object was capable of containing it and dealing with it. He can then reintroject not only his original anxiety but an anxiety modified by having been contained. He also introjects an object capable of containing and dealing with anxiety. The containment of anxiety by an external object capable of understanding is a beginning of mental stability. This mental stability may be disrupted from two sources. The mother may be unable to bear the infant's projected anxiety and he may introject an experience of even greater terror than the one he had projected. It may also be disrupted by excessive destructive omnipotence of the infant's phantasy. In this model the analytic situation provides a container. (Segal, 1975, pp. 134–5)

The analyst is certainly one container, and mother is another, but the theory does not stop there. As is clear, anyone with a maternal aspect to their character who can listen (see Langs, 1978) could function in this way [see REVERIE]. Indeed, society itself may function as an emotional container of one kind or another, more or less defensive. In an early use of this idea, Jaques (1953) explored social institutions, such as funerals, in detail:

> Individuals may put their internal conflicts into persons in the external world, unconsciously follow the course of conflict by means of projective identification, and re-internalize the course and outcome of the externally perceived conflict by means of introjective identification. (p. 21) [see SOCIAL DEFENCE SYSTEMS]

Although this development of the concept of projective identification was partly an effort of the whole Kleinian Group in the 1950s, Bion became its major exponent, harvesting the biggest fruits [see 13. PROJECTIVE IDENTIFICATION]. The maternal mind in this state of 'reverie' performs a function to which Bion gave a neutral term – 'alpha-function' [see REVERIE; ALPHA-FUNCTION].

Mirroring the infant: Winnicott (1967) developed a notion of a maternal state that reflected the infant's. He acknowledged Lacan's (1949) descriptions of the child's discoveries about himself in a mirror, but went further to describe the way in which the mother's face is an emotional 'mirror' for infant and child. He described this as a method of the child's learning about his own internal states. It is clearly related to the kind of projective/introjective cycles that the Kleinians had been developing. However, in describing this visual interaction Winnicott was inevitably focusing on a later period of development. Any interference in this interaction is attributed to the external object only.

The container–contained relation: Bion strove to outline a general theory. He postulated three basic forms of the container–contained relationship – *parasitic, symbiotic* and *commensal*:

> By 'commensal' I mean a relationship in which two objects share a third to the advantage of all three. By 'symbiotic' I understand a relationship in which one depends on another to mutual advantage. By 'parasitic' I mean to represent a relationship in which one depends on another to produce a third which is destructive of all three. (Bion, 1970, p. 95)

Bion's theory of *thinking* consists of the *mating* of a pre-conception and a realization, the result being a conception and a step in the building of thought and theories [see THINKING; PRE-CONCEPTION]. The relation between the terms in this process is that of the container to the contained.

The mystic and the establishment: Bion (1970) applied this theory to social systems, in a radically different way to Jaques [see SOCIAL DEFENCE SYSTEMS]. He regarded the social group as containing the individual. This was an idea considered a long time before by Pichon-Riviere (1931) but without the theoretical back-up that Bion (1970) later possessed. A social group functions to establish a fixed social order of things (the *establishment*). This conflicts with the inspiration and originality of the individual (referred to as the *mystic*, or the genius). He has to be *contained* by the establishment of the group. Often the individual's creativity is crushed by the rigidity of the system 'by compression or denudation'; alternatively certain special individuals erupt in the group, which goes to pieces under their influence (Bion cites Jesus within the constraints of Israel); or a final possibility is the mutual adaptation of one to the other, with a development of both the individual and the group. These ideas expand upon and develop one element of his previous theory of groups [see BASIC ASSUMPTIONS] – the pairing group, in which the pair is the container and the contained.

Thus the outcome is detrimental to the contained, or to the

container, or mutually developing to both. Bion saw this social application of the theory of containers as only one level, with similar patterns of containing recurring at the level of the individual containing himself. As an example of an individual struggling to contain himself, he cited the stammerer attempting to contain his emotions in words. Ultimately Bion was working with the idea of the sexual union of the penis contained in the vagina, experienced in all forms of joining and linking. The problems that such a relationship throws up in the terms of Klein's early stages of the Oedipus complex affect the linking of all mental problems [see LINKING; 4. OEDIPUS COMPLEX; COMBINED PARENT FIGURE].

Reciprocity: Bion also made an elaborate point about the reciprocity of the container–contained relationship. A word may contain a meaning, but '. . . conversely a meaning can contain a word – which may or may not be discovered' (Bion, 1970, p. 106). This cryptic point is a reference to the man who stammers so that the words which should contain his emotions become engulfed and squeezed by the force of the emotion into a stammer or babble. The word in this sense is a container affected and disrupted by the emotion it is supposed to contain, an example which Bion described in other terms:

> . . . he was trying to 'contain' his emotions within a form of words, as one might speak of a general attempting to 'contain' enemy forces within a given zone. The words that should have represented the meaning the man wanted to express were fragmented by the emotional forces to which he wished to give only verbal expression: the verbal formulation could not 'contain' his emotions, which broke through and dispersed it as enemy forces might break through the forces that strove to contain them. (Bion, 1970, p. 94)

Bion was engaged in a characteristic manoeuvre with his reader. On the one hand we see the word as container of meaning; on the other, in the same example, the meaning takes over and contains the word. This sudden change of perspective is a manoeuvre which fascinated Bion. He called it a change of vertex, or a transformation, and gave it great importance; particularly because it results in a psychic 'catastrophe' in the mind of the reader (see below).

Memory: Reciprocity is particularly important for the psychoanalyst when he comes to consider memory – his own memory. He may be filled with memories. Alternatively, memories may be saturated with emotions. In this reciprocally saturated relationship the analyst is not capable of discovery, because of the saturation. Bion wanted to distinguish 'memory' in this sense from something which he called 'remembering'. He made the distinction by considering two situations: one in which the patient comes with a *memory* of a dream to tell the analyst, the second when a dream suddenly appears, as a coherent whole, in the mind of the patient, having been absent the moment before (remembering). The analyst is required to perform the second function – remembering – and must make himself patent for recall to happen without effort (or desire) in the course of a timeless moment [see MEMORY AND DESIRE].

When contact between patient and analyst is stultified, the lack of spontaneous moments – which are replete with catastrophe – is an important cause of failure of a psychoanalytic treament:

> The patient will be at a loss to convey his meaning, or the meaning he wishes to convey will be too intense for him to express properly, or the formulation will be so rigid that he feels that the meaning conveyed is devoid of any interest or vitality. Similarly the interpretations given by the analyst, 'the contained', will meet with the apparently co-operative response of being repeated for confirm-ation, which deprives 'the contained' of meaning either by compression or denudation. Failure to observe or demonstrate the point may produce an outwardly progressive but factually sterile analysis. The clue lies in the observation of the fluctuations which make the analyst at one moment 'the container' and the analysand 'the contained', and at the next reverse the roles ... The more familiar the analyst becomes with the configuration 'container' and 'contained', and with events in the session that approximate to these two representations, the better. (Bion, 1970, p. 108)

Without a recognition of the reciprocity, the damaging aspects of the container–contained relationship are likely to crop up unheeded.

Change: Bion had been interested for a long time in the nature of psychic change. His work on the nature of thinking had established the way in which projective-identification-like linking between mental elements gradually built up a thinking apparatus which effected the transmutation of emotional experience into cognitive activity [see THINKING]. This apparatus for thinking is equally a container of emotional states. It entails the generation of theories with which to think. Development entails the development of this containing, thinking apparatus.

However, he was struck by the need in analysis to understand change, and to recognize that it involved unsettling the container of emotional states. He began to look outside psychoanalysis, to other sciences, to examine the conditions for change to take place in theories. He called theories – and all other entities contained in the mind – *conjunctions* of events: theories are regular conjunctions. Changing the structure of the thinking apparatus therefore demands a destructuring of the theories and a re-establishing of new conjunctions.

This is an activity closely in line with Stokes's (1955) description of the artistic process and might be taken as a general psychic process [see SYMBOL-FORMATION]. Bion did indeed turn this into a general psychic process, and related it to the essentials of Kleinian theory. The destructuring is a process of fragmentation, and Bion designated it as a manifestation of paranoid-schizoid processes. In line with Segal (1952) he placed the restructuring as a part of the depressive position. Change therefore involves oscillations between the paranoid-schizoid and depressive positions – he represented this as Ps-D [see Ps-D]. These oscillations, however, make severe emotional demands. To sustain the destructuring means sustaining anxieties about disintegration of the mind and gives rise to Bion's view that change involves a potential catastrophe. On the other hand, the restructuring entails all the emotions of the depressive position in relation to a damaged object demanding repair. The capacity to develop entails a process of *catastrophic change* and the capacity to withstand and contain the elements of the process which represent annihilation and death.

Bion, Wilfred (1959) 'Attacks on linking', *Int. J. Psycho-Anal.* 30:308–15; republished (1967) in W. R. Bion, *Second Thoughts.* Heinemann, pp. 93–109.

—— (1962) 'A theory of thinking', *Int. J. Psycho-Anal.* 33:306–10; republished (1967) in *Second Thoughts*, pp. 110–19.

—— (1970) *Attention and Interpretation.* Tavistock.

Jaques, Elliott (1953) 'On the dynamics of social structure', *Human Relations* 6:3–23; republished (1955) as 'Social systems as a defence against persecutory and depressive anxiety', in Melanie Klein, Paula Heimann and Roger Money-Kyrle, eds *New Directions in Psycho-Analysis.* Tavistock, pp. 78–98.

Lacan, Jacques (1949) 'La stade du miroir comme formateur de la fonction du Je', *Revue française de Psychanalyse* 20:449–55.

Langs, Robert (1978) *The Listening Process.* New York: Jason Aronson.

Pichon-Riviere, Eduardo (1931) 'Position du problème de l'adaptation réciproque entre la société et les psychismes exceptionnels', *Revue française de Psychanalyse* 2:135–70.

Rosenfeld, Herbert (1952) 'Notes on the analysis of the superego conflict in an acute catatonic schizophrenic', *Int. J. Psycho-Anal.* 33:111–31; republished (1955) in Klein *et al.*, eds *New Directions in Psycho-Analysis.* Tavistock, pp. 180–219; and (1965) in Herbert Rosenfeld, *Psychotic States.* Hogarth, pp. 63–103.

Segal, Hanna (1952) 'A psycho-analytic approach to aesthetics', *Int. J. Psycho-Anal.* 33:196–207; republished (1981) in *The Work of Hanna Segal.* New York: Jason Aronson, pp. 185–206.

—— (1975) 'A psycho-analytic approach to the treatment of schizophrenia', in *The Work of Hanna Segal*, pp. 131–6; previously published in Malcolm Lader, ed. *Studies of Schizophrenia.* Ashford: Headley, pp. 94–7.

Stokes, Adrian (1955) 'Form in art', in Klein *et al.*, eds *New Directions in Psycho-Analysis.* Tavistock, pp. 406–20.

Winnicott, Donald (1967) 'Mirror-role of mother and family in child development', in Peter Lomas, ed. (1967) *The Predicament of the Family*. Hogarth; republished (1971) in D. W. Winnicott, *Playing and Reality*. Tavistock, pp. 111–18.

Contempt

Contempt is one of the triad of key features in the manic defences: the other two are control and triumph (Segal, 1964). It represents the focus of the defensive (manic) denial of the importance of the object (Klein, 1935, 1940). As such it is specifically aimed against gratitude to an object which would, if felt, give rise to feelings of dependence and smallness, a dismantling of the feeling of omnipotence.

See MANIC DEFENCES; 10. DEPRESSIVE POSITION; GRATITUDE

Klein, Melanie (1935) 'A contribution to the psychogenesis of manic-depressive states'. *WMK* 1, pp. 262–89.
—— (1940) 'Mourning and its relation to manic-depressive states'. *WMK* 1, pp. 344–69.
Segal, Hanna (1964) *Introduction to the Work of Melanie Klein*. Heinemann; Hogarth, 1973.

Controversial Discussions (1943–4)

During the 1920s and 1930s the British Psycho-Analytical Society had developed a characteristic style of psychoanalytic theory and practice. This came into conflict with Viennese psychoanalysis. The differences broke out in bitterness in 1926–7 over Klein's practice of child psychoanalysis using play therapy [see 1. TECHNIQUE] but died down with a tendency for the two societies to ignore each other's diverging viewpoints. This was temporarily addressed when Ernest Jones in London and Paul Federn in Vienna began to arrange what were intended to become regular Exchange Lectures between the two Societies. Jones gave the first lecture in 1935 in Vienna (Jones, 1936) and Joan Riviere the second in 1936, also in Vienna (Riviere, 1936); Waelder's lecture in 1936 in London was followed by Waelder's response to Riviere, published in 1937 (Waelder, 1937). But by this time the political situation in Europe was deteriorating and the psychoanalytic conflict arrived literally on the doorstep of the British Society in 1938 when the Viennese psycho-analysts were forced to emigrate. Freud and Anna Freud came to London and formed the focus of a Viennese group of analysts in London who were opposed to Klein's views. They formed an opposition group together with certain British analysts, notably Edward Glover and Melitta Schmideberg (Klein's daughter), who had become disaffected with Klein's theories after the introduction of the concept of the depressive position in 1935 (Steiner, 1985).

At this point the British Society was riven with dispute as Klein and her close associates reacted badly to the criticisms and entrenched themselves in attempts to force their theories and their clinical material upon the newcomers. Committee business in the Society, already hampered by the dislocations of the Second World War in 1940 and 1941, became impossible, especially over the training of new psycho-analysts. A truce was eventually arranged, with an agreement to a series of monthly scientific meetings to discuss the controversial aspects of Klein's theories. Over a period of eighteen months a series of four papers was read by Kleinians on controversial aspects of their theories: in 1943 'On the nature and function of phantasy' by Susan Isaacs, discussed over five meetings; 'Certain functions of projection and introjection in early infancy' by Paula Heimann, discussed at two meetings; and 'Regression' by Paula Heimann and Susan Isaacs, discussed at two meetings; and then in 1944 (though by this time most of the Viennese analysts had ceased to attend the meetings and Glover had resigned from the Society altogether) 'The emotional life of the infant with special reference to the depressive position' by Melanie Klein, discussed at two meetings. These papers were published in rewritten forms in *Developments in Psycho-Analysis* (1952).

The Controversial Discussions resolved no scientific issues. They did concentrate the minds of the Kleinians to produce systematic accounts of their views and also demonstrated, to the surprise of the Viennese, the British analysts' sophistication and power of argument. The outcome was for each side to leave the other alone and to agree to a bureaucratic solution for the committee structure of the British Society and for the training of new psychoanalysts. The final agreement has been known as 'the Gentlemen's Agreement', though it was entered into by three women: Melanie Klein, Anna Freud and the President of the British Society, Sylvia Payne (Grosskurth, 1986). Since then a carefully controlled parity of membership on committees, especially the training committees, has been maintained by designating three groups within the society – the Klein Group, the 'B' Group, now called Contemporary Freudians, and a Middle Group of Independents.

Glover's summaries of his criticisms of the Kleinian papers were subsequently published (Glover, 1945) and Brierley was stimulated to write a number of papers which were collected together as a book on the new form of psychoanalysis (Brierley, 1946). Direct confrontations between Kleinian psychoanalysts and orthodox psychoanalysts (or ego-psychologists, as they have become) have tended to be avoided ever since; the debate between Greenson (1974, 1975) and Rosenfeld (1974) and the conference in 1985 on projective identification (Sandler, 1988) are rare published exceptions.

See 2. UNCONSCIOUS PHANTASY; 4. OEDIPUS COMPLEX

Brierley, Marjorie (1946) *Trends in Psycho-Analysis*. Hogarth.

Glover, Edward (1945) 'An examination of the Klein system of child psychology', *Psychoanal. Study Child* 1:1–43.

Greenson, Ralph (1974) 'Transference: Freud or Klein?', *Int. J. Psycho-Anal.* 55:37–48.

—— (1975) 'Transference: Freud or Klein? A reply to the discussion by Herbert Rosenfeld', *Int. J. Psycho-Anal.* 56:243.

Grosskurth, Phyllis (1986) *Melanie Klein*. Hodder & Stoughton.

Jones, Ernest (1936) 'Early female sexuality', *Int. J. Psycho-Anal.* 16:262–73.

Riviere, Joan (1936) 'On the genesis of psychical conflict in earliest infancy', *Int. J. Psycho-Anal.* 17:395–422; republished (1952) in Klein *et al.*, eds *Developments in Psycho-Analysis*. Hogarth.

Rosenfeld, Herbert (1974) 'Discussion of the paper by Ralph R. Greenson, "Transference: Freud or Klein?"', *Int. J. Psycho-Anal.* 55:49–51.

Sandler, Joseph, ed. (1988) *Projection, Identification and Projective Identification*. Karnac.

Steiner, Riccardo (1985) 'Some thoughts about tradition and change arising from an examination of the British Psycho-Analytical Society's Controversial Discussions 1943–1944', *Int. Rev. Psycho-Anal.* 12:27–71.

Waelder, Robert (1937) 'The problem of the genesis of psychical conflict in earliest infancy', *Int. J. Psycho-Anal.* 18:406–73.

Countertransference

Countertransference underwent a remarkable metamorphosis in the 1950s to become an elegant concept central to modern psychoanalytic techniques. Heimann emphasized the human side of the patient/analyst transaction:

> The aim of the analyst's own analysis is not to turn him into a mechanical brain which can produce interpretations on the basis of a purely intellectual procedure, but to enable him to *sustain* his feelings as opposed to discharging them like the patient. (Heimann, 1960, pp. 9–10)

Her main thesis was that by '. . . comparing the feelings roused in himself with the content of the patient's associations and the qualities of his mood and behaviour, the analyst has the means for checking whether he has understood or failed to understand his patient' (p. 10). Previously Ferenczi (1919) had already described the offputting quality of the analyst who defends himself against any countertransference, and Fenichel (1941) also criticized the 'blank screen' view of the analyst's role. At this time, as well as Heimann and Racker in the Kleinian tradition, there was a widespread movement to take countertransference seriously (Winnicott, 1947; Berman, 1949; Little, 1951; Gitelson, 1952; Annie Reich, 1952; Weigert, 1952).

There are various steps in the history of the Kleinian concept of 'countertransference': (1) The importance of the analyst's feelings as an indicator of the patient's state of mind; (2) the discovery of a normal form of projective identification which is used as a method of *non-symbolic* communication; (3) cycles of introjective and projective identifications as the basis of an intrapsychic understanding of the interpersonal transference/countertransference situation between analyst and patient; (4) the idea of 'normal' countertransference; and (5) the importance of the analyst's mind above all else as the significant aspect of the patient's environment [see 1. TECHNIQUE].

(1) **Countertransference as indicator.** Heimann (1950, 1960) drew attention to the aspect of countertransference that is a *specific* response to the patient, and distinguished it from the intrusion of the analyst's own neurosis and neurotic transference into the psychoanalytic work. The countertransference, because of its potential specificity for the individual patient, may therefore become a precise instrument for probing the patient. This significant idea, though rejected by Klein herself, was specifically acknowledged by Rosenfeld (1952, p. 72) and by Bion (1955, p. 225).

(2) **Normal projective identification.** Subsequently Money-Kyrle (1956) and later Bion (1959) formulated clearer pictures of the analyst as a container for the patient's intolerable experiences, which, through the analytic process of putting experience into words, are thereby *contained*. This arose from distinguishing normal projective identification from the pathological form [see 13. PROJECTIVE IDENTIFICATION] and allowed a theory of the nature of empathy and also of the therapeutic effect of psychoanalytic interpretations to follow. Following the discovery of the phantasies involved in the mechanism of projective identification, it became possible to formulate, in *intrapsychic terms*, the *interpersonal* situation of the analytic setting. The analyst actually has his or her own feelings, just as the patient does (Heimann, 1950). Although Klein never really adopted this way of looking at the analytic session (though her observations of mothers and babies [Klein, 1952] are definitely pointing to the interpersonal interaction at the unconscious level), this 'un-Kleinian' interest in countertransference has become central to Kleinian practice today. And although Heimann never accepted projective identification as a significant concept and eventually broke away from Klein [see HEIMANN; KLEINIAN GROUP] she nevertheless strongly influenced the younger generation of Kleinians, who did relate countertransference to projective identification.

(3) **The analyst as a maternal container.** Bion (1959, 1962) developed these views into a more rigorous theory of maternal and therapeutic containing and used the concept of projective identification to illuminate the interpersonal interaction [see CONTAINING]. In this

view the infant cries, and performs a form of projective communication in which his distress is actually felt (introjected) by mother. If she is a capable mother and in reasonably good form at the moment she can do mental work inside herself to define the problem and what is needed to deal with it. This is an important ego-function involved in mothering [see REVERIE]. Being able to discern something of what is amiss, she can take action to provide for the child in such a way as to relieve something of the distress. The process of defining the distress and dealing with it is communicated in the act of dealing with the infant – say feeding him. This is a form of projecting back (reprojecting) the distress in the form of an understanding action. The child, once the mother has begun to provide and minister to his distress, can then take back his experience of distress – reintroject it – but now in a modified form. It has been modified by mother's function of defining and understanding the distress, expressed to the baby through the appropriate actions that help him. The experience thus bears the marks of mother's understanding imprinted in the modification of the experience. It is now an understood experience and, in the interaction between these two intrapsychic worlds, meaning has been generated. By introjecting this understood experience the infant can come to acquire the understanding that mother has – for example, if mother is accurate, he can realize through her ministrations that a certain experience means hunger (i.e. requires something to be put against his lips for sucking and feeding purposes). The accumulated occasions on which experiences have been understood begin to amount to an acquisition, inside himself, of an internal object that has the capacity to understand his experiences. This, as Segal puts it, '. . . is a beginning of mental stability' (Segal, 1975, p. 135). Segal described this mother–child interaction as a model for the therapeutic endeavour of the analyst [see CONTAINING].

(4) **Normal countertransference**. One of the problems in using countertransference in this way is the status of the analyst's feelings: whether they lead him to understand the patient or whether they result in his defensive evasion of his own feelings, with subsequent harm to the progress of the analysis. Money-Kyrle expressed this problem well when he distinguished 'normal countertransference'. When the process of analysis is going well:

> . . . there is a fairly rapid oscillation between introjection and projection. As the patient speaks, the analyst will, as it were, become introjectively identified with him, and having understood him inside, will reproject him and interpret. But what I think the analyst is most aware of is the projective phase – that is to say, the phase in which the patient is the representative of a former immature or ill part of himself, including his damaged objects, which he can now

understand and therefore treat by interpretation, in the external world. (Money-Kyrle, 1956, pp. 331–2)

Money-Kyrle was describing that familiar experience of realizing that the interpretation one is making may well be made of oneself; and he also recognized the equally familiar possibility that '. . . by discovering new patterns in a patient, the analyst can make "post-graduate" progress in his own analysis' (p. 341).

The countertransference problem: However, this is '. . . normal only in the sense of being an ideal, . . . his [the analyst's] understanding fails whenever the patient corresponds too closely with some aspect of himself which he has not yet learned to understand' (p. 332). In this case the analyst fails, by reason of his own neurosis, to comprehend the patient. This becomes apparent to the analyst as the feeling '. . . that the material has become obscure'. This causes strain for the analyst, and is an event to which the patient also responds. The strain and anxiety tend, Money-Kyrle says, to diminish further the capacity to understand, and a vicious circle has set in. It is at these points that the traditional concept of countertransference comes in – the interference by the analyst's own personal difficulties in the course of his understanding of the patient's difficulties. The analyst:

> . . . may become conscious of a sense of failure as the expression of an unconscious persecutory or depressive guilt . . . when that interplay between introjection and projection breaks down, the analyst may tend to get stuck in one or other of these two positions; and what he does with his guilt may determine the position he gets stuck in. In accepting the guilt, he is likely to get stuck with an introjected patient. If he projects it, the patient remains an incomprehensible figure in the external world. (p. 334)

This framework provides an extremely clear view of what goes wrong with countertransference.

Little (1951), Gitelson (1952) and many others have speculated on a particular method of getting out of this entrapment with one's own unconscious: by confiding one's mistake to the patient. But this method is condemned by Heimann (1960) as burdening the patient with the analyst's own personal matters. Money-Kyrle also argued, with clinical illustration, that the confession may amount to a collusion with the patient's projections. If the analyst has failed to understand, the patient is in a position to project into the analyst an impotent part of himself, so a subsequent attitude of contrition and humility on the analyst's part is not necessarily taken by the patient in the way it is intended by the analyst. The patient may instead take the analyst's attitude as confirmation of the projected impotence. Money-Kyrle described a patient who responded to the analyst's loss of understanding by:

... behaving as if he had taken from me what he felt he had lost, his father's clear, but aggressive, intellect, with which he attacked his impotent self in me. By this time, of course, it was useless to try to pick up the thread where I had first dropped it. A new situation had arisen which had affected us both. And before my patient's part in bringing it about could be interpreted, I had to do a silent piece of self-analysis involving the discrimination of two things which can be felt as very similar: my own sense of impotence at having lost the thread, and my patient's contempt for his impotent self, which he felt to be in me. Having made this interpretation to myself, I was eventually able to pass the second half of it on to my patient, and, by so doing, restored the normal analytic situation. (Money-Kyrle, 1956, pp. 336–7)

This process described by Money-Kyrle is clearly a cycle of projective identification into the analyst followed by the analyst's modification (silent piece of self-analysis), and the reprojection to the patient in the form of the analyst's interpretation, for possible reintrojection by the patient.

Drawing the analyst in: Money-Kyrle's view of countertransference developed the Kleinian idea of transference [see TRANSFERENCE]. With the idea of projective identification the analyst is more than just misperceived by the patient:

We see the patient not only as perceiving the analyst in a distorted way, reacting to this distorted view, and communicating these reactions to the analyst, but as also doing things to the analyst's mind, projecting *into* the analyst in a way which affects the analyst. (Segal, 1977, p. 82) [see 13. PROJECTIVE IDENTIFICATION]

Joseph (1975) has considerably refined the analyst's sensitivity to the patient's enactments in the transference [see ACTING-IN]. She described the analyst's own experience as very important in sensing how the patient is 'drawing the analyst in':

how our patients act on us for many varied reasons; how they try to draw us into their defensive systems; how they unconsciously act out with us in the transference, trying to get us to act out with them; how they convey aspects of their inner world built up from infancy – elaborated in childhood and adulthood, experiences often beyond the use of words, which we can only capture through the feelings aroused in us, through our counter-transference. (Joseph, 1985, p. 62)

This increased sensitivity has enabled analysts to make headway with difficult 'unreachable' borderline patients who seem stuck [see PSYCHIC EQUILIBRIUM; PATHOLOGICAL ORGANIZATIONS].

This view of countertransference is in line with the Kleinian idea of transference [see TRANSFERENCE]. With the idea of projective identification the analyst is more than just misperceived by the patient:

> We see the patient not only as perceiving the analyst in a distorted way, reacting to this distorted view, and communicating these reactions to the analyst, but also as doing things to the analyst's mind, projecting *into* the analyst in a way which affects the analyst. (Segal, 1977, p. 82)

Projective counter-identification: Grinberg (1962), endorsed by Segal (1977), described patients who felt the analyst was making violent projective identifications into them. This sensitivity of the patient is based on the early experience of parents who made massive projective identifications into him during infancy and childhood. Grinberg coined the term 'projective counter-identification' for this occurrence in the analytic situation.

(5) **The analyst's mind as the patient's object.** In recent years it has steadily emerged how sensitive patients are to the analyst's feelings and the analyst's methods of coping with those feelings, defensive or otherwise. Because one of the implications of the cycle of projective and introjective identifications is the process of modification in the analyst, who is required to have the stability of mind to cope with intolerable anxieties without becoming overly disturbed himself, it is in fact the patient's perceptions of the analyst's ability to modify anxiety that is really the important component. Rosenfeld (1987) and many others have drawn attention to this. For example, in discussing timing of interpretations, Rosenfeld wrote:

> In some situations one can interpret *too* quickly what one has recognized, with the result that the patient experiences what is said as a rejection of him ... the analyst has been experienced concretely as expelling the projected feelings and so expelling the patient as well. (Rosenfeld, 1987, p. 16)

Brenman Pick, in a detailed examination of this issue, stated: 'The patient receiving an interpretation will "hear" not only words or their consciously intended meaning. Some patients indeed only listen to the "mood" and do not seem to hear the words at all' (Brenman Pick, 1985, p. 158). Would that it were as straightforward as Money-Kyrle's 'silent piece of self-analysis'! In discussing a very disturbed patient, Brenman Pick emphasized that this problem '... involves a massive effort in managing one's feelings, and that even in so ill a patient, enquiry was, I believe, being made into the question of how I coped with my feelings' (p. 163). The significant external object for the patient is a mental one, not a physical one; it is the analyst's mind and the way it works [see REVERIE; CONTAINING].

Working through in the countertransference: The countertransference is now an important instrument for understanding the transference; the experience of the analyst as having experiences to work through for himself in his own mind has developed, and it is now understood that the mind of the analyst, with its fallibilities as well as its interpretations, is an extremely important aspect of the *total situation* (Joseph, 1985). Previously (in the 1940s and 1950s) the patient's objects were conceptualized as parts of the analyst's body (especially the breast and penis).

Latterly, however, it is realized, the part-objects to which the patient relates and into which he or she projects are parts of the analyst's mind, at least in neurotic patients:

> I have been trying to show that the issue is not a simple one; the patient does not just project into an analyst, but instead patients are quite skilled at projecting into particular aspects of the analyst . . . into the analyst's wish to be a mother, the wish to be all-knowing or to deny unpleasant knowledge, into his instinctual sadism, or into his defences against it. And above all he or she projects into the analyst's guilt, or into the analyst's internal objects. (Brenman Pick, 1985, p. 161)

The patient's acute awareness of the analyst's mind and its contents and functioning led Brenman Pick to describe the psychoanalytic encounter thus: 'If there is a mouth that seeks a breast as an inborn potential, there is, I believe, a psychological equivalent, i.e. a state of mind which seeks another state of mind' (p. 157) [see 1. TECHNIQUE].

Berman, Leo (1949) 'Counter-transferences and attitudes of the analyst in the therapeutic process', *Psychiatry* 12:159–66.

Bion, Wilfred (1955) 'Language and the schizophrenic', in Melanie Klein, Paula Heimann and Roger Money-Kyrle, eds (1955) *New Directions in Psycho-Analysis*. Tavistock, pp. 220–39; previous version published (1954) as 'Notes on the theory of schizophrenia', *Int. J. Psycho-Anal.* 35:113–18; and republished (1967) in W. R. Bion, *Second Thoughts*. Heinemann, pp. 23–35.

—— (1959) 'Attacks on linking', *Int. J. Psycho-Anal.* 40:308–15; republished (1967) in *Second Thoughts*, pp. 93–109.

—— (1962) *Learning from Experience*. Heinemann.

Brenman Pick, Irma (1985) 'Working through in the counter-transference', *Int. J. Psycho-Anal.* 66:157–66.

Fenichel, Otto (1941) *Problems of Psycho-Analytic Technique*. New York: Psycho-Analytic Quarterly Inc.

Ferenczi, Sandor (1919) 'Theory and technique of psycho-analysis', in *Further Contributions to Psycho-Analysis*. Hogarth.

Freud, Sigmund (1912) 'Recommendations to physicians practising psycho-analysis'. *S.E.* 12, pp. 109–20.

Gitelson, M. (1952) 'The emotional position of the analyst in the psycho-analytic situation', *Int. J. Psycho-Anal.* 33:1–10.

Grinberg, Leon (1962) 'On a specific aspect of countertransference due to the patient's projective identification', *Int. J. Psycho-Anal.* 43:436–40.

Heimann, Paula (1950) 'On counter-transference', *Int. J. Psycho-Anal.* 31:81–4.

—— (1960) 'Counter-transference', *Br. J. Med. Psychol.* 33:9–15.

Joseph, Betty (1975) 'The patient who is difficult to reach', in Peter Giovacchini, ed. *Tactics and Techniques in Psycho-Analytic Therapy*, vol. 2. New York: Jason Aronson, pp. 205–16.

—— (1985) 'Transference: the total situation', *Int. J. Psycho-Anal.* 66:447–54.

Klein, Melanie (1952) 'On observing the behaviour of young infants'. *WMK* 3.

Little, Margaret (1951) 'Counter-transference and the patient's response to it', *Int. J. Psycho-Anal.* 32:32–40.

Money-Kyrle, Roger (1956) 'Normal counter-transference and some of its deviations', in (1978) *The Collected Papers of Roger Money-Kyrle*. Perth: Clunie, pp. 330–42; previously published (1956) *Int. J. Psycho-Anal.* 37:360–6.

Racker, Heinrich (1948) 'A contribution to the problem of countertransference', published (1953) *Int. J. Psycho-Anal.* 34:313–24; republished (1968) as 'The countertransference neurosis', in *Transference and Countertransference*. Hogarth, pp. 105–26.

Reich, Annie (1952) 'On counter-transference', *Int. J. Psycho-Anal.* 32:25–31.

Rosenfeld, Herbert (1952) 'Notes on the psycho-analysis of the superego conflict in an acute catatonic schizophrenic', *Int. J. Psycho-Anal.* 33:111–31; republished (1955) in Melanie Klein, Paula Heimann and Roger Money-Kyrle, eds *New Directions in Psycho-Analysis*. Tavistock, pp. 180–219; and in Herbert Rosenfeld (1965) *Psychotic States*. Hogarth, pp. 63–103.

—— (1987) *Impasse and Interpretation*. Tavistock.

Segal, Hanna (1975) 'A psycho-analytic approach to the treatment of schizophrenia', in Malcolm Lader, ed. *Studies of Schizophrenia*. Ashford: Headley Brothers, pp. 94–7; republished (1981) in *The Work of Hanna Segal*. New York: Jason Aronson, pp. 131–6.

—— (1977) 'Counter-transference', *Int. J. Psycho-Anal. Psychother.* 6:31–7; republished (1981) in *The Work of Hanna Segal*, pp. 81–7.

Weigert, E. (1952) 'Contribution to the problem of terminating psycho-analysis', *Psychoanal. Q.* 21:465–80.

Winnicott, Donald W. (1947) 'Hate in the counter-transference', in D. W. Winnicott (1958) *Collected Papers: Through Paediatrics to Psycho-Analysis*. Hogarth, pp. 194–203.

Creativity

The creative achievements of human beings, who are endowed, at the outset of life, with base instincts, were always of interest to Freud. He coined the term 'sublimation' to denote the transmuting of a basic instinct for biological satisfaction into an exalted form of conduct and civilized achievement in the 'sublime' and non-physical world of symbols. For

Klein, creativity was a very much more complex process. It is not the simple transmuting of an instinct. Instead, there are several strands in Kleinian thought relating to creativity.

(i) Reparation: Klein herself wrote a note about the creative process in 1929, describing it *in relation to* a destructive attack on or by persecutors in phantasy. The creative effort was a subsequent attempt to restore the damage to objects felt to be external or internal. In that paper Klein used the term 'reparation' for the first time, and thereafter creativity in Kleinian writings has tended to be seen as a manifestation of reparation. The concept of reparation gained considerably in its significance when Klein introduced the idea of the depressive position [see 10. DEPRESSIVE POSITION; REPARATION]. Much of subsequent Kleinian interest in aesthetics (Segal, 1952, 1974; Stokes, 1955) has focused on the key role of reparation [see SYMBOL-FORMATION].

Creativity represents an essential part of the interaction in which the libidinal drives are brought into prominence over the destructive ones. In the process of investigating the nature of thought and of theory creation, Bion (1962) described, in his own terminology, the kind of unconscious activity that he discerned in Poincaré's account of scientific creativity. That entailed a loosening of all the links that bind the elements into a theory, with a subsequent repatterning around a new focal point, for which Bion took from Poincaré the term 'the selected fact'. In this Bion saw a process which he described as a movement towards the paranoid-schizoid position (loosening of integration) followed by the reorganizing around a new point, a nipple, that brings the parts together again in a movement back towards the depressive position. He represented this by the symbol Ps-D [see Ps-D].

(ii) Play: However, there are other important aspects of creativity, not often referred to directly. In her early work Klein dwelt a great deal on the nature of play as an *externalization of phantasy activity*, particularly unconscious phantasy. Unconscious phantasy is the basic building block of the mind itself [see 2. UNCONSCIOUS PHANTASY] and represents not only the unfolding of instinctual impulses within the mental field, but also the attempts to overcome the conflicts and pain to which the instinctual drives give rise. The process of externalization is part of this activity to create a more congenial psychical world. In the act of play, therefore, the child – and, indeed, the playful adult – is rehearsing, in a public and symbolic way, much of the basic pain of the human situation and exploring new solutions for it. The act of play itself is a creative process. Part of this process is the search for new objects towards which some of the impulses can be turned, thereby diminishing the internal tensions and conflicts.

Klein's notion of play was formed to a major extent from Freud's writings – Little Hans (1909), the *fort-da* game described in *Beyond the*

Pleasure Principle (Freud, 1920) – but especially, in the latter, from the description:

> As the child passes over from the passivity of the game, he hands on the disagreeable experience to one of his playmates and in this way revenges himself on a substitute. (Freud, 1920, p. 17)

Winnicott (1971) emphasized the importance of play, in order to distinguish his views from the Kleinian stress on destructiveness. Referring to Klein's stress on reparation, Winnicott writes: 'In my opinion Klein's important work does not reach to the subject of creativity itself' (Winnicott, 1971, p. 70). Play, in his view, is a joyful activity included within the category of transitional phenomena, whereas with Klein it is a serious business riven by unconscious painful and fearful phantasies.

(iii) Life instincts: In addition, in Freud's recasting of his instinct theory, the libido (life instincts) acquired characteristics beyond just the sexual, and these included a synthetic function of bringing things together – the paradigm, of course, being the coming together of partners in intercourse. This aspect of creativity has been stressed more by Meltzer (1973) in describing the structure of the personality as given by the internal parents in a creative relationship inside the individual. He described this as a godlike presence inside each person from which derives a sense of creativeness which can inspire the individual to his own constructive and creative efforts, and the important aspect of the personality is the relationship the individual has with his internal copulating parental couple [see COMBINED PARENT FIGURE].

Bion, Wilfred (1962) *Learning from Experience*. Heinemann.

Freud, Sigmund (1909) 'Analysis of a phobia in a five-year-old boy'. *S.E.* 10, pp. 1–149.

—— (1920) *Beyond the Pleasure Principle. S.E.* 18, pp. 1–69.

Klein, Melanie (1929) 'Infantile anxiety-situations reflected in a work of art and in the creative impulse'. *WMK* 1, pp. 210–18.

Meltzer, Donald (1973) *Sexual States of Mind*. Perth: Clunie.

Segal, Hanna (1952) 'A psycho-analytic approach to aesthetics', *Int. J. Psycho-Anal.* 33:196–207; republished (1955) in Melanie Klein, Paula Heimann and Roger Money-Kyrle, eds *New Directions in Psycho-Analysis*. Tavistock, pp. 384–405; and (1981) in *The Work of Hanna Segal*. New York: Jason Aronson, pp. 185–206.

—— (1974) 'Delusion and artistic creativity', *Int. Rev. Psycho-Anal.* 1:135–41; republished (1981) in *The Work of Hanna Segal*, pp. 207–16.

Stokes, Adrian (1955) 'Form in art', in Melanie Klein, Paula Heimann and Roger Money-Kyrle, eds (1955) *New Directions in Psycho-Analysis*. Tavistock, pp. 406–20.

Winnicott, D. W. (1971) *Playing and Reality*. Tavistock.

Criminality

In the great disputes over the technique of child analysis (1926–7) [see CHILD ANALYSIS; CONTROVERSIAL DISCUSSIONS], Anna Freud criticized Klein for equating play with verbal free associations [see 1. TECHNIQUE]. Klein had to justify this, and began to understand that play was an activity that could sometimes be compared to the kind of activity Freud (1916) described in certain kinds of characters who persistently behaved in self-defeating ways. Typically he pointed out how *criminality* was an externalization of guilt from unconscious sources [see UNCONSCIOUS GUILT].

Unconscious guilt: Freud (between 1916 and 1924) drew particular attention to unconscious guilt. Klein had been occupied with the exceptional degrees of violence she had found in the play of quite ordinary children, with their responses to it and with their struggles to curb these impulses in themselves. During the fierce dispute with Anna Freud (1927) [see CHILD ANALYSIS] she reported the case of a child who showed strong violent tendencies in his phantasies, together with a harshly inhibiting superego (Klein, 1927) [see UNCONSCIOUS GUILT]. She was interested in the fact that the worst of violent crimes committed by adults often resemble the phantasy wishes of children. In both cases she realized that a process of externalization (into play or into actual crime) often corresponded with Freud's view of criminals from an unconscious sense of guilt, and that this externalization is a method of mitigating the internal violence between the wishes and the superego prohibitions. The external action allows the real world to reassure the ego that the harsh and violent retaliatory threats are not as fearful as the internal ones, that the external superego is not so omnipotent and can be fooled and that, in the case of play, new phantasies can be generated which will ameliorate the violence [see 7. SUPEREGO].

In this Klein also confirmed Freud's view that criminal tendencies did result from an internal situation of guilt arising from a superego of extraordinary harshness; and she remarked on the closeness of these unconscious levels of guilt to the paranoia of psychotic patients [see 3. AGGRESSION; 7. SUPEREGO; PSYCHOSIS].

Freud, Anna (1927) *The Psycho-Analytic Treatment of Children*, published 1946. Imago.

Freud, Sigmund (1916) 'Some character-types met with in psycho-analytic work: III Criminals from a sense of guilt'. *S.E.* 14, pp. 332–3.

—— (1920) *Beyond the Pleasure Principle. S.E.* 18, pp. 1–64.

Klein, Melanie (1927) 'Criminal tendencies in normal children'. *WMK* 1, pp. 170–85.

Death instinct

Freud's early theory of instincts developed from his discovery of childhood sexual impulses. He regarded the libido as in conflict with society; later he saw this conflict as one between the libido and the ego-instincts which seek for love, approval and the physical means of survival from others [see ANXIETY; LIBIDO]. In the course of studying narcissistic conditions such as manic-depressive psychosis, Freud (1914) realized that libidinal attachment and love for an object can be returned to the ego, so the ego becomes the loved object. In this case the ego-instincts are only a version of libido, turned inwards to the ego as the object.

In 1920 he introduced a new dichotomy: between inherently opposed instincts. The libido, now including the ego-instincts (for survival and life) is opposed by a silent, hidden *death instinct* which demands dissolution and the opposite of life. This was a difficult concept for the analytic community to accept, partly because Freud thought that the manifestations of the death instinct were silent. There was no good way of investigating its existence.

The death instinct and the superego: However, Klein (in about 1932) realized that this concept was a powerful instrument for her. It solved her greatest problem. For a long time she had been producing clinical evidence that the superego formed earlier than anyone else had thought, and was harsher than anyone else had thought – in fact the earlier, the harsher [see 7. SUPEREGO]. She had been in direct confrontation over this with Viennese analysts, including Anna Freud, and Freud himself tended to support his daughter. So Klein was in a difficult position, having clinical evidence for something that went directly against Freud himself. What she did was to take Freud's concept of the silent death instinct and to say it is not so silent. It has profound clinical manifestations that are very visible – they are the harsh superego itself. The superego was, then, the manifestation at birth of the death instinct operating a destructiveness towards the individual, as Freud himself had argued (Klein, 1933). She found a way of dealing with two outstanding problems at once – solving the riddle of the early origin of the superego, and putting clinical 'flesh' on the bones of Freud's theory of the death instinct [see 7. SUPEREGO].

Criticisms of Klein's use of the concept of the death instinct: There has been much entrenched criticism of the Kleinian acceptance of the clinical manifestation of the death instinct. Kernberg's forthright but brief dismissal of Kleinian theory on this point (1969), on the grounds that the death instinct was 'clinically silent', was refuted by Rosenfeld (1971), who described, with clinical illustration, the manifestation of an inwardly directed aggression which he then called negative narcissism [see NARCISSISM]. Notwithstanding, Kernberg repeated his tart dismissal in 1980: 'The principal exponents of Kleinian theory have continued to adhere to these concepts, and their failure to respond to criticisms of these concepts bespeaks either their inability to do so or their dogmatism' (Kernberg, 1980, p. 41) – as if he had not noticed the considerable volume of published clinical material from Rosenfeld and other Kleinians (Joseph, 1975; Sidney Klein, 1974; Meltzer, 1968, 1976).

Kleinians have also pointed out that Freud's original descriptions of the death instinct, in 1920, included clinical observations. Freud was concerned with the war neuroses after the First World War. These were repetitions of the trauma, often in the form of repetitive dreaming. He also noted the repetition of trauma in the transference and in the formation of symptoms. He linked this with his own observations of a child 'playing' at losing and refinding an object, and he was impressed by the importance of repeating the play in order to master it. He introduced the concept of the repetition compulsion in this work (Freud, 1920) in order to stress that there is something beyond a simple seeking of pleasure from the satisfaction of libidinal impulses.

In a recent reformulation of the Kleinian concept of the clinical manifestations of the death instinct, Segal (1987) described a number of important features. According to Freud the death instinct is clinically silent; however it is silent only in the respect that pain and anxiety come from the urge to live; pain is in living, death is oblivion.

The experience of personal needs, with which the baby is confronted from the moment of birth onwards, leads to two alternative reactions: (i) the drive to satisfy them which leads on to object-seeking and love; or (ii) a drive to annihilate the need, or the perception of it, or the ego which perceives. The first of these drives is the manifestation of life instincts, the second is that of the death instinct.

The death instinct is manifest in three forms:

(i) destructiveness aimed towards the self is fused with the life instincts and attributed to an object – this is Freud's original notion of 'the deflection of the death instinct', in other words the projection into an object of the wish to harm or kill the subject and therefore a source of deep paranoia [see 7. SUPEREGO];

(ii) a remaining internal element of destructiveness also fused with the life instincts and manifest as rage and aggression is turned towards the object that now, as a result of the 'deflection', threatens the subject from outside; and

(iii) another remaining *internal* element that may threaten and destroy the perceiving self or the perception of the objects directly.

These forms of the death instinct are clinically observable – but in special circumstances. The death instinct is normally in a state of fusion with the libido and life instincts, and health implies that in this fusion the life instincts are in the ascendant. However, in states of *defusion* (some aspects of the schizophrenic disorders of perception and thinking), or when fusion is under the aegis of the death instinct instead of the life instincts, the operation of the death instinct becomes apparent (pathological organizations, masochism and other perversions).

Pleasure in pain: Pain is sought for a complex interaction of reasons. Segal pointed to three factors:

(i) short of death itself, pain and self-destructiveness are a direct satisfaction of the death instinct;

(ii) pain is also inherent in threats to life; so a murderous pleasure is granted to the part of the ego dealing with the death instinct if life and the sources of life are triumphed over;

(iii) when in a fusion of death instincts with libido the death instinct is the stronger, then pain (and death) will have a libidinal and eroticized quality.

The various pathological conditions that derive from an excess of death instinct – psychosis, pathological organizations, perversions – are probably composed of all three factors, though in varying proportions [see PSYCHOSIS; PATHOLOGICAL ORGANIZATIONS; PERVERSIONS].

The death instinct and envy: Klein's original description of envy showed that, in common with the death instinct, both involved attacks on life and the objects of the life instincts. However, more recently, Kleinian analysts have investigated in closer detail the relation between envy and the death instinct (Segal, 1987). Envy is ambivalent since it rests on the recognition of need and satisfaction and represents a fusion of the death instinct with the life instincts [see 12. ENVY], but one in which the death instinct is in the ascendant. So when the experience of need calls out the demand for satisfaction it also calls out a stronger demand to attack and obliterate the need. The particular kind of fusion that is involved in envy is one in which the object is attacked as a satisfaction of the death instinct, and at the same time as a defence against the experiencing of envy by obliterating the object that gives rise to envy.

When there is a dominance of the life instincts, then envious impulses are modified towards jealousy and eventually to healthier forms of competitiveness, ambition and aspiration.

The structural organization of the death instinct: Although many people have accepted the innate potentiality for aggressiveness in human beings, Klein and the subsequent Kleinians have emphasized Freud's original conception that it was a force within the personality that drove towards destruction of the ego. In recent Kleinian thought and practice this has led to an understanding of a personality structure in which an internal organization attacks the good parts of the ego. Rosenfeld, writing with the criticisms of the ego-psychologists very much in mind, investigated with a clinical case study the turning of destructiveness against the self (ego). This he termed negative narcissism, by analogy with Freud's theory of the turning of the libido towards the self in his descriptions of narcissism [see NARCISSISM]:

> When the destructive aspects predominate the envy is more violent and appears as a wish to destroy the analyst as the object who is the real source of life and goodness. At the same time violent self-destructive impulses appear, and these I want to consider in more detail. In terms of the infantile situation the narcissistic patient wants to believe that he has given life to himself and is able to feed and look after himself. When he is faced with the reality of being dependent on the analyst, standing for the parents, particularly the mother, he would prefer to die, to be non-existent, to deny the fact of his birth, and also to destroy his analytic progress and insight representing the child in himself, which he feels the analyst, representing the parents, has created . . . As the individual seems determined to satisfy a desire to die and to disappear into nothing, which resembles Freud's description of 'pure' death instinct, one might consider that we are dealing in these states with the death instinct in complete defusion. However, analytically one can observe that the state is caused by the activity of destructive envious parts of the self which become severely split off and defused from the libidinal caring self which seems to have disappeared. The whole self becomes identified with the destructive self . . . The patient often believes he has destroyed his caring self, his love, for ever . . . It appears that these patients have dealt with the struggle between their destructive and libidinal impulses by trying to get rid of their concern and love for their objects by killing their loving dependent self and identifying themselves almost entirely with the destructive narcissistic part of the self which provides them with a sense of superiority and self-admiration. (Rosenfeld, 1971, pp. 173–4)

There are now numerous papers describing the organization of a part of the personality which is dedicated to destructiveness [see PATHO-LOGICAL ORGANIZATIONS; STRUCTURE; NARCISSISM]; and there are now many descriptions of internal objects, and parts of the self which are felt to be bad and have a perverse and destructive hold over the good parts, exerting on them an intimidating servitude. The individual idealizes his own violence and destructiveness both of himself and towards others.

See INSTINCTS

Freud, Sigmund (1914) 'On narcissism'. *S.E.* 14, pp. 67–102.
—— (1920) *Beyond the Pleasure Principle. S.E.* 18, pp. 3–64.
Joseph, Betty (1975) 'The patient who is difficult to reach', in Peter Giovacchini, ed. *Tactics and Techniques in Psycho-Analytic Therapy*, vol. 2. New York: Jason Aronson, pp. 205–16.
Kernberg, Otto (1969) 'A contribution to the ego-psychological critique of the Kleinian school', *Int. J. Psycho-Anal.* 50:317–33.
—— (1980) *Internal World and External Reality.* New York: Jason Aronson.
Klein, Melanie (1932) *The Psycho-Analysis of Children. WMK* 2.
—— (1933) 'The early development of conscience in the child'. *WMK* 1, pp. 248–57.
Klein, Sidney (1974) 'Transference and defence in manic states', *Int. J. Psycho-Anal.* 55:261–8.
Meltzer, Donald (1968) 'Terror, persecution, dread', in Donald Meltzer (1973) *Sexual States of Mind.* Perth: Clunie, pp. 99–106; previously published *Int. J. Psycho-Anal.* 49:396–400.
—— (1976) 'The delusion of clarity of insight', *Int. J. Psycho-Anal.* 57:141–6.
Rosenfeld, Herbert (1971) 'A clinical approach to the psycho-analytical theory of the life and death instincts: an investigation into the aggressive aspects of narcissism', *Int. J. Psycho-Anal.* 52:169–78.
Segal, Hanna (1987) 'The clinical usefulness of the concept of the death instinct' (unpublished).

Denial

Denial is a very early psychoanalytic idea, originally termed scotomatization by Freud. A piece of perception is obliterated. Denial is specifically involved in the manic defences, and particularly the denial of the reality of some part of the mind, or of psychic reality [see MANIC DEFENCES].

Denying the importance of objects on which the subject actually depends is a key element of the manic defences. Denial is also involved in idealization when the bad aspects of the object are disposed of, leaving an unblemished good object (Rosenfeld, 1983) [see IDEAL OBJECT].

Klein (1946) described the mechanism of denial as connected with the phantasy of annihilation, and an actual loss of part of the ego or object [see ANNIHILATION]. In this sense it differs from repression, which tends to be a removal from consciousness only of the reality of some external event, or memory of it. However, although there is a tendency for Kleinians to use the term 'denial' and for classical Freudians to refer to 'repression', there is in practice little clarity. The distinction is to be made on the degree of violence and omnipotence. Denial is an omnipotent obliteration without reference to actual reality; whereas with repression external reality is respected [see REPRESSION].

Like other primitive defence mechanisms, denial refers to a defensive activity of an early, primitive and typically violent kind in which the ego is contending with psychotic anxieties.

See 9. PRIMITIVE DEFENCE MECHANISMS; REPRESSION

Klein, Melanie (1946) 'Notes on some schizoid mechanisms'. *WMK* 3, pp. 1–24.
Rosenfeld, Herbert (1983) 'Primitive object relations and mechanisms', *Int. J. Psycho-Anal.* 64:261–7.

Denigration See CONTEMPT; MANIC DEFENCES

Depersonalization
The state of the ego in which it has lost the sense of being a substantial person is brought about by excessive projective identification in which, in phantasy, the self has been located in other objects externally. Klein illustrated this process extensively with the help of a novel by Julian Green called *If I Were You* (Klein, 1955).

See 11. PARANOID-SCHIZOID POSITION; 13. PROJECTIVE IDENTIFICATION

Klein, Melanie (1955) 'On identification'. *WMK* 3, pp. 141–75.

Depletion
In cases of excessive (pathological) projective identification, the phantasy of the ego spread around in other objects leaves a sense of depletion. The self feels empty, weak and unable to withstand anxiety leading to further projective defences and cannot introject good and supporting objects in such a way as to assimilate them. Instead, he or she feels overwhelmed by them. 'Depletion' is a term that is descriptive of the patient's experience of the process that results in depersonalization.

See 13. PROJECTIVE IDENTIFICATION; DEPERSONALIZATION

Depressive anxiety
Both Segal (1979) and Grosskurth (1986) suggest that the development of Klein's understanding of the pain of the depressive position was stimulated by her own bereavement at her son's death in 1933.

Loss of the loved object. In two papers (1935, 1940), Klein concerned
herself with manic-depressive states and with mourning. Starting with
the views of Freud and Abraham that these states result from the
experience of losing a loved object, Klein's contribution was to show:

(i) that the loss is felt, in phantasy, to be related to the sadistic impulses
which are felt to have successfully injured or damaged the loved object
[see 10. DEPRESSIVE POSITION]; and

(ii) to elaborate Freud's (1926) description of 'the loss of the loved
object' by describing the experience, in phantasy, of the loss of the
loved *internal* object.

The good internal object arises from the introjection of an external
object and the ego develops an identification with that object
(introjective identification). This is a gradual attainment:

> As the ego becomes more fully organized, the internal imagos (the
> introjected parents and the basis for the superego) will approximate
> more closely to reality and the ego will identify itself more fully with
> 'good' objects. The dread of persecution, which was at first felt on
> the ego's account, now relates to the good object as well and from
> now on preservation of the good object is regarded as synonymous
> with the survival of the ego. (Klein, 1935, p. 264)

The greater appreciation of reality which goes with the relation to
whole objects, at around four to six months of age, creates especially
poignant feelings for the object:

> Hand in hand with this development goes a change of the highest
> importance; namely, from a partial object-relation to the relation to
> a complete object . . . the ego arrives at a new position, which forms
> the foundation of the situation called the loss of the loved object.
> Not until the object is loved *as a whole* can its loss be felt as a whole.
> (Klein, 1935, p. 264)

The fear for the loss of the object, typically in actual mourning, repeats
an infantile loss:

> The poignancy of the actual loss of a loved person is, in my view,
> greatly increased by the mourner's unconscious phantasies of
> having lost his *internal* 'good' objects as well. He then feels that his
> internal 'bad' objects predominate and his internal world is in
> danger of disruption. (Klein, 1940, p. 353)

Fear and guilt. In depressive anxiety:

> . . . there are two sets of fears, feelings and defences [which] can,
> for purposes of theoretical clearness, be isolated from each other.
> The first set of feelings and phantasies are the persecutory ones . . .

The second set of feelings which go to make up the depressive position I formerly described without suggesting a term for them. I now propose to use for these feelings of sorrow and concern for the loved objects, the fear of losing them and the longing to regain them, a simple word derived from everyday language – namely 'pining' for the loved object. In short – persecution (by 'bad' objects) and the characteristic defences against it, on the one hand, and pining for the loved ('good') object, on the other, constitute the depressive position. (Klein, 1940, p. 348)

The term 'pining' has not really caught on, and the two terms 'guilt' or 'depressive anxiety' are normally used instead. It is not in fact clear if they mean exactly the same: 'The question now arises: is guilt an element of depressive anxiety? Are they both aspects of the same process, or is one a result or a manifestation of the other? . . . I cannot at present give a definite answer' (Klein, 1948, p. 36). There is, however, a general acceptance that the anxiety arising from the fear of the attacks on the loved object are in fact guilt. Joseph recently summarized this:

Freud [1926] . . . brought together the various types of anxiety, in relation to the impulses and the superego, thus including feelings of guilt as a type of anxiety. In addition, he stressed that the very existence of the life and death instincts and the awareness of them together, in the form of ambivalence, produced, as he described it, 'the fatal inevitability of a sense of guilt'. (Joseph, 1978, p. 223)

Persecutory and depressive anxieties: The distinction between persecutory and depressive anxieties is, as Klein said, theoretically clear (Grinberg, 1964). However, in practice it is not so clear; depressive anxiety depends on whether the:

anxiety is mainly related to the preservation of the ego – in which case it is paranoiac – or to the preservation of the good internalized objects with which the ego is identified as a whole . . . The anxiety lest the good objects and with them the ego should be destroyed, or that they are in a state of disintegration, is interwoven with continuous and desperate efforts to save the good objects. (Klein, 1935, p. 269) [see 8. EARLY ANXIETY-SITUATIONS; 10. DEPRESS-IVE POSITION]

Persecutory anxiety is a fear for the ego, and depressive anxiety is a fear for the survival of the loved object. The movement between the two is not a sudden once-and-for-all change from persecution to guilt but a gradual one with much to-and-fro (Joseph, 1978), from (i) persecution, to (ii) a persecutory form of guilt, to (iii) a form of guilt which allows reparation [see Ps-D; PARANOID DEFENCE AGAINST DEPRESSIVE ANXIETY].

Because the first onset of guilt is so suffused with a punitive and omnipotent kind of persecution, the depressive position is hard to approach and sustain. It is only when some reparative efforts can get going that the guilt (and the superego) becomes less harsh, a process which entails relinquishing the primitive phantasies of omnipotence [see REPARATION].

Later modifications. Minor modifications to the concepts of guilt were subsequently put forward by Klein herself:

(i) The simple equation of persecutory anxiety with part-objects and depressive anxiety with whole objects cannot be sustained:

> My further work . . . has led me to the conclusion that though in the first stage destructive impulses and persecutory anxiety predominate, depressive anxiety and guilt already play some part in the infant's earliest object-relation, i.e. in his relation to his mother's breast . . . That is to say I now link the onset of depressive anxiety with the relation to part-objects. The modification is the result of . . . a fuller recognition of the gradual nature of the infant's emotional development. (Klein, 1948, pp. 35–6)

> Synthesis between feelings of love and destructive impulses towards one and the same object give rise to guilt and the urge to make reparation to the injured loved object, the good breast. This implies that ambivalence is at times experienced in relation to a part-object – the mother's breast. During the first few months of life, such states of integration are short-lived. (Klein, 1952, p. 65)

These states represent some initial '. . . progress in integration which depends on love-impulses predominating temporarily over destructive impulses' (Klein, 1952, p. 69). This suggests that these moments of integration are the promising beginnings of the diminution in the dominance of persecutory anxiety.

(ii) Subsequently a more sinister state of affairs was described as a result of the pioneering attempts to psychoanalyse schizophrenics using Kleinian concepts. Rosenfeld, acknowledging the transitory states of integration, added, however:

> I wish to make some tentative additions to these concepts, and I suggest that under certain external and internal conditions when aggressive impulses temporarily predominate, states may arise in which love and hate impulses and good and bad objects cannot be kept apart and are thus felt to be mixed up or confused. (Rosenfeld, 1950, p. 53)

This failure of the primary splitting which keeps the good object intact and separate from the bad one in the early paranoid-schizoid position results in *confusion* of impulses and objects.

Klein partially endorsed this and did agree that a particularly persecutory form of guilt results from special circumstances when envy is abnormally high, principally for constitutional reasons, but appeared to prefer to stick to the term guilt to describe the experience:

> It appears that one of the consequences of excessive envy is an early onset of guilt. If premature guilt is experienced by an ego not yet capable of bearing it, guilt is felt as persecution and the object that arouses guilt is turned into a persecutor. The infant then cannot work through either depressive or persecutory anxiety because they become confused with each other. (Klein, 1957, p. 194)

Also Segal (1956), analysing schizophrenics, showed clearly that schizophrenics have a capacity to experience depression in spite of their fixation in the paranoid-schizoid position. Their recourse is immediate fragmentation and projection of the fragments of themselves when they are endangered by depressive feelings. The consequent deterioration of their own mental state is linked with the analyst's experiencing the projected despair and depression for the patient.

Defences against guilt and depressive anxiety. There are various defences that are specific against guilt and depressive anxiety. They are all primitive and related to the psychotic quality of the anxiety.

One of the more frequent forms of defence is the angry *turning away from the object*, a mechanism which may promote the Oedipus situation by the turning away from the breast or from mother, and which may, if the mechanism is performed with excessive anger, lead to considerable problems within the new object-relation. In a milder form, this is the process of deflection. Another common mechanism referred to in Klein's earlier papers is the *externalization* of the superego, as a relief from internal persecution and guilt.

Another defence is the *reversion to a paranoid relation* to the object [see PARANOID DEFENCE AGAINST DEPRESSIVE ANXIETY]. In the earliest stages of the depressive position, guilt is so painful that it is experienced as a deliberate persecution, and is the basis of this reversion.

Manic defences: However, the most important defences specifically ranged against depressive anxiety are gathered together in a group and referred to as the manic defences [see MANIC DEFENCES]. The constancy of the constellation of defences led Klein to use, for a short while, the term 'manic position'. In 1935 she described these comprehensively for the first time. The ego's '... torturing and perilous dependence on its loved objects drives the ego to find freedom. But its identification with these objects is too profound to be renounced ... The sense of omnipotence, in my opinion, is what first and foremost characterizes mania' (Klein, 1935, p. 277). The manic defences comprise:

(i) omnipotence, which tinges all the others;

(ii) denial of psychic reality, with a consequent tendency to denial of external reality;

(iii) denial of the importance of the good objects; and

(iv) control and mastery of objects upon which the ego is dependent.

Reparation: From very early on, Klein was impressed by the reactions of children to damaged objects and the way they sought to deal with them. It was from these observations that she first began to infer the prevalence of guilt. The child's pain about a broken toy may lead him to hide it in a drawer, and to deny therefore what is hurting him, but also he may make more or less effective attempts to restore it.

Early on Klein saw how these reparative attempts related to Freud's notion of sublimation, but as guilt crept more and more into the centre of the Kleinian stage, so reparation became the major form of sublimation of the instincts. It is *how* the instincts are translated into sublimated form.

In her 1940 paper, however, Klein showed that there are various forms of reparation:

(a) manic reparation carries a triumphant note in which the reparation is based on a reversal, humiliating to the parents, of the child–parent relation [see MANIC REPARATION];

(b) obsessional reparation consists of a compulsive repetition of actions of the undoing kind, without a real creative element, designed to placate, often in a magical way; and

(c) a form of reparation grounded in love and respect for the object [see REPARATION].

Freud, Sigmund (1926) *Inhibitions, Symptoms and Anxiety. S.E.* 20, pp. 77–175.

Grosskurth, Phyllis (1986) *Melanie Klein*. Hodder & Stoughton.

Grinberg, Leon (1964) 'On two kinds of guilt: their relation with normal and pathological aspects of mourning', *Int. J. Psycho-Anal.* 45:366–71.

Joseph, Betty (1978) 'Different types of anxiety and their handling in the analytic situation', *Int. J. Psycho-Anal.* 59:223–8.

Klein, Melanie (1930) 'The importance of symbol-formation in the development of the ego'. *WMK* 1, pp. 219–32.

—— (1935) 'A contribution to the psychogenesis of manic-depressive states'. *WMK* 1, pp. 262–89.

—— (1940) 'Mourning and its relation to manic-depressive states'. *WMK* 1, pp. 344–89.

—— (1948) 'On the theory of anxiety and guilt'. *WMK* 3, pp. 25–42.

——— (1952) 'Some theoretical conclusions regarding the emotional life of the infant'. *WMK* 3, pp. 61–93.

——— (1957) *Envy and Gratitude. WMK* 3, pp. 176–235.

——— (1960) 'A note on depression in the schizophrenic'. *WMK* 3, pp. 264–7.

Rosenfeld, Herbert (1950) 'Notes on the psychopathology of confusional states in chronic schizophrenia', in *Psychotic States.* Hogarth, pp. 52–62; previously published *Int. J. Psycho-Anal.* 31:132–7.

Segal, Hanna (1956) 'Depression in the schizophrenic', *Int. J. Psycho-Anal.* 37:339–43; republished (1981) in Hanna Segal, *The Work of Hanna Segal.* New York: Jason Aronson, pp. 121–9.

——— (1979) *Klein.* Fontana.

Development

There are numerous aspects of psychological development: (1) physiological maturation; (2) phases of the libido; (3) the reality principle; (4) the development of object-relations; (5) development of the ego; and (6) the sequence of anxiety-situations. These will be described in turn:

(1) Physiological maturation. There is a natural epigenetic unfolding of the physical body and also of the mind. Bodily development directly underlies the psychological by (a) setting the phases of the libido, (b) determining certain ego-characteristics, and (c) setting a balance between the life and death instincts. It indirectly affects the development of the mind by (d) a development of the perceptual apparatus which offers new kinds of objects (whole objects).

(2) The phases of the libido. Klein accepted the importance of the normal sequence of libidinal phases, but she described how the normal progression is disturbed by the destructive impulses; they either

(i) inhibit progress and prompt regression, or

(ii) promote more rapid progress through stages, perhaps causing premature 'maturity'.

The anxieties and defences of the paranoid-schizoid and depressive positions influence the rate at which the libidinal phases unfold epigenetically:

> The course of libidinal development is thus at every step stimulated and reinforced by the drive for reparation, and ultimately by the sense of guilt. On the other hand, guilt, which engenders the drive for reparation, also inhibits libidinal desires. For when the child feels that his aggressiveness predominates, libidinal desires appear to him as a danger to his loved objects and must therefore be repressed. (Klein, 1945, p. 410) [see LIBIDO]

(3) The reality principle. The infant depends on his neurological development to reach a point at which the receptors can begin to distinguish the reality of external objects. By the time this happens, around the fifth to sixth month of life, there needs to be a significant amount of psychological maturation in order that the depressive anxieties can be tolerated sufficiently for a further maturational process, which depends on the elaboration of the internal world. The ability to relate to a whole object means relinquishing omnipotent projections and introjections, which distort perception. This capacity for tolerating ambivalence [see DEPRESSIVE ANXIETY] is a prerequisite for developing the reality principle.

(4) **The development of object-relations.** Klein, being interested in the relationships with objects, was concerned then with the development of object-relations. In object-relations theory there is an ego that establishes object-relations from birth, as a biological given. The form and development involve the interplay between the paranoid-schizoid and depressive positions.

Development in the paranoid-schizoid position: The earliest ego has to manage intense states of persecution and the fear of annihilation from within and without. In fact, in Freud's view the first act of the ego is to turn the death instinct outwards towards an external object. In addition much of this burden is coped with by the externalization (projection) of bad objects, and the internalization (introjection) of good objects [see 5. INTERNAL OBJECTS]. What this means is that the infant comes to operate phantasies that enable him to recover as quickly as possible the sense that, internal to his ego-boundaries, there is a fullness and a goodness. As with the hungry infant being fed, the sensations of the nipple in his mouth and the milk in his tummy provoke mental representations of unconscious phantasies of a good object going inside (introjection). The result is the progressive ability to sustain, or more rapidly return to, the state in which the infant concretely feels good inside. This is the basis of confidence.

In Klein's view, therefore, the initial defence against the death instinct

(a) involves an important introjective process (of the good containing object) as well as the projective one; and

(b) this first step in development is only gradually achieved.

For Klein this first good object is the mother's breast – that is, the part-object that satisfies the infant's immediate bodily needs. Bick (1968) elaborated further – the first introjected object is one which gives a sense of internal, and therefore an external space for projecting into [see SKIN].

Depressive position: The good object, hitherto experienced as only a part of the mother and omnipotently controlled by primitive mechanisms [see PART-OBJECTS], comes eventually to be experienced as a whole with good and bad aspects. The physical maturation of the nervous system and perception is linked with the development of new phantasies. The good object comes to be felt as damaged or contaminated by the bad one (or by the bad feelings of the ego directed towards the bad elements of the whole object) and seems now to be only partly good. Good objects are now eagerly taken inside or kept inside to sustain the internal state of the ego when anxiety about the state of the internal good object increases. Introjection comes to the fore, with an increased awareness of the internal world and discrimination of it from the external world [see 10. DEPRESSIVE POSITION].

Introjective identification: The development that the depressive position represents rests on a change in the balance of introjective and projective identifications in favour of the former. Omnipotent (pathological) projective identification, characteristic of the paranoid-schizoid position, is gradually relinquished. The acquisition of new objects and their introjection produce an increasingly enriched internal world, with more internal objects providing opportunity for identification and assimilation. An internal object identified with the ego brings with it the skills and attributes of the object which are then at the disposal of the ego to identify with and perform a role in the real external world.

(5) Development of the ego. With the greatly enhanced understanding of the forms of splitting that came with the description of the paranoid-schizoid position and with the work with schizophrenics, the debilitating effect of split-off parts of the self was realized. Development in analysis (as well as during the paranoid-schizoid and depressive positions) has come to be seen increasingly as pulling the splits together into a more integrated ego [see ANNIHILATION; SPLITTING]. Such integration does not mean making the different parts of the self all the same; rather it means the more flexible choice of different aspects of the self, or freer and more flexible identification with the assimilated objects that make up the self [see INTEGRATION].

Structure of the ego: The ego develops structure as well as attributes through the introjective accumulation and assimilation of introjected objects. In Freud's classical theory the ego introjects merely the superego, which becomes a separated-off part of the ego; this is in contrast to the Kleinian descriptions of multiple internal objects in a fluid relationship with the ego [see 5. INTERNAL OBJECTS].

(6) The sequence of anxiety-situations. The important anxieties that beset the human infant and have to be defended against are very numerous, and during the course of the history of psychoanalysis they have been described differently. There is general agreement that the central anxieties revolve around the Oedipus complex; however, the Kleinian work on the very early stages has amplified the catalogue of early anxiety-situations: annihilation, paranoid terror, loss of loved object, neurotic fears [see 8. EARLY ANXIETY-SITUATIONS]. Development entails the evolving of these early anxiety-situations into the later classical situations (Oedipus complex, castration anxiety and penis envy) [see 6. FEMININITY PHASE].

INHIBITION AND ADVANCEMENT OF DEVELOPMENT.

There are several factors that influence the rate of development: the external objects, the constitutional factors involved in ego-development and, in particular, the interference caused by the powerful aggressive impulses. These factors have various effects:

(a) Inhibition of development: Klein (1930, 1931) showed that sadistic impulses could severely inhibit or stop cognitive development. She described how the fears of aggression and retaliation prevented advance of the phases of the libido [see LIBIDO]. This inhibition of development that she could see in her child patients was, she considered, direct evidence for the orthodox theory of fixation in childhood phases of development described by Freud.

(b) Development due to guilt: It is central to Kleinian theory that reparation deriving from guilt and love is the most powerful creative result (Klein, 1929). When the child is able to restore his objects, the important component for development is that he or she reconstitutes an internal situation [see 10. DEPRESSIVE POSITION]. The good object is restored inside, and the internal world becomes more ordered. Repeated sequences of this form of reparation strengthen the sense of a durable internal good object, and therefore a sense of internal security. And:

> . . . when the child's belief and trust in his capacity to love, in his reparative powers and in the integration and security of his good inner world increases . . . manic omnipotence decreases and the obsessional nature of impulses towards reparation diminishes, which means in general that the infantile neurosis has passed. (Klein, 1940, p. 353) [see REPARATION]

(c) Seeking new objects: Part of the response to conflict and disastrous internal situations is to seek out new objects with which there will be less conflictual relationship. Typically, at weaning a child turns from mother (who has disappointed) to father. Processes of this kind spread the impulses, diminishing the intensity of any one, leading to an expansion of object-relations. Thus depressive anxiety '. . . contributes to the need for substitutes' (Klein, 1952, p. 97). In a different form of fleeing from its troubled object-relations, the ego is pushed on from

the pregenital impulses towards genital ones, with their enhancing of the loving impulses. Significant in this move to new objects is the process of substituting symbols for the original objects; this leads into the huge expansion of the symbolic world of civilization, with its enormously expanded opportunities for further search [see SYMBOL-FORMATION].

Interacting with the external world. A view of anxiety as a conflict between the instincts has led to an accusation against Klein that she neglected the external world and repudiated both benevolent and malevolent factors from outside, and also that she adopted a thoroughly pessimistic view of human nature and the impossibility of the therapeutic task of psychoanalysis [see EXTERNAL WORLD; CONSTITUTIONAL FACTOR]. In fact she neither repudiated the importance of external factors nor denied the therapeutic efficacy of psychoanalysis. Her writings are replete with the astonishing effect of interpretations as external events modifying the internal situation of her patients.

Klein viewed the internal world [see INTERNAL REALITY] as a dramatic situation [see POSITION] that was in constant interaction with the external world, through introjection and projection [see CONTAINING]. The process of maturation depends entirely on the progressive modification of anxiety enabled by the environment, which functions as a container of anxiety. Thus the infant's despairing over his anxiety is met by a mother who can first of all interpret it as a need which she can meet [see REVERIE], or secondly can persist in tolerating the infant's anxiety even when the infant cannot [see CONTAINING]. The result is an infant who has the opportunity to introject an object that can tolerate and make sense of anxiety.

Conversely, an environment that does not make sense in terms of satisfying a need, or does not tolerate the infant's anxiety, has a deleterious effect on the infant. Then the opportunity is merely to introject an object that not only does not make sense but adds to the senselessness. The infant then suffers a worsened anxiety of a special kind that Bion termed 'nameless dread' [see NAMELESS DREAD].

Bick, Esther (1968) 'The experience of the skin in early object relations', *Int. J. Psycho-Anal.* 49:484–6; republished (1987) in Martha Harris and Esther Bick, *The Collected Papers of Martha Harris and Esther Bick.* Perth: Clunie, pp. 114–18.

Klein, Melanie (1929) 'Infantile anxiety-situations reflected in a work of art and in the creative impulse'. *WMK* 1, pp. 210–18.

—— (1930) 'The importance of symbol-formation in the development of the ego'. *WMK* 1, pp. 219–32.

—— (1931) 'A contribution to the theory of intellectual development'. *WMK* 1, pp. 236–47.

—— (1940) 'Mourning and its relation to manic-depressive states'. *WMK* 1, pp. 344–69.

—— (1945) 'The Oedipus complex in the light of early anxieties'. *WMK* 1, pp. 370–419.

—— (1952) 'On observing the behaviour of young infants'. *WMK* 3, pp. 94–121.

Dreams

With the development of the idea of unconscious phantasy, the nature of dreams implicitly became moulded anew. Freud's classical theory regarded dreams as the activity of a disturbed mind. In order to preserve sleep the sleeper constructed, in disguised form, a fanciful solution to the disturbing conflict. Dreams thus represented wish-fulfilment. *Anxiety dreams*, however, which wake the dreamer, seem to be a failure of the process as a result of the intensity of the disturbance.

The Kleinian idea of *unconscious phantasy* as the ubiquitous bedrock of all mental processes gives a new view of the nature of dreams. The dream is more clearly an expression (in disguised form) of unconscious phantasy, as well as defences against their conscious appreciation. In this view anxiety dreams are not such a problem for psychoanalytic theory. The dream therefore represents the unconscious phantasy of object-relations which is stimulated by the active impulses (good or bad) of the moment.

Meltzer (1983) regarded dreams and unconscious phantasy as synonymous and thought that conscious, waking life is the manifest content of a dream. In this he followed Bion (1962), who regarded dream thoughts as the first mental product of all experience that derives from raw sense data processed by alpha-function [see ALPHA-FUNCTION]. In this sense dreams are the internal space '. . . where meaning is generated' (Meltzer, 1981, p. 178).

Bion, Wilfred (1962) *Learning from Experience*. Heinemann.
Meltzer, Donald (1981) 'The Kleinian expansion of Freudian meta-psychology', *Int. J. Psycho-Anal.* 62:177–85.
—— (1983) *Dream-Life*. Perth: Clunie.

Economic model

Freud's accumulated psycho-analytic theory, known as metapsychology, comprised a number of separate working models of the mind – topographical, dynamic, developmental, structural and economic. Mostly Klein did nothing to change the overall models, though in some instances she may have elaborated the content: for example, changing the order of infantile development, or elaborating the complexity of internal structure in the structural model. Indeed, her tendency was to deny changing anything much at all in Freud's theories.

It is clear, however, though not generally acknowledged, that Klein's views are a radical change to the idea of the mind as an energy system, operating on closed economic lines. Freud's ideas developed in the wake of nineteenth-century physical science based on the conservation of energy. He introduced this principle into psychoanalytic psychology as a *law of the conservation of mental energy*, and his earliest work concerned the fate of the hypothetical mental energy and its quantitative distribution (Freud, 1895) [see INSTINCTS]. Klein's views developed during the period when the solidity of nineteenth-century science was breaking down. It is probable, too, that Klein had very little scientific background to be influenced by; she was thereby freer from the rigorous scientific baggage Freud carried with him into psychology. Thus Klein's view of the instincts was actually distinctly un-Freudian. She did not respect the conservation principle, and she continually developed her ideas as if some form of loving impulse can spread – multiply, as it were – equally with aggressive impulses. Thus impulses towards external objects always 'spread' to internal objects; and vice versa. As Greenberg and Mitchell perceptively comment about Klein: '. . . love for one object does not limit, but increases love for others. In adult love, for example, the beloved is loved not instead of the original oedipal objects but in addition to them' (Greenberg and Mitchell, 1983, p. 144). There is no law of conservation of love.

Some writers – for example Yorke (1971) – claim that Klein exchanged, for the quantitative distribution of the libido, an interest in the quantitative balance between the life and death instincts. This is not strictly true and is probably encouraged by the equally mistaken view that Klein saw all development as a predetermined (innate) unfolding. In fact, she referred to the way aggressive impulses can bring out a struggle to develop loving impulses, or can be a spur to advance (perhaps prematurely) into the genital position. The fluidity of impulses, their multiplication, the apparently willed manipulation of them to enhance love over aggression, is completely outside the Freudian economic model of quantitative conservation.

These views were allowed to develop as a consequence of Klein's version of the nature of instincts and unconscious phantasy. As Isaacs eventually explicitly stated it, 'Phantasy is (in the first instance) the mental corollary, the psychic representative, of instinct. There is no impulse, no instinctual urge or response which is not experienced as unconscious phantasy' (Isaacs, 1952, p. 83) [see 2. UNCONSCIOUS PHANTASY]. Thus what is in the mind is a 'representation', not a physical quantity or quality. This seems to foreshadow the current interest in communication theory concerned with the distribution of information. Like information, phantasies of relationships with objects are not subject to a law of conservation.

The implicit abandonment of the economic model is a consequence of the emphasis on object-relations. Freud described the aim of the pleasure principle as the discharge of mental energy, and pain (unpleasure) as the build-up of undischarged energy:

> Melanie Klein described something similar to the pleasure principle but from another perspective – an early mechanism of defence which she named projective identification. In her view the young infant defends his ego from intolerable anxiety by splitting off and projecting unwanted impulses and feelings, etc., into his object. This is an object-relations perspective on the discharge of unpleasurable tensions and stimuli. (O'Shaughnessy, 1981, p. 182)

In the framework of Freud's economic model an aim-inhibited drive gives rise to frustration, whereas in the Kleinian framework the same situation gives rise to a state of mourning for an object (aimed towards) which cannot be found. The evacuation of experienced anxiety through projective identification into an object is quite different from the discharge of a hypothetical aim-inhibited mental energy.

Freud, Sigmund (1895) 'Project for a scientific psychology'. *S.E.* 1, pp. 283–397.

Greenberg, Jay and Mitchell, Stephen (1983) *Object Relations in Psycho-Analytic Theory*. Cambridge, MA: Harvard.

Isaacs, Susan (1952) 'The nature and function of phantasy', in Melanie Klein, Paula Heimann, Susan Isaacs and Joan Riviere, eds (1952) *Developments in Psycho-Analysis*. Hogarth, pp. 67–121.

O'Shaughnessy, Edna (1981) 'A commemorative essay on W. R. Bion's theory of thinking', *Journal of Child Psychotherapy* 7:181–92.

Yorke, Clifford (1971) 'Some suggestions for a critique of Kleinian psychology', *Psychoanal. Study Child* 26:129–55.

Ego

Klein did not use the term 'ego' in as precise a way as Freud came to do with his structural model of the ego, the id and the superego. She often used 'ego' interchangeably with 'self'. For Klein the ego exists at birth, has a boundary and identifies objects. It has certain functions of an exceedingly primitive kind – (i) separating 'me' from 'not-me'; (ii) discriminating good (pleasant sensations) from bad; (iii) phantasies of incorporating and expelling (introjection and projection); and (iv) the phantasy of the mating of pre-conceptions and realizations. This is in contrast with ego-psychology and self-psychology which timed the origin of the ego to some months after birth [see EGO-PSYCHOLOGY].

There is considerable debate about the use of the term 'ego', which is a Latinization introduced in the course of translation into English. From the description of the structural model of 'id', 'ego' and 'superego' onwards, there has been a tendency in classical analytic theory and in ego-psychology to describe the ego in terms of mechanisms.

Such a mechanistic stance appears to be in line with the original intentions that Freud set himself in his early 'project' (Freud, 1895) but antagonistic to the more humanistic style of his literary and classical interests, of his language and of the general impulsion during the course of his career towards human experience (Freud, 1925). He came to drop the attempt at a neurological determinism (Schafer, 1976; Bettelheim, 1983; Steiner, 1987). Klein was never at home with the 'scientific' structure for which Freud seemed to be striving [see 7. SUPEREGO]. In any case she was more interested in understanding the *content* of anxiety rather than the energy from which it derived: 'I deviated from some of the rules so far established, for I interpreted what I thought to be most urgent in the material the child presented to me and found my interest focusing on his anxieties and the defences against them' (Klein, 1955, p. 123).

The self: The term 'self', often used synonymously with 'ego' by Klein, would seem to suggest the experience of the subject, his phantasies about himself. If the 'ego' stands for a part of the structure of the mind objectively described, 'self' tends to stand for the subject *in his own phantasies* described from a subjective point of view. The 'self' would then tend to express the relational aspect of Klein's theories, as does 'subject' – which is more consistent with the use of the term 'object'. It is, however, true that 'ego', 'self' and 'subject' are loosely interchangeable in Klein's writings [see SELF]. This is somewhat different from the ego-psychology view, where the 'self' is a representation cathected (invested with mental energy) by the ego (Hartmann, 1950; Sandler and Rosenblatt, 1962). Hartmann's distinction has latterly given rise to a development in ego-psychology known as *self-psychology* (Kohut, 1971) [see EGO-PSYCHOLOGY].

The early ego: The ego, at first, alternates between states of integration and disintegration: '. . . the early ego largely lacks cohesion, and a tendency towards integration alternates with a tendency towards disintegration, a falling to bits' (Klein, 1946, p. 4). This was described later by Bick (1968) in infants in their first week of life [see BICK]. Whereas classical analysis is concerned with the ego as an organ that seeks discharge of the instinctual tensions in some form of satisfaction, and can be described objectively in terms of its structure and function, Klein saw the ego in a different way: as the experience it has of itself. She described this in terms of the phantasies it has of struggling with anxieties experienced in the course of its relations with objects, which, although they are perceived in the colours of the instincts, create a world of experiences, anxieties, loves, hates and fears rather than states of discharge. The ego's struggle is to maintain its own integrity in the face of its painful experiences of objects that threaten annihilation [see DEVELOPMENT].

At first, however, the ego is very unstable, and its earliest functions are desperate efforts to establish stability. Klein conceived of the ego's first act differently at different stages in her theoretical development:

(i) in 1932 the primary function of the ego was the deflection of the death instinct outwards towards an external object that is then feared as a persecutor, the mechanism of projection [see 7. SUPEREGO];

(ii) in 1935 Klein began to view the introjection of the good object as the founding of the ego [see 10. DEPRESSIVE POSITION; 11. PARANOID-SCHIZOID POSITION]; finally,

(iii) in 1957 she described the first ego-function as a form of splitting, the basis of the capacity for judgement (Freud, 1925), though initially of a very narcissistic kind [see 12. ENVY; CONFUSIONAL STATES].

Bettelheim, Bruno (1983) *Freud and Man's Soul.* Hogarth.

Bick, Esther (1968) 'The experience of the skin in early object relations', *Int. J. Psycho-Anal.* 49:484–6; republished (1987) in Martha Harris and Esther Bick, *The Collected Papers of Martha Harris and Esther Bick.* Perth: Clunie, pp. 114–18.

Freud, Sigmund (1895) 'Project for a scientific psychology'. *S.E.* 1, pp. 283–397.

—— (1925) 'Negation'. *S.E.* 19, pp. 235–9.

Hartmann, Heinz (1950) 'Comments on the psycho-analytic theory of the ego', *Psychoanal. Study Child* 5:74–96.

Klein, Melanie (1932) *The Psycho-Analysis of Children.* WMK 2.

—— (1935) 'A contribution to the psychogenesis of manic-depressive states'. *WMK* 1, pp. 262–89.

—— (1946) 'Notes on some schizoid mechanisms'. *WMK* 3, pp. 1–24.

—— (1955) 'The psycho-analytic play technique: its history and significance'. *WMK* 3, pp. 122–40.

—— (1957) *Envy and Gratitude. WMK* 3, pp. 176–235.

Kohut, Heinz (1971) *The Analysis of the Self.* New York: International Universities Press.

Sandler, Joseph and Rosenblatt, B. (1962) 'The concept of the representational world', *Psychoanal. Study Child* 17:128–45.

Schafer, Roy (1976) *A New Language for Psycho-Analysis.* New Haven: Yale.

Steiner, Riccardo (1987) 'A world wide international trade mark of genuineness?', *Int. Rev. Psycho-Anal.* 14:33–102.

Ego-psychology (Classical psychoanalysis)

Classical psychoanalysis, as it developed until the time of Freud's death in 1939, continued as a special study of the ego and resulted in the dominant school of psychoanalysis, *ego-psychology*. Although there are radical departures from the Freudian tradition, ego-psychology has attained a position as inheritor of the tradition in its pure form. This is partly by virtue of numbers. Because the Viennese migrated largely to America, and because of the mushrooming interest in psychoanalysis in the United States between the 1940s and the mid-1970s, the sheer number of psychoanalysts trained in the dominant tradition out-weighed any other group of psychoanalysts anywhere.

Ego-psychology is the study of the development and structure of the ego, after Freud (1923) delineated the structural model. This comprised a model of the mind made up of three interrelated agencies: id, ego and superego. The internal conflict between the instinctual id and the civilized superego places the ego in a crucial position of mediation between them, and ultimately expresses the struggle between the individual and society. So the functioning of the ego was raised to a place of special psychoanalytic interest, a trend that was spearheaded by Anna Freud's (1936) book *The Ego and the Mechanisms of Defence*. The trend became established as a school of psychoanalytic thought and practice with Hartmann's addition of an explicit adapta-tional point of view in his *Ego Psychology and the Problem of Adaptation* (Hartmann, 1939).

This theoretical development was transported out of Vienna as a result of the German Occupation. The consolidation of the school took place in the United States, although the leading figure, Anna Freud, remained in London (without a medical degree she would have been prohibited from practising as a psychoanalyst in the United States but was free to do so in Britain). In the United States the Viennese tradition met two further influences. One was the import-ance of social psychology in America – embodied, in psychiatry, in the cultural orientation of Sullivan, for whom the patient's social, cultural and family context was an important dimension in development and in psychopathology. It is a point of view which found a chord in the adaptational aspect of Viennese psychoanalysis and has tended to strengthen the interpersonal aspect of American psychoanalysis. The other influence was the dominance of behaviourist psychology in the United States, a background which may have brought out the more mechanistic style that the ego-psychology school developed there.

Ego-psychology came to prominence mostly in the 1950s and has since held a position of dominance in the United States. It coincided with certain results of developmental psychology, notably the work of Harlow (Harlow and Zimmermann, 1959; Harlow, 1961) showing important effects on the development of monkeys when they were reared with various mechanical substitutes for a mother. Bowlby (1969) took up this work as demonstrating the importance of affectionate bonding, which was instinctual in a different way from classical oral instincts (hunger) [see LOVE]. Ego-psychology did not come out of this experimental work but out of psychoanalysis, yet its conclusions were in a similar direction: for both there are aspects of the ego and its development that lie outside the classical psychoanalytic theory of drive-reduction. The theory of drives [see LIBIDO] holds that the organism always behaves to reduce the frustration of primary bodily instincts for survival and sex. Apart from drive-reduction, ego-psychology says, there is a whole area of development through which the ego goes autonomously (i.e. independently of the instincts) – there is a realm of psychic development outside the instincts. A special resource of psychic energy within the ego was postulated, which was separate from the – potentially conflictual – instinctual energy of the id.

Since the 1960s, however, there has been an awareness of the limitations of ego-psychology, especially in the area of object-relations, and an interest developed in certain British object-relations psycho-analysts – notably Fairbairn and Rosenfeld (because of the latter's work with schizophrenics) [see FAIRBAIRN; ROSENFELD]. The ego-psychology school of psychoanalysis appears to have passed its peak. Latterly, a degree of balanced criticism has been increasing in the United States, based on the omission of a comprehensive object-relations theory in ego-psychology [see below].

As well as Anna Freud and Hartmann, Kris, Lowenstein and Rapaport have been major exponents of ego-psychology. Rapaport (1958) distilled a brief historical summary of ego-psychology; and Blanck and Blanck (1974) produced a more definitive survey.

The theory of adaptation: The core feature of ego-psychology is the theory of adaptation. Starting with certain aspects of Freud's (1926) theory of anxiety, the notion of autonomous ego-functions (particularly the synthetic ones) was developed, describing the way in which certain features of the ego (motility, perception, memory, etc.) are present without having developed from the id, or the instinctual life, or from the conflicts to which the id gives rise. The ego has the function, independent of the id, to adapt to the environment. In principle, ego-psychology assumes that the normal ego is endowed at the outset with potentialities which progressively unfold, to meet adequately *the average expectable environment*. Thus the meeting of the individual and the social environment (the ego's mediation of the id and superego) is harmonious unless otherwise interfered with by an unexpected environment. This epigenesis of the ego adapting to meet society is quite separate from the epigenetic unfolding of the phases of the libido. It was specifically addressed by Erikson (1951), who defined the serial stages of characteristic ego-development.

The theory

deals with the ego aspect and the social aspect of object-relations. It conceives of the caretaking persons as the representatives of their society, as carriers of its institutional, traditional, caretaking patterns, and thus it focuses attention on the fact that each society meets each phase of the development of its members by institutions (parental care, schools, teachers, occupations, etc.) specific to it, to ensure that the developing individual will be viable in it . . . Thus it is not assumed that societal norms are grafted upon the genetically asocial individual by 'disciplines' and 'socialization', but that the society into which the individual is born makes him its member by influencing the manner in which he solves the tasks posed by each phase of his epigenetic development. (Rapaport, 1958, p. 753)

This contrasts radically with the essentially dynamic mode by which the individual attains membership of a group on the basis of projective and introjective identifications.

Thus ego-psychology views psychoanalysis as concerned with the normative process in which a socially conforming individual is benignly assisted by his society; the psychoanalytic aim is to redress the process when adaptation goes wrong, through supporting the mechanisms that allow the individual to conform to his society and to the manner in which his society expects him to solve his own problems.

The issues that occupied the ego-psychologists were (i) the origins of the ego from a symbiotic primary narcissism; (ii) the ego's particular functions, including those involved in the conflict-free areas of the ego (motility, perception, memory, etc.); (iii) the ego's mechanisms of adaptation as well as defence; (iv) the development of a precise technique of interpreting the preconscious (as opposed to the unconscious); and (v) a loyalty to the spirit of Freud's early search for a scientific (deterministic) psychology (Freud, 1895).

CRITICISMS OF EGO-PSYCHOLOGY. There are a number of specific areas of radical disagreement between the influential American developments and the Kleinian one.

The first year of life and merger: This is the dispute between primary narcissism versus 'object-relations from birth'. The allegiance of ego-psychologists to Freud's theory of narcissism has led to particularly intractable differences with Kleinians. Spitz (1950) and Mahler (Mahler *et al.*, 1975) have been interested in the very early development of the ego as the mind is formed after an initial period of primary narcissism. Spitz recognized true anxiety at only six months. Mahler put the 'psychological birth of the infant' at around nine months or so.

Ego-psychologists deny that the infant is capable of the discrimination of ego-boundaries and of the distinction between good and bad objects, as Klein holds; nor does he or she have any capacity for phantasy before six to nine months [see 2. UNCONSCIOUS PHANTASY].

This is a very important difference of opinion, since Klein's conception of the primitive defence mechanisms in the first six months of life are simply not accepted by ego-psychologists, who view the ego as nonexistent at that stage [see 2. UNCONSCIOUS PHANTASY; GENETIC CONTINUITY].

Primary narcissism: The ego-psychologists based their view that there are no object-relations at birth on Freud's own statements, especially in his paper on narcissism (Freud, 1914). It has been supported by the experimental work of Spitz (1950) and Mahler (Mahler *et al.*, 1975). However, there has recently been some serious questioning of this position by certain ego-psychologists. For instance, Hoffer (1981) remarked: 'If there is any truth in my suggestion that we had here an hallucinatory wish-fulfilment the objectless state of infancy can no longer be considered to be continuous for any great span of time' (quoted in Britton, 1982). Stern (1985), examining recent research results from developmental psychology, has reconsidered the infant's subjective experience in the earliest months after birth, concluding that there is a sophisticated cognitive, affective and socially interactive ego during the period previously designated as that of primary narcissism.

The place of destructiveness: Ego-psychologists have been strict in arguing against the death instinct as a clinically useful entity (Kernberg, 1969; Dorpat, 1983) [see DEATH INSTINCT].

Different vantage points (subjective versus objective): Kleinian metapsychology, by defining the typical experiences and phantasies of the patient and asserting that they have structural and permanent effects on the personality, is criticized for (i) reifying the phenomena, and (ii) confusing the level of description of the patient's experience with the level of psychoanalytic theory. The problem is no minor one, and it cannot simply be dismissed as confused thinking. The science of subjectivity has to take into account the fact that the object of study is subjective and the observer uses his own subjectivity in the form of empathy and intuition in the pursuit of his scientific understanding. This is discussed elsewhere [see SUBJECTIVITY], but briefly the dispute revolves around what status to give the patient's own theories (including his unconscious ones) about the working of his mind – for example, a patient's unconscious phantasy of incorporation may be evidenced in a dream as a taking in of some object represented by the analyst, and this is a picture exactly congruent with the analyst's concept of an introjection of the analyst. The patient's phantasies and the analyst's theories are not easily kept distinct.

Adaptation or integration: The aim of psychoanalytic therapy itself has diverged radically between ego-psychology and Kleinian psycho-analysis. In the Kleinian approach the aim is to integrate aspects of the personality which are either split off from each other or in constant conflict with each other [see DEVELOPMENT]. This is quite different from the ego-psychologist's aim of releasing the inherent unfolding of a normative adaptation to the social world through a mature and conflict-free alliance with the patient.

Segal contended that the ego always develops in relation to its objects and in the context of its impulses in those relations:

> I cannot agree that we neglect autonomous ego-functions like speech. What I said about my work on symbolism and Bion's thinking should indicate how much attention we pay to those processes. The point is that we do not see them as *autonomous* ego-functions, but as functions developed in close connection to object-relationships. (Segal, 1977, pp. 380–1)

Bion has elaborated a theory of thinking based on Freud's two principles of mental functioning in which thoughts and a thinking apparatus are generated *by* an ego in emotional turmoil and conflict struggling to manage its objects (internal and external) [see THINKING].

Radical opinion in the United States has noticed that 'Psychoanalysis has changed its function in the culture of our time' (Marcuse, 1969, p. 190). The development of the adaptational approach represents a conformist strand in American culture, perhaps especially the immigrant sections. The adaptational approach in stressing a normalized and non-conflictual entrance of the individual into society, as Erikson does [see above], has tended to diminish the 'negative' aspects of the human individual that are inherently antagonistic to social conformity, which Freud (1930) detailed (Jacoby, 1975). Defence mechanisms against sexuality have been downgraded as a focus of analysis in favour of adaptational mechanisms.

The treatment alliance: The ego-psychologist addresses the ego of the patient in its plight of having to handle the id-impulses. The ego – and with it the analyst – are, as it were, above the maelstrom of the id-instincts. The ego, with its endowment of autonomous functions, is believed to have conflict-free areas which the psychoanalyst seeks to locate, thus establishing the 'treatment alliance' (Zetzel, 1956).

In contrast, Klein thought that all activities of the ego were inextricably mixed up with the conflicts between love and hate. A positive alliance with the analyst certainly exists, but it is not free from the intrusions of aggressive, destructive and envious parts of the self. Indeed, the part of the ego that engages in an alliance with the analyst may be the dependent infant self – that is to say, the part of the self that is able to accept dependence.

This difference leads to great differences in technique [see 1.

TECHNIQUE]. The ego-psychologist appeals to the patient to acknowledge consciously certain contents of his preconscious, drive derivatives that are nearest to the surface of the patient's mind. In this way the analyst aligns himself with the patient's ego in its struggle with the id-impulses. Klein believed instead that in order to establish and sustain the analytic situation, the analyst must give deep interpretations that locate the level of anxiety.

Representations: Ego-psychologists have given much attention to Freud's descriptions of introjection and the 'alteration of the ego'. However, there is a radical difference in terminology which results in great misunderstanding. Klein viewed perception of an object as acccompanied by a phantasy of incorporation of it to result in an internal object: concrete, real, internal and with its own anthropomorphically conceived intentions. This exists *alongside* the sophisticated memory in which representations of the object exist, and are recognized as separate from the object. The representation of the object in memory and in consciousness is quite different from an internal object that is *not* distinguished from the external one. It is important not to translate 'internal object' into 'object-representation' [see 5. INTERNAL OBJECTS].

Mechanistic psychoanalysis: A particularly objective mechanistic terminology is characteristic of ego-psychology. It seems to have become influenced in the United States by behavioural psychology with its emphasis on the ego as a principle for adaptation to society. A reaction to what feels like a mechanistic view of human beings may have led to the development of humanistic psychology (Hinshelwood and Rowan, 1988). Certain psychoanalysts have also stood out against the apparently dehumanizing quality of American psychoanalysis (Bettelheim, 1960; Fromm, 1971; Schafer, 1976):

> In the United States, of course, 'the cure of mental illness' has been seen as the main task of psychoanalysis, just as the curing of bodily illness is that of medicine. It is expected that anyone undergoing psychoanalysis will achieve tangible results – the kind of results the physician achieves for the body – rather than a deeper understanding of himself and greater control of his life . . . of all the features of Freudian theory, the mechanisms of adjustment had become the most widely accepted in the United States. This reveals the nature of American acceptance of psychoanalysis, particularly since Freud cared little about 'adjustment' and did not consider it valuable. What is true . . . is that the concept of adjustment was injected into the Freudian system because it was of primary importance in the American psychoanalyst's scheme of values, and that this alteration explains the widespread acceptance of psychoanalysis in America. (Bettelheim, 1983, p. 40)

Response to criticisms. Ego-psychology seems to have responded mostly to the last of these criticisms, the mechanistic ring to its terminology. Interest has swung away from ego-mechanisms towards object-relations and representation of the self:

> The core of these challenges [to ego-psychology] is that certain critical issues and features of personality development and of psychopathology, having to do with object-relations and the self, do not easily fit the basic id–ego model of traditional theory. For example, the descriptions of psychological development which have appeared most meaningful to many recent clinicians and theorists are not those having to do with psychosexual development, but accounts that focus on such dimensions as self–other differentiation, the move from separation–individuation, and degree of self-cohesiveness. (Eagle, 1984, p. 18)

Clearly many of these clinical problems are those investigated by Klein and her colleagues in describing the paranoid-schizoid position and projective identification [see 11. PARANOID-SCHIZOID POSITION; 13. PROJECTIVE IDENTIFICATION] but set in a foreign terminology.

A number of analysts in the United States have recognized this and sought to add to ego-psychology with borrowings from object-relations theory [see 13. PROJECTIVE IDENTIFICATION]. Eagle (1984) described four main trends:

(i) The combined approach: Mahler (Mahler *et al.*, 1975) and to some extent Jacobson (1964) retain traditional instinct theory whilst trying to attempt a synthesis with an object-relations theory – for instance Kernberg (1980) and Grotstein (1981). Langs (1978) and Ogden (1982), who have both espoused a strong object-relations emphasis, nevertheless do so in a way that still bears traces of the interpersonal adaptational approach. They specifically used the concept of 'projective identification' to focus understanding on the interpersonal aspect of the psychoanalytic setting.

(ii) The two-factor theory: Kohut (1971) and Modell (1975) work with both instinct theory and an object-relations theory, using each as appropriate with certain patients or at certain stages with a patient.

(iii) A rejection of instinct theory: G. S. Klein (1976) represents a number of United States psychoanalysts who have followed the approach of Fairbairn and thrown out an instinct theory altogether.

(iv) Self-psychology: Kohut's (1971) work with borderline and narcissistic patients developed a psychology of the relations with the self. Arising out of the view that the sense of self is the first psychological struggle the infant is faced with (when primary narcissism gives way to an awareness of an object, and the relation to it), Kohut focused not so

much on the relation to the object, but on the self which is having to do the relating. It is a point of view which resembles in some respects the view developed by Klein and also Winnicott that the infant's first preoccupation is with maintaining its sense of a self against the fear of annihilation. The resemblance here is more to Winnicott, whom Kohut acknowledges in describing the importance of the object as a mirror used to develop a picture of the self.

Bettelheim, Bruno (1960) *The Informed Heart*. Hogarth.

—— (1983) *Freud and Man's Soul*. Hogarth.

Bick, Esther (1964) 'Notes on infant observation during psycho-analytic training', *Int. J. Psycho-Anal.* 45:558–66; republished (1987) in Martha Harris and Esther Bick, *The Collected Papers of Martha Harris and Esther Bick*. Perth: Clunie, pp. 240–56.

Blanck, Gertrude and Blanck, Rubin (1974) *Ego-Psychology: Theory and Practice*. New York: Columbia University Press.

Bowlby, John (1969) *Attachment and Loss*. Hogarth.

Britton, Ronald (1982) 'Review of Hoffer's *Early Development of the Child*', *Int. J. Psycho-Anal.* 63:389–91.

Dorpat, T. L. (1983) 'Book review of Grotstein's *Splitting and Projective Identification*', *Int. J. Psycho-Anal.* 64:116–19.

Eagle, Morris (1984) *Recent Developments in Psycho-Analysis*. New York: McGraw-Hill.

Erikson, Erik (1951) *Childhood and Society*. Imago.

Freud, Anna (1936) *The Ego and the Mechanisms of Defence*. Hogarth.

Freud, Sigmund (1895) 'Project for a scientific psychology'. *S.E.* 1, pp. 283–397.

—— (1914) 'On narcissism'. *S.E.* 14, pp. 67–102.

—— (1923) *The Ego and the Id*. *S.E.* 19, pp. 3–66.

—— (1926) *Inhibitions, Symptoms and Anxiety*. *S.E.* 20, pp. 77–175.

—— (1930) *Civilization and its Discontents*. *S.E.* 21, pp. 59–145.

Fromm, Erich (1971) *The Crisis of Psycho-Analysis*. Jonathan Cape.

Grotstein, James (1981) *Splitting and Projective Identification*. New York: Jason Aronson.

Harlow, H. F. (1961) 'The development of affectional patterns in infant monkeys', in Brian Foss, ed. *The Determinants of Infant Behaviour*, vol. 1. Methuen, pp.75–88.

Harlow, H. F. and Zimmermann, R. R. (1959) 'Affectional responses in the infant monkey', *Science* 130:421–32.

Hartmann, Heinz (1939) *Ego Psychology and the Problem of Adaptation*, published in English (1958). New York: International Universities Press.

Hinshelwood, R. D. and Rowan, John (1988) 'Is psycho-analysis humanistic?', *Br. J. Psychother.* 4:142–7.

Hoffer, Willi (1981) *Early Development and Education of the Child*. Hogarth.

Isaacs, Susan (1948) 'The nature and function of phantasy', *Int. J. Psycho-Anal.* 29:73–97; republished (1952) in Melanie Klein, Paula Heimann, Susan Isaacs and Joan Riviere, eds *Developments in Psycho-Analysis*. Hogarth, pp. 67–121.

Jacobson, Edith (1964) *The Self and the Object World*. New York: International Universities Press.

Jacoby, Russell (1975) *Social Amnesia*. Boston: Beacon Press.

Kernberg, Otto (1969) 'A contribution to the ego-psychological critique of the Kleinian school', *Int. J. Psycho-Anal.* 50:317–33.

—— (1980) *Internal World and External Reality*. New York: Jason Aronson.

Klein, G. S. (1976) *Psycho-Analytic Theory: An Exploration of Essentials*. New York: International Universities Press.

Kohut, Heinz (1971) *The Analysis of the Self*. New York: International Universities Press.

Langs, Robert (1978) *The Listening Process*. New York: Jason Aronson.

Mahler, Margaret, Pine, Fred and Bergman, Anni (1975) *The Psychological Birth of the Human Infant*. Hutchinson.

Marcuse, Herbert (1969) *Eros and Civilization*. Sphere.

Modell, Arthur (1975) 'The ego and the id: 59 years later', *Int. J. Psycho-Anal.* 56:57–68.

Money-Kyrle, Roger (1958) 'On the process of psycho-analytic inference', *Int. J. Psycho-Anal.* 59:129–33; republished (1978) in *The Collected Papers of Roger Money-Kyrle*. Perth: Clunie, pp. 343–52.

Ogden, Thomas (1982) *Projective Identification and Psychotherapeutic Technique*. New York: Jason Aronson.

Rapaport, David (1951) 'The conceptual model of psycho-analysis', *Journal of Personality* 20:56–81.

—— (1958) 'A historical survey of psychoanalytic ego psychology', *Bulletin of the Philadelphia Assn. for Psychoanalysis* 8:105–20; republished in *The Collected Papers of David Rapaport*. New York: Basic, pp. 745–57.

Schafer, Roy (1976) *A New Language for Psycho-Analysis*. New Haven: Yale.

Segal, Hanna (1977) 'Discussion on "Kleinian theory today"', *J. Amer. Psychoanal. Assn* 25:363–85.

Spitz, Rene (1950) 'Anxiety in infancy, a study of its manifestations in the first year of life', *Int. J. Psycho-Anal.* 31:138–43.

Stern, Daniel (1985) *The Interpersonal World of the Infant*. New York: Basic.

Waelder, Robert (1937) 'The problem of the genesis of psychical conflict in earliest infancy', *Int. J. Psycho-Anal.* 18:406–73.

Zetzel, Elisabeth (1956) 'Current concepts of transference', *Int. J. Psycho-Anal.* 37:367–76.

Empathy

Empathy is one of those benign forms of projective identification which can be included in 'normal projective identification' [see 3. PROJECTIVE IDENTIFICATION].

When one talks of 'putting oneself in someone else's shoes' this is a description of empathy, but it is also a description of a process of inserting a part of oneself, some capacity for self-perception, into someone else's position – in particular it is an experiencing part of oneself that is inserted in order to gain, in phantasy, their experience. This is a normal enough activity on the part of sensitive people, and can be loosely included within the group of phantasies of projective identification (Klein, 1959).

One important aspect of this intrusion into someone else is that there is no loss of reality, no confusion of identity. It is characteristic of the omnipotence of *pathological* projective identification [see 13. PROJECTIVE IDENTIFICATION] that the boundaries between the self and the object are destroyed. This differs from empathy, in which a proper, realistic awareness of who and where one is at the time of projecting remains intact.

Meissner (1980) has argued bitterly that it is false to include empathy and other non-psychotic phenomena within the term 'projective identification'. He dismissed as confusing the broadening of the concept of 'projective identification' beyond its reference to the disturbed ego-boundaries of schizophrenics.

See CONCERN; 13. PROJECTIVE IDENTIFICATION

Klein, Melanie (1959) 'Our adult world and its roots in infancy'. *WMK* 3, pp. 247–63.
Meissner, W. W. (1980) 'A note on projective identification', *J. Amer. Psychoanal. Assn* 28:43–67.

Environment   See EXTERNAL WORLD

Epistemophilia
The demand to know about sexuality is a heightened experience for the child since, due to the unbalanced attenuation of human development, the child's instinctual life is available to his or her experience before he or she is physically or socially mature enough for sexual satisfactions. Klein's first psychoanalytic writings demonstrated the close link between sadism and the desire to know. Her first paper was concerned with the inhibition of questions about sexuality and the release of phantasy life consequent on answering those questions. She showed that it was particularly the answers to unasked unconscious questions that produced such a remarkable upsurge of expressed phantasy [see CHILD ANALYSIS]. Klein was interested from then on in the epistemophilic component of the libido, and it came naturally to her to study learning disturbances (e.g. Klein, 1923), and then the intellectual problems of psychotic disorders (Klein, 1930a, 1931). The frustrations and consequent sadistic impulses involved in the child's sexual theories were the most obtrusive clinical material that was displayed to Klein when she sat down with her first child patients. She could link the sexual frustrations, the sadism and then the inhibition of sexual questions and impulses as a causal chain [see 3. AGGRESSION].

The urge to know, as a prominent feature of frustration, led her to stress Freud's (1917) assertion of epistemophilia as a component instinct of the libido, related to scopophilia (voyeurism/exhibitionism). At the same time she also saw that serious problems of learning could arise with inhibitions of epistemophilia which become too suffused with sadistic impulses. From this she developed a theory of intellectual development and symbolization – or rather the disturbance of these processes (Klein, 1930a, 1931). The investigation of these problems in children produced two important results:

(i) the beginnings of the understanding of psychotic disturbances of intellect, and

(ii) the hypothesis that these psychotic disturbances are actually much commoner in children than was then thought (Klein, 1930b) – a hypothesis subsequently proved to be true [see PSYCHOSIS].

The development of Klein's theories brought about major changes in her views on curiosity and knowledge. Because she realized that cognitive development in the very earliest phases was much greater than expected (a capacity, for instance, to distinguish self from other, and also to discriminate between 'good' or 'bad' states and objects), there seemed more and more possibility of there being innate knowledge and *discriminations* of quite a sophisticated degree [see INNATE KNOWLEDGE]. Particularly the knowledge of a penis and vagina and a meeting and relating of the two organs seemed inherent, and not resulting from an actual witnessing of the primal scene [see COMBINED PARENT FIGURE].

One of the problems in comprehending the notion of innate knowledge is that it appears to allow no discovery. At the most primitive stages this may be so. However, the knowledge is an 'emotional' knowing, a recognition of the object's intentional state, benevolent or malevolent, and these states give rise to ego-states of loving and hating. It is the disturbances generated in these states that lead to a manipulative attitude to the world of objects, an omnipotence to bring it into line with a more congenial 'known' world [see 2. UNCONSCIOUS PHANTASY]. In addition, the emerging recognition in the depressive position that these 'known' objects are highly mixed in character, and that the emotional life of the ego is swept by devastating currents of feeling, leads to a developing sense that there is a need to know more.

The epistemophilic link: Bion (1956, 1962a) tackled the problem of the intellectual deficit in schizophrenics in a series of papers, and went on to elaborate a theory of thinking, based on the idea of thoughts being generated by the *containing* of a perception within an expectation (a realization mating with a pre-conception). He discussed in detail, many times, the nature of this 'containing' relationship [see CONTAINING].

The containing link. Bion appeared to elevate the epistemophilic desire for knowledge to the status of love and hate in the human being [see

THINKING]. He described (1962b) the link between the containing mind and its contents as being of three kinds: 'L', 'H' and 'K', representing a loving, a hating and a wanting to know about the contents. These are all emotional links. Of these 'K' is of paramount importance for growth and development of a mind and a personality. A mother must at times find herself trying to understand her infant's experiences and feelings [see REVERIE]. Mother's linking with her infant in this way develops the infant's capacity for thought, through the introjection of an understanding object. However, the 'K'-link may become disturbed through envy and through actual deprivation of this function by the external object.

O'Shaughnessy (1981) described clinical examples of the three important kinds of K-link which Bion offered:

(i) the attempt to get to know the object and the self through projective identifications ('K'): for example, mother's knowing her baby's state of mind;

(ii) the stripping of meaning from the object's projected experience, leading to a denuded and meaningless experience which gives rise to the infant's feeling an internal terror from an introjected envious object that deprives all meaning from experiences (this is referred to as 'minus-K' ('−K')) [see NAMELESS DREAD]; and

(iii) a state of absence of 'K' ('no K') in which the capacity to know has been destroyed, giving rise to a paranoid psychotic condition in which the ego has been severely weakened by splitting and projection of its capacity for 'K' and faces hostile objects into which, in phantasy, bits of the ego have been violently impelled.

(i) The 'K'-link: The capacity to know through the process of learning from one's experience is a function that has to be acquired, and it comes about from introjecting an external object (mother) who can understand the infant's experiences for him and then gradually introduce him to himself [see ALPHA-FUNCTION]. Typically the 'K'-link is represented by the mating of a pre-conception with a realization [see LINKING; THINKING]. Development of this function is beset with problems of an emotional nature. Thought and rationality are dependent upon – and in fact emergent from – the emotional life of the most primitive kind.

(ii) The minus 'K'-link: From *internal* sources, the infant may be suffused by envy, which has the effect of destroying understanding and learning. This is quite distinct from the 'K'-link:

... the infant feels fear that it is dying ... The breast in K would moderate the fear component in the fear of dying that had been projected into it, and the infant in due course would reintroject a now tolerable and growth-stimulating part of the personality. In −K the breast is felt enviously to remove the good or valuable element in the fear of dying and force the worthless residue back into the infant. The infant who started with a fear of dying ends up by containing a nameless dread. (Bion, 1962b, p. 96)

The result is severe depletion of the ego and the internalization of an object that strips and denudes of meaning; this is one version of the extremely harsh superego: 'It is an envious assertion of moral superiority without any morals' (Bion, 1962b, p. 97). Clinical examples of this kind of denuding, moralizing and denigrating object have been given by Brenman (1985).

(iii) No 'K': From *external* sources, the infant may have no actual object that is willing to take in his projective identifications and return them to him in a modified form that is tolerable. The result is continued projective identifications of ever-increasing force, leading to a progressive depletion of the ego and the loss of function, with an accumulation of objects in the external world that have been increasingly violently assaulted by omnipotent projective identifications into them. As lost parts of the mind these objects have a bizarre quality [see BIZARRE OBJECTS] with personal reference to the subject in animosity, hate and envy towards him. The mind is no longer able to develop thoughts or an apparatus for using them in thinking. Instead, the mind becomes '. . . an apparatus for ridding the psyche of accumulations of bad internal objects' (Bion, 1962a, p. 112). A combination of internal and external sources (minus-K and no K) gives rise to psychosis.

Epistemophilia and therapeutic endeavour. Freud made it clear that understanding was the key to psychoanalytic therapy; he thought of this as the conscious awareness of the chaotic unconscious, or 'where id is, there shall ego be'. In Bion's terms this means that 'K' is central to the therapeutic endeavour – the *understanding* of the patient by the analyst is much more important therapeutically than the analyst's love (memory and desire) [see BION] or his hate, or his defensiveness ('−K'). The capacity to take in the patient's projections and render them understandable and bearable is the core of modern Kleinian technique [see 1. TECHNIQUE].

Bion, Wilfred (1956) 'The development of schizophrenic thought', *Int. J. Psycho-Anal.* 37:344–6; republished (1967) in W.R. Bion, *Second Thoughts.* Heinemann, pp. 36–42.

—— (1962a) 'A theory of thinking', *Int. J. Psycho-Anal.* 43:306–10; republished (1967) in *Second Thoughts*, pp. 110–19.

—— (1962b) *Learning from Experience.* Heinemann.

Brenman, Eric (1985) 'Cruelty and narrow-mindedness', *Int. J. Psycho-Anal.* 66:273–81.

Freud, Sigmund (1916–17) *Introductory Lectures. S.E.* 15, 16.

Klein, Melanie (1923) 'The role of the school in the libidinal development of the child'. *WMK* 1, pp. 59–76.

—— (1930a) 'The importance of symbol-formation in the development of the ego'. *WMK* 1, pp. 219–32.

—— (1930b) 'The psychotherapy of the psychoses'. *WMK* 1, pp. 233–5.

—— (1931) 'A contribution to the theory of intellectual development'. *WMK* 1, pp. 236–47.

O'Shaughnessy, Edna (1981) 'A commemorative essay on W. R. Bion's theory of thinking', *Journal of Child Psychotherapy* 7:181–92.

Externalization

Klein used the term 'externalization' extensively in her early attempts to understand the mechanisms in the formation of play. Later the term would be changed to *projection*, with which it is largely synonymous.

See 1. TECHNIQUE; CREATIVITY; PLAY

External object

It is important to distinguish carefully what is meant by the term 'external object'. Its meaning varies with the point of view. The external object looked at from the viewpoint of the subject may be very different from the external object looked at by an objective observer of both subject and object. Different schools of psychoanalysis will give different priorities to the different vantage points.

Kleinians tend to take the first of these vantage points – that is, to understand the external object in terms of the *patient's* own perception of it. This perception will be distorted by the subject's projection on to it of his own expectations, which will be a blend of previous experience and unconscious phantasy expectations arising from the active phantasy of the moment. In addition, depending on the strength of the phantasy, the subject will have a greater or lesser ability to (a) see the external object as it really is, or (b) actually change the object by unconscious provocative manoeuvres to accord with his or her perceptions. The object's actual qualities are important in so far as they match the subject's expectations and in so far as the object has the quality to move into an accord with the patient's perceptions, or to resist.

The primitive defence mechanisms: The early mechanisms are character-ized by omnipotence, so that projective and introjective identifications grossly distort the reality of the external object; this at first is un-hindered until the infant begins to develop distance perception [see DEVELOPMENT]. From the time when distance perception is possible there is a long emotional struggle [see 10. DEPRESSIVE POSITION] to achieve the reality principle.

Reconstruction: In analysis, the creation of the transference is a process in which the external object (in this case the analyst) is viewed in ways that come from the patient's characteristic forms of distortion. The Kleinian view of internal objects [see 5. INTERNAL OBJECTS] is the basis for understanding the distortions of the transference and the reconstruction of the analyst in the form of a perceived figure from the past:

> The patient was responsible for constructing such a culture in the 'here-and-now' and analysis of this structure was my task. What was being relived was an interaction with the internal objects built up in the past, and this needed to be reviewed and integrated. (Brenman, 1980, p. 55)

The analyst's task is to understand and analyse the perceived object continually constructed in the external person of the analyst.

The external object, therefore, is not merely the physical object but is invariably the *psychological presence* of the person (or analyst). For instance, Sandford (1952) described a patient whose object had been a mother who used the infant to project anxiety into, which the child introjected, resulting in an anxious child. In this case the external object was the mother's unconscious – which could be experienced in the transference relationship [see REVERIE].

Grinberg (1962) reported a similar situation referring to projective counter-identification when he described a patient who experienced himself unconsciously as receiving projective identifications from the analyst. It is this recognition that the object is perceived primarily as having motives and attitudes and only secondarily physical attributes which has driven to the fore the interest in countertransference.

See EXTERNAL WORLD; COUNTERTRANSFERENCE; 1. TECHNIQUE

Brenman, Eric (1980) 'The value of reconstruction in adult psychoanalysis', *Int. J. Psycho-Anal.* 61:53–60.
Grinberg, Leon (1962) 'On a specific aspect of counter-transference due to the patient's projective identification', *Int. J. Psycho-Anal.* 43:436–44.
Sandford, Beryl (1952) 'An obsessional man's need to be kept', *Int. J. Psycho-Anal.* 33:144–52; republished (1955) in Melanie Klein, Paula Heimann and Roger Money-Kyrle, eds *New Directions in Psycho-Analysis.* Hogarth, pp. 266–81.

External world

The external world is constructed by the subject out of aspects of the objective world, expectations based on past experience (memories) and unconscious phantasies of projected objects [see EXTERNAL OBJECT].

Klein was – and still is – accused of neglecting the objective features of the external world. This is not, however, correct, since her aim was precisely to understand the patient's problems of objectivity – in other words, to understand the intrusions of the subjective – and this led to only an apparent emphasis on the internal. That emphasis was also partly to counter the opposite tendency of analysts who attended overconscientiously to the actual external objects in the patient's life. In support, Jones lectured the Viennese:

> ... the Viennese would reproach us with estimating the early phantasy life too highly at the expense of external reality. And we should answer that there is no danger of any analyst's neglecting external reality, whereas it is always possible for them to under-estimate Freud's doctrine of the importance of psychical reality. (Jones, 1935, p. 273)

Klein herself described, in some considerable detail, the interactions that she had observed between mothers and their infants (Klein, 1952). This has subsequently been greatly amplified by the development of an infant observation technique [see INFANT OBSERVATION].

Social reality: There is a further problem in the apparently simple dichotomy of reality versus phantasy, external world versus internal. This is to do with the temptation to assume that there is an external reality of the human being in the same way that physicists investigate the physical world of nature. The world of other people, the social world, is a very variable reality, one which changes often as a consequence of individual and collective phantasy [see BASIC ASSUMPTIONS; SOCIAL DEFENCE SYSTEMS]. In the interpersonal world there is no enduring 'thing-in-itself' to be discovered. To a major extent the external world is constructed and continually reconstructed by the individual and by the group. A phantasy projection of an object into the external world is not an innocuous event; that phantasy may bring about an actual alteration of the object in the external world. The infant that screams with a persistent terror may so demoralize his mother that she becomes withdrawn, cold and even persecuting out of her own self-protection, but thereby confirms the infant's phantasy. Within social reality there are occasions when phantasy can actually be omnipotent.

This amenability of the external world to being constructed from phantasy is an important factor to take into account when considering the nature of *reality-testing*. This view of the construction of the social reality has its counterpart in the school of sociology of knowledge represented by Mannheim (1936), and Berger and Luckman (1967).

Berger, Peter and Luckman, Thomas (1967) *The Social Construction of Reality*. Penguin.

Jones, Ernest (1935) 'Early female sexuality', *Int. J. Psycho-Anal.* 16:262–73.

Klein, Melanie (1952) 'On observing the behaviour of young infants'. *WMK* 3, pp. 94–121.

Mannheim, Karl (1936) *Ideology and Utopia*. Routledge & Kegan Paul.

Faeces

Abraham (1924) considered faeces to be the prototype of the internal object – concrete, sensual, internal and yet expellable. Freud (1905) equated them with babies and with a penis. Klein's view of internal objects regarded faeces as one possible source of experiences of internal objects – in that they give rise to anal sensations – and of the expulsion (projection) of something [see 5. INTERNAL OBJECTS].

Faeces therefore represent a part-object whose significance is given by the currently active unconscious phantasy and is one of the infant's earliest defensive manoeuvrings, perhaps before and during birth as well as afterwards. Thus defaecation may be an initial resource of the ego for generating phantasies of expulsion of hostile internal objects. Contriving the physical expulsion produces anal sensations which are then represented mentally as an unconscious phantasy of expelling a bad object [see 2. UNCONSCIOUS PHANTASY]. The passing of faeces occurs in infancy as such a regular conjunction with feeding that it has been endowed with a medical name, the so-called 'gastro-colic reflex'; the experiencing of these regular physiological events will construct equally regular conjunctions of experiencing – taking in a good object and expelling a bad one.

Meltzer (1965) described the infantile use of faeces in an anal form of masturbation to elicit unconscious phantasies in the interest of supporting a narcissistic state [see MASTURBATION PHANTASIES; NARCISSISM].

See PART-OBJECTS

Abraham, Karl (1924) 'A short study of the development of the libido', in Karl Abraham (1927) *Selected Papers on Psycho-Analysis*. Hogarth, pp. 418–501.
Freud, Sigmund (1905) *Three Essays on Sexuality*. S.E. 7, pp. 125–245.
Meltzer, Donald (1965) 'The relation of anal masturbation to projective identification', *Int. J. Psycho-Anal.* 47:335–42.

Ronald Fairbairn

Biography. Fairbairn was an outsider amongst British psychoanalysts. He was born in **1889** and worked all his life in Edinburgh instead of in London. He was originally an academic (in Classics) but after the First World War trained as a doctor and then in psychoanalysis, which he practised in great isolation in his home city until he died in **1964**. Perhaps because of this distance he was the one person outside Klein's own circle whom she allowed to influence her considerably. He did not participate very much in the life of the British Psycho-Analytical Society, being so far removed from it. However, he greatly influenced a number of analysts in Britain (Sutherland, 1963; Guntrip, 1961; Padel, 1987) and in America he is one of the few respected British object-relations analysts, perhaps because he was most fearless in stating *systematically* his objection to Freud's instinct theory while retaining a tripartite structure resembling Freud's structural model.

SCIENTIFIC CONTRIBUTIONS. Fairbairn had been greatly influenced by Klein. He adopted her term 'position', but spoke of the *schizoid position* instead of the paranoid position, as she then (in the 1930s) called it [see PARANOIA]. He investigated deeply the persecutory first stages of life through working with schizoid individuals, whilst at that time Klein was occupied with delineating the depressive position in the slightly later periods of infantile development. As a result, he drew attention to certain things to which Klein, unwilling to be outdone, then moved on. In fact she had herself been interested for a long time in the fragmented states of thinking in psychotic children, but in the early 1940s she interested herself in adult schizophrenics, severely psychiatrically disturbed patients whom she got to know particularly through supervising the work of some psychiatrists who were now joining the Kleinian Group.

Opposition to the depressive position: Fairbairn's criticism had been that Klein had placed too much emphasis on depression and had also followed Abraham's excessive interest in obsessions, in the 'psychotic' early phases. Fairbairn claimed that hysteria had become relatively neglected by psychoanalysts since 1912, when Abraham and Freud began turning their interest to manic-depressive illnesses. Fairbairn linked the states of dissociation in hysteria with the fragmentation of the schizoid personality. If Freud had continued to study the superego through hysteria and schizophrenia, Fairbairn claimed, he would not have pursued the trajectory which later came to be named the 'depressive position' by Klein. The orally formed superego structure is a defensive organization, he believed, against what is beneath. What is repressed is inherently structural and he thought dreams showed this, being dramatizations of '. . . (i) relationships between ego-structures and internalized objects, and (ii) interrelationships between ego-structures themselves' (Fairbairn, 1951, p. 170). In particular, the internalized 'bad' object is split into an exciting one and a rejecting one. So whereas Klein, in her work on the depressive position, had been focusing on anxiety about the fate of the object – how it is damaged, split, etc. – Fairbairn was drawing attention to structural aspects of the splitting and fragmentation of the ego.

Fairbairn argued that there was some abnormality of development in schizophrenia (as opposed to manic-depressive illness) which Klein overlooked. In bringing to the fore states of dissociation in hysteria and schizophrenia, he postulated a 'schizoid position' which, he claimed, preceded the depressive position and was fundamental to it. It explained and determined the future pathology of the personality, and he went on to describe a systematic categorization of conditions on the basis of splits within the ego and the object.

Klein agreed that the onset of the depressive position was on the basis of a prior working-through of another kind of anxiety, not of the depressive type. She had always described the paranoia she found in children and their persecutory anxiety and had used the term 'paranoid position'. Whereas she had then thought of the paranoid position as secondary in importance to the depressive position, she now agreed with Fairbairn that the prior position was of great significance and also that splitting was a crucial element, as were the forms of paranoid projection (externalization) which she had described. She acknowledged Fairbairn's contribution of the term 'schizoid position' by combining it with her own to produce the fair but somewhat cumbersome term 'paranoid-schizoid position'. Klein was, though, at pains to point out her differences with Fairbairn in other respects (especially the abandonment of any theory of instincts):

> It will be seen that some of the conclusions which I shall present in this paper are in line with Fairbairn's conclusions, while others differ fundamentally. Fairbairn's approach was largely from the angle of ego-development in relation to objects, while mine was predominantly from the angle of anxieties and their vicissitudes . . . the particular emphasis he laid on the inherent relation between hysteria and schizophrenia deserves full attention. His term schizoid would be appropriate if it is understood to cover both persecutory fear and schizoid mechanisms. (Klein, 1946, p. 3)

Klein had begun to realize that there were a whole class of primitive defence mechanisms which were specifically directed against sadism and the death instinct, and she now acknowledged with Fairbairn that they were different from the obsessional mechanisms which she had originally pinpointed as the candidate for the specific defences against sadism.

Introjected objects: Fairbairn accepted that the initial stage of the ego resulted in an introjected object, but he thought of this as the bad object. There was no need to introject the good object, only the bad had to be defended against by introjecting and then splitting. This is in contrast to Klein, who thought that from the outset both good and bad objects were introjected; the good object came to establish the stability of the core of the ego and showed the struggles of the infant to protect himself and his good object from the 'bad' object (Klein, 1946).

There is a significant difference of focus to be appreciated. Fairbairn regarded the ego as anchored in external reality, with the introjected and internal objects established to defend against (he says to repress) the external bad object. This contrasted with Klein's focus on the internal world and the development of the ego which, initially at least, results in a construction of the external world based on manoeuvres designed to establish the security of the internal world.

Endopsychic structures: Fairbairn's and Klein's approaches to the phenomena of splitting and fragmentation of the self were quite radically different. Characteristically, Klein's descriptions surveyed multidimensionally a wide panorama of various and varying phantasies, experienced by the person about the state of his 'self'. In contrast, Fairbairn seemed to want to reduce the phenomena to strictly categorizable segments. He described two basic splits which separated two endopsychic structures from a central ego. Each structure comprised (i) a part of the ego, (ii) an internalized object with which part of the ego is identified, and (iii) an internal relationship between the ego-part and the internal object. Each endopsychic structure is composed of such a tripartite 'object-relation system'. One such structure contains a libidinal aspect of the ego (the *libidinal ego*) with its libidinal (*exciting*) object; the second endopsychic structure contains an anti-libidinal ego (the *internal saboteur*, reminiscent of the superego) with an anti-libidinal object (the *rejecting object*). In addition, there remains a *central ego* after these two parts have been split off.

This internal world of three endopsychic structures seems to be fixed and is clearly loosely related to Freud's own tripartite structural model: ego, id (the libidinal ego) and superego (the anti-libidinal ego). However, whereas Freud believed that the various structures of the mind grew directly or indirectly out of the id, Fairbairn contested this and argued that they developed out of the primitive and originally unified ego. The notion that there is an ego at the outset is exactly in line with Klein and against Freud. However, Fairbairn contested Klein because she adhered '. . . uncritically to Freud's hedonistic libido theory' (Fairbairn, 1949, p. 154). In fact Klein did not adhere uncritically to Freud's libido-satisfaction theory [see ECONOMIC MODEL], but Fairbairn thought she did – and in fact she probably thought she did as well, not realizing how much she had modified Freud's models.

Instinct theory: Fairbairn was opposed to instinct theory. According to Guntrip (1961), Fairbairn's great disciple and proselytizer, Fairbairn thought it was mechanistic and was looking for a more humanistic theory. Consequently, he spoke only of objects. He quarrelled with the term 'oral phase', for instance, saying that it might as well be called the 'breast phase' since it is the breast (the object) which is of importance to the child. He regarded the mouth as expressing a particular *strategy* for relating to the object. In this case the mouth is merely the inborn instrument for the strategy (nothing to do with an instinct).

In this way Fairbairn believed he had gone beyond instinct theory and the energy model of the mind which is the cornerstone of classical psychoanalytic theory. Klein, on the other hand, actually went beyond instinct theory in a quite different way. Guntrip (and others – e.g. Sutherland, 1963; Kernberg, 1980; Greenberg and Mitchell, 1983) reiterated the view that Klein's theory was only a way-station, halfway to a full object-relations approach, and that Fairbairn completed this journey. This is not in fact so: the journeys were in different directions. Klein retained an instinct theory only by redefining the meaning of instinct – although making out that she was not doing so – and substituted the notion of unconscious phantasy, a flexible and fluid view of internal structure. Fairbairn, on the other hand, substituted a monolithic and seemingly inflexible system of endopsychic structures (object-relation systems) as an ingenious, object-relations version of the orthodox id/ego/superego structure.

One could say that Klein reinterpreted the concept of 'instinct' to mean the experience of an object 'given by' the bodily sensations of the instinctual impulse; while Fairbairn recast instinct as the 'energy' to seek out objects.

Splitting: The discovery of the importance of splits in the system of ego-part/relationship/object is to be credited to both Fairbairn and Klein, stimulating each other's observations. Klein clearly continued to reflect on the problem, and though she did not acknowledge the similarity with Fairbairn's view, she toyed with a similar idea: a special kind of splitting which left an unmodified primitive object-relation system in a 'deeply unconscious' part of the mind (Klein, 1958, p. 241) [see STRUCTURE].

Love: Fairbairn was most emphatic about the importance of object-relations in human experience. He demonstrated, more critically than Klein, that classical theories of instinctual satisfactions (drive-reduction) view objects as incidental to the subject, merely for the release of tensions. In contrast he emphasized the genuine feeling *for* objects. It is this quality of trying to link human love and concern with scientific understanding which made him of such interest to the Christian minister Guntrip [see LOVE].

Later developments: Fairbairn's ideas have weathered quite well. He had two important followers – Guntrip (1961) and Sutherland (1963) – and he is widely recognized by many American writers (e.g. Ogden, 1983). However, Fairbairn's intricate theoretical probing has not been significantly developed by later adherents.

Fairbairn, Ronald (1949) 'Steps in the development of an object-relations theory of the personality', *Br. J. Med. Psychol.* 22:26–31; republished (1952) in Ronald Fairbairn, *Psycho-Analytic Studies of the Personality*. Routledge & Kegan Paul, pp. 152–61.
—— (1951) 'A synopsis of the development of the author's views regarding

the structure of the personality', republished (1952) in *Psycho-Analytic Studies of the Personality*, pp. 162–79.

Greenberg, Jay and Mitchell, Stephen (1983) *Object Relations in Psychoanalytic Theory*. Cambridge, MA: Harvard.

Guntrip, Harry (1961) *Personality Structure and Human Interaction*. Hogarth.

Kernberg, Otto (1980) *Internal World and External Reality*. New York: Jason Aronson.

Klein, Melanie (1946) 'Notes on some schizoid mechanisms'. *WMK* 3, pp. 1–24.

—— (1958) 'On the development of mental functioning'. *WMK* 3, pp. 236–40.

Ogden, Thomas (1983) 'The concept of internal object relations', *Int. J. Psycho-Anal.* 64:227–41.

Padel, John (1987) 'Positions, stages, attitudes or modes of being', *Bulletin of the European Psycho-Analytical Federation* 12:26–31.

Sutherland, J. D. (1963) 'Object relations theory and the conceptual model of psycho-analysis', *Br. J. Med. Psychol.* 36:109–24.

Father

At birth any experience that later becomes linked with 'father' is wholly a constructed object featuring in unconscious phantasy life. When the infant, in the paranoid-schizoid position, finds there is no object to satisfy it (when mother is absent in some respect), he experiences a bad object [see BAD OBJECT]. This bad object, if genital-level phantasies are operative, will be conceived as a hated and feared couple engaged in an exclusive union, usually of a very violent and damaging kind [see COMBINED PARENT FIGURE]. Part of this union is, then, a part-object that occupies mother (the penis) or occupies mother's breast (the nipple) which will eventually be attributed later to a strict and repressive father when he is known more as an external figure in his own right.

At times there may be protective phantasies that establish the penis as the guardian of the maternal space and serve to diminish the anxiety of excessively violent impulses in the infant.

At a slightly later period, when the infant can establish more figures (whole objects) in his life, father will be an object to turn to out of disappointment with mother (typically at weaning, Klein thought), when he can be loved and identified with. Father is the first chance for exploring new objects, and can then relieve some of the intensity of the depressive position.

Gender: The part-objects 'mother', 'penis', 'breast', 'nipple', etc., arise firstly as objects populating unconscious phantasy and are later attributed to members of the family. It is important to remember that although the social attribution of genders to the actual mother and father seems to sort out the part-objects amongst the parents – 'mother', 'breast' to the actual mother; 'penis' to the father – the child does not do this. Before socialization and the more conscious acceptance of these gender attributes, the infant will experience these part-objects in either parents and thereafter, in spite of socialized attitudes, there may continue to be an ardent search for the maternal aspects of men, or for the masculine ones of women. In fact, the union of the parents remains inside the personality, and maturity consists of a growing capacity to tolerate, welcome and value both aspects embraced together inside the self.

See PART-OBJECTS

Femininity

During the 1920s and 1930s, when there was a good deal of strident debate about the psychology of women in psychoanalytic circles, spearheaded by Karen Horney (1926, 1932), Klein was anxious to show that child analysis could answer the problem, and showed the special contribution she could offer from her work with children [see 6. FEMININITY PHASE]. She showed the importance of little girls' aggressiveness in setting up fearful and persecutory phantasy situations that entailed raiding mother's body for its babies, for father's penis, and to spoil her creativity. This phase, she thought, was important in both boys and girls, and was a special anxiety-situation that enhanced the later oedipal complex, castration anxiety and penis envy described by Freud (Klein, 1932) [see COITUS; COMBINED PARENT FIGURE].

Those early phantasies concern the part-objects – organs, babies, etc. The distribution of these between the actual parents is not in conformity with the later adult expectation of social gender identity. Development of a gender identity requires a considerable readjustment of the early infantile phantasies of the arrangements of organs and part-objects [see FATHER].

There was a great emphasis in Klein's thinking on the interiority of bodies, especially mother's body, and this later became a theory of containing [see CONTAINING]. It is the root of the inward-directedness of femininity, which comes out of anxious concerns and is perhaps femininity's essential quality. This emphasis on the exploration of mother's body and its contents has led to a view that Klein minimized the role of masculinity and the father. This is not entirely so. Father is an object conceived originally within mother and limiting access to her by his own presence. The implication of these views is that these social expectations of mother and father are inherent, though one or other is called out in each individual by social processes and stereotypes.

See 6. FEMININITY PHASE

Horney, Karen (1926) 'The flight from womanhood', *Int. J. Psycho-Anal.* 7:324–9.
—— (1932) 'The dread of women', *Int. J. Psycho-Anal.* 13:348–60.
Klein, Melanie (1932) *The Psycho-Analysis of Children. WMK* 2.

Fragmentation

Severe splitting of the ego, typically in relation to the difficulties encountered in the paranoid-schizoid position, gives rise to a sense of fragmentation, of going to pieces [see 11. PARANOID-SCHIZOID POSITION]. Though a normal experience under stress or exhaustion, it is extremely severe and central to the problems of the schizophrenic [see 8. EARLY ANXIETY-SITUATIONS].

See ANNIHILATION; SPLITTING

Anna Freud

Biography. Freud's youngest daughter was born in 1892 in Vienna and remained his companion until his death, accompanying him to London in 1938 where she remained in the family house after Freud's death until her own in 1982. She was not just Freud's daughter but made significant contributions to psychoanalysis in her own right and carried the banner for orthodox loyalty to Freud's theoretical position (Solnit, 1983; Yorke, 1983).

SCIENTIFIC CONTRIBUTIONS. Anna Freud entered the ring in 1926 as a protagonist of the form of child analysis pioneered by Hug-Hellmuth, and in opposition to Melanie Klein. Although her opposition was later modified (Anna Freud, 1946; Geleerd, 1963) her school of child analysis in London remained quite separate after she arrived in 1938 [see CHILD ANALYSIS; CONTROVERSIAL DISCUSSIONS].

A decade after the beginning of that contest, in 1936, she published her most famous book, *The Ego and the Mechanisms of Defence*, and that, together with Hartmann's work in Vienna and the USA (Hartmann, 1939, 1964) created a whole line of development of psychoanalysis arising out of the specific study of the ego and its relations with the other psychic agencies. Ego-psychology has remained the dominant school of psychoanalysis in the United States [see EGO-PSYCHOLOGY].

Freud, Anna (1936) *The Ego and the Mechanisms of Defence*. Hogarth.
—— (1946) 'Preface' to *The Psycho-Analytic Treatment of Children*. Imago.
Geleerd, Elisabeth (1963) 'An evaluation of Melanie Klein's *Narrative of a Child Analysis*', *Int. J. Psycho-Anal.* 44:493–506.
Hartmann, Heinz (1939) *Ego Psychology and the Problem of Adaptation*. Imago.
—— (1964) *Essays on Ego Psychology*. Hogarth.
Solnit, Albert (1983) 'Anna Freud's contribution to child and applied analysis', *Int. J. Psycho-Anal.* 64:379–90.
Yorke, Clifford (1983) 'Anna Freud and the psycho-analytic study and treatment of adults', *Int. J. Psycho-Anal.* 64:391–400.

Genetic continuity

The term 'genetic continuity' has an important role in psychoanalytic theory and practice. It is the assumption that psychological aspects of the personality in the present have a continuity with preceding stages of development. Thus Freud evolved the view that adult neurosis arose from traumatic occurrences and phantasies in childhood. But more than this, normal features of the personality, such as the superego, develop from its precursors, the oedipal parents in the preceding stage of development.

It was on the basis of genetic continuity that Freud made his inferences, from adults, about the psychological development in children. The theory of genetic continuity was tested when Freud and Little Hans's father investigated the psychoanalytic theory of child development by direct analysis of material from a five-year-old child (Little Hans) during the phases of development that had been hypothesized from the analysis of adults (Freud, 1909).

When Klein came to analyse children she found herself also speculating about earlier stages of development than those she was analysing. Although she analysed children as young as two years and nine months, she found that there was a great deal of fundamental development to be described before that age. Her inferences were therefore also based on the principle of genetic continuity – as well as other evidence, which eventually included direct infant observation [see BICK; INFANT OBSERVATION].

Dishearteningly, Klein found that her contributions to the psycho-analytic theory of development were disputed. Waelder, upholding orthodox psychoanalysis as understood in Vienna, read a headmasterly paper to the British Psycho-Analytical Society in 1936 (a different version was published later – Waelder, 1937), admonishing Klein's developments as deviations from true Freudian theory. He delivered a prolonged debate on what is valid psychoanalytic inference. This produced a retort from Isaacs in defence of the scientific validity of Klein's inferences about the first year of life (Isaacs, 1938). Open controversy broke out during the Controversial Discussions in 1943–4 [see CONTROVERSIAL DISCUSSIONS].

The dispute over what is a valid psychoanalytic inference and what is not has never really been settled, with a tendency to dispute other people's inferences. Agreement that the present had its precursors in the past has not extended to agreement on what exactly those precursors comprise. For example, Klein attributed, partly on the basis of genetic continuity, an early form of the superego to the early pregenital phases of development [see 7. SUPEREGO]. On the grounds of genetic continuity, Fenichel (1931) agreed that there may well be 'precursors of the superego' but that they were quite different from the superego itself and should not be referred to by the same term because those precursors had some different characteristics. The problem arose, therefore, in the terminology – if there is a genetic continuity, how should the continuum be divided up? Answers to that question have rested on a mixture of nonscientific motives, including simply allegiance to a particular preceding theory.

Fenichel, Otto (1931) 'The pregenital antecedents of the Oedipus complex', *Int. J. Psycho-Anal.* 9:47–70.

Freud, Sigmund (1909) 'Analysis of a phobia in a five-year-old boy'. *S.E.* 10, pp. 3–149.

Isaacs, Susan (1938) 'The nature of the evidence concerning mental life in the earliest years', unpublished, but incorporated into Isaacs (1952) 'The nature and function of phantasy', in Klein *et al.*, eds *Developments in Psycho-Analysis*. Hogarth, pp. 67–121.

Waelder, Robert (1937) 'The problem of the genesis of psychical conflict in earliest infancy', *Int. J. Psycho-Anal.* 18:406–73.

Good object

This term denotes a part-object (conceived in unconscious phantasy) which mentally represents the sensation of a need satisfied. There may be a number of 'good' objects, each one associated with the sensation of a particular satisfaction [see also BAD OBJECT], and equally a number of 'bad' objects: 'There are in fact very few people in the young infant's life, but he feels them to be a multitude of objects because they appear to him in different aspects' (Klein, 1952, p. 54). In the earliest phases the good object which is felt to be singular at any one moment is of particular importance, since its secure introjection forms the basis for the ego's stability. As the core of the ego, its loss leads to extreme insecurity in the paranoid-schizoid position. Later, in the depressive position, the loss of the good internal object is threatened by the loss of an external object and gives rise to mourning, guilt and the drive for reparation [see DEPRESSIVE ANXIETY; 10. DEPRESSIVE POSITION; REPARATION].

In the depressive position the good object may be maintained by splitting processes which constantly keep the object free of bad characteristics that would otherwise attract impulses of hatred with the risk of losing the object. Such an object, achieved through splitting, is perfect and known as the 'ideal' (or 'idealized') object. It contributes to insecurity because of its extremely unrealistic quality of perfection. Actual objects always fail to match expectations and in the paranoid-schizoid position lead to catastrophic disappointment (de-idealization), experienced as the sudden appearance of the persecuting 'bad' object. The 'ideal' object is therefore to be distinguished from a 'good' one [see IDEAL OBJECT].

Klein, Melanie (1952) 'The origins of transference'. *WMK* 3, pp. 48–56.

Gratitude

Gratitude is a specific feeling towards an object and needs to be distinguished from gratification, which is the satisfaction of a bodily need. Gratitude is brought out and enhanced towards an object by the gratification that the object gives. It is therefore akin to object-love as described by Abraham (1924). However, Klein viewed this capacity to feel for the object as originating at birth. In her view (Klein, 1957) it was counterpoised to envy, a response which diminishes or kills gratitude to the object.

See LOVE; 12. ENVY

Abraham, Karl (1924) 'A short study of the development of the libido', in Karl Abraham (1927) *Selected Papers on Psycho-Analysis*. Hogarth, pp. 418–501.
Klein, Melanie (1957) *Envy and Gratitude*. *WMK* 3, pp. 176–235.

Greed

Greed is based on a form of introjection carried out in anger. The violence of the oral incorporation, involving biting, leads in phantasy to the destruction of the object. The end state is that there has been no oral satisfaction, since the introjected object is worthless; or, worse, it has turned into a retaliatory persecutor in reaction to the oral sadistic attack carried out in the process of incorporation.

In the paranoid-schizoid position, the internal world may accumulate more and more persecutory and retaliatory objects that threaten the subject; this gives rise to a greater and greater hunger for 'good' objects to alleviate the internal state of dominance by 'bad' objects and by hatred and destructive impulses. This creates an insatiable situation of anxiety and 'destructive introjection' (Klein, 1957, p. 181). Hunger in the context of persecutory anxiety leads, in phantasy, to violent forms of introjection and the fear of destroyed objects inside – destroyed by the bad objects and 'bad' impulses mobilized. Hunger giving rise to more hunger is *greed*.

The end result may be an inhibition of oral impulses and a restriction of introjection, intended to spare the objects that are so hungered for; this may therefore lead to an anorexic state and a depleted internal world.

This introjective violence is a counterpart of the *projective* attack in envy in which the desired object is invaded, in phantasy, in a fit of destructive violence, and spoiled or poisoned [see 12. ENVY].

Klein, Melanie (1957) *Envy and Gratitude*. *WMK* 3, pp. 176–235.

Grid See BION

Guilt Guilt is an anguished state of mind arising out of an internal conflict, particularly over the worth of the self. Freud emphasized over a long period the importance of guilt and realized that unconscious guilt [see UNCONSCIOUS GUILT] was a powerful motive force for self-punishment or for a motivated kind of failure (Freud, 1916, 1924). He eventually made it a central aspect of his final model of the mind, the structural model, in which the ego is in a constant struggle to ward off the attacks of the superego. That conflict between the ego and the superego results in the experience of guilt, as the superego berates the ego for contravening the internal standards embodied in the superego.

Depressive position: Klein took this a step further in describing the depressive position, in which guilt remains the central feature. However, the conflict in the depressive position, which gives rise to guilt, was described in quite different terms from that of the structural model. In Klein's view the conflict between ego and superego is inherent in the mind at birth (that is, it has innate roots in the instinctual endowment) and she linked this with Freud's later instinct theory, in which he postulated a death instinct and a life instinct in conflict. So at birth the ego is set the task of struggling to manage these two opposing instincts (ultimately to achieve a dominance of love over hate) [see 10. DEPRESSIVE POSITION].

Persecutory guilt: The earliest version of this conflict, however, is not a moral sense at all. In the paranoid-schizoid position the conflict is more over the survival of the ego, which feels under threat of death. In the depressive position this threat passes more towards loved objects, and the subject regrets their suffering with an intense remorse that is felt as guilt and responsibility [see DEPRESSIVE ANXIETY]. Guilt as it develops in the depressive position has evolved out of the preceding sense of persecution and fear of death. Guilt therefore has numerous tones to it, strung out along the spectrum from horrendous and persecuting punishment to pained remorse, mourning and reparation.

At the outset, in the paranoid-schizoid position, guilt is a retaliatory persecution of an unmitigated kind. As the depressive position comes into being and the objects become 'whole objects', the violence of the persecution is mitigated with help and concern from the 'good' aspects of the object. This leads to fear for the 'good' object's survival, but part and parcel of this is remorse and guilt. At first this guilt is persecutory and punitive, taking its colour from the preceding paranoid state of persecution. However, with the accumulation of good experiences with the whole object and its tendency to survive, guilt becomes modified by the impulse to put right the good object and to contribute to its survival. At this point guilt comes to be suffused with reparative wishes and contributes to the strength of constructive and creative effort derived from guilt.

See DEPRESSIVE ANXIETY; 8. EARLY ANXIETY-SITUATIONS; REPARA-TION

Freud, Sigmund (1916) *Introductory Lectures on Psycho-Analysis*. *S.E.* 15–16.
—— (1924) 'The economic problem of masochism'. *S.E.* 19, pp. 157–70.

Paula Heimann

Biography. Paula Heimann was born in Danzig in **1899** of Russian parents. She trained in medicine and then psychoanalysis in Berlin. She left, following the Reichstag fire when she was temporarily arrested, and arrived in London, her husband having previously moved to Switzerland. In London Heimann retrained as a psychoanalyst with Melanie Klein and became her staunchest supporter (with Susan Isaacs) all through the difficult times in the 1940s when the Kleinian Group came under attack from the émigré analysts from Vienna. Mysteriously, she and Klein began to disagree, though this never became public, and finally in 1956 Heimann left the Kleinian Group, to the stunned amazement of the rest of the British Psycho-Analytical Society. She was subsequently an important member of the Independent Group of analysts in the Society until her death in **1982**.

SCIENTIFIC CONTRIBUTIONS. Heimann was a crucial prot-agonist in the Controversial Discussions in 1943–4, during which she read a paper spelling out the Kleinian view of internal objects, and also a joint one with Susan Isaacs on regression (both published in 1952). Her work at this stage had been to clarify, both clinically and theoretically, the concepts that Klein had thrown up, especially after the introduction of the concept of the depressive position and the idea of concrete internal objects. This had been the subject of her paper as a student (Heimann, 1942).

Assimilation: Later Heimann followed up one important aspect of that paper, which concerned the fate of the internal object. This was to do with the muddle over whether the object is introjected into the ego or the superego. Heimann described a process of assimilation of the object when it becomes a part of the ego, or is potentially available for introjective identification, in contrast to the process whereby objects remain unassimilable and become hostile internal persecutors (Heimann, 1942) [see ASSIMILATION]. Her work has generated the view of the internal world as an arena of internal object-relationships of varying kinds and was, in embryo, the beginnings of a systematic Kleinian view of the structure of the personality. Klein used the idea of assimilation in her later paper on schizoid mechanisms (Klein, 1946).

Countertransference: The most well-known and developed of Heimann's work is on the use of countertransference as an important aid to the analyst as well as a minefield of risks. Her paper in 1950 is the first detailed, published view of the use of countertransference, and takes issue with the notion of the analyst as a blank screen. Racker's (1948) earlier paper with similar views was not published until 1953 and probably not known to Heimann when she wrote hers. There was a considerable interest in reviewing the nature and possible use of countertransference at this time [see COUNTERTRANSFERENCE].

Heimann was very critical of the attempts by analysts to maintain a cold unresponsiveness in the manner of a surgeon performing an operation (see Freud, 1912). Instead she argued that the analyst's feelings may well have some correspondence to the transference feelings of the patient and are therefore a clue to the transference, or to hidden aspects of it [see 1. TECHNIQUE; COUNTERTRANSFERENCE].

This also has potential dangers, since it could allow analysts free rein to 'accuse' the patient of all the analyst's states of mind. The problem of distinguishing between the analyst's feelings which derive from a position allotted to him by the patient's transference and his feelings that are defensive against the patient and the patient's transference has been a source of considerable debate ever since (Money-Kyrle, 1956; Brenman Pick, 1985; Rosenfeld, 1987) and repeats in some ways the controversy over Ferenczi's *active technique* (Balint, 1968). In fact some analysts took up an interest in the countertransference as a method for justifying active engagement with their patient – physical touching, giving cups of tea, etc. (Little, 1951; Gitelson, 1952; Winnicott, 1971). Heimann subsequently wrote in criticism of these more unorthodox steps (Heimann, 1960).

The disagreement with Klein: Apparently (King, 1983) Klein asked Heimann to withdraw her paper (on countertransference) in 1950, perhaps, like Freud, suspicious of the potential misuse of counter-transference – there are apocryphal stories of Klein's supervisions in which she criticized students with great humour for their use of the countertransference. However, Heimann refused to retract her paper and has taken the credit for an important innovation that others were at the time considering (see Little and Langs, 1981; Racker, 1948). This rejection by Klein may have been a severe blow to Heimann, leading to their break. Nevertheless, Heimann may have been somewhat provocative to Klein. It is noticeable that although Heimann was the great expositor of Klein's theory of the depressive position in the 1940s she never mentioned the paranoid-schizoid position or projective identification, Klein's subsequent theoretical developments of that decade. It is possible that the latter developments were collaborations with others – the younger generation of Herbert Rosenfeld, Hanna Segal, Wilfred Bion – and not with Heimann.

Heimann's 1950 paper may have made Klein angry, as it had been written without reference to her – one of those snowballing retaliatory situations about which Klein had written so much. The final problem for Heimann was Klein's theory of envy (Klein, 1957 – given as a paper in 1955), which Heimann could not accept even though she had accepted the death instinct (King, 1983); later Heimann eventually recanted her Kleinian views on the death instinct (Heimann and Valenstein, 1972).

Balint, Michael (1968) *The Basic Fault*. Tavistock.

Brenman Pick, Irma (1985) 'Working through in the counter-transference', *Int. J. Psycho-Anal.* 66:157–66.

Freud, Sigmund (1912) 'Recommendations to physicians practising psycho-analysis'. *S.E.* 12, pp. 109–20.

Gitelson, M. (1952) 'The emotional position of the analyst', *Int. J. Psycho-Anal.* 33:1–10.

Heimann, Paula (1942) 'A contribution to the problem of sublimation and its relation to processes of internalization', *Int. J. Psycho-Anal.* 23:8–17.

—— (1950) 'On counter-transference', *Int. J. Psycho-Anal.* 31:81–4.

—— (1952) 'Certain functions of introjection and projection in early infancy', in Melanie Klein, Paula Heimann, Susan Isaacs and Joan Riviere, eds (1952) *Developments in Psycho-Analysis*. Hogarth, pp. 122–67.

—— (1960) 'Counter-transference', *Br. J. Med. Psychol.* 33:9–15.

Heimann, Paula and Isaacs, Susan (1952) 'Regression', in Melanie Klein, Paula Heimann, Susan Isaacs and Joan Riviere, eds (1952) *Developments in Psycho-Analysis*. Hogarth, pp. 169–97.

Heimann, Paula and Valenstein, Arthur (1972) 'The psycho-analytic concept of aggression', *Int. J. Psycho-Anal.* 53:31–5.

King, Pearl (1983) unpublished communication.

Klein, Melanie (1946) 'Notes on some schizoid mechanisms'. *WMK* 3, pp. 1–24.

—— (1957) *Envy and Gratitude. WMK* 3, pp. 176–235.

Little, Margaret (1951) 'Counter-transference and the patient's response to it', *Int. J. Psycho-Anal.* 32:32–40.

Little, Margaret and Langs, Robert (1981) 'Dialogue: Margaret Little/Robert Langs', in Little, *Transference Neurosis and Transference Psychosis*. New York: Jason Aronson, pp. 269–306.

Money-Kyrle, Roger (1956) 'Normal counter-transference and some of its deviations', *Int. J. Psycho-Anal.* 57:360–6; republished (1978) in *The Collected Papers of Roger Money-Kyrle*. Perth: Clunie, pp. 330–42.

Racker, Heinrich (1948) 'A contribution to the problem of counter-transference', published (1953) *Int. J. Psycho-Anal.* 34:313–24; republished (1968) as 'The counter-transference neurosis', in Heinrich Racker, *Transference and Counter-Transference*. Hogarth.

Rosenfeld, Herbert (1987) *Impasse and Interpretation*. Tavistock.

Winnicott, D. W. (1971) *Playing and Reality*. Tavistock.

Id Freud (1923) decribed the 'id' as an agency of the mind. Along with the ego and the superego, it comprises *the structural model of the mind*. The 'id' encompasses all the primitive instinctual endowments, and from it grow the ego and the superego. Views divergent from Freud developed particularly in the British Psycho-Analytical Society as a result of the greater emphasis on object-relations; notably:

(i) Fairbairn (1952) dismissed the concept of instincts and replaced it with the idea that impulses are 'strategies' of relating to objects, since the human individual is object-seeking rather than pleasure-seeking. This, he thought, got psychoanalysis out of the difficulty that had led Freud to postulate the death instinct as beyond pleasure [see FAIRBAIRN].

(ii) Klein adopted a clinical approach to the id which not only included the death instinct [see DEATH INSTINCT] but conceived instincts in the form of their mental representation rather than their physiological origins. This directed her attention to phantasy, and unconscious phantasy as the representation of instincts [see 2. UNCONSCIOUS PHANTASY].

By temperament Klein's loyalty was to Freud's 'structural model', but in fact the 'id' changed meaning in her hands as she developed her own theories. She embraced Freud's theory of the death instinct, giving it clinical reference points, and her model of psychic conflict concerned the clash not between the life instinct and the death instinct *per se* but between their representatives in unconscious phantasy. Because psychic conflict results, in her view, from the impact of the death instinct on object-relations, the 'id' has tended to become a representative of the death instinct in her writing. The Freudian conflict between the ego and the id (stimulated by the demands of the superego upon the ego) was replaced, in effect, by Klein's notion of the conflict between the life instinct and the death instinct [see ANXIETY].

See INSTINCTS; DEATH INSTINCT

Fairbairn, Ronald (1952) *Psycho-Analytic Studies of the Personality.* Routledge & Kegan Paul.
Freud, Sigmund (1923) *The Ego and the Id. S.E.* 19, pp. 3–66.

Ideal object Freud (1921) described a process of idealization in the act of love, but developed it in relation to his concept of narcissism and the ego ideal.

For Klein the concepts of 'idealization' and the 'ideal object' are necessarily linked with the concept of the 'bad object' through the mechanism of splitting which gives rise to both kinds of object. When an object is conceived as primordially good then it is said to be 'idealized'; good aspects of the object have been separated off, by splitting, followed by the annihilation (denial) of the bad aspects, and this gives the illusion of perfection.

Idealization and envy: Idealization is a mechanism of defence, linked to a primary form of splitting (Rosenfeld, 1983), aimed at achieving relations with a good object. Bad feelings are inherent in the existence of the death instinct, and lead at first to a risk of confused relationships with objects [see CONFUSIONAL STATES] in which destructive phantasies operate towards good objects, this being the primary form of envy. The splitting aimed at keeping the good object and impulses separate from the bad object and impulses is a defence that is needed at the beginning of life to keep the world safely defined as good or bad. Idealization is an escape from the horrendous persecutory vicious circles in the relations to hostile 'bad' objects [see PARANOIA; 11. PARANOID-SCHIZOID POSITION] and therefore a defence against the emergence of the primary instinctual conflict.

Idealization and the depressive position: Later, splitting an object into two and the idealization of one of the parts can be a response to the painful early anxieties of the depressive position. The depressive anxiety of ambivalence is avoided by a paranoid retreat into separating the good from the bad feelings, through splitting the good from the bad aspects of the object to create an ideal object and a persecutory one again [see PARANOID DEFENCE AGAINST DEPRESSIVE ANXIETY].

Perfection: The perfection aspired to as a result of idealization may itself become quite persecutory and lead to further primitive defence mechanisms. The real object, having its blemishes, comes to represent the persecuting experience of a damaged perfect object that is then '... felt to be unattractive – really an injured, incurable and therefore dreaded person' (Klein, 1935, p. 270).

See GOOD OBJECT

Freud, Sigmund (1921) *Group Psychology and the Analysis of the Ego.* S.E. 18, pp. 67–143.
Klein, Melanie (1935) 'A contribution to the psychogenesis of manic-depressive states'. *WMK* 1, pp. 262–89.
Rosenfeld, Herbert (1983) 'Primitive object relations and mechanisms', *Int. J. Psycho-Anal.* 64:261–7.

Identification

Identification concerns the relating to an object on the basis of perceived similarities with the ego. However, this is a complex phenomenon which has several forms. The simple recognition of a similarity with some other external object that is recognized as having its own separate existence is a sophisticated achievement. At the primitive level of phantasy, objects that are similar are regarded as the same, and this omnipotent form of phantasy gives rise to a confusion between self and object.

The internal objects are phantasies, but at first phantasies are omnipotent, so through these primitive phantasies involved in identification the object *is* the self [see OMNIPOTENCE]. Actual changes in the personality come about on this basis and can be observed objectively. These are primitive processes occurring very early in development [see 11. PARANOID-SCHIZOID POSITION] when there is little distinction between phantasy activity and reality. Phantasy 'is' reality, and phantasy constructs the reality of the internal world on the basis of these primitive forms of introjective and projective identifications.

Introjective identification: The ego contains a whole society of internal objects [see 5. INTERNAL OBJECTS] and any one of them is potentially capable of being identified with [see ASSIMILATION], resulting in 'an alteration of the ego' in the direction of becoming like the object. This is a process of introjective identification.

Projective identification: Projective identification is a phantasy that some part of the ego has been separated off [see SPLITTING] and relocated in an external object [see EXTERNAL WORLD]. In this case the alteration of the ego is a depletion of both energy (sense of life) and of actual abilities (Klein, 1955) – for example the feeling in the presence of a learned and respected teacher that one's own contributions are foolishly silly [see 13. PROJECTIVE IDENTIFICATION].

In recent years some Kleinian analysts (Bick, Meltzer) have described a phenomenon they call adhesive identification (or simply adhesion) [see ADHESIVE IDENTIFICATION]. In this state, which can be seen best in the identification processes of the autistic child or patient, there is an imitative identification in which the ego has no ability to introject anything at all, and no ability to project parts of itself into an object [see SKIN]. The failure appears to be in the development of a sense of space [see INTERNAL REALITY] so there can never be phantasies of projecting into, or introjecting, since there is no possibility of phantasizing about internal spaces. This gives a world lacking in a third dimension, and the only possibility is a form of imitative clinging on to the outside of an inside-less object.

Identity: From the outset, the ego experiences relations with objects [see OBJECTS]. However, the constituents that make up the object and the ego vary considerably, in accord with the phantasies of introjection and projection. These mechanisms are used to adjust the sense of what the ego contains and of what it is (Freud, 1925) and are effective when they are primitively believed to be omnipotent. Such phantasies arise particularly from the need to defend against the fears of the ego being attacked or of attacks on and loss of the good object, which gives security.

Symbolic equation: Symbols are identified with objects not on the basis of similarity but on the basis of collective agreement within a social group. However, there is also a distinction between omnipotence of phantasy when the symbol *is* the object [see SYMBOLIC EQUATION] and symbols proper, when the symbol is recognized as separate and has its identity in its own right as well as functioning as a symbol for some other object.

Freud, Sigmund (1925) 'Negation'. *S.E.* 19, pp. 235–9.
Klein, Melanie (1955) 'On identification'. *WMK* 3, pp. 141–75.

Incorporation

The term 'incorporation' refers to a phantasy of the bodily taking in of an object which is subsequently felt to be physically present inside the body, taking up space and being active there. It is the *subject*'s experience of a mechanism of defence which is objectively described as 'introjection'.

See INTROJECTION

Infant observation

The imperative in child analysis after the First World War was to substantiate Freud's views about childhood, which he had formulated by extrapolating back from adulthood. The same imperative began to be felt about the discoveries of the infant's experiences in the first year of life which had come from Klein's analysis of older children (of about two-and-a-half onwards). In the early 1950s attempts were made to observe this developmental age.

The problem is one of being an outside observer without a direct method of becoming a listener-in to the internal world of the infant. The stage of development is one at which symbolic life is at a minimum; therefore the possibilities of communication (which normally depends on symbols) are equally at a minimum. The method with adults is a mutual verbal communication; with children it is their play, observed and at times participated in [see CHILD ANALYSIS]. With infants, a new method is necessary. The infant conceptualizes everything in terms of objects in relation to his body, its parts and their sensations and direct satisfactions. Without some form of symbolic communication, is any entry into the infant's world possible at all?

This question was furiously debated in the Controversial Discussions in 1943. When Susan Isaacs's 1943 paper ('The nature and function of phantasy') was later published (1948) she included an exhaustive introduction attempting to validate the process of psycho-analytic inference – if Freud had extrapolated back to childhood from adults, then it was valid for Klein to extrapolate to infancy from her work with children.

Klein also made direct observations on infants, interpreting, on the basis of her own discoveries, the kinds of experience in their minds. Interestingly, when her paper was eventually published (Klein, 1952) it showed just how much she paid attention to the environment of mother and mother's state of mind as the primary environment of the child. It effectively supported the dictum 'there is no such thing as an infant' (Winnicott, 1960). Joseph (1948) discussed a brief observation in terms of the problem of making a therapeutic intervention. Apart from these serendipitous observations, the interest in infants made slow progress.

Non-symbolic communication: When it was eventually understood that there are different varieties of projective identification (Bion, 1957) [see 13. PROJECTIVE IDENTIFICATION], a way forward to a method of infant observation became possible. Projective identification is not a symbolic form of communication, but it was realized that the direct impact of one state of mind upon another can have communicative potential outside the world of symbols ('normal projective identification'). At times symbols may even be an instrument used for the purpose of making such a direct impact (nonverbal communications in tone of voice, etc., etc.). Thus analysts who were becoming sensitized to using their own reactions as instruments of understanding [see COUNTERTRANSFERENCE] could come to understand a method that did not require symbolic expressions of the internal world. In the infant-observation method, however, the direct impact of states of mind must be those between the infant and the mother. Thus mother became a vehicle for making manifest the infant's interactions with objects – equivalent to the playthings of the child in analysis.

Infant observation: Bick began this work in 1948, as a training exercise for student child psychotherapists and psychoanalysts (for example Magagna, 1987; Glucksman, 1987; di Ceglie, 1987). She began systematic observations of infants with their mothers in the home on a weekly basis throughout the first year of life (Bick, 1964, 1968 and, posthumously, 1986). As may be expected, the results partly confirmed the results of child analysis and partly contributed new facts and theories, some of which remain at present somewhat outside the mainstream of Kleinian thought [see BICK] – the passive quality of being held together by the first object, and the nature of adhesive identification.

Bick described the very earliest attempts at introjecting an object that would hold the personality together [see 11. PARANOID-SCHIZOID POSITION]. She saw, in the mother–infant interaction, that this first object was particularly experienced through skin contact, and the sense of the skin as a containing object.

See SKIN; ADHESIVE IDENTIFICATION

Bick, Esther (1964) 'Notes on infant observation in psycho-analytic training', *Int. J. Psycho-Anal.* 45:558–66; republished (1987) in Martha Harris and Esther Bick,*The Collected Papers of Martha Harris and Esther Bick*. Perth: Clunie, pp. 240–56.

—— (1968) 'The experience of the skin in early object relations', *Int. J. Psycho-Anal.* 49:484–6; republished (1987) in *The Collected Papers of Martha Harris and Esther Bick*, pp. 114–18.

—— (1986) 'Further considerations of the function of the skin in early object relations', *Br. J. Psychother.* 2:292–9.

Bion, Wilfred (1957) 'Differentiation of the psychotic from the non-psychotic personalities', *Int. J. Psycho-Anal.* 38:266–75; republished (1967) in *Second Thoughts*. Heinemann, pp. 43–64.

di Ceglie, Giovanna (1987) 'Projective identification in mother and baby relationship', *Br. J. Psychother.* 3:239–45.

Glucksman, Marie (1987) 'Clutching at straws: an infant's response to lack of maternal containment', *Br. J. Psychother.* 3:340–9.

Isaacs, Susan (1948) 'The nature and function of phantasy', *Int. J. Psycho-Anal.* 29:73–97; republished (1952) in Melanie Klein, Paula Heimann, Susan Isaacs and Joan Riviere, eds *Developments in Psycho-Analysis*. Hogarth, pp. 66–121.

Joseph, Betty (1948) 'A technical problem in the treatment of the infant patient', *Int. J. Psycho-Anal.* 29:58–9.

Klein, Melanie (1952) 'On observing the behaviour of young infants'. *WMK* 3, pp. 94–121.

Magagna, Jeanne (1987) 'Three years of infant observation with Mrs Bick', *Journal of Child Psychotherapy* 13(1):19–39.

Schmideberg, Melitta (1934) 'The play analysis of a three-year-old girl', *Int. J. Psycho-Anal.* 15:245–64.

Winnicott, D. W. (1960) 'The theory of the infant–parent relationship', *Int. J. Psycho-Anal.* 41:585–95.

Inhibition

Inhibition is an important aspect of psycho-analytic theory describing a blockage to a natural outlet of mental activity. Freud (1900) developed the mechanical theory of a blocking-up of mental energy, but Klein stressed instead the inhibition of symbolic activity and, particularly in her early work, the child's play. This was one of the most prevalent symptoms of disturbed children, and she attributed it to the effects of sadism [see SADISM] (or the retaliation their sadism might provoke) which so frightened these children that they inhibited some mental activity. Sometimes, in psychotic children, all mental activity is inhibited (Klein, 1930; Rodrigue, 1955).

Klein (1932) expanded this idea to show that sadism had the effect of inhibiting development in general and disturbed the natural unfolding (epigenesis) of the libidinal phases [see LIBIDO; DEVELOP-MENT].

Freud, Sigmund (1900) *The Interpretation of Dreams. S.E.* 4, 5.
Klein, Melanie (1930) 'The importance of symbol-formation in the development of the ego'. *WMK* 1, pp. 219–32.
—— (1932) *The Psycho-Analysis of Children. WMK* 2.
Rodrigue, Emilio (1955) 'The analysis of a three-year-old mute schizophrenic',
  in Melanie Klein, Paula Heimann and Roger Money-Kyrle, eds (1955) *New
  Directions in Psycho-Analysis.* Tavistock, pp. 140–79.

Innate knowledge

Klein was impressed at the outset of her work by the enquiring nature of the child's mind, and she relied on Freud's blueprint with Little Hans (Freud, 1909) for the importance of acknowledging their sexual curiosity. It became clear to her how the sadism of children [see SADISM] was linked with the frustration of their enquiries into sexuality, and how the fear of their own sadism led on to an inhibition of enquiry and, further, to a blunting of curiosity in general [see EPISTEMOPHILIA; 3. AGGRESSION]. Because of the criticism of her play technique [see 1. TECHNIQUE; CHILD ANALYSIS] Klein took a prolonged interest in the development of symbolism and its essential role in intellectual development (Klein, 1930, 1931) [see SYMBOL-FORMATION].

Innate phantasy: The interest in symbolism led eventually to the formulation of *unconscious phantasy* (Isaacs, 1948) [see 2. UNCON-SCIOUS PHANTASY]. Instincts are represented in the mind as unconscious phantasies of relationships with objects. The various instincts give rise to phantasies of objects and active relationships with them that are not as yet known in external reality. The primitive conceptions of objects are based on the bodily sensations involved in the instincts. This was a point of contention, and the theory of unconscious phantasy was criticized because it implied that the infant could phantasize about biting, burning, cutting up, restoring, etc., without ever having had prior experience.

In the instance of the newborn turning his head for the nipple to suckle when he or she receives a physical stimulus on the cheek, there is simply a reflex. However, the theory suggested that the infant will have some *mental representation* of this event. That is, there will be a phantasy of an object to turn to and suck from. Isaacs (1948), in her key paper, goes to some lengths to try to convey the idea of a somatic knowledge actually embedded in the physical sensations. Freud had already concerned himself briefly with this debate in his reflections on Little Hans: '. . . the sensations of his penis had put him on the road to postulating a vagina' (Freud, 1909, p. 135). Klein was more explicit: '. . . the quite small child, which seemingly knows nothing about birth, has a very distinct "knowledge" of the fact that children grow in the womb' (Klein, 1927, p. 173). There was considerable resistance among Klein's critics to accepting innate knowledge.

Innate cognitive endowment: In the formulation that Isaacs began it would seem that one has to postulate certain innate capacities to make distinctions:

(i) to distinguish something that is motivated for the good ('good object') from something motivated for the bad ('bad object');

(ii) to distinguish the self from not-self (objects).

These endowed capabilities [see EGO] are inherent in bodily sensations. In the process of mental representation [see ALPHA-FUNCTION] these sensations are experienced as affective relationships with objects. The objects that are then phantasized are not physical, or in fact concrete in the normal sense; they are endowed with a primitive sense of place, within or without the self, and with affective motivations of benevolence or malevolence. In the first instance, therefore, they are *affective objects* [see PART-OBJECTS].

Kleinians described this innate knowledge of objects and of activities performed on them or by them as a form of knowledge very different from the adult's. The infant does not have proper use of the distance receptors, hearing and seeing, and his knowledge is therefore limited to his skin inwards; knowledge is confined to a sense of separate identity from an object. This kind of knowledge, though very different, enters into and forms the basis for the later *experience* (as opposed to the perception) of objects when the eyes and ears, etc., are mastered properly.

Alpha-function: Bion (1962) was interested in further study of the process by which sense data are converted to usable mental contents. He terms the elaboration of sense data into the unconscious phantasy of an object *alpha-function* [see ALPHA-FUNCTION]. The innate knowledge he called a *pre-conception* [see PRE-CONCEPTION; THINKING], and it is available at the outset to 'mate' with a realization of this object. The result of a mating is, in Bion's terms, a *conception*. He was trying to convey that the reality of objects has to meet a function of the ego that will *give the realizations meaning*. The quality of having meaning is an innate endowment that is progressively elaborated in the world of external objects.

See CONSTITUTIONAL FACTOR

Bion, Wilfred (1962) *Learning from Experience*. Heinemann.

Freud, Sigmund (1909) 'Analysis of a phobia in a five-year-old boy'. *S.E.* 10, pp. 3–149.

Isaacs, Susan (1948) 'The nature and function of phantasy', *Int. J. Psycho-Anal.* 29:73–97; republished (1952) in Melanie Klein, Paula Heimann, Susan Isaacs and Joan Riviere, eds *Developments in Psycho-Analysis*. Hogarth, pp. 67–121.

Klein, Melanie (1927) 'Criminal tendencies in normal children'. *WMK* 1, pp. 170–85.

—— (1930) 'The importance of symbol-formation in the development of the ego'. *WMK* 1, pp. 219–32.

—— (1931) 'A contribution to the theory of intellectual development'. *WMK* 1, pp. 236–47.

Instincts

In the heyday of nineteenth-century science, Freud was impelled to look for a 'scientific' psychology that would conform to laws of psychic determinism analogous to the laws of physics (Freud, 1895).

Psychic determinism: The basis of Freud's mechanistic theory was the mental energy of the instincts. The origins of mental life and activity can be considered to lie in the biological body and the genetic inheritance expressed in bodily development. Instincts remain the link between the biological origins of the individual and his or her psychological strivings and development. Freud originally regarded the instincts as arising from stimulation of the so-called 'erogenous' zones (the mouth, the anus and the genitals), all of which gave rise to a special form of neurological stimulation. That stimulation was the significant component of mental energy. He then proceeded to analyse its dissipation and discharge like the charge from an electrical condenser.

Freud's theory of instincts continued to change during his lifetime, and at his instigation. Especially as he began to be forced away from his neurological theories (from 1914 onwards) his interest in the nature and activity of the ego began to predominate over his interest in the instincts. The speculative theory of the instincts announced in 1920 (*Beyond the Pleasure Principle*) were those taken up by Klein.

Much effort has been devoted over the years to moving away from the constraints of Freud's instinct theory. Object-relations theory has emphasized the vicissitudes of the object rather than the instincts. Fairbairn, for instance, abolished all references to instincts [see FAIRBAIRN; ID]. Ego-psychology has described aspects of the ego independent of the instinctual endowment [see EGO-PSYCHOLOGY].

Unconscious phantasy: Klein took over the idea of the biological origins of the instincts. However, she modified the idea of mental energy and the mechanistic approach to its discharge [see ECONOMIC MODEL]. Instead she regarded stimulation of the body as giving rise to the primary mental events which were subjective interpretations of bodily stimuli as provoked by an object. Susan Isaacs showed how these interpretations, known as 'unconscious phantasies', make up, in effect, the substance of the mind [see 2. UNCONSCIOUS PHANTASY].

INSTINCT AND CONFLICT. Freud had originally evolved the theory that the stimulation of the erogenous zones, demanding immediate and total discharge, had brought the ego into a conflict with the civilized standards of society. Such a conflict was essentially between the sexual demands of the person and the restraints of society, and it formed the basis of early psychoanalytic theory. The problem with this is that it does not explain why society happens in the first place, nor the civilizing influence in mankind.

In attempting to solve this problem, Freud postulated that social conformity is important because it means personal survival. Mankind cannot survive without an imposed social co-operation. To introduce this notion meant that there was some driving force in the human being to survive, and he postulated a set of ego-instincts. These ensured that the person looked after his or her own interests when threatened by social condemnation and the loss of love, nutrition, etc. The ego-instincts were thus a different category from those arising from the erogenous zones, which had the specially impelling quality of erotism in their stimulation. He tended to take the ego-instincts rather for granted and did not deal with them in much detail. They certainly did not interest him as much as the libido. In this view, conflict was between two sets of instincts, one involving survival of the individual, the other the survival of the species. It was a notion which fitted in well with a specifically Germanic interpretation of the theory of evolution (for instance Weissman's germplasm versus somatoplasm).

Reinforcing this view was Freud's theory of castration anxiety. The conflict with society entailed a threat (especially intense in phantasy) to the child's own genitals. The conflict remained one with the external world, which opposes the libidinal aspects of the body. Freud never really seems to have resolved which priorities to give to these separate views of the impact of society [see SYMBOL-FORMATION]. From 1914 he was unsure of the distinction between libido and the ego-instincts – the latter appeared to be a narcissistic withdrawal of libido on to the ego as the loved object (Freud, 1914).

The death instinct: Freud's instinct theory changed radically in 1920. He must have been impressed by the scale of destruction in the First World War. He may also have been more relaxed after Jung left the psychoanalytic movement in 1919, and he no longer had to defend so rigidly his sexual theory of neurosis and of civilization. He raised aggression to the same level of importance as the sexual drives – in a strange way: by imputing to the human being an innate aggressive drive against his or her own existence, the death instinct. This existed parallel to those instincts devoted to the promotion of life. Now he set aside the opposition of ego and sexual instincts and aligned them together against the death instinct. He made this theoretical venture on various grounds: for instance, the stubborn resistance of some patients to benefit from good psychoanalytic interpretations – the negative therapeutic reaction; and the propensity for neurotic patients to repeat continually and to re-experience new versions of a trauma from their childhoods (or, in the case of war neurosis, from their adulthoods, especially in dreams). He set the theory (and perhaps this shows the remnants of his argument with Jung's religiousness) in an intensely biological and physical framework, so much so that it was dismissed as mystical biology [see DEATH INSTINCT].

Plasticity: Crucial to Freud's instinct theory and to all the psycho-analytic theories that have followed from his is the view that human instincts are especially plastic. They can be channelled into a remarkable variety of derivative impulses. Society responds, as it were, by offering channels for the diverted derivatives of instincts. This is a process known as sublimation. Typically the plasticity is in the change from physical and biological satisfactions into cultural and symbolic channels [see SYMBOL-FORMATION].

The change from biological organism to social being is largely a mystery and Freud's views offer no solution, merely a description. Fairbairn avoided the question by denying that the mind is biological in any way that is psychoanalytically relevant. By saying that mankind is object-seeking, he established that the biological arena was no longer to be considered. Klein, too, made the question redundant but, without denying instincts, viewed the infant as establishing object-relations at birth [see 5. INTERNAL OBJECTS; 2. UNCONSCIOUS PHANTASY]. In this way it was established that there was a psycho-logical and social being at the outset, not simply emergent from the biological level. The problem of understanding how the social being comes about no longer exists, as it is there at the beginning. The question is therefore removed from psychology and referred back to philosophy [see MIND–BODY PROBLEM].

The new theories: The great watershed in Klein's theoretical develop-ment came around 1932 and concerned her view of sadism. During her early work, as sadism came to have more and more emphasis it became a separate entity, a set of impulses that, though linked with oral and anal phases of the libido, gave rise to a separate clinical phenomenology and separate sets of defences [see SADISM]. Klein finally abandoned the link between sadism and the libido and switched explicitly to Freud's own later theory of instincts, which other analysts had not really developed. In 1932 she accepted that she was observing the clinical manifestations of a conflict between the life and death instincts: '. . . in the early stages of development, the life instinct has to exert its power to the utmost in order to maintain itself against the death instinct' (Klein, 1932, p. 150). Embracing the newer theory of instincts allowed her more freedom of thought to develop her own theories: of the nature and development of the superego; of sadism, persecution and paranoia, as coherent phenomena deriving from the death instinct, interacting with the development of the libido; and of the distinct quality of anxiety and guilt in the depressive position.

Freud, Sigmund (1895) 'Project for a scientific psychology'. *S.E.* 1, pp. 283–397.
—— (1914) 'On narcissism'. *S.E.* 14, pp. 67–102.
—— (1920) *Beyond the Pleasure Principle. S.E.* 18, pp. 3–64.
Klein, Melanie (1932) *The Psycho-Analysis of Children. WMK* 2.

Integration

Klein, from very early on, viewed the mind as operating in split and unintegrated ways. More than any other analyst, Klein relinquished the integrity of the mind. Instead of the interrelated structure of id, ego and superego, she saw integration as *the developmental task*. This task was conceived differently at various stages in her work:

(i) (up to about 1932) she was preoccupied with the struggle to integrate the internal imagos of the parents into a mature superego;

(ii) then (1935–46) came the depressive position: with the integration of good and bad objects during development, splitting becomes progressively more realistic [see 10. DEPRESSIVE POSITION]; and

(iii) finally (from 1946 onwards) she was concerned with the integration of the ego itself [see 11. PARANOID-SCHIZOID POSITION].

Integration is promoted by the push of anxiety to move on to a new level of maturity, combined with the pull of biological development. In clinical practice Kleinian technique has emphasized more and more the last of these forms of integration – the integration of splits within the ego. The transference relationship is viewed as being split into various aspects, many of which are projected outside the analytic consulting room and are experienced in relation to apparently extra-analytic objects. This dispersal of relationships and of experience results from the processes of splitting together with projective identification [see 1. TECHNIQUE].

See DEVELOPMENT

Internal reality

Freud's momentous starting point was to take seriously what neurotic and psychotic patients said to him, and he started with the assumption that they were conveying something comprehensible that was real for themselves. Internal or psychic reality is the conviction of the reality of the psychic world that exists unconsciously and is felt as inside the person.

Klein elaborated this with the theory of internal objects; she

> made a discovery that created a revolutionary addition to the model of the mind, namely that we do not live in one world, but in two – that we live in an internal world which is as real a place to live as the outside world . . . Psychic reality could be treated in a concrete way. (Meltzer, 1981, p. 178)

Internal objects are experienced as concretely real and inside the ego, which means an experience of inside the body [see SKIN]. They are different from images and representations which, when we experience them, retain an ephemeral quality in themselves (though they may be representations of concrete things). Such a bizarre idea derived ultimately from work with psychotic patients but was regarded as the infant's initial state of experiencing himself and his world at birth, and before he can know anything objectively about the world around him. This is felt concretely as an internal world of actual objects (not images or representations) engaging in relations with each other and with the subject.

This quality of concrete internal realness is very hard to capture consciously in adulthood, and it took many years of debate throughout the 1930s and 1940s for the distinction between internal (introjected) objects and representations to become graspable. The distinction is not, at bottom, a conceptual one but a distinction in quality of experiencing oneself and one's own mental activity

Rapaport (1957) tried to distinguish the 'inner' world of mental representations from the 'internal' world of psychic structure. Thus the patient has a world of memories, ideas, phantasies which he 'represents' to himself – the representational world (Sandler and Rosenblatt, 1962) – which has a quality of being mental and different from a physical quality. The contrasting world of psychic structure is what the analyst constructs for himself to give an *objective* picture of the patient's mind in the framework of a metapsychology. Rapaport's distinction fails, however, but in an important way. One category of phantasy that patients have is about the structure of their own minds, and the functions that have structured it in the way they believe it is. This may be simply the patient's own idiosyncratic phantasy. The problem, however, is that such phantasies can be shown to have an important effect in producing a mind that appears, to analytic observation, to be structured according to the patient's belief. Abraham (1924) gave as a touching personal example the way his hair turned white on his father's death. The example was intended to show that the introjection of the lost object was so intense (omnipotent) that it did cause actual change to the ego. His father did not just enter the representational world of mental objects but became an actual physical change, as if his father had actually entered his head and changed it physically.

If, therefore, the patient's phantasies of the structure and functioning of his own mind have a real correspondence to the objectively conceived psychic structure and function, then the distinction between the patient's subjective and the analyst's objective perspectives breaks down. The observation reported by Abraham is typical of the Kleinian descriptions of the patient's communications about the structuring of his or her mind. This has led to the criticism of Klein that she (i) reified the phantasy phenomena, and (ii) confused the levels of description with those of theory [see 2. UNCONSCIOUS PHANTASY]. However, the internal reality of the patient is reified because it is the patient who reifies it and functions as if there really were physical objects going in and out of his ego. It is this inside world which has the quality of a physical existence which is meant by the 'internal world'; it is perceptible to the patient, not just to the analyst.

See 5. INTERNAL OBJECTS; 2. UNCONSCIOUS PHANTASY

Abraham, Karl (1924) 'A short study of the development of the libido', in Karl Abraham (1927) *Selected Papers on Psycho-Analysis*. Hogarth, pp. 418–501.
Meltzer, Donald (1981) 'The Kleinian expansion of Freudian meta-psychology', *Int. J. Psycho-Anal.* 62:177–85.
Rapaport, David (1957) 'A theoretical analysis of the superego concept', in (1967) *The Collected Papers of David Rapaport*. New York: Basic.
Sandler, Joseph and Rosenblatt, Bernard (1962) 'The concept of the representational world', *Psychoanal. Study Child* 17:128–45.

Introjection

Surprisingly, for a term that is linked with – and a mirror image of – 'projection', the history and meaning of 'introjection' are very different and much less problematic.

Ferenczi: The term was first coined by Ferenczi in 1909, when psychoanalysts (Freud, Abraham) were being induced, by the association with Jung, to look at psychotic patients. Ferenczi made a distinction between neurosis and psychosis on the basis that neurotic problems were based on excessive introjection, as a mirror of the problem of psychotics, whose problems focused around their excessive projection. Ferenczi was one of the first to point out the correlation between oral impulses and introjection, and anal ones and projection, which Abraham was to take up extensively later in his work with manic-depressives.

Freud: When Freud first stumbled on the importance of the vicissitudes of the object in 1917 and later in 1921, he used the term identification [see IDENTIFICATION]. By this, however, he quite clearly meant a process by which an object was relocated within the ego-boundaries that had once been experienced as external. For him it was a mysterious and mystifying process: on the one hand it is a phantasy activity [see 2. UNCONSCIOUS PHANTASY], yet it truly causes 'an alteration of the ego' in objective reality. The personality as perceived by other people is changed.

Abraham: Abraham, also impressed by this demonstration of a mechanism by which the ego develops, claimed the possibility of physical changes and described as an example a *physical* change in himself, when his own father died and his hair turned white overnight! There was clearly a process of identification going on as well as introjection. In his example, his white hair was in identification with his father's. Thus the introjection is of an object into the ego, causing the change in the ego.

Abraham showed that the process of introjection of a loved object was very frequent – indeed, a *normal process* in human relations. People carry their loved ones in their heart and continue an internal dialogue with them [see 5. INTERNAL OBJECTS].

Introjection and the superego: However, in 1923, Freud modified the concept of introjection when he worked out the development of the superego. With the giving up of the loved oedipal objects (mother and father) they are introjected to form the superego, which becomes a true internal object. It is not identified with, and remains a separate internal structure. There appear, then, to be two possibilities:

(i) the introjection of an object once external, which is identified with (introjective identification) [see ASSIMILATION], and

(ii) the introjection of an object which is not identified with, such as the superego.

Internal objects. For Klein, introjected objects that are not identified with become internal objects, and she conceived of a varied and continuous process which populates the internal world with very many internal objects. This internal society becomes, on one hand, a resource of objects for identification [see INTERNAL REALITY] and, on the other, a set of experiences about what the ego consists of and contains (good or bad).

Introjection as a defence mechanism: Although 'introjection' is used to describe the mental representation of an oral instinctual impulse, it is also a defence mechanism [see PSYCHOSIS]. That means, in Klein's framework, an unconscious phantasy engineered for the purpose of defending against certain experiences [see 2. UNCONSCIOUS PHANTASY]. For Freud, introjection is a defence against the loss of the external object, but for Klein the typical experience is an anxiety about the world inside, which feels terrifying. If the internal world is believed, in phantasy, to contain very bad or persecuting objects that seem to endanger the ego, then one phantasy is to internalize the external good object. For example, the hungry child (who believes there is a bad object gnawing at his tummy from the inside) can experience the internalization of mother's milk as a good object going into him and replacing the bad one and, indeed, saving him [see ANXIETY]. However, the fear of persecutors inside may eventually make it seem better not to let the good object inside in case it is damaged by what is in there – one cause of anorexia, for instance.

Introjection and development: Introjection as a phantasy is a defence adopted to preserve the ego or the good objects. In the longer term it is one of the most important mechanisms used to build up a secure personality through the experience of having good objects introjected and safely located inside, with the ensuing experience of an internal sense of goodness, or self-confidence and mental stability. At the origins of the depressive position, at about four to six months of age, introjection comes to the fore with the building-up of the internal world separate and distinct from the external world. Introjection takes over from projection, which was the more dominant process in the earlier paranoid-schizoid position (Klein, 1946). In this sense Klein is close to Ferenczi's original hypothesis.

Because these are descriptions of the subject's own phantasies, there is a confusion between technical terms; 'introjection' (an objective description of the observing psychologist) and terms like 'incorporation', which names the patient's phantasies, are difficult to distinguish. Although the solution has been to designate one term to refer to the patient's unconscious phantasy and another for the analyst's (objective) description of the same process in his patient, there is still a strong tendency to use the terms interchangeably in Kleinian literature. This is to do with the problem of the two levels: an *objective* science of the *subjective* [see SUBJECTIVITY].

Ferenczi, Sandor (1909) 'Introjection and transference', in *First Contributions to Psycho-Analysis*. Hogarth, pp. 30–79.
Freud, Sigmund (1917) 'Mourning and melancholia'. *S.E.* 14, pp. 237–60.
—— (1921) *Group Psychology and the Analysis of the Ego. S.E.* 18, pp. 67–143.
—— (1923) *The Ego and the Id. S.E.* 19, pp. 3–66.

Klein, Melanie (1946) 'Notes on some schizoid mechanisms'. *WMK* 3, pp. 1–24.

Susan Isaacs

Biography. Susan Isaacs was born (1885) and brought up in Lancashire and retained her provincial accent all her life (Gardner, 1969). She was academically outstanding, and remained an eminent educationalist throughout her psychoanalytic career. She taught generations of teachers at the Institute of Education in the University of London, and for a brief period ran an experimental progressive school for very young children (Malting House School in Cambridge). She was an enormous asset to the Kleinian Group in its early days and later during the trials of the Controversial Discussions, because she brought the rigour of academic debate to the clinical intuitions of the practitioners. She died in the prime of her career in **1948**.

SCIENTIFIC CONTRIBUTIONS. Isaacs's written work is spread between psychoanalysis and education. Like Klein she was anxious to distinguish the two. Her psychoanalytic work is largely rigorous exposition of Klein's ideas, with much clinical illustration. Isaacs and Heimann were the main protagonists in the Controversial Discussions (Isaacs, 1948; Isaacs and Heimann, 1952). Isaacs's sharp wit and quick thinking on her feet gave the Kleinian Group the advantage in these debates, winning points though rarely convincing the opposition [see CONTROVERSIAL DISCUSSIONS].

Her great lasting contribution was her thorough exposition of the concept of unconscious phantasy (Isaacs, 1948). It is hard to know how much of the concept, with all its deep philosophical as well as psychoanalytic significance, was Isaacs's work, but it seems likely that the initial idea, coming from the clinician Klein, was taken up by the academic thinker Isaacs in partnership [see 2. UNCONSCIOUS PHANTASY].

Gardner, D. E. M. (1969) *Susan Isaacs*. Methuen.

Isaacs, Susan (1948) 'The nature and function of phantasy', *Int. J. Psycho-Anal.* 29:73–97; republished (1952) in Melanie Klein, Paula Heimann, Susan Isaacs and Joan Riviere, eds *Developments in Psycho-Analysis*. Hogarth, pp. 67–121.

Isaacs, Susan and Heimann, Paula (1952) 'Regression', in Melanie Klein, Paula Heimann, Susan Isaacs and Joan Riviere, eds (1952) *Developments in Psycho-Analysis*. Hogarth, pp. 169–97.

Jealousy

Whereas jealousy is the cornerstone of classical Freudian theory in the form of the Oedipus complex, Klein took the concept and gave it a new depth. She showed how the earliest experiences of antagonism are almost pure violence and persecution, and then how jealousy crystallizes out of that as a more specific affect that allows admiration of the person towards whom the jealousy is felt. As in guilt [see GUILT], there is a spectrum of affects from persecution through various degrees of intensity of jealousy as the depressive position is encountered and worked through, and then leading off towards healthy competition at the other end. This description was enhanced when, in 1957, Klein described primary envy, and distinguished it as a wanton invasion and spoiling of the good object and how it contributes to the persecuting end of the jealousy spectrum [see 12. ENVY].

Melanie Klein

Biography. Melanie Klein was born in Vienna in **1882** but seemingly never heard of Freud until about 1914–15, when in Budapest she was advised to consult Ferenczi, who took her into her first analysis. Uwe Peters (1985) noted that shortly before the First World War Melanie Klein's husband, Arthur, worked in the same office as Ferenczi's brother. It is possible that this was Melanie Klein's path to her first analysis. It seems she was depressed at the time, in the aftermath of her mother's death and during the puerperium of her third child (Grosskurth, 1986). Due to the political turmoil in Europe she eventually (1920) went to live in Berlin, where she continued to study psychoanalysis; and her earlier experiments with analysing her own children along the lines of Little Hans (Freud, 1909) developed into her rigorous play technique. She was encouraged by Abraham, whom she eventually persuaded to take her into analysis in 1924 (Segal, 1979). He died eighteen months later, bringing her second analysis to an abrupt halt. Abraham was interested in Klein's attempts to corroborate the psychological events of early childhood from direct analysis of children, because he was discovering the importance of early sadism in his work with psychotic patients. There is no doubt that Klein was influenced by his views, but it is not inconceivable that Abraham himself was also encouraged and influenced by her own clinical results. Apart from Abraham's powerful patronage she seems to have been disliked and dismissed by the rest of the Berlin Psycho-Analytical Society.

In Berlin she came in contact with some English analysts who had come there to train with Abraham. These included Edward Glover and Alix Strachey (James Strachey's wife). As a result she was invited to lecture in England, where her views were suddenly applauded. She was tempted to stay in London and accepted Ernest Jones's invitation readily (he was the elder statesman of the British Psycho-Analytical Society and her patron in Britain). Part of this deal seems to have been that she should analyse one of his children. Her difficult and unyielding personality, together with her unparalleled clinical abilities, made her an exacting colleague, and many of those who associated with her later drew away. Only the most talented and robust stayed with her, and she seems to have had several differently composed groups of supporters at different times [see KLEINIAN GROUP]. These groups were therefore always small but their standards, cohesiveness and activity gave others the impression of a large and powerful Kleinian group. She died in London in **1960** and bequeathed a rich tradition of ideas and practice which, like Freud's own, has constantly developed ever since.

Freud, Sigmund (1909) 'Analysis of a phobia in a five-year-old boy', *S.E.*10, pp. 3–149.

Grosskurth, Phyllis (1986) *Melanie Klein: Her World and her Work*. Hodder & Stoughton.

Peters, Uwe (1985) *Anna Freud: A Life Dedicated to Children*. Weidenfeld & Nicolson.

Segal, Hanna (1979) *Klein*. Fontana.

Kleinian Group

Klein's colleagues fall into separate groups, from different stages of her career (Grosskurth, 1986). There was no clearly bounded Kleinian group until the mid-1940s.

(i) Her earliest supporters were eminent members of the British Psycho-Analytical Society, such as Ernest Jones and Edward Glover, who decided to adopt Klein in spite of the poor reputation she had gathered on the Continent. A number of people supported her views. Notable were Edward Glover, Marjorie Brierley and Alix and James Strachey (Strachey and Strachey, 1986); and also Klein's own daughter, Melitta Schmideberg.

(ii) At first, in London, she attracted a number of adherents who were particularly loyal to her and supported her through the moment of independence in 1932 when others, notably Glover and her own daughter, fell away. These included Joan Riviere, Susan Isaacs, Mina Searl and, a little later, Paula Heimann.

These initial groups supported her up to the war years and shortly after and were responsible for all the work on the nature of phantasy, the mysterious internal objects, and the theoretical framework of the depressive position. However, these supporters faded away soon after that. Susan Isaacs died in 1948, Joan Riviere took a waning interest in the work as she grew older and was particularly disconcerted by the virulence of the rivalry with the classical analysts from Vienna, and Paula Heimann eventually sought a greater degree of professional independence in 1956 [see HEIMANN].

(iii) When Klein's work on psychosis came out during the early thirties, an interest developed within adult and child psychiatry (previously most interest in the 1920s and 1930s had been amongst educationalists and the literary intelligentsia). In the years before 1940, therefore, several doctors sought training with Klein – W. Clifford M. Scott, John Bowlby, Donald Winnicott. They were all important people for her cause because they were medically qualified and therefore more influential within the institutions that were important, but they had all established reputations of their own and were unpromising as new acolytes for the beleaguered position of the group in the 1940s. Nevertheless it seems certain that these were people from whom Klein gathered some of the important experience for understanding schizoid mechanisms and the mechanism of projective identification. Most of these broke from – or never saw themselves as fully members of – the Kleinian Group as it was forming under the pressures of the disputes in the 1940s after Anna Freud's arrival in London.

(iv) Shortly after the war a number of young doctors, some émigrés who had not previously been analysts, came for training with Klein. They were perhaps the true second generation, and they stuck with the group: notable were Hanna Segal, Herbert Rosenfeld and Wilfred Bion. It was these people, together with the solid support of the more retiring Roger Money-Kyrle and the later addition of Donald Meltzer, who pushed forward Kleinian thought, almost wholly on the basis of extending the concept of projective identification.

(v) Finally there was a considerable interest in 'training as a Kleinian' from the 1950s onwards and many people have come from other countries for psychoanalytic training, especially from South America and more recently Italy. Since Bion's brief period in the United States, a small group of Klein-orientated analysts has developed in North America.

Grosskurth, Phyllis (1986) *Melanie Klein: Her World and her Work.* Hodder & Stoughton.
Strachey, James and Strachey, Alix (1986) *Bloomsbury Freud: The Letters of James and Alix Strachey.* Chatto & Windus.

Libido

Freud's original intention was to develop a quasi-physics of the mind. The details of the theory of the libido that he developed and the continual modifications to it in his writings and in those of psychoanalytic theorists who came after him is one of the more complex stories in the development of psychoanalysis (Laplanche and Pontalis, 1973).

Freud, in effect, described an economics of the libido, which was subject to quantitative conservation. He conceptualized a *mental energy* exactly analogous to a physical energy and regarded it as generated by stimulus of the *erogenous zones* (mouth, anus, genitals). This theory of libido (Freud, 1905) regarded all mental energy as deriving from sexual sources, even if in the course of its flow through the mental apparatus it became 'desexualized'. He called this energy *libido*. In short, the mind works by directing the libido towards some object (which could also be the subject's own ego); that is to say, the object is invested with attention and interest (cathexis). When someone is in love, for instance, their loved one (object) is invested with huge amounts of interest, absorbing enormous quantities of mental energy [see INSTINCTS; ECONOMIC MODEL].

Phases of the libido: At each stage of the infant's development the libido is organized rather differently. There were three main phases of infantile libido development: the oral stage, with the mouth as the primary focus of interest; the anal stage, in which potty training and symbolic substitutes are the preoccupying interest; and the genital stage, when the genitals begin their long hegemony as the source of avid and compulsive instinctual interest [see 3. AGGRESSION].

Abraham, with extreme precision, elaborated these phases by working out a timetable of sub-phases. Each of Freud's stages was divided into two, resulting in six altogether: (i) early oral stage (sucking), pre-ambivalent; (ii) later oral stage, sadistic (cannibalistic); (iii) earlier anal-sadistic stage, retentive (excess of sadism); (iv) later anal-sadistic stage, expulsive; (v) earlier genital stage, phallic and sadistic; (vi) later genital stage, post-ambivalent, with true object-love (whole objects) (see Abraham, 1924).

Klein's view of the libido. Klein's theories of the libido fall into two phases – before and after the period 1932–5, at which point she adopted Freud's theory of the death instinct as a *clinical* concept.

1920–32: Klein, building on encouragement from Abraham, began by checking his findings with children. She found that these phases were by no means as marked as Freud and Abraham described. In fact, she showed that from the beginning there was mostly a mixture of all these phases – that is to say, there were oral, anal and genital impulses and sadistic impulses occurring together. This did not mean that she threw out the sequence altogether; in fact she (and increasingly many other analysts) began to think of a primacy of impulses *over* other impulses. All kinds of impulses exist in the oral phase, but the oral ones are dominant, and likewise with the other phases [see 4. OEDIPUS COMPLEX; 7. SUPEREGO].

Klein was continually impressed by the strength of the sadistic impulses and she realized that an important part of pressure to progress through the sequence of dominance was the effect of the sadism, the fear of retaliation, and the anguished wish to restore damage [see SADISM]. Thus she thought that some impulses would be deliberately inhibited unconsciously by the child, possibly slowing down the libidinal sequence. She also thought of the genital phase as representing a particular upsurge of libidinal feelings, and that there may therefore be a precocious surge towards the genital phase as a reassurance against the sadistic impulses of the pregenital phases. Thus the libido had an important place during this phase of Klein's work. The development of the instincts was the important aspect of infantile development [see DEVELOPMENT], together with the ways in which development was affected by the manipulation of the various kinds of impulses to ensure the lowest level of anxiety.

After 1935: Klein's emphasis changed with the introduction of the depressive position in 1935 [see 10. DEPRESSIVE POSITION]. At that point Klein came to see the developmental history of the infant in terms of the *quality* of object-relations. From then on her emphasis was on the accumulation of the internal objects: of what kind, in what condition, and in what relation to the self. This theory of internal objects was buttressed further by the theory of unconscious phantasy. With unconscious phantasy, the theory of instincts moved further into the background [see 2. UNCONSCIOUS PHANTASY]. Unconscious phantasies, being the mental representation of instincts, could then be talked about without reference to the instincts, since there was a one-to-one translation of them from the phases into the unconscious phantasy. However, because phantasies can be generated, in a defensive, reparative and creative manner, the quantitative aspect of the instincts became lost [see ECONOMIC MODEL]. The elaboration of unconscious phantasy implied that instinct derivatives can be contrived by the ego rather than merely allowed to emerge [see MASTURBATION PHANTASIES; PSYCHOLOGICAL DEFENCE].

See INSTINCTS

Abraham, Karl (1924) 'A short study of the development of the libido', in Karl Abraham (1927), *Selected Papers on Psycho-Analysis*. Hogarth, pp. 418–501.
Freud, Sigmund (1905) *Three Essays on Sexuality*. S.E. 7, pp. 125–245.
Laplanche, J. and Pontalis, J.-B. (1973) *The Language of Psycho-Analysis*. Hogarth.

Linking
In Bion's (1959) theory of schizophrenia he described the attacks on the ego itself, which represented the experiences that Klein (1946) regarded as the effects of the death instinct acting within – the feeling of falling to pieces. Bion described particularly an attack on the awareness of internal reality [see 11. PARANOID-SCHIZOID POSITION; ANNIHILATION].

Severance: The severance of thoughts within the mind is characteristic of schizophrenics and was described by Rosenfeld (1947) and by Segal (1950):

The fact that many things are tolerated in consciousness in the schizophrenic must not blind one to the necessity of interpreting what is repressed. Schizophrenics, more than others, repress the links between different trends of thought. They often tolerate in their ego thoughts and phantasies which would probably be repressed in the neurotic; but on the other hand they repress the links between the various phantasies and between phantasy and reality. (Segal, 1950, p. 118)

It is the *links* between mental contents which are dealt with by the schizophrenic. Freud also described this kind of process when he was interested in severe obsessional neurosis:

in this disorder, as I have already explained, repression is effected not by means of amnesia but by a severance of causal connections brought about by withdrawal of affect. These repressed connections appear to persist in some kind of shadowy form, and they are thus transferred, by a process of projection, into the external world, where they bear witness to what has been effaced from consciousness. (Freud, 1909, pp. 231–2)

Violence: Although Freud and Segal described the process in terms of repression, Bion described its violent quality:

It is to be expected that the deployment of projective identification would be particularly severe against thought, of whatsoever kind, that turned to the relations between object-impressions, for if this link could be severed, or better still never forged, then at least consciousness of reality would be destroyed even though reality itself could not be. (Bion, 1957, p. 50)

The end result is that the schizophrenic lives in a fragmented world of violence, with primitive ideas unusable in his mind:

All these are now attacked till finally two objects cannot be brought together in a way which leaves each object with its intrinsic qualities intact and yet able, by their conjunction, to produce a new mental object. (Bion, 1957, p. 50) [see PSYCHOSIS]

The destruction of these connections and conjunctions leads to the patient feeling 'surrounded by minute links which, being impregnated now with cruelty, link objects together cruelly' (Bion, 1957, p. 50) [see BIZARRE OBJECTS]. Bion called these particles 'beta-elements' [see BETA-ELEMENTS]. The effect is well on the way to what Freud called a 'world catastrophe' (Freud, 1911, p. 70):

This is a disaster for mental life which is then not established in the normal mode. Instead of thinking based on the reality principle and symbolic communication within the self and with other objects, an anomalous enlargement of the pleasure ego occurs, with excessive use of splitting and projective identification as its concrete mode of relating to hated and hating objects. Omnipotence replaces thinking and omniscience replaces learning from experience in a disastrously confused, undeveloped and fragile ego. (O'Shaughnessy, 1981, p. 183) [see THINKING]

Added to the narcissistic withdrawal of the libido from objects in reality, which Freud had described as the world catastrophe, is the idea of an omnipotent violent splitting up and projection of the ego. The ego is the focus of aggression, not just of libidinal love [see NARCISSISM].

Oedipal linking: Bion (1959) took these observations further and established a formal theory. He regarded this coupling activity as based on an innate predisposition to conceive of the link between a container and its contents, typically the nipple in the breast or the penis in the vagina. The attack on the link between two internal mental objects is an attack on the internal parental couple [see COMBINED PARENT FIGURE]. Because of the connotation of the oedipal couple, the conjoining of two mental objects is felt not only to arouse envy but to be the basis for internal, mental creativity.

Container and contained: The coupling of penis and vagina, or mouth and nipple, is taken by Bion (1962) as a prototype of the way mental objects are put together, one inside the other. Thus putting experiences into thoughts, and thoughts into words, entails a repeated chain of linking processes modelled on physical intercourse between two bodily parts [see CONTAINING]. With this model Bion went on to investigate the nature of thought itself and described its basis in the linking together of thoughts, in the mating of pre-conceptions (expectations) with realizations [see THINKING]. The particular kind of links that go to make up thinking are designated by the notation 'K' and exist alongside other kinds of links, 'L' and 'H' representing loving and hating the object [see EPISTEMOPHILIA].

Bion, Wilfred (1957) 'Differentiation of the psychotic from the non-psychotic personalities', *Int. J. Psycho-Anal.* 38: 266–75; republished (1967) in W. R. Bion, *Second Thoughts*. Heinemann, pp. 43–64.
—— (1959) 'Attacks on linking', *Int. J. Psycho-Anal.* 40:308–15; republished (1967) in *Second Thoughts*, pp. 93–109.
—— (1962) *Learning from Experience*. Heinemann.
Freud, Sigmund (1909) 'Notes upon a case of obsessional neurosis'. *S.E.* 10, pp. 153–320.
—— (1911) 'Psycho-analytic notes on an autobiographical account of a case of paranoia'. *S.E.* 12, pp. 3–82.
Klein, Melanie (1946) 'Notes on some schizoid mechanisms'. *WMK* 3, pp. 1–240.

O'Shaughnessy, Edna (1981) 'A commemorative essay on W. R. Bion's theory of thinking', *Journal of Child Psychotherapy* 7:181–92.

Rosenfeld, Herbert (1947) 'Analysis of a schizophrenic state with depersonalization', *Int. J. Psycho-Anal.* 28:130–9; republished (1965) in Herbert Rosenfeld, *Psychotic States*. Hogarth, pp. 13–33.

Segal, Hanna (1950) 'Some aspects of an analysis of a schizophrenic', in (1981) *The Work of Hanna Segal*. New York: Jason Aronson, pp. 101–20; previously published *Int. J. Psycho-Anal.* 31:268–78.

Loss   Both Freud and Abraham were interested in the experiences of psychotic patients and worked for a decade on the analysis of manic-depressive patients. Freud (1917) eventually described the similarity between depressive illnesses and mourning and the central aspect of loss in the nature of the problem. These losses linked up with his preceding views about the special importance of castration in childhood development. In 1926, when he investigated the nature of anxiety, he saw a number of situations of loss: the loss at birth, weaning, castration and so on through the developmental cycle [see 8. EARLY ANXIETY-SITUATIONS].

Loss of the internal object: Klein added to this by describing these losses as having a crucial similarity in that they all arouse anxiety through creating a sense of an insecure *internalized good object* (Klein, 1940) [see 10. DEPRESSIVE POSITION]. In this she added significantly to Freud's theory (expounded in 1917) in which he was impressed by the melancholic's aberrant mourning reaction when the external object had not actually been lost; and developed Abraham's work in which he described the manic-depressive's preoccupation with lost objects represented by faeces.

Thus Klein developed the direction in which Abraham and Freud had been pointing. For this she was criticized by Fairbairn, who admonished all three for being too absorbed in the depressive position and for neglecting splitting processes manifest in schizophrenia (the other major psychosis), characteristics that are similar to hysteria with which, of course, psychoanalysis had started [see FAIRBAIRN; 11. PARANOID-SCHIZOID POSITION].

See DEPRESSIVE ANXIETY

Freud, Sigmund (1917) 'Mourning and melancholia'. *S.E.* 14, pp. 237–60.
Klein, Melanie (1940) 'Mourning and its relation to manic-depressive states'. *WMK* 1, pp. 344–69.

Love   Klein followed Abraham in trying to understand the kind of love which *feels for* the object rather than the love described in classical psychoanalysis, in which the object is merely what the subject satisfies himself upon. The latter form of satisfaction is an anaclitic love, a cupboard love. In contrast, Klein described, from direct observation of infants, how 'gratification is as much related to the object which gives the food as to the food itself' (Klein, 1952, p. 96). Wisdom (1970) struggled to make this distinction clear, as also did Fairbairn (1952).

Eagle (1984), reviewing the evidence Bowlby (1969) had also interpreted, showed that experiences of objects are not just in terms of the gratification of instincts – hunger, for example: 'These findings present a serious challenge to "homeostatic drive-reduction" models'; and with respect to Harlow's monkey-rearing experiments (Harlow and Zimmermann, 1969),

> If attachment to an object is derived from its role in drive gratification, why didn't the infant monkeys become attached to the milk-dispensing mother who provided gratification more closely fitting a drive discharge model than the 'contact comfort' gratification provided by the terrycloth mother? (Eagle, 1984, p. 11)

In Klein's view there is a generous love from the beginning. Gratification brings out a gratitude towards the object.

The paranoid-schizoid position: However, from the beginning gratification brings not only gratitude but also envy. In so far as the infant can sustain an attitude of gratitude to the loved object, and in so far as the actual external object (mother) can help to bring out gratitude, the infant can grow stronger in his belief in love and the good parts of himself.

It is in the balance of envy versus gratitude that the security of the infant lies, since envy destroys love and gratitude. For the most part the infant deals with this by splitting off an 'ideal' gratifying object, towards whom gratitude is felt, from an envied and hated persecutor. However, this splitting brings a form of insecurity in itself, since any degree of frustration results in an abrupt switch in the impulses to hatred, and in the object, which suddenly becomes a persecuting one.

To avoid these insecurities the infant sometimes engages in excessive projective identification. The more intense the relationship, the greater the projective identification, and this leads to an emptying of the ego. Schizoid love depletes.

Love in the depressive position: When Klein described the depressive position she entered upon descriptions of quite new affective states – new, that is, to the descriptive pens of psychoanalysts. In fact they are much closer to the affects that are the preoccupation of the novelist and the ordinary person. She sought to convey the qualities of a particular, poignant kind of love: a pining. Klein was here following up Abraham's notion of 'true object-love', the experience of whole objects. Love in the depressive position is for the non-ideal object, the good object that is also blemished and flawed [see 10. DEPRESSIVE POSITION]. As this becomes established, the love, in spite of the flaws, tends not to switch so violently to hatred and a degree of emotional stability begins to develop. There is here the capacity for tolerance and forgiveness. Love in the depressive position is marked indelibly with concern and forgiveness.

However, the flawed whole object gives rise to the experience that the good object is, or was, perfect and has been injured and damaged, with the arousing of an anguished concern. In turn this concern gives rise to the wish to restore and repair [see GUILT; REPARATION].

See CONCERN; WHOLE OBJECT

Bowlby, John (1969) *Attachment and Loss*. Hogarth.

Eagle, Morris (1984) *Recent Developments in Psycho-Analysis*. New York: McGraw-Hill.

Fairbairn, Ronald (1952) *Psycho-Analytic Studies of the Personality*. Routledge & Kegan Paul.

Harlow, H. F. and Zimmermann, R. R. (1969) 'Affectional responses in the infant monkey', *Science* 130:412–32.

Klein, Melanie (1952) 'On observing the behaviour of young infants'. *WMK* 3, pp. 94–121.

Wisdom, J. O. (1970) 'Freud and Melanie Klein: psychology, ontology and *Weltanschauung*', in Charles Hanly and Morris Lanzerowitz, eds (1970) *Psycho-Analysis and Philosophy*. New York: International Universities Press, pp. 327–62.

Manic defences

The pain of the depressive position occurs throughout life, and is met at times by a defensiveness in most people [see 10. DEPRESSIVE POSITION]. Of paramount importance are the defences which go to make up the states of mania and hypomania – states which in minor degree are common in everyone. The manic defences are typically omnipotent: 'The *sense of omnipotence* is what first and foremost characterizes mania and, further, mania is based on the mechanism of *denial* . . .' (Klein, 1935, p. 277). The defences comprise:

(i) Denial: Omnipotence is based on denial, 'first of all denied is psychic reality' (Klein, 1935, p. 277);

(ii) Disparagement:

> The ego is unwilling and unable to renounce its good internal objects and yet endeavours to escape from the perils of dependence on them . . . Its attempt to detach itself from an object without at the same time renouncing it [is accomplished] by denying the importance of its good objects. (Klein, 1935, p. 277)

The ego:

> denies that it feels concern for it. 'Surely,' argues the ego, 'it is not a matter of such great importance if this particular object is destroyed. There are so many others to be incorporated.' This *disparagement* of the object's importance and the contempt of it is, I think, a specific characteristic of mania. (Klein, 1935, p. 278)

(iii) Control: 'At the same time, however, it endeavours ceaselessly to *master and control* all its objects' (Klein, 1935, p. 277). 'This is necessary for two reasons: (a) in order to deny the dread of them [the objects depended upon] which is being experienced, and (b) so that the mechanism of making reparation to the object may be carried through' (Klein, 1935, p. 278);

(iv) Idealization: 'Idealization is an essential part of the manic position' (Klein, 1940, p. 349) [see IDEAL OBJECT].

So important are the mechanisms involved in mania that Klein, for a period in the late 1930s, referred to the *manic position*.

These defences protect the subject from experiencing the painful consequences of dependence on good loved objects and the painful consequences of such dependence. Manic defences, however, lead to further problems:

> sadistic gratification of overcoming and humiliating it, of getting the better of it, the *triumph* over it, may enter so strongly into the act of reparation that the 'benign circle' started by this act becomes broken. The objects which were to be restored change again into persecutors . . . As a result of the failure of the act of reparation, the ego has to resort again and again to obsessional and manic defences. (Klein, 1940, p. 351) [see REPARATION]

Relation of manic to obsessional defences. In 1940 Klein stated that the manic defences evolve out of the obsessional defences employed against persecutory anxiety (they 'bind' persecutory anxiety). In this sense, she emphasized the omnipotent control, calling it 'triumph' and saying: 'I wish to stress the importance of *triumph*, closely bound up with contempt and omnipotence' (Klein, 1940, p. 351). The relation appears to be tenuous, and although the obsessional defences were of great interest to Klein in her early work as specific defences against persecutory feelings, after the influence of Fairbairn in 1946 the obsessional defences drop out of Kleinian literature [see OBSESSIONAL DEFENCES]. This is one of the many instances where the Kleinian concepts have grown so far away from the classical terminology that the classical ones have dropped out of Kleinian usage, yet have never been clearly stated to be redundant.

Klein, Melanie (1935) 'A contribution to the psychogenesis of manic-depressive states'. *WMK* 1, pp. 262–89.
—— (1940) 'Mourning and its relation to manic-depressive states'. *WMK* 1, pp. 344–69.

Manic reparation

In the early stages of development, the infant employs omnipotent mechanisms to establish the security of the ego. Consequently, when the depressive position first bears down on him [see 10. DEPRESSIVE POSITION], he may experience the loved object as irreparably damaged – mirroring the extreme violence of his omnipotent phantasies. The anguish of wanting to repair so totally damaged an object stems from the fact that this is experienced as a vastly demanding task. As a result the whole situation has to be belittled and the task made light of as if it can be accomplished by magic.

Later in life even normal stresses can provoke the contemptuous phantasy that anyway the object is not worth bothering about. But the contempt and belittling are manic defences against the severity of the anguish, and assist the subject to feel less helpless and dependent on his important good objects that appear to him damaged and bring out such an onerous responsibility [see DEPRESSIVE ANXIETY]. The end result, however, is that the contempt damages the objects even more, and may therefore lead to a vicious circle.

See REPARATION

Masculinity See FATHER; FEMININITY

Masturbation phantasies

Klein was interested from the beginning of her work in the phantasy content of anxiety, and she concentrated upon the sexual phantasies. She employed the idea of masturbation phantasies which once accompanied physically stimulating activity, but which had subsequently become unconscious:

> . . . an unconscious phantasy has a very important connection with the subject's sexual life; for it is identical with the phantasy which served to give him sexual satisfaction during a period of masturbation. At that time the masturbatory act was compounded of two parts. One was the evocation of a phantasy and the other some active behaviour for obtaining self-gratification at the height of the phantasy. Originally the action was a purely autoerotic procedure for the purpose of obtaining pleasure from some particular part of the body, which could be described as erotogenic. Later, this action

became merged with a wishful idea from the sphere of object-love. (Freud, 1908, p. 161)

Klein elaborated this idea of the concrete and physical nature of these phantasies into an object-relational form.

Although Abraham (1921) and Ferenczi (1921) both used the symptom of tic as evidence for an autoerotic phase, Klein bluntly challenged them (Klein, 1925). Instead she described a case of tic in which phantasies accompanied the various physical movements; each movement, she noted, represented symbolically a part of a sexual act with an object. She used this to mark out her own approach, concentrating upon the *object-relations* involved in instinctual impulses [see NARCISSISM; 2. UNCONSCIOUS PHANTASY]. It challenged the view of a primary phase of autoerotism and narcissism and asserted that unconscious masturbation phantasies were embedded in all activity:

> Let me give an illustration of the effect of masturbation phantasies on sublimation. Felix, aged thirteen, produced the following phantasy in analysis. He was playing with some beautiful girls who were naked and whose breasts he stroked and caressed. He did not see the lower parts of their bodies. They were playing football with one another. This single sexual phantasy . . . was succeeded during the analysis by many other phantasies, some in the form of daydreams, others coming to him at night as a substitute for onanism and all concerned with games. These phantasies showed how some of his fixations were elaborated into an interest in games. In the first sexual phantasy . . . coitus had already been replaced by football. This game, together with others, had absorbed his interest and ambition entirely. (Klein, 1923, p. 90)

Klein was demonstrating that embedded in the process of narcissistic gratification there were phantasies of objects associated with the 'masturbation'. Later Heimann, in developing the Kleinian view of narcissism [see NARCISSISM], described masturbation as a phantasy of an erotic relation with an *internal* object:

> autoerotism is based on phantasies concerning an inner gratifying 'good' breast (nipple, mother) which is projected on to, and thus represented by, a part of the infant's own body. This process is, as it were, met halfway by the erotogenic quality of the child's organs. (Heimann, 1952, pp. 147–8)

The erogenous zones allow the use of the body for generating unconscious phantasies especially intensely through masturbatory manipulation. Erotic sexuality is therefore a commonly contrived set of unconscious phantasies elaborated defensively against persecutory or depressive anxieties. Meltzer (1966) described a case in which anal masturbation was employed to engender unconscious phantasies.

Abraham, Karl (1921) 'Contribution to a discussion on tic', in Karl Abraham (1927) *Selected Papers on Psycho-Analysis*. Hogarth, pp. 322–5.

Ferenczi, Sandor (1921) 'Psycho-analytic observations on tic', in *Further Contributions to the Theory and Technique of Psycho-Analysis*. Hogarth, pp. 142–74.

Freud, Sigmund (1908) 'Hysterical phantasies and their relation to bisexuality' *S.E.* 9, pp. 155–66.

Heimann, Paula (1952) 'Certain functions of projection and introjection in early infancy', in Melanie Klein, Paula Heimann, Susan Isaacs and Joan Riviere, eds (1952) *Developments in Psycho-Analysis*. Hogarth, pp. 122–68.

Klein, Melanie (1923) 'Infant analysis'. *WMK* 1, pp. 77–105.

—— (1925) 'A contribution to the psychogenesis of tic'. *WMK* 1, pp. 106–27.

Meltzer, Donald (1966) 'The relation of anal masturbation to projective identification', *Int. J. Psycho-Anal.* 47:335–42.

Donald Meltzer

Biography. Donald Meltzer trained in medicine and in child psychiatry in the United States, but came to London in 1954 specifically to train in psychoanalysis with Melanie Klein. He remained in analysis with her until her death in 1960. His brilliant evocation of clinical material has made him a leading member of the Kleinian Group, though his interest in child analysis diverged from the contemporary interest of the group in psychosis and borderline personality disorders. He was influential in developing the training in child psychotherapy that had been started by Esther Bick at the Tavistock Clinic and he worked closely there with her and with Martha Harris, his second wife. Latterly his views on technique and the training of psychoanalysts have brought him into conflict with the Institute of Psycho-Analysis in London.

SCIENTIFIC CONTRIBUTIONS. Meltzer's contributions to Kleinian psychoanalysis are many and outstanding, in particular (i) his extremely detailed understanding of the psychoanalytic process during the session (Meltzer, 1967) and (ii) his powerful exegesis of the work of Freud, Klein and Bion (Meltzer, 1978, 1987).

His description of a borderline personality in 1968 was an early discussion of a personality structure organized around the destructive impulses – a point of view also held by Rosenfeld (1971) and developed more recently by many others [see STRUCTURE]. Meltzer amplified his views on these perverse kinds of personalities in a series of papers published in 1973. His continuing interest in psychotic children led him to run a research seminar on childhood autism in which he used the concepts of Esther Bick [see SKIN] and Frances Tustin [see AUTISM] (Meltzer *et al.*, 1975).

Latterly Meltzer's interest in teaching has led to several major commentaries on Kleinian writings. *The Kleinian Development* (Meltzer, 1978) is a major attempt to present the relevant strands of Freud's writings, Klein's detailed case history (*Narrative of a Child Analysis*, 1961) and the work of Bion as a continuous thread of intellectual and clinical development. The growing point of Kleinian thought, in Meltzer's view, is the consolidation of Bion's work on thinking and experiencing (Meltzer, 1987) and he has worked towards creating a psychoanalytic epistemology from this.

Klein, Melanie (1961) *Narrative of a Child Analysis*. Hogarth.

Meltzer, Donald (1967) *The Psycho-Analytic Process*. Heinemann.

—— (1968) 'Terror, persecution, dread', *Int. J. Psycho-Anal.* 49:396–400; republished (1973) in Donald Meltzer, *Sexual States of Mind*. Perth: Clunie, pp. 99–106.

—— (1973) *Sexual States of Mind*. Perth: Clunie.

—— (1978) *The Kleinian Development*. Perth: Clunie.

—— (1987) *Studies in Extended Metapsychology*. Perth: Clunie.

Meltzer, Donald, Bremner, John, Hoxter, Shirley, Weddell, Doreen and Wittenberg, Isca (1975) *Explorations in Autism*. Perth: Clunie.

Rosenfeld, Herbert (1971) 'A clinical approach to the psycho-analytical theory of the life and death instincts: an investigation into the aggressive aspects of narcissism', *Int. J. Psycho-Anal.* 52:169–78.

Memory and desire

Freud's advice in his papers on technique to develop an 'evenly-suspended attention' (Freud, 1912) was enhanced by Bion's recommendations in the form of two strict rules to abolish memory and desire (Bion, 1967). Bion described how, in particular, the attempt to drag past sessions back into one's conscious recall will distract from the present session. He also described how an ambitious desire to wring progress out of the analysis or out of the patient can equally cast a distorting influence over the capacity to observe the present. Reference to the past (memory) or to the future (desire) means that 'the evolution of the session will not be observed at the only time when it can be observed – while it is taking place' (Bion, 1967, p. 18).

He thought that his rules would lead to less cluttering of the analyst's mind and its greater openness to the patient. The consequences of adopting this strict mental regime would be that progress would be measured in terms of

the increased number and variety of moods, ideas and attitudes seen in any given session . . . [and] less clogging of the sessions by the repetition of material which should have disappeared and, consequently, a quickened tempo within each session every session. (Bion, 1967, p. 18)

See CONTAINING; BION; REVERIE

Bion, Wilfred (1967) 'Notes on memory and desire', in Elizabeth Spillius, ed. (1988) *Melanie Klein Today: Volume 2: Mainly Practice*. Routledge; previously published (1967) in *The Psycho-Analytic Forum* 2:272–3 and 279–80.
Freud, Sigmund (1912) 'Recommendations to physicians practising psycho-analysis'. *S.E.* 12, pp. 111–20.

Mind–body problem

The relation between the mind and the body is a philosophical question, an issue in the history of ideas. However, it is inevitably also a problem for psychologists and has profound implications for psychiatric treatments, chemotherapy and psychotherapy. Unfortunately the problem has remained stubbornly insoluble for philosophers, and psychology may be in a position to inform philosophy.

From the beginning of the great Cartesian dichotomy psychologists have floundered and quarrelled helplessly at the bottom of this 'great rift valley' of philosophy. Freud was no exception. He was formed in the mould of nineteenth-century science, which had achieved remarkable results in the natural sciences, including physiology. On the other hand there was the Romantic tradition of German 'Naturphilosophie' which emphasized a Hegelian metaphysical and introspective approach to philosophical problems. The dichotomy is whether to approach the mind from an objective point of view – i.e. the workings of the brain – or from a subjective point of view: a psychology of personal experiences. The former viewed the mind as an epiphenomenon perched on top of the basic physical and physiological processes that determine the working of the brain – mind as a side-effect, as it were, of neurophysiology. Freud was tempted by this physiological psychology when he began thinking about the unconscious and the discoveries he had been making in the 1890s. He sought to construct physical explanations for the missing ideas and memories from which his hysterical patients suffered. His post-humously published 'Project for a scientific psychology' (Freud, 1895 [1940]) was an attempt to work out a physiological model for these psychologically missing events. However, that project was abandoned because 'Freud the neurologist was being overtaken by Freud the psychologist' (Strachey, 1957, p. 163).

Freud was uncomfortable with a physiological view of the relation between mind and body because it went against his personal experiences of the patients he spent his life working with; it also went against the German philosophical tradition of humanism, which according to Bettelheim is clearly to be found seeping through in the German-language originals of Freud's writings (Bettelheim, 1983). Freud never quite found his way out of the physiological psychology with which he started, and the mixture of Freud the neurologist and Freud the psychologist is sufficiently blended for Sulloway (1979) to campaign for the biological Freud while Bettelheim does equally well with the humanist Freud; both are equally convinced, and neither is really convincing (Young, 1986). As Young (1986) has argued, what Freud lacked (and we still do today) is a language with which we can speak about the mind and the body, in fact 'the person' (Strawson, 1959).

Psychophysical parallelism: Freud's position on the mind–body problem is technically known, in philosophy, as psychophysical parallelism: there is a mind and there is a brain. Both work in their own ways. The working of one is not translatable exactly into the workings of the other. Neither one nor the other is primary and determining, yet they must interrelate. For practical purposes the two exist in parallel (psychophysical parallelism) without specifying which produces which. In order to get by as a psychologist Freud, influenced by Hughlings Jackson, took the phenomenon of the mind and left aside the problem of how it related to the brain.

Interactionism: It is possible to take a further philosophical position and to say that the mind emerges from the activity of the brain, which in turn may be manipulated by the mind. Members of the Kleinian Group, who were considering unconscious phantasy in the late 1930s and early 1940s, come close to adopting this psychophysical *interactionism.*

Biological processes are mirrored in activities of the mind called *unconscious phantasies.* Equally, unconscious phantasies mould both the person and his or her social world. Neither the physical nor the psychological events are primary, and it is clear from Kleinian writings that there is an assumption that they can each influence the other. Thus instinctual stimuli from an empty stomach, say, are mentally represented as an unconscious phantasy of a relation with an object (one that causes hunger). The mind may also elaborate unconscious phantasy as a defensive manoeuvre against strong phantasy anxieties (Segal, 1964). Such elaborated defensive phantasies are initiated by manipulation of the body (masturbation), especially in the early phases of infancy – for example, the expulsion of faeces can be used to initiate the phantasy of expelling a bad internal object [see FAECES]. Later the manipulation of symbolic representations retains somatic (bodily) links.

Biology and psychology: Phantasies of expulsion or incorporation create the sense of self and identity and the specific phantasies put together the particular character of the self. Projective processes also create the perceptions of the social world around which in turn, through introjective processes, they precipitate social forms in the individual. The development of the human infant is a movement out of a world of bodily satisfaction into a world of symbols and symbolic satisfaction. There is a progressive movement out of the body into the symbolic world of the mature mind [see ALPHA-FUNCTION]. That movement occurs in the generation of thoughts, as well as being the process of psychological development. Such a process is not explained by the Kleinian notion of unconscious phantasy, but it is well described.

Symbols, being inherent in the experience of parts of the body, are therefore an inherent capacity of the human infant from birth. He represents for himself his own sensations as relationships with objects [see 2. UNCONSCIOUS PHANTASY]. Since the object has a presence for the infant irrespective of the actual objective situation, it is in a mental world of conceptions, already a symbol. When the infant can come to perceive the objective realities, the meaningfulness of that reality is generated by an investment from the mental representations.

At some glittering moment in the history of each individual, a mental event comes to manipulate a bodily event. This is so tightly concealed in our pasts that it appears impossible, a miracle. The symbolic representation in the mind results in the manipulation of the body to create further bodily sensations and ultimately mental events. Perhaps the supernatural quality to such an idea is mitigated by the fact that the objects we investigate physically are not initially experienced as physical [see 5. INTERNAL OBJECTS]. At the infantile level the object is not physically present; the infant and his world are emotional objects – that is, locations that are given primitive emotional significance. Their non-physicalness in no way detracts from their quality of realness for the infant. The distinction between mind and body comes about in the course of development; it is generated psychologically. In Kleinian terms an initial splitting process takes place to distinguish, in primitive infantile space, the body from the mind (Scott, 1948). We should not take it for granted that such a fundamental differentiation of the person is invariable in its character, as it seems likely that different socialization in different cultures gives rise to variations in the early conceptions of body and mind (Marsella *et al.*, 1987).

Bettelheim, Bruno (1983) *Freud and Man's Soul.* Hogarth.

Freud, Sigmund (1895) 'Project for a scientific psychology'. *S. E.* 1, pp. 283–397.

Marsella, Anthony, Devos, George and Hsu, Francis (1987) *Culture and Self: Asian and Western Perspectives.* Tavistock.

Scott, W. Clifford M. (1948) 'Some embryological, neurological, psychiatric and psychosomatic implications of the body schema', *Int. J. Psycho-Anal.* 29:141–55.

Segal, Hanna (1964) *Introduction to the Work of Melanie Klein.* Heinemann.

Strachey, James (1957) 'Editor's note to "The Unconscious"'. *S.E.* 14, pp. 161–5.

Strawson, P. F. (1959) *Individuals: An Essay in Descriptive Metaphysics.* Methuen.

Sulloway, Frank (1979) *Freud: Biologist of the Mind.* Burnett.

Young, Robert (1986) 'Freud: scientist and/or humanist', *Free Assns* 6:7–35.

Mother

'Mother' is the first object in the infant's life, but Klein was concerned to understand how the mother is related to from the earliest moments and what sort of distortions get into the infant's appreciation of her. At the first stage of development the infant has no distance perception and knows of mother only from sensations arising from the skin inwards. The experience of the infant when appreciating his own bodily sensation is that an object, felt to have motivations towards him, has caused his own bodily sensations [see 5. INTERNAL OBJECTS]. This primary object is sometimes called the 'breast' [see BREAST] and is appreciated according to whether it is (a) well or badly intentioned towards the infant; and (b) whether the object is experienced inside or outside the infant.

There are in fact at the outset numerous 'mothers', each one connected to the gratification that the infant is receiving or is lacking, giving rise to a 'good' mother and a 'bad' mother respectively, for each need. These 'mothers' correspond to separate 'infants' – that is, separately experienced states of the infant split from each other and kept separate for defensive purposes [see 11. PARANOID-SCHIZOID POSITION; SPLITTING].

See FATHER

Mother-with-penis

See COMBINED PARENT FIGURE; 4. OEDIPUS COMPLEX

Mourning

See 10. DEPRESSIVE POSITION; LOSS

Nameless dread

This is a term first used by Karin Stephen (1941) to describe the extreme extent of anxiety in infancy: 'a dread of powerlessness in the face of instinct tension in childhood' (p. 181). 'Nameless dread' was later given a fuller and specific meaning by Bion to describe a state of meaningless fear that comes about in the context of an infant with a mother incapable of 'reverie' [see REVERIE], a concept that derives from Bion's theory of containing [see CONTAINING]. When the mother fails to contain the infant's terrors and make them meaningful, this 'projective identification-rejecting-object' [see THINKING] is felt to strip the meaning from the experience and the baby: he 'therefore reintrojects, not a fear of dying made tolerable, but a nameless dread' (Bion, 1962a, p. 116). With repeated recurrence of this projective failure, an internal object is formed through introjection on the same lines; this object destroys meaning and leaves the subject in a mysterious meaningless world:

> In practice it means that the patient feels surrounded not so much by real objects, things-in-themselves, but by bizarre objects that are real only in that they are the residue of thoughts and conceptions that have been stripped of their meaning and ejected. (Bion, 1962b, p. 99) [see CONTAINING]

An internal object that strips meaning gives rise to a superego that issues meaningless injunctions about behaviour.

Bion, Wilfred R. (1962a) 'A theory of thinking', *Int. J. Psycho-Anal.* 43:306–10; republished (1967) in W. R. Bion, *Second Thoughts*. Heinemann, pp. 110–19.
—— (1962b) *Learning from Experience*. Heinemann.
Stephen, Karin (1941) 'Aggression in early childhood', *Br. J. Med. Psychol.* 18:178–90.

Narcissism

Klein made a radical departure from Freud over the nature of narcissism. Freud (1914) discerned several aspects to narcissism:

(i) Primary narcissism as a stage early in infancy before there is a recognition by the infant of an object, and when the infant's own ego is taken as the object of libidinal love;

(ii) Secondary narcissism, a regression from an object-relationship which has disappointed through either loss of the object, or some kind of slight by the object, back to a narcissistic love of the ego; and

(iii) Narcissistic object-relations, when the ego loves an object in so far as the object resembles the ego.

Klein disagreed and asserted that there was no primary narcissism. This is perhaps her most fundamental theoretical difference from classical psychoanalysis and ego-psychology [see EGO-PSYCHOLOGY]. There are a number of stages in the development of the Kleinian concept of narcissism:

(1) narcissism and object-relations coexist;
(2) narcissistic states as opposed to a narcissistic stage;
(3) narcissism and envy;

(4) negative narcissism; and

(5) narcissistic character structure.

(1) Coexistence of narcissism and object-relations. Klein collapsed the various forms of narcissism that Freud had described into her single theory of internal objects [see 5. INTERNAL OBJECTS]. First, in 1925, she challenged Ferenczi and Abraham over their view of the objectless nature of tic [see MASTURBATION PHANTASIES]; she '. . . held the view that autoerotism and narcissism are in the young infant contemporaneous with the first relation to objects' (Klein, 1952, p. 51).

Narcissistic object-relations: 'The phase in which the onset of the Oedipus conflict and its accompanying sadistic masturbation phantasies arise is the phase of narcissism' (Klein, 1932, p. 171). On the face of it a stage which is both objectless (autoerotic or narcissistic) and in which there are object-relations (the Oedipus complex) appears contradictory. At this time Klein wrote about this as if it were not contradictory but entirely a development of orthodox theories. Later, however, she agreed that this '. . . hypothesis contradicts Freud's concept of autoerotic gratification and narcissistic *stages*' (Klein, 1952, p. 51); and she distinguished between Freud's narcissistic *stage*, and narcissistic *states*. She clarified that it '. . . is to this internalized object that in auto-erotic gratification and narcissistic states a withdrawal takes place' (Klein, 1952, p. 51).

Narcissism and introjective identification: Heimann (1952) stated the Kleinian theory of narcissism most explicitly at this time:

> The essential difference between infantile and mature object-relations is that, whereas the adult conceives of the object as existing independently of himself, for the infant it always refers in some way to himself. It exists by virtue of its function for the infant. (Heimann, 1952, p. 142)

She was describing part-object-relations [see PART-OBJECTS] in which the object represents simply the phantasized cause of the infant's own sensations [see 2. UNCONSCIOUS PHANTASY]. The world as it actually is, impinging on the infant, is moulded by the infant's own phantasies of the object's motivations towards him (good motives or bad ones).

These objects are not only orientated towards the infant's own ego but are also introjected and identified with (assimilated), so that the object becomes identified with a part of him and the relation to the object becomes a relation to himself or a part of himself. Heimann's illustration is the infant who, in sucking his thumb,

> . . . feels himself in contact with the desired breast, although in

reality he or she merely sucks his own finger. His phantasies of incorporating the breast, which form part of his oral experiences and impulses, lead him to identify his finger with the incorporated breast. He can independently produce his own gratification . . . he turns to his internalized good breast. (Heimann, 1952, p. 146)

A narcissistic state has become, for Klein, an 'autoerotic' gratification by an internal object identified with a part of the ego and loved as such. It is a defensive response.

The concept of narcissism was modified by the understanding of the omnipotent quality of the phantasies that underlie the primitive defence mechanisms [see OMNIPOTENCE; 9. PRIMITIVE DEFENCE MECHANISMS].

The narcissistic *stages* that Freud talked of have become, for Klein and Heimann, narcissistic *states* (Segal, 1983) in which there is a retreat to a mental state in which omnipotent phantasies of identification come to the fore. Narcissistic object-choice is a more permanent organization of omnipotent phantasies in the structure of the object-relations and the personality. Klein at first regarded it, along with Freud, as the identification of an external object to be loved with a part of the self: typically in homosexuality the penis of another male represents the lover's own masculinity, which he loves.

(2) **Narcissistic states.** The further development of the Kleinian concept of narcissism came with Klein's descriptions of projective identification [see 13. PROJECTIVE IDENTIFICATION]. The process of identifying a part of the self with an object became completely recast, elaborated, and installed as the hub of Kleinian thinking [see 11. PARANOID-SCHIZOID POSITION]: '. . . the relation to another person on the basis of projecting bad parts of the self into him is of a narcissistic nature' (Klein, 1946, p. 13), because the object '. . . is not felt to be a separate individual but is felt to be *the* bad self' (Klein, 1946, p. 8). Good parts of the self are also put into objects in projective identification. However, the emphasis that Klein gives to projective identification as a means, in the paranoid-schizoid position, of dealing with persecutory anxiety and the death instinct links narcissistic object-relations to anxiety, aggression and the death instinct.

Omnipotence and narcissism: The use of projective identification has become almost synonymous with narcissism in Kleinian literature, and the paranoid-schizoid position has been referred to as the 'narcissistic position' (Segal, 1983). It is important, however, to distinguish between 'normal projective identification' and 'pathological projective identification' [see 13. PROJECTIVE IDENTIFICATION]. Bion (1959) and Rosenfeld (1964) distinguished two kinds of projective identification on the basis of the degree of omnipotence in the phantasy. When the phantasy is omnipotent the identification of a part of the self with the object results in the boundary between them dissolving so that one *is* the other [see OMNIPOTENCE]. This is similar to Segal's descriptions of the primitive form of symbol which she calls a 'symbolic equation' [see SYMBOLIC EQUATION].

Rosenfeld (1964) also made the point that omnipotent identification through introjection resulted in similar loss of boundaries, in which the introjected object is merged omnipotently, in phantasy, with a part of the self. The hallmark of narcissistic states is *omnipotent* identification by projection or introjection with a violence that disperses the boundary between the ego and the object, with a consequent loss of awareness of internal and external reality [see 11. PARANOID-SCHIZOID POSITION].

(3) Narcissism and envy. Segal (1983) pointed out that Klein, in *Envy and Gratitude* (1957):

> . . . describes fully the deployment of projective identification as an implementation of envious aims and also as a defence against envy – for instance getting into an object and taking over the object's qualities. She does not in that connection refer to narcissism, yet in this work it is implicit that there must be an intimate relation between narcissism and envy. Freud's description of primary narcissism is that the infant feels himself to be the source of all satisfaction. The discovery of the object gives rise to hate.

On the other hand, primary envy as described by Klein is:

> a spoiling hostility at the realization that the source of life and goodness lies outside. To me envy and narcissism are two sides of a coin. Narcissism defends us against envy. The difference would lie in this. If one believes in a prolonged narcissistic stage, envy would be secondary to disillusionment. If, with Melanie Klein, one contends that awareness of an object-relation, and therefore envy, exist from the beginnning, narcissism could be seen as a defence against envy and therefore to be more related to the death instinct and envy than to libidinal forces. (Segal, 1983, pp. 270–1)

Narcissism – the omnipotent identification by projection or introjection – is thus more or less equated with the whole of the struggles of the ego in the opening moments of life to organize against the threat of the death instinct (originally manifest as primary envy).

(4) Negative narcissism. Rosenfeld (1964) thought that '. . . the strength and persistence of omnipotent narcissistic object-relations are closely related to the strength of the infant's envy' (p. 171). He took the idea of the aggressive aspect of narcissism due to envy and the death instinct further (Rosenfeld, 1971). He recognized a symmetry between the withdrawal of the libido on to the ego (as Freud described) on the one hand, and the withdrawal of death instinct on to the ego, on the other. The latter he termed *negative narcissism* and also related it to the negative therapeutic reaction:

> In studying narcissism in greater detail it seems to me essential to differentiate between the libidinal and the destructive aspects of narcissism. In considering narcissism from the libidinal aspect one can see that the overvaluation of the self plays a central role, based mainly on the idealization of the self. Self-idealization is maintained by omnipotent introjective and projective identifications with good objects and their qualities. In this way the narcissist feels that everything that is valuable relating to external objects and the outside world is part of him or is omnipotently controlled by him. Similarly, when considering narcissism we find that the destructive aspects of self-idealization again play a central role, but now it is the idealization of the omnipotent destructive parts of the self. They are directed both against any positive libidinal object-relationship and any libidinal part of the self which experiences need for an object and the desire to depend on it. (Rosenfeld, 1971, p. 173)

In the course of his clinical material in this paper, Rosenfeld described the organization of objects and relations internally under the dominance of self-directed aggressive impulses – hangovers of the original death instinct that had not been fully dealt with by the primary 'externalization' described by Freud and Klein [see DEATH INSTINCT; STRUCTURES].

(5) **Narcissistic character structure.** Rosenfeld's dissection of two kinds of narcissism is of considerable practical significance and has been endorsed by others. The structuring of the personality, as described by Rosenfeld, between an omnipotent 'bad' self and an entrapped 'good' self had previously been described by Meltzer (1968) and Money-Kyrle (1969), but Rosenfeld showed the stability of this organization in certain types of personality, usually referred to as borderline.

Segal (1983) emphasized the distinction between a simple narcissistic withdrawal, on the one hand, and on the other the permanent personality structure of a narcissistic personality of whom we '. . . see increasing numbers' (p. 270). The structure is built up by the '. . . re-internalization of the projectively possessed object' (p. 270). The personality structure is defensively organized against envy. More recent work on the pathology of borderline personalities demonstrates the struggle against 'bad' parts of the self that are composed of mechanisms and object-relations connected with the death instinct. This is one method by which the ego attempts to organize the phantasies expressing the death instinct, and it contrasts with the more typical mode of projecting a 'bad' *object* which Klein described:

> I hold that anxiety arises from the operation of the death instinct within the organism, is felt as fear of annihilation (death) and takes the form of persecution. The fear of the destructive impulse seems to attach itself at once to an object – or rather it is experienced as the fear of an uncontrollable overpowering object. (Klein, 1946, p. 4)

The pathological structures which organize the death instinct in this way have been described subsequently by many others (Joseph, 1982; Steiner, 1982; Brenman, 1985; Sohn, 1985) [see STRUCTURE].

Bion, Wilfred (1957) 'Differentiation of the psychotic from the non-psychotic personalities', *Int. J. Psycho-Anal.* 38:266–75; republished (1967) in W. R. Bion, *Second Thoughts*. Heinemann, pp. 43–64.

—— (1959) 'Attacks on linking', *Int. J. Psycho-Anal.* 40:308–15; republished (1967) in *Second Thoughts*, pp. 93–109.

Brenman, Eric (1985) 'Cruelty and narrow-mindedness', *Int. J. Psycho-Anal.* 66:273–81.

Freud, Sigmund (1914) 'On narcissism'. *S.E.* 14, pp. 67–102.

—— (1925) 'Negation'. *S.E.* 19, pp. 235–9.

Heimann, Paula (1952) 'Certain functions of introjection and projection in early infancy', in Melanie Klein, Paula Heimann, Susan Isaacs and Joan Riviere, eds (1952) *Developments in Psycho-Analysis*. Hogarth, pp. 122–68.

Joseph, Betty (1982) 'Addiction to near death', *Int. J. Psycho-Anal.* 63:449–56.

Klein, Melanie (1925) 'A contribution to the psychogenesis of tics'. *WMK* 1, pp. 106–27.

—— (1932) *The Psycho-Analysis of Children. WMK* 2.

—— (1946) 'Notes on some schizoid mechanisms'. *WMK* 3, pp.1–24.

—— (1952) 'The origins of transference'. *WMK* 3, pp. 48–56.

—— (1957) *Envy and Gratitude. WMK* 3, pp. 176–235.

Meltzer, Donald (1968) 'Terror, persecution, dread', *Int. J. Psycho-Anal.* 49:396–400; republished (1973) in Donald Meltzer, *Sexual States of Mind.* Perth: Clunie, pp. 99–106.

Money-Kyrle, Roger (1969) 'On the fear of insanity', in (1978) *The Collected Papers of Roger Money-Kyrle*. Perth: Clunie, pp.434–41.

Rosenfeld, Herbert (1964) 'On the psychopathology of narcissism', *Int. J. Psycho-Anal.* 45:332–7; republished (1965) in Herbert Rosenfeld, *Psychotic States*. Hogarth, pp. 169–79.

—— (1971) 'A clinical approach to the psycho-analytical theory of the life and death instincts: an investigation into the aggressive aspects of narcissism', *Int. J. Psycho-Anal.* 52:169–78.

Segal, Hanna (1983) 'Some clinical implications of Melanie Klein's work', *Int. J. Psycho-Anal.* 64:269–76.

Sohn, Leslie (1985) 'Narcissistic organization, projective identification and the formation of the identificate', *Int. J. Psycho-Anal.* 66:201–13.

Steiner, John (1982) 'Perverse relationships between parts of the self', *Int. J. Psycho-Anal.* 63:15–22.

Negative narcissism

Rosenfeld (1971), in response to criticism of the Kleinian acceptance of the death instinct (for instance Kernberg, 1969), looked at clinical material that suggested there was a destructive process working within the personality that was felt to be 'bad' and which dominated 'good' parts of the personality in the way a Mafia gang may control a whole society. Similar to this internal intimidation was a kind of malevolent form of internal seduction, described by Meltzer (1968).

On the basis that Freud described narcissism as the turning of the libido towards the ego in an act of self-love, Rosenfeld introduced the phrase 'negative narcissism' to describe an internal state of the ego's destructiveness towards itself.

See NARCISSISM; DEATH INSTINCT

Kernberg, Otto (1969) 'A contribution to the ego-psychological critique of the Kleinian School', *Int. J. Psycho-Anal.* 50:317–33.

Meltzer, Donald (1968) 'Terror, persecution, dread', *Int. J. Psycho-Anal.* 49:396–400; republished (1973) in Donald Meltzer, *Sexual States of Mind.* Perth: Clunie, pp. 99–106.

Rosenfeld, Herbert (1971) 'A clinical approach to the psycho-analytical theory of the life and death instincts: an investigation into the aggressive aspects of narcissism', *Int. J. Psycho-Anal.* 52:169–78.

Negative therapeutic reaction

Freud became aware, to his consternation, that there were some patients who reacted badly to analytic interpretations – they got worse with good interpretations, rather than better. He was affronted by the Wolf man's '. . . habit of producing transitory "negative reactions"; every time something had been conclusively cleared up, he attempted to contradict the effect' (Freud, 1917, p. 69). Since then there has been a prolonged effort to understand this problem. The general assumption has been that however right the interpretation that provoked a negative reaction in the patient, there must be a 'more correct' one that would understand this negative reaction.

There have been various attempts to understand this reaction:

(i) Guilt: Freud (1923) attributed it to guilt, especially to unconscious guilt, which leads to a need for punishment; the patient achieves punishment in the form of suffering ill-health [see 2. UNCONSCIOUS PHANTASY];

(ii) Death instinct: in 1924 Freud speculated on the role of the death instinct in the negative therapeutic reaction;

(iii) Depressive position: Riviere (1936) drew some conclusions in the light of Klein's depressive position, which showed the importance of object-relations involved in the unconscious guilt – a fear of being responsible for the damage or death of the good object, especially the internalized good object [see 10. DEPRESSIVE POSITION]. She pointed out that if one interprets to a guilty patient what is wrong with him, then it makes him feel more guilty still for being wrong in that way. She advocated balancing interpretations of the bad parts of the self with interpretations of the good parts – a view endorsed by Rosenfeld (1987);

(iv) Envy: In the same year, Horney (1936) argued that the negative therapeutic reaction resulted from envy of the analyst – that is, a wish to spoil the analyst's work. In many respects this harks back to a brief paper by Abraham (1919) about patients who cannot stand the analyst's successful work.

When Klein (1957) brought precision into the term 'envy' [see 12. ENVY], the destructiveness was clearly seen as an extremely primitive impulse against the analyst's interpretations. So, the best interpretations bring out the strongest envious reaction. In addition the envious patient envies the analyst's *capacity to make interpretations* as well as the interpretations themselves – i.e. he or she envies an aspect of the analyst's mind.

Bion (1962) described the patient's use of projective identification to invade the analyst's mind with intolerable parts of his own as a result of envy of the analyst's *capacity for containing his own experiences* and those of his patients.

Rosenfeld (1975) and also Etchegoyen *et al.* (1987) pointed out the need to distinguish the negative therapeutic reaction deriving from the envious impulse to spoil the analyst's best efforts and the reaction (maybe equally negative) to the analyst whose interpretations are just wrong because they are defensive on the analyst's part.

Ego-structure: Rosenfeld (1971) described negative narcissism and the organization of the personality in borderline states, in which the negative impulses are directed against the best part of the self and against any object (including the analyst) who relates to the co-operative side of the personality. This structure of borderline personalities has been described frequently since then [see STRUC-TURE]. The undermining of the analysis, often with a *hidden* negative therapeutic reaction, leads to frequent impasse of apparently unknown cause – the patient

> ... takes over the analyst's capacities by omnipotent projective identification which implies a very concrete feeling of being inside

the analyst and thus controlling him so that all the analyst's creativity and understanding can be attributed to the patient's ego. (Rosenfeld, 1975, p. 223)

The whole structure of the personality is organized around envy and the defences against a recognition of the separate capacity of the analyst [see NARCISSISM].

Abraham, Karl (1919) 'A particular form of neurotic resistance against the psycho-analytic method', in Karl Abraham (1927) *Selected Papers on Psycho-Analysis*. Hogarth, pp. 303–11.

Bion, Wilfred (1962) *Learning from Experience*. Heinemann.

Etchegoyen, Horatio, Lopez, Benito and Rabih, Moses (1987) 'Envy and how to interpret it', *Int. J. Psycho-Anal.* 68:49–61.

Freud, Sigmund (1917) 'From the history of an infantile neurosis'. *S.E.* 17, pp. 3–123.

—— (1923) *The Ego and the Id. S.E.* 19, pp. 3–66.

—— (1924) 'The economic problem of masochism'. *S.E.* 19, pp. 157–70.

Horney, Karen (1936) 'The problem of the negative therapeutic reaction', *Psychoanal. Q.* 5:29–44.

Klein, Melanie (1957) *Envy and Gratitude. WMK* 3, pp. 176–235.

Riviere, Joan (1936) 'A contribution to the analysis of the negative therapeutic reaction', *Int. J. Psycho-Anal.* 17:304–20.

Rosenfeld, Herbert (1971) 'A clinical approach to the psycho-analytical theory of the life and death instincts: an investigation into the aggressive aspects of narcissism', *Int. J. Psycho-Anal.* 52:169–78.

—— (1975) 'Negative therapeutic reaction', in Peter Giovacchini, ed. *Tactics and Techniques in Psycho-Analytic Therapy*, vol. 2. New York: Jason Aronson, pp. 217–28.

—— (1987) *Impasse and Interpretation*. Tavistock.

Steiner, John (1987) 'Interplay between pathological organizations and the paranoid-schizoid and depressive positions', *Int. J. Psycho-Anal.* 68:69–80.

Objects

The term 'object' is a technical one, used originally in psychoanalysis to denote the object of an instinctual impulse. It is the person, or some other thing, that is of interest for the satisfaction of a desire. The notion of an object comes directly from Freud's early scientific theories. In that view, the object had very little about its character that was personal. It was something upon which impulses of energy were discharged, recognized only for the purposes of the subject's pleasure-seeking, satisfaction and relief.

In the 1930s object-relations became the major focus for the school of psychoanalysis developed particularly within Britain [see OBJECT-RELATIONS SCHOOL]. Klein gave it an initial observational basis with her play technique [see 1. TECHNIQUE], and the concept of the 'object' has become modified as a result [see 5. INTERNAL OBJECTS]. In Klein's framework, the object is a component in the mental representation of an instinct.

Objects and phantasy. What is represented in unconscious phantasy is a relationship between the self and an object in which the object is motivated with certain impulses, good or bad, related to the instinctual drives – oral, anal, genital, etc. – of the subject [see 2. UNCONSCIOUS PHANTASY]. In their origins unconscious phantasy is *omnipotent* and the object is felt to have real existence – inside or outside the subject. The object is related to on the basis of its supposed impulses towards the ego. Typically, these very primitive interpretations of the instinctual sensations lead to intense love and gratitude or hatred and envy. They are the inherent mental activity of the infant from birth. At the outset, Klein believed, the infant exists in relation to objects that are primitively distinguished from the ego – there are object-relations from birth.

We can take, for example, the infant who is hungry. His bodily sensations given by his physiology are also experienced subjectively and psychologically. The discomfort is attributed to the motivation of a malevolent object actually located in his tummy that intends to cause the discomfort of hunger. Bion ambiguously refers to this object as a 'no-breast', recognizing that objectively there is an absence, but for the infant there is no such thing as an absence, but the presence of something causing the pain of the frustration – hunger actually gnaws.

In this example the object is attributed to the inside of the ego, in the tummy. It is referred to as an *internal object*. A good internal object is experienced when the infant is fed and feels the warm milk giving satisfying sensations in his tummy [see 5. INTERNAL OBJECTS].

The infant lives in a world of bad object-relations and good object-relations, depending on the bodily sensations that are at the centre of attention at the moment. The object has the characteristic of being motivated to cause the bodily sensation, together with a slowly accumulating set of sense data from the skin contact and other distance receptors experienced at first within the primitive object-relationships. Being drastically reduced to a single motivated entity these objects are, from an objective point of view, partial, and known as *part-objects* [see 11. PARANOID-SCHIZOID POSITION; PART-OBJECTS].

Whole object. The experience of part-objects is in contrast to *whole objects*, whose characteristics are markedly different. The infant, with his limited capacity to see, hear and perceive, has minimal recognition of the actual source of his sensations. That capacity develops with maturation of the nervous system and the distance receptor organs (eyes and ears), as well as the presentation by the personal environment of the social *meanings* of what we apprehend. With the increased capacity to recognize the external world, the objects that appear to the infant become modified, a modification whose success depends on the emotional capacity to tolerate ambivalence [see

DEPRESSIVE ANXIETY]. There is no longer the 'bad' mother who is believed to cause the hunger, nor exactly the simplistically 'good' mother who satisfies hunger. Something of each is present in the same object. The object comes to be seen more as a *whole*, becomes two-toned, having a complexity of motives and attracting mixed feelings from the ego [see DEPRESSIVE ANXIETY]. This constellation is known as the *depressive position* [see 10. DEPRESSIVE POSITION]. The development of the capacity to perceive whole objects is not just dependent on the greater sophistication of perception. It is largely determined by the capacity to tolerate these states of anxiety introduced by encountering a mixed (or contaminated) object. This emotional development is crucial and if this step is not secured the individual easily retreats to the paranoid-schizoid position [see 11. PARANOID-SCHIZOID POSITION] and to a distorted perception of a world of starkly 'good' and 'bad' objects. Kleinian analysts conceive of the relation to whole objects as one of the therapeutic targets of psychoanalysis [see DEVELOPMENT].

The characteristics of objects. Although Klein was not systematic in her theoretical views, her descriptions of objects can in fact be categorized on several dimensions:

(i) Good versus bad: In the very primitive state the object related to has uncontaminated qualities of either goodness or badness, in the sense of doing good or bad to the subject and at the same time commanding a relationship in which the ego is filled with loving or hostile feelings which are themselves felt by the ego to be good or bad. This kind of object is thus 'split' from an objective point of view [see SPLITTING], leading to a split in the state of the ego and its feelings.

(ii) Instinctual drives: In principle each impulse gives rise to an object specific for the bodily sensations characteristic of the drive: a mother who 'causes' hunger, a mother who 'satisfies' hunger, one who causes cold and one who warms, one who holds in a precarious way and one who holds firmly, etc. [see INSTINCTS; 2. UNCONSCIOUS PHANTASY]. These objects referred to as 'mother' are in no way to be confused with the actual mother as perceived by an outside observer, since the infant's perceptions are so radically different and based on internal states of his body. At the outset of life there is also barely a recognition of time and of one object superseding another. It is also to be noted that these objects come in pairs: those that frustrate and those that satisfy. Each pair corresponds to the good versus bad distinction in (i) above [see PART-OBJECTS].

(iii) Part- versus whole object: These primitive states [see 11. PARANOID-SCHIZOID POSITION] in which the baby fears bad objects, inside or

out, give way to the new state of mixed (contaminated good objects) exciting mixed feelings and ambivalent relations [see AMBIVALENCE]. The new state, which is as painful as the first, but in a different way [see DEPRESSIVE ANXIETY], is thus connected with the experience of more complete objects, known as whole objects. Reversion to part-object-relations and progress to whole-object-relations is a constant fluctuating dynamic through the course of life. It is represented by Bion with the sign 'Ps-D', referring to an oscillation between the paranoid-schizoid position and the depressive position [see Ps-D].

(iv) Internal/external: The ego has a boundary from birth onwards and experiences itself in relation to the outside world which is inherently experienced as outside. Objects experienced as the result of bodily sensations from the inside of the body are felt to be inside the ego and are thus internal objects: for instance, the 'hunger-causing-object' which is interpreted as inside the tummy where the hunger pains are. Conversely, objects experienced through the skin are experienced as outside (external objects). It has appeared from the work of some of Klein's collaborators, especially Bick, that the distinction between inside and outside can be catastrophically disrupted [see ADHESIVE IDENTIFICATION]. Very early in life, the location of objects as inside or outside can be changed: an internal object comes to be expelled into the outside, or an external object – the breast from which the infant sucks – comes to be experienced as lying inside the tummy giving the warm full sensations. Such movements of objects in relation to ego-boundaries are interpretations of bodily sensation [see 2. UNCON-SCIOUS PHANTASY] and eventually of induced bodily sensations, like sucking a thumb [see MASTURBATION PHANTASIES]. The purpose of such relocations in phantasy and the bodily stimulation which may be employed to give rise to these phantasies is to protect the infant from fearful objects: for example, a bad and hurting internal hunger-producing object that is motivated to hurt or damage the baby's tummy [see 9. PRIMITIVE DEFENCE MECHANISMS].

(v) Physical versus mental: In the course of development the world of internal objects changes and a quality of mental becomes separate from a quality of physical (Scott, 1948). Internal objects retain a physical quality; but now a possibility of representation occurs which is not felt to be a physical presence but is acknowledged as 'mere' representation. This brings in the possibilities of the 'representational world' (Sandler and Rosenblatt, 1962) and 'self' and 'object' representations, terms used in the ego-psychology framework [see EGO-PSYCHOLOGY].

Internal objects and representations. It is frequently difficult to grasp the distinction between the concept of 'internal objects' as described by Kleinians and 'representations' described by orthodox Freudians such as Sandler and Rosenblatt. Because of the omnipotence of early phantasy there is an experience of an actual physically present object inside the ego, felt as physically inside the body and usually identified with a part of the body: a lump in the throat, butterflies in the stomach, etc., are common experiences in which such concrete thinking percolates through to conscious awareness. The theory of internal objects is that such a belief in a concrete presence inside the ego (self or body) is the currency of unconscious processes [see 2. UNCONSCIOUS PHANTASY]; the omnipotence of phantasy actually brings about experiences and visible manifestations of the person's personality that conform to their beliefs. They are what they believe they are.

There is therefore a similarity with the kind of description of mental structure and psychic objects that Freud gave when he formulated the model of ego, id and superego. Whereas Freud put that model forward as a conceptual tool for psychoanalysts to use in their work, the Kleinian approach is that the patients, too, have models of what their mind and body actually consist of, and actually believe in them. Segal (1964) reported the dream of a naval officer which was:

> . . . a pyramid. At the bottom of this pyramid there was a rough crowd of sailors bearing a heavy gold book on their heads. On this book stood a naval officer of the same rank as himself, and on his shoulders an admiral. The admiral, he said, seemed in his own way to exercise as great a pressure from above and to be as awe-inspiring as the crowd of sailors who formed the base of the pyramid and pressed up from below. (p. 21)

The patient went on to describe how his dream represented himself, his instincts from below and his conscience from above. As that patient had no knowledge or reading of psychoanalysis he was using a model of himself that would have heartened Freud. Other patients have very varied views of their structure and of the processes which go on to create this structure (especially introjection and projection) [see INTERNAL REALITY].

In contrast, representations and images are mental contents which lack that sense of concreteness and are recognized as representations, just as a true symbol is recognized as an object that represents something and is not actually confused with the thing it stands for [see SYMBOL-FORMATION].

Although the contrast is made for purposes of clarification, both internal objects and representations coexist in the mental life of individuals. The representational world is the mental activity that becomes increasingly prominent from early on in life and develops as the sense of internal reality becomes more tested and accurate with the onset of the depressive position [see 10. DEPRESSIVE POSITION]. It would be true to say, however, that probably no representation exists without there being an internal object, and no mental manipulation of representations without a corresponding unconscious phantasy of relationships involving internal objects. In normal circumstances the concreteness of internal objects does not prevent the more realistic appreciation of the world given by representations and images. However, as unconscious phantasies are the psychological manifestations of the instincts they give colour, energy, passion and meaning to mental activity; it is therefore the unconscious phantasies of the internal world of objects that give significance to representations and images that are handled in the conscious mind. The world of internal objects loosely corresponds to the concept of 'affective cathexis' of representations as used by orthodox psychoanalysts (see Sandler, 1987).

See 5. INTERNAL OBJECTS; INTERNAL REALITY

Sandler, Joseph (1987) *From Safety to Superego*. Karnac.
Sandler, Joseph and Rosenblatt, Bernard (1962) 'The concept of the representational world', *Psychoanal. Study Child* 17:128–45.
Scott, W. Clifford M. (1948) 'Some embryological, neurological, psychiatric and psycho-analytic implications of the body schema', *Int. J. Psycho-Anal.* 29:141–55.
Segal, Hanna (1964) *Introduction to the Work of Melanie Klein*. Heinemann; republished (1973) Hogarth.

Object-Relations School

The term 'object - relations' surreptitiously creeps up on the reader of Klein. It eventually gave rise to a whole strand of psychoanalytic theory, centred especially within the British Psycho-Analytical Society. The lack of precise definition has been important because it has given free licence for multiple uses of the term.

The Object-Relations School includes a number of different theoretical points of view, and generally indicates those British analysts who focus primarily on the state and character of the objects. It is to be contrasted with the Classical or Ego-Psychology School, which focuses more on the instinctual impulses that make up the energy of the interest [see EGO-PSYCHOLOGY].

The Object-Relations School includes Fairbairn, Winnicott and Balint particularly, and in general the so-called Independent Psycho-analysts (Kohon, 1986) of the British Psycho-Analytical Society. What they have in common is a tendency to ignore the 'economic' aspects of instinctual energy that distinguish them from the ego-psychologists. Klein was marked out as different by her acceptance of the death instinct. There are two strands in the British Psycho-Analytical Society: (i) the Fairbairnian framework which categorically states that man is not pleasure-seeking at all, but object-seeking; (ii) various intermediate positions – two-factor theories (Eagle, 1984) combining an emphasis on objects with an instinct theory. All these derive their inspiration from Klein.

However, there are many British psychoanalysts who would claim now that Klein is not truly part of the Object-Relations School (e.g. Kohon, 1986). They reserve the term for Fairbairn, Balint and Winnicott. Guntrip (1961), for instance, in promoting Fairbairn, drew a particular map of progress in psychoanalytic theory in the last fifty years. It reaches out along a dimension starting with Freud's scientific neurology, towards a psychological theory, whole and uncontaminated by biology. This idea is temptingly straightforward, though it can be argued that it is a spurious picture, more seductive than substantial. It is indeed true that there has been a pendulum swing away from scientific neurology and biology towards pure psychology, and this is surely evident, but the mellifluous style of Guntrip's pen tends to overswing the pendulum. Nevertheless the dimension that Guntrip emphasizes is a prominent feature of the map. It was also described by Greenberg and Mitchell (1983) as the contrast between a 'drive/structure model' and a 'relational/structure model'.

Both the scientific 'biologism' with which Freud started and the pure 'psychologism' of Fairbairn (and Guntrip) are extreme points. Human beings are both biological and psychological at the same time, and a tightly biological interpretation of Freud and the instinct-rejecting psychology of Fairbairn end up suffering from the same fallacy: both try to reduce the whole dimension (biology–psychology) to a single, and simple, area of study. Unfortunately, the human mind is poised tantalizingly right across that dimension [see MIND–BODY PROBLEM] and psychoanalytic theory needs to reflect this dialectic. Klein, of course, was equally divided in this dilemma as she constantly attempted to balance her loyalty to her patients' experience with a loyalty to Freud's scientific purpose. She remained uncomfortably stretched between biology and psychology.

Kohon (1985) has suggested redrawing the map along a dimension in which the tension in Freud's approach between a scientific biology of the mind and a literary and humanistic psychology became divided, after the dispersion from Vienna, into a tension between American and British psychoanalysis characterized by British psychoanalysts developing a theory which 'concerns itself with the relation of the subject to his object, not with the relationship between the subject and the object, which is an interpersonal relationship' (Kohon, 1985, p. 27).

The beginnings of object-relations theory. As Freud was forced more and more to give importance to transference [see TRANSFERENCE], so the patient's relationships gained more and more prominence. The transference relationship is the cornerstone of the practice of psychoanalysis, and theory based in actual practice (seemingly a special characteristic of British psychoanalysis) inevitably moved the transference relationship increasingly towards the centre of theory as well as practice; this entailed moving the ego's relationships with its objects into the foreground.

Enacted transference: The Dora case [see TRANSFERENCE] threw up a difficult problem for Freud, since he had intended it as an exemplary case for future publication. Since Dora dropped out of her treatment very prematurely after three months, he had to think hard about what had gone wrong. He realized that he had not been alive to the negative transference, nor to how intensely relations are felt as actually real in their *enactment* with the analyst (Freud, 1905).

However, it was his problem with another kind of patient that put him more firmly on the road that would lead (others) eventually to the object-relations approach. These patients were the psychotic ones who, he found, did not make a proper transference with him. From the Dora case onwards, he might have been wary that he was missing transference, but he actually thought it was in the nature of schizophrenia that these patients failed to invest the analyst with instinctual energy. This could not then be used to engage the patient to overcome his resistances. He 'analysed' Judge Schreber from the published memoirs the judge left behind, since he thought this was the only way to understand the mind of a schizophrenic (Freud, 1911). He found that the patient had suffered a 'world disaster', by which he meant that the world as a whole had completely lost its interest for him – that is, no instinctual energy was invested (cathected) in the world. Instead, the schizophrenic reconstructs an imaginary world of delusions and hallucinations to fill in, as it were, the place where the actual world had once been. This separation of two worlds, actual and personal, is of importance as a forerunner of an object-relations point of view [see INTERNAL REALITY].

Narcissism: At this point (about 1913) Freud brought together certain ideas of an entirely new kind. He was spurred on by his wish to confront and demolish Jung's assertions of non-libidinal experiences. Jung had been a psychiatrist with experience of psychotic patients, while Freud had not. Freud had worked in a neurological sanatorium with hysterical (neurotic) patients and so, as Jung began to pull away from the psychoanalytic movement, Freud was determined to keep his end up in understanding schizophrenics and to lay down a libidinal theory of their disorders. As a result of all this Freud really began to see that in some sense the person himself, or some part of his self or his own ideas, could become the object of his own instinctual energies. Thus was born the concept of narcissism (Freud, 1914), and out of this would eventually come an interest in the object itself (self or other) that is invested with libidinal interest.

Introjection of objects: The second great and innovatory step took place in 1917 with Freud's paper 'Mourning and melancholia'. For some time, Freud had been working with Abraham on trying to understand the psychoses. In fact Abraham (1911) had also written a paper on the topic at about the same time as Freud's paper on the schizophrenic Judge Schreber. However, Abraham's paper was on manic-depressive psychosis, and he was at some advantage over Freud. The interesting thing about manic-depressive psychosis is that it is intermittent. The patient goes through phases when the condition remits and he comes to appear approximately normal. Abraham then set out to try analysing these patients during the periods of remission. Could he work then as he would with a neurotic patient? The answer, he found, was that he could (Abraham, 1924). This created an interest in manic-depressive illness rather than schizophrenia, and Freud's paper on mourning and melancholia constituted his own reflections upon this disorder. It is a paper with some beautiful descriptions of the conditions of mourning and of melancholia (manic-depressive psychosis), and in it he also produced an extraordinary development in his conceptual thinking. He showed that the work of mourning is a slow, step-like giving up of the cathexis of a loved object that has been lost. He showed too that the condition of melancholia is clinically similar in many respects to mourning and that it entails a similar giving up of a lost loved object. The difference, he argued, was that the melancholic does not give up the object but does something quite different with it. He re-establishes the object inside his own ego and goes on relating to it there. Freud argued that the reason for doing this is a particularly strong element of hate and fury towards the loved object, and that the outcome is a strong hatred and fury focused on the ego as if it were the object. 'The shadow', he said, 'of the object falls on the ego' (Freud, 1917, p. 249). He called this 'identification' [see INTROJECTION; IDENTIFICATION].

At this point Freud was describing a phenomenology of the object and had left aside the economics of the instinctual drives. Having discovered this highly interesting process of identification, which actually causes an 'alteration of the ego', he showed four years later (Freud, 1921) that group psychology is based on identification. He had by this time performed the familiar trick which has been the fate of so many psychoanalytic concepts – having been discovered as patho-logical phenomena in patients, they come to be seen everywhere as an essential ingredient of normal psychology.

The parting of the ways: Freud's way forward was to show the development of the superego as based on this identification process which entails the setting up internally of the oedipal loved objects that had to be given up by the young child (Freud, 1923). The boundary of the ego was now seen as permeable to objects instead of just to directed instinctual energy.

Abraham, in the short time that was allowed him before his premature death in 1925, developed Freud's understanding of the internalizing process, especially in pointing to the connection with pregenital impulses. He followed up Freud's hints that introjection had something to do with 'cannibalism' and the oral and sadistic impulses and that there was a mirror process in 'projection' or expulsion, which was related to the anal impulses. The confluence of some basic defence mechanisms [see 9. PRIMITIVE DEFENCE MECHANISMS], with component instincts and their corresponding erogenous zones, must have seemed very elegant and suggestive of a theory rounding out into completion. He was drawn into the realization that introjection and projection primarily concern the fate of the objects, their location inside or outside the ego and the movement between the two sites. He began filling in this theory with meticulous and detailed examples vividly expressed in the psychopathology of his manic-depressive patients.

Child analysis: After Abraham's death the impetus really passed to Klein, whom he had encouraged to analyse children and to develop her play technique, which by a happy chance gave her a wonderfully clear window into the whole arena of object-relations. She gave her children a collection of objects (toys) and watched them arrange the toys in all sorts of relationships to each other. She could then see the instinctual wishes played out visually in front of her as relationships between objects in the most natural way possible – as the play of children [see 1. TECHNIQUE; CHILD ANALYSIS].

Kleinian object-relations theory. What Klein found straight away with her play technique was that her patients played with objects – their toys – and also enacted dramas with the person of the analyst. Very young children seem to have feelings *for* the object itself, however imaginary [see LOVE]. Thus Klein noticed that from the child's point of view, his objects appeared alive, lovable and loving, menacing, pitiable and so on – quite different from the objects in Freud's descriptions. In short, in the child's mind there is a full and intense relation with the object conceived in the most animistic and anthropomorphic way. The objects, even toys, lived and felt and died.

Anyone can make these simple observations on children's play, and they stand in contrast to the descriptions of instinctual discharges upon passive objects.

Objects and instincts: Her loyalty to Freud's theory of instincts always gave Klein a sense of being firmly and securely embedded within Freudian psychoanalysis. But she set out to describe the patient's experience of his objects and the psychological content of the anxieties about them. She found she could keep both the concepts 'object' and 'instinct' when she saw that the relations with objects were exactly defined by the impulses from libidinal sources (oral, anal, genital). She found that the child believed the object to be suffused with intents and motivations aligned with the child's own particular libidinal impulses active at the moment. The oral infant could believe that the object was another who might itself bite the infant in frustration or retaliation. The child's relation to the object is a phantasy with participant actors and a narrative. Objects, therefore, were the stuff of a child's phantasy life, rather than merely a means to instinctual satisfactions. Yet they are also the latter.

The theoretical links between object-relations and instincts seemed difficult to attain, and in 1939 a study group was set up, known as the Internal Objects Group, which met intermittently during the war years, to try to understand and find ways of making these views on objects credible. Several papers resulted from this work (contributions to the Controversial Discussions) [see CONTROVERSIAL DISCUSSIONS]. The most important paper was by Susan Isaacs (1948) in which she described how the instincts find a mental expression as a phantasy in the unconscious mind (unconscious phantasy) – *a phantasy of a relation with an object* [see 2. UNCONSCIOUS PHANTASY]. This is a tie-up of biological, psychological and ultimately social dimensions in the object-relations stance of Klein.

Abraham, Karl (1911) 'Notes on the psycho-analytic treatment of manic-depressive insanity and allied conditions', in Karl Abraham (1927) *Selected Papers on Psycho-Analysis*. Hogarth, pp. 137–56.

—— (1924) 'A short study of the development of the libido', in (1927) *Selected Papers on Psycho-Analysis*, pp. 418–501.

Eagle, Morris (1984) *Recent Developments in Psycho-Analysis*. New York: McGraw-Hill.

Freud, Sigmund (1905) 'Fragment of an analysis of a case of hysteria'. *S.E.* 7, pp. 3–122.

—— (1911) 'Psycho-analytic notes on an autobiographical account of a case of paranoia'. *S.E.* 12, pp. 3–82.

—— (1914) 'On narcissism'. *S.E.* 14, pp. 67–102.

—— (1917) 'Mourning and melancholia'. *S.E.* 14, pp. 237–60.

—— (1921) *Group Psychology and Analysis of the Ego. S.E.* 18, pp. 67–143.

—— (1923) *The Ego and the Id. S.E.* 19, pp. 3–66.

Greenberg, Jay and Mitchell, Stephen (1983) *Object Relations in Psycho-Analytic Theory*. Cambridge, MA: Harvard.

Guntrip, Harry (1961) *Personality Structure and Human Interaction*. Hogarth.

Isaacs, Susan (1948) 'The nature and function of phantasy', *Int. J. Psycho-Anal.* 29:73–97; republished (1952) in Melanie Klein, Paula Heimann, Susan Isaacs and Joan Riviere, eds *Developments in Psycho-Analysis*. Hogarth, pp. 67–121.

Kohon, Gregorio (1985) 'Objects are not people', *Free Assns.* 2:19–30.

—— (1986) *The British School of Psychoanalysis: The Independent Tradition*. Free Association Books.

Obsessional defences

Obsessional defences are repetitious acts or thoughts usually devoted to some act of controlling – displaced from anxiety about controlling an internal state, an impulse or an emotion – ritually reversing an impulse to damage. Klein followed Freud (1909) and Abraham (1924) in regarding obsessional defences as specific against sadistic impulses:

> . . . obsessional mechanisms and symptoms in general serve the purpose of binding, modifying and warding-off anxiety belonging to the earliest levels of the mind; so that obsessional neuroses are built up upon the anxiety of the first danger-situations. (Klein, 1931, p. 246)

So great was her emphasis that she referred on one or two occasions to the 'obsessional position'. Repetitive undoing (a key defence in the obsessional mechanisms) was particularly prominent in her clinical material of young children, and she attributed it, at that stage, to the effects of guilt: '. . . of greatest importance in the development of obsessional neurosis . . . is the feeling of guilt engendered by the superego' (Klein, 1927, p. 179).

However, the status of the obsessional mechanisms began to diminish in later years when her descriptions of the depressive position revised her view of guilt. The prominent defences she described then were the manic ones [see MANIC DEFENCES], and it became difficult to distinguish them from the obsessional defences:

> . . . where obsessional neurosis was the most powerful factor in the case, such mastery betokened a forcible separation of two (or more) objects; whereas, where mania was in the ascendant, the patient had recourse to methods more violent. That is to say the objects were killed but, since the subject was omnipotent, he supposed he could also immediately call them to life again. (Klein, 1935, p. 278)

This hairline distinction was bolstered further on:

> The very fact that manic defences are operating in such close connection with the obsessional ones contributes to the ego's fear that the reparation attempted by obsessional means has also failed. (Klein, 1940, p. 351).

The specific obsessional defence of *undoing* was displaced by the discovery of reparation, which in some respects it resembles; reparation is the attempt to right a wrong [see REPARATION].

The down-grading of the obsessional defences was complete by 1946 when Klein turned to study the splitting processes that came to the fore in the work she and her psychiatric colleagues were doing with schizophrenics. Fairbairn's criticism had influenced Klein, who agreed that she had placed too much emphasis on depression and on Abraham's interest in obsessional mechanisms in the 'psychotic' early phases. She had begun to realize that there were a whole class of primitive defence mechanisms against sadism and paranoid anxiety of a quite different nature which underlay the 'neurotic defences' [see 9. PRIMITIVE DEFENCE MECHANISMS].

From then on the obsessional defences were regarded as neurotic defence mechanisms made up of elements of the primitive defence mechanisms which are developmentally prior. In a footnote in 1957 (p. 221) she remarked casually that the obsessional mechanisms are specific in the second year of life – long after the crucial first six months of life that span the paranoid-schizoid position and the onset of the depressive position.

To all intents and purposes the obsessional defences were divided between the manic defences (controlling and isolating) and reparation (undoing). They are largely absorbed into the omnipotent forms of reparation [see MANIC REPARATION]; though there are also important projective aspects to the obsessional defences which give the 'sphincter activity' quality to so many obsessional symptoms.

Abraham, Karl (1924) 'A short account of the development of the libido', in Karl Abraham (1927) *Selected Papers on Psycho-Analysis.* Hogarth, pp. 418–501.

Freud, Sigmund (1909) 'Notes upon a case of obsessional neurosis'. *S.E.* 10, pp. 153–320.

Klein, Melanie (1927) 'Criminal tendencies in normal children'. *WMK* 1, pp. 170–85.

—— (1931) 'A contribution to the theory of intellectual development'. *WMK* 1, pp. 236–47.

—— (1935) 'A contribution to the psychogenesis of manic-depressive states'. *WMK* 1, pp. 262–89.

—— (1940) 'Mourning and its relation to manic-depressive states'. *WMK* 1, pp. 344–69.

—— (1946) 'Notes on some schizoid mechanisms'. *WMK* 3, pp. 1–24.

—— (1957) *Envy and Gratitude. WMK* 3, pp. 176–235.

Omnipotence

The early stages of infancy are characterized by omnipotent thoughts, feelings and phantasies. For Klein the importance of omnipotence was linked to fears of an omnipotent destructiveness and to the fact that certain phantasy activities, especially those involved in the primitive defence mechanisms (taking in, expelling, annihilating) have profound and permanent effects on the development of the ego and on its characteristic object-relations. Klein regarded these omnipotent phantasies [see 9. PRIMITIVE DEFENCE MECHANISMS] as defences against the experience of separateness, dependence and envy.

Omnipotence of phantasy. The early phantasies of taking in and expelling are experienced by the infant as real and giving rise to an actual 'alteration of the ego'. These early omnipotent mechanisms are therefore responsible for actual developments in the self and the ego. Certain objects are believed, in phantasy, to reside inside and to form a part of the self: for instance, an introjected 'good' object with a consequent actual development of a sense of security and confidence. The concretely felt loss of the good internal object has opposite effects. The bad object experienced internally is felt as a paranoid threat to life [see 5. INTERNAL OBJECTS; OBJECTS].

Omnipotent phantasies enter into the psychological make-up in various ways:

(i) Omnipotence as a defence: The sense of omnipotence is important in the primitive defence mechanisms which are involved in breaking down the ego-boundaries so that the experiences of separateness and envy are avoided [see 9. PRIMITIVE DEFENCE MECHANISMS];

(ii) Narcissistic states: The omnipotent defences can also create confusion between self and object, which persists as 'omnipotent narcissistic object-relations' (Rosenfeld, 1987) leading to an enduring *state of narcissism* (Segal, 1983) [see NARCISSISM];

(iii) Narcissistic organization: These omnipotent states may become organized in the personality to create a form of negative narcissism, described by Rosenfeld (1987) in terms of omnipotent bad parts of the self that engage in intimidating or seductive relations entrapping the good parts of the self [see STRUCTURE].

Development. Normally the movement out of this sense of omnipotence comes through the experience of helplessness in a way that is mediated by external containing objects, which can be introjected and identified with. The giving up of the narcissistic invasion or incorporation of objects is an essential step in the development of the depressive position [see 10. DEPRESSIVE POSITION] and the recognition of the reality of the objects in their own right.

Omnipotence and impingement. In contrast, Winnicott regarded omnipotence as a protected area from the start that must resist impingement, a view which resembled the classical theory of primary narcissism [see NARCISSISM]. Without a distinction between himself and mother the infant exists in a state of 'primary omnipotence'. Mother's role, in Winnicott's view, is to provide for the infant in such a way as to allow him to continue his delusional belief in his own omnipotence. She therefore provides the needed satisfaction (the breast) in exactly the place and at the moment when the infant is hallucinating his own satisfaction of his hunger. The second main task of a mother, according to Winnicott, is to pinpoint the moments when the infant begins to be ready to move out of his omnipotence. Then she can introduce a moment of frustration, a lack of satisfaction, at the right moment and at the right time. The 'good-enough mother' is the right degree. The transition from infantile omnipotence to a more accurate reality fails if the confrontation with mother is made too brutally and too early. The infant then suffers an experience Winnicott termed *impingement*.

Winnicott (1953) described how the infant does get out of the state of primary narcissism through an intermediate step: he seeks and creates transitional objects as halfway stages so that infantile omnipotence never has to be fully given up. Winnicott appears to revert to a more orthodox view of primary narcissism, whilst calling it primary omnipotence. The ego, if such it can be called in Winnicott's view, has the single primary function of experiencing no sense of itself in a world. The ego has no defence mechanisms of its own and the environment is charged to defend that mental state of undifferentiated omnipotence.

Rosenfeld, Herbert (1987) *Impasse and Interpretation*. Tavistock.
Segal, Hanna (1983) 'Some clinical implications of Melanie Klein's work', *Int. J. Psycho-Anal.* 64:269–76.
Winnicott, Donald (1953) 'Transitional objects and transitional phenomena', *Int. J. Psycho-Anal.* 34:89–96; republished (1971) in D. W. Winnicott, *Playing and Reality*. Tavistock.

Paranoia

From the outset of her work Klein was impressed by the violent quality of children's play and human phantasy life. She soon saw that inhibitions and neurotic problems in children arose out of intense fear, which came from the phantasies of aggression. The prevalence of the paranoid feelings and object-relations led her, in 1935, to contrast the depressive position to a prior *paranoid position* – the latter term dropped out in 1946 when Klein introduced the term 'paranoid-schizoid position' [see 11. PARANOID-SCHIZOID POSITION].

The paranoid vicious circle: Klein was always occupied with the source of this aggression. Aggressive phantasies lead to the intense fear of retaliation. Fear provokes further hate and violence which in turn provoke further fear of retaliation. She pictured this as a '. . . vicious circle dominated by the death instinct, in which aggression gives rise to anxiety and anxiety reinforces aggression' (Klein, 1932, p. 150). She described the way children could be trapped in this vicious circle leading to panic and *pavor nocturnus* (night terrors) and found herself wondering about the relation between these states and paranoid psychosis in adults. Eventually she found, in a severely inhibited child, that these paranoid fears were so intense that they inhibited all activity, including the ability to create symbols. Klein then realized that these crescendos of aggression and fear were indeed the basis for psychoses (Klein, 1930).

Although Klein was very aware of the importance of loving and good feelings [see LOVE], she always viewed the aggressive impulses and the vicious circles to which they gave rise as the crucial disturbance that interrupted the capacity to love.

See 12. ENVY; DEATH INSTINCT; PSYCHOSIS

Klein, Melanie (1930) 'The importance of symbol-formation in the development of the ego'. *WMK* 1, pp. 219–32.
—— (1932) *The Psycho-Analysis of Children. WMK* 2.

Paranoid defence against depressive anxiety

Klein's evidence that the depressive position occurs so close to – and arises out of – the preceding states of paranoia [see 11. PARANOID-SCHIZOID POSITION; 13. PROJECTIVE IDENTIFICATION] suggested to her a fluctuating process, in which there is repeatedly a retreat from the depressive position when depressive anxieties become too strong. In that case '. . . paranoid fears and suspicions were reinforced as a defence against the depressive position' (Klein, 1935, p. 274). Later there may be a further advance towards the depressive position and other attempts to sustain depressive anxiety (Joseph, 1978).

See 10. DEPRESSIVE POSITION; Ps-D

Joseph, Betty (1978) 'Different types of anxiety and their handling in the analytic situation', *Int. J. Psycho-Anal.* 59:223–8.
Klein, Melanie (1935) 'A contribution to the psychogenesis of manic-depressive states'. *WMK* 1, pp. 262–89.

Part-objects

The notion of part-objects came from Abraham. Speaking of manic-depressive patients, he reported:

> ... one of the patients used very often to have the phantasy of biting off the nose or the lobe of the ear or the breast, of a young girl who he was very fond of. At other times he used to play with the idea of biting off his father's finger ... We may thus speak of *partial incorporation* of the object. (Abraham, 1924, p. 487)

Abraham saw the biting and incorporation of a part of the object as a manifestation of the earliest – oral – form of loving relationship with an object. He thought that the biting, with the loving, was an ambivalence. In Abraham's theory part-objects represent a stage of ambivalence before the gaining of the post-ambivalent true object-love (whole objects).

Klein developed this quite differently. By analysing children directly she showed that Abraham's neat sequences of phases [see LIBIDO] were not accurate. In 1935 she described how attaining a whole-object-relationship results in the painful difficulties of ambivalence rather than resolving ambivalence; part-object-relationships entailed the freeing of the ego from ambivalence [see OBJECTS]. So for her, the phantasy of biting off a finger, or other part-object, carried the sense of incorporating a good object, the 'good' penis.

The emotional object: Though represented in the phantasies of children and psychotic patients as anatomical parts, part-objects have very little physical presence and few physical qualities:

> ... the object of all these phantasies is, to begin with, the breast of the mother. It may seem curious that the tiny child's interest should be limited to a part of a person rather than to the whole but one must bear in mind first of all that the child has an extremely underdeveloped capacity for perception, physical and mental, and then ... the tiny child is only concerned with his immediate gratifications. (Klein, 1936, p. 290)

The part-object is firstly an emotional object, having a function rather than a material existence: '... the part-object-relationship is not with the anatomical structures only but with function, not with anatomy but with physiology, not with the breast but with feeding, poisoning, living, hating' (Bion, 1959, p. 102).

Because the infant cannot perceive the true nature and cause of his own sensations, they are interpreted according to innate experiences (and knowledge) [see 2. UNCONSCIOUS PHANTASY; INNATE KNOWLEDGE]. In particular, the object has a feeling state – good or bad – and has intentions or motives towards the infant. The object, at the outset, is sensual, emotional and intentional rather than physical. Thus 'the breast' cannot conjure up the varied images or the penumbra of associated meanings that it will have later in life. It is an object with a simpler relationship to the baby. It touches his cheek, intrudes a nipple into his mouth for good or bad purposes. In spite of having only these ephemeral qualities it is completely real for the infant. Such objects are called 'part-objects' – although, from the infant's point of view, the part is all there is to the object.

Omnipotence: A part-object exists, in the paranoid-schizoid position, in relation to the bodily sensations of the subject. Through projection into the object it becomes a narcissistic extension of the ego's own experiences and the separateness of the good object is not acknowledged. Only when the object comes to be recognized as whole does it properly take on a separate existence from the subject, and this entails the angry narcissistic response which enhances the fears of the depressive position in which the infant is trying to keep the good object safe from damage.

The infant's capacity to perceive people as *whole objects* gradually develops as the visual apparatus comes into use. This capacity to see people as wholes is not just a capacity of the perceptual apparatus; it represents an emotional accomplishment as well. Since separate objects are defined for the infant largely in terms of their benevolent or malevolent feelings and intentions towards him, then to bring the parts together into something more integrated or whole means merging into one object, with a mixture of feelings and intentions, the separate objects that represented distinct feelings and intentions. This step towards mixed feelings poses an emotional situation that is quite new and very painful for the infant [see 10. DEPRESSIVE POSITION]. He has to give up an omnipotent view of a world created by his own interpretation of his bodily sensations.

Part-objects and synthesis: The parts of the personality can be separated and expelled into the external world: 'The fact that in George's phantasies parts were played by helpful figures distinguished his type of personifications from those of Erna's play. Three principal parts were represented in his play' (Klein, 1929a, p. 201). The internal world was described, then, in terms of parts which may be represented separately and which interacted as if in a drama on a stage. In fact, Klein specifically related the dramas occurring internally in the phantasy world of internal objects to a performance on a stage (see Klein, 1929b):

I believe these mechanisms (splitting-up and projection) are a principal factor in the tendency to personification in play. By their means the synthesis of the superego, which can be maintained only with more or less effort, can be given up for the time being. (Klein, 1929a, p. 205)

But the superego as a whole is made up of the various identifications adopted on the different levels of development whose stamp they bear ... Already during the process of its construction the ego employs its tendency to synthesis by endeavouring to form a whole out of these various identifications. (1929a, p. 204)

It is the coming together in a realistic way of some of these identifications that Klein, in 1935, described in an entirely new theoretical way as the *depressive position*.

Depressive position: This is a new relation to mother, in which the very and exceptionally good and wholly well-intentioned mother (a part-object) comes to be a mixed – even contaminated – figure and no longer the source of perfection the child desires. It is this new relation to mother that is the core of the depressive position: '. . . only when the ego has introjected the object as a whole . . . is it able to fully realize the disaster created through its sadism' (Klein, 1935, p. 269). The infant has to contend with the fact that he hates, with the most unrestrained and paranoid intensity, the mother who is now seen also as the loved one who feeds and cares for and loves him. Such a confluence of emotions is extremely disturbing and may be resisted. Klein's observations led her to the view that the infant fluctuates between the paranoid relations and the depressive position. The constant approaches towards the depressive position gradually allow the emotional turmoil to be mastered [see 10. DEPRESSIVE POSITION].

A catalogue of part-objects would include: 'babies', 'bad object', 'breast', 'buttocks', 'child', 'combined parent figure', 'faeces', 'father', 'good object', 'milk', 'mother', 'mother-with-penis', 'penis', 'womb'.

See FATHER; BAD OBJECT; COMBINED PARENT FIGURE

Abraham, Karl (1924) 'A short history of the development of the libido', in Karl Abraham (1927) *Selected Papers on Psycho-Analysis*. Hogarth, pp. 418–501.

Bion, Wilfred (1959) 'Attacks on linking', *Int. J. Psycho-Anal.* 40:308–15; republished (1967) in W. R. Bion *Second Thoughts*. Heinemann, pp. 93–109.

Klein, Melanie (1927) 'Criminal tendencies in normal children'. *WMK* 1, pp. 170–85.

—— (1929a) 'Personification in the play of children'. *WMK* 1, pp. 199–209.

—— (1929b) 'Infantile anxiety-situations reflected in a work of art and in the creative impulse'. *WMK* 1, pp. 210–18.

—— (1935) 'A contribution to the psychogenesis of manic-depressive states'. *WMK* 1, pp. 262–89.

—— (1936) 'Weaning'. *WMK* 1, pp. 290–305.

Pathological organizations

In recent years patients with severe personality disorders have come under close investigation (Rey, 1979). Joseph (1975, 1978) has described the technical problems of working with such patients [see TRANSFERENCE; COUNTERTRANSFERENCE; 1. TECHNIQUE]. These patients appear not too psychotically handicapped but stuck in a level of disorder which does not shift, or only slowly with very long analyses (Spillius, 1988). As with the work with psychotic patients in the previous generation of psychoanalysts, and with children in the generation before that, this work has given rise to certain theoretical developments.

From a Kleinian point of view borderline personalities have three major characteristics:

(i) they have become stuck in some in-between position between the paranoid-schizoid and depressive positions, with a complex defensiveness against both the fragmentation of the paranoid-schizoid position and the guilt and responsibility of the depressive position (Joseph, 1989) [see PSYCHIC EQUILIBRIUM];

(ii) they have developed in the context of an excess of death instinct and envy, but have managed to develop certain kinds of stable object-relations, though these are organized around the dominance of the 'bad' parts of the self over the 'good' parts [see STRUCTURE; NEGATIVE NARCISSISM];

(iii) the stability of the personality is especially fragile and they have struggled beyond the paranoid-schizoid position only by the development of a rigid system of defences, known originally as narcissistic organization (Rosenfeld, 1964), then delusional defence system (Segal, 1972), defensive organization (O'Shaughnessy, 1981) and then more recently as *pathological organization* (Steiner, 1982; Spillius, 1988) since their function is clearly not just defensive but also a rigid adherence to certain kinds of object-relations and a source of considerable pleasure of a pathological and usually perverse kind [see NARCISSISM; STRUCTURE].

Various writers have researched these 'patients with a weak ego who, with more persecution than normal, arrive in infancy at the borders of the depressive position as defined by Klein (1935) but are then unable to negotiate it, and instead form a defensive organization' (O'Shaughnessy, 1981, p. 359) [see DEPRESSIVE ANXIETY; ANXIETY]. O'Shaughnessy distinguished defences in a more normal development from the defensive organization:

> Unlike defences – piecemeal, transient to a greater or lesser extent, recurrent – which are a normal part of development, a defensive

organization is a fixation, a pathological formation . . . Expressed in Kleinian terms, defences are a normal part of negotiating the paranoid-schizoid and depressive positions; a defensive organization, on the other hand, is a pathological fixed formation in one or other position, or on the borderline between them. (O'Shaughnessy, 1981, p. 363)

She emphasized 'the controlling and static transference characteristic of the operation of a defensive organization' (O'Shaughnessy, 1981, p. 363) aimed at 'a total and perpetual organization of his relationships internal and external to exclude all disturbance' (O'Shaughnessy, 1981, p. 366).

The idea of a fixed structure of defences comes, directly or indirectly, from the Schreber case and Freud's description of the construction of an organized delusion in place of a fragmented and annihilated reality (Freud, 1911). Riesenberg-Malcolm (1970) described a case in which a sado-masochistic fantasy was continually employed to reconstruct an organized mental activity and internal world following a psychotic fragmentation of the personality. Segal (1972) described a similar rigid defensive system that was designed to avert psychosis following a childhood psychotic breakdown. However, Kleinians have subsequently added to Freud's formulation with two concepts (strands as Spillius (1988) described):

(a) *Psychic equilibrium:* the stasis in the normal fluctuation between the paranoid-schizoid position and the depressive position [see Ps-D]. Though the early writers (Riesenberg-Malcolm, 1970; Segal, 1972) described cases in which the defensive organization combats a psychotic breakdown it is now regarded as a retreat from the anxieties of both the paranoid-schizoid position and the depressive position. Development of the personality slows to a halt before the depressive position has been properly reached and the organized defences are aimed at maintaining immobility and retaining an omnipotent character.

(b) *Aggressive aspects of narcissism:* under the dominance of the death instinct the personality is structured around the organization of omnipotent defences.

Personality structure. Bion's (1957) paper distinguished between a psychotic part of the personality and the non-psychotic part [see PSYCHOSIS; 13. PROJECTIVE IDENTIFICATION]. This paper was seminal within and without the Kleinian Group. Later he described an internal world in which alpha-function fails; it is one dominated by the stripping of meaning from all experience and production of extremely persecuting missiles (beta elements) expelled in order to eliminate all experience (Bion, 1962) [see THINKING; ALPHA-FUNCTION]. The idea of separate parts of a single personality divided according to the psychosis–neurosis axis has gained considerable weight and has been central to ideas concerning the structuring of the personality [see STRUCTURE]. Meltzer (1968) described internal conflicts between a part of the self that was capable of experiencing dependency and more realistic object-relations, and another part that took a mocking attitude to the benefits of object-relations and constantly twisted the individual towards futile, despairing, destructive or self-destructive attitudes [see STRUCTURE]. Money-Kyrle (1969) at this time also described the internal struggle between sane and insane parts of the self.

Idealization of 'bad' parts of the self: Rosenfeld (1971) described idealization of the 'bad' self as a 'negative narcissism' which is generally found in these 'borderline' patients [see NARCISSISM; NEGATIVE NARCISSISM]. He described a structure in which, like Meltzer's, the death instinct is organized within the personality as an object, or group of objects, that dominate the rest of the personality. The destructive and self-destructive parts of the personality demand to be idealized and intimidate or seduce the loving, constructive and more realistic parts of the personality into the idealization. At about this time, 1970, Brenman (1985a and b) described a cruel superego internally dominating the personality in the way described by Bion (1962) – see above. In order to maintain an idealized belief in the cruel, vengeful and destructive aspects of the personality, Brenman argued, a gross restriction of perception, a narrow-mindedness, is necessary. This eliminates human understanding and demands 'the worship of omnipotence which is felt to be superior to human love and forgiveness, the clinging to omnipotence as a defence against depression, and the sanctification of grievance and revenge' (Brenman, 1985a, p. 280). This suppression of perception is also illustrated by Steiner (1985). Sidney Klein re-emphasized in 1980 the importance of Bion's original description of the psychotic-nonpsychotic contrast within the personality and he described clinically his patients' unconscious knowledge of structures within themselves which he termed 'autistic'. Areas of the personality are dominated by the death instinct and are encapsulated and separated from the rest of the personality which maintains a more 'normal' (neurotic) state. These capsules emerged in dreams as hard-shelled objects, molluscs, etc., and he referred to Rosenfeld's (1978) concept of 'islets' of psychosis which may be converted to somatic pathology.

The identificate: Sohn (1985) described the core feature of pathological organizations as an identification with a particular object; and in particular the identification is by omnipotent projection [see 13. PROJECTIVE IDENTIFICATION]. Rosenfeld (1964) thought that this omnipotent identification was by simultaneous introjective identification as well (the ego identifies with the good attributes and denies them in the object). Sohn describes how becoming the object induces the sense of omnipotence, or enhances it, and the self can enjoy being a new object [see OMNIPOTENCE]. However the dominance of the destructive-ness brings consequences: (i) the devaluation of the object whose qualities are expropriated through this invasive identification; and (ii) the splitting, and therefore weakening of the self. The ego splits between the needy and dependent self and a more omnipotent part. It is the latter that takes over the object, adopts its qualities as its own, inflates the omnipotence further, denies the existence of other and weaker parts of the ego and can then believe itself to be the whole ego and an enhanced ego. It dominates over the rest of the internal world and obliterates the existence of a separate external world. The invasion and control of the object, which is then incorporated as a sort of satellite of the self, is a composite of the properties of the object and the arrogance of the self; a precipitate which Sohn calls *the identificate*.

The ego, depleted by splitting, and the object, devalued by appropriating its attributes, gives rise to a hollowness which is enhanced because the omnipotent self may frequently change its object, becoming new objects repeatedly in order to sustain the splitting, projection, control and omnipotence. This falseness has elsewhere been described as a pseudo-alliance (Joseph, 1975), a pseudo-compli-ance (Riesenberg-Malcolm, 1981a) or a pseudo-integration (Steiner, 1987). Brenman (1985b) further explored the multiple and rapidly changing identifications, with ideal objects 'an ostensibly whole object used as a part object' (Brenman, 1985b, p. 424) [see PART-OBJECTS].

Points of on-going research. These descriptions are sufficiently frequent and consistent to suggest a valid addition to Kleinian thought. However, there remain a number of points where the various workers do not coincide.

Splitting or liaison: Steiner (1982) debated whether there is really a clear split between 'good' and 'bad' parts of the personality. He concluded that 'we are dealing here not with a split between good and bad, but with the consequences of a breakdown in splitting and a reassembling of the fragments into a complex mixture under the dominance of an omnipotent narcissistic structure' (Steiner, 1982, p. 250). In both the narcissistic, defensive part and the more healthy part there is evidence of fusion of the instincts, a 'liaison':

> If we assume that a primitive destructive part of the self exists in all individuals, an important determinant of the outcome will be the way this destructiveness is dealt with by the remaining parts of the personality. In psychotic patients this destructive part of the self dominates the personality, destroying and immobilising the healthy

parts. In the normal individual the destructive part is less split off so that it can to a greater extent be contained and neutralised by the healthy parts of the personality. There remains an intermediate situation in which the balance is more even, which results clinically in borderline and narcissistic states. Here the destructive part of the self cannot completely ignore the healthy parts and is forced to take account of them and enter into a liaison with them. (Steiner, 1982, p. 242)

The liaison creates a complex affair in which healthy parts of the personality are induced into colluding knowingly with purposes that are felt to be destructive, and thus are perversely used to *masquerade* as health [see PERVERSION].

Excitement: In many of these descriptions the pathological organization offers perverse gratifications of an excited kind in which objects are omnipotently and sado-masochistically controlled (Meltzer, 1968; Riesenberg-Malcolm, 1970; O'Shaughnessy, 1981; Joseph, 1975, 1982, 1983; Brenman Pick, 1985). The excitement lures the co-operative parts of the personality away from normal development and from 'good' and healing object-relations:

It is technically extremely important to be clear as to whether the patient is telling us about and communicating to us real despair, depression or fear and persecution, which he wants us to understand and help him with, or whether he is communicating in such a way as primarily to create a masochistic situation in which he can get caught up. (Joseph, 1982)

The operation of a pathological organization distorts internal and external reality (Riesenberg-Malcolm, 1981b; Joseph, 1983) so much that these patients have sometimes been called 'character perversions' [see PERVERSIONS], even though the patients may not exhibit explicit sexual perversions. However, the sado-masochistic excitement in these defences is not invariably reported. It remains to be seen whether it is an integral element of the pathological organization.

Internal relations of the pathological organizations: In Sidney Klein's (1980) description of autistic parts of the self the patient appears unreachable because so much of the personality is locked away within the encapsulated psychotic part of the personality. In contrast others have regarded the pathological organization as deeply implicated in an internal conflict, arising from the 'bad' parts of the self intimidating 'good' parts (Rosenfeld, 1971) or seducing them (Meltzer, 1968; Riesenberg-Malcolm, 1970). And Steiner (1982) postulated a *liaison* between the 'bad' and 'good' parts of the self. Therefore three possible inter-relations between 'good' and 'bad' parts of the self have been reported:

(i) the parts remain relatively non-interacting through the creation of a hard capsule;

(ii) the parts are engaged, under the dominance of the 'bad' ones, in avoiding all emotional movement; or

(iii) the 'good' part of the self knowingly and willingly colludes with the 'bad'.

It is not yet clear if these are different theoretical formulations of the same pathology, or if they are formulations of different clinical phenomena.

Object and self: These descriptions of the splitting of the ego, or self, and their resulting conflictual relationship sometimes comes very close to sounding like an internal conflict between the self and a 'bad' internal object. Bion (1962) for instance made a specific link between the apparatus for evacuating experience in the psychotic's mind, and the persecutory superego. This link is also referred to by Brenman: 'the primitive harsh superego is linked with a powerful pathological organization' (Brenman, 1982, p. 304).

Although the organization is clearly derived from ego defences and impulses its exact object-relations status is unclear. Partly this comes from the omnipotent quality of the phantasies that are involved which create a confusion between self and object [see CONFUSIONAL STATES]. Meltzer's (1973) description of projective identification into *internal* objects may be a way of describing this apparently obscure occurrence in which separated parts of the self become seemingly unassimilated internal objects.

Bion, Wilfred (1957) 'Differentiation of the psychotic from the non-psychotic personalities', *Int. J. Psycho-Anal.* 38:266–75; republished in W.R. Bion (1967), *Second Thoughts.* Heinemann, pp. 43–64.
—— (1962) *Learning from Experience.* Heinemann.
Brenman, Eric (1982) 'Separation: a clinical problem', *Int. J. Psycho-Anal.* 63:303–10.
—— (1985a) 'Cruelty and narrowmindedness', *Int. J. Psycho-Anal.* 66:273–81.
—— (1985b) 'Hysteria', *Int. J. Psycho-Anal.* 66:423–32.
Brenman Pick, Irma (1985) 'Male sexuality: a clinical study of forces that impede development', *Int. J. Psycho-Anal.* 66:415–22.
Freud, Sigmund (1911) *Psycho-Analytic Notes on an Autobiographical Account of a Case of Paranoia. S.E.* 12, pp. 9–82.
Joseph, Betty (1975) 'The patient who is difficult to reach', in Peter Giovacchini, ed. *Tactics and Techniques in Psycho-Analytic Therapy,* vol. 2. New York: Jason Aronson, pp. 205–16.
—— (1978) 'Different types of anxiety and their handling in the analytic situation', *Int. J. Psycho-Anal.* 59:223–8.
—— (1982) 'On addiction to near-death', *Int. J. Psycho-Anal.* 63:449–56.

—— (1983) 'On understanding and not understanding: some technical issues', *Int. J. Psycho-Anal.* 64:291–8.

—— (1989) *Psychic Change and Psychic Equilibrium.* Routledge.

Klein, Melanie (1935) 'A contribution to the psychogenesis of manic-depressive states', in *The Writings of Melanie Klein* 1, pp. 282–310.

Klein, Sidney (1980) 'Autistic phenomena in neurotic patients', *Int. J. Psycho-Anal.* 61:395–402; republished (1981) in James Grotstein, ed. *Do I Dare Disturb the Universe?* pp. 103–14.

Meltzer, Donald (1968) 'Terror, persecution, dread', *Int. J. Psycho-Anal.* 49:396–400; republished (1973) in Donald Meltzer *Sexual States of Mind.* Perth: Clunie, pp. 99–106.

—— (1973) *Sexual States of Mind.* Perth: Clunie.

Money-Kyrle, Roger (1969) 'On the fear of insanity', in (1978) *The Collected Papers of Roger Money-Kyrle.* Perth: Clunie, pp. 434–41.

O'Shaughnessy, Edna (1981) 'A clinical study of a defensive organization', *Int. J. Psycho-Anal.* 62:359–69.

Rey, Henri (1979) 'Schizoid phenomena in the borderline', in Joseph LeBoit and Atilio Capponi, eds *Advances in Psychotherapy of the Borderline Patient.* New York: Jason Aronson, pp. 449–84.

Riesenberg-Malcolm, Ruth (1970) 'The mirror: a perverse sexual phantasy in a woman seen as a defence against psychotic breakdown', in Elizabeth Bott Spillius, ed. (1988) *Melanie Klein Today: Volume 2: Mainly Practice.* Routledge, pp. 115–37; previously published (1970) in Spanish as 'El espejo: Una fantasia sexual perversa en una mujer, vista como defensa contra un derrume psicotico', *Revista de Psicoanálisis* 27:793–826.

—— (1981a) 'Technical problems in the analysis of a pseudo-compliant patient', *Int. J. Psycho-Anal.* 62:477–84.

—— (1981b) 'Expiation as a defence', *Int. J. Psycho-Anal. Psychother.* 8:549–70.

Rosenfeld, Herbert (1964) 'On the psychopathology of narcissism: a clinical approach', *Int. J. Psycho-Anal.* 45:332–7.

—— (1971) 'A clinical approach to the psycho-analytical theory of the life and death instincts: an investigation into the aggressive aspects of narcissism', *Int. J. Psycho-Anal.* 52:169–78.

—— (1978) 'The relationship between psychosomatic symptoms and latent psychotic states' (unpublished).

Segal, Hanna (1972) 'A delusional system as a defence against re-emergence of a catastrophic situation', *Int. J. Psycho-Anal.* 53:393–403.

Sohn, Leslie (1985) 'Narcissistic organization, projective identification and the formation of the identificate', *Int. J. Psycho-Anal.* 66:201–13.

Spillius, Elizabeth Bott (1988) *Melanie Klein Today: Volume 2: Mainly Practice.* Routledge.

Steiner, John (1982) 'Perverse relationships between parts of the self: a clinical illustration', *Int. J. Psycho-Anal.* 63:241–52.

—— (1985) 'Turning a blind eye: the cover-up for Oedipus', *Int. Rev. Psycho-Anal.* 12:161–72.

—— (1987) 'Interplay between pathological organization and the paranoid-schizoid and depressive positions', *Int. J. Psycho-Anal.* 68:69–80.

Penis The 'penis' is a part-object, initially conceived in unconscious phantasy as a part of the combined parent figure. It is believed by the infant to reside inside the mother's body, abdomen or breast [see COMBINED PARENT FIGURE].

The violence of the initial conception may be attributed to the external father when he is eventually met [see FATHER]. With the onset of the depressive position, the penis may be regarded as an ally in restoring the damaged mother. As the development of the little boy progresses, he may find great reassurance from his penis if it is identified with the restoring penis or father. On the other hand, it may be greatly feared and even disowned if it is identified with the violent object of the initial phantasy.

As with other part-objects, the characteristics seem in some measure to be innately determined, and work has to be done to distinguish the external objects (in this case father) more as he really is [see INNATE KNOWLEDGE].

See FATHER; PART-OBJECTS; MASCULINITY

Persecution Klein was amazed at the outset of her work to see the level of violence in children's play and soon realized that the states of anxiety she found in her children, for example *pavor nocturnus*, were connected with a fear of this violence. The sense of an impending retaliation greatly affected the child, and she thought of this as a state of persecution which was not much less than the paranoia of psychotic patients [see PARANOIA].

When she discovered that the level of sadism [see SADISM] and fear of retaliation inhibited play, symbolization and other forms of intellectual development in the child, she made the connection with the thought disorder of schizophrenic patients. She traced this fear of violence and persecution back to the early months of life by analysing the *pavor nocturnus* of children whose symptoms had started in their first months, and confirmed that Abraham and Freud were right in inferring that fixation points for the psychoses exist very early in the pregenital phases.

She later (1946) placed the persecution in the context of the paranoid-schizoid position, a fear of annihilation, but made it clear that people constantly return to these persecutory anxieties, under certain circumstances, throughout life. However, the persecutory tone to object-relations dies only gradually and the early experiences of the depressive position are suffused with a persecutory form of guilt. Only gradually does the tone change to a more clearly concerned and reparative form of guilt [see DEPRESSIVE ANXIETY]. Indeed, this early form of guilt may encourage a retreat to the paranoid-schizoid position, where the fear of persecution is less anguished than the onset

of guilt in the depressive position [see PARANOID DEFENCE AGAINST
DEPRESSIVE ANXIETY].

See 11. PARANOID-SCHIZOID POSITION; PARANOIA

Klein, Melanie (1946) 'Notes on some schizoid mechanisms'. *WMK* 3,
  pp. 1–24.

Personification

Klein showed that in their play
children turned their toys into per-
sons, imaginary or real, who were of importance in their actual life [see
1. TECHNIQUE], and they worried about the relations between those
personified objects.

Personification, ubiquitous in all play, led Klein to the view that all
mental activity is conceived with relationships between personified
objects. She was impressed with the fluidity and ease with which
relations, affects and conflicts could be transferred to new objects [see
SYMBOL-FORMATION]. Klein's belief in the capacity to represent
persons, to symbolize and to make a transference was in contrast with
Anna Freud's view [see 1. TECHNIQUE].

See PLAY

Perversion

In his earlier theories, Freud (1905) regarded
the sexual instinct as having various compon-
ents – sadism and masochism, voyeurism, homosexuality. A child's
sexuality is multiply perverse (polymorphous perverse sexuality of
childhood). He thought that this died out of conscious interest during
normal maturation. However, in people who enjoy perversions the
infantile instinct remains, and in neurosis a perverse component
impulse expresses itself indirectly, representing a poorly repressed
perverse sexual interest.

Although classical theory laid great emphasis on perverse sexuality
and the consequences of its repression, Klein says little about the
perversions in particular. It is true that she found that one of the
component instincts, sadism, was especially important, but she did not
follow through with an investigation of sado-masochistic perversions
[see SADISM]. She left her ubiquitous findings of sadism in children
curiously unconnected to adult sexual sadism.

Adult perversions: However, Klein (1927) found that the sadistic
components, greatly to the fore in children, matched the kinds of
sadism found in adult criminality. Subsequently Kleinians tended to
regard all perversions as a manifestation of the death instinct – impulses
that distort sexuality.

Klein described the precocious development of genital feelings as a
means of dealing with the terrors of the pregenital impulses. The

genital erotization of pregenital impulses mobilizes the reassuring genital impulses of love and creativity, but the process of premature genitalizing runs the risk of creating adult sexual perversions and excited states of destructiveness. Sado-masochism and other perversions, and the addictions, represent one way of struggling to develop object-relations beyond the paranoid-schizoid position, when an excess of destructiveness dominates the personality [see PATHO-LOGICAL ORGANIZATIONS].

Hunter (1954) and Joseph (1971) analysed sexual perversions (both cases of fetishism) and showed the importance of turning to a new object or, rather, away from an old object that had given rise to too much anxiety. Joseph's patient showed pathological omnipotent projective identifications into his fetish, by physically getting his body into it. Moreover, Meltzer (1973) described the enormous variety of phantasy contents of the envious and sadistic impulses involved in sexual perversions. He distinguished infantile perverse sexuality from adult and regarded polymorphous perversity as an exploration, in so far as the child is capable, of the mystery of his own sexuality, his parents' sexuality and the possibilities of identifying with them. In contrast, adult perversion is driven by destructive impulses to damage sexuality, especially that of the parents and their coitus.

Homosexuality: Freud (1911) viewed the human being as innately bisexual, but that an undue degree of homosexuality could be responsible for the development (defensively) of paranoia. However, Rosenfeld (1949) explored the possibility that particularly acute problems in the paranoid-schizoid position resulted in a genital turning away, in hostility, from mother to father. Thus homosexuality is a means of coping with undue paranoia.

Perversion of the transference: Kleinian interest has moved to a technical interest in the manifestation of sadistic impulses towards the analyst (Etchegoyen, 1978; Spillius, 1983). Joseph (1975, 1982) has taken a close interest in the perversion of the transference relationship, a form of perversity that is closely linked with the negative therapeutic reaction [see NEGATIVE THERAPEUTIC REACTION]. She (1982) showed how important it is to spot if the manifestations that appear to be anxiety are really a form of masochistic enjoyment of suffering, and what appears to be a paranoid reaction is really a pseudo-paranoia aimed at creating an exciting situation.

Character perversion: Joseph (1975) also showed the way in which patients engage only partially, and get great enjoyment from keeping the more lively parts of the personality at an unreachable distance from the analyst. Sometimes these perverse relationships in the transference may be accompanied by transient acting out of actual perverse sexual impulses (Gallwey, 1979).

Rosenfeld (1971) and others have drawn repeated attention to the manifestations of wanton destructiveness and sadism towards the analyst, and the ways this is organized as a part of the personality – a *perversion of character* [see NARCISSISM; STRUCTURE]. The internal organization of the death instinct may result in 'bad' parts of the self intimidating the 'good' parts (for example Money-Kyrle, 1969; Rosenfeld, 1971) or the perverse parts of the self may seduce the 'good' parts (Meltzer, 1968; Steiner, 1982) [see STRUCTURE].

Steiner (1982) described detailed case material demonstrating Joseph's (1975) more general descriptions of the way in which apparently good parts of the self could be taken over and used in order to seduce, distort and pervert the relationship with the analyst so that what appeared as co-operative and loving impulses hid secret attempts to control and invade [see PATHOLOGICAL ORGANIZATIONS].

Etchegoyen, Horatio (1978) 'Some thoughts on transference perversion', *Int. J. Psycho-Anal.* 59:45–53.

Freud, Sigmund (1905) *Three Essays on the Theory of Sexuality. S.E.* 7, pp. 125–245.

—— (1911) 'Psycho-analytic notes on an autobiographical account of a case of paranoia'. *S.E.* 12, pp. 3–82.

Gallwey, Patrick (1979) 'Symbolic dysfunction in the perversions: some related clinical problems', *Int. Rev. Psycho-Anal.* 6:155–61.

Hunter, Dugmore (1954) 'Object relation changes in the analysis of fetishism', *Int. J. Psycho-Anal.* 35:302–12.

Joseph, Betty (1971) 'A clinical contribution to the analysis of a perversion', *Int. J. Psycho-Anal.* 52:441–9.

—— (1975) 'The patient who is difficult to reach', in Peter Giovacchini, ed. *Tactics and Techniques in Psycho-Analytic Therapy*, vol. 2. New York: Jason Aronson, pp. 205–16.

—— (1982) 'On addiction to near death', *Int. J. Psycho-Anal.* 63:449–56.

Klein, Melanie (1927) 'Criminal tendencies in normal children'. *WMK* 1, pp. 170–85.

Meltzer, Donald (1968) 'Terror, persecution, dread', *Int. J. Psycho-Anal.* 49:396–400; republished (1973) in Donald Meltzer, *Sexual States of Mind.* Perth: Clunie, pp. 99–106.

—— (1973) *Sexual States of Mind.* Perth: Clunie.

Money-Kyrle, Roger (1969) 'On the fear of insanity', in (1978) *The Collected Papers of Roger Money-Kyrle.* Perth: Clunie, pp. 434–41.

Rosenfeld, Herbert (1949) 'Remarks on the relation of male homosexuality to paranoia, paranoid anxiety and narcissism', *Int. J. Psycho-Anal.* 30:36–47; republished (1965) in Herbert Rosenfeld, *Psychotic States.* Hogarth, pp. 34–51.

—— (1971) 'A clinical approach to the psycho-analytical theory of the life and death instincts', *Int. J. Psycho-Anal.* 52:169–78.

Spillius, Elizabeth Bott (1983) 'Some developments from the work of Melanie Klein', *Int. J. Psycho-Anal.* 64:321–32.

Steiner, John (1982) 'Perverse relationships between parts of the self: a clinical illustration', *Int. J. Psycho-Anal.* 63:241–52.

Play

Klein developed a method of analysing children based on observing their play which she analysed as if it were comparable to the free associations of adults and to dreams [see 1. TECHNIQUE]. She was criticized for this by Anna Freud on the grounds that the child has a different purpose behind his play from the adult's purpose in free association. The latter, Anna Freud contended, resulted from a co-operation with the analyst in the psychoanalytic venture, whereas the child cannot understand the purpose of psychoanalysis. Klein responded to this by showing (a) that both play and free associations are comparable symbolic expressions of the content of the mind, and (b) that the child, from the first interpretation, has an understanding (an unconscious understanding) of the nature of psychoanalysis [see CHILD ANALYSIS].

At the outset she modelled her views on Freud's interest in children's play:

> in their play children repeat everything that has made a great impression on them in real life, and in doing so they abreact the strength of the impression and, as one might put it, make themselves masters of the situation. But on the other hand it is obvious that all their play is influenced by a wish that dominates them the whole of the time – the wish to be grown up and to be able to do what grown-up people do. It can also be observed that the unpleasurable nature of an experience does not always unsuit it for play. If a doctor looks down a child's throat or carries out some small operation on him, we may be quite sure that these frightening experiences will be the subject of the next game; but we must not in that connection overlook the fact that there is a yield of pleasure from another source. As the child passes over from the passivity of the experience to the activity of the game, he hands on the disagreeable experience to one of his playmates and in this way revenges himself on a substitute. (Freud, 1920, p. 17)

The emphasis here is upon the importance of play in mastering the internal world of the child. That aspect of Freud's descriptions that recognized the turning of a passive experience into an active one was taken up by Waelder (1933) and Anna Freud (1936).

Under the stimulus of controversy with Anna Freud, Klein (1926, 1929) was at pains to elucidate the processes involved in child's play. She regarded the urge to play as composed of a number of ingredients, most of which are indicated or hinted at in the passage from Freud above:

(i) the human mind thinks from the outset in terms of objects in relation to each other and to the subject;

(ii) the child seeks relief from the disasters of his internal world through externalizing the worst persecuting situations into the external world;

(iii) part of the child's natural development is to seek new objects as substitutes for earlier ones, and toys and playmates are one of the forms of practising symbolization of this kind; and

(iv) the turning to new objects is also driven by the conflicts with the early object, so that respite is gained by finding a new object (a symbol).

These processes are unconscious ones and represent the mind of the child struggling with the difficulties posed by its impulses and its objects. Play, in Klein's view, was a serious business for the child and not merely a trivial enjoyment, nor just an exercise in mastering the physical environment.

See PERSONIFICATION; CRIMINALITY; EXTERNALIZATION; CREAT-IVITY

Freud, Anna (1936) *The Ego and the Mechanisms of Defence.* Hogarth.
Freud, Sigmund (1920) *Beyond the Pleasure Principle. S.E. 18*, pp. 7–64.
Klein, Melanie (1926) 'The psychological principles of early analysis'. *WMK 1*, pp. 128–38.
—— (1929) 'Personification in the play of children'. *WMK 1*, pp. 199–209.
Waelder, Robert (1933) 'The psycho-analytic theory of play', *Psycho-Anal. Q.* 2:208–24.

Play technique See 1. TECHNIQUE

Poisoning
One of the innate unconscious phantasies at the oral level is of poisoning mother's milk (or creativity) by attacking and invading her breasts [see 13. PROJECTIVE IDENTIFICATION]. It is also then feared that the object will put poison into the subject in retaliation [see PARANOIA].

See 12. ENVY; BAD OBJECT

Position
Klein adopted the term 'position' to give a different emphasis to her model of development. She wanted to get away from the idea of stages or phases of development, which she had shown were not clear-cut but overlapping and fluctuating. A position is a constellation of anxieties, defences, object-relations and impulses. She first began to use the term in this sense in 1935 when

she described the *depressive position* [see 10. DEPRESSIVE POSITION].
Previously the term had referred to libidinal positions [see LIBIDO] –
homosexual, heterosexual, etc. (see, for instance, Klein, 1928, p. 186).

Position and object-relations: The term 'position' describes the characteristic posture that the ego takes up with respect to its objects.
Although Klein continued to use the terms 'oral', 'anal', 'phallic', etc.,
these refer increasingly to kinds of instinctual impulses rather than
stages – to typical unconscious phantasies [see 2. UNCONSCIOUS
PHANTASY] rather than strict periods of development. In fact her
observations had led her to modify considerably the classical timetable
of development by putting the origins of the Oedipus complex and the
superego way back into the first year of life. She wanted to convey, with
the idea of position, a much more flexible to-and-fro process between
one and the other than is normally meant by regression to fixation
points in the developmental phases [see Ps-D]. She wanted also to
convey, with the term 'position', an emphasis on relationships.
Working with children, she was much more familiar with the way in
which objects were placed and manipulated by the ego.

Position or defensive structure: At first Klein used the term 'position'
freely and described a paranoid position, a manic position and an
obsessional position as well as the depressive position. Later, however,
she restricted the use of the term: the 'paranoid', 'manic' and
'obsessional' positions were dropped as she recognized that they
referred simply to typical structures of defences against anxieties; for
Klein these 'positions' denoted pathological configurations (Meltzer,
1978). Later the two fundamental positions – the depressive position,
with depressive anxiety, and the paranoid-schizoid position [see 11.
PARANOID-SCHIZOID POSITION], with persecutory anxiety – had
developmental significance.

Psychotic positions: The change of the term from a pathological to a
developmental use led to confusions over Klein's meaning. Many read
her as suggesting that children were normally psychotic. She was at
pains to correct this:

> In my former work I have described the psychotic anxieties and
> mechanisms of the child in terms of phases of development . . . But
> since in normal development the psychotic anxieties and mechan-
> isms never solely predominate (a fact which, of course, I have
> emphasized) the term psychotic phases is not really satisfactory. I
> am now using the term 'position' . . . It seems to me easier to
> associate with this term . . . the differences between the develop-
> mental psychotic anxieties of the child and the psychoses of the
> adult: e.g. the quick changeover that occurs from a persecution-

anxiety or depressed feeling to a normal attitude – a changeover
that is so characteristic for the child. (Klein, 1935, p. 276n)

The term position, she thought, would indicate a point of regressive
attraction in the psychotic rather than frank psychosis. Thus she called
these the psychotic positions to be contrasted with the libidinal
positions, because they were concerned with the primitive and violent
methods of dealing with the manifestations of the death instinct.

Klein, Melanie (1928) 'Early stages of the Oedipus complex'. *WMK* 1,
   pp. 186–98.
—— (1935) 'A contribution to the psychogenesis of manic-depressive states'.
   WMK 1, pp. 262–89.
Meltzer, Donald (1978) *The Kleinian Development: Part II, Richard Week-by-
   Week*. Perth: Clunie.

Pre-conception

Though much less so than the
young of other species, the human
infant is born with inherent capabilities [see INNATE KNOWLEDGE].
One of these is the ability to have psychological experiences. When a
baby's face is touched his head turns, and he sucks. This potentiality is
available from the start, and any potentiality to experience those events
psychologically will be equally inherent. What sort of psychological
entity is that inherent potentiality? Assuming that the newborn is
capable of experiences, what is the experience of the suckling reflex
before it has happened for the first time? Bion introduced the idea of a
pre-conception, a psychological entity waiting for a realization that will
'mate' with it. The 'unexperienced' pre-conception mated with a
realization produces a *conception*, and from this thoughts and thinking
can develop.

See CONTAINING; BION; 13. PROJECTIVE IDENTIFICATION; THINK-
ING

Primal scene

Freud used the term 'primal scene' to
denote the infant or child's experience
of the parental couple in intercourse. Typically, he was concerned with
the actual witnessing by the child of the parents' copulation. The
exhaustive detail in his analysis of the Wolf man (Freud, 1918)
concerned the patient's trauma at sleeping in his parents' bedroom on
holiday, the mystifying phantasies that the patient had about it, the
wishes to identify with one or the other or both parents and, in
particular, the attempts actually to date it in the patient's infancy. This
case history was published at about the time when Klein was becoming
interested in analysis, and must have had a deep influence on her.

Klein's earliest work was concerned exclusively with the child's
sexual theories; she soon came to realize the profound distress caused

by mystification, frustration and exclusion and the intense sadistic
response in even the pleasantest child. For the child's conception of
the primal scene she coined her own term, *the combined parent figure*
[see COMBINED PARENT FIGURE].

This figure is entirely a phantasy, but the effects of the phantasy of
attacking mother's body, where the child believes that father (or his
penis) constantly resides, are actual in the normal and abnormal
development of the child [see 6. FEMININITY PHASE].

See EXTERNAL WORLD

Freud, Sigmund (1918) 'From the history of an infantile neurosis'. *S.E.* 17,
    pp. 3–13.

Projection

Projection was first described by Freud in 1895
and there has been a long history to its meaning
since then. The term first came from optics and the new science of
map-making in the sixteenth century, arriving in the nineteenth
century in the psychology of perception, whence Freud introduced it
into psychoanalysis.

There are various senses in which the the term 'projection' is used:
(i) perception; (ii) projection and expulsion; (iii) externalizing conflict;
(iv) projection and identity; and (v) projection of parts of the self.

(i) Perception: In the physiological sense, certain experiences are
interpreted as projected out beyond the actual extension of the
perceptual organ. Thus although the impact of light rays happens
physiologically at the retina, the visual interpretation is attributed to
some greater or lesser distance in front of the eyes. Similarly, the blind
man walking along with his white stick will encounter an obstacle
through the tactile sensations in the palm of his hand which is grasping
the stick. Nevertheless, he accurately projects his awareness of an
object to the other end of the stick. This is 'projection' as normally
used in the psychology of perception. On the basis of bodily sensations,
the infant projects in the same way an object causing those sensations
[see INSTINCTS; 5. INTERNAL OBJECTS]. Projection is therefore part
of a normal process of interpreting the sense data of the perceptual
system [see ALPHA-FUNCTION].

(ii) Projection and expulsion: Freud (1895) had already noted the link
between projection and paranoia. Abraham (1924), in investigating
melancholia and the importance in this condition of the 'lost object' or
the fear of losing it, recognized that an important phantasy was the anal
one of expelling an object physically from the body. He linked the
impulse for anal expulsion with the mechanism of projection.

(iii) Externalizing conflict: Klein found the mechanism of projection

important in the externalization of internal conflicts in play with external objects (Klein, 1927). This form of projection in delinquent acts confirmed Freud's view of criminals who act out of an unconscious sense of guilt (Freud, 1916).

(iv) Projection and identity: Projection has a primary role in the existence of the ego: 'Projection . . . originates from the deflection of the death instinct outwards and in my view helps the ego to overcome anxiety by ridding it of danger and badness' (Klein, 1946, p. 6). Projection is one of the elemental phantasy activities that locate objects within or without the ego:

> expressed in the language of the oldest – the oral – instinctual impulses, the judgement is: 'I should like to eat this', or 'I should like to spit it out'; and put more generally, 'I should like to take this into myself and to keep that out'. That is to say: 'It shall be inside me' or 'it shall be outside me'. As I have shown elsewhere, the original pleasure-ego wants to introject into itself everything that is good and to eject from itself everything that is bad. (Freud, 1925, p. 237)

(v) Projection of parts of the self: Another sense in which the term 'projection' was used by both Freud (1895) and Klein (1946) was to attribute certain states of mind to someone else. Something of the ego is perceived in someone else. This is characteristic of the way in which homosexual feelings are avoided. They are typically attributed to someone else, and Freud constructed a complex chain of 'vicissitudes': 'I love him' becomes 'I hate him' becomes 'he hates me'. Hatred is thus attributed to the other person. Freud (1914) began a study of the phenomenology of this kind of relating in his paper on narcissism when he described narcissistic object-choice, in contrast to an anaclitic object-choice. However, because Freud had not clearly delineated the object as a field of study in its own right, the use of the term 'projection' became confused; and Klein's usage embodied this confusion.

Klein's usage of 'projection'. Klein used the term 'projection' with many of the above meanings: (a) projection of the internal object; (b) deflection of the death instinct; (c) externalization of internal conflict; and (d) projection of parts of the self.

(a) Projection of the internal object: This use of the term was taken over from Abraham (1924); for example, an infant crying with hunger experiences the absent mother/breast/bottle as an active presence of a hostile bad object causing the hunger pains [see 2. UNCONSCIOUS PHANTASY] in his tummy. Through screaming and crying (and often defecating), the object comes to be experienced as expelled outside the infant's body, where it is slightly less terrifying.

(b) Projection of the death instinct: Klein's view of the death instinct projected (or deflected) outwards means that there is a primary inwardly directed aggression which turns outward against some outside object. The projection of an object (that is, a *relocation of the object*) to the outside is a different use of the term 'projection' from the projection outwards of an impulse (*redirection of an instinct*) towards an external object.

(c) Externalization of conflict: Klein's original observations were of children acting out a relationship between toys in the external world in which it is the internal conflict or internal relationship that is projected into the external world. Prurient interest in criminal behaviour and its legal prosecution may be a common case of externalizing internal conflicts over certain impulses [see SOCIAL DEFENCE SYSTEMS].

(d) Projective identification: This is the more traditional view of projection in which part of the self is attributed to an object. Thus part of the ego – a mental state, for instance, such as unwelcome anger, hatred or other bad feeling – is seen in another person and quite disowned (denied). Klein termed this 'projective identification' [see 13. PROJECTIVE IDENTIFICATION].

Many of these uses cannot be completely distinguished; the projection of the object, the impulse, the relationship or the part of the self involved are all inextricable aspects of the object-relationship.

Omnipotence: Bion (1959) distinguished two forms of projective identification on this basis: a pathological form conducted with omnipotence and violence, and a 'normal' form, without that degree of violence and with a consequent maintenance of a sense of internal and external reality. The pathological form of projective identification, in which there is confusion of self with an object, is to be contrasted with empathy, in which the projector remains aware of his own separate identity [see 13. PROJECTIVE IDENTIFICATION; EMPATHY].

Abraham, Karl (1924) 'A short study of the development of the libido', in Karl Abraham (1927) *Selected Papers on Psycho-Analysis*. Hogarth, pp. 418–501.
Bion, Wilfred (1959) 'Attacks on linking', *Int. J. Psycho-Anal.* 40:308–15; republished (1967) in W. R. Bion, *Second Thoughts*. Heinemann, pp. 93–109.
Freud, Sigmund (1895) 'Draft H – paranoia'. *S.E.* 1, pp. 206–12.
—— (1914) 'On narcissism'. *S.E.* 14, pp. 67–102.
—— (1916) 'Some character-types met with in analytic work: III Criminals from a sense of guilt'. S.E. 14, pp. 332–3.
—— (1925) 'Negation'. *S.E.* 19, pp. 235–9.
Klein, Melanie (1927) 'Criminal tendencies in normal children'. *WMK* 1, pp. 170–85.
—— (1946) 'Notes on some schizoid mechanisms'. *WMK* 3, pp. 1–24.

Ps-D In following Klein's (1923, 1931) view that intellectual development is greatly dependent upon emotional development, Bion (1963) established a theory of thinking [see THINKING] based on the linking of thoughts, which has the significance for the subject of the linking of parents and their organs in the primal scene [see COMBINED PARENT FIGURE]. He developed the model of a container [see CONTAINING]. The conjunction of mental contents forms a network that serves as a container.

In the creative process, thinking involves the dismantling of previous views and theories, with the development of new views. In changing one's way of thinking, the container has to be dissolved before it is reformed. Bion regarded the effort of dissolution as having the quality of a small psychic catastrophe, a going to pieces. It was therefore a movement into the paranoid-schizoid position (Ps). The re-forming of a new set of views and theories is a synthesizing move reminiscent of the depressive position (D). Creative effort can therefore be viewed as a process, on a small scale, of movements to and fro between the paranoid-schizoid and depressive positions. Bion represented this *to-and-fro* process by the symbol Ps-D.

When this happened, Bion thought, it caused intense emotional experiences – so intense that he used the term *catastrophe* about the mental event of having a new thought. His case rests heavily on the evidence of Poincaré's personal account of scientific creativity, one element of which was the search for a *selected fact* around which a cloud of as yet unorganized facts could be organized. Bion thought this an excellent description of the movement into the depressive position with the internalization of the breast (nipple) around which the personality of the infant can become organized.

Klein had described the movements from the depressive position to the paranoid-schizoid position as a paranoid defence against depressive anxiety [see PARANOID DEFENCE AGAINST DEPRESSIVE ANXIETY]. Bion, armed with his view that projective identification may be normal as well as pathological, was able to conceive of a non-pathological move towards the paranoid-schizoid position. The tolerance of a degree of disintegration without resorting to omnipotent primitive defence mechanisms is essential for creative thinking.

Latterly Kleinian analysts in working with severe borderline personality disorders have investigated in much closer detail the fluctuations between the paranoid-schizoid and depressive positions (Joseph, 1978, 1989) [see PSYCHIC EQUILIBRIUM; PSYCHIC CHANGE]. An equilibrium exists between these two positions around which fluctuations constantly reverberate; they are not to be conceived as stages of development through which the personality progresses to maturity or through which it regresses towards fixation points. Instead there is a constant fluctuation between the two positions all through development; and at each stage of development Ps-D fluctuations occur. Development and maturation, therefore, exist in another dimension.

That dimension is the relinquishing of omnipotence, and an acknowledgement of reality external and internal. Though these developmental steps are commonly associated with the depressive position, there are moments of paranoid-schizoid functioning in which omnipotence does not play a large part and normal projective identification (empathy) for instance replaces the pathological form [see 13. PROJECTIVE IDENTIFICATION]. All through life there may be realistic anxieties about the survival of the self (the persecutory anxiety typical of the paranoid-schizoid position) and these may be tackled without omnipotence, an aspect of the personality that is known as *normal narcissism*. Equally situations occur in which the depressive position may revert to omnipotent functioning, in for example pathological states of mourning [see DEPRESSIVE ANXIETY]. One can conceive of the whole Ps-D fluctuation moving forward developmentally as a whole, or at times backwards towards omnipotence and an unrealistic loss of separateness.

See LINKING.

Bion, Wilfred (1963) *Elements of Psycho-Analysis*. Heinemann.

Joseph, Betty (1978) 'Different types of anxiety and their handling in the analytic situation', *Int. J. Psycho-Anal.* 59:223–8.

—— (1989) *Psychic Change and Psychic Equilibrium*. Routledge.

Klein, Melanie (1923) 'The role of the school in the libidinal development of the child'. *WMK* 1, pp. 59–76.

—— (1931) 'A contribution to the theory of intellectual development'. *WMK* 1, pp. 236–47.

Psychic change

All contact in an analysis has an impact on the emotional and inner life of the patient, and it changes his state of mind.

When two characters or personalities meet, an emotional storm is created. If they make a sufficient contact to be aware of each other, or even sufficient to be *un*aware of each other, an emotional state is produced by the conjunction of these two individuals ... The analysand or the analyst says something. The curious thing about this is that it has an effect, it disturbs the relationship between two people. This would also be true if nothing was said, if they remained silent ... The result of remaining silent, or the result of intervening with a remark, or even saying: 'Good morning' or:

'Good evening', again sets up what appears to be an emotional storm. (Bion, 1979)

Betty Joseph (1985) emphasized that there is constantly something 'going on' [see ACTING-IN]. The transference is not a static affair but a lived sequence of conflicts, anxieties and defences. The patient continually attempts to restore his balance [see PSYCHIC EQUILIBRIUM] from this multitude of minute influences that push and pull his inner life:

> The shifts towards taking more responsibility for one's impulses, or away from it; the emerging of concern or guilt, and the wish to put things right, or going into flight from it; the awareness of part of the personality, the ego, feeling able to look at and struggle with what is going on and face anxiety, or starting to deny it – these movements are the very stuff that is inherent in our understanding of psychic change. (Joseph, 1989, p. 195)

The analyst follows these movements in the transference as each new one throws up new anxieties, new defences and uses of the analyst. The meticulous following of the patient's shifts must be non-judgemental.

> We as analysts need to be able to find and follow the moment-to-moment changes in our patients, without concerning ourselves as to whether they are positive, or signs of progress or retreat, but seeing them as our patient's own individual method of dealing with his anxieties and relationships in his own unique way. Otherwise we cannot hope to help our patients to achieve real, long-term, positive psychic change as a result of treatment. If we get caught up in preoccupations about whether the shifts show progress or not, looking for evidence to support this, we may become enthusiastic for what we feel to be progress or disappointed when there is apparent regression; we shall find that we get thrown off course and unable to listen fully; or we may well bring unconscious pressure on our patients to fit in, to comply with our felt wishes, our needs; or our patients may just feel misunderstood. (Joseph, 1989, p. 192)

This follows Bion's (1967) prescription [see MEMORY AND DESIRE]: to have an object that simply follows, gives the patient insight and understanding of his habitual patterns of relationships and defences, and not just a critique of them:

> I think one cannot help patients to break out of the old methods of operating and emerge to the experiencing of this type of psychic reality and the beginnings of suffering psychic pain and get through it, except by following minute movements of emergence and retreat,

experiencing and avoiding within the transference. (Joseph, 1981, p. 101)

The aim is to make more secure an *understanding* internal object; a judgemental function strengthens internal objects of a persecutory nature and the paranoid-schizoid position [see TECHNIQUE; CONTAINING].

This function of a supportive, understanding object enables the patient to face and comprehend the reality of his internal world of impulses and of the state of his objects; and it achieves 'long-term psychic change, in terms of movement towards and into the depressive position; in terms of greater integration of the self and a more whole and realistic relation to objects' (Joseph, 1989, p. 202). It will be 'indicated not only by a broadening and deepening of emotions but by signs of parts of the ego engaging in a new way in the analytic work' (Joseph, 1983, p. 296).

Bion, Wilfred (1967) 'Notes on memory and desire', *Psycho-Analytic Forum* 2:272–3 and 279–80; republished (1988) in Elizabeth Bott Spillius *Melanie Klein Today: Volume 2: Mainly Practice*. Routledge, pp. 17–21.
—— (1979) 'Making the best of a bad job.'
Joseph, Betty (1981) 'Toward the experiencing of psychic pain', in James Grotstein, ed. *Do I Dare Disturb the Universe?* Beverly Hills: Caesura.
—— (1983) 'On understanding and not understanding: some technical issues', *Int. J. Psycho-Anal.* 64: 291–8.
—— (1985) 'Transference – the total situation', *Int. J. Psycho-Anal.* 66:291–8.
—— (1989) 'Psychic change and the psycho-analytic process', in Betty Joseph *Psychic Change and Psychic Equilibrium*. Routledge.

Psychic equilibrium

Arising from work with severe borderline personality disorders, Betty Joseph (1989) has concluded that all patients are attempting to preserve a balance that gives respite from the disturbances of the paranoid-schizoid and depressive positions [see PSYCHIC CHANGE].

The disturbed patients she described have become stuck in some in-between position between the disintegration of the paranoid-schizoid position and the guilt and responsibility of the depressive position [see Ps-D].

These personalities develop in the context of an excess of death instinct. They have managed to struggle beyond the fragmentation and projective dispersal of the personality which is characteristic of the psychotic and the paranoid-schizoid position, to develop certain kinds of stable object-relations. But they have not properly achieved the depressive position and have got stuck in a precarious balance, as Joseph (1981) has called it. Her alternative term, *psychic equilibrium*, has been taken up by Spillius (1988) and Feldman and Spillius (1989). Any form of psychic change [see PSYCHIC CHANGE] or development is threatening and these patients direct their efforts to the maintenance of their equilibrium. The equilibrium is rigidly maintained giving a very flat transference which is difficult to bring to life in the analysis and the patient seems 'unreachable'.

These disturbed patients feel very precarious, being threatened on one side by fragmentation and on the other by the pain of the depressive position. The latter has a very special quality according to Joseph (1981) [see PSYCHIC PAIN]. They resist psychic movement, or change, with strong and highly organized defences [see PATHO-LOGICAL ORGANIZATIONS] which are dominated by 'bad' parts of the self (Rosenfeld, 1971) [see NEGATIVE NARCISSISM].

With Joseph's (1978) careful observation of the material and of the quality of the countertransference, she could detect how the patient exerts a subtle pressure on the analyst to draw him into an *acting-out* with the patient [see ACTING-IN; TRANSFERENCE; COUNTERTRANS-FERENCE; 1. TECHNIQUE].

Feldman, Michael and Spillius, Elizabeth (1989) 'Introduction', in Betty Joseph *Psychic Change and Psychic Equilibrium*. Routledge.
Joseph, Betty (1978) 'Different types of anxiety and their handling in the analytic situation', *Int. J. Psycho-Anal.* 59:223–8.
—— (1981) 'Toward the experiencing of psychic pain', in James Grotstein, ed. *Do I Dare Disturb the Universe?* Beverly Hills: Caesura.
—— (1989) *Psychic Change and Psychic Equilibrium*. Routledge.
Rosenfeld, Herbert (1971) 'A clinical approach to the psycho-analytical theory of the life and death instincts: an investigation into the aggressive aspects of narcissism', *Int. J. Psycho-Anal.* 52:169–78.
Spillius, Elizabeth Bott (1988) *Melanie Klein Today: Volume 2: Mainly Practice*. Routledge.

Psychic pain

Certain patients become stuck in between the paranoid-schizoid and depressive positions and try to sustain a precarious balance there [see PSYCHIC EQUILIBRIUM]. If movement occurs out of the fragile equilibrium, the 'slow emergence from this state brings extreme pain of an incomprehensible type, great distress which the patient often attempts to silence concretely with drugs or alcohol, believing there is no other way of dealing with it' (Joseph, 1981, p. 98). It is often experienced as physically located in the body, yet quite definitely felt as psychic pain. The pain has specific qualities: (a) incomprehensibility; (b) on the borderline between physical and mental; and (c) derived from emergence out of the delicate mental balance towards the depressive position. Psychic pain has a special unknown-ness 'which is unable to be put under headings. The pain is not experienced as guilt in relation to impulses, concern about objects or the loss of an object; it has not this clarity . . . it is more connected with emerging into the real world' (Joseph, 1981, pp. 99–100). It seems to be the kind of problem that is posed with whole-object relations, when development is under the dominance of the destructive impulses (death instinct) [see 10. DEPRESSIVE POSITION].

The immediate response to this pain, by the patient, is to treat it as a signal anxiety and withdraw back into the stuckness and triumph of an unreachability [see TRANSFERENCE; ACTING-IN].

Joseph, Betty (1981) 'Toward the experiencing of psychic pain', in James Grotstein, ed. *Do I Dare Disturb the Universe?* Beverly Hills: Caesura.

Psychic reality See INTERNAL REALITY

Psychological defence
Klein's interest in defences was secondary to understanding the anxiety which underlay them and which drove the defensiveness. She was particularly interested in the way children produced or inhibited their phantasies and play. The inhibition of phantasy was a resistance in the analysis and therefore a defence against those phantasies that were the source of anxiety. She showed how apt interpretation of the anxiety beneath promptly mobilized the phantasy life of the child (Klein, 1920) [see 1. TECHNIQUE].

Defences and psychosis: Klein became particularly aware, probably under Abraham's influence, that the defensiveness involved in these young children resembled the defences Abraham (1924) and Freud (1917) were describing in psychotic patients – projection, introjection and identification.

Between 1924 and 1926, in one particular analysis (the six-year-old girl Erna), Klein found that the presenting obsessional neurosis covered over a real paranoia, and she began to realize that the degree of sadism that she was finding in so many children was not far from the kind of violence hypothesized as fixation points for the psychoses. This idea was confirmed later in the analysis of Dick, a four-year-old boy, in 1929 (Klein, 1930) [see PSYCHOSIS]. In 1932 and 1933 Klein began to regard a certain class of defence as specific against the manifestation of the death instinct, destructive impulses. These were especially implicated in paranoid fears and were therefore linked with incipient processes of psychoses and represented early fixation points for schizophrenia and paranoia (Klein, 1930).

Impulse and defence: Klein's strict distinction between the anxious phantasies that made up the content of the anxiety and the defences against them was not a simple one. She did not elucidate this complexity clearly but closely followed Abraham's clinical discoveries that the primitive defences involved the activity of instinctual impulses – projection depending on anal expelling, and introjection on oral incorporating. Abraham (1924) described these processes clinically in terms of the phantasies acted out by psychotic patients, and Klein could see the parallels in her material as her children acted out their phantasies in the playroom. Phantasies therefore came to be involved in both the content of the anxiety defended against and the processes of defence against these anxieties. On this basis the theory of the ubiquitous nature of *unconscious phantasy* as the basic function of the mind itself gradually developed [see 2. UNCONSCIOUS PHANTASY].

Thus phantasies are developed, unconsciously, to defend against other phantasies – a confusion pointed to and elucidated by Segal (1964). The manipulation of phantasies that protect against anxiety may at first be through stimulating somatic sensations [see 5. INTERNAL OBJECTS; MASTURBATION PHANTASIES]. As Bick observed, these manipulated phantasies may, in the first instance, be provoked by the external object, mother, especially through skin contact [see SKIN]. Joseph showed how these defensive phantasies are mobilized in the transference relationship:

> We can observe phantasies being attached to the analyst, as if forcing him into a particular role, as a constant process going on in the analytic situation, so that anxieties arise, defences are mobilized, the analyst is in the mind of the patient drawn into the process, continually being used as part of his defensive system. (Joseph, 1981, p. 24)

Defences and development: Klein also took up the line of thought started by Freud in 1917 in which he showed that as a result of an experience of a particular psychic pain (loss of a loved object), some individuals incorporate objects into their ego. Later (1921) he recognized this as a more general occurrence and a typical feature of social life. It leads, however, to the interesting result that a defence (introjection) stimulates development of the ego – in fact, with Abraham's work (1924), introjection formed the basis for a theory of ego-development (Heimann, 1952). The ego is composed of a 'precipitate of object-relations'.

There is the risk of some confusion here if a defence is also a developmental step. As Klein proceeded to elaborate the theory of internal objects, the distinction between a defensive aspect and a developmental aspect of introjection slowly became clearer, though the concept of an 'internal object' was, and still is, extremely difficult to grasp [see 5. INTERNAL OBJECTS; OBJECTS]. Heimann (1942) began to distinguish internal objects that become assimilated to the ego and those that remain, as it were, foreign bodies within the ego [see ASSIMILATION] and Klein wrote extensively on the importance of the good internal object as the core of the ego and its stability.

The early ego: These mechanisms are fundamental to the earliest stages in the ego's existence and its experiencing, and they concern the development, or evasion, of awareness of the internal world and the external world, the good and bad in each. Processes of projection and introjection contribute to the building up of a fundamental picture of the internal and external worlds. Processes of splitting and denial have a great influence, too, on the sense of integrity and fullness of the self, or the lack of those feelings. These are object-related processes occurring at a time when classical psychoanalysis, or ego-psychology, holds that the personality is in a state of primary narcissism [see EGO-PSYCHOLOGY]. Primitive mechanisms are thus responsible for the way in which the earliest stages of the ego develop and therefore have a significant role in psychological development as well as defence.

Primitive defence mechanisms and perception: The personality can be said to be taking in from the environment all the time. In the adult this is a process of perception and thought. However, Klein saw the roots of these processes in the most primitive stages as depending on the process of introjection. Because of the omnipotence with which the infant believes his mind works, these introjections have lasting effects by contributing to the sense of actual things being taken in by the primitively functioning mind [see OMNIPOTENCE]. Although in the course of development this level of functioning is overlaid by symbolic thinking, there is a level at which experiences do give rise to actual senses of taking in or giving out which leave the person feeling better or worse for those experiences. Such primitive meanings to experiences live on as part of the personality performed by these primitive functions. Later, Bion (1957) showed that the perceptual apparatus can be the organ for projection (expulsion) in psychotic functioning.

See 9. PRIMITIVE DEFENCE MECHANISMS

Abraham, Karl (1924) 'A short study of the development of the libido', in Karl
   Abraham (1927) *Selected Papers on Psycho-Analysis*. Hogarth, pp. 418–501.
Bion, Wilfred (1957) 'Differentiation of the psychotic from the non-psychotic

personalities', *Int. J. Psycho-Anal.* 38:266–75; republished (1967) in
W. R. Bion, *Second Thoughts*. Heinemann, pp. 543–64.

Freud, Sigmund (1917) 'Mourning and melancholia'. *S.E.* 14, pp. 237–60.

—— (1921) *Group Psychology and the Analysis of the Ego. S.E.* 19, pp. 67–143.

Heimann, Paula (1942) 'A contribution to the problem of sublimation and its
relation to internalization', *Int. J. Psycho-Anal.* 23:8–17.

—— (1952) 'Certain functions of introjection and projection in early infancy',
in Melanie Klein, Paula Heimann, Susan Isaacs and Roger Money-Kyrle,
eds (1952) *Developments in Psycho-Analysis*. Hogarth, pp. 122–68.

Joseph, Betty (1981) 'Defence mechanisms and phantasy in the psycho-
analytic process', *Bulletin of the European Psycho-Analytical Federation*
17:11–24.

Klein, Melanie (1920) 'The development of a child'. *WMK* 1, pp. 1–53.

—— (1930) 'The importance of symbol-formation in the development of the
ego'. *WMK* 1, pp. 219–32.

—— (1932) *The Psycho-Analysis of Children. WMK* 2.

—— (1933) 'The early development of conscience in the child'. *WMK* 1,
pp. 248–57.

Segal, Hanna (1964) *Introduction to the Work of Melanie Klein*. Heinemann.

Psychosis

Freud considered the psychotic conditions (schizophrenia, including paranoia, and manic-depressive psychosis) un-analysable. Such patients occupied themselves narcissistically with their own thoughts and psychic constructions to the complete neglect of the external world, including the analyst. Klein, however, had a different view of narcissism [see NARCISSISM] and could demonstrate the object-relations that are typical of psychotics (Klein, 1930a). These involved enormous degrees of sadism [see SADISM] and confirmed Abraham's detailed work on the fixation points of the psychoses [see ABRAHAM]. There are two phases of Kleinian work on psychosis:

(1) Klein's discovery of paranoia in children; and
(2) the exploration by her and her colleagues of the descriptions of schizoid mechanisms (Klein, 1946) by working directly with adult schizophrenics [see 11. PARANOID-SCHIZOID POSITION; 13. PROJECTIVE IDENTIFICATION].

(1) **Childhood paranoia.** Children's play is full of violent deeds done to enemies and the fear of the same torture and death at the hands of those enemies. Klein took this seriously and viewed it as representing a real sadism in the early years of the child. The analysis of little Erna, around 1925, showed Klein that small children can suffer from psychotic illness: 'As the analysis went on I discovered that the severe obsessional neurosis masked a paranoia' (Klein, 1927, p. 160n). In that analysis, Klein herself, in play,

> . . . had to undergo fantastic tortures and humiliations. If in the game anyone treated me kindly, it generally turned out that the kindness was only simulated. The paranoiac traits showed in that I was constantly spied upon, people divined my thoughts. (Klein, 1929, p. 199)

This is a picture of the world of the child, in which there is no helpful person, only potential persecutors. Retaliatory attacks on the persecutors render them more harmful rather than less, because they are supposed, in phantasy, to be enraged further to retaliatory violence. This kind of vicious circle represents a paranoid state of hostility, with intense suspicion of any 'good' figures:

> . . . a phantasy about how he could manage to achieve a better place in class. He phantasied how he would catch up those above him, remove and kill them, and discovered to his astonishment that now they no longer appeared to him as companions, as they had just previously, but as enemies. (Klein, 1923, p. 61)

The nub of the problem which the psychotic faces and fails to overcome is the quality of excessive sadism, which leads to phantasies of fearful retaliation from the objects and a partial or total cessation of phantasy life (and internal life) altogether. This view of the extreme emotional state of the psychotic was followed up a year later (Klein, 1930a) with a paper on the inhibition of intellectual development, in which she showed that certain words become the nub (fixation point) of crucial aggressive phantasies that frighten the child to the degree that these words could not be learned [see SYMBOL-FORMATION].

Inhibition of symbolization: Being beyond the young ego, the task of coping with the sadistic vicious circles of paranoia may lead to an inhibition of the process of expulsion and therefore of symbolization. The inhibition of symbolization distorts or stops the whole process of ego-development and of the intellect:

> In Dick there was a complete and apparently constitutional incapacity of the ego to tolerate anxiety . . . The ego had ceased to develop phantasy-life and to establish a relation to reality. After a feeble beginning, symbol-formation in this child had come to a standstill. (Klein, 1930a, p. 224)

The degree of sadism that she was finding in so many children was not far from the kind of violence hypothesized as fixation points for the psychoses. Dick's severe inhibition in his use of symbols is a typical phenomenon found in the clinical picture of schizophrenia:

> . . . it was characterized by an almost complete absence of affect and

anxiety, a very considerable degree of withdrawal from reality, and of inaccessibility, a lack of emotional *rapport*, negativistic behaviour, alternating with signs of automatic obedience, indifference to pain, perseveration – all symptoms which are characteristic of dementia praecox. (Klein, 1930a, p. 230)

Klein was enthusiastic that these discoveries were important for psychiatry and the eventual treatment of severe mental illness (psychosis). She asserted that psychosis in children is much commoner than hitherto realized and that it frequently passes the notice even of parents:

In my opinion schizophrenia is more common in childhood than is usually supposed . . . and I think that one of the chief tasks of the children's analyst is to discover and cure psychosis in children. (Klein, 1930b, p. 235)

Psychotic defences: Because of the intensity and primitiveness of the paranoia Klein believed she had discovered a new level of mental operation and the earliest of developmental problems. She thought there were specific defences that operate against this level of anxiety, aggression and fear (as opposed to defences against the libido). She called these the primitive defence mechanisms or psychotic defences [see 9. PRIMITIVE DEFENCE MECHANISMS]. These mechanisms include splitting, denial, idealization, projection, introjection and identification. They are mostly suffused with omnipotence and carried out with great violence in phantasy [see OMNIPOTENCE].

When Klein described 'psychotic' *phases* in the development of children she was accused of regarding all children as psychotic. However, her descriptions are clear – children suffering from childhood schizophrenia are in the grip of sadistic impulses, and inextricably caught in the endless vicious circles to which the omnipotent defences against sadism give rise [see PARANOIA]. She defended herself against the criticism with the assertion that she was merely describing the *fixation points* for psychosis.

(2) **Schizophrenia.** Klein's original emphasis on manic-depressive illness was rectified by Fairbairn's challenge to understand the schizoid conditions (Klein, 1946). During the course of her ensuing interest in adult schizophrenics she described projective identification and the paranoid-schizoid position. All these conditions were particularly connected with the problem of sadism and retaliation.

During the 1940s Klein, together with certain colleagues, studied schizophrenia. Rosenfeld (1947) reported in full the first psychoanalysis of a schizophrenic conducted in a Kleinian manner. He used a rigorous technique, restricting himself to interpretation of the transference (although some of the normal features of the analytic situation, like using the couch, were declined by the patient), and Segal (1950) followed soon after with the analysis of a hospitalized schizophrenic. These patients demonstrated the importance of under-standing the mechanisms of splitting and projective identification that are involved in the instability of the ego and its sense of identity, in the loss of affect, in cognitive defects, and in the impairment of normal symbol-formation – as well as the importance of a strict technique of analysis of the transference [see 13. PROJECTIVE IDENTIFICATION; SYMBOL-FORMATION].

Splitting and psychosis: Rosenfeld described a schizoid patient who became involved with the husband of her best friend, when he had a breakdown while his wife was away having a second child. When the man friend tried to seduce the patient, there was some conscious wish in the patient for this, but:

> Her whole anxiety turned on whether she could control *his* wishes and arguments. She repeated some of his arguments to me, and it was clear that Dennis stood for her own greedy sexual wishes which she had difficulty in dealing with and which she therefore projected on to him. (Rosenfeld, 1947, p. 18)

Rosenfeld described other examples of splitting, this time a fragment-ing kind. In talking of an appointment the patient had with a hairdresser, she had muddled up the time:

> ... by leaving home at the time she was due there. She had not forgotten that the journey took thirty minutes, but this fact and the action of travelling had become completely dissociated from one another ... it seemed as if all thought processes, actions and impulses were split into innumerable parts, isolated from one another and kept in a state of division. The patient referred spontaneously to their condition as 'I am split up again' ... The splitting of thoughts and actions showed itself particularly in relation to the analytic situation; for example, her frequent lateness for analysis arose from her dividing up her coming to analysis into many isolated part-actions. Getting up, dressing, having breakfast, the bus-ride to the analysis and the analytic session itself were all acts which did not seem to her to have anything to do with one another. (Rosenfeld, 1947, p. 27) [see SPLITTING]

Confusion: Rosenfeld (1965) showed the extreme degrees to which schizophrenic patients become confused with the analyst or with other individuals and was very explicit in his demonstration of the patient's concrete experiences of getting into the analyst or being ejected. Parts of the patient were experienced as being omnipotently located in – and thus confused with – the object in which they were located.

Projected depression: Similarly, Segal (1956) described affects that have been split off and projected:

> ... in the course of development, schizophrenics reach the depressive position and, finding it intolerable, deal with it by projective identification... Often it will be found that the depressive part of the patient's ego is projected into the analyst, and in order to achieve that projection the patient resorts to careful stage-managing of the analytical situation. (Segal, 1956, p. 121)

This observation was strongly endorsed by Klein (1960), who commented that this is why depression is so difficult to detect in the schizophrenic – and presumably other affects as well. This explains the apparent lack of transference that Freud noted, and his own pessimism about schizophrenics may have been to do with feeling the depression that the patients projected into him.

The damaged ego: With the excessive splitting of the ego, its impulses and its experiences, there are a number of consequences: 'As far as the ego is concerned the excessive splitting-off and expelling into the outer world of parts of itself considerably weaken it' (Klein, 1946, p. 8).

The conjunction of introjection and splitting was equally important for Klein, as the resultant phantasy is typically a flight to the internal idealized object, which, if excessive, hampers ego-development: '... the ego may be felt to be entirely subservient to and dependent on the internal object – only a shell for it' (Klein, 1946, p. 9).

'This weakened ego ... becomes also incapable of assimilating its internal objects, and this leads to a feeling of being overwhelmed by them ... [and] incapable of taking back into itself the parts which it projected into the external world' (Klein, 1946, p. 11). The unbalanced interplay between splitting and introjective and projective processes results in gross disturbances of the ego which make further development very insecure and give a propensity for schizophrenia in later life.

Containing and alpha-function: Bion took some major theoretical steps on the basis of his experience of analysing schizophrenics (Bion, 1967). These utterly original formulations are described in detail under other entries [see BION], since the advance in theory from the work with schizophrenics has had a profound effect on the whole body of Kleinian theory and practice. Bion distinguished a pathological form of projective identification, to be found in schizophrenics and other seriously disturbed patients, from a more normal form [see 13.

PROJECTIVE IDENTIFICATION; EMPATHY]. Together with others, Bion established that projective identification is the basis for an extremely primitive, nonverbal and non-symbolic communication between mother and infant. This has become known as 'containing' [see CONTAINING] and has been important in the development of psychoanalytic technique [see 1. TECHNIQUE; COUNTER-TRANS-FERENCE]. Bion investigated the processes involved in the containing function of the mother [see REVERIE; ALPHA-FUNCTION] or of the analyst in detail and showed what could go wrong with projective-identification-rejecting objects [see 13. PROJECTIVE IDENTIFICATION; CONTAINING; THINKING; ALPHA-FUNCTION].

Bion, W. R. (1967) *Second Thoughts*. Heinemann.
Klein, Melanie (1923) 'The role of the school in the libidinal development of the child'. *WMK* 1, pp. 59–76.
—— (1927) 'Symposium on child analysis'. *WMK* 1, pp. 139–69.
—— (1929) 'Personification in the play of children'. *WMK* 1, pp. 199–209.
—— (1930a) 'The importance of symbol-formation in the development of the ego'. *WMK* 1, pp. 219–32.
—— (1930b) 'The psychotherapy of the psychoses'. *WMK* 1, pp. 233–5.
—— (1946) 'Notes on some schizoid mechanisms'. *WMK* 3, pp. 1–24.
—— (1960) 'A note on depression in the schizophrenic'. *WMK* 3, pp. 264–7.
Rosenfeld, Herbert (1947) 'Analysis of a schizophrenic state with depersonalization', *Int. J. Psycho-Anal.* 28:130–9; republished (1965) in Herbert Rosenfeld, *Psychotic States*. Hogarth, pp. 13–33.
—— (1965) *Psychotic States*. Hogarth.
Segal, Hanna (1950) 'Some aspects of the analysis of a schizophrenic', *Int. J. Psycho-Anal.* 31:268–78; republished (1981) in *The Work of Hanna Segal*. New York: Jason Aronson, pp. 101–20.
—— (1956) 'Depression in the schizophrenic', *Int. J. Psycho-Anal.* 37:339–43; republished (1981) in *The Work of Hanna Segal*, pp. 121–9.

Realization See PRE-CONCEPTION; THINKING

Reparation
Reparation is the strongest element of the constructive and creative urges. Right from the beginning Klein noticed children's distress at their own aggressiveness: '. . . he showed in phantasy as well as in his games a shrinking from, an alarm at, his own aggressiveness' (Klein, 1920, p. 58n). The capacity for pity and the wish to restore everything was clear to Klein all the way through her work – in describing an opera which represented remarkably the typical infantile anxiety-situation, she wrote: '. . . when the boy feels pity for the wounded squirrel and comes to its aid, the hostile world changes into a friendly one' (Klein, 1929, p. 214).

In her 1940 paper Klein showed there to be various forms of reparation: (i) manic reparation, which carries a note of triumph, as the reparation is based on a reversal of the child–parent relation, which is humiliating to the parents [see MANIC REPARATION]; (ii) obsessional reparation, which consists of a compulsive repetition of actions of the undoing kind without a real creative element, designed to placate, often in a magical way; and (iii) a form of reparation grounded in love and respect for the object, which results in truly creative achievements.

Remorse and love: It was a great surprise and of considerable importance to Klein, and indeed quite poignant, when she recognized early on, in her very youngest patients, that there was a lot of feeling for the people, toys, objects with which they played:

> The impression I get of the way in which even the quite small child fights his unsocial tendencies is rather touching . . . One moment after we have seen the most sadistic impulses, we meet with performances showing the greatest capacity for love and the wish to make all possible sacrifices to be loved . . . It is impressive to see in analysis how these destructive tendencies can be used for sublimation . . . how the phantasies can be liberated for most artistic and constructive work. (Klein, 1927, p. 176)

This did not confirm the view that children use objects for the simple satisfactions of needs, exploitatively for the discharge of instinctual energy. Instead children feel for their objects, and their play tells exactly what feelings and why [see LOVE].

It was equally surprising – perhaps alarming – for her to note the enormous degree of violence and cruelty with which children deal with their objects, which give rise to the subsequent remorse and concern:

> . . . we might see the mother cooked and eaten and the two brothers dividing the meal between them . . . But such a manifestation of primitive tendencies is invariably followed by anxiety, and by performances which show how the child now tries to make good and to atone for that which he has done. Sometimes he tries to mend the very same men, trains and so on he has just broken. Sometimes drawing, building and so on express the same reactive tendencies. (Klein, 1927, p. 175)

Klein showed that the impulses of cruelty are turned to pity and remorse. Play is an attempt at restoring the damaged object in phantasy, or often in reality in the case of a small toy:

> . . . where before a small boy has done nothing but chop bits of wood to pieces he will now begin to try to make those bits of wood into a pencil. He will take pieces of lead he has got from pencils he

has cut up, and put them in a rough crack in the wood, and then sew a piece of stuff round the rough wood to make it look nicer . . . this home-made pencil represents his father's penis, which he has destroyed in phantasy and his own whose destruction he dreads . . . When in the course of analysis, the child begins to show stronger constructive tendencies in all sorts of ways in its play and its sublimations it also exhibits changes in its relation to its father or mother . . . and these changes mark the beginning of an improved object-relationship in general, and a growth of social feeling. (Klein, 1933, p. 255)

Obsessional mechanisms: So often did the child show obsessional rituals to prevent or restore that Klein came to the conclusion at first that the obsessional mechanisms were specifically developed against the manifestations of aggressiveness – a view which agreed with Freud's. However, the impulse to restore seemed a good deal more than obsessional prevention and undoing. It entailed great *concern* and activity to put things right, and to mobilize extraordinary creative drives. She came to think of reparation as a significant root in all creative activity: '. . . the desire to make reparation, to make good the injury psychologically done to the mother and also to restore herself was at the bottom of the compelling urge to paint these portraits of her relatives' (Klein, 1929, p. 218). To a significant extent the concept of reparation took over, in Klein's thinking, from the obsessional defences.

Reparation and sublimation: Sublimation is the conversion of libidinal impulses into sophisticated and creative skills. Reparation, on the other hand, is not seen in this way. Characteristically, Klein was interested in the psychological content of the conversion process to which Freud was referring. Reparation is certainly concerned with the impulses but consists of the phantasy of putting right the effects of the aggressive components. There is some suggestion, too, that Klein viewed reparation as a phantasy brought out particularly by aggression, whereas the emphasis in sublimation is on the libidinal or sexual components. However, it was important for her to point out the interaction between the aggressive impulses and the libidinal ones: 'The course of libidinal development is thus at every step stimulated and reinforced by the drive for reparation, and ultimately by the sense of guilt' (Klein, 1945, p. 410). Reparation is a result of the confluence of the opposing instinctual drives rather than merely a displacement of an impulse on to some socially acceptable representative, as in sublimation.

Later, when Klein relaxed her commitment to classical theory, the idea of sublimation fell away somewhat, whereas the idea of reparation developed and became the cornerstone of the maturational processes that forge a way out of the depressive position.

The altruism inherent in reparation is a diversion of the instinctual impulses [see INSTINCTS] into social channels. It is therefore a category of sublimation, a process Freud identified as the means by which instinctual impulses can be channelled into socially constructive applications – in this case guilt channelled into repair.

The depressive position: In the depressive position, reparation moves into a central role. Primarily it is a repair of the internal world that is intended, through repairing the external. It is a powerhouse for mature energy and creativity in the actual external world [see CREATIVITY].

Reparation is called out specifically by the anxieties of the depressive position and, together with reality-testing, forms one of the main methods of getting over depressive anxiety. In the depressive position, the concern is about the fate of the 'good', loved object and is more than just needing to ensure the child's own survival through maintaining a mother to support and care for it – though that is one aspect of the anxiety. Reparation comes out of real concern for the object, a pining for it. It may involve great self-sacrifice in the external world into which damaged objects have been projected. Powerful reparative urges are often responsible for lives devoted to humanitarian ends and lived in great hardship. It is a phantasy that may be acted out with external objects – for instance through going into one of the helping professions.

Failed reparation: Reparation itself may also be interfered with. Where manic defences against the depressive anxieties are operating forcefully there may be extremely omnipotent phantasies, and reparation will therefore be conceived with comparable omnipotence. This is a recipe for failure, since huge efforts are called out to restore extremely damaged objects. States of clinical depression may possibly supervene as the damaged object is identified with and the sense of failure is projected into friends, relatives and the helping agencies.

Such efforts may result in considerable devaluation of the importance of the object and a denial of dependence [see MANIC REPARATION] or an obsessional, forceful control and mastery of the objects. With devaluation or excessive control, the object may be felt to have suffered further damage, giving rise to further depressive anxiety about harming and about the destructive impulses, and hindering the development of the child.

Reparation and development: Reparation, though it is concerned primarily with the state of the internal world and the good object that forms the core of the personality, is usually expressed in action towards objects in the external world which represent the damaged internal object, or which can be introjected in phantasy to support the internal world. It is thus a force for constructive action in the external world. It supplements or supplants the positive attitudes of a simple love relationship, since it is concerned with the troubles or difficulties of the loved object, and it is so in a way which approaches more realism than the simple love relationship with an idealized uncontaminated loved one.

See 10. DEPRESSIVE POSITION

Klein, Melanie (1920) 'Inhibitions and difficulties at puberty'. *WMK* 1, pp. 54–8.
—— (1927) 'Criminal tendencies in normal children'. *WMK* 1, pp. 170–85.
—— (1929) 'Infantile anxiety-situations reflected in a work of art and in the creative impulse'. *WMK* 1, pp. 210–18.
—— (1933) 'The early development of conscience in the child'. *WMK* 1, pp. 248–57.
—— (1940) 'Mourning and its relation to manic-depressive states'. *WMK* 1, pp. 344–69.
—— (1945) 'The Oedipus complex in the light of early anxieties'. *WMK* 1, pp. 370–419.

Repression

Originally repression was *the* defence mechanism Freud described. However, he later (1926) began to distinguish others: 'The significance of repression is reduced to that of "a special method of defence". This new conception of the role of repression suggests an enquiry into the other specific modes of defence' (Anna Freud, 1936, p. 46). A range of defence mechanisms operated by the ego became a major field of study in psychoanalysis (A. Freud, 1936; Fenichel, 1945). Klein's clinical material also drew attention to the operation of other mechanisms, but she was confronted particularly with defence mechanisms that were concerned with the contents of the child's ego and body and the kinds of objects in the world around. She began to think of these as the primitive defence mechanisms and distinguished them from repression. By 1930, she claimed specifically:

It is only in the later stages of the Oedipus conflict that the defence against libidinal impulses makes its appearance; in the earlier stages it is against the accompanying destructive impulses that the defence is directed ... This defence is of a violent character, different from the mechanism of repression. (Klein, 1930, p. 220) [see 9. PRIMITIVE DEFENCE MECHANISMS]

When, in the course of the next couple of years, Klein adopted the distinction between the death instinct and libido, she marked out a comparable distinction between primitive defence mechanisms (ranged against anxiety deriving from the death instinct) and repression (dealing with libidinal conflicts and anxieties).

Violence of defences: Primitive defence mechanisms differ from 'neurotic' ones in the degree of violence in the obliteration of that part of the conscious mind. Klein's emphasis was on the repression (or splitting or denial) of *parts* of the personality, while in classical psychoanalysis repression tends more to affect the *contents* – affective or cognitive – of the mind, rather than its structure. The primitive defence mechanisms severely distort or impoverish the ego. Because they are omnipotent phantasies, there is an actual 'alteration of the ego' when they operate. In repression, which is much less violent, the awareness of internal and external reality is much better maintained.

However, the primitive defences may affect the eventual quality of repression:

> The early methods of splitting fundamentally influence the ways in which, at a somewhat later stage, repression is carried out and this in turn determines the degree of interaction between conscious and unconscious. In other words the extent to which the various parts of the mind are 'porous' in relation to one another is determined largely by the strength or weakness of the early schizoid mechanisms. (Klein, 1952, p. 66)

In her most explicit passage on repression, she stated:

> The mechanism of splitting underlies repression (as is implied in Freud's concept); but in contrast to the earliest forms of splitting which lead to states of disintegration, repression does not normally result in a disintegration of the self. Since at this stage there is greater integration, within both the conscious and the unconscious parts of the mind, and since in repression the splitting predominantly effects a division between conscious and unconscious, neither part of the self is exposed to the degree of disintegration which may arise in previous stages. However, the extent to which splitting processes are resorted to in the first few months of life vitally influences the use of repression at a later stage. For if early schizoid mechanisms and anxieties have not been sufficiently overcome, the result may be that instead of a fluid boundary between the conscious and unconscious, a rigid barrier between them arises. (Klein, 1952, p. 87)

The relation between repression and splitting may be illuminated by the idea of vertical and horizontal splitting. The more severe defence, splitting, divides the mind into two minds, as it were (object, relationship and self in each part) with each separate relationship coexisting side by side (horizontally); whereas repression consigns part of the mind, now more integrated, to an unconscious realm without destroying the integrity (vertical division).

The severity of the splitting lessens as the depressive position takes over, with the consequent greater acceptance of external and internal reality: '... as the adaptation to the external world increases, the splitting is carried out on planes which gradually become increasingly nearer and nearer to reality' (Klein, 1935, p. 288). Repression gradually emerges with the greater impact of reality and the nature of the actual external objects.

Alpha- and beta-elements: Bion's (1962) distinction between alpha- and beta-elements [see ALPHA-FUNCTION; BETA-ELEMENTS] is an altern-ative theoretical framework for examining the distinction between repression and the primitive defence mechanisms, in this case projective identification. Alpha-function is the psychological process that generates meaning from the raw sense data. It gives rise to mental contents which can be used for thinking and dreaming, and are dealt with by repression. However, if alpha-function fails to operate the mind accumulates quantities of beta-elements, unthinkable mental contents suitable only for discharge by means of projective identifica-tion (pathological), and the mind develops as an apparatus for discharging such accumulations [see THINKING].

Bion, Wilfred (1962) *Learning from Experience*. Heinemann.

Fenichel, Otto (1945) *The Psycho-Analytic Theory of the Neurosis*. Routledge & Kegan Paul.

Freud, Anna (1936) *The Ego and the Mechanisms of Defence*. Hogarth.

Klein, Melanie (1930) 'The importance of symbol-formation in the develop-ment of the ego'. *WMK* 1, pp. 219–32.

——(1935) 'A contribution to the psychogenesis of manic-depressive states'. *WMK* 1, pp. 262–89.

—— (1952) 'Some theoretical conclusions regarding the emotional life of the infant'. *WMK* 3, pp. 61–93.

—— (1957) *Envy and Gratitude. WMK* 3, pp. 176–235.

Resistance

Klein described resistance in analysis as the manifestation of a negative transference. In contrast, classical psychoanalysis regarded resistance as a repression of libido. This is a crucial difference, giving rise to radically different kinds of interpretations and radically different expectations of thera-peutic effectiveness. In Klein's view, resistance showed itself as the avoidance of a relationship with herself, or an avoidance of play with toys:

My experience has confirmed my belief that if I construe the dislike at once as anxiety and negative transference feeling and interpret it as such in connection with the material which the child at the same time produces and then trace it back to its original object, the mother, I can at once observe that the anxiety diminishes. This manifests itself in the beginning of a more positive transference and, with it, of more vigorous play . . . By resolving some part of the negative transference we shall then obtain, just as with adults, an increase in the positive transference and this, in accordance with the ambivalence of childhood, will soon in its turn be succeeded by a re-emerging of the negative. (Klein, 1927, pp. 145–6)

Such interpretations were '. . . against the usual practice' (Klein, 1955, p. 124), and she was in dispute with Anna Freud over the handling of resistance and the negative transference [see CHILD ANALYSIS].

Klein studied inhibitions in play in great detail, and she became aware of the enormous impact of aggressive feelings on the development of symbolization and therefore on the whole of intellectual functioning [see SYMBOL-FORMATION]. Through her understanding of the personification of internal objects, and eventually of parts of the ego [see 13. PROJECTIVE IDENTIFICATION], she realized that she was dealing with the kind of defensiveness adopted by psychotics. Psychotic resistance is an attack upon the capacity of the mind to think and know (the epistemophilic instinct) which Bion (1959) referred to as 'attacks on linking' [see LINKING; EPISTEMOPHILIA].

Resistance, equated with the negative transference, represented clinical manifestations of the death instinct [see 3. AGGRESSION]. The concept has come to be more or less merged with the negative therapeutic reaction [see NEGATIVE THERAPEUTIC REACTION].

Bion, Wilfred (1959) 'Attacks on linking', *Int. J. Psycho-Anal.* 30:308–15; republished (1967) in W.R. Bion, *Second Thoughts*. Heinemann, pp. 110–19.
Klein, Melanie (1923) 'The role of the school in the libidinal development of the child'. *WMK* 1, pp. 59–76.
—— (1927) 'Symposium on child analysis'. *WMK* 1, pp. 139–69.
—— (1955) 'The psycho-analytic play technique: its history and significance'. *WMK* 3, pp. 122–40.

Restitution/restoration
These terms were used by Klein in her earlier work, and followed Abraham's (1924) descriptions of the impulse to make good after aggression. Later the term 'reparation' became accepted.

See REPARATION; 10. DEPRESSIVE POSITION

Abraham, Karl (1924) 'A short account of the development of the libido', in Karl Abraham (1927) *Collected Papers on Psycho-Analysis*. Hogarth, pp. 418–501.

Reverie

This term was adopted by Bion (1962) to refer to a state of mind that the infant requires of the mother. Mother's mind needs to be in a state of calm receptiveness to take in the infant's own feelings and give them meaning [see CONTAINING]. The idea is that the infant will, through projective identification, insert into the mother's mind a state of anxiety and terror which he is unable to make sense of and which is felt to be intolerable (especially the fear of death). Mother's reverie is a process of making some sense of it for the infant, a function known as 'alpha-function' [see ALPHA-FUNCTION]. Through introjection of a receptive, understanding mother the infant can begin to develop his own capacity for reflection on his own states of mind.

When, for some reason, mother is incapable of this reverie for reflective meaning, the infant is unable to receive a sense of meaning from her; instead, he experiences a sense of meaning having been stripped away, resulting in a terrifying sense of the ghastly unknown [see NAMELESS DREAD]. There may be various reasons for an inadequate state of reverie:

(i) The inadequate external object: The mother's mind may in fact be cluttered with other worries, and she is thus absent for the infant. Thus the mother's mind is the important component of the external world for the infant [see EXTERNAL OBJECT].

(ii) Envy: The infant may attack the containing function upon which he depends [see 12. ENVY] and thus restrict his introjective opportunities of a good and understanding object.

(iii) The stripping container: The infant may have an abnormally large component of envy which, projected into the object, renders it, in phantasy, an envious container that deprives his projections of any meaning [see CONTAINING; NAMELESS DREAD; EPISTEMOPHILIA].

(iv) Unlimited projections: The mother may be a fragile container of projections and collapse under the force of omnipotent projective identifications from the infant. A function of limiting the projections is performed, in phantasy, by the 'penis inside mother'. If an adequate limiting function is present, it might in turn lead to increased envy, with the consequences described in (ii) and (iii) above [see FATHER].

Holding. Winnicott (1960) described a maternal mental state of readiness for the infant which in many respects resembled Bion's description of 'reverie' [see OMNIPOTENCE; CONTAINING]. However, there are clear differences between the functions of 'holding' and of 'reverie', which derive from quite different theoretical frameworks. The function of Winnicott's holding is to support the infant's unwavering belief in his own omnipotence; Bion's concept of reverie is the maternal attempt to provide a containing function of understanding the infant's reality in order to support his loss of omnipotence.

Bion, Wilfred (1962) 'A theory of thinking', *Int. J. Psycho-Anal.* 43:306–10; republished (1967) in W.R. Bion, *Second Thoughts*. Heinemann, pp. 110–19.
Winnicott, Donald (1960) 'The theory of the parent–infant relationship', in Donald Winnicott (1965) *The Maturational Processes and the Facilitating Environment*. Hogarth, pp. 37–55.

Herbert Rosenfeld

Biography. Rosenfeld, born in 1909 in Germany, arrived as a refugee in Britain in 1935. His interest in chronic schizophrenic patients in British mental hospitals led him towards seeking his own analysis with Klein. He soon became an important supporter of Klein, especially in his ability to make sense of psychotic patients in terms of her later theory. Much of the contents of Klein's paper on schizoid mechanisms in 1946 depended on the work she did with students and analysands of hers who were also psychiatrists, such as Rosenfeld. He established himself as one of the foremost Kleinian authorities on schizophrenia and made continuous scientific developments up to his death in 1986.

SCIENTIFIC CONTRIBUTIONS. In 1947 Rosenfeld published the first detailed case history of the analysis of a schizophrenic, demonstrating the importance of Klein's concepts of splitting of the ego and projective identification, with the characteristic schizoid depersonalization which she had described in 1946. He investigated the confusional states in schizophrenia (Rosenfeld, 1950, 1965), which was a precursor of Klein's concept of envy. In 1952 Rosenfeld described in outline the therapeutic action of psychoanalysis based on projective identification, which was subsequently elaborated by Money-Kyrle (1956), Bion (1959, 1962) and many others.

Narcissism: From the 1960s onwards Rosenfeld was concerned with the nature of narcissism, which in Kleinian theory diverged from Freud's view of a primary state to which the ego may regress. In Klein's view, there is no objectless state (Klein, 1925), and narcissism is a withdrawal into a preoccupation with internal rather than external objects. Rosenfeld later explored the clinical manifestations of the death instinct and the negative narcissism that results [see NARCISSISM]. His 1971 paper was a response to a considerable objection to the concept of the death instinct (e.g. Kernberg, 1969) based on Freud's original view that the death instinct is clinically silent. Rosenfeld's important paper is an account of the *clinical evidence* of the death instinct [see SADISM]. He describes an extremely important ego-structure in which part of the personality is organized for the expression of death-instinct impulses and is manifest clinically as an idealization of destructiveness and an attack on the subject's own good parts. In this he followed Meltzer (1968) but introduced the term *negative narcissism*. This sinister organization of the ego, which perverts the transference and all human relations (Rosenfeld, 1987), has been an element of much recent clinical investigation by Kleinians.

For many years Rosenfeld supervised analysts and psychotherapists in Britain and abroad and developed an intense sensitivity to the capacity of the analyst to understand the patient. He was very interested in sorting out the negative reactions of patients to interpretations which they felt did not quite understand them from their destructive reactions (envy) to interpretations which they felt *did* demonstrate the analyst's capacity to understand and tolerate the patient (Rosenfeld, 1987).

Bion, Wilfred (1959) 'Attacks on linking', *Int. J. Psycho-Anal.* 30:308–15; republished (1967) in W.R. Bion, *Second Thoughts*. Heinemann, pp. 93–109.
—— (1962) *Learning from Experience*. Heinemann.
Kernberg, Otto (1969) 'A contribution to the ego-psychological critique of the Kleinian school', *Int. J. Psycho-Anal.* 50:317–33.
Klein, Melanie (1925) 'A contribution to the psychogenesis of tics'. *WMK* 1, pp. 106–27.
Meltzer, Donald (1968) 'Terror, persecution, dread', *Int. J. Psycho-Anal.* 49: 396–400; republished (1973) in Donald Meltzer, *Sexual States of Mind*. Perth: Clunie, pp. 99–106.
Money-Kyrle, Roger (1956) 'Normal counter-transference and some of its deviations', *Int. J. Psycho-Anal.* 57:360–6; republished (1978) in *The Collected Papers of Roger Money-Kyrle*. Perth: Clunie, pp. 330–42.
Rosenfeld, Herbert (1947) 'Analysis of a schizophrenic state with depersonalization', *Int. J. Psycho-Anal* 28:130–9; republished (1965) in Herbert Rosenfeld, *Psychotic States*. Hogarth, pp. 13–33.
—— (1950) 'Notes on the psychopathology of confusional states in chronic schizophrenia', *Int. J. Psycho-Anal.* 31:132–7; republished (1965) in *Psychotic States*, pp. 52–62.
—— (1952) 'Notes on the analysis of the superego conflict in an acute catatonic patient', *Int. J. Psycho-Anal.* 33:11–131; republished (1965) in *Psychotic States*, pp. 63–103.
—— (1965) *Psychotic States*. Hogarth.
—— (1971) 'A clinical approach to the psycho-analytical theory of the life and death instincts: an investigation of the aggressive aspects of narcissism', *Int. J. Psycho-Anal.* 52:169–78.
—— (1987) *Impasse and Interpretation*. Tavistock.

Sadism

Klein's earliest works (1922, 1923), refer a great deal to the sadism of children and infants. She was shocked by the quality of violence which she found in children's play. Like Freud she took the expressions of her patients seriously and she noted that play, exhibiting powerfully cruel forms of aggression, was often followed by attempts to restore or put right the harm caused by the violence [see REPARATION]. She construed this evidence of violence in young children in terms of the psychoanalytic theories that were current at the time when she was beginning to practise psychoanalysis. Abraham's views were particularly important, and this was one of the factors that made her settle in Berlin in 1919 when she had to leave Hungary. Both Abraham (1911) and Freud (1917) had begun to show the prevalence of aggression in manic-depressive psychosis and had emphasized that the psychodynamics of psychotic patients pointed to a phase in childhood characterized by a very high degree of violence. Both called this violence 'sadism' and connected varieties of it to the oral, anal and genital phases of development [see LIBIDO]. Klein followed their terminology.

The term 'sadism', however, suggests a pathological extreme of aggression, especially sexually linked, but since the early phases of sadism came to be regarded as part of normal development, the use of the term has tended to drop the severely pathological connotation. Instead extreme cruelty is attributed, in Kleinian thought, to the basic instinctual endowment of human beings [see 3. AGGRESSION; INSTINCTS]. The prevalence, therefore, of these impulses of cruel aggression is extremely wide and Klein (1927) thought that criminal behaviour was the tip of an iceberg: merely the part of human aggression that is actually enacted, as opposed to the aggressive wishes and phantasies that exist in everyone. This view was strengthened in 1932 when Klein adopted the death instinct as a clinical phenomenon, and aggression was severed from its direct sexual connections. The term 'sadism' has therefore lost its pathological connotation and tends now to be used in rather a nontechnical sense in order to emphasize the scale of hidden cruelty that lies behind the more ordinary aggressiveness in human experience and behaviour.

Abraham, Karl (1911) 'Notes on the psycho-analytic treatment of manic-depressive insanity and allied conditions', in Karl Abraham (1927) *Selected Papers in Psycho-Analysis*. Hogarth, pp. 137–56.

Freud, Sigmund (1917) 'Mourning and melancholia'. *S.E.* 14, pp. 237–60.

Klein, Melanie (1922) 'Inhibitions and difficulties at puberty'. *WMK* 1, pp. 54–8.

—— (1923) 'The role of the school in the libidinal development of the child'. *WMK* 1, pp. 59–76.

—— (1927) 'Criminal tendencies in normal children'. *WMK* 1, pp. 170–85.

—— (1932) *The Psycho-Analysis of Children*. *WMK* 2.

Hanna Segal

Biography. Born in Poland Segal trained as a doctor in Britain and then as a psychoanalyst, becoming a particularly important member of the later Kleinian Group. She is accredited with the first analysis of a hospitalized schizophrenic with a largely unmodified psychoanalytic technique. She has worked particularly to organize and establish more soundly the Kleinian Group after Klein's death, and has been extremely active in making Kleinian concepts known to those outside the Kleinian Group and outside psychoanalysis.

SCIENTIFIC CONTRIBUTIONS. Segal contributed to the pioneering of the psychoanalysis of schizophrenics in the 1940s and 1950s together with Scott, Rosenfeld and Bion. She was particularly struck by the importance of the disturbance to symbol-formation in schizophrenics (Segal, 1950) [see SYMBOLIC EQUATION]. However, her original observations on these problems had to await proper elucidation until her crucial paper in 1957. She showed that the capacity to use symbols entailed constructing a relationship between the symbol and what is symbolized (at root, a part of the body) which could leave room for a distinction to be made between them. She contrasted this with the *symbolic equation*, in which the symbol and the thing symbolized are not distinguished. Equating symbols and their referents interferes with thought and behaviour in serious ways because of the disturbance of the ability to recognize reality. Symbolic equation results from the use of pathological projective identification, which confuses objects with parts of the self. The whole phenomenon of disturbed symbol-formation, pathological projective identification and a damaged sense of reality is a feature of the paranoid-schizoid position. These papers (Segal, 1950, 1957) were confirmation of Klein's original working hypothesis that the fixation points for the psychoses lie in the paranoid-schizoid position.

Related to the investigation of symbol-formation was an investigation of aesthetics (Segal, 1952). Again, Segal employed the distinction between the paranoid-schizoid and depressive positions to powerful effect [see SYMBOL-FORMATION]. Artistic creation requires a relatively stable attainment of the depressive position, from which the drive for reparation is mobilized into constructive activity. This view was taken seriously and elaborated by the art critic Adrian Stokes (Stokes, 1963). Segal subsequently wrote a series of papers on aspects of creativity (Segal, 1974, 1977, 1981, 1984).

Not least of Segal's important work has been the writing of definitive summaries of Klein's own ideas (Segal, 1964, 1979). In recent years she has been interested in and outspoken about nuclear armaments (Segal, 1987).

Segal, Hanna (1950) 'Some aspects of the analysis of a schizophrenic', *Int. J. Psycho-Anal.* 31:268–78; republished (1981) in Hanna Segal, *The Work of Hanna Segal*. New York: Jason Aronson, pp. 101–20.

—— (1952) 'A psycho-analytic approach to aesthetics', *Int. J. Psycho-Anal.* 33: 196–207; republished (1955) in Melanie Klein, Paula Heimann and Roger

Money-Kyrle, eds *New Directions in Psycho-Analysis*. Hogarth, pp. 384–405; and (1981) in *The Work of Hanna Segal*, pp. 185–206.

—— (1957) 'Notes on symbol formation', *Int. J. Psycho-Anal.* 38:391–7; republished (1981) in *The Work of Hanna Segal*, pp. 49–65.

—— (1964) *Introduction to the Work of Melanie Klein*. Heinemann; republished (1973) Hogarth.

—— (1974) 'Delusion and artistic creativity', *Int. J. Psycho-Anal.* 1:135–41; republished (1981) in *The Work of Hanna Segal*, pp. 207–16.

—— (1977) 'Psycho-analysis and freedom of thought'. H. K. Lewis; republished (1981) in *The Work of Hanna Segal*, pp. 217–27.

—— (1979) *Klein*. Fontana.

—— (1981) 'Manic reparation', in *The Work of Hanna Segal*, pp. 147–58.

—— (1984) 'Joseph Conrad and the mid-life crisis', *Int. Rev. Psycho-Anal.* 11: 3–9.

—— (1987) 'Silence is the real crime', *Int. Rev. Psycho-Anal.* 14:3–12.

Stokes, Adrian (1963) *Painting and the Inner World*. Tavistock.

Self Following Freud's description of the structural model (id, ego and superego) there was a major move towards a study of the ego rather than the id, and the ways in which the ego relates to and uses its objects. Klein's emphasis was on the importance of relationships with objects. She tended to use the terms 'self', 'ego' and 'subject' interchangeably. The term 'ego' (also 'subject') is used as the complement of 'object'. Whereas 'self', she later contended, '. . . . is used to cover the whole of the personality, which includes not only the ego but the instinctual life which Freud called the id' (Klein, 1959, p. 249), the ego is '. . . the organized part of the self'.

Ego-psychology, by contrast, has taken an interest in the ego's role in the structure, and less in the instinctual life from which the objects stem [see 2. UNCONSCIOUS PHANTASY]. The difference between 'ego' and 'self' was sharply made by Hartmann (1950) when he distinguished between the ego as a mental organization objectively described and self as the representation that is cathected in narcissism. The term 'ego' is a technical term thought up by the pragmatic English translators of Freud to enhance the objectivity of psychoanalytic science; it is therefore a distortion of the German 'ich' (I or me) used by Freud, which gives a much more personal or subjective connotation (Bettelheim, 1983).

See EGO

Bettelheim, Bruno (1983) *Freud and Man's Soul*. Hogarth.

Hartmann, Heinz (1950) 'Comments on the psycho-analytic theory of the ego', *Psychoanal. Study Child* 5:74–96.

Klein, Melanie (1959) 'Our adult world and its roots in infancy'. *WMK* 3, pp. 247–63.

Skin

Bick (1964) introduced infant observation as part of the training for student child psychotherapists and psychoanalysts [see INFANT OBSERVATION]. In the course of this she began to notice specific phenomena in the mother–infant interaction which concerned skin stimulation. It seemed that skin contact was the most prominent element in the earliest relationship and in the earliest introjections of the ego.

The first object is the one which gives to the infant the feeling of being in existence – having an identity, we might say, at a later stage of development. Observations of the interaction of the mother–infant pair led her to understand two opposite states of mind for the infant – either a feeling of being in existence with some coherence, or the opposite, a feeling of dissolution, incoordination, annihilation. In the very early days and weeks after birth certain events can be seen to be associated with uncoordinated, restless movements with the limbs and grunting or crying and screaming. These occur typically when the baby is undressed, his face is washed, he is held precariously when feeding is interrupted. Other events reduce the apparent incoordination and distress: when he is carried, dressed after a bath, while feeding or when wrapped in blankets in the cot. These fairly clearly distinguished states are held to correspond to later states of mind which Bick identified as the feeling of going to pieces (annihilation) or containment [see CONTAINING].

For Klein the infant at birth has an ego that can distinguish objects separate from itself, but Bick was much less certain of that as an endowed cognitive ability: the whole ego could collapse, and frequently did in the early days and weeks. Although Klein (1946) did describe the falling to bits of the ego, she did not explain how such an extremely fragile ego could introject and project; these are functions which require a firm degree of ego-stability and boundary. After all, Klein had described the fear of annihilation as a primary experience of the infant. In 1946 she had shown the intricate details of the projections and introjections engaged in by the infant in the process of sustaining the ego and a sense of identity, and protecting himself from the fear of annihilation [see 11. PARANOID-SCHIZOID POSITION]. Bick, however, described this in another framework.

The first object: Keeping the personality together and saving it from falling apart in fragments is experienced *passively* as a function performed initially from outside:

> ... in its most primitive form the parts of the personality are felt to have no binding force amongst themselves and must therefore be held together in a way that is experienced by them passively, by the skin functioning as a boundary. (Bick, 1968, p. 484)

In fact, Bick drew attention to and expanded the very earliest moment of the ego's existence. Klein had variously described the earliest moment and function of the ego as (i) a projection of the death instinct (Klein, 1932); (ii) an introjection of the good object to form the core of the ego (Klein, 1935, 1946) [see 11. PARANOID-SCHIZOID POSITION]; and (iii) primary splitting of the ego to prevent undue envy (Klein, 1957). Bick showed that the baby has to struggle for the capacity to introject and that this capacity is an achievement of both infant and mother: 'The stage of primal splitting and idealization of self and object can now be seen to rest on this earlier process of containment of self and object by their respective "skins" ' (Bick, 1968, p. 484).

The internal good object, described by Klein as the core of the ego in the paranoid-schizoid and depressive positions, has a preceding condition – the capacity to introject at all:

> ... this internal function of containing the parts of the self is dependent initially on the introjection of an external object experienced as capable of fulfilling this function ... Until the containing functions have been introjected, a concept of a space within the self cannot arise. Introjection, the construction of an object in an internal space, is therefore impaired. (Bick, 1968, p. 484)

The first achievement is to win the concept of a space that holds things. This concept is gained in the form of the experience of an object which holds the personality together.

The skin: The infant, in gaining the nipple in his mouth, has an experience of acquiring such an object – an object which closes the hole in the boundary that the mouth seems to represent. With this first introjection comes the sense of a space into which objects can be introjected. Through her observations of the infant, it became clear to Bick that once he has introjected such a primary containing object, he identifies it with his skin – or, to put it another way, skin contact stimulates the experience (unconscious phantasy) of an object containing the parts of his personality as much as the nipple in the mouth does. The skin is an extremely important receptor organ in the young infant: '... sometimes we think of our skin as our most intimate possession, while sometimes it is merely the envelope of our true self and of what is inside us' (Schilder and Wechsler, 1935, p. 360).

In addition, there are nipple 'substitutes':

> The need for a containing object would seem in the infantile unintegrated state to produce a frantic search for an object – a light, a voice, a smell, or other sensual object – which can hold the attention and thereby be experienced, momentarily at least, as holding the parts of the personality together. (Bick, 1968, p. 484)

Leaking: Bick described occasions in which this first achievement of the ego goes wrong; and she gave to Meltzer and his co-workers with autistic children (Meltzer *et al.*, 1975) a theory of the lack of internal space that is characteristic of autism.

Without an internal object capable of holding the personality together, the infant cannot project *into* an external object to act as a container. Then the personality simply leaks uncontainedly out into a limitless space. The infant experiences a dissolution or annihilation which Bick specifically related to the horrors of outer space:

> When the baby is born he is in the position of an astronaut who has been shot out into outer space without a space suit ... The predominant terror of the baby is of falling to pieces or liquefying. One can see this in the infant trembling when the nipple is taken out of his mouth, but also when his clothes are taken off. (Bick, 1986, p. 296)

Schmideberg, in the first fully reported case of a child analysis, had also noted the important '... role of clothing in overcoming paranoid anxiety' (Schmideberg, 1934, p. 259).

Leaking and pathological projective identification: There is a contrast with Bion's hypothesis in which the first object is one that receives primitive communications from the infant, brought about by projective identification [see LINKING; CONTAINING]. Bick described a prior situation in which the capacity to generate phantasies of a containing space is itself acquired from an object. So the communicative form of projective identification would, in Bick's view, depend on the experience of an object that holds the personality together, derived from skin and mouth sensations. Where Bion described the later experiences of an infant attempting to project into a mother who resisted the projections, Bick described not a crescendo of ever more violent projections to force the object to open up and contain but instead a situation where there is no object to give the idea of a container, and projective identification of all kinds is disabled. There is then a phantasy of complete, formless, total dissolution of identity and existence.

There is not an absolute distinction to be drawn between the two states described by Bion and by Bick, and it seems that Bick regarded the one problem as running into the next, depending on how securely the internal containing object has been established; conversely it may be felt by the infant as a partial skin, one that tends to develop 'holes'.

The second skin: Bick thought there was a specific reaction to which the infant resorted when the containing object was particularly uncertainly established. To develop a method of holding himself together the infant generates omnipotent phantasies that avoid the need for the passive experience of the object:

> Disturbance of the primal skin function can lead to development of a 'second-skin' formation through which dependence on the object is replaced by a pseudo-independence, by the inappropriate use of certain mental functions, or perhaps innate talents, for the purpose of creating a substitute for this skin container. (Bick, 1968, p. 484)

Precocious development of speech – providing the sound of his own voice – and a muscular development so that the body is held palpably rigid and 'together' are typical examples. Symington (1983) and Dale (1983), for instance, have shown how important these concepts have recently become in modern child psychotherapy, and Symington (1985) has described some of these manifestations in an adult patient. Work with severely disturbed children (Bick, 1986) and with autistic children (Meltzer, 1975; Meltzer *et al.*, 1975) has led to the discovery of a peculiar phenomenon of 'sticking to' objects in the absence of spaces to project into. This was called *adhesion* or adhesive identification [see ADHESIVE IDENTIFICATION].

There is a similarity between the second-skin phenomenon described by Bick and the phenomenon of the 'false self' described by Winnicott (1960). The false self is a set of personality characteristics, often rather rigid, which are experienced by the individual as not really true to himself but are developed to conceal his own lack of sense of a true being. This underlying lack of identity is related to the experience of annihilation [see ANNIHILATION]. In Winnicott's view that experience comes from a premature experiencing of an external object as separate. In Bick's view the same experience of annihilation comes from a deficient experience of an external object that can help the infant by holding his personality together. The terms 'second skin' and 'false self' come from quite different theoretical backgrounds and therefore point to different implications for clinical practice.

Bick, Esther (1964) 'Notes on infant observation in psycho-analytic training', *Int. J. Psycho-Anal.* 45:558–66; republished (1987) in Martha Harris and Esther Bick, *The Collected Papers of Martha Harris and Esther Bick*. Perth: Clunie, pp. 240–56.

—— (1968) 'The experience of the skin in early object relations', *Int. J. Psycho-Anal.* 49:484–6; republished (1987) in *The Collected Papers of Martha Harris and Esther Bick*, pp. 114–18.

—— (1986) 'Further considerations of the function of the skin in early object relations', *Br. J. Psychother.* 2:292–9.

Dale, Francis (1983) 'The body as bondage', *Journal of Child Psychotherapy* 9: 33–44.

Klein, Melanie (1932) *The Psycho-Analysis of Children*. WMK 2.

—— (1935) 'A contribution to the psychogenesis of manic-depressive states'. *WMK* 1, pp. 262–89.

—— (1946) 'Notes on some schizoid mechanisms'. *WMK* 3, pp. 1–24.

—— (1957) *Envy and Gratitude. WMK* 3, pp. 176–235.

Meltzer, Donald (1975) 'Adhesive identification', *Contemporary Psycho-Analysis* 11:289–310.

Meltzer, Donald, Bremner, John, Hoxter, Shirley, Weddell, Doreen and Wittenberg, Isca (1975) *Explorations in Autism*. Perth: Clunie.

Schilder, Paul and Wechsler, David (1935) 'What do children know about the interior of the body?', *Int. J. Psycho-Anal.* 16:355–60.

Schmideberg, Melitta (1934) 'The play analysis of a three-year-old girl', *Int. J. Psycho-Anal.* 15:245–64.

Symington, Joan (Cornwall) (1983) 'Crisis and survival in infancy', *Journal of Child Psychotherapy* 9:25–32.

—— (1985) 'The survival function of primitive omnipotence', *Int. J. Psycho-Anal.* 66:481–7.

Tustin, Frances (1981) *Austistic States in Children*. Routledge & Kegan Paul.

Winnicott, Donald (1960) 'Ego distortion in terms of true and false self', in D.W. Winnicott, *The Maturational Processes and the Facilitating Environment*. Hogarth, pp. 140–52.

Social defence systems
In the 1940s, during the social mobilization of the British nation for war, there was considerable interest in social psychology. A number of analysts became interested in the way in which the discoveries of psychoanalysis manifested themselves in the phenomena of social psychology. These analysts included Bion, Bridger, Foulkes, Main and Rickman.

After the war these ideas moved in various directions to create *group-analysis* (Pines, 1983, 1985), the *therapeutic community* (Main, 1946, 1977), and a school of *organizational studies* based at the Tavistock Clinic (later the Tavistock Institute) (Rice, 1963, 1965).

The problem of a social psychology based on the concepts of individual psychology is normally that the social group is conceived in terms of an individual. For instance, Freud's early attempt to understand society (Freud, 1913) was as an aggregate of individuals, a sort of super-individual engaged with the phantasies typical of individuals; but he later (1921) laid the foundations of understanding the aggregating bonds in individual psychology with social phenomena growing out of them (Gabriel, 1983). Jaques (1953) took up Freud's ideas of the aggregating bonds: '. . . one of the primary cohesive elements binding individuals into institutionalized human association is defence against psychotic anxiety' (Jaques, 1953, p. 4); and he showed how this results from identifications of introjective and projective kinds:

Individuals may put their internal conflicts into persons in the external world, may unconsciously follow the course of the conflict by means of projective identification, and may re-internalize the course and outcome of the externally perceived conflict by means of introjective identification. (Jaques, 1953, p. 21)

Elliott Jaques's work was central to the development of the Tavistock Institute, as was that of Bion [see BASIC ASSUMPTIONS] and Isabel Menzies, and they exploited Klein's (1946) views on the primitive defence mechanisms of projection and introjection in conjunction with identification.

Collective defences: Jaques (1953) described the way in which individuals may use social institutions in order to support their own psychic defences, so that these institutional methods are collective forms of defence which Jaques called *the social defence system*. They come to be incorporated into the routine life of the institution. Human institutions, therefore, have a sub-culture which is unconscious in the true Freudian sense and which is highly determinant of the manner in which the institution conducts its business and the efficiency with which the individuals address their conscious tasks.

Menzies (1960) used the idea of the social defence system in the 'psychoanalysis' of a hospital system, and showed how certain mechanisms have been installed into the nursing routines of the hospital (the *defensive techniques*) which each new recruit has to learn. These mechanisms, in defending against anxieties in the work, often undermine the therapeutic goals of the institution – in this case, care of patients. The idea of collective defensiveness has proved to be a fertile application of Kleinian thought (Rice, 1963; Miller and Gwynne, 1973; de Board, 1979; Hinshelwood, 1987; Menzies Lyth, 1988, 1989). The 'social defence system' is an important notion that demonstrates the insertion of the individual unconscious, unconscious phantasy and defence mechanisms into social processes without reducing the latter to individual psychology.

de Board, Robert (1979) *The Psycho-Analysis of Organizations.* Tavistock.
Freud, Sigmund (1913) *Totem and Taboo. S.E.* 13, pp. 1–162.
—— (1921) *Group Psychology and the Analysis of the Ego. S.E.* 18, pp. 67–143.
Gabriel, Yannis (1983) *Freud and Society.* Routledge & Kegan Paul.
Hinshelwood, R.D. (1987) *What Happens in Groups.* Free Association Books.
Jaques, Elliott (1953) 'On the dynamics of social structure', *Human Relations* 6:3–23; republished (1955) as 'Social systems as a defence against persecutory and depressive anxiety', in Melanie Klein, Paula Heimann and Roger Money-Kyrle, eds *New Directions in Psycho-Analysis.* Tavistock, pp. 478–98.
Main, Thomas (1946) 'The hospital as a therapeutic institution', *Bulletin of the Menninger Clinic* 19:66–70.
—— (1977) 'The concept of the therapeutic community: variations and

vicissitudes', *Group-Analysis 10, Supplement*; republished (1983) in Malcolm
Pines, ed. *The Evolution of Group-Analysis*. Routledge & Kegan Paul,
pp. 197–217.

Menzies (Lyth), Isabel (1960) 'The functioning of a social system as a defence
against anxiety', *Human Relations* 13:95–121; republished (1970) as
Tavistock Pamphlet No. 3. Tavistock Institute of Human Relations.

—— (1988) *Containing Anxiety in Institutions*. Free Association Books.

—— (1989) *The Dynamics of the Social*. Free Association Books.

Miller, E. and Gwynne, G.V. (1973) *A Life Apart*. Tavistock.

Pines, Malcolm (1983) *The Evaluation of Group-Analysis*. Routledge & Kegan
Paul.

—— (1985) *Bion and Group Psychotherapy*. Routledge & Kegan Paul.

Rice, A.K. (1963) *The Enterprise and its Environment*. Tavistock.

—— (1965) *Learning for Leadership*. Tavistock.

Society

Although Kleinian psychoanalysis has been particularly rigorous about focusing on the intrapsychic
world and has often been criticized for a neglect of the external world
[see EXTERNAL WORLD], it has given rise to a remarkably persistent
tendency to generate theories about the external world and society. In
fact there are no fewer than three major attempts to develop a
psychoanalytic theory of society based on Kleinian concepts. They all
rely on the concept of projective identification, perhaps because
projective identification can be used as an intrapsychic theory of the
interpersonal world. The three theories are: (i) Jaques's (1953) theory
of social defence systems [see SOCIAL DEFENCE SYSTEMS], (ii) Segal's
(1957) theory of symbol-formation [see SYMBOL-FORMATION], and
(iii) Bion's (1962a, 1962b) theory of containing [see CONTAINING].

In addition Bion's theory of basic-assumption groups [see BASIC
ASSUMPTIONS] has strong leanings towards a Kleinian perspective
(Bion, 1961). He wrote his papers describing the basic assumptions
before he became a trained Kleinian psychoanalyst and he did not
pursue the ideas in that form. Part of the basic-assumption idea
(especially the 'pairing' assumption) was transformed in 1970 into a
theory of social containing (Bion, 1970).

Bion, Wilfred (1961) *Experiences in Groups*. Tavistock.

—— (1962a) 'A theory of thinking', *Int. J. Psycho-Anal.* 43:306–10;
republished (1967) in W.R. Bion, *Second Thoughts*. Heinemann,
pp. 110–19.

—— (1962b) *Learning from Experience*. Heinemann.

—— (1970) *Attention and Interpretation*. Tavistock.

Jaques, Elliott (1953) 'On the dynamics of social structure', *Human Relations*
6:10–23; republished as 'The social system as a defence against persecutory
and depressive anxiety', in Melanie Klein, Paula Heimann and Roger
Money-Kyrle, eds (1955) *New Directions in Psycho-Analysis*. Tavistock,
pp. 478–98.

Segal, Hanna (1957) 'Notes on symbol-formation', *Int. J. Psycho-Anal.* 38: 391–7; republished (1981) in *The Work of Hanna Segal*. New York: Jason Aronson, pp. 49–65.

Splitting

The integrity of the human mind was called into question by Freud's theory of the unconscious. It was only very late that he acknowledged the more severe forms of splitting of the mind (Freud, 1940). Klein, however, was confronted very early on in her work with children by the importance of the various forms of splitting. She showed that it was centrally involved in the very earliest defensive manoeuvres of the ego [see 9. PRIMITIVE DEFENCE MECHANISMS].

The experience of the ego going to pieces in this way is a manifestation of the death instinct [see 11. PARANOID-SCHIZOID POSITION].

Early usage. The concept of splitting was taken over by Freud from the older idea of dissociation. The mind was considered to exist in separate parts, explaining the phenomenon of multiple personality. These ideas of dissociation from eighteenth-century philosophy were used by Bleuler in describing, and naming, schizophrenia.

However, Freud moved away from associationist psychology as he discovered the unconscious and the theory of repression. From this very early time psychoanalysis was a conflict theory of the mind. Most mental events could, for Freud, be theoretically understood with the concept of repression without recourse to any further idea of splitting. Very belatedly, however, in a paper written in 1938, he reported that he was aware of the phenomenon of splitting of the ego. In that paper he clearly described the adoption by the mind of two separate points of view. His example was the male fetishist who both believed that the woman had lost her penis and at the same time believed that the woman had a penis (represented by the fetish object). This mechanism is not the result of repression, though one of the points of view may be repressed. It is like the child who believes in Father Christmas and has all the excitement and appropriate emotional response on Christmas night, even though he has learned the reality that it is 'only Dad dressed up'. Equally, the prejudiced comment 'Some of my best friends are foreigners' displays a similar split attitude.

There are various forms of splitting: (i) splitting of the object, and (ii) splitting of the ego.

(i) Splitting of the object: Klein's early work concentrated upon the objects and their vicissitudes. She showed that from extremely early in life objects are not objectively perceived and understood – in fact they are frequently given unnaturally good natures or unnaturally bad ones [see PART-OBJECTS]. Children split their objects so that parental

imagos are separately endowed in their child's imaginative play with wholly good and benign qualities and intentions, or else with wholly bad ones. As a result, splitting became a term employed to describe the way in which objects come to be separated into their good aspects and their bad ones.

Then the introjection and projection of the good or bad version of the object comes to play a major role in the development of the personality [see INTERNAL REALITY]. The integration of such splits in objects into a realistic form of discrimination became, for Klein, the key feature of childhood development. The increasingly realistic perception of objects brings about the depressive position [see 10. DEPRESSIVE POSITION].

(ii) Splitting of the ego: Freud described a division in the ego when he referred to a 'differentiating grade in the ego' (Freud, 1921, p. 130) resulting from identification with a lost object. This explanation of melancholia later became the basis for understanding the division of the primitive ego into the later ego and the superego (Freud, 1923). Abraham, and then Klein, made a different use of Freud's 1917 descriptions and, with the introjection of external objects into the ego as a regular aspect of perception itself, they based the whole development of the ego upon modifications ('alteration of the ego', as Freud called it) resulting from the introjection and then identification of a part of the ego with new internal objects [see ASSIMILATION].

After 1946 Klein became more interested in the *splitting of the ego*. In particular she described the splitting-off of aspects of the self which were feared as bad, usually with the projective invasion of them into an object [see 13. PROJECTIVE IDENTIFICATION]. She also described the minute splitting of objects which brings with it attendant fragmentation of the ego. This latter splitting process, which gives rise to the fear of annihilation [see ANNIHILATION], may have an active quality to it – that is, the ego may fragment itself [see BION] or it may be more passive and dependent on the presence or absence of an integrating object [see SKIN].

Fragmentation. In the 1940s, Klein and her co-workers were studying schizophrenics and were taken back to the phenomena that had induced Bleuler to invent the term to designate a state of multiple splitting of thoughts. Klein had always been more interested in the splitting of emotional states. This came out of her work with the split objects that represented the relationships dominated by good or bad feelings: 'I believe that the ego is incapable of splitting the object without a corresponding splitting taking place within the ego' (Klein, 1946, p. 6). However, Bion (1959) referred to this kind of phenomenon as attacks on the linking of thoughts.

Klein described the schizophrenic fragmentation as connected with a splitting of objects. In this case there is not a clean division of the object into good or bad; there is a multiple splitting. It is a defensive attempt, engineered in phantasy, to obliterate a feared object by fragmenting it to bits. This fragmenting kind of attack on the object results in the ego falling into a corresponding number of bits, each in relation to the bits of the object. She viewed this as the origin of the psychotic's perceived *fear of annihilation*.

Types of splitting. There are therefore many complex types of splitting which can be systematically grouped into four types with the help of two discriminations:

(a) a splitting of the object or of the ego

(b) a coherent split (as in good versus bad) or a fragmenting one.

Thus the four possible types of split are: a coherent split in the object, a coherent split in the ego, a fragmentation of the object, and a fragmentation of the ego. Clearly some of these go along with each other.

Splitting and repression. Klein declared that the primitive defence mechanisms she was describing do not replace the concepts of the neurotic defences, but merely underlie them. She described vertical and horizontal splitting [see REPRESSION]. The splitting apart of parts of the self becomes, in the course of development, a split between the conscious and the unconscious – i.e. repression. In Klein's view the more severe forms of splitting eventually give rise to particularly rigid and impervious forms of repression.

Bion, Wilfred (1959) 'Attacks on linking', *Int. J. Psycho-Anal.* 40:308–15; republished (1967) in W. R. Bion, *Second Thoughts*. Heinemann, pp. 93–109.
Freud, Sigmund (1917) 'Mourning and melancholia'. *S.E.* 14, pp. 237–60.
—— (1921) *Group Psychology and the Analysis of the Ego. S.E.* 18, pp. 67–143.
—— (1923) *The Ego and the Id. S.E.* 19, pp. 3–66.
—— (1940) 'Splitting of the ego in the process of defence'. *S.E.* 23, pp. 271–8.
Klein, Melanie (1946) 'Notes on some schizoid mechanisms'. *WMK* 3, pp. 1–24.

Structure

Freud produced several models of the structure of the mind, notably: (i) the topographical model of unconscious, preconscious and conscious; and (ii) the structural model of id, ego and superego. Following the introduction of the last model (Freud, 1923), ego-psychology concentrated on the structure of the ego's mechanisms of defence (Anna Freud, 1936) and of adaptation (Hartmann, 1939).

A Kleinian structural model: In contrast, Klein paid less attention to Freud's structural model of ego, id and superego. The Kleinian view of the normal structure of the personality concerned the population of internal objects, which is loosely related to Freud's view of the relations between the ego and the superego. Heimann (1942, 1952) began to elaborate the structuring of this internal world in terms of the degree of assimilation – or lack of assimilation – of objects into the ego [see ASSIMILATION]. In normality there is a fluid structure of the personality in which the self (ego) is in relation to its internal objects, identifying with them for shorter or longer periods as may be realistic in the circumstance of the external world at the time.

In 1946, however, Klein drew attention to the structure of the ego as it is affected by splitting. This may conform to the divisions between internal objects identified with, or it may be another form of splitting and dispersal into the external world which is accomplished through projective identification into external objects.

Structure in the paranoid-schizoid and depressive positions: In the paranoid-schizoid position the internal world, both objects and ego, is split and may be fragmented, and the ego's preoccupation is to form an integration of the various part-objects and of the parts of the self.

When the depressive position comes in, the personality structure radically alters to become more integrated, with a good object at the core of the ego. That good object may be damaged or dead and is in relation to helpful or harmful objects populating the internal and external worlds. This more integrated structure – less reliant upon spreading the internal world into external objects, as in the paranoid-schizoid position – forms a more consistent ego-boundary and a more realistic and therefore stable sense of identity and of the contents of the self.

Meltzer (1973) described the development of psychic structure as it moves from the paranoid-schizoid to the depressive position in terms of the increased use of introjection and the establishment of the *combined parents* as a couple in the core of the internal world [see COMBINED PARENT FIGURE].

Internal organization. The development of the personality tends to bring about fairly stable constellations of characteristic object-relations, embodying impulses, anxieties and defences typical of the personality.

In recent years Kleinian psychoanalysts have been interested in the internal organization of aspects of the death instinct (Segal, 1972; O'Shaughnessy, 1981; Riesenberg-Malcolm, 1981; Steiner, 1982; Brenman, 1985). Certain kinds of patients, usually referred to as borderline, exhibit particularly clear stable organizations of death-instinct impulses and defences against them [see PATHOLOGICAL ORGANIZATIONS].

The bad self: These developments have come about as a result of recognizing that the ego can come to organize a *bad self* which is endowed with especially large quantities of death-instinct impulses, which can then dominate the 'good self' by intimidation or seduction.

Meltzer (1968) described an internal seduction of the good part of the self away from a respect for external reality and into a 'voluptuous despair' by a bad part of the self that idealized violence. This idea was elaborated by Money-Kyrle (1969) and particularly by Rosenfeld (1971), who described in further clinical detail this internal 'Mafia gang' that intimidated the good parts of the personality so that the subject identified with a triumphant violence. Good parts of the personality, which could tolerate dependence, gratitude, love and forgiveness, were imprisoned and in hiding, often having apparently disappeared. This overwhelming of the personality by an omnipotent narcissistic organization is typical, Rosenfeld believed, of borderline and frankly psychotic individuals (Rosenfeld, 1987) [see NARCISSISM].

Spillius (1983) has connected this with Bion's (1959) projective-identification-rejecting object [see CONTAINING]. Bion described infantile experiences in which the infant, filled with intense anxiety, attempts to communicate to the mother by projective identification. Part of maternal function is to accept and contain such unpleasant alarm, a state of mind Bion called reverie [see REVERIE]. However, some mothers constantly give their infants the experience of rejecting these communications, which are effected by projective identification. The infant, Bion said, experiences his own projected feelings stripped of meaning and forced back into him. Thus mother comes to be introjected as an internal object [see NAMELESS DREAD]. When identified with, this object becomes the 'bad self' which triumphs in destroying meaning and undermining the capacity to learn from experience.

Character perversion: Joseph (1975), in a now classical exposition, described the structure of certain 'hard to reach' patients who continually reserved their position as observers of aspects of themselves [see PSYCHIC EQUILIBRIUM]. Such a distancing from the vulnerable, dependent parts of their personality presented itself as a stable, permanent feature. Joseph showed, and later reiterated (Joseph, 1981), the quality of perverse excitement at these thwarting and enticing manoeuvres towards the analyst and towards the part of the self that wished to co-operate with the analyst [see PERVERSION].

Similarly perverse internal relations between the parts of the personality were described by Steiner (1982), who showed that the good parts of the personality could be exploited by the bad parts as a kind of masquerade behind which the bad parts could hide. Loving relations hide a perverse quality of secret cruelty in which the bad or perverse part of the personality can take pleasure.

Split-off psychosis: Separating off bad or psychotic aspects of the internal world into a separate compartment was described by Bion in 1957. In this frame of reference the early psychotic objects and anxieties remain deeply split off ' . . . terrifying figures . . . relegated to the deep layers of the unconscious' (Klein, 1958, p. 241). They are apparently out of contact with the non-psychotic self yet remain always available for reactivation in certain circumstances.

Sidney Klein (1980) described evidence in dreams of hard encapsulated objects that contain split-off psychotic parts of the personality, which may occur even in neurotic patients. Bick described the preservation, in the very young infant, of an external rigid 'façade' to the personality. She described 'second-skin phenomena' [see SKIN], the purpose of which was to protect the infant from the experience of a catastrophic going to pieces or dissolving (Symington, 1983, 1985) [see ANNIHILATION]. In order to protect himself from the lack of a holding object to which the infant could adequately relate, various methods of muscular or verbal activity provide a form of focusing his attention into an integrated state – this would normally be achieved by mother's nipple and breast.

Rosenfeld showed how the encapsulated elements of psychosis could be identified with physical organs within the body – 'psychotic islands' (Rosenfeld, 1978). This restricted domain of psychosis was not in fact a new idea, since Freud had described it clearly:

> The sharp distinction between neurosis and psychosis, however, is weakened by the circumstance that in neurosis, too, there is no lack of attempts to replace a disagreeable reality by one which is more in keeping with the subject's wishes. This is made possible by the existence of a *world of phantasy*, of a domain which became separated from the real external world at the time of the introduction of the reality principle. This domain has since been kept free from the demands of the exigencies of life. (Freud, 1924, p. 187)

Bion, Wilfred (1957) 'Differentiation of the psychotic from the non-psychotic personalities', *Int. J. Psycho-Anal.* 38:266–75; republished (1967) in W. R. Bion, *Second Thoughts.* Heinemann, pp. 43–64.

—— (1959) 'Attacks on linking', *Int. J. Psycho-Anal.* 40:308–15; republished (1967) in *Second Thoughts*, pp. 93–109.

Brenman, Eric (1985) 'Hysteria', *Int. J. Psycho-Anal.* 66:423–32.

Freud, Anna (1936) *The Ego and the Mechanisms of Defence.* Hogarth.

Freud, Sigmund (1923) *The Ego and the Id. S.E.* 19, pp. 3–66.

—— (1924) 'The loss of reality in neurosis and psychosis'. *S.E.* 19, pp. 183–7.

Hartmann, Heinz (1939) *Ego Psychology and the Problem of Adaptation*, English translation, 1958. Imago.

Heimann, Paula (1942) 'A contribution to the problem of sublimation and its relation to the process of internalization', *Int. J. Psycho-Anal.* 23:8–17.

—— (1952) 'Preliminary notes on some defence mechanisms in paranoid states', *Int. J. Psycho-Anal.* 33:208–13; republished (1955) as 'A combination of defence mechanisms in paranoid states', in Melanie Klein, Paula Heimann and Roger Money-Kyrle, eds *New Directions in Psycho-Analysis*. Tavistock, pp. 240–65.

Joseph, Betty (1975) 'The patient who is difficult to reach', in Peter Giovacchini, ed. *Tactics and Techniques in Psycho-Analytic Therapy*, vol. 2. New York: Jason Aronson, pp. 205–16.

—— (1981) 'Defence mechanisms and phantasy in the psycho-analytic process', *Bulletin of the European Psycho-Analytic Federation* 17:11–24.

Klein, Melanie (1946) 'Notes on some schizoid mechanisms'. *WMK* 3, pp. 1–24.

—— (1958) 'On the development of mental functioning'. *WMK* 3, pp. 236–46.

Klein, Sidney (1980) 'Autistic phenomena in neurotic patients', *Int. J. Psycho-Anal.* 61:395–402; republished (1981) in James Grotstein, ed. *Do I Dare Disturb the Universe?* Beverly Hills: Caesura, pp. 103–13.

Meltzer, Donald (1968) 'Terror, persecution, dread', *Int. J. Psycho-Anal.* 49: 396–400; republished (1973) in Donald Meltzer, *Sexual States of Mind*. Perth: Clunie, pp. 99–106.

—— (1973) *Sexual States of Mind*. Perth: Clunie.

Money-Kyrle, Roger (1969) 'On the fear of insanity', in (1978) *The Collected Papers of Roger Money-Kyrle*. Perth: Clunie, pp. 434–41.

O'Shaughnessy, Edna (1981) 'A clinical study of a defence organization', *Int. J. Psycho-Anal.* 62:359–69.

Riesenberg-Malcolm, Ruth (1981) 'Technical problems in the analysis of a pseudo-compliant patient', *Int. J. Psycho-Anal.* 52:477–84.

Rosenfeld, Herbert (1971) 'A clinical approach to the psycho-analytical theory of the life and death instincts: an investigation into the aggressive aspects of narcissism', *Int. J. Psycho-Anal.* 52:169–78.

—— (1978) 'The relationship between psychosomatic symptoms and latent psychotic states' (unpublished).

—— (1987) *Impasse and Interpretation*. Tavistock.

Segal, Hanna (1972) 'A delusional system as a defence against the re-emergence of a catastrophic situation', *Int. J. Psycho-Anal.* 53:393–403.

Spillius, Elizabeth Bott (1983) 'Some developments from the work of Melanie Klein', *Int. J. Psycho-Anal.* 64:321–2.

Steiner, John (1982) 'Perverse relationships between parts of the self: a clinical illustration', *Int. J. Psycho-Anal.* 63:241–53.

Symington, Joan (Cornwall) (1983) 'Crisis and survival in infancy', *Journal of Child Psychotherapy* 9:25–32.

—— (1985) 'The survival function of primitive omnipotence', *Int. J. Psycho-Anal.* 66:481–7.

Subjectivity

Within Kleinian thought there is a conflation of concepts referring to the objective experience of the analyst and the subjective experience of the patient. There have been many criticisms of this position – perhaps no other aspect of Klein's work has been dismissed so often. Brierley (1942) pointed out: 'We must distinguish between the patients' language (describing their phantasies) and scientific language – between living experience and our theoretical inferences' (p. 110) [see INTERNAL REALITY].

The confusion of unconscious phantasies of good and bad objects with scientific formulations of Freud's mental structure led Glover (1945) to refer to the invention of ' . . . a new religious biology' (p. 31). Glover's excoriating tract against Klein was occupied with a defence of orthodox theory. He summarized many of the criticisms that he voiced in the Controversial Discussions 1943–4 [see CONTROVERSIAL DISCUSSIONS].

Objective and subjective: The mind–body problem leaves psychologists hesitant about choosing an objective or subjective approach to the mind. We can know a brain by objective research inside someone's head, and to an extent by measuring parameters of their behaviour. However, we can also know about a brain by being, as it were, inside it and experiencing subjectively our own mind. These two portals of entry into knowledge of our 'selves' are not congruent with each other and cannot be mapped one on to the other [see MIND–BODY PROBLEM]. When we come to a psychology of personal experience, as psychoanalysis is, we are caught between (i) describing the phenomena of the patient's mind as we observe someone objectively, or (ii) recording *their* experience through *our* experience as we identify with them subjectively [see EMPATHY]. The first of these is called metapsychology, which is a structure of technical terms forming a theory about human minds. It is the activity of an ordinary science based on the theories of natural sciences such as physics.

The second approach, recording some individual person's experiences (phenomenology), is different in several respects: (i) it is the psychology of that individual person and not necessarily generalizable (or quantifiable); (ii) it is open to interpretation by the observer, who listens to the account of the experiences given to him by the subject; and (iii) when it comes to psychoanalysis, the interest is not merely in the conscious experience that is reported but in the unconscious experiences that are inferred. There are therefore very extensive problems of validity, generalizability and communicability in a 'science of the subjective'.

Phantasy and mechanism: Kleinians use the terms 'introjection' and 'projection' to refer to the subjective experiences of their patients, yet the terms were originally developed to refer to psychological features and processes objectively described in a scientific manner – i.e. Freudian metapsychology. 'Introjection' is an objective term which is akin to the subjective experience of 'incorporation', or 'internalization'; similarly, 'projection' is linked to 'expulsion' and 'externalization'; an objectively described 'ego' is experienced as a 'self'.

A merging of the objective and the subjective is unsettling for scientists accustomed to consider the object as separate from the observer. 'We forfeit', said Brierley, in heated discussion, 'our claim to be scientists and revert to the primitive state of the Chinese peasant who interprets an eclipse as the sun being swallowed by a dragon' (Brierley, 1943).

Two parallel languages appear to exist: (i) metapsychological terms about the objectively known 'facts'; and (ii) a phenomenological language of the patient's personal meaning and phantasy. The term 'introjection' refers to the objective scientific description of a psychological event in which some aspect of an external object becomes part of the ego; the term 'incorporation' refers to the individual's phantasy of taking something in from the object.

It might seem that confusion between different categories of language could be cleared up by a rigorous use of terms: metapsychological terms for objective scientific description, phenomenological terms for subjective experience. However, this does not seem to work properly.

A collapse of the distinction: Any separation of the objective description of the ego from the subjective experience of the world of unconscious phantasy leads to paradoxical questions such as:

> . . . she [Klein] often treats phantasy as constitutive of psychic reality: in it is built up the superego, ego and in it exist all these parts of the self. Yet on the other hand she employs the structural language of Freudian metapsychology, treats phantasy as one ego-activity. (Mackay, 1981, p. 196)

Thus: is introjection part of the ego-functions; or is the ego a product of introjection (the phantasy of incorporating an object)?

When we talk about psychic reality, which language should we use? Psychic reality is the world that is real for the patient, yet how can his subjective world be real for another person? Meltzer claimed that Klein's discoveries meant that 'Psychic reality could be treated in a concrete way as a place . . . where the meaning of life is generated for deployment to the outside world' (Meltzer, 1981, p. 178); and he distinguished the new kind of knowledge that is implied:

> This transformation to a Platonic view is implicit in Mrs Klein's earliest work and it transformed her psychoanalysis at that point

from a Baconian science, aiming at explanations and hoping to arrive at absolute truths, or laws, into a descriptive science, observing and describing phenomena that were infinite in their possibilities because they were phenomena of imagination. (p. 178)

It becomes difficult to keep the languages separate. 'Ego' is a metapsychological term (language [i]), but it is created out of the acts of personal phantasy (language [ii]). The phantasy of incorporating an object has the effect of an objective 'alteration of the ego', experienced by the subject and visible to the observer. The description that the ego is formed from incorporating objects sounds like an objective explanation of what happens – like 'the solar system is formed from whirling eddies of matter'. But describing the formation of the ego by incorporating objects is also a personal phantasy activity about oneself. Even if we keep the term 'ego' (a metapsychological term) distinct from 'self' (a personal term of subjective experience) and reconstruct the phrase as 'the self is formed from the incorporation of objects', we arrive at a description which is not distinct from the phrase 'the ego is formed by the introjection of objects'. The distinction between the languages appears to become redundant. An act of phantasy is itself an objective theory.

The collapse of the distinction between phantasy and objective science arises from the situation in which (a) phantasy is, at this level, omnipotent so that, objectively, an ego that phantasizes is also, subjectively, a self that is in a moment of creating itself; and (b) phantasy is the subjective world where meaning is generated, and the meanings that reside in objective explanations result from the activity of phantasy no less than the meanings of subjective phantasy. Meaning, in the subjective and objective worlds, is the same meaning, even if the knowledge of the subjective and objective worlds becomes two different knowledges and creates two different languages.

The science of the subjective: It is a problem that there is no psychological process or event which is not also experienced subjectively, and in fact formed and moulded by subjective experience and phantasy: 'A phantasy is both a figment and a function' (Isaacs, 1943). This makes the science of subjective experience a peculiar one – one that cannot describe its field of research as distant from, or distinct from, the experience of the researched person: '... we know that in psycho-analysis there is an organic relation between material and technique, and this is something that other scientists reproach us with' (Segal, 1972, p. 159).

'Objective' versus 'subjective' is a simplistic dichotomy when it comes to the human sciences:

... when the mind itself, which is the domain of the subjective, is the object of study, we still have to be objective in our attitude towards the phenomena we are studying; but we have to accept and remember that the nature of the object is to be 'subjective'. (Heimann, 1943)

Mackay (1981) has explored the possibility that Klein's meta-psychology is a phenomenological one, an exclusive concentration upon the individual's own subjective perceptions and experiences. Undoubtedly the Kleinian approach starts there, but psychological experiences and bodily processes are not theoretically separated out. It is not necessary to assert, as Mackay does, that a 'mechanism–phenomenology' dichotomy is inevitable.

Countertransference: The inability to make the scientific language and the subjective experience distinct means inevitably that 'introjection' and 'incorporation' amount to the same thing; but further, to separate the language artificially does a violence to the subject, since it conveys that there is some agent outside the subject and his experience which operates with processes other than those belonging to the human subject which he is studying. The psychoanalyst uses subjective methods (empathy and intuition) for gathering his material. Following Bion (1962) [see THINKING] the thinking work which the psychoanalyst does upon the subjectively gathered data about his patient is also a subjectively determined process of unconscious phantasy.

Validity and reliability: The analyst subjectively experiences his patient and the interaction of two subjective, intrapsychic worlds needs to be explored through the complexities of the transference–countertransference relationship [see COUNTERTRANSFERENCE]. The features of this form of communication between two people about subjective experiences are extraordinarily complicated – a complication which has, to a degree, been put into some order by the concept of containing [see CONTAINING] and by understanding the non-symbolic communication conducted by means of projective identification.

We reach another situation when we have to think about the communication of subjective experiences between one analyst and another. It has been natural to assume that such communications would be conducted, like those in other sciences, by means of a professionally adapted special language of words, the terminology of metapsychology. It is probable, however, that when it comes to a science of the subjective we have to be careful about this by allowing for the same kind of complexity as occurs in the communications (transference–countertransference) between analyst and patient. For the latter part of his career as a psychoanalyst, Bion (1970) was deeply occupied with the problems of communication between analysts about their experiences, as analysts, of the unconscious subjective worlds of their patients [see BION].

The reliability of a psychoanalyst's observations and interpretations are subjectively determined by his own personality. Testing the validity therefore rests upon his own personal analysis which he has received in his own training or subsequently. Such a process of validity is private and he is validated only in the coarsest way by being accepted into a Psycho-Analytical Society. It is understandable, therefore, that validity and reliability are publicly restricted to the membership of a Society or of a lineage of analysts from a particular founding figure. Bion (1963) attempted to establish different and objective criteria for discussing what happens in a psychoanalysis and singled out a number of 'elements' – the grid [see BION], 'L', 'H' and 'K' [see EPISTEMO-PHILIA] and the container–contained relationship [see CONTAINING]. However, Bion does not seem to have been followed in developing this as a method of communication between psychoanalysts. Instead, his concepts have been applied more to clinical practice with patients.

Bion, Wilfred (1962) 'A theory of thinking', *Int. J. Psycho-Anal.* 43:306–10; republished (1967) in W.R. Bion, *Second Thoughts*. Heinemann, pp. 110–19.
—— (1963) *Elements of Psycho-Analysis*. Heinemann.
—— (1970) *Attention and Interpretation*. Tavistock.
Brierley, Marjorie (1942) 'Internal objects and theory', *Int. J. Psycho-Anal.* 23: 107–20.
—— (1943) 'Contribution to the Controversial Discussions 1943–1944 of the British Psycho-Analytical Society' (unpublished).
Glover, Edward (1945) 'An examination of the Klein system of child psychology', *Psychoanal. Study Child* 1:1–43.
Heimann, Paula (1943) 'Contribution to the Controversial Discussions 1943–1944 of the British Psycho-Analytical Society' (unpublished).
Isaacs, Susan (1943) 'Contribution to the Controversial Discussions 1943–1944 of the British Psycho-Analytical Society' (unpublished).
Mackay, Nigel (1981) 'Melanie Klein's metapsychology: phenomenological and mechanistic perspective', *Int. J. Psycho-Anal.* 62:187–98.
Meltzer, Donald (1981) 'The Kleinian expansion of Freud's metapsychology', *Int. J. Psycho-Anal.* 62:177–85.
Segal, Hanna (1972) 'The role of child analysis in the psycho-analytic training', *Int. J. Psycho-Anal.* 53:157–61.
—— (1979) *Klein*. Fontana.

Symbol-formation

Freud's (1900) undeveloped view of symbolization, based on sublimation, was elaborated by Jones (1916) and others. Freud thought that human instincts were particularly modifiable, so that the psychic energy derived from them could be restrained from direct bodily satisfactions by social and superego prohibitions and converted towards social ends – this was the process of sublimation.

The psychoanalytic technique of talking emphasized the importance of verbal symbols: words. In the memory, he said, there are two kinds of representation: the memory of a thing (or experience); and the memory of its name (or verbal designation). He gave a great deal of emphasis to this distinction – the key feature of the preconscious mind (word-presentations) distinguished it from the unconscious (thing-presentation only). In practice it is an important feature of schizophrenics that they cannot keep an adequate distinction between thing-and word-presentations; they thus erode the proper distinction between the unconscious and the conscious systems of the mind.

However, Freud's work was actually only descriptive of the distinction between the thing and its verbal symbol and was more or less all he needed, whilst his technique was a verbal one. Klein's reliance on words was supplemented by the symbolic value of children's play. Thus she regarded children's discharge in play as highly symbolic, a fact that was not properly catered for in Freud's theories, where physical action is equated with a direct discharge of instinctual energy. Klein regarded play as equivalent to dreams:

> In their play children represent symbolically phantasies, wishes and their experiences. Here they are employing the same language, the same archaic, phylogenetically acquired mode of expression as we are familiar with in dreams. (Klein, 1926, p. 134) [see 1. TECHNIQUE]

Dreams were allowed by Freud as a symbolic alternative to words for the discharge of mental energy – allowed, because both words and dreams avoid the recourse to muscular action. Klein, however, showed that play was as symbolic as words, even though it involved muscular discharge. Thus phantasy was not necessarily a method of discharge that is alternative to bodily action, as Freud had been contented to leave it; but phantasy was a profoundly important concomitant, if not mainspring, of physical discharge of energy. The relation between direct discharge and symbolic activity had been reversed.

Klein herself did not make large inroads into understanding the difference between these two worlds (physical or symbolic satisfactions), but she did point implicitly to the importance of further study of symbol-formation as a uniquely human achievement.

Substitution: Klein never made the discrepancy with Freud explicit, since she wished to avoid provoking the orthodox psychoanalytic world. Even so, many people did subsequently complain of Klein's so-called 'un-Freudian' view of phantasy (e.g. Glover, 1945; Yorke, 1971) [see 2. UNCONSCIOUS PHANTASY]. In the earlier part of her career she charted the vicissitudes of symbol-formation and the causes and effects of defective symbolization (Klein, 1929a, 1929b, 1930, 1931).

She showed that from the earliest stages the infant begins to search for symbols and does so in order to relieve himself of painful experiences [see PLAY]. The conflicts and persecution in the phantasy with primal objects (i.e. mother's body) promote a search for new, conflict-free relationships with substitute objects (symbols). Nevertheless, these conflicts tend to follow and often affect the relationship with the substitute object (the symbol), which eventually promotes further search for yet another substitute. In this case she described a process of substitution similar to displacement, which Freud also thought was one of the factors underlying the process of dream symbolization.

Substitution of one object for another becomes symbol-formation in the narrower sense when a non-material object of satisfaction is substituted, by common social acceptance, for a physical object of direct somatic gratification.

Symbols and defences: Klein's interest in symbolization waned as she became more involved in the intricate process of defining the *contents* of phantasies, rather than in the nature of the process of their expression. However, implicit in her earlier work is an embryo theory of symbol-formation. Symbols are a *primary resource* of the ego in expressing, both internally and externally, the unconscious phantasy activity at any given moment. Externalization of these phantasies in symbolic play and personifications was driven by the need to put internal states of persecution away at a distance. Thus Klein was showing that symbols, as substitutes, are a defensive strategy, and the analysis of the process of symbolization is an analysis of defences.

Psychoanalysis was originally an analysis of symbols – typically in Freud's own self-analysis (Freud, 1900). Later the analysis of defences or resistance was emphasized (Freud, 1915). Klein's view of symbolization as itself a defensive manoeuvre profoundly affected Kleinian technique and the understanding of the transference [see 1. TECHNIQUE]. In adult analysis, even the act of verbalizing can itself be a defensive form of acting out in the transference. Thus symbols represent both a primary creative expressiveness [see CREATIVITY] and also a defence against anxiety. The confluence of a developmental step with a defence mechanism is a common finding in Klein's work [see 9. PRIMITIVE DEFENCE MECHANISMS; DEVELOPMENT].

Symbols and bodily parts: The first activity of symbolization – play – is a particularly personal and idiosyncratic process. It does not have the social quality of true symbols. This might imply that Klein was not really describing a true process of symbolization. However, the implication in her work is that though the child spontaneously, without respect to a socially conventional set of symbols, uses his own, they do in fact have social validity through being common. They are common to human beings because they are ultimately understandable as the experiences of the parts of the human body and their relations with each other [see 2. UNCONSCIOUS PHANTASY]. This accepts Ferenczi's view, which Klein acknowledged (1930): 'Ferenczi holds that identification, the forerunner of symbolism, arises out of the baby's endeavour to rediscover in every object his own organs and their functioning' (p. 220). The body parts we have in common therefore act as the basis of the commonality of original symbolic expression, and then as the basis of all further commonality of symbols.

Biology and psychology: Since bodily sensations (giving rise to drives) are represented as relationships with objects [see 2. UNCONSCIOUS PHANTASY] the experiences of parts of the body are objects for the infant irrespective of the actual cause of the sensation. This is a mental world of conceptions, already symbols. When the infant eventually perceives the external world objectively, the meaningfulness of those external objects comes from the investment of the mentally conceived relationships. External objects are already symbols and have meaning only because of the internal ones – for instance, a baby who has waited in a state of mounting frustration to be fed may be seen to turn from the breast when it eventually approaches; what happens is that with his rage and terror he perceives the external object approaching and gives meaning to it by identifying it as the 'bad' persecutor, intending pain and harm.

Inhibition of symbol-formation: The capacity to live in a world of symbols remote from the world of physical and biological objects is the hallmark of human development. The ability to move on to new, substitute objects (symbols) is a move out of anxiety, but it is also a developmental move.

Klein understood for the first time that the schizophrenic's difficulty in forming and using symbols was an inhibition of this *process* of symbol-formation. The capacity to identify objects in a symbolic way with quite different things is of great importance and is the underlying mechanism for the development of intellect. Or – to put it the other way round – as Klein found, the failure to symbolize results in a lack of intellectual development which resembles schizophrenia in adults (Klein, 1930).

Symbolic equation. Segal (1950, 1957), working within the Kleinian tradition, used elegant clinical examples to make an important distinction between two phenomena:

(i) Symbolic representation, in which a true symbol is substituted in the place where the original had been; its special feature is that the symbol is recognized as having its own characteristics separate from that which it symbolizes; and

(ii) Symbolic equation, involving an unrealistic form of projection into an innocent object (the symbol). In the symbolic equation the symbol *becomes* the original, and attracts the same conflicts and inhibitions as the original because of the fusion of the self and the object that comes about with pathological projective identification [see SYMBOLIC EQUATION].

As omnipotent identifications diminish with progress towards the depressive position and towards recognizing a whole object, objects are experienced as having their own qualities and recognized as standing *for* some other object with quite different properties and attributes. Movement away from symbolic equations towards symbolic representation takes place with the depressive position and the increasing awareness of the difference between the internal and external worlds. It is a process of giving up the external objects and therefore of mourning their loss.

Epistemophilia and alpha-function: Later Bion took up the idea of an epistemophilic instinct [see 3. AGGRESSION] and put it alongside the life and death instincts by designating the three with comparable symbols – 'L', 'H' and 'K'. 'L' and 'H' represent loving and hating links with objects. 'K' is the capacity to make sense or give meaning to an experience – or rather, the capacity to experience a sense of meaning in something, to link with it through learning from the experience with it [see EPISTEMOPHILIA]. For Bion, human beings have an innate ability to realize their physical/physiological events as events in a world of meaning – a capacity which he referred to, in as neutral a way as possible, as 'alpha-function' [see ALPHA-FUNCTION].

Bion eventually recast Segal's views on symbol-formation in his own mould. Segal herself says, as a recent postscript to her own paper (Segal, 1979), that she would now see the *kind* of projective identification as important, and that we can look at that in terms of the container and the contained [see CONTAINING]. Thus the function of symbols can be seen as the container for the projective identification of emotional states. Typically Bion, in his later exposition, wrote of the way words are used; for instance a man who stammers, trying to express himself:

> The words that should have represented the meaning the man wanted to express were fragmented by the emotional forces to which he wished to give verbal expression; the verbal formulation could not 'contain' his emotions, which broke through and dispersed it as enemy forces might break through the forces that strove to contain them. (Bion, 1970, p. 94)

The relation between the symbol and what it is supposed to contain may have various modes, including the two that Segal distinguished.

The development of symbolization. There are thus several stages and two directions in which the development of symbols can go. The stages were set out by Money-Kyrle (1968):

> The theory of conceptual development has to be extended to include, not only growth in the number and scope of concepts, but also the growth of each single concept through at least three stages: a stage of concrete representation, which strictly speaking is not representational at all, since no distinction is made between the representation and the object or situation represented; a stage of ideographic representation as in dreams; and a final stage of conscious, and predominantly verbal, thought. (Money-Kyrle, 1968, p. 422)

The progression through these steps is part and parcel of the advance of the subject towards and through the depressive position.

(i) Concrete representation: The moment of awareness of a bodily sensation results in a concrete (unconscious) phantasy of an object that has a full reality.

(ii) Ideographs: The conversion of beta-elements into usable mental contents results in what Bion regarded as 'ideographs' or the 'furniture of dreams' (alpha-elements).

(iii) Verbalization: Ideographs (alpha-elements), if they have been formed, are suitable for creating dreams with, but also for further symbolic development into verbal representations.

Nameless dread. The two steps – between (i) and (ii) and between (ii) and (iii) – depend on whether alpha-function is working adequately. When it is, the above stages may be followed; however, with a failure of alpha-function (Meltzer, 1978) it is replaced by a different function in which meaning is progressively stripped from the objects, which become more and more persecutory; this gives rise to a state of terror referred to as nameless dread [see NAMELESS DREAD].

Alpha-function may fail because of excessive frustration by the actual external world, when there is so little mating of pre-conceptions with realizations that no development of conceptions and a capacity for thought properly occurs at all; or, alternatively, the individual may have such a high degree of innate envy that he cannot link with 'K' but only with a cruel form ('−K') that creates extremely persecutory objects of thought [see LINKING]. In these cases there is a 'reversal of alpha-function' (Meltzer, 1978), and the concepts retrace the three steps from verbal thought to dream ideographs, to concrete representation and perhaps (in psychosomatic disorders) finally to bodily states. This retreat is the cognitive aspect of a retreat from the depressive position to the paranoid-schizoid position [see PARANOID DEFENCE AGAINST DEPRESSIVE ANXIETY].

Psychotic symbol-equations. This phenomenon, explained by Segal and well known in psychotic patients, clearly results from the kind of projective identification, arising from the excessive fragmentation of the mind associated with the reversal of alpha-function. This form of projective identification being suffused with aggression, destroys the boundaries between self and object, depletes the self, and reduces thinking to the concrete stage of discharging beta-elements. This is the *pathological* form of projective identification [see 13. PROJECTIVE IDENTIFICATION]. Autistic states, in which symbolization does not apparently occur, are regarded by Bion (1962) and Meltzer (Meltzer *et al.*, 1975) as the inability to establish alpha-function at all [see AUTISM] or to engage in a process of 'reversal of alpha-function' (Meltzer, 1978).

Aesthetics. Closely related to symbol-formation is the whole philosophical field of aesthetics and how to distinguish what is a beautiful representation from what is ugly or merely pretty. In 1940 Rickman related the disgust at ugliness to feelings about damage to, and death of, objects in the depressive position. He groped towards the idea that artistic creativity is linked with the endeavour to restore life to objects.

This link between the aesthetic experience and the depressive position was greatly refined by Segal (1952). Whereas Rickman had described ugliness as due to the destructiveness, Segal described the depressive position of the artist as one in which there is a depressive pining over the damaged object and at the same time an effort to re-create it through the medium of his art. Art is an *other* world, and Segal says it is the internal world as described by Melanie Klein. Reparation to the object which is pined for gives rise to aesthetically beautiful art [see 10. DEPRESSIVE POSITION]. Or, to put it the other way, the effort to repair the internal object which is the essence of the depressive position is an artistic endeavour, only expressed and made directly communicable in physical form by the artist [see REPARATION]. The piece of art is an externalization into physical reality that becomes a symbolic expression of the state of the internal world and of the work that has been put into it.

Segal contrasted this with manic reparation [see MANIC REPARATION], which gives rise to a slick quality of prettiness, in which the artist demonstrates an easy triumph over the state of his internal world and thus his evasion of the pining and guilt. In contrast to the depth of art that contemplates and mourns the damaged object, prettiness is an apparently easy performance of creativity that does not involve mourning the destruction; it is based on a denial of damage and destruction.

Stokes (1955), an art critic, followed Segal's approach fairly closely and decided that the essence of good art is the peculiar conjunction of fusion with differences. This is an abstract notion of the psychic situation to which Segal was pointing when she described beauty as a quality of struggle to restore an object broken in bits and mourned. The oscillation between fragments and whole is a theme which was later taken up by Bion in describing oscillations between the paranoid-schizoid position and the depressive position which underlay all creative endeavour, not just artistic but scientific as well (Bion, 1962) [see Ps-D].

Bion, Wilfred (1962) *Learning from Experience*. Heinemann.
—— (1970) *Attention and Interpretation*. Tavistock.
Ferenczi, Sandor (1912) 'Symbolism', *Imago* 1:276–84.
Freud, Sigmund (1900) *The Interpretation of Dreams*. *S.E.* 4, 5.
—— (1915) 'Repression'. *S.E.* 14, pp. 141–58.
Glover, Edward (1945) 'An examination of the Klein system of child psychology', *Psychoanal. Study Child* 1:3–43.
Jones, Ernest (1916) 'The theory of symbolism', *British Journal of Psychology* 9: 181–229.
Klein, Melanie (1926) 'The psychological principles of early analysis'. *WMK* 1, pp. 128–38.
—— (1929a) 'Personification in the play of children'. *WMK* 1, pp. 199–209.
—— (1929b) 'Infantile anxiety-situations in a work of art and in the creative impulse'. *WMK* 1, pp. 210–18.
—— (1930) 'The importance of symbol-formation in the development of the ego'. *WMK* 1, pp. 219–32.
—— (1931) 'A contribution to the theory of intellectual development'. *WMK* 1, pp. 262–89.
Meltzer, Donald (1978) 'A note on Bion's concept "reversal of alpha-function"', in *The Kleinian Development*. Perth: Clunie, pp. 110–26; republished (1981) in James Grotstein, ed. *Do I Dare Disturb the Universe?* Beverly Hills: Caesura, pp. 529–35.
Meltzer, Donald, Bremner, John, Hoxter, Shirley, Weddell, Doreen and Wittenberg, Isca (1975) *Explorations in Autism*. Perth: Clunie.
Money-Kyrle, Roger (1968) 'Cognitive development', *Int. J. Psycho-Anal.* 49: 691–8; republished (1978) in *The Collected Papers of Roger Money-Kyrle*. Perth: Clunie, pp. 416–33.
Rickman, John (1940) ' On the nature of ugliness and the creative impulse', *Int. J. Psycho-Anal.* 21:294–313.
Segal, Hanna (1950) 'Some aspects of the analysis of a schizophrenic', *Int. J. Psycho-Anal.* 31:268–78; republished (1981) in *The Work of Hanna Segal*. New York: Jason Aronson, pp. 101–20.
—— (1952) 'Psycho-analytic approach to aesthetics', *Int. J. Psycho-Anal.* 33: 196–207; republished (1955) in Melanie Klein, Paula Heimann and Joan Riviere, eds *New Directions in Psycho-Analysis*. Tavistock, pp. 384–405; and (1981) in *The Work of Hanna Segal*, pp. 185–206.

—— (1957) 'Notes on symbol formation', *Int. J. Psycho-Anal.* 38:391–7; republished (1981) in *The Work of Hanna Segal*, pp. 49–65.

—— (1979) 'Postscript to "Notes on symbol-formation" ', in (1981) *The Work of Hanna Segal*, pp. 60–5.

Stokes, Adrian (1955) 'Form in art', in Melanie Klein, Paula Heimann and Roger Money-Kyrle, eds *New Directions in Psycho-Analysis*. Tavistock, pp. 406–20.

Yorke, Clifford (1971) 'Some suggestions for a critique of Kleinian psychology', *Psychoanal. Study Child* 26:129–55.

Symbolic equation

Jones (1916) and others (Ferenczi, 1912; Milner, 1953) have discerned a particular form of symbolism [see SYMBOL-FORMATION] in which there is an equation of the symbol with the thing symbolized, resulting in the symbol being dealt with as if it really were the original. However, Segal's (1950) description is vivid. For one of her schizophrenic patients:

> ... there was no distinction between the symbol and the thing symbolized ... He blushed, stammered, giggled and apologized after bringing a canvas stool. He behaved as if he had offered me an actual faecal stool. It was not merely a symbolic expression of his wish to bring me his stool. He felt that he had actually offered it to me. (Segal, 1950, p. 104)

> Once formed, however, the symbol did not function as a symbol but became in all respects equivalent to the object. (p. 105)

Segal (1957) later used elegant clinical examples to demonstrate *symbolic representation*, in which the symbol is substituted in the place where the original had been but without losing the real difference of the symbol; and *symbolic equation*, in which the symbol is not distinguished and the innocent object is believed to *be* the thing symbolized:

> Patient A ... was once asked by his doctor why he had stopped playing the violin since his illness. He replied with some violence, 'Why? Do you expect me to masturbate in public?' Another patient, B, dreamed one night that he and a young girl were playing a violin duet. He had associations to fiddling, masturbating, etc., from which it emerged clearly that the violin represented his genital and playing the violin represented a masturbatory phantasy of a relation with the girl. Here then are two patients who apparently use the same symbols in the same situation: a violin representing the male genital, and playing the violin representing masturbation. The way in which the symbols function, however, is very different. For A the violin had become so completely equated with his genital that to touch it in public became impossible. (Segal, 1957, pp. 49–50)

Patient A's equation of the object with the thing symbolized was part of a habitual disturbance to his reality that resulted from the use of the concrete, pathological form of projective identification [see 13. PROJECTIVE IDENTIFICATION]. The result was that the symbol lost its distinction from the original and attracted the same conflicts and inhibitions as the original.

Segal, like Klein and Ferenczi, acknowledged the place of identification in the process. When there is a failure to distinguish between the thing symbolized and the symbol, it

> . . . is part of a disturbance in the relation between the ego and the object. Parts of the ego and internal objects are projected into an [external] object and identified with it. The differentiation between the self and object is obscured. Since a part of the ego is then confused with the object, the symbol – which is a creation and a function of the ego – becomes, in turn, confused with the object which is symbolized. (Segal, 1957, p. 53)

The term *symbolic equation* arises from a defensive fusion of self and object, and object and symbol – a fusion brought about by pathological projective identification.

SYMBOLS IN THE DEPRESSIVE POSITION. As the depressive position takes over from the paranoid-schizoid, the object begins to be a whole object, recognized more realistically for what it is. Thus the object becomes more distinguished from the ego and there is a growing differentiation of the internal and external worlds and objects. This gives rise to the curiously ambiguous quality of symbols in which they are recognized as having their own qualities but *at the same time* recognized as standing for some other object with quite different properties and attributes.

The important steps in this movement to recognize the symbol as separate are:

(i) the giving up of omnipotent forms of identification which deny separateness;

(ii) the consequent mourning of objects that disappear, with the willing result that representations of them can be tolerated; and

(iii) the increased awareness of internal reality and external reality and the actual identity of objects.

Thus the object that *represents* can be distinguished from an object omnipotently *identified with*.

The internalization of these true symbols, Segal indicated, is a great asset in the depressive position, because they assist in re-creating the damaged internal object and therefore have a key relation to reparation, being a support to the repair of the internal world, which, in the course of the depressive position, is so radically converted to an internal world of symbols, and of verbal thought and relations. We now know the mature internal world to be greatly influenced by the structure of language.

Symbolic equation and containing: In 1978 Segal explicitly showed how true symbols and the symbolic equation relate respectively to normal and pathological projective identification and to successful and unsuccessful containment: 'The symbolic equation is used to deny the separateness between the subject and the object. [Whereas the true] symbol is used to overcome an *accepted* loss' (Segal, 1978, p. 316). The defensive (pathological) use of projective identification is carried on to such an extent that the self and object fuse, with the subsequent equation of symbol and object symbolized (symbolic equation).

Segal went on to show how this affects the development of verbal symbols:

> Verbalization can be looked at from the angle of the relation between the container and contained. Unlike other forms of symbolism, speech has to be learned, though the baby begins by making onomatopoeic sounds. Those sounds have to be taken up by the environment to be converted into speech and later on words have to be learned from the environment. The infant has had an experience and mother provides the word or phrase which circumscribes this experience. It contains, encompasses and expresses the meaning. It provides a container for it. The infant can then internalize this word or phrase containing the meaning. (Segal, 1978, p. 318)

Thus verbal containment, being learned from the social environment, requires the projection into the environment (mother) of the situation to be symbolized [see SYMBOL-FORMATION].

Pathological projective identification into mother fuses the infant with her, and her responses (protesting actions, sounds, etc.) will be re-internalized as hostile objects equated with the situation itself. With a particular patient, Segal reported: 'Strange things happened to my interpretations. They could become a pain in her belly or a sexual excitement' (Segal, 1978, p. 318). The failure of the containing function of mother stripped the experience of meaning and it was reduced to a somatic sensation.

The psychodynamic situation is that the relation between the symbol and the object symbolized is one of great violence that destroys separation and meaning in the symbol. Playing the violin was reduced in Segal's patient to a masturbatory somatic sensation in which the communicative voice of the violin, the meaning of its music, was violently obliterated in order to destroy the sense of boundary between the ego and the listening world around.

PALAEOLOGICAL THINKING. The relation between concrete representation and projective identification has been challenged by Meissner (1980):

> The example [in Segal (1957) of penis *equated* with violin because both can be played with] may represent a case of projective identification, in so far as the projected part (penis) becomes identified with the object (violin), but then again it may not. We may simply be dealing with a case of what Arieti (1974) described as a form of palaeologic thought, the logic of predicates following Von Domarus's principle. In other words penis and violin are equated simply because they share a common attribute, namely, that each is something that one can play with. It can therefore be questioned whether any instance of symbolic equation can be taken *prima facie* as evidence for projective identification. (p. 60)

This is an interesting challenge.

Von Domarus (1944) described schizophrenic logic as pre-Aristotelian in that two subjects with the same predicate are regarded as identical – men die: grass dies: therefore men are grass. This contrasts with the normally formed syllogism described by Aristotle – living organisms die: men are living organisms: therefore men die.

The identification arising from the so-called palaeological (pre-Aristotelian) form of logic is clearly prevalent in schizophrenics. But Meissner's argument is not really relevant, since Segal is describing the *psychodynamic production* of this form of thinking, whereas Meissner is drawing attention to the *formal structure* of palaeological thought. As Arieti says, 'Von Domarus's principle and the other palaeologic laws that will be mentioned shortly do not explain these phenomena dynamically but only formally' (Arieti, 1974, p. 235). Meissner's claim that projective identification may not always be the psychodynamic explanation is a quibble, since he does not give alternative cases.

In normal circumstances the standing hypothesis is allowed to stand until alternative evidence is actually found.

There is a further problem with Meissner's criticisms. Arieti, in discussing this primitive form of logic, compares it with the so-called primitive thinking of children and primitive cultures and relies on the opinions of the anthropologist Heinz Werner (1940), whom he quoted: '. . . the advanced form of thinking characteristic of Western civilization is only one form among many, and . . . more primitive forms are not so much lacking in logic as based on logic of a different kind' (Werner, 1940, p. 15). This does not make all members of primitive cultures schizophrenic. The whole argument is based on stereotyped views of 'primitives'. Many later anthropologists have noted the interesting logical forms of non-Western cultures (Radcliffe-Brown, 1952; Lévi-Strauss, 1966) without diagnosing them as composed of psychotic individuals. The point is that palaeological thinking (like so-called modern thinking) may itself be of two kinds: (a) schizophrenic or delusional, or (b) non-psychotic and mythical; it is not unreasonable, therefore, to claim that pathological projective identification is specifically implicated in the delusional type, as Segal described.

Arieti, Silvano (1974) *Interpretation of Schizophrenia*. New York: Basic.

Ferenczi, Sandor (1912) 'Symbolism', *Imago* 1:276–84.

Jones, Ernest (1916) 'The theory of symbolism', *British Journal of Psychology* 9: 181–229.

Klein, Melanie (1930) 'The importance of symbol-formation in the development of the ego'. *WMK* 1, pp. 219–32.

Lévi-Strauss, Claude (1966) *The Savage Mind*. Weidenfeld & Nicolson.

Meissner, W.W. (1980) 'A note on projective identification', *J. Amer. Psychoanal. Assn.* 28:43–68.

Milner, Marion (1953) 'The role of illusion in symbol-formation', *Int. J. Psycho-Anal.* 34:181–95; republished (1955) in Melanie Klein, Paula Heimann and Roger Money-Kyrle, eds *New Directions in Psycho-Analysis*. Tavistock, pp. 82–108.

Radcliffe-Brown, A.R. (1952) *Structure and Function in Primitive Society*. Cohen & West.

Segal, Hanna (1950) 'Some aspects of the analysis of a schizophrenic', *Int. J. Psycho-Anal.* 31:268–78; republished (1981) in *The Work of Hanna Segal*. New York: Jason Aronson, pp. 101–20

—— (1957) 'Notes on symbol formation', *Int. J. Psycho-Anal.* 38:391–7; republished (1981) in *The Work of Hanna Segal*, pp. 49–65.

—— (1978) 'On symbolism', *Int. J. Psycho-Anal.* 59:315–19.

Von Domarus, E. (1944) 'The specific laws of logic in schizophrenia', in Jacob Kasanin, ed. *Language and Thought in Schizophrenia*. Berkeley: University of California Press, pp. 104–14.

Werner, Heinz (1940) *Comparative Psychology of Mental Development*. New York: International Universities Press.

Symptom

Klein's main interest was in anxiety, so when Freud (1926) wrote his comprehensive paper on anxiety, Klein felt vindicated in selecting it out as somehow different from other symptoms, more directly related to the instinctual endowments of the individual. Klein analysed her patients and described her findings in terms of the object-relations of the struggling ego attempting to master anxiety. Thus other symptoms took a secondary place and were interpreted in terms of object-relations [see ANXIETY].

A crucial point was reached in 1925, when Klein contradicted both Ferenczi and Abraham over the nature of the symptom of a tic. They

(Ferenczi, 1921; Abraham, 1921) regarded the tic as a primary narcissistic phenomenon, whereas Klein challenged them by asserting that it had a basis in an object-relationship [see MASTURBATION PHANTASIES].

Klein's discussion of symptoms normally concerned very little other than anxiety itself. She regarded symptoms as symbolizing the underlying object-relations which give rise to anxiety; interpretation required '. . . uncovering the object-relations on which it is based' (Klein, 1925, p. 121). Consequently, the particular mode by which a symptom forms was of less interest than the hidden meaning, just as in psychoanalytic practice it is the latent content of the dream which is interpreted rather than the final dream symbols.

Conversion symptoms, hypochondria and psychosomatic illness: Riviere (1952) and Heimann (1952) discussed certain bodily symptoms in the context of narcissism. The relationship with an internal object can reach delusional proportions in which the individual develops bizarre conscious beliefs about his body based on the unconscious phantasies of a malignant object inside. Such a development is based on identifying a part of the body with a 'bad' persecuting object that has been introjected. Meltzer (1987), in noting the difference between psychosomatic illness, when there are actual pathological changes in the body itself, and the other two conditions (hypochondria and conversion symptoms), hypothesized (after Bion) a link between certain psychic phenomena (the accumulation of unprocessed sense data) and bodily pathology. The disorder, he suggested, is at the level of the translation from bodily instinct to mental representation when alpha-function fails [see ALPHA-FUNCTION].

Abraham, Karl (1921) 'Contribution to a discussion on tic', in Karl Abraham (1927) *Selected Papers on Psycho-Analysis*. Hogarth.

Ferenczi, Sandor (1921) 'Psycho-analytic observations on tic', in *Further Contributions to the Theory and Technique of Psycho-Analysis*. Hogarth.

Freud, Sigmund (1926) *Inhibitions, Symptoms and Anxiety*. S.E. 20, pp. 77–175.

Heimann, Paula (1952) 'Certain functions of introjection and projection in early infancy', in Melanie Klein, Paula Heimann, Susan Isaacs and Joan Riviere, eds (1952) *Developments in Psycho-Analysis*. Hogarth, pp. 128–68.

Klein, Melanie (1925) 'A contribution to the psychogenesis of tics'. *WMK* 1, pp. 106–27.

Meltzer, Donald (1987) *Studies in Extended Metapsychology*. Perth: Clunie.

Riviere, Joan (1952) 'General introduction', in Melanie Klein, Paula Heimann, Susan Isaacs and Joan Riviere, eds (1952) *Developments in Psycho-Analysis*. Hogarth, pp. 1–36.

Teeth

The teeth represent the organs of oral sadism [see SADISM]. Growing the teeth produces pain in the mouth which gives rise to the *unconscious phantasy* of persecutors in the mouth, biting the infant, who fears retaliatory aggression. The tooth is a terrifying realization for the infant of a hostile internal (part-) object.

See 5. INTERNAL OBJECTS

Thinking

In her earliest work Klein's classical position led her to emphasize the importance of the infantile struggles to accept the primal scene, and the painful and surreptitious thinking about the mysteries of parental sexuality (Klein, 1923). Her interest in the epistemophilic component of the libido brought about some major changes in understanding curiosity and knowledge, both inherent from the outset of life (Klein, 1930, 1931) [see EPISTEMOPHILIA; INNATE KNOWLEDGE].

Although Klein's interest in this aspect of her work waned for a time, it gained a new impetus when several of her co-workers began analysing schizophrenics. They were confronted with severe disorders of cognition. Rosenfeld and Segal produced case material analysing the fractured thinking and personality splitting of these patients [see LINKING]. Bion, however, took this further and began an extensive theoretical voyage, taking as his starting point the difficulties schizophrenics have in making intellectual links (Bion, 1959) [see LINKING]. The abnormal ways in which schizophrenics use their mental apparatus led him to an understanding of normal thinking.

Bion's work described several different views of thinking (Spillius, 1988) which were all delivered in his two publications in 1962: (1) the mating of a pre-conception with a realization; (2) the mating of a pre-conception with an absence; and (3) a process depending on alpha-function, originally provided by the maternal mind in a state of 'reverie'; the maternal mind forms an object capable of understanding, which can be introjected to form the basis of the function of thinking. The last of these models was the one he chose to elaborate further (Bion, 1970) and others have adopted it as a Kleinian theory of thinking.

(1) **The mating of a pre-conception with a realization.** In developing his theory of thinking, Bion relied on the Kleinian concepts of the paranoid-schizoid position and projective identification. His idea about the linking of objects is that there is an innate grasp of the linking of two objects and the relationship between them, based on the innate expectation of the relationship between mouth and nipple, and between penis and vagina. Bion attempted a mathematical degree of rigour in his terms:

(a) Pre-conception. This term represents a state of expectation. The term is the counterpart of a variable in mathematical logic or an unknown in mathematics. It has the quality that Kant ascribes to an empty thought in that it can be thought but cannot be known. (b) Conception. Conception is that which results when a pre-conception mates with the appropriate sense impressions. (Bion, 1962b, p. 91)

There is an inherent expectation of a union of two objects to make a third which is more than a sum of the two parts. Such a relationship he sees as the underlying property of the construction of thoughts. He described 'a developmental history' of a thought (Bion, 1962a,b) which goes as follows: an innate *pre-conception*, like the neural and anatomical expectancy of the mouth for a nipple, meets a *realization* (the real nipple enters the mouth), and the result is a conception. Conceptions are the results of satisfying conjunctions [see PRE-CONCEPTION].

(2) **The mating with an absence.** In deference to Freud, who viewed the development of thought as arising from the absence of a satisfaction, Bion considered the situation in which a pre-conception has to mate with the absence of a realization:

> Is a 'thought' the same as an absence of a thing? If there is no 'thing', is 'no thing' a thought and is it by virtue of the fact that there is 'no thing' that one recognizes that 'it' must be a thought? (Bion, 1962b, p. 35)

For the infant the absence of a breast is as concretely a presence as the present breast, the absent one being known as the 'no-breast' [see BAD OBJECT; OBJECTS]. Bion is trying to discover the source of the quality that alerts consciousness to the fact that 'it' is a thought rather than a reality or a hallucination. This depends on the ability of the ego to tolerate the experience of the bad object that threatens it and the experience of the loss of the good object. If tolerance is possible, then the ego is capable of experiencing the 'thought' of an object while acknowledging its actual absence. The capacity to distinguish the thought from the object itself, or from the hallucination of the object, is a prerequisite for thinking [see SYMBOLIC EQUATION; OBJECTS].

The creation of a thought, then, necessitates the development of 'an apparatus for thinking it'; and thinking is defined, by reference to Freud, as the ability 'to bridge the gulf of frustration between the moment when a want is felt and the moment when action appropriate to satisfying the want culminates in its satisfaction' (Bion, 1962a, p. 112). Such relationships between objects can be grossly disrupted by the early oedipal attacks, by envy or by serious actual deprivation.

The bad object: In the circumstance that tolerance of frustration is not sufficient to bridge the gap, then 'Incapacity for tolerating frustration tips the scale in the direction of frustration' (Bion, 1962a, p. 112). Instead of a union of pre-conception with negative realization, something else develops, termed a 'bad' object, which is then evacuated by means of the mechanism of projective identification. Thus frustration and pain are avoided by the expulsion of the frustration and a conjoined bit of the ego (the pre-conception). This

> is a significant departure from the events that Freud describes as characteristic of thought in the phase of dominance of the reality principle. What should be a thought, a product of the juxtaposition of pre-conception and negative realization, becomes a bad object, indistinguishable from a thing-in-itself, fit only for evacuation. (Bion, 1962a, p. 112)

An apparatus for thinking then fails to develop; instead it is the use of projective identification which develops:

> The model I propose for this development is a psyche that operates on the principle that evacuation of a bad breast is synonymous with obtaining sustenance from a good breast. The end result is that all thoughts are treated as if they were indistinguishable from bad internal objects; the appropriate machinery is felt to be, not an apparatus for thinking thoughts but an apparatus for ridding the psyche of accumulations of bad internal objects. (Bion, 1962a, p. 112)

Alpha-function: Thus, if all goes well, sense impressions are converted, through mating with pre-conceptions, into usable thoughts; this distinguishes those tolerable frustrations which can be used to develop thinking (alpha-elements) from other mental contents which are felt to be fit only for evacuation (beta-elements) [see ALPHA-FUNCTION; BETA-ELEMENTS]. Alpha-function is the (unspecified) process by which meaning accrues to sense data.

Higher-level thinking: Conceptions, once established, can repeat the history of pre-conceptions: that is to say, they become pre-conceptions for further realizations (or negative, absence-of, realizations) in a hierarchical way that generates sophisticated thinking and theory-building. At each step the functions of satisfaction and frustration play their part in furthering – or otherwise – the developing apparatus for thinking. This is one dimension of Bion's grid (Bion, 1963) which was itself a systematic theory (pre-conception), elaborated to meet the realizations of actual types of thoughts [see BION].

(3) **Containing.** The third model of the development of thought is that the capacity to develop an apparatus for thinking depends upon the introjection of an object capable of understanding the infant's experience and giving it meaning. Bion's concept of normal projective identification [see CONTAINING] was distinguished from 'excessive' projective identification used to evacuate accumulations of bad internal

objects. In fact, normal projective identification is the expected occurrence given an adequate experience of a containing external object:

> As a realistic activity it [projective identification] shows itself as behaviour reasonably calculated to arouse in the mother feelings of which the infant wishes to be rid. If the infant feels it is dying it can arouse fears that it is dying in the mother. A well-balanced mother can accept these and respond therapeutically: that is to say in a manner that makes the infant feel it is receiving its frightened personality back again but in a form that it can tolerate – the fears are manageable by the infant personality. (Bion, 1962a, p. 115)

The mother is the apparatus for the infant to tolerate the conjunction of the pre-conception with a negative realization, the no-breast [see CONTAINING]. To perform this function, mother's mind must be in a state of 'reverie' [see REVERIE] which approximates to the free-floating state of attention described by Freud and also, in Bion's description, to the mind that has abolished memory and desire [see MEMORY AND DESIRE; BION]. When things go wrong, and mother fails to take in the infant's sensations, then the infant resorts to increasingly violent attempts to project into mother and thus develops the 'apparatus for ridding the psyche of bad internal objects'. In this case of failure, the infant has a mother, an internal object in the making, which Bion described as a 'projective-identification-rejecting object', and for the infant this is a wilfully misunderstanding object with which he is destined to identify. Instead of the infant having his frustrations made comprehensible, he feels they become actively denuded of meaning, a 'nameless dread' [see NAMELESS DREAD].

The containing link: Bion (1962) started to investigate the vicissitudes of the containing relationship by describing the quality of the link between the containing mind and the contents put into it. These links have three potentialities: 'L', 'H' and 'K', which represent loving, hating and a wanting to know about the contents. Thus mother at times will love her child, hate him or find herself trying to understand how he is experiencing, feeling and thinking. For purposes of the development of thought, the K-link is the most important. Mother's linking with the infant in this way develops the capacity of the child through the introjection of the K-linking object. However, there are disturbances to the K-link. O'Shaughnessy (1981) has described, with clinical examples, the three important kinds of K-link: (i) the attempt to get to know the object through its projective identifications; (ii) the stripping of meaning from the object's projected experience, leading to a denuded and meaningless experience which gives rise to the infant feeling an internal terror from an introjected envious object that deprives it of meaning for its experiences (this is referred to as 'minus-K' (or '−K'); and (iii) a state of absence of 'K' ('no K') in which the capacity to know has been destroyed, giving rise to a paranoid psychotic condition in which the ego has been severely weakened by splitting and projection of its capacity for K and faces hostile objects into which, in phantasy, bits of the ego have been violently expelled [see EPISTEMOPHILIA].

Bion's theory of thinking is, in the main, adopted by Kleinians as a whole. There is a variation in the extent to which it is used (even understood) and some people have researched it further in their own right. The most ambitious of these is Meltzer (1987).

Bion, Wilfred (1959) 'Attacks on linking', *Int. J. Psycho-Anal.* 40:308–15; republished (1967) in W.R. Bion, *Second Thoughts*. Heinemann, pp. 93–109.
—— (1962a) 'A theory of thinking', *Int. J. Psycho-Anal.* 43:306–10; republished (1967) in *Second Thoughts*, pp. 110–19.
—— (1962b) *Learning from Experience*. Heinemann.
—— (1963) *Elements of Psycho-Analysis*. Heinemann.
—— (1970) *Attention and Interpretation*. Tavistock.
Klein, Melanie (1923) 'The role of the school in the libidinal development of the child'. *WMK* 1, pp. 59–76.
—— (1930) 'The importance of symbol-formation in the development of the ego'. *WMK* 1, pp. 219–32.
—— (1931) 'A contribution to the theory of intellectual development'. *WMK* 1, pp. 236–47.
Meltzer, Donald (1987) *Studies in Extended Metapsychology*. Perth: Clunie.
O'Shaughnessy, Edna (1981) 'A commemorative essay on W. R. Bion's theory of thinking', *Journal of Child Psychotherapy* 7:181–92.
Spillius, Elizabeth Bott (1988) *Melanie Klein Today, Volume 1: Mainly Theory*. Routledge.

Transference

Transference was known from the very beginning of psychoanalysis. The way it is understood and its impact on theoretical development have constantly changed. The concept of transference is really several concepts that have unfolded over the course of more than a century: (1) it was an unethical, untoward event; (2) it was then the psycho-analyst's ally in overcoming resistances, when hypnotic methods showed themselves to be limited and only transiently beneficial; (3) it could present a form of resistance to analysis by making the working relationship into an emotional one; (4) then it came to be seen as the re-enactment of the past, giving a new clarity to the psychoanalytic reconstruction of the details of childhood traumas; (5) alternatively, the enactment in the consulting room could be seen as the externalization of current unconscious phantasy; and (6) finally, a multiply split set of relationships with the analyst were described.

(1) An untoward event. When Breuer first reported to Freud what was termed by them 'an untoward event' (Jones, 1953), it was in fact the realization that Anna O. had fallen in love with Breuer. Breuer then decided straight away that his method was unethical for a medical practitioner, and he left the field for Freud to struggle on alone. Freud was more circumspect. He looked around the edges of the ethical problem and, being a well-brought-up natural scientist, he adopted the characteristic neutrality to ethical questions. He decided to look at Anna O.'s love as a phenomenon for study. This meant abstaining from any personal satisfaction in the relationship. The love was to be held as a phenomenon which was entirely remote from the actual person of the analyst, and when he found the anxious affections of his other young lady patients turning towards him in the same way, he refused to accept that it was due to his own personal charms.

Thus, transference was looked at anew – from being an untoward and unethical happening it could become a phenomenon for study, and then for use in practice.

(2) Overcoming resistances. At the time when Freud began to relinquish the hypnotic method for gaining access to the patient's unconscious, he had ready to hand the transference as an alternative means for overcoming the resistances to psychoanalytic exploration. Transference at that stage (in the 1890s) was simply the positive affection of the patient for the analyst which the analyst used as if it were a charge of energy [see LIBIDO] to set against the resistance to recalling memories from the past. He simply played on the positive and fantastical loyalty of the patient to press him or her to relax the repressive forces – the 'pressure technique'.

(3) Transference resistance. Transference was abruptly brought to Freud's attention again by the Dora case. In a general sense, Freud had already realized that the patient could harbour unnaturally hostile feelings towards the analyst, as well as unnaturally positive feelings. However, he delayed acknowledging their importance until Dora broke off her analysis very prematurely and with a good deal of unkindness. Freud was especially hurt as he had started the Dora analysis in order to write up an exemplary case that would be a model for all future practice. She made him swallow his pride and recognize that this had been a model of how not to practise – at least a model of how not to deal with transference. His overcoming of his disappointment was only part of the adjustment he had to make.

The importance of the negative transference meant a revision of both his practice of psychoanalysis and of his theories. Freud tended to take two views of this occurrence in the case of Dora. First, he regarded the transference, in which the whole analysis was broken off, as a form of resistance against the work of analysis and the recovery of memories and phantasies from the past (Freud, 1912). By engaging in an intensity of feeling towards the analyst the patient was attempting, through seduction or hostility, to thwart the process of understanding the past. Then secondly, Freud also thought of the relationship between Dora and himself as an enactment of a *specific* relationship of some kind (Freud, 1915).

(4) Repetition in the transference. Freud could see how Dora's negative transference recapitulated certain feelings she had previously felt towards a certain Herr K. He had in fact known that transference was linked to the early traumas in the patient's history. Now he had a real lesson in how the trauma is relived, re-experienced, re-enacted, as real life – in the transference to the analyst. And Freud was able to write up his case – not as an exemplary one but as a cautionary tale that demonstrated in a new way the importance of transference: the very detailed way in which the past could be witnessed. It was no longer a case of retrieving hazy memories confused by the efforts to keep them repressed.

In spite of this painful lesson in transference, Freud remained, as always, reluctant to give up completely his earlier views. Even today descriptions of transference imply that it is both a force for or against the resistance to analysis and a dangerous re-enactment of the past.

(5) Enacting unconscious phantasy. Over the years since then, the transference as a *re-enactment* has been further developed. A new meaning has supervened on the idea of a re-enactment of the past. This further development has resulted from the work of Klein. Perhaps one of the important factors in her revision of transference was the fact that she was working with children, some as young as two, and therefore at a time when the traumatizing events were assumed to be taking place. Thus the re-enactments of children were not from the far-gone past, but from their immediate present. The whole of their play was a series of enactments of all kinds of happenings and relationships. The vivacity and vigour of the re-enactment were astonishing to her. What, then, were the children enacting in their play? Clearly children enact their phantasy life. Klein took this seriously. Play, she thought, was in earnest; it was not just for amusement. It was the child's own way of relating to himself his own worst fears and anxieties. The relationships enacted in the consulting room were, then, the expressions of the child's efforts to encompass the traumatic way he experiences his daily life.

Reverting to the practice of adult psychoanalysis, this new realization had a profound effect on both theory and practice. Transference, already regarded as an enactment in the consulting room, was now regarded as a re-enactment of current phantasy experiences in the way the child's play is a re-enactment of his phantasy elaboration of his traumas [see ACTING-IN]. This view of transference, as coming out of the here-and-now difficulties actually during the session of the analysis, was bolstered by the development of, and emphasis upon, the notion of unconscious phantasy [see 2. UNCONSCIOUS PHANTASY]. The practice of Kleinian psychoanalysis has become an understanding of the transference as an expression of unconscious phantasy, active right here and now in the moment of the analysis. The transference is, however, moulded upon the infantile mechanisms with which the patient managed his experiences long ago:

> . . . the patient is bound to deal with his conflicts and anxieties re-experienced towards the analyst by the same methods he used in the past. That is to say, he turns away from the analyst as he attempted to turn away from his primal objects. (Klein, 1952, p. 55)

This view of transference came, in turn, to bolster the concept of unconscious phantasy. These two concepts have developed reciprocally as the core of Kleinian practice.

Acting-out in the transference: More recently there has been increasing interest in the way the patient acts out in the transference. This development, particularly connected with the work of Betty Joseph [see PSYCHIC EQUILIBRIUM], has demonstrated that patients use the transference not just for the gaining of satisfaction of their impulses but also for the support of their defensive positions [see ACTING-IN]. The patient attempts to 'use us – analysts – to help them with anxiety' (Joseph, 1978, p. 223). She describes extremely subtle ways in which the patient attempts 'to draw us into their defensive systems' (Joseph, 1985). By emphasizing the transference as the total situation (Joseph, 1985) she has investigated difficult and intractable borderline patients whose personalities are constructed around a rigid system of defences, a pathological organization [see PATHOLOGICAL ORGANIZATIONS].

Ego-psychology techniques: One of the differences in the approach to transference is that ego-psychologists will look at the material for the evidence of impulses, instinct derivatives and the defences against these, while others will look for objects and the relationships to them.

However, there is a deeper layer to this difference. What Klein started was a different emphasis in looking at the material the patients produced. She was concerned with the *content* of anxieties, and in this she was stepping aside from the prior interest in the instincts and the discharge of their energy. Analysts are either interested in approaching the structure of the patient's mind in objective terms, building a model of that structure and working to modify it, or, on the other hand, analysts enter the subjective world of the patient and attempt to find words to grasp it. These approaches to psychoanalytic practice, which brought their protagonists into such conflict in the 1920s over the technique of child analysis, remain in clear contrast today in the analysis of adults [see 1. TECHNIQUE; CHILD ANALYSIS].

(6) Split transferences. From the 1940s onwards, Klein introduced a further development in the understanding and therapeutic interpretation of transference. Abraham (1919) and subsequently many other analysts pointed to hidden aspects of the patient's relationship to the analyst: usually it is negative aspects that are concealed. Klein could embrace this with her developing theory in the 1940s when she began to understand the importance of splitting. She could show that all material given in the course of free association in an analytic session may show aspects of the immediate transference to the analyst now, even when the material does not refer explicitly to the analyst or even when it apparently consists of childhood memories:

> For instance reports of patients about their daily life, relations, and activities not only give an insight into the functioning of the ego, but also reveal – if we explore the unconscious content – the defences against the anxieties stirred up in the transference situation . . . he tries to split the relations to him [the analyst], keeping him either as a good or as a bad figure: he deflects some of the feelings and attitudes experienced towards the analyst on to other people in his current life, and this is part of 'acting out'. (Klein, 1952, p. 56) [see 1. TECHNIQUE]

The sequence of associations in the material is really an account of the (unconsciously) splintered set of remnants of the relationship with the analyst, often very immature aspects of that relationship. The task of the analyst is to understand how he is represented in this myriad of conflicting ways, and that they must be brought back together in a 'gathering of the transference' (Meltzer, 1968).

Countertransference: In the course of this historical journey of the concept of 'transference', a somewhat similar journey was traversed by the concept 'countertransference'. This too started as an interference and something off-putting of which the analyst was very wary. Psychoanalysts sheltered behind the idea that they could present a blank screen to their patients because they may actually have been frightened of how much they were stirred by their patients (Fenichel, 1941). However, from about 1950 onwards the idea of the analyst as a blank and mechanical operator fairly quickly fell into disrepute, for two reasons: (a) an analyst cannot, in practice, keep his own personality secret; (b) the feelings that an analyst discovers in himself in the course of his sessions have, if carefully processed, considerable importance in understanding the state of mind of the patient he has with him at the moment [see COUNTERTRANSFERENCE].

Abraham, Karl (1919) 'A particular form of neurotic resistance against the psycho-analytic method', in Karl Abraham (1927) *Selected Papers on Psycho-Analysis*. Hogarth, pp. 303–11.

Fenichel, Otto (1941) *Problems in Psycho-Analytic Practice*. New York: The Psycho-Analytic Quarterly Inc.

Freud, Sigmund (1912) 'The dynamics of transference'. *S.E.* 12, pp. 97–108.
—— (1915) 'Remembering, repeating and working through'. *S.E.* 14, pp. 121–45.

Jones, Ernest (1953) *The Life and Work of Sigmund Freud*, vol. 1. Hogarth.

Joseph, Betty (1978) 'Different types of anxiety and their handling in the analytic situation', *Int. J. Psycho-Anal.* 59:223–8.
—— (1985) 'Transference – the total situation', *Int. J. Psycho-Anal.* 66:447–54

Klein, Melanie (1952) 'The origins of transference'. *WMK* 3, pp. 48–56.

Meltzer, Donald (1968) *The Psycho-Analytic Process*. Perth: Clunie.

The unconscious

The notion of the unconscious is one of the few concepts that have remained relatively unchanged in the course of the development of all the schools of psychoanalysis. The unconscious system is conceived of as primitively active from the beginning – as unknown, but nevertheless a dominating influence on the life of the person. It is a fact in psychoanalysis that most of mental life is not accessible to the conscious mind (Freud, 1915).

Freud explored the symbolic aspects of the unconscious and came up with certain rules of unconscious mental activity – displacement and condensation. These terms describe the way in which symbols are handled in the unconscious. Klein and her followers respected these concepts by adding to and elaborating them. In particular, Kleinians have developed the notion of unconscious phantasy [see 2. UNCONSCIOUS PHANTASY].

The unconscious is structured like a small society. That is to say, it is a mesh of relationships between objects. An unconscious phantasy is a state of activity of one or more of these 'internal' object-relations. Isaacs says that instincts, when active physiologically, are mentally represented as relationships with objects. Thus a somatic sensation tugs along with it a mental experience of a relationship with an object that causes the sensation, is believed to be motivated to cause that sensation and is loved or hated by the ego according to whether the sensation is pleasant or unpleasant. In this way a sensation that hurts becomes a mental representation of a relationship with a 'bad' object that is intending to hurt and damage the ego.

The unconscious – and, indeed, the mind – is constructed of sensations interpreted as relationships with objects. This concept eventually departed from the classical psychoanalytic theory of mental energy [see ECONOMIC MODEL].

Freud, Sigmund (1915) 'The unconscious'. *S.E.* 14, pp. 159–215.

Unconscious guilt
Freud had drawn attention to the importance of unconscious guilt in 1916, in his views on criminality and a will to fail. The idea gained impetus in 1923, when he introduced the concept of the superego and made guilt central to character development; or rather, the importance of guilt prompted him to make the agency provoking guilt the central factor in character development.

Following that change in theory, there was intense interest in guilt and the need for punishment. In 1924 Freud linked it with masochism, then others soon began examining the issue (for instance Glover, 1926; Fenichel, 1928).

Klein, always interested in showing that child analysis was important in throwing light on the topics of the day, contributed significantly to this problem. She had, in any case, much material showing the early occurrence of remorse, regret and guilt in children and its origins in aggressive and sadistic object-relations [see 3. AGGRESSION; 7. SUPEREGO]. In 1927 she followed up Freud's views on the place of unconscious guilt in criminal behaviour with her paper on criminal tendencies in children [see CRIMINALITY].

She confirmed Freud's view that criminal *behaviour* is dealt with by an externalization of the guilt that is felt unconsciously. The external situation reflects the form of the violent *internal* attacks on the ego by a harsh superego, represented as hostile internal objects. She confirmed that the mechanism behind this was the substitution of an external punishment to alleviate the sadistic and terrifying internal states which provoke complete helplessness. A harsh but external substitute punishment is felt to be less terrifying for being real in this way rather than phantastic; it can also be evaded by concealment or by discrediting the accuser.

This use of Freud's theory of externalizing the internal state also became important for Klein in understanding the process of play [see 1. TECHNIQUE] and of symbol-formation [see SYMBOL-FORMATION]. The externalization was a defence against a terrifying internal persecution (unconscious guilt) and at the same time created the possibility of using symbols (Klein, 1929, 1930). The movement from one object to another, which in this case was from an internal object to an external one, also became a cornerstone of her theories of development in the child (Klein, 1932). When the relationship with one object becomes too hostile, new objects are sought: for instance, the movement from mother, who disappoints the infant at weaning and creates a crisis of sadism and persecution, towards a search for a new object, father; or, alternatively, the sadistic object-relations of the pregenital phases may provoke a move towards genital impulses and objects (perhaps premature genitality) [see DEVELOPMENT].

Fenichel, Otto (1928) 'The clinical aspect of the need for punishment', *Int. J. Psycho-Anal.* 9:47–70.

Freud, Sigmund (1916) 'Some character-types met with in psycho-analytic work: III Criminals from a sense of guilt'. *S.E.* 14, pp. 332–3.

—— (1923) *The Ego and the Id. S.E.* 19, pp. 3–66.

—— (1916) 'The economic problem of masochism'. *S.E.* 19, pp. 157–70.

Glover, Edward (1926) 'The neurotic character', *Int. J. Psycho-Anal.* 7:11–29.

Klein, Melanie (1927) 'Criminal tendencies in normal children'. *WMK* 1, pp. 170–85.

—— (1929) 'Personification in the play of children'. *WMK* 1, pp. 199–209.

—— (1930) 'The importance of symbol-formation in the development of the ego'. *WMK* 1, pp. 219–32.

—— (1932) *The Psycho-Analysis of Children. WMK* 2.

Whole object

This is a term implied in Abraham's work on the vicissitudes of the object and its relation to the development of the libido (Abraham, 1924). Abraham's theory of partial objects and 'partial love' was given a radically new meaning by Klein [see PART-OBJECTS].

The depressive position: The capacity to perceive a person 'as he really is' is an achievement that demands more than the maturing of the perceptual apparatus. The 'good' object that satisfies the infant's needs and the 'bad' object that keeps him waiting come to be recognized as one and the same person, a *whole object* (Klein, 1935) [see 10. DEPRESSIVE POSITION]. It is not just the physical presence but its *emotional reality* that comes to be recognized. The whole object has (i) its own very mixed set of feelings and motives, and (ii) in addition, the object is recognized as *being able to suffer*, like the subject. Objects are no longer defined by the subject's own feelings and needs.

Love and concern: Abraham had described part-objects as merely those giving gratification to the subject, by satisfying his needs; and 'true object-love' arose only when the object was appreciated as a whole. Klein, however, thought that love and gratitude occurred from the start. Any object that gratifies enhances gratitude and love, and one that frustrates provokes hate and paranoia. In the case of part-objects there is an abrupt switch between love and hate according to the infant's state of need or satisfaction, but in the depressive position feelings for the object acquire a stability and the new dimension of *concern* for the object. It is an achievement to reach a capacity for concern because it is painful to the subject – the object's pain is the subject's pain.

See LOVE; 10. DEPRESSIVE POSITION; PART-OBJECTS

Abraham, Karl (1924) 'A short study of the development of the libido', in Karl Abraham (1927) *Selected Papers in Psycho-Analysis*. Hogarth, pp. 418–501.
Klein, Melanie (1935) 'A contribution to the psychogenesis of manic-depressive states'. *WMK* 1, pp. 262–89.

BIBLIOGRAPHY OF KLEINIAN PUBLICATIONS

The place of publication is London unless otherwise indicated.

1920

Klein, Melanie 'Der Familienroman in Statu Nascendi', *Internationale Zeitschrift für Psychoanalyse* 6: 151–5.

Riviere, Joan 'Three notes', *Int. J. Psycho-Anal.* 1: 200–3.

1921

Klein, Melanie 'Eine Kinderentwicklung', *Imago* 7: 251–309; (1923) 'The development of a child', *Int. J. Psycho-Anal.* 4: 419–74.

Rickman, John 'An unanalysed case: anal erotism, occupation and illness', *Int. J. Psycho-Anal.* 2: 424–6.

1922

Klein, Melanie 'Hemmungen und Schwierigkeiten im Pubertätsalter', in *Die Neue Erziehung*, vol. 4; (1975) 'Inhibitions and difficulties at puberty', in *The Writings of Melanie Klein*, vol. 1. Hogarth, pp. 54–8.

1923

Isaacs, Susan, 'A note on sex differences from a psycho-analytic point of view', *Br. J. Med. Psychol.* 3: 288–308.

Klein, Melanie 'Die Rolle der Schule für die libidinöse Entwicklung des Kindes', *Internationale Zeitschrift für Psychoanalyse* 9: 323–44; (1924) 'The role of the school in the libidinal development of the child', *Int. J. Psycho-Anal.* 5: 312–31.

—— 'Zur Frühanalyse', *Imago* 9: 222–59; (1926) 'Infant analysis', *Int. J. Psycho-Anal.* 7: 31–63.

1924

Riviere, Joan 'A castration symbol', *Int. J. Psycho-Anal.* 5: 85.

1925

Klein, Melanie, 'Zur Genese des Tics', *Internationale Zeitschrift für Psychoanalyse* 11: 332–49; (1948) 'A contribution to the psychogenesis of tics', in *Contributions to Psycho-Analysis*. Hogarth, pp. 117–39.

1926

Klein, Melanie 'Die Psychologischen Grundlagen der Frühanalyse', *Imago* 12: 365–76; (1926) 'The psychological principles of early analysis', *Int. J. Psycho-Anal.* 8: 25–37.

Rickman, John 'A psychogical factor in the aetiology of descensus uteri, laceration of the perineum and vaginismus', *Int. J. Psycho-Anal.* 7: 363–5; (1926) *Internationale Zeitschrift für Psychoanalyse* 12: 513–16.

—— (1926–7) 'A survey: the development of the psycho-analytical theory of the psychoses', *Br. J. Med. Psychol.* 6: 270–94; 7: 321–74.

1927

Klein, Melanie 'Criminal tendencies in normal children', *Br. J. Med. Psychol.* 7: 177–92.

—— 'Symposium on child analysis', *Int. J. Psycho-Anal.* 7: 339–70.

Riviere, Joan 'Symposium on lay analysis', *Int. J. Psycho-Anal.* 8: 370–7.

Searl, N.M. 'Symposium on lay analysis', *Int. J. Psycho-Anal.* 8: 377–80.

1928

Isaacs, Susan 'The mental hygiene of pre-school children', *Br. J. Med. Psychol.* 8: 186–93; republished (1948) in Isaacs, *Childhood and After*, pp. 1–9.

Klein, Melanie 'Frühstadien des Ödipuskonfliktes', *Internationale Zeitschrift für Psychoanalyse* 14: 65–77; (1928) 'Early stages of the Oedipus conflict', *Int. J. Psycho-Anal.* 9: 167–80.

—— 'Notes on "A dream of forensic interest" by D. Bryan', *Int. J. Psycho-Anal.* 9: 255–8.

Money-Kyrle, Roger 'The psycho-physical apparatus', *Br. J. Med. Psychol.* 8: 132–42; republished (1978) in *The Collected Papers of Roger Money-Kyrle*, pp. 16–27.

—— 'Morals and super-men', *Br. J. Med. Psychol.* 8: 277–84; republished (1978) in *The Collected Papers of Roger Money-Kyrle*, pp. 28–37.

Rickman, John *Index Psycho-Analyticus 1893–1926*. Hogarth.

—— *The Development of the Psycho-Analytical Theory of the Psychoses 1893–1926*. Baillière, Tindall & Cox.

1929

Isaacs, Susan 'Privation and guilt', *Int. J. Psycho-Anal.* 10: 335–47; republished (1948) in Isaacs, *Childhood and After*, pp. 10–22.

Klein, Melanie 'Personification in the play of children', *Int. J. Psycho-Anal.* 19: 193–204; (1929) *Internationale Zeitschrift für Psychoanalyse* 15: 171–82.

—— 'Infantile anxiety-situations reflected in a work of art and in the creative impulse', *Int. J. Psycho-Anal.* 10: 436–43; (1931) 'Fruhe Angstsituationen im Spiegel künstlerischer Darstellungen', *Internationale Zeitschrift für Psychoanalyse* 17: 497–506.

Riviere, Joan 'Womanliness as a masquerade', *Int. J. Psycho-Anal.* 10: 303–13.

—— 'Magical regeneration by dancing', *Int. J. Psycho-Anal.* 10: 340.

Searl, N.M. 'The flight to reality', *Int. J. Psycho-Anal.* 10: 280–91.

—— 'Danger situations of the immature ego', *Int. J. Psycho-Anal.* 10: 423–35.

1930

Klein, Melanie 'The importance of symbol-formation in the development of the ego', *Int. J. Psycho-Anal.* 11: 24–39; (1930) 'Die Bedeutung der Symbolbildung für die Ichentwicklung', *Internationale Zeitschrift für Psychoanalyse* 16: 56–72.

—— 'The psychotherapy of the psychoses', *Br. J. Med. Psychol.* 10: 242–4.

Schmideberg, Melitta 'The role of psychotic mechanisms in cultural development', *Int. J. Psycho-Anal.* 11: 387–418.

Searl, N.M. 'The role of ego and libido in development', *Int. J. Psycho-Anal.* 11: 125–49.

Sharpe, Ella Freeman 'Certain aspects of sublimation and delusion', *Int. J. Psycho-Anal.* 11: 12–23.

—— 'The technique of psycho-analysis', *Int. J. Psycho-Anal.* 11: 251–77, 361–86; republished (1950) in Sharpe, *Collected Papers in Psycho-Analysis*, pp. 9–106.

Strachey, James 'Some unconscious factors in reading', *Int. J. Psycho-Anal.* 11: 322–31.

1931

Klein, Melanie 'A contribution to the theory of intellectual inhibition', *Int. J. Psycho-Anal.* 12: 206–18.

Money-Kyrle, Roger 'The remote consequences of psycho-analysis on individual, social and instinctive behaviour', *Br. J. Med. Psychol.* 11: 173–93; republished (1978) in *The Collected Papers of Roger Money-Kyrle*, pp. 57–81.

Schmideberg, Melitta 'A contribution to the psychology of persecutory ideas and delusions', *Int. J. Psycho-Anal.* 12: 331–67.

—— 'The role of psychotic mechanisms in cultural development', *Int. J. Psycho-Anal.* 12: 387–418.

1932

Isaacs, Susan 'Some notes on the incidence of neurotic difficulties in young children', *British Journal of Educational Psychology* 2: 71–91, 184–95.

Klein, Melanie *The Psycho-Analysis of Children*. Hogarth; (1930) *Die Psychoanalyse des Kindes*. Vienna: Internationaler Psychoanalytischer Verlag.

Rickman, John 'The psychology of crime', *Br. J. Med. Psychol.* 12: 264–9.

Riviere, Joan 'Jealousy as a mechanism of defence', *Int. J. Psycho-Anal.* 13: 414–24.

Searl, N.M. 'A note on depersonalization', *Int. J. Psycho-Anal.* 13: 329–47.

1933

Isaacs, Susan *Social Development in Young Children*. Routledge & Kegan Paul.

Klein, Melanie 'The early development of conscience in the child', in Sandor Lorand, ed. *Psycho-Analysis Today*. New York: Covici-Friede, pp. 149–62.

Money-Kyrle, Roger 'A psycho-analytic study of the voices of Joan of Arc', *Br. J. Med. Psychol.* 13: 63–81; republished (1978) in *The Collected Papers of Roger Money-Kyrle*, pp. 109–30.

Schmideberg, Melitta 'Some unconscious mechanisms in pathological sexuality and their relation to normal sexuality', *Int. J. Psycho-Anal.* 14: 225–60.

Searl, N.M. 'The psychology of screaming', *Int. J. Psycho-Anal.* 14: 193–205.

—— 'Play, reality and aggression', *Int. J. Psycho-Anal.* 14: 310–20.

—— 'A note on symbols and early intellectual development', *Int. J. Psycho-Anal.* 14: 391–7.

1934

Isaacs, Susan 'Rebellious and defiant children', in Isaacs (1948) *Childhood and After*. Routledge & Kegan Paul, pp. 23–35.

Klein, Melanie 'On criminality', *Br. J. Med. Psychol.* 14: 312–15.

Middlemore, Merrell 'The treatment of bewitchment in a puritan community', *Int. J. Psycho-Anal.* 15: 41–58.

Money-Kyrle, Roger 'A psychological analysis of the causes of war', *The Listener*; republished (1978) in *The Collected Papers of Roger Money-Kyrle*, pp. 131–7.

Schmideberg, Melitta 'The play analysis of a three-year-old girl', *Int. J. Psycho-Anal.* 15: 245–64.

Stephen, Karin 'Introjection and projection: guilt and rage', *Br. J. Med. Psychol.* 14: 316–31.

Strachey, James 'The nature of the therapeutic action of psycho-analysis', *Int. J. Psycho-Anal.* 15: 127–59; republished (1969) *Int. J. Psycho-Anal.* 50: 275–92.

1935

Isaacs, Susan 'Bad habits', *Int. J. Psycho-Anal.* 16: 446–54.

——— *The Psychological Aspects of Child Development.* Evans Bros.

——— 'Property and possessiveness', *Br. J. Med. Psychol.* 15: 69–78; republished (1948) in Isaacs, *Childhood and After*, pp. 36–46.

Klein, Melanie 'A contribution to the psychogenesis of manic-depressive states', *Int. J. Psycho-Anal.* 16: 145–74.

Schmideberg, Melitta 'The psycho-analysis of asocial children', *Int. J. Psycho-Anal.* 16: 22–48; previously published (1932) *Internationale Zeitschrift für Psychoanalyse* 18: 474–527.

——— 'Zum Verständnis massenpsychologischer Erscheinungen', *Imago* 21: 445–57.

——— 'The psychological care of the baby', *Mother and Child* 6: 304–8.

Sharpe, Ella Freeman 'Similar and divergent unconscious determinants underlying the sublimation of pure art and pure science', *Int. J. Psycho-Anal.* 16: 186–202; republished (1950) in Sharpe, *Collected Papers on Psycho-Analysis*, pp. 137–54.

1936

Isaacs, Susan 'Personal freedom and family life', *New Era* 17: 238–43.

Isaacs, Susan, Klein, Melanie, Middlemore, Merrell, Searl, Mina and Sharpe, Ella (ed. John Rickman) *On the Bringing up of Children*. Kegan Paul.

Klein, Melanie 'Weaning', in J. Rickman, ed. *On the Bringing up of Children*. Kegan Paul, pp. 31–6.

Rickman, John, ed. *On the Bringing up of Children*. Kegan Paul.

Riviere, Joan 'On the genesis of psychical conflict in earliest infancy', *Int. J. Psycho-Anal.* 17: 395–422; republished (1952) in Melanie Klein, Paula Heimann, Susan Isaacs and Joan Riviere *Developments in Psycho-Analysis*, pp. 37–66.

——— 'A contribution to the analysis of the negative therapeutic reaction', *Int. J. Psycho-Anal.* 17: 304–20.

1937

Isaacs, Susan *The Educational Value of the Nursery School*. The Nursery School Association; republished (1948) in Isaacs, *Childhood and After*. Routledge & Kegan Paul, pp. 47–73.

Klein, Melanie 'Love, guilt and reparation', in Melanie Klein and Joan Riviere, *Love, Hate and Reparation*. Hogarth, pp. 57–91.

Money-Kyrle, Roger 'The development of war', *Br. J. Med. Psychol.* 17: 219–36; republished (1978) in *The Collected Papers of Roger Money-Kyrle*, pp. 138–59.

Rickman, John 'On "unbearable" ideas and impulses', *American Journal of Psychology* 50: 248–53.

Riviere, Joan 'Hate, greed and aggression', in Melanie Klein and Joan Riviere, *Love, Hate and Reparation*. Hogarth, pp. 3–56.

Strachey, James 'Contribution to a symposium on the theory of the therapeutic results of psycho-analysis', *Int. J. Psycho-Anal.* 18: 139–45.

1938

Isaacs, Susan 'Psychology and the school', *New Era* 19: 18–20.

Schmideberg, Melitta 'Intellectual inhibition and disturbances in eating', *Int. J. Psycho-Anal.* 19: 17–22.

Thorner, Hans A. 'The mode of suicide as a manifestation of phantasy', *Br. J. Med. Psychol.* 17: 197–200.

1939

Isaacs, Susan 'Modifications of the ego through the work of analysis', in Isaacs (1948) *Childhood and After*. Routledge & Kegan Paul, pp. 89–108.

—— 'Criteria for interpretation', *Int. J. Psycho-Anal.* 20: 148–60; republished (1948) in Isaacs, *Childhood and After*, pp. 109–21.

—— 'A special mechanism in a schizoid boy', *Int. J. Psycho-Anal.* 20: 333–9; republished (1948) in Isaacs, *Childhood and After*, pp. 122–8.

Money-Kyrle, Roger *Superstition and Society*. Hogarth.

Strachey, James 'Preliminary notes upon the problem of Akhnaton', *Int. J. Psycho-Anal.* 20: 33–42.

1940

Isaacs, Susan 'Temper tantrums in early childhood in their relation to internal objects', *Int. J. Psycho-Anal.* 21: 280–93; republished (1948) in Isaacs, *Childhood and After*, pp. 129–42.

Klein, Melanie 'Mourning and its relation to manic-depressive states', *Int. J. Psycho-Anal.* 21: 125–53.

Rickman, John 'On the nature of ugliness and the creative impulse', *Int. J. Psycho-Anal.* 21: 294–313.

1941

Middlemore, Merrell *The Nursing Couple*. Hamish Hamilton.

Strachey, Alix 'A note on the use of the word "internal" ', *Int. J. Psycho-Anal.* 22: 37–43.

Winnicott, D.W. 'The observation of infants in a set situation', *Int. J. Psycho-Anal.* 22: 229–49.

1942

Heimann, Paula 'A contribution to the problem of sublimation and its relation to processes of internalization', *Int. J. Psycho-Anal.* 23: 8–17.

Klein, Melanie 'Some psychological considerations', in Waddington *et al.* *Science and Ethics*. Allen & Unwin.

Money-Kyrle, Roger 'The psychology of propaganda', *Br. J. Med. Psychol.* 42: 82–94; republished (1978) in *The Collected Papers of Roger Money-Kyrle*. Perth: Clunie, pp. 160–75.

1943

Bion, Wilfred and Rickman, John 'Intra-group tensions in therapy: their study as a task of the group', *The Lancet* (ii) 27.11.43:678–81; republished (1961) in W.R. Bion, *Experiences in Groups*. Tavistock, pp. 11–26.

Isaacs, Susan 'An acute psychotic anxiety occurring in a boy of four years', *Int. J. Psycho-Anal.* 24: 13–32; republished (1948) in Isaacs, *Childhood and After*. Routledge & Kegan Paul, pp. 143–85.

1944

Milner, Marion 'A suicidal symptom in a child of three', *Int. J. Psycho-Anal.* 25: 53–61.

Money-Kyrle, Roger 'Towards a common aim: a psycho-analytical contribution to ethics', *Br. J. Med. Psychol.* 20: 105–17; republished (1978) in *The Collected Papers of Roger Money-Kyrle*. Perth: Clunie, pp. 176–97.

—— 'Some aspects of political ethics from the psycho-analytic point of view', *Int. J. Psycho-Anal.* 25: 166–71.

1945

Isaacs, Susan 'Notes on metapsychology as process theory', *Int. J. Psycho-Anal.* 26: 58–62.

—— 'Fatherless children', in Peggy Volkov, ed. *Fatherless Children*. NEF Monograph No. 2; republished (1948) in Isaacs, *Childhood and After*. Routledge & Kegan Paul, pp. 186–207.

—— 'Children in institutions', in Isaacs (1948) *Childhood and After*, pp. 208–36.

Klein, Melanie 'The Oedipus complex in the light of early anxieties', *Int. J. Psycho-Anal.* 26: 11–33.

Milner, Marion 'Some aspects of phantasy in relation to general psychology', *Int. J. Psycho-Anal.* 26: 143–52.

Riviere, Joan 'The bereaved wife', in Peggy Volkov, ed. *Fatherless Children*. NEF Monograph No. 2.

Winnicott, D.W. 'Primitive emotional development', *Int. J. Psycho-Anal.* 26: 137–42.

1946

Bion, Wilfred 'The leaderless group project', *Bulletin of the Menninger Clinic* 10: 77–81.

Klein, Melanie 'Notes on some schizoid mechanisms', *Int. J. Psycho-Anal.* 27: 99–110; republished (1952) in Melanie Klein, Paula Heimann, Susan Isaacs and Joan Riviere, *Developments in Psycho-Analysis*. Hogarth, pp. 292–320.

Scott, W. Clifford M. 'A note on the psychopathology of convulsive phenomena in manic-depressive states', *Int. J. Psycho-Anal.* 27: 152–5.

1947

Money-Kyrle, Roger 'Social conflict and the challenge to psychology', *Br. J. Med. Psychol.* 27: 215–21; republished (1978) in *The Collected Papers of Roger Money-Kyrle*. Perth: Clunie, pp. 198–209.

Rosenfeld, Herbert 'Analysis of a schizophrenic state with depersonalization', *Int. J. Psycho-Anal.* 28: 130–9; republished (1965) in Rosenfeld, *Psychotic States*. Hogarth, pp. 13–33.

Scott, W. Clifford M. 'On the intense affects encountered in treating a severe manic-depressive disorder', *Int. J. Psycho-Anal.* 28: 139–45.

Stephen, Adrian 'The superego and other internal objects', *Int. J. Psycho-Anal.* 28: 114–17.

Thorner, Hans A. 'The treatment of psychoneurosis in the British Army', *Int. J. Psycho-Anal.* 27: 52–9.

1948

Bion, Wilfred 'Psychiatry in a time of crisis', *Br. J. Med. Psychol.* 21: 81–9.

Isaacs, Susan 'On the nature and function of phantasy', *Int. J. Psycho-Anal.* 29: 73–97; republished (1952) in Melanie Klein, Paula Heimann, Susan Isaacs and Joan Riviere, *Developments in Psycho-Analysis*. Hogarth, pp. 67–121.

—— *Childhood and After*. Routledge & Kegan Paul.

Joseph, Betty 'A technical problem in the treatment of the infant patient', *Int. J. Psycho-Anal.* 29: 58–9.

Klein, Melanie *Contributions to Psycho-Analysis*. Hogarth.

—— 'A contribution to the theory of anxiety and guilt', *Int. J. Psycho-Anal.* 29: 114–23.

Munro, Lois 'Analysis of a cartoon in a case of hypochondria', *Int. J. Psycho-Anal.* 29: 53–7.

Scott, W. Clifford M. 'Some embryological, neurological, psychiatric and psycho-analytic implications of the body schema', *Int. J. Psycho-Anal.* 29: 141–55.

—— 'Notes on the psychopathology of anorexia nervosa', *Br. J. Med. Psychol.* 21: 241–7.

—— 'Some psychodynamic aspects of disturbed perception of time', *Br. J. Med. Psychol.* 21: 111–20.

—— 'A psycho-analytic concept of the origin of depression', *British Medical Journal*, vol. I: 538; republished (1955) in Melanie Klein, Paula Heimann and Roger Money-Kyrle, eds *New Directions in Psycho-Analysis*. Tavistock, pp. 39–47.

1949

Heimann, Paula 'Some notes on the psycho-analytic concept of introjected objects', *Int. J. Psycho-Anal.* 22: 8–17.

Rosenfeld, Herbert 'Remarks on the relation of male homosexuality to paranoia, paranoid anxiety and narcissism', *Int. J. Psycho-Anal.* 30: 36–47; republished (1965) in Rosenfeld, *Psychotic States*. Hogarth, pp. 34–51.

Scott, W. Clifford M. 'The "body scheme" in psycho-therapy', *Br. J. Med. Psychol.* 22: 139–50.

Thorner, Hans A. 'Notes on a case of male homosexuality', *Int. J. Psycho-Anal.* 30: 31–5.

1950

Bion, Wilfred 'The imaginary twin', in W.R. Bion (1967) *Second Thoughts*. Heinemann, pp. 3–22.

Heimann, Paula 'On counter-transference', *Int. J. Psycho-Anal.* 31: 81–4.

Klein, Melanie 'On the criteria for the termination of a psycho-analysis', *Int. J. Psycho-Anal.* 31: 78–80, 204.

Money-Kyrle, Roger 'Varieties of group formation', *Psychoanalysis and the Social Sciences* 2: 313–30; republished (1978) in *The Collected Papers of Roger Money-Kyrle*. Perth: Clunie, pp. 210–28.

Rosenfeld, Herbert 'Note on the psychopathology of confusional states in chronic schizophrenia', *Int. J. Psycho-Anal.* 31: 132–7; republished (1965) in Rosenfeld, *Psychotic States*. Hogarth, pp. 52–62.

Segal, Hanna 'Some aspects of the analysis of a schizophrenic', *Int. J. Psycho-Anal.* 31: 268–78; republished (1981) in *The Work of Hanna Segal*. New York: Jason Aronson, pp. 101–20; and (1988) in Bott Spillius, ed. *Melanie Klein Today: Developments in Theory and Practice, Volume 2, Mainly Practice*, pp. 96–114.

Sharpe, Ella Freeman *Collected Papers in Psycho-Analysis*. Hogarth.

Winnicott, D.W. 'Hate in the counter-transference', *Int. J. Psycho-Anal.* 30: 69–74.

Winnicott, D.W. 'Hate in the counter-transference', *Int. J. Psycho-Anal.* 30: 69–74.

1951

Jaques, Elliott *The Changing Culture of a Factory*. Routledge & Kegan Paul.

Klein, Sidney 'Contribution to a symposium on group therapy', *Br. J. Med. Psychol.* 24: 223–8.

Langer, Marie *Maternidad y Sexo*. Buenos Aires: Editorial Nova.

Money-Kyrle, Roger *Psycho-Analysis and Politics*. Duckworth.

—— 'Some aspects of state and character in Germany', in George Wilbur and Warner Munsterberger, eds *Psycho-Analysis and Culture*. New York: International Universities Press, pp. 280–92; republished (1978) in *The Collected Papers of Roger Money-Kyrle*, pp. 229–44.

1952

Bion, Wilfred 'Group dynamics: a review', *Int. J. Psycho-Anal.* 33: 235–47; republished (1955) in Melanie Klein, Paula Heimann and Roger Money-Kyrle, eds *New Directions in Psycho-Analysis*, pp. 440–77; and (1961) in W.R. Bion, *Experiences in Groups*, pp. 141–91.

Evans, Gwen 'Early anxiety situations in the analysis of a boy in the latency period', *Int. J. Psycho-Anal.* 33: 93–110; republished (1955) in Melanie Klein, Paula Heimann and Roger Money-Kyrle, eds *New Directions in Psycho-Analysis*, pp. 48–81.

Heimann, Paula 'Certain functions of projection and introjection in early infancy', in Melanie Klein, Paula Heimann, Susan Isaacs and Joan Riviere, *Developments in Psycho-Analysis*. Hogarth, pp. 122–68.

—— 'Notes on the theory of the life and death instincts', in Melanie Klein, Paula Heimann, Susan Isaacs and Joan Riviere, *Developments in Psycho-Analysis*, pp. 321–37.

—— 'A contribution to the re-evaluation of the Oedipus complex – the early stages', *Int. J. Psycho-Anal.* 33: 84–93; republished (1955) in Melanie Klein, Paula Heimann and Roger Money-Kyrle, eds *New Directions in Psycho-Analysis*, pp. 23–38.

—— 'Preliminary notes on some defence mechanisms in paranoid states', *Int. J. Psycho-Anal.* 33: 208–13; republished (1955) as 'A combination of defence mechanisms in paranoid states', in Melanie Klein, Paula Heimann and Roger Money-Kyrle, eds *New Directions in Psycho-Analysis*, pp. 240–65.

Heimann, Paula and Isaacs, Susan 'Regression', in Melanie Klein, Paula Heimann, Susan Isaacs and Joan Riviere, *Developments in Psycho-Analysis*, pp. 169–97.

Klein, Melanie 'Some theoretical conclusions regarding the emotional life of the infant', in Melanie Klein, Paula Heimann, Susan Isaacs and Joan Riviere, *Developments in Psycho-Analysis*, pp. 198–236.

—— 'On observing the behaviour of young infants', in Melanie Klein, Paula Heimann, Susan Isaacs and Joan Riviere, *Developments in Psycho-Analysis*, pp. 237–70.

—— 'The origins of transference', *Int. J. Psycho-Anal.* 33: 433–8.

—— 'The mutual influences in the development of the ego and the id', *Psychoanal. Study Child* 7: 51–3.

Klein, Melanie, Heimann, Paula, Isaacs, Susan and Riviere, Joan *Developments in Psycho-Analysis*. Hogarth.

Milner, Marion 'Aspects of symbolism in comprehension of the not-self', *Int. J. Psycho-Anal.* 34: 181–95; republished (1955) as 'The role of illusion in symbol formation', in Melanie Klein, Paula Heimann and Roger Money-Kyrle, eds *New Directions in Psycho-Analysis*, pp. 82–108.

Money-Kyrle, Roger 'Psycho-analysis and ethics', *Int. J. Psycho-Anal.* 33: 225–34; republished (1955) in Melanie Klein, Paula Heimann and Roger Money-Kyrle, eds *New Directions in Psycho-Analysis*, pp. 421–40; and (1978) in *The Collected Papers of Roger Money-Kyrle*, pp. 264–84.

Munro, Lois 'Clinical notes on internalization and identification', *Int. J. Psycho-Anal.* 33: 132–43.

Riviere, Joan 'General introduction' to Melanie Klein, Paula Heimann, Susan Isaacs and Joan Riviere, *Developments in Psycho-Analysis*, pp. 1–36.

—— 'The unconscious phantasy of an inner world reflected in examples from English literature', *Int. J. Psycho-Anal.* 33: 160–72; republished (1955) in Melanie Klein, Paula Heimann and Roger Money-Kyrle, eds *New Directions in Psycho-Analysis*, pp. 346–69.

—— 'The inner world in Ibsen's *Master-Builder*', *Int. J. Psycho-Anal.* 33: 173–80; republished (1955) in Melanie Klein, Paula Heimann and Roger Money-Kyrle, eds *New Directions in Psycho-Analysis*, pp. 370–83.

Rosenfeld, Herbert 'Notes on the psycho-analysis of the superego conflict in an acute catatonic patient', *Int. J. Psycho-Anal.* 33: 111–31; republished (1955) in Melanie Klein, Paula Heimann and Roger Money-Kyrle, eds *New Directions in Psycho-Analysis*, pp. 180–219; and (1965) in Rosenfeld *Psychotic States*, pp. 63–103; and (1988) in Bott Spillius, ed. *Melanie Klein Today: Developments in Theory and Practice, Volume 1, Mainly Theory*, pp. 14–51.

—— 'Transference-phenomena and transference-analysis in an acute catatonic schizophrenic patient', *Int. J. Psycho-Anal.* 33: 457–64; republished (1965) in Rosenfeld, *Psychotic States*, pp. 104–16.

Sandford, Beryl 'An obsessional man's need to be kept', *Int. J. Psycho-Anal.* 33: 144–52; republished (1955) in Melanie Klein, Paula Heimann and Roger Money-Kyrle, eds *New Directions in Psycho-Analysis*, pp. 266–81.

—— 'Some psychotherapeutic work in maternity and child welfare clinics', *Br. J. Med. Psychol.* 25: 2–15.

Segal, Hanna 'A psycho-analytic approach to aesthetics', *Int. J. Psycho-Anal.* 33: 196–207; republished (1955) in Melanie Klein, Paula Heimann and Roger Money-Kyrle, eds *New Directions in Psycho-Analysis*, pp. 384–407; and (1981) in *The Work of Hanna Segal*, pp. 185–206.

Thorner, Hans A. 'Examination anxiety without examination', *Int. J. Psycho-Anal.* 33: 153–9; republished (1955) as 'Three defences against inner persecution', in Melanie Klein, Paula Heimann and Roger Money-Kyrle, eds *New Directions in Psycho-Analysis*, pp. 384–407.

—— 'The criteria for progress in a patient during analysis', *Int. J. Psycho-Anal.* 33: 479–84.

1953

Davidson, Audrey and Fay, Judith *Phantasy in Childhood*. Routledge & Kegan Paul.

Garma, Angel 'The internalized mother as harmful food in peptic ulcer patients', *Int. J. Psycho-Anal.* 34: 102–10.

Jaques, Elliott 'On the dynamics of social structure', *Human Relations* 6: 10–23; republished (1955) as 'The social system as a defence against persecutory and depressive anxiety', in Melanie Klein, Paula Heimann and Roger Money-Kyrle, eds *New Directions in Psycho-Analysis*, pp. 478–98.

Money-Kyrle, Roger *Toward a Rational Attitude to Crime.* The Howard League; republished (1978) in *The Collected Papers of Roger Money-Kyrle*, pp. 245–52.

Racker, Heinrich 'A contribution to the problem of counter-transference', *Int. J. Psycho-Anal.* 34: 313–24; republished (1968) as 'The counter-transference neurosis', in Racker, *Transference and Counter-Transference*, pp. 105–26.

Segal, Hanna 'A necrophilic phantasy', *Int. J. Psycho-Anal.* 34: 98–101; republished (1981) in *The Work of Hanna Segal*, pp. 165–71.

1954

Bion, Wilfred 'Notes on the theory of schizophrenia', *Int. J. Psycho-Anal.* 35: 113–18; expanded (1955) as 'Language and the schizophrenic', in Melanie Klein, Paula Heimann and Roger Money-Kyrle, eds *New Developments in Psycho-Analysis*, pp. 220–39; and republished (1967) in W.R. Bion, *Second Thoughts*, pp. 23–35.

Heimann, Paula 'Problems of the training analysis', *Int. J. Psycho-Anal.* 35: 163–8.

Hunter, Dugmore 'Object relation changes in the analysis of fetishism', *Int. J. Psycho-Anal.* 35: 302–12.

Munro, Lois 'Steps in ego-integration observed in play analysis', *Int. J. Psycho-Anal.* 35: 202–5; republished (1955) in Melanie Klein, Paula Heimann and Roger Money-Kyrle, eds *New Directions in Psycho-Analysis*, pp. 109–39.

Racker, Heinrich 'Notes on the theory of transference', *Psychoanal. Q.* 23: 78–86; republished (1968) in Racker, *Transference and Counter-Transference*, pp. 71–8.

—— 'On the confusion between mania and health', *Samiska* 8: 42–6; republished (1968) as 'Psycho-analytic technique and the analyst's unconscious mania', in Racker, *Transference and Counter-Transference*, pp. 181–5.

Rosenfeld, Herbert 'Considerations regarding the psycho-analytic approach to acute and chronic schizophrenia', *Int. J. Psycho-Anal.* 35: 138–40; republished (1965) in Rosenfeld, *Psychotic States*. Hogarth, pp. 117–27.

Segal, Hanna 'A note on schizoid mechanisms underlying phobia formation', *Int. J. Psycho-Anal.* 35: 238–41; republished (1981) in *The Work of Hanna Segal*, pp. 137–44.

1955

Bion, Wilfred 'Language and the schizophrenic', in Melanie Klein, Paula Heimann and Roger Money-Kyrle, eds *New Directions in Psycho-Analysis*. Tavistock, pp. 220–39.

Klein, Melanie 'The psycho-analytic play technique: its history and significance', in Melanie Klein, Paula Heimann and Roger Money-Kyrle, eds *New Directions in Psycho-Analysis*, pp.3–22.

—— 'On identification', in Melanie Klein, Paula Heimann and Roger Money-Kyrle, eds *New Directions in Psycho-Analysis*, pp. 309–45.

Klein, Melanie, Heimann, Paula and Money-Kyrle, Roger, eds *New Directions in Psycho-Analysis*. Tavistock.

Money-Kyrle, Roger 'An inconclusive contribution to the theory of the death instinct', in Melanie Klein, Paula Heimann and Roger Money-Kyrle, eds *New Directions in Psycho-Analysis*, pp. 409–59.

Rodrigue, Emilio 'The analysis of a three-year-old mute schizophrenic', in Melanie Klein, Paula Heimann and Roger Money-Kyrle, eds *New Directions in Psycho-Analysis*, pp. 140–79.

—— 'Notes on menstruation', *Int. J. Psycho-Anal.* 36: 328–34.

Stokes, Adrian 'Form in art', in Melanie Klein, Paula Heimann and Roger Money-Kyrle, eds *New Directions in Psycho-Analysis*, pp. 406–20.

1956

Bion, Wilfred 'Development of schizophrenic thought', *Int. J. Psycho-Anal.* 37: 344–6; republished (1967) in W.R. Bion, *Second Thoughts*, pp. 36–43.

Heimann, Paula 'Dynamics of transference interpretations', *Int. J. Psycho-Anal.* 37: 303–10.

Jaques, Elliott *Measurement of Responsibility*. Tavistock.

Money-Kyrle, Roger 'The world of the unconscious and the world of common sense', *British Journal of the Philosophy of Science*, 7: 86–96; republished (1978) in *The Collected Papers of Roger Money-Kyrle*, pp. 318–29; and (1988) in Bott Spillius, ed. *Melanie Klein Today: Volume 2, Mainly Practice*, pp. 22–33.

—— 'Normal counter-transference and some of its deviations', *Int. J. Psycho-Anal.* 37: 360–6; republished (1978) in *The Collected Papers of Roger Money-Kyrle*, pp. 330–42.

Rodrigue, Emilio 'Notes on symbolism', *Int. J. Psycho-Anal.* 37: 147–58.

Segal, Hanna 'Depression in the schizophrenic', *Int. J. Psycho-Anal.* 37: 339–43; republished (1981) in *The Work of Hanna Segal*, pp. 121–30; and (1988) in Bott Spillius, ed. *Melanie Klein Today: Volume 1, Mainly Theory*, pp. 52–60.

1957

Bion, Wilfred 'Differentiation of the psychotic from the non-psychotic personalities', *Int. J. Psycho-Anal.* 38: 266–75; republished (1967) in W.R. Bion, *Second Thoughts*, pp. 43–64; and (1988) in Bott Spillius, ed. *Melanie Klein Today: Volume 1, Mainly Theory*, pp. 61–78.

Klein, Melanie *Envy and Gratitude*. Tavistock.

Racker, Heinrich 'A contribution to the problem of psychopathological stratification', *Int. J. Psycho-Anal.* 38: 223–39; republished (1968) as 'The meanings and uses of counter-transference' in Racker, *Transference and Counter-Transference*, pp. 127–73.

—— 'Analysis of transference through the patient's relations with the interpretation', in Racker (1968) *Transference and Counter-Transference*, pp. 79–104.

Segal, Hanna 'Notes on symbol formation', *Int. J. Psycho-Anal.* 38: 391–7; republished (1981) in *The Work of Hanna Segal*, pp. 49–64; and (1988) in Bott Spillius, ed. *Melanie Klein Today: Volume 1, Mainly Theory*, pp. 87–101.

Strachey, Alix *The Unconscious Motives of War*. George Allen & Unwin.

1958

Bion, Wilfred 'On hallucination', *Int. J. Psycho-Anal.* 39: 144–6; republished (1967) in W.R. Bion, *Second Thoughts*, pp. 65–85.

—— 'On arrogance', *Int. J. Psycho-Anal.* 39: 341–9; republished (1967) in Bion, *Second Thoughts*, pp. 86–93.

Garma, Angel 'Peptic ulcer and pseudo-peptic ulcer', *Int. J. Psycho-Anal.* 39:104–7.

Jaques, Elliott 'Psycho-analysis and the current economic crisis', in John Sutherland, ed. *Psycho-Analysis and Contemporary Thought*. Hogarth, pp. 125–44.

Klein, Melanie 'On the development of mental functioning', *Int. J. Psycho-Anal.* 39: 84–90.

Langer, Marie 'Sterility and envy', *Int. J. Psycho-Anal.* 39: 139–43.

Money-Kyrle, Roger 'Psycho-analysis and philosophy', in John Sutherland, ed. *Psycho-Analysis and Contemporary Thought*, pp. 102–24; republished (1978) in *The Collected Papers of Roger Money-Kyrle*, pp. 297–317.

—— 'On the process of psycho-analytical inference', *Int. J. Psycho-Anal.* 59: 129–33; republished (1978) in *The Collected Papers of Roger Money-Kyrle*, pp. 343–52.

Pichon-Riviere, Arminda 'Dentition, walking and speech in relation to the depressive position', *Int. J. Psycho-Anal.* 39: 167–71.

Racker, Heinrich 'Psycho-analytic technique', in Racker (1968) *Transference and Counter-Transference*, pp. 6–22.

—— 'Classical and present techniques in psycho-analysis', in Racker (1968) *Transference and Counter-Transference*, pp. 23–70.

—— 'Psycho-analytic technique and the analyst's unconscious masochism', *Psychoanal. Q.* 27: 555–62; republished (1968) in Racker, *Transference and Counter-Transference*, pp. 174–80.

—— 'Counterresistance and interpretation', *J. Amer. Psychoanal. Ass.* 6: 215–21; republished (1968) in Racker, *Transference and Counter-Transference.* pp. 186–92.

Riviere, Joan 'A character trait of Freud's', in John Sutherland, ed. *Psycho-Analysis and Contemporary Thought*, pp. 145–9; republished in Hendrik Ruitenbeek, ed. *Freud as We Knew Him.* Detroit: Wayne State University Press.

Rosenfeld, Herbert 'Some observations on the psychopathology of hypochondriacal states', *Int. J. Psycho-Anal.* 39: 121–8.

—— 'Contribution to the discussion on variations in classical technique', *Int. J. Psycho-Anal.* 39: 238–9.

—— 'Discussion on ego distortion', *Int. J. Psycho-Anal.* 39: 274–5.

Segal, Hanna 'Fear of death: notes on the analysis of an old man', *Int. J. Psycho-Anal.* 39: 187–91; republished (1981) in *The Work of Hanna Segal*, pp. 173–82.

1959

Bion, Wilfred 'Attacks on linking', *Int. J. Psycho-Anal.* 40: 308–15; republished (1967) in W.R. Bion, *Second Thoughts*, pp. 93–109; and (1988) in Bott Spillius, ed. *Melanie Klein Today: Volume 1, Mainly Theory*, pp. 87–101.

Heimann, Paula 'Bemerkungen zur Sublimierung', *Psyche* 13: 397–414.

Joseph, Betty 'An aspect of the repetition compulsion', *Int. J. Psycho-Anal.* 40: 213–22; republished (1989) in Betty Joseph, *Psychic Equilibrium and Psychic Change.* Routledge, pp. 16–33.

Klein, Melanie 'Our adult world and its roots in infancy', *Human Relations* 12: 291–303; republished (1963) in Klein, *Our Adult World and Other Essays.* Heinemann.

Rosenfeld, Herbert 'An investigation into the psycho-analytic theory of depression', *Int. J. Psycho-Anal.* 40: 105–29.

Taylor, James N. 'A note on the splitting of interpretations', *Int. J. Psycho-Anal.* 40: 295–6.

1960

Jaques, Elliott 'Disturbances in the capacity to work', *Int. J. Psycho-Anal.* 41: 357–67.

Joseph, Betty 'Some characteristics of the psychopathic personality', *Int. J. Psycho-Anal.* 41: 526–31; republished (1989) in Betty Joseph *Psychic Equilibrium and Psychic Change*, pp. 34–43.

Klein, Melanie 'On mental health', *Br. J. Med. Psychol.* 40: 237–41.

—— (published 1961) *Narrative of a Child Analysis.* Hogarth.

—— (published 1963) *Our Adult World and Other Essays.* Heinemann.

—— 'Some reflections on the Oresteia', in Klein (1963) *Our Adult World and Other Essays.*

—— 'On the sense of loneliness', in Klein (1963) *Our Adult World and Other Essays.*

Menzies (Lyth), Isabel 'The functioning of a social system as a defence against anxiety', *Human Relations* 11: 95–121; republished (1970) as Tavistock Pamphlet No. 3. Tavistock Institute of Human Relations; and (1988) in Isabel Menzies Lyth *Containing Anxiety in Institutions: Selected Essays Volume 1*, pp. 43–85.

Money-Kyrle, Roger 'On prejudice – a psycho-analytical approach', *Br. J. Med. Psychol.* 33: 205–9; republished (1978) in *The Collected Papers of Roger Money-Kyrle*, pp. 353–60.

Racker, Heinrich 'A study of some early conflicts through their return in the patient's relation with the interpretation', *Int. J. Psycho-Anal.* 41: 47–58.

Rosenfeld, Herbert 'A note on the precipitating factor in depressive illness', *Int. J. Psycho-Anal.* 41: 512–13.

—— 'On drug addiction', *Int. J. Psycho-Anal.* 41: 467–75.

Soares de Souza, D. 'Annihilation and reconstruction of object-relationships in a schizophrenic girl', *Int. J. Psycho-Anal.* 41: 554–8.

Stokes, Adrian 'A game that must be lost', *Int. J. Psycho-Anal.* 41: 70–6.

Williams, Hyatt W. 'A psycho-analytic approach to the treatment of the murderer', *Int. J. Psycho-Anal.* 41: 532–9.

1961

Bion, Wilfred *Experiences in Groups*. Tavistock.

Bion, Wilfred, Segal, Hanna and Rosenfeld, Herbert 'Melanie Klein', *Int. J. Psycho-Anal.* 42: 4–8.

Klein, Melanie *Narrative of a Child Analysis*. Hogarth.

Money-Kyrle, Roger *Man's Picture of his World*. Duckworth.

1962

Bick, Esther 'Child analysis today', *Int. J. Psycho-Anal.* 43: 328–32; republished (1987) in *The Collected Papers of Martha Harris and Esther Bick*, pp. 104–13; and (1988) in Bott Spillius, ed. *Melanie Klein Today: Developments in Theory and Practice, Volume 2, Mainly Practice*, pp. 168–76.

Bion, Wilfred *Learning from Experience*. Heinemann.

—— 'A theory of thinking', *Int. J. Psycho-Anal.* 43: 306–10; republished (1967) in W.R. Bion, *Second Thoughts*, pp. 110–19; and (1988) in Bott Spillius, ed. *Melanie Klein Today: Developments in Theory and Practice, Volume 1, Mainly Theory*, pp. 178–86.

Grinberg, Leon 'On a specific aspect of countertransference due to the patient's projective identification', *Int. J. Psycho-Anal.* 43: 436–40.

Langer, Marie 'Selection criteria for the training of psycho-analytic students', *Int. J. Psycho-Anal.* 43: 272–6.

Rosenfeld, Herbert 'The superego and the ego-ideal', *Int. J. Psycho-Anal.* 43: 258–63.

Segal, Hanna 'The curative factors in psycho-analysis', *Int. J. Psycho-Anal.* 43: 212–17; republished (1981) in *The Work of Hanna Segal*, pp. 69–80.

Stokes, Adrian 'On resignation', *Int. J. Psycho-Anal.* 43: 175–81.

1963

Bion, Wilfred *Elements of Psycho-Analysis*. Heinemann.

Grinberg, Leon 'Relations between psycho-analysts', *Int. J. Psycho-Anal.* 44: 363–7.

Meltzer, Donald 'A contribution to the metapsychology of cyclothymic states', *Int. J. Psycho-Anal.* 44: 83–97.

—— 'Concerning the social basis of art', in Adrian Stokes, ed. *Painting and the Inner World*. Tavistock.

Money-Kyrle, Roger 'A note on migraine', *Int. J. Psycho-Anal.* 44: 490–2; republished (1978) in *The Collected Papers of Roger Money-Kyrle*, pp. 361–5.

Rosenfeld, Herbert 'Notes on the psychopathology and psycho-analytic treatment of depressive and manic-depressive patients', in *Psychiatric Research Report No. 17*. Washington: The American Psychiatric Association.

—— 'Notes on the psychopathology and psycho-analytic treatment of schizophrenia', in *Psychiatric Research Report No. 17*.

Segal, Hanna and Meltzer, Donald 'Narrative of a child analysis', *Int. J. Psycho-Anal.* 44: 507–13.

1964

Bick, Esther 'Notes on infant observation in psycho-analytic training', *Int. J. Psycho-Anal.* 45: 558–66; republished (1987) in *The Collected Papers of Martha Harris and Esther Bick*, pp. 240–56.

Bicudo, Virginia Leone 'Persecuting guilt and ego restriction', *Int. J. Psycho-Anal.* 45: 358–63.

Grinberg, Leon 'On two kinds of guilt: their relation with normal and pathological aspects of mourning', *Int. J. Psycho-Anal.* 45: 366–71.

Hoxter, Shirley 'The experience of puberty', *Journal of Child Psychotherapy* 1(2): 13–26.

Langer, Marie, Puget, Janine and Teper, Eduardo 'A methodological approach to the teaching of psycho-analysis', *Int. J. Psycho-Anal.* 45: 567–74.

Meltzer, Donald 'The differentiation of somatic delusions from hypochondria', *Int. J. Psycho-Anal.* 45: 246–50.

O'Shaughnessy, Edna 'The absent object', *Journal of Child Psychotherapy* 1(2): 134–43.

Rosenfeld, Herbert 'On the psychopathology of narcissism: a clinical approach', *Int. J. Psycho-Anal.* 45: 332–7; republished (1965) in Rosenfeld, *Psychotic States*. Hogarth, pp. 169–79.

—— 'The psychopathology of hypochondriasis', in Rosenfeld (1965) *Psychotic States*, pp. 180–99.

—— 'An investigation into the need of neurotic and psychotic patients to act out during analysis', in Rosenfeld (1965) *Psychotic States*, pp. 200–16.

—— 'The psychopathology of drug addiction and alcoholism', in Rosenfeld (1965) *Psychotic States*, pp. 217–42.

—— 'Object relations of the acute schizophrenic patient in the transference situation', in P. Solomon and B.C. Glueck, eds *Recent Research on Schizophrenia*. Washington: American Psychiatric Association.

Segal, Hanna *Introduction to the Work of Melanie Klein*. Heinemann; republished (1973) Hogarth.

—— 'Phantasy and other mental processes', *Int. J. Psycho-Anal.* 45: 191–4; republished (1981) in *The Work of Hanna Segal*, pp. 41–8.

Williams, Arthur Hyatt 'The psychopathology and treatment of sexual murderers', in Ismond Rosen, ed. *The Pathology and Treatment of Sexual Deviation*. Oxford: Oxford University Press, pp. 351–77.

1965

Bion, Wilfred *Transformations*. Heinemann.

Harris, Martha 'Depression and the depressive position in an adolescent boy', *Journal of Child Psychotherapy* 1(3): 33–40; republished (1987) in *The Collected Papers of Martha Harris and Esther Bick*, pp. 53–63; and (1988) in Bott Spillius, ed. *Melanie Klein Today: Developments in Theory and Practice, Volume 2, Mainly Practice*, pp. 158–67.

Jaques, Elliott 'Death and the mid-life crisis', *Int. J. Psycho-Anal.* 46: 502–14; republished (1988) in Bott Spillius, ed. *Melanie Klein Today: Developments in Theory and Practice, Volume 2, Mainly Practice*, pp. 226–48.

Klein, Sidney 'Notes on a case of ulcerative colitis', *Int. J. Psycho-Anal.* 46: 342–51.

Lush, Dora 'Treatment of depression in an adolescent', *Journal of Child Psychotherapy* 1(3): 26–32.

Money-Kyrle, Roger 'Success and failure in mental maturations', in (1978) *The Collected Papers of Roger Money-Kyrle*, pp. 397–406.

Rosenbluth, Dina 'The Kleinian theory of depression', *Journal of Child Psychotherapy* 1(3): 20–5.

Rosenfeld, Herbert *Psychotic States*. Hogarth.

Stokes, Adrian *The Invitiation to Art*. Tavistock.

1966

Grinberg, Leon 'The relation between obsessive mechanisms and states of self-disturbance: depersonalization', *Int. J. Psycho-Anal.* 46: 177–83.

Harris, Martha, and Carr, Helen 'Therapeutic consultations', *Journal of Child Psychotherapy* 1(4): 13–31; republished (1987) in *The Collected Papers of Martha Harris and Esther Bick*, pp. 38–52.

Joseph, Betty 'Persecutory anxiety in a four-year-old boy', *Int. J. Psycho-Anal.* 47: 184–8.

Malin, Arthur S. and Grotstein, James S. 'Projective identification in the therapeutic process', *Int. J. Psycho-Anal.* 47: 26–31.

Meltzer, Donald 'The relation of anal masturbation to projective identification', *Int. J. Psycho-Anal.* 47: 335–42; republished (1988) in Bott Spillius, ed. *Melanie Klein Today: Developments in Theory and Practice, Volume 1, Mainly Theory*, pp. 102–16.

Money-Kyrle, Roger 'A note on the three caskets', in (1978) *The Collected Papers of Roger Money-Kyrle*, p. 407.

—— 'British schools of psycho-analysis', in Silvano Arieti, *American Handbook of Psychiatry*; republished (1978) in *The Collected Papers of Roger Money-Kyrle*, pp. 408–25.

Racker, Heinrich 'Ethics and psycho-analysis and the psycho-analysis of ethics', *Int. J. Psycho-Anal.* 47: 63–80.

Rodrigue, Emilio 'Transference and a-transference phenomena', *Int. J. Psycho-Anal.* 47: 342–8.

Stokes, Adrian 'On being taken out of one's self', *Int. J. Psycho-Anal.* 47: 523–30.

1967

Bion, Wilfred 'Notes on memory and desire', *Psycho-Analytic Forum* 2: 272–3, 279–80; republished (1988) in Bott Spillius, ed. *Melanie Klein Today: Developments in Theory and Practice, Volume 2, Mainly Practice*, pp. 17–21.

—— *Second Thoughts*. Heinemann.

Bleger, J. 'Psycho-analysis of the psycho-analytic frame', *Int. J. Psycho-Anal.* 48: 511–19.

—— *Simbiosis y Ambiguedad*. Buenos Aires: Paidos.

Boston, Mary 'Some effects of external circumstances on the inner experience of two child patients', *Journal of Child Psychotherapy* 2(1): 20–32.

Grinberg, Leon, Langer, Marie, Liberman, David and de Rodrigue, Emilio and Genevieve 'The psycho-analytic process', *Int. J. Psycho-Anal.* 48: 496–503.

Meltzer, Donald *The Psycho-Analytic Process*. Heinemann.

Pick, Irma 'On stealing', *Journal of Child Psychotherapy* 2(1): 67–79.

Rodrigue, Emilio 'Severe bodily illness in childhood', *Int. J. Psycho-Anal.* 48: 290–3.

Segal, Hanna 'Melanie Klein's technique', in Benjamin Wolman, ed. *Psycho-Analytic Techniques*. New York: Basic, pp. 188–90; republished (1981) in *The Work of Hanna Segal*, pp. 3–24.

1968

Bick, Esther 'The experience of the skin in early object relations', *Int. J. Psycho-Anal.* 49: 484–6; republished (1987) in *The Collected Papers of Martha Harris and Esther Bick*, pp. 114–18; and (1988) in Bott Spillius, ed. *Melanie Klein Today: Developments in Theory and Practice, Volume 1, Mainly Theory*, pp. 187–91.

Gosling, Robert 'What is transference?', in John Sutherland, ed. *The Psycho-Analytic Approach*. Baillière, Tindall & Cassell, pp. 1–10.

Grinberg, Leon 'On acting-out and its role in the psycho-analytic process', *Int. J. Psycho-Anal.* 49: 171–8.

Harris, Martha 'The child psychotherapist and the patient's family', *Journal of Child Psychotherapy* 2(2): 50–63; republished (1987) in *The Collected Papers of Martha Harris and Esther Bick*, pp. 18–37.

Jaques, Elliott 'Guilt, conscience and social behaviour', in John Sutherland, ed. *The Psycho-Analytic Approach*, pp. 31–43.

Meltzer, Donald 'Terror, persecution, dread', *Int. J. Psycho-Anal.* 49: 396–400; republished (1973) in Meltzer, *Sexual States of Mind*, pp. 99–106; and (1988) in Bott Spillius, ed. *Melanie Klein Today: Developments in Theory and Practice, Volume 1, Mainly Theory*, pp. 230–8.

Money-Kyrle, Roger 'Cognitive development', *Int. J. Psycho-Anal.* 49: 691–8; republished (1978) in *The Collected Papers of Roger Money-Kyrle*, pp. 416–33; and (1981) in James Grotstein, ed. *Do I Dare Disturb the Universe?*, pp. 537–50.

Munro, Lois 'Comment on the paper by Alexander and Isaacs on the psychology of the fool', *Int. J. Psycho-Anal.* 49: 424–5.

Racker, Heinrich *Transference and Counter-Transference*. Hogarth.

Rodrigue, Emilio 'The fifty thousand hour patient', *Int. J. Psycho-Anal.* 50: 603–13.

Rosenbluth, Dina ' "Insight" as an aim of treatment', *Journal of Child Psychotherapy* 2(2): 5–19.

Spillius, Elizabeth Bott 'Psycho-analysis and ceremony', in John Sutherland, ed. *The Psycho-Analytic Approach*, pp. 52–77; republished (1988) in Bott Spillius, ed. *Melanie Klein Today: Developments in Theory and Practice, Volume 2, Mainly Practice*, pp. 259–83.

1969

Brenman, Eric 'The psycho-analytic point of view', in Sidney Klein, ed. *Sexuality and Aggression in Maturation: New Facets*. Ballière, Tindall & Cassell, pp. 1–13.

Grinberg, Leon 'New ideas: conflict and evolution', *Int. J. Psycho-Anal.* 50: 517–28.

Meltzer, Donald 'The relation of aims to methodology in the treatment of children', *Journal of Child Psychotherapy* 2(3): 57–61.

Menzies (Lyth), Isabel E.P. 'The motor-cycle: growing up on two wheels', in Sidney Klein, ed. *Sexuality and Aggression in Maturation: New Facets*. Baillière, Tindall & Cassell, pp. 37–49; republished (1989) in Menzies Lyth *The Dynamics of the Social: Selected Essays, Volume 2*, pp. 142–57.

—— 'Some methodological notes on a hospital study', in Foulkes and Stewart-Price, eds *Psychiatry in a Changing Society*. Tavistock, pp. 99–112; republished (1988) in Isabel Menzies Lyth *Containing Anxiety in Institutions: Selected Essays, Volume 1*, pp. 115–29.

Money-Kyrle, Roger 'On the fear of insanity', in (1978) *The Collected Papers of Roger Money-Kyrle*, pp. 434–41.

Rosenfeld, Herbert 'On the treatment of psychotic states by psycho-analysis: an historical approach', *Int. J. Psycho-Anal.* 50: 615–31.

Williams, Arthur Hyatt 'Murderousness', in Louis Blom-Cooper, ed. *The Hanging Question*. Duckworth.

1970

Bion, Wilfred *Attention and Interpretation*. Tavistock.

Brenner, John 'Some factors affecting the placement of a child in treatment', *Journal of Child Psychotherapy* 2(4): 63–7.

Grinberg, Leon 'The problem of supervision in psycho-analytic education', *Int. J. Psycho-Anal.* 51: 371–83.

Jackson, Judith 'Child psychotherapy in a day school for maladjusted children', *Journal of Child Psychotherapy* 2(4): 54–62.

Jaques, Elliott *Work, Creativity and Social Justice*. Heinemann.

Menzies (Lyth), Isabel E.P. 'Psychosocial aspects of eating', *Journal of Psychosomatic Research* 14: 223–7; republished (1989) in Menzies Lyth *The Dynamics of the Social: Selected Essays, Volume 2*, pp. 142–57.

Riesenberg-Malcolm, Ruth 'The mirror: a perverse sexual phantasy in a woman seen as a defence against psychotic breakdown', in (1988) Bott

Spillius, ed. *Melanie Klein Today, Volume 2: Mainly Practice*, pp. 115–37; previously published (1970) in Spanish as 'El espejo: una fantasia sexual perversa en una mujer, vista como defensa contra un derrume psicotico', *Revista de Psicoanálisis* 27: 793–826.

Rioch, Margaret J. 'The work of Wilfred Bion on groups', *Psychiatry* 33: 56–66.

Rosenbluth, Dina 'Transference in child psychotherapy', *Journal of Child Psychotherapy* 2(4): 72–87.

Szur, Ruth 'Acting-out', *Journal of Child Psychotherapy* 2(4): 23–38.

Thorner, Hans A. 'On compulsive eating', *Journal of Psychosomatic Research* 14: 321–5.

Wittenberg, Isca *Psycho-Analytic Insight and Relationships: A Kleinian Approach*. Routledge & Kegan Paul.

1971

Harris, Martha 'The place of once weekly treatment in the work of an analytically trained child psychotherapist', *Journal of Child Psychotherapy* 3(1): 31–9.

Joseph, Betty 'A clinical contribution to the analysis of a perversion', *Int. J. Psycho-Anal.* 52: 441–9; republished (1989) in Joseph *Psychic Equilibrium and Psychic Change*, pp. 51–6.

Money-Kyrle, Roger 'The aim of psycho-analysis', *Int. J. Psycho-Anal.* 52: 103–6; republished (1978) in *The Collected Papers of Roger Money-Kyrle*, pp. 442–9.

Rosenfeld, Herbert 'A clinical approach to the psycho-analytical theory of the life and death instincts: an investigation into the aggressive aspects of narcissism', *Int. J. Psycho-Anal.* 52: 169–78; republished (1988) in Bott Spillius, ed. *Melanie Klein Today: Developments in Theory and Practice, Volume 1, Mainly Theory*, pp. 239–55.

—— 'Contribution to the psychopathology of psychotic states: the importance of projective identification in the ego structure and the object relations of the psychotic patient', in Pierre Doucet and Camille Laurin, eds *Problems of Psychosis*. Amsterdam: Excerpta Medica, pp. 115–28; republished (1988) in Bott Spillius, ed. *Melanie Klein Today: Developments in Theory and Practice, Volume 1, Mainly Theory*, pp. 117–37.

Rustin, Margaret 'Once-weekly work with a rebellious adolescent girl', *Journal of Child Psychotherapy* 3(1): 40–8.

Wittenberg, Isca 'Extending fields of work', *Journal of Child Psychotherapy* 3(1): 22–30.

1972

Boston, Mary 'Psychotherapy with a boy from a children's home', *Journal of Child Psychotherapy* 3(2): 53–67.

Hoxter, Shirley 'A study of a residual autistic condition and its effects upon learning', *Journal of Child Psychotherapy* 3(2): 21–39.

Rosenfeld, Herbert 'A critical appreciation of James Strachey's paper on the nature of the therapeutic action of psycho-analysis', *Int. J. Psycho-Anal.* 53: 455–61.

Segal, Hanna 'The role of child analysis in the general psycho-analytic training', *Int. J. Psycho-Anal.* 53: 147–61.

—— 'A delusional system as a defence against re-emergence of a catastrophic situation', *Int. J. Psycho-Anal.* 53: 393–403.

—— 'Melanie Klein's technique of child analysis', in Benjamin Wolman, ed. *Handbook of Child Psycho-Analysis*. New York: Van Nostrand Rheinhold; republished (1981) in *The Work of Hanna Segal*, pp. 25–37.

—— 'A note on internal objects' (published as 'A propos des objets internes', *Nouvelle Revue de Psychanalyse* 10: 153–7).

1973

Etchegoyen, R. Horatio 'A note on ideology and technique, *Int. J. Psycho-Anal.* 54: 485–6.

Harris, Martha 'The complexity of mental pain seen in a six-year-old child following sudden bereavement', *Journal of Child Psychotherapy* 3(3): 35–45; republished (1987) in *The Collected Papers of Martha Harris and Esther Bick*, pp. 89–103.

Meltzer, Donald *Sexual States of Mind*. Perth: Clunie.

1974

Bion, Wilfred *Bion's Brazilian Lectures 1*. Rio de Janeiro: Imago Editora Ltda.

Grinberg, Leon and Grinberg, R. 'The problem of identity and the psycho-analytic process', *Int. Rev. Psycho-Anal.* 1: 499–507.

Henry, Gianna 'Doubly deprived', *Journal of Child Psychotherapy* 3(4): 15–28.

Hughes, Athol 'Contributions of Melanie Klein to psycho-analytic technique', in V.J. Varma, ed. *Psychotherapy Today*. Constable.

Klein, Sidney 'Transference and defence in manic states', *Int. J. Psycho-Anal.* 55: 261–8.

Meltzer, Donald 'Mutism in infantile autism, schizophrenia and manic-depressive states: the correlation of clinical psychopathology and linguistics', *Int. J. Psycho-Anal.* 55: 397–404.

Rosenfeld, Herbert 'Discussion on the paper by Greenson on transference: Freud or Klein?', *Int. J. Psycho-Anal.* 55: 49–51.

Segal, Hanna 'Delusion and artistic creativity', *Int. Rev. Psycho-Anal.* 1: 135–41; republished (1981) in *The Work of Hanna Segal*, pp. 207–16; and (1988) in Bott Spillius, ed. *Melanie Klein Today: Developments in Theory and Practice, Volume 2, Mainly Practice*, pp. 249–58.

1975

Bion, Wilfred *Bion's Brazilian Lectures 2*. Rio de Janeiro: Imago Editora Ltda.

—— *A Memoir of the Future: 1. The Dream*. Rio de Janeiro: Imago Editora Ltda.

Grinberg, Leon, Sor, Dario and Tabak de Bianchedi, Elizabeth *Introduction to the Work of Bion*. Perth: Clunie.

Harris, Martha 'Some notes on maternal containment in "good enough" mothering', *Journal of Child Psychotherapy* 4: 35–51; republished (1987) in *The Collected Papers of Martha Harris and Esther Bick*, pp. 141–63.

Joseph, Betty 'The patient who is difficult to reach', in Peter Giovacchini, ed. *Tactics and Techniques in Psycho-Analytic Therapy*, vol. 2. New York: Jason Aronson, pp. 205–16; republished (1988) in Bott Spillius, ed. *Melanie Klein*

Today: Developments in Theory and Practice, Volume 2, Mainly Practice, pp. 48–60; and (1989) in Joseph *Psychic Equilibrium and Psychic Change*, pp. 75–87.

Meltzer, Donald 'Adhesive identification', *Contemporary Psycho-Analysis* 11: 289–310.

Meltzer, Donald, Bremner, John, Hoxter, Shirley, Weddell, Doreen and Wittenberg, Isca *Explorations in Autism*. Perth: Clunie.

Menzies (Lyth), Isabel E.P. 'Thoughts on the maternal role in contemporary society', *Journal of Child Psychotherapy* 4: 5–14; republished (1988) in *Containing Anxiety in Institutions: Selected Essays, Volume 1*, pp. 208–21.

Rey, Henri 'Intra-psychic object-relations: the individual and the group', in Lewis Wolberg and Marvin Aronson, eds *Group Therapy: An Overview*. New York: Stratton, pp. 84–101.

Rosenfeld, Herbert 'The negative therapeutic reaction', in Peter Giovacchini, ed. *Tactics and Techniques in Psycho-Analytic Therapy*, vol. 2, pp. 217–28.

Segal, Hanna 'A psycho-analytic approach to the treatment of schizophrenia', in Malcolm Lader, ed. *Studies of Schizophrenia*. Ashford: Headley Bros, pp. 94–7.

Turquet, Pierre 'Threats to identity in the large group', in Lionel Kreeger, ed. *The Large Group*. Constable, pp. 87–144.

1976

Bion, Wilfred 'Emotional turbulence' in Bion (1987). 'On a quotation from Freud' in Bion (1987). 'Evidence' in Bion (1987).

Grinberg, Leon, Gear, M.C. and Liendo, E.C. 'Group dynamics according to a semiotic model based on projective identification and counter-identification', in L.R. Wolberg *et al.*, eds, *Group Therapy*, New York: Stratton, pp. 167–79.

Harris, Martha 'Infantile elements and adult strivings in adolescent sexuality', *Journal of Child Psychotherapy* 4(2): 29–44; republished (1987) in *The Collected Papers of Martha Harris and Esther Bick*, pp. 121–40.

Jaques, Elliott *A General Theory of Bureaucracy*. Heinemann.

Meltzer, Donald 'The delusion of clarity of insight', *Int. J. Psycho-Anal.* 57: 141–6.

Orford, Eileen 'Some effects of the absence of his father on an eight-year-old boy', *Journal of Child Psychotherapy* 4(2): 53–74.

1977

Alvarez, Anne 'Problems of dependence and development in an excessively passive autistic boy', *Journal of Child Psychotherapy* 4(3): 25–46.

Bion, Wilfred *A Memoir of the Future: 2. The Past Presented*. Rio de Janeiro: Imago Editora .

—— *Seven Servants*. New York: Jason Aronson.

—— 'Emotional disturbance', in Peter Hartocollis, ed. *Borderline Personality Disorders*. New York: International Universities Press; republished (1977) in W.R. Bion, *Two Papers: The Grid and Caesura*. Rio de Janeiro: Imago Editora.

—— 'On a quotation from Freud', in Peter Hartocollis, ed. *Borderline Personality Disorders*; republished (1977) in Bion, *Two Papers: The Grid and Caesura*.

—— *Two Papers: The Grid and Caesura*. Rio de Janeiro: Imago Editora Ltda.

Grinberg, Leon 'An approach to the understanding of borderline patients', in Peter Hartocollis, ed. *Borderline Personality Disorders*.

Grotstein, James S. 'The psycho-analytic concept of schizophrenia', *Int. J. Psycho-Anal.* 58: 403–52.

Harris, Martha 'The Tavistock training and philosophy', in Dilys Daws and Mary Boston, eds *The Child Psychotherapist*. Aldershot: Wildwood; republished (1987) in *The Collected Papers of Martha Harris and Esther Bick*, pp. 259–82.

Segal, Hanna 'Counter-transference', *Int. J. Psycho-Anal. Psychother.* 6: 31–7; republished (1981) in *The Work of Hanna Segal*, pp. 81–8.

—— 'Psycho-analysis and freedom of thought', [Inaugural Lecture, Freud Memorial Professor, University College, London, H.K. Lewis; republished (1981) in *The Work of Hanna Sega*, pp. 217–27; and (1989) in Sandler, ed. *Dimensions of Psychoanalysis*, pp. 51–63.

Segal, Hanna and Furer, Manuel 'Psycho-analytic dialogue: Kleinian theory today', *J. Amer. Psychoanal. Assn.* 25: 363–85.

1978

Bion, Wilfred *Four Discussions with W.R. Bion*. Perth: Clunie.

Elmhurst, Susanna Isaacs 'Time and the pre-verbal transference', *Int. J. Psycho-Anal.* 59: 173–80.

Etchegoyen, R. Horatio 'Some thoughts on transference perversion', *Int. J. Psycho-Anal.* 59: 45–53.

Grinberg, Leon 'The "razor's edge" in depression and mourning', *Int. J. Psycho-Anal.* 59: 245–54.

Grotstein, James S. 'Inner space: its dimensions and its co-ordinates', *Int. J. Psycho-Anal.* 59: 55–61.

Jaques, Elliott, ed. *Health Services*. Heinemann.

Joseph, Betty 'Different types of anxiety and their handling in the analytic situation', *Int. J. Psycho-Anal.* 59: 223–8; republished (1989) in Joseph *Psychic Equilibrium and Psychic Change*, pp. 106–15.

Meltzer, Donald *The Kleinian Development*. Perth: Clunie.

—— 'A note on Bion's concept "reversal of alpha-function" ', in Meltzer (1978) *The Kleinian Development*, pp. 119–26; republished (1981) in James Grotstein, ed. *Do I Dare Disturb the Universe?* pp. 529–35.

—— 'Routine and inspired interpretations', *Contemporary Psycho-Analysis* 14: 210–25.

Money-Kyrle, Roger *The Collected Papers of Roger Money-Kyrle*. Perth: Clunie.

—— 'On being a psycho-analyst'; republished (1978) in *The Collected Papers of Roger Money-Kyrle*, pp. 457–65.

Rosenfeld, Herbert 'Notes on the psychopathology and psycho-analytic treatment of some borderline states', *Int. J. Psycho-Anal.* 59: 215–21.

Saunders, Kenneth 'Shakespeare's "The Winter's Tale", and some notes on the analysis of a present-day Leontes', *Int. Rev. Psycho-Anal.* 5: 175–8.

Segal, Hanna 'On symbolism', *Int. J. Psycho-Anal.* 55: 315–19.

Tustin, Frances 'Psychotic elements in the neurotic disorders of children', *Journal of Child Psychotherapy* 4(4): 5–17.

Williams, Arthur Hyatt 'Depression, deviation and acting-out', *Journal of Adolescence* 1: 309–17.

Wittenberg, Isca Salzberger 'The use of "here and now" experiences in a teaching conference on psychotherapy', *Journal of Child Psychotherapy* 4(4): 33–50.

1979

Bion, Wilfred *A Memoir of the Future: 3. The Dawn of Oblivion*. Perth: Clunie.

—— 'Making the best of a bad job', in Bion (1987), pp. 247–57.

Gallwey, P.L.G. 'Symbolic dysfunction in the perversions: some related clinical problems', *Int. Rev. Psycho-Anal.* 6: 155–61.

Grinberg, Leon 'Counter-transference and projective counter-identification', *Contemporary Psycho-Analysis* 15: 226–47.

Grotstein, James S. 'Who is the dreamer who dreams the dream and who is the dreamer who understands it?', *Contemporary Psycho-Analysis* 15: 110–69; republished (1981) in Grotstein, ed. *Do I Dare Disturb the Universe?*, pp. 357–416.

Harris, Martha 'L'apport de l'observation de l'interaction mère–enfant', *Nouvelle Revue de Psychanalyse* 19: 99–112; republished (1987) in *The Collected Papers of Martha Harris and Esther Bick*. Perth: Clunie, pp. 225–39.

Hinshelwood, R.D. 'The community as analyst', in R.D. Hinshelwood and Nick Manning, eds *Therapeutic Communities: Reflections and Progress*. Routledge & Kegan Paul, pp. 103–12.

Menzies (Lyth), Isabel E.P. 'Staff support systems: task and anti-task in adolescent institutions', in Hinshelwood and Manning, eds *Therapeutic Communities: Reflections and Progress*, pp. 197–207; republished (1988) in Isabel Menzies Lyth *Containing Anxiety in Institutions: Selected Essays, Volume 1*, pp. 222–35.

Money-Kyrle, Roger 'Looking backwards – and forwards', *Int. Rev. Psycho-Anal.* 60: 265–72.

Rey, Henri 'Schizoid phenomena in the borderline', in Joseph LeBoit and Attilio Capponi, eds *Advances in Psychotherapy of the Borderline Patient*. New York: Jason Aronson, pp. 449–84; republished (1988) in Bott Spillius, ed. *Melanie Klein Today: Developments in Theory and Practice, Volume 1, Mainly Theory*, pp. 203–29.

Rhode, Maria 'One life between two people', *Journal of Child Psychotherapy*, 5: 57–68.

Rosenfeld, Herbert 'Difficulties in the psycho-analytic treatment of the borderline patient', in Joseph LeBoit and Attilio Capponi, eds *Advances in Psychotherapy of the Borderline Patient*, pp. 187–206.

—— 'Transference psychosis in the borderline patient', in LeBoit and Capponi, eds *Advances in Psychotherapy of the Borderline Patient*, pp. 485–510.

Segal, Hanna *Klein*. Fontana.

Steiner, John 'The border between the paranoid-schizoid and the depressive positions in the borderline patient', *Br. J. Med. Psychol.* 52: 385–91.

1980

Alvarez, Anne 'Two regenerative situations in autism: reclamation and becoming vertebrate', *Journal of Child Psychotherapy* 6: 69–80.

Bion, Wilfred *Bion in São Paulo and New York*. Perth: Clunie.

—— *Bion's Brazilian Lectures 3*. Rio de Janeiro: Imago Editora; republished in Bion (1987) pp. 1–220.

Brenman, Eric 'The value of reconstruction in adult psycho-analysis', *Int. J. Psycho-Anal.* 61: 53–60.

Elmhirst, Susanna Isaacs 'Bion and babies', *The Annual of Psycho-Analysis* 8: 155–67 (New York: International Universities Press); republished (1981) in James Grotstein, ed. *Do I Dare Disturb the Universe?*, pp. 83–91.

—— 'Transitional objects and transition', *Int. J. Psycho-Anal.* 61: 367–73.

Gammil, James 'Some reflections on analytic listening and the dream screen', *Int. J. Psycho-Anal.* 61: 375–81.

Grinberg, Leon 'The closing phase of the psycho-analytic treatment of adults and the goals of psycho-analysis', *Int. J. Psycho-Anal.* 61: 25–37.

Grotstein, James S. 'A proposed revision of the psycho-analytic concept of primitive mental states', *Contemporary Psycho-Analysis* 16: 479–546.

—— 'The significance of the Kleinian contribution to psycho-analysis', *International Journal of Psycho-Analytic Psychotherapy* 8: 375–498.

Klein, Sidney 'Autistic phenomena in neurotic patients', *Int. J. Psycho-Anal.* 61: 395–402; republished (1981) in James Grotstein, ed. *Do I Dare Disturb the Universe?*, pp. 103–14.

Wilson, Stephen 'Hans Andersen's nightingale', *Int. Rev. Psycho-Anal.* 7: 483–6.

1981

Etchegoyen R. Horatio 'Instances and alternatives of the interpretative work', *Int. Rev. Psycho-Anal.* 8: 401–21.

Gosling, Robert 'A study of very small groups', in James Grotstein, ed. *Do I Dare Disturb the Universe?*, pp. 633–45.

Grinberg, Leon 'The "Oedipus" as a resistance against the "Oedipus" in psycho-analytic practice', in James Grotstein, ed. *Do I Dare Disturb the Universe?* pp. 341–55.

Grotstein, James S., ed. *Do I Dare Disturb the Universe?* Beverly Hills: Caesura.

—— *Splitting and Projective Identification*. New York: Jason Aronson.

—— 'Wilfred R. Bion: the man, the psycho-analyst, the mystic', in Grotstein, ed. *Do I Dare Disturb the Universe?*, pp. 1–35.

Harris, Martha 'The individual in the group: on learning to work with the psycho-analytic method', in James Grotstein, ed. *Do I Dare Disturb the Universe?*, pp. 647–60; republished (1987) in *The Collected Papers of Martha Harris and Esther Bick*, pp. 332–9.

Jaques, Elliott 'The aims of psycho-analytic treatment', in James Grotstein, ed. *Do I Dare Disturb the Universe?*, pp. 417–25.

Joseph, Betty 'Toward the experiencing of psychic pain', in James Grotstein, ed. *Do I Dare Disturb the Universe?*, pp. 93–102; republished (1989) in Joseph *Psychic Equilibrium and Psychic Change*, pp. 88–99.

—— 'Defence mechanisms and phantasy in the psychological process', *Bulletin of the European Psycho-Analytical Federation* 17: 11–24; republished (1989) in Joseph *Psychic Equilibrium and Psychic Change*, pp. 116–26.

Mancia, Mauro 'On the beginning of mental life in the foetus', *Int. J. Psycho-Anal.* 62: 351–7.

Mancia, Mauro and Meltzer, Donald 'Ego-ideal functions and the psycho-analytic process', *Int. J. Psycho-Anal.* 62: 243–9.

Mason, Albert 'The suffocating superego: psychotic break and claustro-phobia', in James Grotstein, ed. *Do I Dare Disturb the Universe?*, pp. 139–66.

Meltzer, Donald 'The relation of splitting of attention to splitting of self and objects', *Contemporary Psycho-Analysis* 17: 232–8.

—— 'The Kleinian expansion of Freudian metapsychology', *Int. J. Psycho-Anal.* 62: 177–85.

Menzies (Lyth), Isabel E.P. 'Bion's contribution to thinking about groups', in James Grotstein, ed. *Do I Dare Disturb the Universe?*, pp. 661–6; republished (1989) in Isabel Menzies Lyth *The Dynamics of the Social: Selected Essays, Volume 2*, pp. 19–25.

O'Shaughnessy, Edna 'A clinical study of a defensive organization', *Int. J. Psycho-Anal.* 62: 359–69; republished (1988) in Bott Spillius, ed. *Melanie Klein Today: Developments in Theory and Practice, Volume 1, Mainly Theory*, pp. 292–310.

—— 'A commemorative essay on W.R. Bion's theory of thinking', *Journal of Child Psychotherapy* 7: 181–92; republished (1988) in Bott Spillius, ed. *Melanie Klein Today: Developments in Theory and Practice, Volume 2, Mainly Practice*, pp. 177–90.

Riesenberg-Malcolm, Ruth 'Expiation as a defence', *Int. J. Psycho-Anal. Psychother.* 8: 549–70.

—— 'Melanie Klein: achievements and problems', *Revista de Psicoanálisis* 3: 52–63; republished (1986) in English in Robert Langs, ed. *The Yearbook of Psychoanalysis and Psychotherapy*, vol. 2, pp. 306–21.

—— 'Technical problems in the analysis of a pseudo-compliant patient', *Int. J. Psycho-Anal.* 62: 477–84.

Rosenfeld, Herbert 'On the psychopathology and treatment of psychotic patients', in James Grotstein, ed. *Do I Dare Disturb the Universe?*, pp. 167–79.

Segal, Hanna *The Work of Hanna Segal.* New York: Jason Aronson.

—— 'The function of dreams', in James Grotstein, ed. *Do I Dare Disturb the Universe?*, pp. 579–87; republished in *The Work of Hanna Segal*, pp. 89–97.

—— 'Manic reparation', in *The Work of Hanna Segal*, pp. 147–58.

Thorner, Hans A. 'Notes on the desire for knowledge', in James Grotstein, ed. *Do I Dare Disturb the Universe?*, pp. 589–99.

—— 'Either/or: a contribution to the problem of symbolization and sublimation', *Int. J. Psycho-Anal.* 62: 455–64.

Tustin, Frances *Autistic States in Children.* Routledge & Kegan Paul.

—— 'Psychological birth and psychological catastrophe', in James Grotstein, ed. *Do I Dare Disturb the Universe?*, pp. 181–96.

1982

Bion, Wilfred *The Long Weekend, 1897–1919.* Abingdon: Fleetwood.

Brenman, Eric 'Separation: a clinical problem', *Int. J. Psycho-Anal.* 63: 303–10.

Etchegoyen, R. Horatio 'The relevance of the "here and now" transference interpretation for the reconstruction of early development', *Int. J. Psycho-Anal.* 63: 65–75.

Harris, Martha 'Growing points in psycho-analysis inspired by the work of Melanie Klein', *Journal of Child Psychotherapy* 8: 165–84.

Jaques, Elliott *The Form of Time*. Heinemann.

Joseph, Betty 'On addiction to near death', *Int. J. Psycho-Anal.* 63: 449–56; republished (1988) in Bott Spillius, ed. *Melanie Klein Today: Developments in Theory and Practice, Volume 1, Mainly Theory*, pp. 293–310; and (1989) in Joseph *Psychic Equilibrium and Psychic Change*, pp. 127–38.

Meltzer, Donald, Milana, Giuliana, Maiello, Susanna and Petrelli, Diomine 'The conceptual distinction between projective identification (Klein) and container–contained (Bion)', *Journal of Child Psychotherapy* 8: 185–202.

Rustin, Margaret 'Finding a way to the child', *Journal of Child Psychotherapy* 8: 145–50.

Segal, Hanna 'Early infantile development as reflected in the psycho-analytical process: steps in integration', *Int. J. Psycho-Anal.* 63: 15–22.

Steiner, John 'Perverse relationships between parts of the self: a clinical illustration', *Int. J. Psycho-Anal.* 63: 241–52.

Williams, Arthur Hyatt 'Adolescence, violence and crime', *Journal of Adolescence* 5: 125–34.

Wittenberg, Isca 'On assessment', *Journal of Child Psychotherapy* 8: 131–44.

1983

Alvarez, Anne 'Problems in the use of the counter-transference: getting it across', *Journal of Child Psychotherapy* 9: 7–23.

Boston, Mary and Szur, Rolene, eds *Psychotherapy with Severely Deprived Children*. Routledge & Kegan Paul.

Cornwall, Joan (Symington) 'Crisis and survival in infancy', *Journal of Child Psychotherapy* 9: 25–32.

Dale, Francis 'The body as bondage', *Journal of Child Psychotherapy* 9: 33–45.

Etchegoyen R. Horatio 'Fifty years after the mutative interpretation', *Int. J. Psycho-Anal.* 64: 445–59.

Folch, Terttu Eskelinen de 'We – versus I and you', *Int. J. Psycho-Anal.* 64: 309–20.

Hinshelwood, R.D. 'Projective identification and Marx's concept of man', *Int. Rev. Psycho-Anal.* 10: 221–6.

Joseph, Betty 'On understanding and not understanding: some technical issues', *Int. J. Psycho-Anal.* 64: 291–8; republished (1989) in Joseph *Psychic Equilibrium and Psychic Change*, pp. 139–50.

Mancia, Mauro 'Archaeology of Freudian thought and the history of neurophysiology', *Int. Rev. Psycho-Anal.* 10: 185–92.

O'Shaughnessy, Edna 'On words and working through', *Int. J. Psycho-Anal.* 64: 281–9; republished (1988) in Bott Spillius, ed. *Melanie Klein Today: Developments in Theory and Practice, Volume 2, Mainly Practice*, pp. 138–51.

Rosenfeld, Herbert 'Primitive object relations and mechanisms', *Int. J. Psycho-Anal.* 64: 261–7.

Segal, Hanna 'Some clinical implications of Melanie Klein's work', *Int. J. Psycho-Anal.* 64: 269–76.

Sohn, Leslie 'Nostalgia', *Int. J. Psycho-Anal.* 64: 203–11.

Spillius, Elizabeth Bott 'Some developments from the work of Melanie Klein', *Int. J. Psycho-Anal.* 64: 321–32.

Taylor, David 'Some observations on hallucinations: clinical applications of some developments of Melanie Klein's work', *Int. J. Psycho-Anal.* 64: 299–308.

Williams, Meg Harris ' "Underlying pattern" in Bion's *Memoir of the Future*', *Int. Rev. Psycho-Anal.* 10: 75–86.

Wilson, Stephen '*Experiences in Groups*: Bion's debt to Freud', *Group Analysis* 16: 152–7.

Wittenberg, Isca, Henri, Gianna and Osbourne, Elsie, *The Emotional Experience of Learning and Teaching*. Routledge & Kegan Paul.

1984

Barrows, Kate 'A child's difficulties in using his gifts and imagination', *Journal of Child Psychotherapy* 10: 15–26.

Bianchedi, Elizabeth, Antar, Riccardo, Fernandez Bravo de Podetti, M. Ruth, Grassano de Piccolo, Elsa, Miravent, Irene, Pistiner de Cortinas, Lia, T. Scalozub de Boschan, Lidia and Waserman, Mario 'Beyond Freudian metapsychology: the metapsychological points of view of the Kleinian School', *Int. J. Psycho-Anal.* 65: 389–98.

Grinberg, Leon and Rodriguez, Juan Francisco 'The influence of Cervantes on the future creator of psycho-analysis', *Int. J. Psycho-Anal.* 65: 155–68.

Klein, Sidney 'Delinquent perversion: problems in assimilation: a clinical study', *Int. J. Psycho-Anal.* 64: 307–14.

Meltzer, Donald *Dream Life*. Perth: Clunie.

—— 'A one-year-old goes to nursery', *Journal of Child Psychotherapy* 19: 89–104.

Segal, Hanna 'Joseph Conrad and the mid-life crisis', *Int. Rev. Psycho-Anal.* 11: 3–9.

Tustin, Frances 'Autistic shapes', *Int. Rev. Psycho-Anal.* 11: 279–90.

Waddle, Margot 'The long weekend', *Free Assns* Pilot Issue: 72–84.

Wilson, Stephen 'Character development in *Daniel Deronda*: a psycho-analytic view', *Int. Rev. Psycho-Anal.* 11: 199–206.

1985

Alvarez, Anne 'The problem of neutrality: some reflections on the psycho-analytic attitude in the treatment of borderline and psychotic children', *Journal of Child Psychotherapy* 11: 87–103.

Bion, Wilfred *All My Sins Remembered* and *The Other Side of Genius*. Abingdon: Fleetwood.

Brenman, Eric 'Cruelty and narrow-mindedness', *Int. J. Psycho-Anal.* 66: 273–81; republished (1988) in Bott Spillius, ed. *Melanie Klein Today: Developments in Theory and Practice, Volume 1, Mainly Theory*, pp. 256–70.

—— 'Hysteria', *Int. J. Psycho-Anal.* 66: 423–32.

Brenman Pick, Irma 'Working through in the counter-transference', *Int. J. Psycho-Anal.* 66: 157–66; republished (1988) in Bott Spillius, ed. *Melanie Klein Today: Developments in Theory and Practice, Volume 2, Mainly Practice*, pp. 34–47.

—— 'Development of the concepts of transference and counter-transference', *Psychoanalytic Psychotherapy* 1: 13–23.

—— 'Breakdown in communication: on finding the child in the analysis of an adult', *Psychoanalytic Psychotherapy* 1: 57–62.

—— 'Male sexuality: a clinical study of forces that impede development', *Int. J. Psycho-Anal.* 66: 415–22.

Dresser, Iain 'The use of transference and counter-transference in assessing emotional disturbance in children', *Psychoanalytic Psychotherapy* 1: 95–106.

Etchegoyen, R. Horatio 'Identification and its vicissitudes', *Int. J. Psycho-Anal.* 66: 3–18.

Etchegoyen, R. Horatio, Barutta, Ricardo, Bonfanti, Luis, Gazzaro, Alfredo, de Santa Colan, Fernan, Suguier, Guillermo and de Berenstein, Sloin 'On the existence of two working levels in the process of working through', *The Journal of the Melanie Klein Society* 12(1): 58–81.

Etchegoyen, R. Horatio and Ribah, Moises 'The psycho-analytic theory of envy', *The Journal of the Melanie Klein Society* 13(1): 50–80.

Gallwey, Patrick 'The psychodynamics of borderline personality', in D.E. Farrington and J. Gunn, eds *Aggression and Dangerousness*. Chichester: Wiley.

Goldie, Lawrence 'Psycho-analysis in the National Health Service general hospital', *Psychoanalytic Psychotherapy* 1: 23–34.

Grinberg, Leon 'Bion's contribution to the understanding of the individual and the group', in Malcolm Pines, ed. *Bion and Group Psychotherapy*. Routledge & Kegan Paul.

Herman, Nini *My Kleinian Home*. Quartet.

Hinshelwood, R.D. 'Questions of training', *Free Assns* 2: 7–18.

Hughes, Athol, Furgiuele, Piera and Bianco, Margherita 'Aspects of anorexia nervosa in the therapy of two adolescents', *Journal of Child Psychotherapy* 11(1): 17–33.

Jackson, Judith 'An adolescent's difficulties in using his mind: some technical problems', *Journal of Child Psychotherapy* 11(1): 105–19.

Jackson, Murray 'A psycho-analytical approach to the assessment of a psychotic patient', *Psychoanalytic Psychotherapy* 1: 11–22.

Joseph, Betty 'Transference: the total situation', *Int. J. Psycho-Anal.* 66: 447–54; republished (1988) in Bott Spillius, ed. *Melanie Klein Today: Developments in Theory and Practice, Volume 2, Mainly Practice*, pp. 61–72; and (1989) in Joseph *Psychic Equilibrium and Psychic Change*, pp. 156–67.

Klein, Sidney 'The self in childhood: a Kleinian point of view', *Journal of Child Psychotherapy* 11(2): 31–47.

Lucas, Richard 'On the contribution of psycho-analysis to the management of psychotic patients in the National Health Service', *Psychoanalytic Psychotherapy* 1: 2–17.

Menzies (Lyth), Isabel E.P. 'The development of the self in children in institutions', *Journal of Child Psychotherapy* 11: 49–64; republished (1989) in Isabel Menzies Lyth *Containing Anxiety in Institutions: Selected Essays, Volume 1*, pp. 236–58.

Segal, Hanna 'The Klein–Bion model' in Arnold Rotherstein ed. *Models of the Mind*. New York: International Universities Press.

Segal, Julia *Phantasy in Everyday Life*. Penguin.

Sohn, Leslie 'Narcissistic organization, projective identification and the formation of the identificate', *Int. J. Psycho-Anal.* 66: 201–13; republished (1988) in Bott Spillius, ed. *Melanie Klein Today: Developments in Theory and Practice, Volume 1, Mainly Theory*, pp. 271–92.

—— 'Anorexic and bulimic states of mind in the psycho-analytic treatment of anorexic/bulimic patients and psychotic patients', *Psychoanalytic Psychotherapy* 1: 49–55.

Steiner, John 'Turning a blind eye: the cover-up for Oedipus', *Int. Rev. Psycho-Anal.* 12: 161–72.

—— 'The training of psychotherapists', *Psychoanalytic Psychotherapy* 1: 56–63.

Steiner, Riccardo 'Some thoughts about tradition and change arising from an examination of the British Psycho-Analytical Society's Controversial Discussions 1943–1944', *Int. Rev. Psycho-Anal.* 12: 27–71.

Symington, Joan (Cornwall) 'The establishment of female genital sexuality', *Free Assns* 1: 57–75.

—— 'The survival function of primitive omnipotence', *Int. J. Psycho-Anal.* 66: 481–7.

Thorner, Hans A. 'On repetition: its relationship to the depressive position', *Int. J. Psycho-Anal.* 66: 231–6.

Williams, Meg Harris 'The tiger and "O": a reading of Bion's *Memoir* and autobiography', *Free Assns* 1: 33–56.

1986

Bick, Esther 'Further considerations of the function of the skin in early object relations: findings from infant observation integrated into child and adult analysis', *Br. J. Psychother.* 2: 292–9.

Britton, Ronald 'The infant in the adult', *Psychoanalytic Psychotherapy* 2: 31–44.

Grosskurth, Phyllis *Melanie Klein*. Hodder & Stoughton.

Hinshelwood, R.D. 'A "dual" materialism', *Free Assns* 4: 36–50.

—— 'Electicism: the impossible project', *Free Assns* 5: 23–7.

Joseph, Betty 'Envy in everyday life', *Psychoanalytic Psychotherapy* 2: 23–30; republished (1989) in Joseph *Psychic Equilibrium and Psychic Change*, pp. 181–91.

Meltzer, Donald *Studies in Extended Metapsychology*. Perth: Clunie.

—— 'On first impressions', *Contemporary Psycho-Analysis* 22: 467–70.

Menzies (Lyth), Isabel E.P. 'Psycho-analysis in non-clinical contexts: on the art of captaincy', *Free Assns* 5: 65–78.

O'Shaughnessy, Edna 'A three-and-a-half-year-old boy's melancholic identification with an original object', *Int. J. Psycho-Anal.* 67: 173–9.

Piontelli, Alessandra *Backwards in Time*. Perth: Clunie.

Rey, J. Henri 'Reparation', *Journal of the Melanie Klein Society* 4(1): 5–11.

—— 'The schizoid mode of being and the space-time continuum', *Journal of the Melanie Klein Society* 4(2): 12–52.

—— 'Psycholinguistics, object relations theory and the therapeutic process', *Journal of the Melanie Klein Society* 4(2): 53–72.

—— 'The psychodynamics of psycho-analytic and psycholinguistic structures', *Journal of the Melanie Klein Society* 4(2): 73–92.

—— 'Psychodynamics of depression', *Journal of the Melanie Klein Society* 4(2): 93–116.

Riesenberg-Malcolm, Ruth 'Interpretation: the past in the present', *Int. Rev. Psycho-Anal.* 13: 433–43; republished in Bott Spillius, ed. *Melanie Klein Today: Developments in Theory and Practice, Volume 2, Mainly Practice*, pp. 73–89.

Steiner, Riccardo 'Responsibility as a way of hope in the nuclear era: some notes on F. Fornari's *Psycho-Analysis of War*', *Psychoanalytic Psychotherapy* 2: 75–82.

Tustin, Frances *Autistic Barriers in Neurotic Patients*. Karnac.

Waddell, Margot 'Concept of the inner world in George Eliot's work', *Journal of Child Psychotherapy* 12: 109–24.

Williams, Arthur Hyatt 'The ancient mariner: opium, the saboteur of self-therapy', *Free Assns* 6: 123–44.

1987

Bion, Wilfred *Clinical Seminars and Four Papers*. Abingdon: Fleetwood Press.

Etchegoyen, R. Horatio, Lopez, Benito and Rabih, Moses 'Envy and how to interpret it', *Int. J. Psycho-Anal.* 68: 49–61.

Harris, Martha 'Depressive paranoid and narcissistic features in the analysis of a woman following the birth of her first child and the death of her own mother', in *The Collected Papers of Martha Harris and Esther Bick*. Perth: Clunie, pp. 53–63.

—— 'Towards learning from experience in infancy and childhood', in *The Collected Papers of Martha Harris and Esther Bick*, pp. 164–78.

—— 'The early basis of adult female sexuality and motherliness', in *The Collected Papers of Martha Harris and Esther Bick*, pp. 185–200.

—— 'A baby observation: the absent mother', in *The Collected Papers of Martha Harris and Esther Bick*, pp. 219–24.

—— 'Bion's conception of a psycho-analytic attitude', in *The Collected Papers of Martha Harris and Esther Bick*, pp. 340–4.

Herman, Nini *Why Psychotherapy?* Free Association Books.

Hinshelwood, R.D. 'The psychotherapist's role in a large psychiatric institution', *Psychoanalytic Psychotherapy* 2: 207–15.

—— *What Happens in Groups*. Free Association Books.

Mason, Albert 'A Kleinian perspective on clinical material presented by Martin Silverman', *Psycho-Analytic Inquiry* 7: 189–97.

Meltzer, Donald 'On aesthetic reciprocity', *The Journal of Child Psychotherapy* 13(2): 3–14.

Obholzer, Anton 'Institutional dynamics and resistance to change', *Psycho-analytic Psychotherapy* 2: 201–6.

Pasquali, Gabrielle 'Some notes on humour in psycho-analysis', *Int. Rev. Psycho-Anal.* 14: 231–6.

Piontelli, Alessandra 'Infant observation from before birth', *Int. J. Psycho-Anal.* 68: 453–63.

Rhode, Eric *On Birth and Madness*. Duckworth.

Rosenfeld, Herbert *Impasse and Interpretation*. Tavistock.

Segal, Hanna 'Silence is the real crime', *Int. Rev. Psycho-Anal.* 14: 3–12;

republished (1987) *The Journal of the Melanie Klein Society* 5(1): 3–17.

Steiner, John 'Interplay between pathological organization and the paranoid-schizoid and depressive positions', *Int. J. Psycho-Anal.* 68: 69–80; republished (1988) in Bott Spillius, ed. *Melanie Klein Today: Developments in Theory and Practice, Volume 1, Mainly Theory*, pp. 324–42.

Steiner, Riccardo 'A world wide trade mark of genuineness', *Int. Rev. Psycho-Anal.* 14: 33–102.

Tognoli Pasquali, Laura 'Reflections on Oedipus in Sophocles' tragedy and in clinical practice', *Int. Rev. Psycho-Anal.* 14: 475–82.

1988

de Bianchedi, Elizabeth T., Scalozub de Boschan, Lidia, de Cortinas, Lia P. and de Piccolo, Elsa G. 'Theories on anxiety in Freud and Melanie Klein: their metapsychological status', *Int. J. Psycho-Anal.* 69: 359–68.

Dresser, Iain 'An adopted child in analysis', *Psychoanalytic Psychotherapy* 3: 235–46.

Elmhirst, Susanna Isaacs 'The Kleinian setting for child analysis', *Int. Rev. Psycho-Anal.* 15: 5–12.

Etchegoyen, R. Horatio 'The analysis of Little Hans and the theory of sexuality', *Int. Rev. Psycho-Anal.* 15: 37–43.

Folch, Terttu Eskelinen de 'Communication and containing in child analysis: towards terminability', *Int. J. Psycho-Anal.* 69: 105–12; republished (1988) in Bott Spillius, ed. *Melanie Klein Today: Developments in Theory and Practice, Volume 1, Mainly Theory*, pp. 206–17.

—— 'Guilt bearable and unbearable: a problem for the child in analysis', *Int. Rev. Psycho-Anal.* 15: 13–24.

Hughes, Athol 'The use of manic defence in the psycho-analysis of a ten-year-old girl', *Int. Rev. Psycho-Anal.* 15: 157–64.

Joseph, Betty 'Projection and projective identification: clinical aspects', in Bott Spillius, ed. *Melanie Klein Today: Developments in Theory and Practice, Volume 1, Mainly Theory*, pp. 138–150; republished (1988) in Sandler, ed. *Projection, Identification, Projective Identification*. Karnac, pp. 65–76; and (1989) in Joseph *Psychic Equilibrium and Psychic Change*, pp. 168–80.

—— 'Object relations and clinical practice', *Psychoanal. Q.* 57: 626–42; republished (1989) in Joseph *Psychic Equilibrium and Psychic Change*, pp. 203–15.

Mancia, Mauro 'The dream as religion of the mind', *Int. J. Psycho-Anal.* 69: 419–26.

Meltzer, Donald and Williams, Meg Harris *The Apprehension of Beauty*. Perth: Clunie.

Menzies Lyth, Isabel *Containing Anxiety in Institutions: Selected Essays, Volume 1*. Free Association Books.

—— 'A psychoanalytic perspective on social institutions', in Bott Spillius, ed. *Melanie Klein Today: Developments in Theory and Practice, Volume 2, Mainly Practice*, pp. 284–99.

Pick, Irma Brenman 'Adolescence: its impact on patient and analyst', *Int. Rev. Psycho-Anal.* 15: 187–94.

Piontelli, Alessandro 'Pre-natal life and birth as reflected in the analysis of a two-year-old psychotic girl', *Int. Rev. Psycho-Anal.* 15: 73–81.

Rey, Henri 'That which patients bring to analysis', *Int. J. Psycho-Anal.* 69: 457–70.

Riesenberg-Malcolm, Ruth 'The constitution and operation of the super-ego', *Psychoanalytic Psychotherapy* 3: 149–59.

—— 'Construction as reliving history', *Bulletin of the European Psycho-Analytical Federation* 31: 3–12.

Rustin, Margaret 'Encountering primitive anxieties: some aspects of infant observation as a preparation for clinical work with children and families', *The Journal of Child Psychotherapy* 14(2): 15–28.

Sanders, Kenneth *A Matter of Interest*. Perth: Clunie.

Spillius, Elizabeth Bott *Melanie Klein Today: Developments in Theory and Practice, Volume 1, Mainly Theory*; *Volume 2, Mainly Practice*. Routledge.

Steiner, Riccardo ' "Paths to Xanadu . . ." Some notes on the development of dream displacement and condensation in Sigmund Freud's *Interpretation of Dreams*', *Int. Rev. Psycho-Anal.* 15: 415–54.

Symington, Joan 'The analysis of a mentally handicapped youth' *Int. Rev. Psycho-Anal.* 15: 243–50.

Tustin, Francis 'The "black hole" – a significant element in autism', *Free Assns* 11: 35–50.

—— 'Psychotherapy with children who cannot play', *Int. Rev. Psycho-Anal.* 15: 93–106.

Waddell, Margot 'Infantile development: Kleinian and post-Kleinian theory, infant observation practice', *British Journal of Psychotherapy* 4: 313–28.

· 1989

Berke, Joseph *The Tyranny of Malice*. New York: Simon & Schuster.

Britton, Ronald 'The missing link: parental sexuality and the Oedipus complex', in Britton, Feldman and O'Shaughnessy *The Oedipus Complex Today: Clinical Implications*, pp. 83–101.

Britton, Ronald, Feldman, Michael and O'Shaughnessy, Edna *The Oedipus Complex Today: Clinical Implications*. Karnac.

Feldman, Michael 'The Oedipus complex: manifestations in the inner world and the therapeutic situation', in Britton, Feldman and O'Shaughnessy *The Oedipus Complex Today: Clinical Implications*, pp. 103–28.

Herman, Nini *Too Long a Child*. Free Association Books.

Hinshelwood, R.D. 'Little Hans's transference', *Journal of Child Psychotherapy* 15(1): 63–78.

—— 'Social possession of identity', in B. Richards, ed. *Crises of the Self*. Free Association Books, pp. 75–83.

Jackson, Murray 'Treatment of the hospitalized borderline patient: A Kleinian perspective', *Psycho-Analytic Inquiry* 9: 554–69.

Jackson, Murray and Tarnopolsky, Alex 'The borderline personality', in Blueglass and Bowden, eds *The Principles and Practice of Forensic Psychiatry*. Churchill Livingston.

Joseph, Betty *Psychic Equilibrium and Psychic Change*. Routledge.

—— 'Psychic change and the psycho-analytic process', in Joseph *Psychic Equilibrium and Psychic Change*, pp. 192–202.

—— 'On passivity and aggression: their interrelationship', in Joseph *Psychic Equilibrium and Psychic Change*, pp. 67–74.

Meltzer, Donald 'Concerning the stupidity of evil', *Melanie Klein and Object Relations* 7(1): 19–21.

Menzies Lyth, Isabel *The Dynamics of the Social: Selected Essays, Volume 2*. Free Association Books.

Obholzer, Anton 'Psycho-analysis and the political process', *Psychoanalytic Psychotherapy* 4: 55–66.

O'Shaughnessy, Edna 'The invisible Oedipus complex', in Britton, Feldman and O'Shaughnessy, *The Oedipus Complex Today: Clinical Implications*, pp. 129–50.

—— 'Seeing with meaning and emotion', *The Journal of Child Psychotherapy* 15(2): 27–31.

Piontelli, Alessandro 'A study on twins before birth', *Int. Rev. Psycho-Anal.* 16: 413–26.

Sandler, J., ed. *Dimensions of Psychoanalysis*. Karnac.

Sayers, Janet 'Melanie Klein and mothering', *Int. Rev. Psycho-Anal.* 16: 363–76.

Steiner, Deborah 'The internal family and the facts of life', *Psychoanalytic Psychotherapy* 4: 31–42.

Steiner, John 'The psycho-analytic contribution of Herbert Rosenfeld', *Int. J. Psycho-Anal.* 70: 611–17.

Steiner, Riccardo ' "It's a new kind of diaspora . . ." ', *Int. Rev. Psycho-Anal.* 16: 35–78.

Temperley, Jane 'Psychoanalysis and the threat of nuclear war', in B. Richards, ed. *Crises of the Self*. Free Association Books, pp. 259–67.

Waddell, Margot 'Living in two worlds: psychodynamic theory and social work practice', *Free Associations* 15: 11–35.

—— 'Experience and identification in George Eliot's novels', *Free Assns* 17: 7–27.

—— 'Growing up', *Free Assns* 17: 90–105.

This second edition of
A DICTIONARY OF KLEINIAN THOUGHT
was finished in November 1990.

It was set in 10/12½pt Ehrhardt

The book was commissioned by Robert M. Young,
edited by him and Karl Figlio,
copy-edited by Gillian Beaumont,
designed by Carlos Sapochnik,
and produced by Selina O'Grady
and Martin Klopstock for
Free Association Books.